Canadian Politics

Canadian

Politics

SEVENTH EDITION

Edited by
James Bickerton and
Alain-G. Gagnon

UNIVERSITY OF TORONTO PRESS
Toronto Buffalo London

Toronto Buffalo London
utorontopress.com
Printed in Canada

ISBN 978-1-4875-8811-3 (cloth)
ISBN 978-1-4875-8810-6 (paper)
ISBN 978-1-4875-8812-0 (EPUB)
ISBN 978-1-4875-8813-7 (PDF)

Library and Archives Canada Cataloguing in Publication

Title: Canadian politics / edited by James Bickerton and Alain-G. Gagnon.
Names: Bickerton, James, editor. | Gagnon, Alain-G. (Alain-Gustave), 1954– editor.
Description: Seventh edition. | Includes bibliographical references and index.
Identifiers: Canadiana (print) 20200256017 | Canadiana (ebook) 20200256025 | ISBN 9781487588113 (hardcover) | ISBN 9781487588106 (softcover) | ISBN 9781487588120 (EPUB) | ISBN 9781487588137 (PDF)
Subjects: LCSH: Canada – Politics and government – Textbooks. | LCGFT: Textbooks.
Classification: LCC JL65.C35 2020 | DDC 320.971–dc23

We welcome comments and suggestions regarding any aspect of our publications – please feel free to contact us at news@utorontopress.com or visit us at utorontopress.com.

Every effort has been made to contact copyright holders; in the event of an error or omission, please notify the publisher.

University of Toronto Press acknowledges the financial assistance to its publishing program of the Canada Council for the Arts and the Ontario Arts Council, an agency of the Government of Ontario.

Canada Council for the Arts
Conseil des Arts du Canada

Funded by the Government of Canada
Financé par le gouvernement du Canada
Canada

The editors would like to dedicate this seventh edition of *Canadian Politics* to three colleagues who have recently passed away: Alan C. Cairns, Robert Young, and Michael Burgess. Eminent political scientists, they have left us with a rich intellectual legacy as well as an inspiring example of dedication and unstinting service to their profession and the broader community. In the domains of constitutional politics, federalism, and urban politics, they have inspired generations of students and scholars. We have enjoyed the great fortune of working with them and learning from them over many years. They will be greatly missed by the Canadian political science community.

– J.B. and A.G.G.

Contents

Part Six: Contemporary Issues

Preface and Acknowledgments

The seventh edition of *Canadian Politics* continues the work of earlier editions in bringing together a highly respected group of scholars to offer a comprehensive account of Canadian government and politics.

For this new edition, the editors have organized the book into six parts. The first part covers the origins and foundations of Canada as a political entity, while Part Two focuses on government, Parliament, and the courts. Part Three examines matters pertaining to federalism and the Canadian Charter of Rights and Freedoms. Part Four casts new light on electoral politics and political communications, whereas Part Five examines citizenship, diversity, and social movements. The last part concentrates on political issues that merit the special attention of political actors and decision-makers, namely the evolving relationship between Canada and Indigenous peoples, immigration and refugees, environment and climate change, and relations between Canada and the United States.

This new edition counts on the continued participation of several scholars who we would like to thank for their generous collaboration. We also would like to take this opportunity to welcome new contributors Amanda Clarke, Andrew Heard, Guy Laforest, Douglas Macdonald, Jacquetta Newman, Naiomi Walqwan Metallic, Mireille Paquet, Laura Stephenson, Lori Turnbull, Debora VanNijnatten, and Graham Wilson. Of the twenty-three chapters in the seventh edition of *Canadian Politics*, those retained from earlier editions have been revised and updated to offer the most up-to-date comprehensive analyses. This edition includes twelve new chapters, with ten new contributing authors and coverage of six new subjects.

A special word of thanks is extended to Catherine Viens, doctoral candidate in the Department of Political Science at Université du Québec à Montréal, who assisted us in preparing the manuscript. Finally, we would like to acknowledge Mat Buntin and Marilyn McCormack of the University of Toronto Press for their support and gentle prodding throughout the preparation of this new edition. As usual, the editorial team there has been excellent. Our final thanks go to Ian MacKenzie, who has accompanied us in the final editing of this book.

Contributors

About the Editors

James Bickerton is a professor of political science at St. Francis Xavier University. His books include *Nova Scotia, Ottawa and the Politics of Regional Development* (University of Toronto Press), co-authorship of *Ties That Bind: Parties and Voters in Canada* (Oxford University Press) and *Freedom, Equality, Community: The Political Philosophy of Six Influential Canadians* (McGill-Queen's University Press), and co-editorship of *Governing: Essays in Honour of Donald J. Savoie* (McGill-Queen's University Press).

Alain-G. Gagnon holds the Canada Research Chair in Quebec and Canadian Studies, is the director of the newly established *Centre d'analyse politique: Constitution et Fédéralisme,* and is professor in the Department of Political Science at the Université du Québec à Montréal. His publications include, with Routledge, *The Case for Multinational Federalism* and *Federal Democracies*, and with Palgrave Macmillan, *Political Autonomy and Divided Societies* and *Multinational Federalism*. He has also authored *Minority Nations in the Age of Uncertainty* (University of Toronto Press), which has been translated into 18 languages. In 2017, he was elected president of the Academy of Social Sciences of the Royal Society of Canada for a two-year term.

About the Contributors

Yasmeen Abu-Laban is a professor of political science and Canada Research Chair in the Politics of Citizenship and Human Rights at the University of Alberta. Her published research addresses ethnic and gender politics; nationalism, globalization, and racialization; immigration policies and politics; surveillance and border control; and multiculturalism and anti-racism. She served as president of the Canadian Political Science Association and in 2018 became vice-president of the International Political Science Association.

Raymond Bazowski teaches in the Department of Political Science at York University. His research interests include the philosophy of law, comparative constitutionalism, and the effect of law on public policy. Among his recent publications is *The Charter at Twenty* (with Charles Smith).

Mark R. Brawley is a professor of political science at McGill University. His area of expertise is international political economy (IPE); he is interested in both trade and international financial relations. His interests in IPE often make connections between security policy and economics. He has written books on hegemonic leadership in the international system: *Liberal Leadership* (Cornell University Press) and *Afterglow or Adjustment?* (Columbia University Press), as well as several articles on the subject. Several of his articles examine the rise of the BRICS (Brazil, Russia, India, and China), though his most recent book is *Political Economy and Grand Strategy: A Neoclassical Realist View* (Routledge).

Amanda Clarke is an assistant professor and Public Affairs Research Excellence Chair at Carleton University's School of Public Policy and Administration. Her research examines public-sector reform, policy-making and civic engagement, focusing in particular on the impact of digital technologies in these domains. She is published in *Canadian Public Administration, Governance,* and *Policy and Internet.* Dr. Clarke is co-editor of *Issues in Canadian Governance* and author of *Opening the Government of Canada: The Federal Bureaucracy in the Digital Age.*

Lyne Deschatelêts received her master's degree in political science from the Université du Québec à Montréal in 2013. Her research focuses on media and politics. More specifically, her master's thesis provided an in-depth case study of how gender rights discourses were used in the press during the reasonable accommodation debates in Quebec.

Allison Harell is an associate professor at the Université du Québec à Montréal. She holds the UQAM Chair on the Political Psychology of Social Solidarity and is co-director of the Political Communication and Public Opinion Laboratory at UQAM. She is also a member of the Canadian Election Study team and the Centre for the Study of Democratic Citizenship. Her research focuses on public opinion and political behaviour in Canada and other advanced industrialized democracies.

Andrew Heard is a professor of political science at Simon Fraser University. His research interests relate to Canadian constitutional and institutional questions. He is the author of *Canadian Constitutional Conventions: The Marriage of Law and Politics.* In addition, he has published articles and chapters on constitutional conventions, Senate reform, the Crown, federalism, judicial behaviour, parliamentary privilege, the electoral system, and the Charter of Rights and Freedoms.

Will Kymlicka holds the Canada Research Chair in Political Philosophy at Queen's University. His books include *Finding Our Way: Rethinking Ethnocultural Relations in Canada* and, most recently, *Zoopolis: A Political Theory of Animal Rights* co-authored with Sue Donaldson (both are with Oxford University Press).

Guy Laforest's title is directeur général, École nationale d'administration publique (ÉNAP, Quebec). His main research areas are political theory and intellectual history in Canada and Quebec. He has published extensively. Among his publications are *Interpreting Quebec's Exile within the Federation* (Peter Lang) as well as *The Constitutions That Shaped Us* and *The Quebec Conference of 1864: Understanding the Emergence of the Canadian Federation* (with E. Brouillet and A.-G. Gagnon, both through McGill-Queen's University Press).

Samuel LaSelva is a professor of political science at the University of British Columbia. He is the author of *Canada and the Ethics of Constitutionalism: Identity, Destiny and Constitutional Faith* (McGill-Queen's University Press). He has published in the *Canadian Journal of Political Science, Review of Constitutional Studies*, and *BC Studies.*

Douglas Macdonald is a senior lecturer emeritus with the School of the Environment, University of Toronto. He is the author of *The Politics of Pollution: Why Canadians Are Failing Their Environment* and *Business and Environmental Politics in Canada*, which was awarded the Canadian Political Science Association's Donald Smiley Prize as the best book published that year on Canadian politics and government. He is the author of a number of peer-reviewed articles and professional reports on Canadian environmental politics and policy, including climate change policy. His recent book, *Carbon Province, Hydro Province: The Challenge of Canadian Energy and Climate Federalism* (University of Toronto Press, 2020), is based on research done over the past decade.

Alex Marland is a professor of political science at Memorial University of Newfoundland. He researches communication, marketing, and electioneering in Canadian politics and government. His book *Brand Command: Canadian Politics and Democracy in the Age of Message Control* (UBC Press) won the Donner Prize for best public policy book by a Canada.

Naiomi Walqwan Metallic is from the Listuguj Mi'gmaq First Nation in Gespe'gewa'gi. Naiomi W. Metallic is an assistant professor at the Schulich School of Law at Dalhousie University, where she holds the Chancellor's Chair in Aboriginal Law and Policy. She holds a BA (Dalhousie), an LLB (Dalhousie), an LLL (Ottawa), and an LLM (Osgoode). She was also a law clerk to Michel Bastarache of the Supreme Court of Canada in 2006–7. She has been named to the Best Lawyer in Canada® list in Aboriginal law since 2015 and was chosen for *Canadian Lawyer* magazine's 2018 Top 25 Most Influential Lawyers in Human Rights, Advocacy, and Criminal Law.

Éric Montpetit is a professor in the Political Science Department at the Université de Montréal and vice-dean at the Faculty of Arts and Sciences. His current research centres on the behaviour of policy actors (interest groups, civil servants, politicians, the media) and on the politics of scientific expertise in the context of government regulation-making. His work covers subject areas that include contaminated soil, biotechnology, energy, and climate change and has appeared in reputed public policy and political science journals, including *Policy Sciences*, the *Journal of Public Policy*, the *Journal of European Public Policy, Policy Studies Journal, Comparative Political Studies, Public Administration*, and *Political Studies*. His latest book, *In Defense of Pluralism: Policy Disagreement and Its Media Coverage*, was published by Cambridge University Press.

Jacquetta Newman is an associate professor at King's University. She is interested in what is now referred to as "governance" and the sort of politics that emerge out of the relationship between state and society. Her published research addresses themes relating to political sociology, social movements, political identities, comparative politics (in industrial states), women's politics and public policy, democratic structures and practices, and neo liberal feminism.

Michael Orsini is a professor in the School of Political Studies, University of Ottawa. From January to June 2016, he was Fulbright Visiting Research Chair at Vanderbilt University's Center for Medicine, Health, and Society. His main areas of research are in health politics and policy, as well as the role of social movements in policy processes. His substantive areas of interest include autism, HIV/AIDS, and illnesses that affect marginalized people. Professor Orsini is starting work on a project that explores the roles of emotions and stigma in three key policy fields, as well as a Canadian Institutes of Health Research-funded project on the impact of criminalization discourse on HIV/AIDS advocacy.

Martin Papillon is an associate professor and director of the Centre de recherche sur les politiques et le développement social in the Department of Political Science at the Université de Montréal. His academic work focuses on the intersection of Indigenous self-determination and Canadian federalism. He is interested in emerging dynamics of multilevel governance in the context of modern treaty implementation and in the transformative potential of the United Nations Declaration on the Rights of Indigenous Peoples in Canada, with a focus on the principle of free, prior, and informed consent. He co-edited a number of volumes on these topics, including *The State of the Federation: Aboriginal Multilevel Governance* (McGill-Queen's); *The Global Promise of Federalism* (University of Toronto Press); *Comparing Canada* (UBC Press); and *Les autochtones et le Quebec* (Presses de l'Université de Montréal).

Mireille Paquet is an associate professor at Concordia University and holds the Concordia University Research Chair on the Politics of Immigration. Her research focuses on immigration policy-making in Canada and in North America. She has published a number of journal articles and book chapters on immigration politics. She is the author of *Province-Building and the Federalization of Immigration in Canada* (University of Toronto Press) and co-edited *Citizenship as a Regime: Canadian and International Perspectives* (with N. Nagels and A.-C. Fourot, McGill-Queen's University Press).

Donald J. Savoie holds the Canada Research Chair in Public Administration and Governance at the Université de Moncton. He has published numerous books on public policy, public administration, and federalism and was awarded the Killam Prize in Social Sciences in 2015. His book *What Is Government Good At? A Canadian Answer* won the 2015 Donner Prize.

Laura Stephenson specializes in political behaviour, both Canadian and comparative. Her research is focused on understanding how institutions and context influence attitudes, electoral preferences, and engagement with politics.

A. Brian Tanguay is a professor of political science and a member of the North American Studies Program at Wilfrid Laurier University. His main research interests are Quebec and Ontario politics, political parties, and electoral reform. In 2003–4, he drafted the Law Commission of Canada's report, *Voting Counts: Electoral Reform for Canada*. He is the co-editor, with Alain-G. Gagnon, of *Canadian Parties in Transition* (several editions). Among his recent publications (co-authored with L.B. Stephenson) is "Ontario's Referendum on Proportional Representation," *IRPP Choices*.

Lori Turnbull joined Dalhousie University's Department of Political Science as a faculty member in July 2005. She teaches courses in introductory politics, Canadian parliamentary government, and pressure politics. Her major areas of research are Canadian parliamentary governance, political ethics, elections, electoral systems, and public engagement. Prof. Turnbull's work has been published in the *Canadian Public Administration* journal, the *Canadian Political Science Review*, the *Journal of Parliamentary and Political Law*, and *How Ottawa Spends*. Recently, she worked as a policy researcher for the Commission of Inquiry into Certain Allegations Respecting Business and Financial Dealings between Karlheinz Schreiber and the Right Honourable Brian Mulroney.

Debora VanNijnatten is a professor of political science and North American studies at Wilfrid Laurier University. She has a particular interest in Canada-US climate change cooperation as well as Canada's international climate policy. She is the co-author/co-editor of several books, including successive editions of *Canadian Environmental Politics and Policy* (Oxford University Press) and *Climate Change Policy in North America: Designing Integration in a Regional System* (University of Toronto Press), and she has authored numerous articles and book chapters that explore Canada's climate policy challenges.

Jennifer Wallner is an associate professor with the School of Political Studies at the University of Ottawa. Her research focuses on intergovernmental relations and public policy in a comparative context, with a particular emphasis on education policy, fiscal federalism, and institutions. While on sabbatical, she worked with the Privy Council Office in the Intergovernmental Affairs Secretariat. She has published multiple academic and policy papers, been a contributing co-editor of two books with UBC Press, and written a book on federalism and education policy in Canada published by the University of Toronto Press.

Graham Wilson has published several books and has authored numerous articles and chapters. His work has focused primarily on interest groups and their relationship with government and policy-making. He edited the *Oxford Handbook of Business and Government* (Oxford University Press), and he has published extensively on the relationship between bureaucrats and politicians. In 2012, Wilson published his newest book, *The Consequences of the Global Financial Crisis: The Rhetoric of Reform and Regulation* (with Wyn Grant), with Oxford University Press. The same year, Wilson was awarded the Ulrich Kloti Award for Lifetime Achievement from the Structure and Organization of Government Research Committee of the International Political Science Association.

PART ONE

Canadian Politics: Origins and Foundations

one

Understanding Canada's Origins: Federalism, Multiculturalism, and the Will to Live Together

SAMUEL V. LASELVA

> More than most other countries, Canada is a creation of human will. It has been called a "geographical absurdity," an "appendage of the United States," a "4,000-mile main street" with many bare stretches. Nevertheless this country has existed for a long time, because its people have never stopped willing that there be a Canada.
> – Royal Commission on Bilingualism and Biculturalism (1965)

Introduction: The Canadian Enigma

Canada has existed for a long time, but Canada is a difficult country to understand and also a difficult country to govern both in times of constitutional crisis and in periods of constitutional stability. Even if Canadians "have never stopped willing that there be a Canada," the nearly successful sovereignty referendum in Quebec and the Supreme Court secession reference suggest that Canada's continued existence cannot be taken for granted. The 1995 sovereignty referendum and the 1998 secession reference focused on Quebec and reveal its complex relationship to the rest of Canada, a relationship that is not fully nor easily encapsulated within Parliament's ambiguous and aspirational declaration in 2006 that the Québécois form a nation within a united Canada. The difficulties that confront Canadians are by no means confined to the French-English question. Aboriginal nationalism, with its demand for Aboriginal sovereignty and social justice, raises equally difficult questions as the Idle No More movement and the Final Report of the Truth and Reconciliation Commission illustrate. There are also multicultural groups, which – together with women, LGBTQ+ people, and those with disabilities – do not threaten the unity of Canada, but they seek to shape its identity, and their demands can conflict with those of other political actors. The failed Meech Lake and Charlottetown Constitutional Accords demonstrate that the very pluralism of Canada can sometimes result in "mosaic madness" and may yet compel Canadians to "look into the abyss" (Bibby 1990; Cairns 1997). When the focus shifts from mega-constitutional matters to issues like interprovincial trade or the Canadian welfare state or federal spending power, problems of disunity and fragmentation are just as evident, and Canada continues to be both a difficult country to understand and a difficult country to govern.

Consequently, Canada is often regarded as a "geographical absurdity" or even an "impossible country." Canada, it has been argued, "preserves nothing of value. It is literally nothing. It is the *absence* of a sense of identity, the *absence* of a common life" (Horowitz 1985, 363). When such a view is taken, Canada is regarded as a country without a future and Canadians are urged to begin the process of de-confederation. But not everyone favours the fragmentation of Canada or believes that it is inevitable, or supports the creation of regional and ethnic solitudes, or absorption into the United States. Many Canadians believe that Canada does preserve something of value and that the Canadian experiment differs from the American union. But why is Canada worth preserving? Historically, one of the most evocative expressions of Canadian distinctiveness has been the motto "True north, strong and free" (Russell 2017, 454). As a northern country, Canada was held to differ from the United States and to express unique character values. Canada's cold climate was also used to explain its adherence to British liberty and its rejection of American-style democracy (Berger 1966, 15). Just as evocative is the celebration of Canadian multiculturalism that often occupies pride of place in contemporary accounts of Canada's uniqueness. In his *Conversation with Canadians* (1972), Pierre Trudeau contrasted Canada with the American melting pot and insisted that a vigorous policy of multiculturalism formed the basis of fair play for all Canadians. Of course, Trudeau attached even greater significance to the Canadian Charter of Rights and Freedoms. In his *Memoirs*, he emphasized that his search for the Canadian identity "had led [him] to insist on the charter" (Trudeau 1993, 323).

However, the adoption of the Charter has not settled the most difficult questions about the Canadian identity. In fact, Charter patriotism has come into conflict with the other particularisms that define Canada, with the result that Canada has become an even more difficult country to govern and to understand. Trudeau believed that the Charter would provide Canadians with a new beginning and a strong foundation for the future. Yet Canada existed for a long time before the Charter was adopted in 1982, and Trudeau took too little account of this fact. The Canadian nation, a distinguished historian has written, "is fragile indeed, and one reason … might well be the lack of a history that binds Canadians together. It is not that we do not have such a history. It is simply that we have chosen not to remember it" (Granatstein 1998, xvii, xviii). Others, like Janet Ajzenstat, are more specific. They warn that "we have lost the Fathers' insight"; they pray that Canada will not "be wracked by the terrible passions that have inflicted such damage on European nations in the twentieth century"; and they hope "that our shortsightedness never catches up with us" (Ajzenstat 2007, xii, 109).

Indeed, not only do Canadians have a past, but their past has demonstrated their will to live together. If they assume, as Trudeau often did, that "the past is another country," they lose the opportunity to reflect more deeply on the distinctiveness of their country, the values it has come to represent, and the challenges that bedevil it. Canada may never become an easy country to govern, but it can become a less difficult country to understand.

Confederation and Canadian Federalist Theory

Unlike Canadians, Americans do not need to be told about the importance of their history; they revere their past and draw sustenance from it even in times of crisis. In the Gettysburg Address, delivered during the American Civil War, Abraham Lincoln prayed for a "new birth" of freedom so that government by the people would not perish (Current 1967, 284–5). But Lincoln began his address by invoking the Declaration of Independence and by remembering that the American founders had brought forth a new nation conceived in liberty and dedicated to equality. The paradox of Lincoln is that he was able to utter "the words that remade America" by appealing to the spirit of its most important founding document (Wills 1992, 120).

In contrast, no theme of Canadian history seems better established or more often retold than the failure of the original Macdonald constitution. In textbook accounts, the Confederation Settlement of 1867 is identified almost exclusively with John A. Macdonald and his failed dream of creating a highly centralized state that reduced the provinces to little more than administrative units and that conferred almost imperial powers on Ottawa. Where constitutional scholars diverged is on the reasons for the failure. Some blame the Judicial Committee of the Privy Council (JCPC) and believe that its decentralizing judicial decisions undermined the original understanding of Confederation. Others insist that Macdonald's vision was flawed from the outset because it underestimated the pluralism of Canada, a pluralism that initially manifested through a strong provincial rights movement, though it eventually incorporated Quebec's Quiet Revolution as well as the demands of new Canadians. If such accounts of Confederation are sound, then Canada's constitutional past is little more than a lesson in failure and, unlike American history, hardly worth remembering.

But there is more to the Constitutional Settlement of 1867 than Macdonald's understanding of it (Gwyn 2007, 5, 322–33). Nor is the failure of his vision tantamount to the defeat of Confederation. In the debates of 1865, Macdonald announced that he favoured a strong unitary state for

Canada because "it would be the best, the cheapest, the most vigorous, and the strongest system of government we could adopt" (Canada 1865, 29). Macdonald was, after all, a Tory and he had a Tory vision of Canada. As a Tory, he celebrated the British connection, admired the unlimited sovereignty of the British Parliament, and exalted the nation. "The nation," Donald Creighton wrote in his account of Macdonald's idea of union, "transcends the group, the class, or section" (Creighton 1972, 217). Macdonald dreamed of Canada as "a great nationality, commanding the respect of the world, able to hold our own against all opponents" (Canada 1865, 41). But even Macdonald had to admit that his dream of a Tory union was "impracticable." It was impractical, he said in the debates of 1865, because it did not gain the assent of Quebec, which feared that its nationality, language, religion, and code of law might be assailed in a legislative union. And even the Maritime provinces rejected the idea of a unitary state. As a result, Macdonald modified his views and accepted the project of a federal union. However, Macdonald still claimed victory: Canada would be a federal union, but the Parliament of Canada would have all the great powers of legislation as well as the residual power covering matters not enumerated in the 1867 Act. By so strengthening the central government, he insisted, "we make … the Confederation one people and one government" (Canada 1865, 41).

For Macdonald, the important contrast was with the United States and its federal experiment. Federalism is often regarded as an American invention. It is just as often praised for guaranteeing freedom. But in 1865, many Canadians viewed federalism with suspicion, partly because it was regarded as inconsistent with parliamentary institutions and partly because of its association with the American Civil War. In response, Macdonald's bold tactic was both to praise the United States Constitution and to insist that its framers "had commenced at the wrong end." They had made each state "a sovereignty in itself" and had conferred too limited powers on the general government. By so doing, they made "states' rights" the defining feature of their federation and prepared the way for the Civil War. Moreover, the American president, Macdonald added, was merely a party leader and incapable of representing the whole of the American people. In contrast, Canadian Confederation accepted the monarchical principle and elevated the sovereign above the rivalry of political parties. Confederation would also confer the power of criminal law on the central government, thereby correcting the American mistake of allowing every state to enact its own criminal code. It would establish lieutenant-governors for the provinces and create a unified judicial system controlled primarily by the central government. Macdonald even boasted that Canadian Confederation so successfully arranged the powers of government that, unlike the American union, it would eliminate "all conflict of jurisdiction and authority." By centralizing power rather than dispersing it, Confederation would create a new dominion of the north, one demonstrably superior to that of its southern neighbour because it solved the problems of federalism (Canada 1865, 33).

Such, in outline, was Macdonald's understanding of Confederation. Its importance is difficult to exaggerate. Canada's first century was, in constitutional terms, little more than an engagement with it. Moreover, its eventual failure made a second constitutional beginning almost inevitable. But why did the Macdonald constitution fail? Macdonald himself provided one answer. Less than two years after Confederation, he complained, "It is difficult to make the local Legislatures understand that their powers are not so great as they were before the Union." He then added, "In fact, the question that convulsed the United States and ended in Civil War, commonly known as the 'States' Rights' question, has already made its appearance in Canada" (Rogers 1933, 17–18). For Macdonald, it was the refusal of the provinces to accept the subordinate position assigned to them that shattered the original understanding of Confederation and, if pressed still further, would spell the failure of the Constitution.

Not only did the provinces press their demands, but the JCPC was often sympathetic to them, so much so that in 1937 it struck down much of Prime Minister Bennett's "New Deal" legislation. Critics of the JCPC believe that its decentralizing decisions were largely responsible for the failure of the Macdonald constitution, a failure that had severe economic and social consequences during the Great Depression of the 1930s. Its decisions also facilitated "province-building," which countered Macdonald's project of nation-building. Writing in 1979, Alan Cairns believed that province-building had produced "big governments" in Canada capable of embarking on policies usually reserved for sovereign nations. Province-building, he insisted, had turned the Canadian Constitution into "a lame-duck constitution." It had made Canadian federalism into a game similar to "eleven elephants in a maze" and just as self-defeating (Cairns [1979] 1988, 183, 188).

The defeat of the Macdonald constitution can also be explained in a way that does not privilege Macdonald's understanding of Confederation. In the debates of 1865, Macdonald's vision of Canada met with skepticism and even derision from critics of Confederation. Christopher Dunkin rejected Macdonald's boast that there would be no conflicts of jurisdiction and authority under Confederation. He not only accused Macdonald of failing to respect the distinction between a legislative and a federal union, he also predicted the early demise of Confederation. The allocation of powers under the proposed constitution, he said, would fuel quarrels rather than quell them. The Senate would not perform the functions assigned to it, and if lieutenant-governors acted to control provincial legislatures, they would provoke open resistance. Nor would judges appointed by the central government earn the confidence of the local legislatures. The provinces, he added, "cannot possibly work harmoniously together long; and so soon as they come into collision … the fabric is at an end" (Canada 1865, 487, 508, 530).

Dunkin was not alone in refusing to "prophesy smooth things" (Canada 1865, 543). Joseph Perrault warned that although French and English had come to a new world, they had brought their old hostilities with them. He recalled Lord Durham's assimilation proposals and complained that the real object of Confederation was, like Durham's, the obliteration of the French-Canadian nationality. He warned that French-Canadian patriots would defend their cultural heritage and predicted that racial tensions would disrupt Confederation (Canada 1865, 596, 600, 612). For the critics of Confederation, it was the very pluralism of Canada that rendered Macdonald's constitutional vision untenable. For them, the Macdonald constitution had failed even before it was adopted.

The story of Canada is a story of failure so long as Confederation is understood as Macdonald's attempt to find a remedy for "states' rights" and other errors of American federalism by creating a highly centralized Canadian state. But there is more to Confederation. Confederation was also intended as a solution to Canadian problems, and it was hardly achieved by Macdonald alone. "Canadians," wrote Carl J. Friedrich, "had a very special problem to deal with which found no parallel in the American experience: that was how to arrange a federal system that would satisfy their French speaking citizens" (Friedrich 1967, 60–1). In the debates of 1865, Dunkin surmised that "the two differences of language and faith … were the real reasons" for the supposed federal union, whose purpose was to meet a "probable clashing of races and creeds" (Canada 1865, 509). If French Canadians provided the "real" reason, the Maritime provinces were the "other" reason, for they too rejected Macdonald's initial plea for a unitary state based on their concern to preserve their local identities and distinct destinies. Not the spectre of the American Civil War but the deep pluralism of Canada was the problem that most engaged Canadians in 1867. Moreover, when Confederation is understood as a response to the pluralism of Canada, pride of place belongs not to Macdonald but to his political co-equal, George-Étienne Cartier. It was Cartier who, despite Macdonald's misgivings, insisted on significant autonomy for Quebec, and thereby guaranteed that Quebec and the other provinces would have exclusive and substantial powers of their own. Without him, Confederation would have remained a political dream.

In Cartier's understanding of it, Confederation represented a novel engagement with the pluralism of Canada, one that rejected both assimilation and cultural solitudes and envisaged the creation of a new political nationality (LaSelva 1996, 39–41, 156–60; Ajzenstat 2007, 88–109). In response to Lord Durham and other advocates of assimilation, Cartier insisted that the project of racial unity was not only utopian but impossible, because diversity was "the order of the physical world and of the moral world." He also rejected the creation of cultural solitudes and the belief that cultural peace was impossible without them. On the contrary, he insisted that the racial, cultural, and religious diversity of Canada was a benefit rather than otherwise. "We were of different races," he observed, "not for the purpose of warring against each other, but in order to emulate for the general welfare." Moreover, unlike Macdonald, Cartier was an unequivocal federalist; he believed that federalism, when responsive to cultural and local differences and combined with a suitable scheme of minority rights, made Canada possible. In his view, Canadian federalism did not presuppose the Canadian nation but created it. Confederation, he said, would bring into existence a new Canada and a new nationality, "a political nationality with which neither the national origin, nor the religion of any individual, would interfere" (Canada 1865, 60). While Macdonald worried about "states' rights" and the American Civil War, Cartier reflected on the pluralism of Canada and imagined a new kind of nationality. But Cartier died in 1873, and his understanding of Confederation was nearly forgotten. Macdonald lived until 1891 and struggled to realize his vision of Canada, only to witness the emergence of a strong provincial rights movement as well as the compact theory of Confederation, both of which countered his view of the Constitution and worked to defeat it.

A Second Beginning: Charter Canadians, Multicultural Citizenship, and Trudeau's Canada

In contemporary Canada, almost no one worries much about the fate of the Macdonald constitution. The past – and certainly Macdonald's idea of Tory union – almost does seem a different country, and the Canadian model is now increasingly identified with multiculturalism and the Charter of Rights (Igartua 2006, 1, 164–92). That such a change has occurred is due in no small measure to Pierre Elliott Trudeau. For more than a century, Canadians struggled with Macdonald's vision of Confederation. But with the adoption of the Charter of Rights and the other constitutional changes of 1982, they increasingly live in a world reshaped by the liberal universalism of Pierre Trudeau.

Trudeau's constitutional world is not Macdonald's. Philosophically, Macdonald was a Tory; Trudeau, a Liberal. Macdonald cherished the past and valued the British connection; Trudeau looked to the future and admired the American constitutional system. For Macdonald, sovereignty clearly resided in Parliament; for Trudeau, in the individual. Macdonald feared federalism and attempted to fetter it; Trudeau celebrated the pluralism that federalism enables and accommodates. Moreover, Trudeau also embraced multiculturalism, and multiculturalism bears no resemblance at all to Macdonald's idea of Tory union. If Canadians increasingly neglect their past, only part of the reason is the failure of the Macdonald constitution. Just as important is the extent to which Trudeau's vision of the future has captured the public imagination of Canadians. In Trudeau's constitutional vision, the past *is* another country and the future is a liberal utopia (LaSelva 2007, 11–18). But Trudeau's constitutional vision has not been embraced by all Canadians and it has not produced a more harmonious Canada. His vision has replaced Macdonald's, but Canadians struggle with it just as much.

Trudeau is an enigmatic figure, and revelations after his death about his youthful political activities have made him even more so (Nemni and Nemni 2006, 173–4, 266–73). A philosopher turned politician, he initially warned against fundamental constitutional change, but then, as prime minister, introduced the most important innovations since Confederation. His motto was "Reason over passion," yet he had passionate commitments to a reconstructed federalism, to a charter of human rights, and to Canada itself. In his earlier years, he rejected patriotism only to embrace it when he felt in his bones the vastness of his country. He regarded the Canadian mosaic as superior to the American melting pot and insisted that no such thing as a model citizen or ideal Canadian existed. For him, multiculturalism made Canada "a very special place" because it offered every Canadian "the opportunity to fulfil his own cultural instincts and to share those from other sources" (Trudeau 1972, 32). Moreover, he regarded Canadian federalism as a profound experiment of major proportions. If French and English cooperated to create a truly multinational state, Canada could serve as an example for the world on "how to govern their polyethnic populations with … justice and liberty." Such a Canada, he insisted, would have the best reason possible for rejecting "the lure of annexation to the United States" (Trudeau 1968b, 178–9). Trudeau's commitment was to a Canada that differed fundamentally from the United States, yet Trudeau also believed that Canada required a constitutionally entrenched Charter of Rights and Freedoms that, like the American Bill of Rights, secured the "primacy of the individual" and the sovereignty of "we the people" (Johnston 1990, 77). For Trudeau, such a Charter would secure "inalienable rights" and be an expression of the "purest liberalism." It would provide "a new beginning for the Canadian nation" and bring into existence a Canada with which all Canadians could identify (Trudeau 1990, 363).

Trudeau attached the utmost importance to his proposed Charter and pinned virtually all his hopes for Canada on it. Even before he entered politics, he strongly favoured the adoption of a Charter of Rights while warning Canadians that other constitutional changes, such as modification of the division of powers or a reformed Senate, were either not pressing or too perilous to undertake. When he became minister of justice, he called on both Ottawa and the provinces to restrict their powers in favour of the basic human values of all Canadians – political, legal, egalitarian, and linguistic. With such a constitutional innovation, he said, "we will be testing – and, hopefully establishing – the unity of Canada" (Trudeau 1968a, 54). Shortly after becoming prime minister, he renewed his call for an entrenched Charter and insisted that constitutional reform should take as its starting point the rights of the people rather than the prerogatives of government. The principal objective of constitutional reform, he said, should be to "construct a Canada in which the prime strength is ... in the people; a country which is knit [together] by persons confident of their individual rights wherever they might live; a Canada with which the people may identify" (Trudeau 1972, 91, 94).

After the Charter was adopted, but well before such incidents as the Maher Arar terrorism case exposed additional concerns about the protection of rights in Canada, Trudeau reminded Canadians of its crucial importance: it embodied a set of common values and ensured that all Canadians had the same rights. "All Canadians," he wrote, "are equal, and that equality flows from the Charter" (Johnston 1990, 34). In his *Memoirs* (1993), Trudeau even surmised that the adoption of the Charter had solved the long-standing problem of the Canadian identity.

In Trudeau's conception of it, the Charter embodies common values and guarantees the equality of Canadians, thereby expressing the identity of Canada and securing its unity. But the fundamental fact about Canada is its many-sided pluralism, and Trudeau knew as much. Why else did he sponsor official bilingualism and multiculturalism or, in a speech on Louis Riel, remind Canadians that a democracy is ultimately judged by the way the majority treats the minority? Trudeau went further still. "Canada's population distribution," he noted as early as 1971, "has now become so balanced as to deny any one racial or linguistic component an absolute majority. Every single person in Canada is now a member of a minority group" (Trudeau 1972, 32).

What, then, is to be done about minority rights? And how are minority rights to be reconciled with the equality of all Canadians? Trudeau provided an answer to these questions, and his answer is rooted in his commitment to liberalism. Trudeau said that because Canada was a mosaic rather than a melting pot, the Charter protected both individual rights and minority rights. In protecting the rights of minorities, however, the Charter sought, whenever possible and even in the case of the official languages, "to define rights exclusively as belonging to a person rather than a collectivity." Trudeau went on to say, "The spirit and substance of the Charter is to protect the individual against tyranny – not only that of the state but also any other to which the individual may be subjected by virtue of his belonging to a minority group" (Trudeau 1990, 365). Put in another way, the Charter treats all Canadians equally because it does not privilege minority rights but treats them as derived of individual rights. Had Trudeau's liberalism solved the problem of minority rights and created a Canada with which all Canadians could identify?

This is a difficult question. The answer can be partly gleaned from Trudeau's opposition to the 1987 Meech Lake Constitutional Accord, which had as its basic purpose the recognition of Quebec as a distinct society within Canada. Such recognition was deemed necessary partly because the government of Quebec regarded the Charter as unduly restrictive of its autonomy. The Accord was almost ratified, but eventually failed. In rejecting it, Trudeau both defended the Charter and reformulated his long-standing opposition to special status for Quebec. According to Trudeau, the Meech Lake Accord would require Canadians to "say goodbye to the dream of one Canada." He wrote, "For Canadians who dreamed of the Charter as a new beginning for Canada … where citizenship [is based on] commonly shared values, there is to be nothing left but tears" (Johnston 1990, 10). He felt that the spirit of the Meech Lake Accord conflicted with the spirit of the Charter and that special status *of any kind* for Quebec destroyed the dream of one Canada (Strayer 2013, 129–30). But such a position encounters a host of difficulties, not the least of which is the fact that the Confederation Settlement of 1867 accommodated Quebec and even used Quebec's distinctiveness to shape the Canadian federation. If Trudeau's vision of the Charter cannot accommodate a distinct Quebec, then his conception of minority rights is problematic: Trudeau's Canada is not a Canada with which all Canadians can identify (Laforest 2009, 252–60).

Trudeau's vision of Canada contains several unsettling ironies. His most basic objective was to delegitimate Québécois separatism by creating a truly pluralistic Canada with which Quebeckers and other Canadians could identify. The formula he initially embraced was "multiculturalism within a bilingual framework" (Trudeau [1971] 1985, 350). What his Charter adds to the formula is the theme of equality: Canadians are equal citizens in a multicultural society that exists within a bilingual framework. If the revised formula captures Trudeau's vision of Canada, then the first irony is that it does nothing at all to satisfy the historic demand of Quebec – the recognition of

Quebec's distinctiveness so that the French-Canadian homeland can flourish within Canada (Gagnon and Schwartz 2015, 244–5).

And even if Canada were to be conceived without Quebec, the formula remains untenable because it does not adequately accommodate Aboriginal Canadians. In its 1969 *Statement on Indian Policy*, the Trudeau government had asked Aboriginals to move off their reserves and become full members of Canada's multicultural society. They were told that different status for Aboriginal peoples was "a blind alley" (Government of Canada 1969, 5, 9; Trudeau 1972, 13–15). But Aboriginal peoples rejected this proposal. As Canada's First Nations with historic entitlements to self-government, they struggled as Indigenous peoples to have their rights recognized first by the courts and then again in sections 25 and 35 of the Constitution Act, 1982 (Borrows 2016, 103–27). Later, the Government of Canada apologized to Indigenous peoples for the treatment they received in residential schools, sponsored the Truth and Reconciliation Commission, and took other measures to counter the legacy of colonialism (Truth and Reconciliation Commission of Canada 2015, 369–71). Taken together, these facts created the second irony for Trudeau's vision of Canada. The process of accommodating Aboriginal peoples within Canada began only when their claim to special status was recognized; but if their claim was recognized (as I agree it should have been), then Quebec's claim to distinct status is and should be no less imperative and no less capable of explicit recognition and accommodation in the text of the constitution.

Trudeau said that the Charter protects minority rights; it would be more accurate to say that Charter patriotism brings minorities into conflict and thereby challenges the dream of one Canada. The Charter does not protect the right of French Canadians to a homeland within Canada or the explicit right of Aboriginal Canadians to self-government. But it does protect the rights of "Charter Canadians" (women, LGBTQ+ people, and those with disabilities) and multicultural citizens (new immigrants). In *The Charter Revolution and the Court Party,* Fred Morton and Rainer Knopff argue that the Charter has transformed the Canadian constitutional system by transferring power from legislatures to courts. Moreover, although Trudeau often portrayed the Charter as a victory for minority rights over majority tyranny, they insist that the Charter revolution is not about tyranny at all. Canada, they write, would remain a liberal democracy, "regardless of the outcome of such Charter issues as whether Sikhs in the RCMP are allowed to wear turbans or the legal definition of spouse is read to include homosexuals" (Morton and Knopff 2000, 36). For them, the most sinister aspect of Charter litigation is that it enables special interest groups to advance their agendas under the guise of inalienable rights and at the expense of democratic politics (see also Petter 2010, 218–27).

Will Kymlicka takes a more benign view than Morton and Knopff. In *Multicultural Citizenship*, he argues that the recognition of multicultural or polyethnic rights is nothing less than a requirement of liberal justice. Such minority rights deserve recognition, he insists, partly because individual choices are made in a cultural context and partly because to deny them is to unfairly privilege the dominant culture. But Kymlicka stops short of saying that the recognition of multicultural or polyethnic rights has made Canada an easier country to understand or govern. In fact, he believes that Canadians lack a theory of what holds their country together (Kymlicka 1995, 76, 109, 192). In a later essay, Kymlicka reflected again on Canada and insisted that the Canadian model of pluralism should be judged a success, at least when compared to European nations, where ethnic and cultural pluralism has frequently resulted in reactionary policies, secession, and even civil war (Kymlicka 2007, 69, 79–81).

As for Trudeau, with time he became less sanguine about Canada's future, as can be seen from his reflections on the Charlottetown Constitutional Accord of 1992, which provided him with a final opportunity to discuss minority rights and to explain his vision of Canada (English 2009, 624–7). If the Charter is, as he called it, the "people's package," then the Charlottetown Accord was the "Canada round." Its purpose was to recognize the rights of Charter Canadians and multicultural citizens alongside the right of Indigenous peoples to self-government and Quebec's status as a distinct society. The Accord also contained provisions for the reform of central institutions such as an elected Senate, outlined a comprehensive social and economic union for Canada, and modified aspects of the division of powers as well as the amending formula. When Canadians voted on the Accord, they rejected it, and Trudeau believed that they made the only choice possible. In a speech delivered before its defeat, Trudeau described the Accord as "a mess that deserves a big 'no.'" He insisted that the Accord was nothing less than a recipe for dictatorship and a prelude to civil war because it undermined equality, established a hierarchy among citizens, and privileged collective rights over individual rights. Moreover, he reminded Canadians that his own constitutional vision was based on inalienable rights, and he reiterated his admiration for the American Constitution. He urged Canadians to read Madison's *Federalist Paper* No. 10, informed them that the American Supreme Court had been established to defend individual rights, and reminded them that the American system had "worked out well" (Trudeau 1992, 57–8, 44, 47–8). Trudeau regarded the Charlottetown Accord as such a mess that it almost drove him to abandon the Canadian mosaic and embrace the American model.

The Will to Live Together: Pluralism and the Canadian Constitution

What followed the defeat of the Charlottetown Accord was a near successful sovereignty referendum in Quebec and then a landmark reference case in the Supreme Court on the secession question and the breakup of Canada. The Secession Reference is now part of Canadian constitutional history, but it also has an enduring and practical relevance because of the fundamental constitutional principles that the Supreme Court announced in it. In the Secession Reference, the most immediate and pressing question was whether or not Quebec had a unilateral right of secession under the Canadian Constitution. The Supreme Court ruled that Quebec had no such right, but it also insisted on the duty of all concerned parties to negotiate constitutional change, including the possible dissolution of Canada. The federalism principle, together with the democratic principle, the Court held, "dictates that the clear repudiation of the existing constitutional order ... would give rise to a reciprocal obligation on all parties to Confederation to negotiate constitutional changes" (Supreme Court of Canada 1998, 424).

The Court's ruling is important, partly because it denies that secession is purely a political matter and brings it within the pale of the Constitution. It is also important for a different reason. To arrive at its decision, the Court had to analyze the Canadian Constitution, but instead of adopting a narrow or legalistic approach, it attempted to uncover nothing less than the Constitution's "internal architecture" and its fundamental principles. In fact, the Court identified four such principles: federalism, democracy, constitutionalism and the rule of law, and respect for minorities. The Court insisted that these four principles of Canadian constitutionalism were as new as the Charter and as old as Confederation (Supreme Court of Canada 1998, 424, 410, 403). The Court's opinion is much more than a discussion of the secession question. It is also an innovative exploration of the Canadian constitution and the pluralism of Canada.

In the Secession Reference, the Court quietly corrected several widespread fallacies of Canadian constitutionalism and attempted to replace them with sounder positions. The first fallacy did not originate with Trudeau but he best exemplifies it. Trudeau never tired of insisting that the Charter provided a new beginning for the Canadian people. Others have described Canada before the advent of the Charter as a "lost constitutional world" (Cairns 1995, 97). The Court did not deny the importance of the Charter or underestimate the changes that had come with it. The Court recognized that the Charter significantly restricted Parliament and the provincial legislatures while considerably enhancing the authority of the judicial branch. But it also insisted that, in minority rights, the Charter represented a continuance of Canada's constitutional past rather than a break with it. "Although Canada's record of upholding the rights of minorities is not a spotless one," the Court wrote, "that goal is one towards which Canadians have been striving since Confederation, and the process has not been without successes." The Court insisted that even the "recent and arduous" achievement of Indigenous rights was "consistent with this long tradition of respect for minorities, which is at least as old as Canada itself" (Supreme Court of Canada 1998, 422). In the opinion of the Court, the goal of protecting minority rights did not suddenly emerge with the adoption of the Charter but was an integral part of the Confederation Settlement of 1867 and a defining feature of the Canadian identity.

The second fallacy corrected by the Court also relates to Confederation and, in particular, Macdonald's Tory interpretation. When the focus is on Macdonald, the emphasis is on the unitary features of the Canadian Constitution and the dream of a Tory union. What is remembered is the desire of the Fathers of Confederation to create a constitution similar in principle to that of the United Kingdom, and it is almost forgotten that, in the very same preamble to the Constitution, they first expressed their desire to be federally united. Canada becomes lost in the British connection, and the Canadian identity becomes almost impossible to comprehend. The Court did not so much deny Macdonald's influence as largely ignore it and draw attention instead to the importance of Cartier and his goal of creating a Canadian federal state that solved Canadian problems. The Court quoted at length Cartier's belief that Canadians had come together to contribute to the common welfare and to create a new political nationality with which neither the national origins nor the religion of any individual would interfere. Far from regarding federalism as an aberrant or incidental feature of the Canadian Constitution, the Court insisted that "the significance of the adoption of a federal form of government cannot be exaggerated." Federalism was the "lodestar" of the Constitution. The federal-provincial division of powers was "a legal recognition of the diversity that existed among the initial members of Confederation, and manifested a concern to accommodate that diversity within a single nation" (Supreme Court of Canada 1998, 405, 412, 407).

By thus focusing on Cartier's vision of federalism and Canada, the Court reinterpreted Confederation and revealed its significance as the foundational event of Canadian constitutionalism and the defining moment in the evolution of Canadian pluralism. When so interpreted, Confederation is not a lost constitutional world, nor is it part of a past that is another country. Macdonald's idea of a Tory union may be a failed constitutional experiment, but Cartier's vision of Canada has yet to be achieved or even fully understood.

For Cartier, the existence of Canada represented the will of Canadians to live together under a common political nationality that presupposed mutual obligations and collective goals but did not require them to submerge their allegiances and identities in a monolithic and all-embracing nationalism. Canadian federalism, with its scheme of minority rights, allowed multiple loyalties and multiple identities to flourish; it thereby enabled Canadians both to live together and to live apart in one country.

Conclusion: Understanding Canada

To understand Canada it is necessary to comprehend the challenges that confront Canadians and the values that have ground the Canadian experiment at least since Confederation and possibly, though very tentatively, as early as the Royal Proclamation of 1763 or the Quebec Act of 1774. For Canadians, the most basic challenge is to come to terms with their own diversity. Writing in 1946, W.L. Morton insisted that "the Canadian state cannot be devoted to absolute nationalism [because] the two nationalities and the four sections [regions] of Canada forbid it" (Morton [1946] 1967, 49). Contemporary Canada is even more pluralistic, because it now also contains self-governing territories as well as provinces, multicultural citizens and Charter Canadians, French- and English-speaking Canadians as well as Aboriginal and Québécois nationalists.

For some Canadians, this explosion of pluralism has called the long-term viability of Canada into question; at the very least, it has made Canada an even more difficult country to govern. Other Canadians seek to reimagine Canada. They imagine a three-nations Canada composed of English Canada, Quebec, and Indigenous peoples. Or, believing that strong fences make for good neighbours, they have called for the creation of a more autonomous Quebec, as well as sovereign Indigenous nations within a highly decentralized Canada. Some also concentrate on articulating a theory of multicultural justice and redesigning the Canadian state to meet its quite different requirements. Reflecting on the explosion of pluralism, Robert Fulford has called the country a postmodern dominion and has insisted that it can be best understood as a postmodern state. The key to postmodernism, he suggests, is the absence of a master narrative and the questioning of any notion of a coherent, stable, autonomous identity (Fulford 1993, 118). "What," he asks, "could be more Canadian than that?"

But Canada is not merely an ever-changing association of particularisms. Its very existence presupposes values that are seldom made explicit or fully understood (LaSelva 2017, 1075–9). In *Lament for a Nation*, George Grant insisted that Canada was a country without a future because its foundational values conflicted with modernity. "To be a Canadian," he said, "was to build a more ordered and stable society than the liberal experiment in the United States." Grant identified Canada with the values of British conservatism; he also insisted that Canada could not survive the encounter with technological progress and the American dream. For Grant, modernity meant the disappearance of local cultures and the emergence of an homogeneous universal state centred on the American empire (Grant [1965] 1970, 4, x, 54).

Five decades after Grant wrote his book, a world state has not appeared, local cultures flourished, and Canada has not been absorbed into the United States. Grant did not simply fail to predict the future; he also misunderstood Canada's past and foundational values. Grant identified Canada with Macdonald's idea of a Tory union, yet it was Cartier's rejection of cultural assimilation and his faith in a new kind of political nationality that grounded the Canadian experiment (Smiley 1967). Macdonald identified Canada with order and stability; Cartier viewed it in terms of mutual recognition, the cooperative virtues, and the many faces of amity or fraternity. Cartier's vision is deeply rooted in Canada's past, but it also speaks to the complex issue of mutual recognition that confronts Canadians as they attempt to come to terms with an Aboriginal Truth and Reconciliation Commission, new experiments in Indigenous self-government, demands for even more provincial autonomy and decentralized federalism, and the multicultural anxiety that non-Western ways of life can create, not only for Quebec but for all of Canada.

Canada may yet disappear, if Canadians fail to overcome the limitations inherent in Trudeau's constitutional vision or if they experience a failure of political will to remain together in the face of new challenges of diversity. If constitutional pluralism combined with federal comity, Michael Ignatieff writes, "can't work in my Canada, it probably can't work anywhere" (Ignatieff 1993, 147). In a postmodern world increasingly characterized by aggressive nationalisms and competing multicultural identities, the fate of the Canadian experiment concerns more than just Canadians.

References and Suggested Readings

Ajzenstat, Janet. 2007. *The Canadian Founding: John Locke and Parliament.* Montreal and Kingston: McGill-Queen's University Press.

Bailyn, Bernard. 1967. *The Ideological Origins of the American Revolution.* Cambridge, MA: Harvard University Press.

Berger, Carl. 1966. "The True North Strong and Free." In *Nationalism in Canada*, edited by Peter Russell, 3–26. Toronto: McGraw-Hill.

Bibby, Reginald W. 1990. *Mosaic Madness.* Toronto: Stoddart.

Bissoondath, Neil. 1994. *Selling Illusions: The Cult of Multiculturalism in Canada.* Toronto: Penguin.

Borrows, John. 2016. *Freedom and Indigenous Constitutionalism*. Toronto: University of Toronto Press.

Cairns, Alan C. [1979] 1988. "The Other Crisis of Canadian Federalism." In *Constitution, Government and Society in Canada*, 171–91. Toronto: McClelland and Stewart.

———. 1995. "The Constitutional World We Have Lost." In *Reconfigurations*, 97–118. Toronto: McClelland and Stewart.

———. 1997. *Looking into the Abyss*. Ottawa: C.D. Howe Institute.

Canada. 1865. *Parliamentary Debates on the Subject of the Confederation of British North American Provinces*. Quebec: Hunter, Rose. Photographically reproduced, 1951. Ottawa: King's Printer.

Cook, Ramsay. 1969. *Provincial Autonomy, Minority Rights and the Compact Theory, 1867–1921*. Ottawa: Information Canada.

Creighton, Donald. 1972. *Towards the Discovery of Canada*. Toronto: Palgrave Macmillan.

Current, Richard N., ed. 1967. *The Political Thought of Abraham Lincoln*. Indianapolis: Bobbs-Merrill.

English, John. 2009. *Just Watch Me: The Life of Pierre Elliott Trudeau 1968–2000*. Toronto: Knopf.

Friedrich, Carl J. 1967. *The Impact of American Constitutionalism Abroad*. Boston: Boston University Press.

Fulford, Robert. 1993. "A Post-Modern Dominion: The Changing Nature of Canadian Citizenship." In *Belonging*, edited by William A. Kaplan, 104–19. Montreal and Kingston: McGill-Queen's University Press.

Gagnon, Alain-G., and Alex Schwartz. 2015. "Canadian Federalism since Patriation: Advancing a Federalism of Empowerment." In *Patriation and Its Consequences*, edited by Lois Harder and Steve Patten, 244–66. Vancouver: UBC Press.

Government of Canada. 1969. *Statement on Indian Policy, 1969*. Ottawa: Queen's Printer.

Granatstein, J.L. 1998. *Who Killed Canadian History?* Toronto: Harper Collins.

Grant, George. [1965] 1970. *Lament for a Nation: The Defeat of Canadian Nationalism*. Toronto: McClelland and Stewart.

Gwyn, Richard. 2007. *John A.: The Man Who Made Us*. Vol. 1 of *The Life and Times of John A. Macdonald, 1815–1867*. Toronto: Random House Canada.

Horowitz, Gad. 1985. "Mosaics and Identity." In *Canadian Political Thought*, edited by H.D. Forbes, 359–64. Toronto: Oxford University Press.

Igartua, Jose E. 2006. *The Other Quiet Revolution: National Identities in English Canada, 1945–71*. Vancouver: UBC Press.

Ignatieff, Michael. 1993. *Blood and Belonging: Journeys into the New Nationalism*. Toronto: Penguin.

Johnston, Donald, ed. 1990. *Pierre Trudeau Speaks Out on Meech Lake*. Toronto: General Paperbacks.

Kymlicka, Will. 1995. *Multicultural Citizenship*. Oxford: Clarendon.

———. 2007. "The Canadian Model of Multiculturalism in a Comparative Perspective." In *Multiculturalism and the Canadian Constitution*, edited by Stephen Tierney, 61–90. Vancouver: UBC Press.

Laforest, Guy. 1995. *Trudeau and the End of a Canadian Dream*. Montreal and Kingston: McGill-Queen's University Press.

———. 2009. "The Internal Exile of Quebecers in the Canada of the Charter." In *Contested Constitutionalism*, edited by James B. Kelly and Christopher P. Manfredi, 251–62. Vancouver: UBC Press.

LaSelva, Samuel V. 1996. *The Moral Foundations of Canadian Federalism: Paradoxes, Achievements and Tragedies of Nationhood*. Montreal and Kingston: McGill-Queen's University Press.

———. 2007. "To Begin the World Anew: Pierre Trudeau's Dream and George Grant's Canada." *Supreme Court Law Review* 36 (2): 1–30.

———. 2017. "The Canadian Charter, the British Connection, and the Americanization Thesis." *Canadian Journal of Political Science* 50: 1061–81.

McPherson, James M. 1991. *Abraham Lincoln and the Second American Revolution.* New York: Oxford University Press.

Morton, F.L., and Rainer Knopff. 2000. *The Charter Revolution and the Court Party.* Toronto: Broadview.

Morton, W.L. [1946] 1967. "Clio in Canada: The Interpretation of Canadian History." In *Approaches to Canadian History*, edited by Carl Berger, 42–9. Toronto: University of Toronto Press.

Nemni, Max, and Monigue Nemni. 2006. *Young Trudeau: Son of Quebec, Father of Canada, 1919–1944.* Toronto: McClelland and Stewart.

Petter, Andrew. 2010. *The Politics of the Charter.* Toronto: University of Toronto Press.

Rogers, Norman McL. 1933. "The Genesis of Provincial Rights." *Canadian Historical Review* 14: 9–23.

Royal Commission on Bilingualism and Biculturalism. 1965. *Preliminary Report of the Royal Commission on Bilingualism and Biculturalism.* Ottawa: Queen's Printer.

Russell, Peter. 2017. *Canada's Odyssey: A Country Based on Incomplete Conquests.* Toronto: University of Toronto Press.

Smiley, Donald V. 1967. *The Canadian Political Nationality.* Toronto: Methuen.

Strayer, Barry L. 2013. *Canada's Constitutional Revolution.* Edmonton: University of Alberta Press.

Supreme Court of Canada. 1998. Reference re Secession of Quebec 161 DLR (4th) 385.

Sweeney, Alastair. 1976. *George-Étienne Cartier.* Toronto: McClelland and Stewart.

Taylor, Charles. 1993. *Reconciling the Solitudes: Essays on Canadian Federalism and Nationalism.* Montreal and Kingston: McGill-Queen's University Press.

Trudeau, Pierre Elliott. 1968a. *A Canadian Charter of Human Rights.* Ottawa: Queen's Printer.

———. 1968b. *Federalism and the French Canadians.* Toronto: Palgrave Macmillan.

———. [1971] 1985. "Statement on Multiculturalism." In *Canadian Political Thought*, edited by Hugh Donald Forbes, 349–51. Toronto: Oxford University Press.

———. 1972. *Conversation with Canadians.* Toronto: University of Toronto Press.

———. 1990. "The Values of a Just Society." In *Towards a Just Society*, edited by Thomas S. Axworthy and Pierre Elliott Trudeau, 357–85. Markham, ON: Penguin.

———. 1992. *A Mess That Deserves a Big NO.* Toronto: Robert Davies.

———. 1993. *Memoirs.* Toronto: McClelland and Stewart.

Truth and Reconciliation Commission of Canada. 2015. *Final Report: Honouring the Truth, Reconciling the Future.* Toronto: James Lorimer.

Waite, Peter. 1962. *The Life and Times of Confederation.* Toronto: University of Toronto Press.

Wills, Garry. 1992. *Lincoln at Gettysburg: The Words That Remade America.* New York: Simon & Schuster.

two
The Canadian Political Regime from a Quebec Perspective[1]

GUY LAFOREST AND ALAIN-G. GAGNON

Introduction

At the international level, there is increasing interest in the political systems of Canada and Quebec because of their relevance in a world where the stakes related to the diversity of populations are growing, but also because of the stability and good management of Canadian institutions, not to mention the contrast with the United States in the time of Trump. In the era of digital technology, new social media, and politics as entertainment, interest in Canadian politics grew in 2015 with the arrival in power of Justin Trudeau, who charmed many people around the world with his mastery of the new media and his discourse on openness to diversity (Trudeau 2015). The uniqueness of the Canadian-Quebec experience comes from the fact that history has led them to integrate many layers of deep diversity: territorially bounded minority nations within Canada (Quebec, the Inuit, and Acadia); a "homeland minority" within Quebec (Canadian anglophones); immigrant populations seeking a more inclusive citizenship through multiculturalism (à la canadienne) or interculturalism (à la québécoise); and Indigenous peoples engaged in reconstructing their nations and on a quest for self-government. As a result, the most up-to-date work on plural identities, federalism, and citizenship is subjecting the developments in the Canada-Quebec laboratory to careful scrutiny (Gagnon 2014, 129; Gagnon and Keating 2012).

In this chapter, we begin by suggesting a number of answers to questions on the nature and principal elements of Canada's political identity. Though we will provide our own answer, we will also consider the views of important players in Canada's political and intellectual life. Next, we will proceed with an overview of key historical events (see the annex at the end of the chapter), focusing on the theme of foundation. In conclusion, we will offer an interpretation of the conflict between Canadian and Quebec nation-building (Gagnon and Iacovino 2007), which has been the primary dividing line in Canadian politics since World War II.

The Canadian Political Identity

Canada, encompassing ten million square kilometres, is an imposing country in geographical terms. Yet for its English-speaking population (and particularly its central Canadian establishment concentrated in the Toronto-Ottawa-Montreal corridor) this immense land mass shelters a vulnerable nation, one that has been obsessed with its relationship with (and defencelessness against) the United States of America, the greatest power in history. Having the United States next door has always meant peril looming over the creation of a distinct Canadian identity. In the mid-1960s, George Grant's reflections in *Lament for a Nation: The Defeat of Canadian Nationalism* reveal a visceral fear in the face of its domineering neighbour. Domestically, over the last fifty years, the sovereigntist threat emanating from Quebec has been the only real danger to preservation of territorial integrity. Twice, first in May 1980 and then even more significantly in October 1995, referendums on sovereignty held by the government of Quebec shook Canada to its very foundations. Already under Stephen Harper's majority government (2011–15), and perhaps even more so after Justin Trudeau arrived to power, the threat of Quebec secession has been fading as a priority concern in Canadian politics, yielding to the more broadly encompassing problem of diversity and the renewal of nation-to-nation partnerships with Indigenous peoples.

As an initial overview of Canadian political identity, we will look to the Supreme Court of Canada. In 1998, in its landmark opinion in Reference re Secession of Québec, Canada's highest court identified four principles that are the political-normative foundations of the Canadian constitutional edifice: federalism, democracy, constitutionalism[2] and the rule of law, and respect for minority rights. By placing federalism first in its list, the Supreme Court clearly assigned to it the leading role in Canada's political-constitutional architecture, although we think that this was more of a pious wish for the future than an accurate description of the past. While the Court's opinion is now precedent, it is still possible to criticize it in a "free and democratic society," an expression that is also found in the first section of the Canadian Charter of Rights and Freedoms.

Certainly, for its entire existence as a country, Canada has been a *federal* regime in which the powers and competencies enshrined in its Constitution are divided between the central (federal) government and the member states (provinces) of the federation. It is also a *democratic* regime in which citizens enjoy political rights, including those that require elections in a representative system, and the principle of political equality inscribed in the right to vote. Canada is also a constitutional monarchy in which sovereignty is shared between Parliament, the Constitution (as interpreted by the courts), and the residual prerogatives of the Crown, which in modern times have been inherited by the prime minister. This last characteristic is found in the third principle identified by the Supreme Court: constitutionalism and the rule of law. A constitutionally limited monarchy in the British tradition, Canada is also defined by its respect for the principle of the rule of law. That principle places it in the category of democratic states in the world that adhere to the main political tenets of liberalism, in which the empire of law provides a framework for and limits the authority of governments so as to provide protection for individual rights and equality among citizens. In its articulation of the underlying principles that define the Canadian political system, particularly the primacy given to the principle of respect for minority rights, the Supreme Court has increased Canada's reputation as a champion of diversity in the world. Justin Trudeau reinforces that reputation when he declares, as he often does, that it is in its diversity, precisely, that Canada's strength lies.

When Canadian diplomats go abroad, they take with them the official "portrait" of the country that is quite similar to that drawn by the Supreme Court: a constitutional monarchy, representative liberal democracy, and federal parliamentary regime; and an independent, bilingual, multicultural nation-state. But where does Quebec fit into this Canadian political identity? The only majority French-speaking province (over 80 per cent of Quebecers are of French-speaking or French-Canadian heritage, and 96 per cent of the province's 8.4 million inhabitants speak French), Quebec has made a substantial contribution to Canada's unique configuration. While Canada may be considered to be in the vanguard of a new type of civilization open to diversity and plural identities, it can be argued that it owes this distinction to Quebec (Kymlicka 1998). In 1971, Canada became the first country to embrace multiculturalism, a policy that Pierre Trudeau's government "twinned" with institutional bilingualism (adopted in 1969 and updated in 1988). These policies were a means to develop rules for living together for two linguistic and cultural communities, one English-speaking and the other French-speaking.

Some nineteen years ago, Michael Ignatieff (later leader of the federal Liberal Party), tried to identify how the panoply of rights that we find in Canada made the country a unique legal environment in the family of liberal democratic states. He argued that it was due to a combination of four types of rights: liberal rights with respect to moral issues, such as abortion; social-democratic entitlements, as seen in programs for redistribution of wealth to less advantaged communities and individuals; collective rights for certain groups; and, lastly, the possibility – tested in two Quebec referendums – that a member state could leave the federation in a legal and peaceful manner (Ignatieff 2001, 25–6). A major contributor to the evolution of this unique political-legal scheme was political pressure exerted by Quebec, the nature of the shared social values and public culture in that province, and the key role played by its political actors, federally and provincially. Yet, and from a Quebec perspective this is the dark side of Canadian politics, the country has still not managed to state in its Constitution that Quebec – as a people, nation, distinct society, minority nation, autonomous political community (words for expressing it have not been lacking) – is a political and cultural entity different from the rest of the country, and that this difference has major political and legal consequences. The resolution passed by the House of Commons, in November 2006, that Quebecers constitute a nation within a united Canada has little political or legal weight. To properly understand Canada, we cannot simply close our eyes to the historical experiences of Quebec.

While Canada may be obsessed by its relationship with the United States, Quebec suffers from an obsession with demographics and anxiety over its francophone identity, which manifests itself in a sometimes melancholic nationalism over the fact that it is the only European offspring in the Americas that has not become independent (Bouchard 2000). To begin with, Quebec is a demographic miracle. From Napoleonic times to today, the population of France has grown from 25 to 67 million inhabitants. During that same period, Quebec has seen its population explode from a mere 70,000 to 8.4 million. A Catholic, conservative, rural society that still had inordinately huge families in 1920, Quebec needed only two generations to go through a sudden and rather late metamorphosis that turned it into a modern secular society. It turned its back on the Catholic Church, became urbanized and open to all modern social trends and innovations, and fell from top to bottom in birth rates (Grégoire, Montigny, and Rivest 2016). And to think that sociologists called this a Quiet Revolution! The expression is more accurately used to refer to the government's institutional "catching up" (*rattrapage*) and the reconfiguration of French-Canadian nationalism that occurred between 1960 and 1970. Because this provincial government, urged on by widespread nationalist mobilization within the population, rapidly took over education, health care, social services, and substantial swaths of the economy (most notably with the creation of Hydro-Québec and the nationalization of electricity). In this sense, the expression *nation without a state* (Guibernau 1999) that is often applied to minority nations in the European context is not an accurate description of Quebec's situation.[3] The division of powers between the orders of government in the Canadian federation gave Quebec a significant margin of autonomy that its political leaders had left in the hands of the church and charities until the second half of the twentieth century. The dynamic of rapid change that overtook this social arrangement was spurred on by the huge baby boom cohort, which was – ideologically speaking – fuelled by the spread of nationalism associated with the world-wide decolonization movement of the post–World War II period (Monière 2001; Keating 2001a). It was this suddenly modern, innovative Quebec (as symbolized by the World Exposition in Montreal in 1967) that fostered both a strong independentist movement and the political and identity changes that gave birth to contemporary Canada (Ralston Saul 1997).

In its reconstruction of the foundational principles of Canada's political-constitutional edifice, the Supreme Court emphasized what it perceived to be the country's key normative elements, thereby producing a highly idealized narrative of Canadian history (Racine 2012, 143). Our approach, which takes into consideration the geopolitical framework and political conflict dynamics, is somewhat different. We will conclude this section by identifying four interrelated dimensions of Canadian politics: the central role of the state, the British inheritance, the federal principle, and Quebec's defining contribution to Canadian diversity.

The State's Inescapable Key Role

In Canada's history, the state has always been a strong identity marker, initially to achieve emancipation from London's control, and then, most importantly, in order to differentiate Canada from its American neighbour. While the American dream is constructed on extreme individualism and deep distrust of the state, in a more Tory Canada, the ideal has always been clothed as a benevolent protector of the community. In the United States, the founding texts enshrine the individualist aspirations of protection of life, liberty, and the pursuit of happiness. In Canada, as early as 1867, the federal dominion was established to promote peace, order, and good government (Brouillet, Gagnon, and Laforest 2018). The tone was set. To build and develop a distinct autonomous country north of the United States, it has been necessary to count on the willingness of a number of regional communities strung out along an east-west axis. This has been implemented and renewed through five major national policies: the construction of the railroads in the nineteenth century; the establishment of a tariff wall to protect and promote national economic integration; the immigration and settlement policy to populate western Canada; the establishment of a welfare state after World War II (in particular with respect to the equalization principle); and, closer to us in 1982, the advent of the Canadian Charter of Rights and Freedoms. In Canada, the central government's tutelary role has taken on a special colour in the protection of minority communities: Catholics and Protestants, the Anglo-Quebecer minority, official language minorities across Canada, Aboriginal peoples, and groups attached to the multicultural heritage of the country.

The Historical Importance and Contemporary Significance of Canada's British Heritage

Canada is a country with a "strong state" backbone. However, after 1867, it needed more than a century to really assert its independence from the British imperial motherland. That spirit of moderation dominated in the British manner of merging parliamentary supremacy into a regime retaining strong monarchical symbolism and continuing to attribute limited but very real legislative and executive powers to those who exercised the authority of the Crown. That heritage thus contributed an anti-radicalist aspect to the political culture of Canada, distinguishing it from both France and the United States. The history of Canada's movement towards autonomy can be described as "quiet decolonization." That spirit also characterized constitutional transformation. In the European continental tradition, especially in France, changing the constitution means moving into a new house after demolishing the old one. With its British heritage, Canada acts differently. In Canada, constitutional engineering involves renovation of the old house, with some recycling of materials. The state was strong, first and foremost, in order to remain distinct from the United States and to develop a subcontinent, but its British filiation also ensured that it would be a limited liberal state. The principle British customs and political traditions are referred to as constitutional conventions. They include the rule of law, constitutional monarchy limited by parliamentary supremacy, and a responsible government in which the head of the government is the leader of the political party with the majority in the House of Commons. Adherence to these conventions protected Canada from state authoritarianism long before the Canadian Charter of Rights and Freedoms came into effect.

There would be an element lacking in our understanding of Canadian politics if we failed to establish a link between British heritage and the political culture of the Canadian public service. Throughout the long gestation of the Canadian state, the predominantly English-speaking federal public service maintained close contact with the British imperial bureaucracy. This is another aspect of the strong state in Canadian history: a competent central administrative elite devoted to British traditions, cultivating the virtues of public service and considering itself naturally superior to its counterparts working in the provincial capitals. In effect, the federal government bureaucracy headquartered in Ottawa transferred to itself the presumption of superiority that long characterized the British imperial bureaucracy that preceded it (Owram 1986). This often overlooked aspect of Canadian federalism belongs not only to the sphere of political culture; it retains all of its relevance in the dynamic of intergovernmental relations at work in Canada today.

The Federal Principle: Autonomy and Non-Subordination of Powers

We agree with the Supreme Court of Canada's 1998 opinion, according to which federalism is a key pillar of Canada's political identity. However, if we take into account the totality of the Canadian historical and political experience, it is difficult to abstract from two other fundamental dimensions: statism and the British heritage. The landmark work by Donald Smiley (1987) has already established the limits of federalism's importance during the period from the emergence of the Dominion of Canada in 1867 to the advent of a new constitutional order in 1982. More recently, the work of jurist José Woehrling and by Eugénie Brouillet and Jean Leclair (even though they belong to different schools of interpretation) shares the same vision of the Supreme Court's reluctance in its constitutional jurisprudence to give the federal principle decisive importance in a consistent, ongoing manner (Brouillet 2005; Woehrling 2009; Leclair 2007).

Most Quebecers have placed more importance on federalism in their understanding of Canada than have the inhabitants of the other Canadian provinces and territories. However, it would be perfectly unreasonable to think that Quebec French-speakers (considered to be living in Lower Canada during the constitutional regime of 1791 and in Canada East after 1840) were alone in their desire for a federal union at the time of the discussions among the North American British colonies in the 1860s (Laforest, Brouillet, Gagnon, and Tanguay 2015; Brouillet, Gagnon, and Laforest 2018). In the Maritime provinces of Charles Tupper and in the Ontario of George Brown, a strong autonomy current, wishing to preserve both the freedom of those political communities and their distinct identity, joined forces with George-Étienne Cartier and his allies in Canada East in favour of a federal approach. It is just as true that in Quebec, the plan for a Canadian federal union was presented as a form of sovereignty-association. While it is accurate to think, as Marie Bernard-Meunier (2007) wrote, that federalism must reconcile the two fundamental needs of remaining oneself and uniting, it is just as fair to recognize that, at that key moment, it was the desire to remain oneself that was the dominant sentiment in Quebec. Elsewhere in British North America, it was the desire to unite that was most often as strong as the desire to remain oneself. Perhaps we must see in this one of the very first explanations for political leaders, intellectuals, and academics studying or practising federalism in Quebec tending to give federalism more moral, normative, and existential importance than their counterparts elsewhere in Canada. This has recently been shown convincingly by François Rocher. In Quebec, generations of stakeholders and interpreters have viewed the union of 1867 as a pact (or compact) between political communities (some prefer to speak of colonies or provinces) or even between peoples, and it has consistently been asserted that the purpose of this pact was to preserve Quebec's autonomy. That autonomy was in the service of a higher end: the preservation and promotion of what continues to make Quebec different (Rocher 2009, 93–146). Elsewhere in Canada, the dominant view has tended to disregard the moral foundations of federalism, instead focusing on its functional and instrumental aspects: the bureaucratic language of performance and efficiency.

Quebec's Contribution to Canada's Uniqueness and the State's Key Role in Shaping the Quebec Difference

Quebec is not quite the geographical centre of Canada, but arguably it remains its historical heart. It is the simple fact of Quebec's massively French-speaking presence that strongly distinguishes Canada from the United States of America. In addition to the part Quebec has played in the genesis and development of federalism, we will take into consideration here only a few aspects that give an authentically dualist dimension to public life, though constitutional recognition of it is lacking. That dimension of duality – unimaginable without Quebec's place in Canada and its historic role – can be found in a number of political and social features: official bilingualism; the presence of two legal systems (British-inspired common law and French-inspired Quebec civilist tradition); two host societies for immigrants, one mainly in French and the other in English; the complex fabric of two distinct civil societies, including two separate communications networks; and two autonomous intellectual and research communities.

Like Canada as a whole, Quebec needed the strong presence of the state in the second half of the twentieth century to update and affirm its difference. That dynamic of social modernization, known as the Quiet Revolution, led to greater conflict between the Canadian and Quebec national identities, between two attempts at nation-building that are at the same time similar and rival projects, creating the basis for a more-or-less permanent political tension (Gagnon and Iacovino 2007).

Multiple Foundations

To interpret the history of a country is to perform a purposeful political action for which we must take responsibility. Where and when did Canada start? Today, no one would venture onto this terrain without referring to an initial, complex, and multiform foundation established by the First Peoples – that is, the Indigenous peoples – over some ten thousand years of occupation of the land that is now Canada. That foundation has acquired new importance over the last forty years, thanks to the political-social and cultural resurgence of Indigenous peoples in Canada, in the moral conscience of humanity, and even in the functioning of international organizations.

When it comes time to interpret the first European explorations, the classical lines demarcating the English-language and French-language historiographies quickly become apparent. Was the discoverer John Cabot (Newfoundland, 1497) or Jacques Cartier (Gaspé and Quebec, 1534)? In itself, the answer has little importance because it was not until the seventeenth century that the European colonization of Canada began in earnest.

No one would criticize the Acadians for insisting on the great effort the French put into occupying the eastern region of Canada in the very early years of the seventeenth century. However, as the celebrations surrounding the commemoration of the 400th anniversary of the founding of the city of Quebec by Champlain in 1608 showed, it is still possible to see that event as the main catalyst leading to the emergence of contemporary Quebec and Canada. Beginning in 1608, the organization of political life, in the European or Western sense of the term, began to take on an air of permanence. In the wake of the founding of the city of Quebec, Canadian history became paradoxical. On one hand, as early as 1663, the Sovereign Council of New France represented the French ancien régime in its most absolutist form (Bouchard 2000, 85–6). That was in addition to the religious absolutism of the Catholic Church, lord of souls and often of the land, even more authoritarian than it was in France at the same period. If we add to this the imposition of a seigneurial regime drawn straight from French feudalism (until it was abandoned in 1854), we find in this first iteration of Canada institutions inspired by old and decaying European systems. Moreover, New France evolved as a highly homogenous place on the linguistic and cultural level (90–1). This homogeneity, the result of the hegemony of the Catholic Church and ancien régime institutions, significantly limited the French settlers' contact with the First Peoples while blocking the settlement of a substantial number of French non-Catholics in the colony. However, this homogeneity was also the consequence of a more "modern" process.

Above all, the colony of New France was a vast territory, and, like all the other great swaths of land in America, it was subjected to the mercantile greed of powerful European states. The destiny of New France owes much to the fact that it was never much more than an outpost for the market exploitation of natural resources. Its fate was closely tied to that of France, to its military success, and the mercantile vision of its interests. This suggests that it was less the military clashes in the St. Lawrence Valley that led to its final appropriation by the British Crown (which in actual fact conquered

Quebec several times) than France's choice to yield control of New France in exchange for its Caribbean colonies, which were considered more profitable. And so the Treaty of Paris in 1763 sealed Canada's political fate. The famous battle on the Plains of Abraham in 1759 took on great importance when France calculated that it was in its interest to transfer or sell its Canadian colony to Great Britain. Some see in this period (1759–63) the origins of a more liberal, modern British political regime; others prefer to remember that it was first and foremost a military conquest; still others recall the Royal Proclamation of 1763 delimiting the British Crown's fiduciary obligations to Indigenous peoples. Nonetheless, as the newest subjects of the powerful British Empire, the seventy thousand Catholic French-speaking inhabitants and four thousand Indigenous peoples concentrated in the St. Lawrence Valley had new political masters (Bouchard 2000, 85, 90). Paradoxically, the British Canada that replaced New France would engender, in the twentieth century, the only majority French-speaking society in North America: the Province of Quebec.

The complexity of the founding of Canada further increased with the British Parliament's adoption of the Quebec Act of 1774. Under the British imperial policy, the Act replaced the Royal Proclamation of 1763, which had established a legal, cultural, and religious regime that entailed a strict policy of assimilation "of the French Canadians by an English colony, governed by English laws, in an English spirit" (Wade 1966, 80; our translation). To the great displeasure of Britain's American colonies, and thereby hastening their rebellion, the Quebec Act essentially re-established the historic borders of New France extending far into the continental interior. On the religious, cultural, and identity fronts, London had essentially abandoned the assimilationist plan. The seigneurial system of land ownership and organization, as well as the French customs and civil law came back into force. The Catholic religion was safeguarded, including the church's right to collect tithes, and a new oath of allegiance allowed Catholics to hold public office (Lamonde 2000, 24–5). The spirit and the letter of the Quebec Act are not without grey areas: the preponderant status of the French language, undeniable on the ground (where the colony spoke French in a proportion of thirty to one), was not constitutionalized. Whereas the Proclamation of 1763 had combined a regime of identity assimilation with the promise of an English-style legislative assembly, the Quebec Act combined a regime that was generous with respect to identity but with a political framework founded on the arbitrary authority of the British-appointed executive, with no promise of an elected assembly in the near future. Still, one inescapable fact remains: the Quebec Act is the founding document for identity recognition in Quebec and Canada, in much the same manner as the Magna Carta in England.

Seventeen years after the Quebec Act, following the tumultuous years of the American Revolution and the Loyalist migration into Canada, the Constitutional Act of 1791 implanted democratic practices in Canada by creating Upper and Lower Canada and establishing two separate houses of political deliberation. However, the powers devolved to these assemblies were not very strong. Each of the new colonies had its own elected legislative assembly, legislative council, and governor. Control of the elected legislature over public spending and the principle of ministerial responsibility was slow to take root. Indeed, the quest for that responsibility was a major factor contributing to the conflict between British authorities and the Patriote Party on the eve of the Patriote Rebellion of 1837–8 in Lower Canada, as well as the rebellion in Upper Canada. Reacting to the disturbances, London revived the broad lines of the 1840 Durham Report, which recommended anglicizing the French Canadians and imposing a loyal English-speaking majority across the whole territory. To this end it proceeded to merge Upper and Lower Canada with the Act of Union, which came into effect in 1841, thereby creating one House of Assembly and a single government. The governor and members of the executive council continued to be appointed by London; the legislative council had twenty-four members appointed for life; to Lower Canada's disadvantage, half the eighty-four members of the House of Assembly were elected from Canada East (though its population was greater) and half from Canada West. Initially, English was the only official language in the legislature, but in 1844 French was recognized. The Act of Union also was used as an opportunity to consolidate the debts of the territories, which again was to Lower Canada's disadvantage.

According to John Ralston Saul (1997), the true political foundation of modern Canada is to be found in the rapid evolution of the Act of Union political regime toward de facto recognition of the principle of responsible government in 1848. From then on, the colonial governors appointed by London exercised their powers only on the advice of an executive cabinet or council, which had to be chosen from among the representatives elected to the legislative assembly by the population or from among the members of the legislative council. Crucial to this democratic evolution, according to Ralston Saul, was the political partnership between the French-Canadian leader Louis-Hippolyte Lafontaine and his reformist colleague from Upper Canada, Robert Baldwin. Their joint achievements during that crucial decade – spanning legalization of the use of the French language in parliamentary life to significant economic-social changes – established a durable political culture of collaboration and mutual trust between French- and English-speakers. The country of Canada would emerge as a democratic federation twenty years later.

As jurist Eugénie Brouillet has written, "The Québec Act laid the first legal groundwork for the Quebec nation's deep rooting in a distinct culture" (2005, 111; our translation). The 1867 British North America Act (officially the Constitution Act, 1867 since 1982) can be seen as a logical, consistent continuation of the spirit of the Quebec Act, strengthening the roots of Canada in a plurality of shared identities and sovereignties. This opened a new chapter in the history of the modern state since a hybrid structure was invented. The Dominion of Canada created by Confederation would be largely autonomous with respect to the British Empire, though subordinate to it on certain fundamental issues such as foreign affairs and constitutional decisions. Within the dominion, relations between the central government and the provinces would reproduce this colonial hierarchy. At the same time, the new system of government established a complex form of federalism in which the federated entities (provinces) were sovereign in their exclusive areas of jurisdiction, while also recognizing the "right to difference" for the intertwined national, cultural, religious, and linguistic communities.

For contemporary Quebec, the political regime established by Confederation is the founding pillar of its existence as an autonomous political community and a distinct national society. In 1867, the federal principle was chosen to accommodate Quebec's insistence that it could not consent to the dissolution of its national identity. This is why the Civil Code of Québec and the British common law used in the other Canadian provinces were both recognized (Burelle 2005). This is also why, in the division of powers, the provinces were made responsible for most of the so-called local issues associated with cultural and community identities: social, civil, family, school, and municipal organization. The regime also gave solid legal guarantees to the English-speaking Protestant minority living in Quebec. It was a regime of complex diversity across Canada, but also within Quebec. Brouillet summarizes the spirit of Confederation by establishing its link with the Quebec Act:

> In 1867 … an initially federating regime came into being. It was certainly infused with certain elements with centralizing connotations, but, all in all, it mirrored the socio-cultural and political situation in the communities. More specifically, the regime that was adopted satisfied the essential aspects of the Quebec nation's identity concerns: its political autonomy acquired constitutional status and extended to all the matters that, at the time, were considered to be related to its special cultural identity. As Professor Jean-Charles Bonenfant wrote, "The spirit of 1867 is therefore the definitive acceptance of the existence of French Canadians; it is the logical continuation of the *Québec Act*.… They [the founding fathers] truly

intended to ensure the French Canadians' survival and they accepted the means that, at the time, seemed to be the best suited to achieve it." (Brouillet 2005, 197; our translation)

Towards a New Constitutional Regime

A number of plans for constitutional reform have been proposed over the years. They have often been accompanied by royal commissions or working groups looking for ways to adapt institutions and answers to the tensions of the day. During the Great Depression in the early 1930s, the time was ripe for re-evaluation of the division of powers. The central government therefore launched the Rowell-Sirois Commission to study the relations between the central government and the provinces and sought to take advantage of the crisis by centralizing powers in Ottawa over the following decades. There was a strong reaction in Ontario, but a mitigated one at first in Quebec, in particular under the leadership of Adélard Godbout. Ottawa continued its centralizing momentum during World War II by exercising increased power in the fields of taxation and social policy. This centralizing process is to be seen as leading to the Judicial Committee of the Privy Council (which favoured a more decentralized vision of the Constitution) being replaced by the Supreme Court of Canada as the court of last resort in 1949.

Quebec initially responded very timidly to the central government's steps by creating the Tremblay Commission in 1953. That commission, mandated to study the constitutional problems in the Canadian federation, produced a very important report that provided most of the political parties active on the provincial level with their line of conduct for a long time. The report emphasized the notions of provincial autonomy, non-subordination of one order of government to the other, and subsidiarity with a view to healthy collaboration between Quebec and Ottawa.

The tensions between Quebec and Ottawa became palpable with the start of the Quiet Revolution and French-speaking Quebecers' gradual takeover of the Quebec economy and public institutions. Naturally, the rapid development of the social sciences helped to give French-speakers the tools needed for that reconquest. In the face of these tensions, the government of Lester B. Pearson launched the Laurendeau-Dunton Commission on bilingualism and biculturalism in 1963. That commission's work helped to bring more French Canadians into the federal public service, even though the report's conclusions were used to substitute the multiculturalism policy for the biculturalism policy initially envisaged to attenuate the impending constitutional crisis and meet the Quebec demands inspired by the principle of Canadian duality.

All of Canada's habits and customs pertaining to constitutional legislation were about to be revolutionized, and the Quebec government's frequently expressed opposition would be no obstacle. In reaction to that reorientation, but also in the process of achieving a parallel goal of more substantial autonomy, Quebec held two referendums: the first on sovereignty-association in 1980, and a second on sovereignty-partnership in 1995. The goal of the Canadian constitutional revolution was to confirm the principle of the equality of the provinces (at the expense of Quebec, which defined itself as a founding nation), the major regions (the Atlantic region, Quebec, Ontario, the west, and the north), ethnic-cultural groups (French Canadians were one group among so many others), and individuals, through the enshrinement of the Canadian Charter of Rights and Freedoms in the Constitution Act. The Charter and Act formed the cornerstone of the new legal edifice designed to make the Supreme Court the institution par excellence for all Canadians by changing the ties between citizens and their political leaders. In short, it was a question of transforming the *demoi*, characteristic of all federal states, into a single *demos*, thereby confirming the impoverishment of Canada's federal practices. This major transformation of the Canadian legal system was not accomplished without bumps along the way or without weakening the trust meant to be a feature of the relations between the national communities at the origin of the pact federating Canada (Karmis and Rocher 2012).

The Conflict between Canadian and Quebec Nation-Building

In contemporary political science and philosophy, authors such as Alain-G. Gagnon, Michael Keating, Will Kymlicka, Wayne Norman, Michel Seymour, and James Tully have suggested conceptual frameworks for studying countries where politics are defined by complex, multi-faceted conflicts generated by attempts to build distinct, autonomous national communities (Gagnon and Tully 2001; Gagnon 2014; Gagnon and Keating 2012; Keating 2001a, 2001b; Norman 2006; Seymour 2017; Kymlicka 1995, 2007). The nation-building goal may be an encompassing, legally independent nation-state (for example, Canada) or a non-sovereign nation (for example, Quebec). In his work on the challenges of modern nationalism, Keating defines the concept of "nation-building" as follows:

> In this new context, autonomy is no longer a question of establishing a state, or using it to pursue a strategy of economic autarky. Rather it involves the creation of a national project, mobilization around it and an ability to engage in policy making in a complex and interdependent world. A stateless nation requires of self government

> to provide an arena for debate and decision, to frame policies, to legitimize decisions, and to define the collective interest in the state and international arenas. It also requires autonomous government capacity in the form of bureaucratic resources and finance. (Keating 2001a, 64)

Keating notes that nation-building will seek concrete results in all areas of public policy: economic, social and cultural, as well as political. He introduces the concepts of "plurinationalism" and "post-sovereignty" to describe contexts in which several national identities coexist within a political order (separated and parallel, but also intertwined to various degrees, both in people's heads and territorially within the state). This also signals the end of the independent state's claims to the territorial monopoly of authority and legitimacy (Keating 2001b). Wayne Norman's work complements Keating's by delving deeper into the conditions for championing more than one nation within the same territorial and political space and the normative acceptability of the ensuing nation-building and engineering (Norman 2006).

The twentieth century in Canada and the twentieth century in Quebec have been traversed by nation-building: attempts to consolidate or fortify national identity as Keating might put it. From the perspective of Canadian nation-building since 1945, there have been many achievements: Canadian citizenship and the Canadian passport; the welfare state and the implementation of a social union across the country; the establishment of the Supreme Court as the court of last resort; the consolidation of a pan-Canadian communications network; a national anthem and a new flag; the establishment of institutional bilingualism and multiculturalism, as well as cultural and scientific policies; the promotion of a pan-Canadian network of civil society institutions; a distinctive foreign policy; the repatriation of the Constitution and the adoption of the Canadian Charter of Rights and Freedoms; and, in general, the consolidation of a liberal-democratic regime, which aspires to the ideal of genuine pluralist democratic deliberation.

From the perspective of Quebec nation-building, since the start of the Quiet Revolution in 1960, there have been many achievements, indicative of the enormity of its "projet de société," in other words, the consolidation and maintenance of a complete, modern society. It has constructed a welfare state in parallel with (and in juxtaposition to) the Canadian welfare state; indeed, the health insurance card – the "carte soleil" – is perhaps the best Quebec nation-building has to offer to rival with the passport of Canadian nation-building. The long list of additional achievements would include the nationalization of hydroelectric resources; the consolidation of a French-language Quebec communications network; government action on the creation and development of a public education system; the establishment of a major network of Crown corporations; the Quebec Charter of Human Rights and Freedoms; the institution of language policies making French the official national common language (and including measures giving immigrants access to French-language public schools); the promotion of a network of Quebec civil society institutions; the establishment of a Quebec international policy; various components of a Quebec citizenship regime, including a normative framework and practices associated with an intercultural approach; the development of Quebec cultural and scientific policies; the establishment of a daycare system; the institution of community entrepreneurship (social economy) in all regions of Quebec; and, like Canada, the consolidation of a liberal-democratic regime that aspires to genuine pluralist democratic deliberation. In a certain way, it can be seen that nothing more closely resembles Canadian nation-building than Quebec nation-building. Aside from a few controversial differences, the two approaches look strikingly similar.

The tension between these two nation-building enterprises is the element missing from the Supreme Court of Canada's narrative on Canada's political identity. The passage of time cannot erase the memory that the Court's interpretive reconstruction would never have occurred without the huge pressure exerted by the 1980 Quebec referendum. Since that seminal event, in the public spheres of both nations, many people have argued in favour of a political and constitutional approach in accord with a "monist" conception of the nation-state based on the concentration of sovereignty, citizenship, and national identity in a single political entity (either Canada or Quebec). Others have embraced and extolled pluralist federal thought that is open to diversity, asymmetries, and multiple cultural and national identities. In many sectors there has been collaboration between the two nation-building enterprises and their institutions, such as on the work Canada and Quebec have put into advancing the cause of cultural diversity on the international level.

The model of pluralist federalism open to asymmetries and multiple identities has legal roots in Canada's federal Constitution. For brevity, we will simply borrow André Burelle's perspective to summarize the Canadian spirit of 1867: union without merger between the founding communities of Canada (in which the federated entities retain their full sovereignty over local concerns), ascending subsidiarity, recognition of two orders of equally legitimate sovereign government, respect for the principle of non-subordination and management through joint decision-making when there are overlaps, and equivalence in law and treatment of individuals and the founding communities as a rejection of the melting pot (Burelle 2005, 459). In 1982, and very specifically in the context of escalating conflict between Canadian and Quebec nation-building, Canada made its constitutional regime more complex by completing its independence from Great Britain and enshrining the Canadian Charter of Rights and Freedoms. In doing so, Canada succumbed to the temptation to embody, in its own manner, the modern, monist, homogenizing nation-state. Burelle sees this as an example of "one nation" federalism sliding towards a unitary model, with its rhetorical justification based on the philosophy of individualistic liberalism. In its pure form, this type of regime seeks to merge individuals into a single civic nation by delegating the totality of its national sovereignty to the central parliament, which can, for pragmatic reasons, delegate certain powers to the provinces. A descending subsidiarity beginning from the central government is practised, expressing the existence of a single "senior" national government and "junior" provincial governments. Under this model, the central power can enter the areas of jurisdiction of the federated entities to protect the "national interest." Lastly, this model promotes the idea of identical – symmetrical and uniform – law and treatment of individuals and provinces, given their merger into a single nation (459–60).

Under the 1982 constitutional regime, Canada does not resemble or conform to a monochromatic, individualistic liberalism that is blind to differences. We find instead a conception of equality that is generous to the underprivileged and less advantaged, with a commitment to redistribute economic wealth to poorer provinces (including Quebec), and open to recognition of many forms of difference, such as with respect to Indigenous peoples, the multicultural heritage of all Canadians, the strengthening of language rights for territorially concentrated French-speaking and English-speaking minorities and the guarantee of gender equality. Yet, the 1982 constitutional regime adopts a hard line on Quebec's national difference, which it does not acknowledge or integrate into any of its categories. Adopted by nine provinces and the federal Parliament without the consent of Quebec, this regime is viewed in Quebec as equivalent to the imposition of Canadian nationalism, compelling Quebec to demonstrate a standard Canadian patriotism (Keating 2001b; Ignatieff 2001; Taylor 1992). It consolidates the central government's role as promoter of Canadian national identity, while undermining the autonomy of the Quebec government, thereby weakening its capacity to promote the Quebec national identity (Kymlicka 1998, 166).

There are ways of going beyond the modern nation-state model today, ways that reject the monist, unitary model of sovereignty, notably through plurinational federalism (Gagnon 2010; Gagnon and Iacovino 2007; Gagnon 2014; Requejo 2005). Canadian and Quebec nation-building can both correspond to authentic communities with shared destinies, where people feel responsible for the fate of their fellow citizens but do not conflate patriotism to country with attachment to a single national identity. This will require that Quebecers come to accept that Canadian nation-building is legitimate, including within Quebec, and that they rediscover their own form of pan-Canadian solidarity (Pratte 2007; Parekh 2000; Laforest 2014). A valuable illustration of this attitude is offered by the Sécrétariat du Québec en relations canadiennes (2017).

On their part, it requires Canadians to rediscover the principle of independence at the heart of federalism. They will need to accept the legitimacy of Quebec nation-building by seeing that the Quebec difference is an important component of the Charter of Rights and Freedoms that is at the heart of Canadian constitutionalism. If authentic reconciliation of Canadian and Quebec nation-building is to take place, Canadians and Quebecers need to expand the space within their federation for asymmetry and redefine justice as equivalence in treatment rather than in terms of a standardized moral framework (Gagnon and Laforest 2012; McGarry 2007; Burelle 2005).

There has been modest progress in recent years on expanding the non-constitutional space for the asymmetrical treatment of Quebec. Examples are the signing of the federal-provincial agreement on health care in 2004 and the 2006 resolution by the Canadian Parliament recognizing that Quebecers are a nation within a united Canada. However, in Quebec, political actors of all stripes agree that there is still a long way to go before there will be true reconciliation between Canadian and Quebec nation-building (Laforest 2014; Gagnon 2010, 2014; Gagnon and Iacovino 2007). Since he became prime minister in 2015, Justin Trudeau has exhibited less tendency than his father to react viscerally to the conflict between Canadian and Quebec nation-building. However, while he has shown himself to be no stranger to the language of reconciliation, he seems content for now to limit his understanding and pursuit of it to the goal of establishing a nation-to-nation partnership with Canada's Indigenous peoples.

Conclusion

This review of the foundations of the Canada–Quebec relationship has brought us into fertile terrain for social scientists (Gagnon and Chokri 2005; Bickerton, Brooks, and Gagnon 2006; Laforest and Gagnon 2013) and for moral philosophers in that it has helped to retrace the lines of current debates about what seemed to be a bygone time.

In our own analysis, we have tried to highlight two understandings of the historical and constitutional principles and normative contours of Canadian political identity: the one adopted by the Supreme Court of Canada in its 1998 judgment on Quebec's right to secede and an alternative interpretation from a Quebec perspective that we have formulated ourselves. Next, we explored the nature and meaning of the plural foundations that have marked the Canadian and Quebec political experiences. Last, we have sought to clarify the fundamental cleavage between – and the tensions that arise from – Canadian and Quebec nation-building.

This study of the Canadian political regime has allowed us to place the contributions of Canada and Quebec in terms of diversity management within their societies in the broader context of advanced liberal democracies. In London and Edinburg during the referendum on Scottish independence in 2014, as in Madrid and Barcelona, where the future of the Catalonia region of Spain dominated political debate from 2010 to 2020, the Canada-Quebec situation remains highly topical and pertinent. Canadian and Quebec political specialists are recognized for their valuable experience and expertise on plurinationalism and diversity management.[4] The ongoing discussion of the Quebec-Canada relationship proves that identity issues need not be considered dangerous but instead can be efficient democratic mobilization tools essential for national communities to find mutually beneficial ways to live together in a context of shared community-of-fate and identity pluralism.

Annex

Important Dates in the History of Canadian Politics, 1492–2020

1492	Christopher Columbus arrives in America
1497	John Cabot explores the east coast of North America and probably the Gulf of St. Lawrence
1534	The explorer Jacques Cartier takes possession of Canada in the name of the king of France
1608	Founding of the city of Quebec by Samuel de Champlain
1629–1632	First English conquest (the city of Quebec in the hands of the Kirkes)
1634	Founding of Trois Rivières by Laviolette
1642	Founding of Montreal (Ville-Marie) by Maisonneuve
1654–1667	Acadia passes into the hands of the English
1663	New France becomes a royal colony (establishment of the Sovereign Council)
1689–1697	First colonial war between France and England
1755	Beginning of the deportation of the Acadians
1759	Surrender of the city of Quebec
1760	Capitulation of Montreal
1760	Establishment of the military regime

1763	Treaty of Paris
	Royal Proclamation
1774	Quebec Act
1791	Constitutional Act
1810	First attempt to unite the two Canadas
1822	Second attempt to unite the two Canadas
1834	The 92 Resolutions
1837	Russell's resolutions
	Rebellion: the battles of Saint-Denis, Saint-Charles, and Saint-Eustache
1838	Declaration of the independence of Lower Canada (Nelson)
	12 Patriotes hung in Montreal
1840	Act of Union
1848	Baldwin-Lafontaine ministry
	Introduction of responsible government
1854	End of the seigneurial regime
1864	Charlottetown and Quebec conferences
1867	British North America Act enacted
1876	Indian Act
1899	Canada sends troops abroad for the first time to participate in the Boer War
1905	Creation of the provinces of Alberta and Saskatchewan
1931	Statute of Westminster
1939	Creation, by the federal authorities, of the Rowell-Sirois Commission on dominion-provincial relations
1949	End of recourse to the Judicial Committee of the Privy Council. The Supreme Court becomes the court of last appeal for all types of cases in Canada
1953	Creation, by the Quebec authorities, of the Tremblay Commission on constitutional issues
1963	Creation, by the federal authorities, of the Laurendeau-Dunton Commission on bilingualism and biculturalism
1976	Election of the Parti Québécois
1980	First Quebec referendum on sovereignty
1982	Repatriation of the Constitution and enshrinement of the Canadian Charter of Rights and Freedoms in the Constitution
1987	Signature of the agreement in principle at Meech Lake
1990	Defeat of the Meech Lake Accord
1992	Charlottetown Accord defeated by referendum
1995	Second Quebec referendum on sovereignty

1999 Social Union Framework Agreement advocated by the central government received the support of all provinces but cannot secure the support of Quebec government
2002 Romanow Commission on the Future of Health Care in Canada tabled its report, *Building on Values*
2006 Recognition of the Quebec nation by the House of Commons
2011 Election of the Stephen Harper's Conservative Party in Canada and formation of a majority government
2012 Election of Pauline Marois's Parti Québécois in Quebec and formation of a minority government
2014 Election of Philippe Couillard's Liberal Party in Quebec and formation of a majority government
2015 Election of Justin Trudeau's Liberal Party in Canada and formation of a majority government
Report of the Truth and Reconciliation Commission of Canada
2018 Election of François Legault's Coalition Avenir Québec and formation of a majority government
2019 Re-election of Justin Trudeau's Liberal Party in Canada and formation of a minority government

Notes

1 This chapter is an enhanced version of a text that appeared in *Le parlementarisme canadien*. It is published here with the permission of the Presses de l'Université Laval. We would like to express our warmest thanks to the editor, Denis Dion. Our thanks goes especially to Mary Baker, who has assumed the translation from French into English. Our colleague Jim Bickerton has also provided us with important suggestions to enrich our chapter.

2 For the complete ruling, consult Supreme Court of Canada, "Supreme Court Judgments," https://scc-csc.lexum.com/scc-csc/scc-csc/en/item/1643/index.do

3 In relation to the title of his work, *Nations without States* (1999). Nonetheless, we consider the author justified in writing that for autonomous political communities that are, however, not sovereign, such as Quebec, Catalonia, and Scotland, the management of internal diversity is a fundamental stake, as the work of the Bouchard-Taylor Commission demonstrated clearly.

4 For example, the work done by the members of the Groupe de recherche sur les sociétés plurinationales and the Centre de recherche interdisciplinaire sur la diversité et la démocratie, both based at the Université du Québec à Montréal, has advanced research in this area in recent years.

References and Suggested Readings

Ajzenstat, J., P. Romney, I. Gentles, and W.D. Gairdner, eds. 2003. *Canada's Founding Debates*. Toronto: University of Toronto Press.

———. 2004. *Débats sur la fondation du Canada*. French edition prepared by S. Kelly and G. Laforest. Quebec City: Presses de l'Université Laval.

Bernard-Meunier, M. 2007. "Apprendre à jouer le jeu. Le défi du Québec au sein du Canada." In *Reconquérir le Canada. Un nouveau projet pour la nation québécoise*, edited by A. Pratte, 115–40. Montreal: Voix parallèles.

Bickerton, J.S. Brooks, and A.-G. Gagnon. 2006. *Freedom, Equality, Community: The Political Philosophy of Six Influential Canadians*. Montreal and Kingston: McGill-Queen's University Press.

Bouchard, G. 2000. *Genèse des nations et cultures du Nouveau Monde: essai d'histoire comparée*. Montreal: Boréal.

Brouillet, E. 2005. *La négation de la nation: l'identité culturelle québécoise et le fédéralisme canadien*. Quebec City: Septentrion.

Brouillet, E., A.-G. Gagnon, and G. Laforest, eds. 2018. *The Quebec Conference of 1864: Understanding the Emergence of the Canadian Federation*. Montreal and Kingston: McGill-Queen's University Press.

Burelle, A. 2005. *Pierre Elliott Trudeau: l'intellectuel et le politique*. Montreal: Fides.

Cour suprême du Canada. 1998. *Renvoi relatif à la sécession du Québec*.

Fournier, J.-M. 2014. "Le Canada que nous souhaitons en 2020." Speech given in Ottawa, 2 October.

Gagnon, A.-G., ed. 2004. *Québec: State and Society*, 3rd ed. Toronto: University of Toronto Press.

———, ed. 2009. *Contemporary Canadian Federalism: Foundations, Traditions, Institutions*. Toronto: University of Toronto Press.

———. 2010. *The Case for Multinational Federalism: Beyond the All-Encompassing Nation*. Abingdon: Routledge.

———. 2014. *Minority Nations in the Age of Uncertainty: New Paths to National Emancipation and Empowerment*. Toronto: University of Toronto Press.

Gagnon, A.-G., and L.-M. Chokri. 2005. "Le régime politique canadien: histoire et enjeux." In *Le parlementarisme canadien*, edited by R. Pelletier and M. Tremblay, 3rd ed., 9–35. Quebec City: Presses de l'Université Laval.

Gagnon, A.-G., and R. Iacovino. 2007. *Federalism, Citizenship, and Quebec: Debating Multinationalism*. Toronto: University of Toronto Press.

Gagnon, A.-G., and M. Keating, eds. 2012. *Political Autonomy and Divided Societies: Imagining Democratic Alternatives in Complex Settings*. Basingstoke, UK: Palgrave Macmillan.

Gagnon, A.-G., and G. Laforest. 2012. "The Moral Foundations of Asymmetrical Federalism: Normative Considerations." In *Federalism, Plurinationality and Democratic Constitutionalism: Theory and Cases*, edited by F. Requejo and M. Caminal, 85–107. London: Routledge.

Gagnon, A.-G., and James Tully, eds. 2001. *Multinational Democracies*. Cambridge: Cambridge University Press.

Grant, G. 1965. *Lament for a Nation: The Defeat of Canadian Nationalism*. Toronto: McClelland and Stewart.

Grégoire, M., É. Montigny, and Y. Rivest. 2016. *Le cœur des Québécois. L'évolution du Québec de 1976 à aujourd'hui*. Quebec City: Presses de l'Université Laval.

Guibernau, M. 1999. *Nations without States: Political Communities in a Global Age*. London: Polity.

———. 2007. *The Identity of Nations*. Cambridge: Polity.

Ignatieff, M. 2001. *La révolution des droits*. Montreal: Boréal.

Karmis, D., and W. Norman. 2005. *Theories of Federalism: A Reader*. London: Palgrave Macmillan.

Karmis, D., and F. Rocher, eds. 2012. *La dynamique confiance/méfiance dans les démocraties multinationales. Le Canada sous l'angle comparatif*. Québec: Presses de l'Université du Québec.

Keating, M. 2001a. *Nations against the State: The New Politics of Nationalism in Quebec, Catalonia and Scotland*. 2nd ed. Basingstoke, UK: Macmillan.

———. 2001b. *Plurinational Democracy: Stateless Nations in a Post-Sovereignty Era*. Oxford: Oxford University Press.

Kymlicka, W. 1995. *Multicultural Citizenship: A Liberal Theory of Minority Rights*. New York: Oxford University Press.

———. 1998. *Finding Our Way: Rethinking Ethnocultural Relations in Canada*. Toronto: Oxford University Press.

———. 2007. *Multicultural Odysseys: Navigating the New International Politics of Diversity*. New York: Oxford University Press.

Laforest, G. 2010. "What Canadian Federalism Means in Québec." *Review of Constitutional Studies* 15 (1): 1–33.

———. 2014. *Interpreting Quebec's Exile within the Canadian Federation*. Brussels: Peter Lang.

Laforest, G., E. Brouillet, A.-G. Gagnon, and Y. Tanguay. 2015. *The Constitutions That Shaped Us: A Historical Anthology of Pre-1867 Canadian Constitutions*. Montreal and Kingston: McGill-Queen's University Press.

Laforest, G., and A.-G. Gagnon. 2013. "Comprendre la vie politique au Canada et au Québec." In *Le parlementarisme canadien*, edited by R. Pelletier and M. Tremblay, 5th ed., 9–39. Quebec City: Presses de l'Université Laval.

Laforest, G. with the collaboration of Oscar Mejia Mesa. 2014. *Interpreting Quebec's Exile within the Federation: Selected Political Essays*. Brussels: Peter Lang.

Lamonde, Y. 2000. *Histoire sociale des idées au Québec*. Montreal: Fides.

Leclair, J. 2007. "Vers une pensée politique fédérale: la répudiation du mythe de la différence québécoise 'radicale.'" In *Reconquérir le Canada. Un nouveau projet pour la nation québécoise*, edited by A. Pratte, 39–83. Montreal: Voix parallèles.

McGarry, J. 2007. "Asymmetry in Federations, Federacies and Unitary States." *Ethnopolitics* 6 (1): 105–16.

McLachlin, B. 2002. "Les droits et les libertés au Canada; vingt ans après l'adoption de la Charte." Speech given at the National Arts Centre, Ottawa.

Monière, D. 2001. *Pour comprendre le nationalisme au Québec et ailleurs*. Montreal: Les Presses de l'Université de Montréal.

Norman, W. 2006. *Negotiating Nationalism: Nation-Building, Federalism, and Secession in the Multinational State*. Oxford: Oxford University Press.

Owram, D. 1986. *The Government Generation: Canadian Intellectuals and the State, 1900–1945*. Toronto: University of Toronto Press.

Parekh, B. 2000. *Rethinking Multiculturalism: Cultural Diversity and Political Theory*. London: Macmillan.

Pelletier, R. 2008. *Le Québec et le fédéralisme canadien: un regard critique*. Quebec City: Presses de l'Université Laval.

Pisani, E. 1995. "Après le référendum: et maintenant?," *Le Devoir*, 14 December.

Pratte, A., ed. 2007. *Reconquérir le Canada. Un nouveau projet pour la nation québécoise* Montreal: Voix-parallèles.

Racine, J.-C. 2012. *La condition constitutionnelle des Canadiens. Regards comparés sur la réforme constitutionnelle de 1982*. Quebec City: Presses de l'Université Laval.

Ralston Saul, J. 1997. *Reflections of a Siamese Twin: Canada at the End of the Twentieth Century*. Toronto: Viking.

———. 2000. Inaugural LaFontaine-Baldwin Lecture, March 23, Toronto. https://archive.gg.ca/media/doc.asp?lang=e&DocID=1374.

Requejo, F. 2005. *Multinational Federalism and Value Pluralism: The Spanish Case*. London: Routledge.

Rocher, F. 2009. "The Quebec-Canada Dynamic or the Negation of the Ideal of Federalism." In *Contemporary Canadian Federalism: Foundations, Traditions, Institutions*, edited by A.-G. Gagnon, 81–131. Toronto: University of Toronto Press.

Sécrétariat du Québec en relations canadiennes. 2017. "Quebecers: Our Way of Being Canadian." https://www.sqrc.gouv.qc.ca/documents/relations-canadiennes/politique-affirmation-en.pdf.

Seymour, M. 2017. *A Liberal Theory of Collective Rights*. Montreal and Kingston, McGill-Queen's University Press.

Simard, J.-J. 1999. "Ce siècle où le Québec est venu au monde." In *Québec 2000: rétrospective du XXe siècle*, edited by R. Côté. Montreal: Fides.

Smiley, D. 1987. *The Federal Condition in Canada*. Toronto: McGraw-Hill Ryerson.

Supreme Court of Canada, *Reference re Secession of Quebec* – SCC Cases (Lexum): https://scc-csc.lexum.com/scc-csc/scc-csc/en/item/1643/index.do.

Taylor, C. 1992. *Rapprocher les solitudes. Écrits sur le fédéralisme et le nationalisme au Canada*. Quebec City: Presses de l'Université Laval.

Trudeau, J. 2015. "La diversité, force du Canada." Speech 26 November, London. http://pm.gc.ca/fra/nouvelles/2015/11/26/la-diversite-force-du-canada.

Tully, J. 1995. *Strange Multiplicity: Constitutionalism in an Age of Diversity*. Cambridge: Cambridge University Press.

Wade, M. 1966. *Les Canadiens français de 1760 à nos jours*. Tome 1, *1760–1914*. Ottawa: Cercle du livre de France.

Woehrling, J. 2009. "The Canadian Charter of Rights and Freedoms and Its Consequences for Political and Democratic Life and the Federal System." In *Contemporary Canadian Federalism: Foundations, Traditions, Institutions*, edited by A.-G. Gagnon, 224–49. Toronto: University of Toronto Press.

Zarka, Y.-C. 2005. "Langue et identité." *Cités: Philosophie, histoire, politique* 23: 3–5.

PART TWO

Government, Parliament, and the Courts

three
The Centre Rules: Executive Dominance

DONALD J. SAVOIE

Introduction

The executive has long held a dominant position in Westminster-style parliamentary governments. In formal constitutional terms, power is concentrated in the hands of the prime minister and Cabinet. Recent developments in Canada, however, suggest that the hand of the prime minister has been considerably strengthened. Indeed, when it comes to the political power inherent in their office, it remains that Canadian prime ministers have no equals in the West. If anything, Canadian prime ministers have been able to strengthen their power still further at the expense of other political, policy, and administrative actors over the past several years.

Gordon Robertson, former secretary to the Cabinet and once described as the gold standard for the position of clerk of the Privy Council, wrote forty-five years ago that in our system "ministers are responsible. It is their government" (Robertson 1971, 497). The Privy Council Office (PCO) argued in its 1993 publication on the machinery of government that "we operate under the theory of a confederal nature of decision-making where power flows from ministers" (Canada 1993). I maintain, to the contrary, that power no longer flows from ministers, but from the prime minister, and unevenly at that.

The above speaks to the evolution of how policies are struck and decisions are made in Ottawa. J.S. Dupré argued that "institutionalized" Cabinet replaced the "departmentalized" Cabinet in the late 1960s and early 1970s. Individual ministers and their departments lost a great deal of autonomy to full Cabinet as well as shared knowledge and collegial decision-making (Dupré 1987, 238–9). But, I argue, this era did not last very long before court government started to take root. To be sure, information was gathered at the centre. However, it was gathered for the benefit of the prime minister and a handful of senior advisors operating in the PCO and the Prime Minister's Office (PMO), not for collegial decision-making. Court government took root in Ottawa under Pierre Trudeau and, if anything, it has grown stronger under Mulroney, Chrétien, Martin, Harper, and Justin Trudeau. It will be recalled that Paul Martin said in his leadership campaign that under his predecessor, Jean Chrétien, the key to getting things done was the PMO. He made the point that "Who you know in the PMO" has become what matters in Ottawa. However, according to observers, once in power his government was "more centralized than anything seen in the Chrétien era" (Simpson 2005, A15).

Stephen Harper continued in the tradition of centralizing power in his office. It will be recalled that he tabled a motion in Parliament in 2006 that read "that this House recognize that the Québécois form a nation within a united Canada" after consulting only a handful of his closest advisors. Cabinet was left outside the loop. Even the minister responsible for intergovernmental affairs was not informed, let alone consulted, before the decision was made and before full caucus was told (*Globe and Mail* 2006, A1, A4). Justin Trudeau went further than his predecessors. He did away with regional ministers, a concept that dates back to Canada's first prime minister, Sir John A. Macdonald.

There are other still more recent examples. Senator Lowell Murray, a highly respected minister in the Mulroney Cabinet, maintains that Cabinet government is now dysfunctional. How could it not be, given that the key decisions regarding Canada's military deployments in Afghanistan (one by a Liberal government and another by a Conservative government) were made by the prime minister with the help of only a handful of political advisors and civilian and military officials? The two relevant ministers – National Defence and Foreign Affairs – were not even in the room. They, like Cabinet, were informed after the fact (Murray 2013).

This chapter reports on the forces that have strengthened the hand of the prime minister in government. It then reviews the levers of power available to the prime minister and new developments that have made his or her office and central agencies the dominant actors within the federal government — in short, the arrival of court government.

The Forces

An important development that gave rise to court government in Ottawa was the 1976 election to office of the Parti Québécois (PQ), a provincial party committed to taking Quebec out of Canada. The impact was felt in every government building in Ottawa, but nowhere was it more strongly felt than in the Langevin Building, home to both the PMO and the PCO.

One's place in history matters a great deal to prime ministers. No Canadian prime minister wants the country to break up under his or her watch. Thus, the main task at hand is keeping the country united. No other politician in Canada feels so directly responsible for Canadian unity as does the prime minister. Indeed, should Canada break up, the prime minister will be the first to be held to account.

The preoccupation with national unity tends to recast substantive policy issues into the question of their impact on Quebec and the likelihood of securing federal-provincial agreements. There are plenty of examples. Andrew Cooper, in his comparative study of Canadian and Australian foreign affairs, writes, "A tell-tale sign of how Canada's economic and diplomatic strategy were subordinated to political tactics on agricultural trade was the routing of all the important decisions in this issue-area … through the central agencies of the Prime Minister's Office and the Privy Council Office. The decisive impact of the constitutional issue in this manner inevitably stymied the government's ability to perform effectively in the concluding phase of the Uruguay Round" (Cooper 1997, 217). The participants directly involved in recasting or rerouting the issues are for the most part political strategists or generalists operating at the centre and are not usually specialists in health care, social or economic development policy, and so on (Cameron and Simeon 2000). They are also often directly tied to the prime minister and the PMO in one fashion or another.

Provincial premiers have direct access to the prime minister and do not hesitate to pursue an issue. If the prime minister decides to support the premier, then the issue is brought to the centre of government in Ottawa for resolution. Commitments are made between two first ministers for whatever reasons, and the prime minister cannot take the risk of seeing the system or the process not producing the right decision. As a result, someone at the centre will monitor the decision until it is fully implemented. When that happens, ministers and their departments inevitably lose some of their power to the prime minister and advisors.

The program review exercises of the mid-1990s and 2011–12 brought home the point that Cabinet is not able to make spending decisions and that the decision-making power had to be concentrated in the hands of a few individuals, notably the prime minister, the minister of finance, and the president of the Treasury Board. It is accepted wisdom in Ottawa that the reason the federal government lost control of its expenditure budget was that ministers in Cabinet were unwilling to say no to the proposed spending plans of colleagues, knowing full well that their time would come when they too would come forward with their own spending proposals (Savoie 1990). One can hardly overstate the importance of the expenditure budget to public policy and government operations. It steals the stage. When the prime minister and courtiers decide to bring both fiscal policy and key spending decisions to the centre of government, they are also bringing the key policy-making levers. The prime minister, with the minister of finance, has kept tight control over all program review exercises since 1978. In brief, none have been Cabinet-driven exercises.

The Media

All important files have the potential of bringing the centre of government into play. But what makes a file important is not at all clear. It depends on the circumstances. Media attention can, on very short notice, turn an issue, however trivial, into an important file. When this happens, there is no distinction made between policy and administration. A file that receives media attention becomes political, and at that point the prime minister and advisors will want to oversee its development. Without putting too fine a point on it, the front page of the *Globe and Mail*, *Le Devoir*, or a CBC or CTV news report can make a file important, no matter its scope or nature.

Today, the media, much like society itself, are far less deferential to political leaders and political institutions. Nothing is off limits anymore, and political leaders and government officials must continually be cautious about letting their guard down when meeting the press. Twenty-four-hour news channels and social media have made controlling the message still more important than in years past. This too has strengthened the hand of the prime minister and close advisors.

The media will also focus on party leaders at election time rather than on selected party candidates, even those enjoying a high profile. Journalists buy seats on the chartered aircraft of party leaders and follow them everywhere. In Canada, the media, and by extension the public, focus on the clash of party leaders. For one thing, there are the leaders' debates on national television, in both English and French. How well a leader does in the debates can have an important impact, or at least be perceived to have an important impact, on the election campaign, if not the election itself (Johnston et al. 1992, 244). It is now widely accepted in the literature, however, that "debates are more about accidents and mistakes than about enlightenment on the capabilities of candidates to govern" (Polsby and Wildavsky 1991, 246).

Increasingly, Canadian political leaders would appear to be the only substantial candidates in the election race. In the past, Canada had powerful Cabinet ministers with deep roots in the party or strong regional identification and support. One can think of Jimmy Gardiner, Chubby Power, Jack Pickersgill, Ernest Lapointe, Louis St-Laurent, Don Jamieson, and Allan MacEachen. We no longer seem to have powerful regional figures able to carry political candidates at the regional level to victory on their coattails or speak to the prime minister from an independent power base in the party.

In Canada, winning candidates on the government side are aware that their party leader's performance in the election campaign explains in large measure why they themselves were successful. The objective of national political parties at election time is more to sell their leaders to the Canadian electorate than it is to sell their ideas or their policies. Canadian elections invariably turn on the question of who — which individual — will form the government (Savoie 2013). It should come as no surprise, then, that if the leader is able to secure a majority mandate from voters, the party is in the leader's debt, and not the other way around. In brief, Justin Trudeau rather than the Liberal Party is responsible for his 2015 victory.

National political parties, at least the Canadian variety, are not much more than election-day organizations, providing the fund raising and poll workers needed to fight an election campaign. They are hardly effective vehicles for generating public policy debates, for staking out policy positions, or for providing a capacity to ensure their own party's competence once in office. Robert Young once argued that "the Pulp and Paper Association has more capacity to do strategic analytical work than the Liberal and [Progressive] Conservative parties combined" (quoted in Sutherland 1996, 5). Regional cleavages in Canada, as is well known, dominate the national public policy agenda, and national political parties shy away from attacking regional issues head on for fear they will split the party along regional lines and hurt its chances at election time. The thinking goes, at least in the parties that have held power, that regional issues are so sensitive and politically explosive that they are best left to party leaders and a handful of advisors.

The Centre of Government

The centre of government has remained largely intact, despite a management delayering exercise in the early 1990s, a massive government restructuring introduced in 1993, and the program review exercises in the mid-1990s and again in 2011–12. It has remained intact even though the workload of central agencies should have decreased substantially, given that PCO has far fewer Cabinet committees to service than in the 1970s and 1980s under Trudeau and Mulroney.

One might well ask, then, what officials at the centre do. When Trudeau decided to enlarge the size and scope of the PMO in the late 1960s, his first principal secretary sought to reassure critics and Cabinet ministers that the office would remain essentially a service-oriented organization. He explained that it existed to "serve the prime minister personally, that its purpose is not primarily advisory but functional and the PMO is not a mini-Cabinet; it is not directly or indirectly a decision-making body and it is not, in fact, a body at all" (quoted in Sutherland 1996, 5). It is, of course, not possible to distinguish between a service function and a policy advisory function in this context. Drafting a letter or preparing a speech for the prime minister can constitute policy-making, and many times it does. There is also no doubt that several senior officials in the PMO do provide policy advice to the prime minister, and if some in Pierre Trudeau's early PMO denied this, present-day advisors and assistants certainly do not (Savoie 2013).

PMO staffers have the prime minister's ear on all issues they wish to raise, be it political, policy, administrative, or the appointment of a minister or deputy minister. They can also work hand-in-hand with a minister to initiate a proposal, and the minister will feel more secure, knowing that someone close to the prime minister supports the proposal. They can also, however, quickly undercut a proposal when briefing the prime minister. In short, senior PMO staff members do not consider themselves simply a court of second opinion. They are in the thick of it and do not hesitate to offer policy advice or to challenge a Cabinet minister.

The role of the PCO has also changed in recent years. Arnold Heeney, the architect of the modern Cabinet office in Ottawa, wrote after his retirement that he had successfully resisted Mackenzie King's desire to make the secretary to the Cabinet "a kind of deputy minister to the Prime Minister" or "the personal staff officer to the Prime Minister" (Heeney 1967, 367). It is interesting to note, however, that no secretaries to the Cabinet since Gordon Robertson have described their main job as secretary to the Cabinet. In 1997, the PCO produced a document on its role and structure whose very first page makes it clear that the secretary's first responsibility is to the prime minister. The document has not been revised to this day. It states that the "Clerk of the Privy Council and Secretary to the Cabinet" has three primary responsibilities:

1. As the Prime Minister's Deputy Minister, provides advice and support to the Prime Minister on a full range of responsibilities as head of government, including management of the federation.
2. As the Secretary to the Cabinet, provides support and advice to the Ministry as a whole and oversees the provision of policy and secretariat support to Cabinet and Cabinet committees.
3. As Head of the Public Service, is responsible for the quality of expert, professional and non-partisan advice and service provided by the Public Service to the Prime Minister, the Ministry and to all Canadians. (Canada 1997, 1)

It is also important to recognize that the prime minister no longer needs to rely on regional ministers to understand how government policies are being received. Public opinion surveys are more reliable, more objective, less regionally biased, more to the point, and easier to cope with than are ministers. As already noted, Justin Trudeau decided to do away with regional ministers. Pierre Trudeau had Martin Goldfarb; Mulroney had Allan Gregg; Chrétien had Michael Marzolini; Paul Martin had David Herle; Stephen Harper had Ottawa-based Praxicus Public Strategies; while Justin Trudeau has David Herle. Surveys can enable prime ministers and their advisors to challenge the views of ministers. After all, how can even the most senior ministers dispute what the polls say?

A pollster in court always at the ready with data can be particularly helpful in dealing with the problem of political overload. "Political overload" refers to a pervasive sense of urgency and an accompanying feeling of being overwhelmed both by events and the number of matters needing attention. A pollster can also advise the prime minister on "hot button" issues.

Prime ministers, at least since Trudeau, have decided that the best way to deal with the overload problem is to focus on a handful of policy issues and to rely on central agencies to manage the rest. All of the major policy initiatives in Trudeau's last mandate (1980–4), including the national energy program, the Constitution, and the "six and five" wage restraint initiative, were organized outside of the government's formal decision-making process (*Globe and Mail* 1997, A1). Similarly, Mulroney sidestepped Cabinet in pursuing constitutional reform, the Canada-US Free Trade Agreement, and the establishment of regional economic development agencies. At a considerable cost to the Treasury, Chrétien paid no attention to the formal decision-making process when he decided to introduce the millennium scholarship fund for low-to-moderate income students. The Cabinet was not consulted before the fund was unveiled, even though Chrétien called it "the government's most significant millennium project" (Savoie 1999, 297). Chrétien, like Mulroney and Trudeau before him, also did not consult Cabinet before striking a number of important bilateral deals with provincial premiers. Martin negotiated a costly health care agreement with the provinces without consulting Cabinet, and Harper, as already noted, decided to recognize Quebec as a nation within Canada without consulting Cabinet and decided to deploy military personnel to Afghanistan without consulting the relevant ministers, let alone Cabinet.

So what actually goes on in Cabinet meetings? The first item is "General Discussion," which the prime minister opens and leads. He can raise any matter he chooses, ranging from a letter he may have received from a premier, to a purely partisan matter, to diplomacy. The PCO prepares a briefing note of possible talking points for the prime minister to speak from. But he can, of course, completely ignore it. However, the "General Discussion" can be particularly useful to prime ministers as a cover to make it appear that Cabinet has indeed considered an important issue, which could be, for example, life threatening or require military intervention. Mulroney, for instance, agreed to participate in the first Gulf War in a discussion with President George H. Bush, but raised the matter in Cabinet so that he could report that Cabinet had indeed reviewed the situation.

The second item on the Cabinet agenda is called "Presentations." On occasions ministers, at times accompanied by their deputy ministers, are invited to give briefing sessions on various issues. The minister of finance and her deputy minister might present a "deck" on the government's fiscal position. Or the minister of industry and her deputy might make a presentation on Canada's productivity in relation to the United States. At the end of the presentation, ministers are free to raise any question or to ask for further clarification or explanation. But actual decisions rarely, if ever, flow out of these discussions. The purpose is to brief Cabinet, not to secure decisions.

The third item is "Nominations." Government appointments, ranging from a Supreme Court judge, to a senator, to a deputy minister, to a member of the board of a Crown corporation, all require an order-in-council. There is always a list of appointments to be confirmed at every Cabinet meeting. However, the nominations have all been sorted out well in advance of the meeting. The PMO and the PCO manage the appointment process, and they consult with others only to the extent they want to.

To be sure, prime ministers do not seek Cabinet consensus when appointing Supreme Court judges or even senators – suffice to note that the *Ottawa Citizen* had it right when it wrote that "Mulroney's Supreme Court may soon become Jean Chrétien's court" because of "an unusual confluence of expected retirements" (*Ottawa Citizen* 1997). Nor do prime ministers seek Cabinet consensus when appointing deputy ministers or the administrative heads of government departments. Frequently, they do not even consult the relevant minister when appointing his or her deputy. I asked a former senior PCO official why it was that Jean Chrétien when minister of, say, justice or energy in Trudeau's government could not be trusted to appoint his own deputy minister, but that the moment he became prime minister he could be trusted to appoint all the deputy ministers? His response was simply, "Because he became king" (Savoie 1999, 283).

The fourth item is "Cabinet Committee Decisions," presented as appendices on the agenda. In overhauling the Cabinet decision-making process, Trudeau made it clear that all decisions taken in Cabinet committees could be reopened for discussion in Cabinet. A former Trudeau minister reports that in his early years in office Trudeau was quite willing to let ministers reopen a Cabinet committee decision in full Cabinet. In time, however, he became annoyed with the practice and did not hesitate to show his displeasure whenever a minister sought to review an appendix item. Cabinet, he felt, simply did not have time available to discuss Cabinet committee decisions. In any event, by the late 1970s and the early 1980s, Trudeau automatically sent a Cabinet committee decision back to the committee for review whenever a minister raised questions about it in full Cabinet. Mulroney did much the same or relied on the operations committee of Cabinet, chaired by Don Mazankowski, to sort out problems with Cabinet committee decisions. Chrétien did not react well when a Cabinet committee decision was challenged and, like Trudeau in his later years, he automatically referred it back to the Cabinet committee without any discussion in full Cabinet. Harper was much like Chrétien, as is Justin Trudeau. The result is that Cabinet committee decisions are now very rarely challenged in full Cabinet.

Mulroney, we now know, had little patience for the Cabinet process and at one point said that he "favoured any decision-making system that minimized the time he spent in cabinet" (Kroeger 1998, 10). He preferred to deal with the big issues outside of Cabinet. The telephone and face-to-face conversation were his stock in trade. Indeed, we are now informed that "under Mulroney, important matters such as energy mega-projects were often decided without benefit of any cabinet documents at all" (10). The point is that Trudeau *père*, Mulroney, Chrétien, Martin, Harper, and now Justin Trudeau have all preferred to deal with major issues outside of the constraints imposed by the system. The result is that we now have policy-making by announcements. The prime minister makes a major policy announcement, for example, as Chrétien did in the case of the Kyoto Accord, and the system scrambles to implement it.

On the heels of his 2008 re-election, Harper sent a directive to his minister of finance to scrap the $28 million in public subsidies that political parties receive for each vote they garner in a federal election. Word soon circulated around Ottawa and in the media that the decision was Harper's alone. His Cabinet was not consulted, nor obviously his caucus. He simply sent, at the last minute, a directive to the minister of finance to include it in his economic update statement "without ministers or deputy ministers knowing." This, in turn, the media argued, demonstrated that he was a "ferociously partisan leader" with a profound desire to centralize "everything in his own hands" (Simpson 2008). Justin Trudeau pledged, during the 2015 election campaign, to return to Cabinet government. There is plenty of evidence that Cabinet government is not back and that, if anything, he and his office have strengthened their hands further in dealing with Cabinet (MacDougall 2017).

To be sure, prime ministers do not always bypass their Cabinets or consult them only after the fact. They pick and choose issues they want to direct and in some circumstances may decide to let the Cabinet's collective decision-making process run its course. They may even let the government caucus have its day from time to time and permit a government proposal or legislation to be pulled back and reworked to accommodate the views of caucus members. Mulroney, for example, attached a high priority to working with his caucus. There are also issues on which a prime minister may hold no firm view and decide that it is best to keep one's political capital in reserve for another day and another issue.

Globalization

"Globalization" has also served to strengthen the hand of the prime minister. In hindsight, we may well have overstated the probability that globalization would spell gloom and doom for nation-states (Savoie 1995). Many national governments are discovering that the international environment can actually enhance their own power. The 2008 financial crisis, for example, forced the hand of national governments to intervene in financial markets and introduce new measures to stimulate economic growth.

In any event, Canadian prime ministers belong to a series of recently created international clubs of heads of government, from the Group of Eight (G8) to Asia-Pacific Economic Cooperation (APEC) and the International Organization of La Francophonie. Deals, even bilateral ones, between heads of governments are struck at these meetings. The globalization of the world economy means that many more issues or files are placed in the prime minister's in-basket. Everything in a government department now seems to connect to other departments and other governments, whether at the provincial level or internationally. In Canada, prime ministers and premiers sit at the centre of the public policy process, and when they decide to focus on a policy issue, they can very easily make it their own.

National governments, precisely because of global economic forces, now need to work increasingly with each other and with regional and international trade agreements. They also need a capacity to move quickly to strike new deals when the time is right or to change course because of emerging political and economic circumstances and opportunities. The focus will be on the heads of national governments. It is also they, not their ministers, who lead the discussions at G8, at Commonwealth meetings, at La Francophonie, and at the APEC conference, to name several of the international fora in which the prime minister participates.

That said, the global economy and the interconnected world of public policy issues have caused some power to move away from national governments, drifting up to international or regional trade agreements or organizations and down to local governments (Rose 1984). Perhaps because there may now be somewhat less power to go around in the national government, the prime minister and courtiers can rule with a heavy hand.

The Canadian prime minister, unlike the American president, who has to deal with Congress, or the Australian prime minister, who has to deal with a powerful and elected Senate, has a free hand to negotiate for his or her government and to make firm deals with foreign heads of government. The final hours of negotiations on NAFTA between prime minister-elect Chrétien and the American president, through his ambassador to Canada, are telling. At one point, the American ambassador wondered about Chrétien's political authority to agree to a final deal, given that he had yet to appoint his Cabinet. The ambassador put the question to Chrétien. "What happens if we work all this out and then your new trade minister doesn't agree?" Chrétien replied, "Then I will have a new trade minister the following morning" (Greenspon and Wilson-Smith 1996, 48). It is hardly possible to overemphasize the fact that the Canadian prime minister has few limits defining his or her political authority within the government. The prime minister's power is limited by the court of public opinion because the government has to seek a new mandate every four years, and by the scarcity of time because one cannot possibly attend every important meeting and deal with every issue.

The Workings of Court Government

Canadian prime ministers have in their hands all the important levers of power. Indeed, one way or another all major national public policy roads lead to their doorstep. They are elected leader of their party by party members; they chair Cabinet meetings, establish Cabinet processes and procedures, set the Cabinet agenda, establish the consensus for Cabinet decisions; they appoint and fire ministers and deputy ministers, establish Cabinet committees and decide on their membership; they exercise virtually all the powers of patronage and act as personnel manager for thousands of government and patronage jobs; they articulate the government's strategic direction as outlined in the Speech from the Throne; they dictate the pace of change and are the main salespersons promoting the achievements of their government; they have a direct hand in establishing the government's fiscal framework; they represent Canada abroad; they establish the proper mandate of individual ministers and decide all machinery of government issues; and they are the final arbiter in interdepartmental conflicts. Prime ministers are the only politicians with a country-wide constituency, and unlike MPs and even Cabinet ministers, they do not need to search out publicity or national media attention, since attention is invariably focused on their office and their residence, 24 Sussex Drive. Each of these levers of power taken separately is a formidable instrument in its own right, but when they are all added up and placed in the hands of one individual, they constitute an unassailable advantage.

There is nothing new about this; Canadian prime ministers have enjoyed these avenues of power for some time. However, other developments have lately consolidated further the position of prime ministers and their advisors even further. Indeed, this is now evident even before they and their party assume office. Transition planning has become a very important event, designed to prepare a new government to assume power. Transition planning also strengthens the hand of prime ministers and their courtiers, given that by definition it is designed to serve the prime minister. It is the PCO, however, that leads the process, and it is clear that "transition services are for the incoming prime minister" (Savoie 1993, 8). Indeed, the focus of the PCO transition planning process is entirely on party leaders or would-be prime ministers. In any event, it would be difficult for it to be otherwise since, in the crucial days between the election victory and formally taking power, the only known member of the incoming Cabinet is the prime minister-elect. For other potential Cabinet ministers, it is a "moment of high anxiety," waiting to see if they will be invited to sit in Cabinet, and if so, in what portfolio (8).

The central purpose of transition planning is to equip incoming prime ministers to make their mark during the government's first few weeks in office. It is now widely recognized that these early weeks can be critical in setting the tone for how the new government will govern. It is also the period when prime ministers, as recent history shows, will make important decisions on the machinery of government and decide which major policy issues their government will tackle during its mandate. These and such key decisions as whether to try to amend the Constitution or fight the deficit are taken or set in motion during the transition period.

In the late 1970s, the PCO began the practice of preparing mandate letters for delivery to ministers on the day of their appointment. It has since become an integrated part of the Cabinet-making process. Mandate letters are also now handed to all ministers when they are assigned to a new portfolio. All ministers in the Chrétien government, for example, were given a mandate letter at the time he formed the government in 1993, again when his second mandate began in 1997, and yet again in his third mandate in 2000. The same was true for Paul Martin in 2003 and 2004 and Stephen Harper in 2006, 2008, and 2011. Justin Trudeau continued the practice and added a new "deliverology" unit in the Privy Council Office to ensure that ministers and their departments deliver on what the prime minister asked (Curran 2016).

What are the contents of these mandate letters? In most cases, they are brief, only about two to three pages long. They are also tailored to the recipient. That is, a mandate letter to a newly appointed minister will be different from one to a veteran minister. In the first instance, it will outline basic information about becoming a Cabinet minister, including conflict-of-interest guidelines, and the need to respect the collective nature of Cabinet decisions. In all cases, the letters will delineate issues the minister should attend to and identify priority areas, if any, to be pursued. Here, again, there are two basic mandate letters. One states, in effect, "Don't call us, we'll call you." That is, the prime minister has decided that the department in question should not come up with a new policy agenda or legislative program. In these cases, the message is essentially to keep things going, cause no ripples, and keep out of trouble (Savoie 1999, 138). In other instances, the letter will refer to particular policy objectives and major challenges. In these cases, it can be quite specific, singling out proposed legislation, a special concern that needs attending to, or a program that needs to be overhauled. Mandate letters are now also prepared for newly appointed deputy ministers. Here again the purpose is to outline the main challenges the new deputy ministers will be confronting and the priorities they will be expected to follow.

Are mandate letters taken seriously? The answer is yes. Indeed, ministers consulted said that it is the very first thing that they read after leaving the swearing-in ceremony at Rideau Hall and that they take their contents quite seriously. They know, as one observed, that "the prime minister can always dig out his copy and ask about the status of a particular point" (personal communication). More importantly, the letters reveal what the prime minister expects from them during their stay in their departments. Both present and former PMO and PCO officials report that all prime ministers, from Trudeau *père* to Trudeau *fils*, take the mandate letters seriously and that they spend the required time to ensure that each says what they wish it to say.

Ministers, leaving aside a few exceptions, no longer leave Cabinet over a policy disagreement. Much more often, ministers leave after receiving a patronage appointment from the prime minister – a Senate, judicial, or diplomatic appointment. The notable exceptions recently include Lucien Bouchard (1990) from the Mulroney Cabinet and Michael Chang (2006) from the Harper Cabinet. Both resigned over national unity questions.

The budget has become the government's major policy statement and defines in very specific terms what the government will do in the coming months and where it will be spending new money. Traditionally, the government's budget process pitted guardians (e.g., the prime minister and minister of finance) against spenders (ministers of line departments and regional ministers) (Savoie 1990). Efforts were made under Trudeau and Mulroney to establish various systems to allocate the spending of new money, but they all fell far short of the mark.

The prime minister, the minister of finance and their advisors have, for some time now, combined the guardian and spender roles. This has not changed under Justin Trudeau. The budget exercise is no longer strictly concerned with the country's broad economic picture, projecting economic growth, establishing the fiscal framework, and deciding which taxes ought to be introduced, increased, or decreased. It now deals with both "big" and "small" decisions, revenue projections, and spending decisions (Good 2007). For example, when senior military officials in Canada sought to replace their armoured vehicles, they bypassed Cabinet to appeal directly to the prime minister. Lieutenant-General Andrew Leslie told the media that he hoped "Stephen Harper will replace the old tanks," adding that he expected "the Prime Minister's decision within about a week" (*Globe and Mail* 2007, A1). In addition, when the centre decides to sponsor new initiatives, it will much more often than not secure the required funding outside of the Cabinet process (Savoie 2013).

The role of the clerk of the Privy Council and secretary to the Cabinet has changed a great deal in recent years, and the clerk's influence in Ottawa is readily apparent to everyone inside the system. Outsiders, however, know very little about the clerk's role and responsibilities. One of the main challenges confronting a clerk is to establish a proper balance between representing the public service as an institution to the prime minister and Cabinet and representing the prime minister to the public service. The balance appears to have shifted to the latter with the appointment of thirty-seven-year-old Michael Pitfield as clerk-secretary in 1975 by Pierre Trudeau. The balance may well have shifted even further in favour of the prime minister when Paul Tellier decided, as clerk-secretary under Mulroney, to add the title of prime minister's deputy minister to his job.

Tellier's decision, however, simply reflected the reality of his day-to-day work. Indeed, the clerk-secretary is accountable to the prime minister, not to Cabinet, and the great majority of his daily activities are now designed to support the prime minister, not Cabinet. The prime minister, not Cabinet, appoints the clerk; the prime minister, not Cabinet, evaluates the clerk's performance; and the prime minister, not Cabinet, will decide if he or she stays or should be replaced. All this is to say that not only does the secretary to Cabinet wear the hat of deputy minister to the prime minister, it is without doubt the hat that fits best and the one he or she wears nearly all the time. A former senior PCO official observed that "all clerks since Pitfield have done an excellent job at being deputy minister to the prime minister. As far as secretary to the Cabinet, the performance has been spotty."[1]

The Charter of Rights and Freedoms has shifted some power to the courts. It has also strengthened the centre of government in its dealings with line departments. The Department of Justice (DOJ) officials are now part of the centre where, in concert with senior central agency officials, they have essentially pushed aside line departments in the scrutiny of legislation in the name of Charter vetting. James B. Kelly points to the moment when DOJ became part of the centre,: it was when "the clerk of the Privy Council, on the instruction of the prime minister, directed line departments to consult the DOJ" in dealing with potential Charter issues (Kelly 2005, 224).

The way to govern in Ottawa – at least since Pierre Trudeau – is for prime ministers to focus on three or four priority issues while also always keeping an eye on Quebec and national unity concerns. Thomas Axworthy, former principal secretary to Pierre Trudeau, in his appropriately titled article, "Of Secretaries to Princes," wrote that "only with maximum prime ministerial involvement could the host of obstacles that stand in the way of reform be overcome." The prime minister "must choose relatively few central themes, not only because of the time demands on the prime minister, but also because it takes a herculean effort to coordinate the government machine" (Axworthy 1998, 247). To perform a herculean effort, a prime minister needs carefully selected individuals in key positions to push his or her agenda. Cabinet, the public service as an institution, or even government departments, are not always helpful.

The result is that important decisions are no longer made in Cabinet. They are now made in the PMO, in the PCO, in the Department of Finance, in international organizations, and at international summits. There is no indication that the one person who holds all the cards, the prime minister, and the central agencies that enable him or her to bring effective political authority to the centre, are about to change things. Canadian prime ministers have few internal institutional checks to inhibit their ability to have their way.

In Canada, national unity concerns, the nature of federal-provincial relations, and the role of the media tend, in a perverse fashion, to favour the centre of government in Ottawa. The prime minister's court dominates the policy agenda and permeates government decision-making to such an extent that it is only willing to trust itself to oversee the management of important issues. In a sense, the centre of government has come to fear ministerial and line department independence more than it deplores line department paralysis. As a result, court government is probably better suited to manage the political agenda than is Cabinet government. The prime minister, like the European monarchs of yesterday, decides, at least within the federal government, who has standing at court. Prime Minister Chrétien left little doubt that Canada had made the transition to court government when he observed, "The Prime Minister is the Prime Minister and he has the cabinet to advise him. At the end of the day, it is the Prime Minister who says 'yes' or 'no'" (*Globe and Mail* 2000, A4).

Advisors, much like courtiers of old, have influence, not power. Jean Chrétien made his view clear that ministers have influence, not power in

Cabinet, when he wrote that a "minister may have great authority within his department, but within Cabinet he is merely part of a collectivity, just another advisor to the prime minister. He can be told what to do and on important matters his only choice is to do or resign" (Chrétien 1985, 85). One of Chrétien's former senior policy advisers unwittingly described court government well when he wrote, "Everything a prime minister says is unfortunately taken by some as coming from the fount of all wisdom. Often the prime minister is just throwing out an idea or suggestion for debate and discussion; yet, inevitably to his surprise, it is solemnly transcribed as if it were one of the Ten Commandments" (Goldenberg 2006, 83). He was referring to both elected politicians and senior civil servants. Henry VIII and his ilk, the absolute monarchs of yore, would have expected nothing less from their courtiers.

Note

1 Consultation with a former senior PCO official, Ottawa, November 1997.

References and Suggested Readings

Axworthy, Thomas S. 1998. "Of Secretaries to Princes." *Canadian Public Administration* 31 (2): 247–64.

Cameron, David, and Richard Simeon. 2000. "Intergovernmental Relations and Democratic Citizenship." In *Revitalizing the Public Service: A Governance Vision for the XXIst Century*, edited by B. Guy Peters and Donald J. Savoie, 58–118. Montreal and Kingston: McGill-Queen's University Press.

Canada, Privy Council Office. 1993. *Responsibility in the Constitution*. Ottawa: Government of Canada.

———. 1997. *The Role and Structure of the Privy Council Office*. Ottawa: Government of Canada.

Chrétien, Jean. 1985. *Straight from the Heart*. Toronto: Key Porter Books.

Cooper, Andrew F. 1997. *In Between Countries: Australia, Canada and the Search for Order in Agricultural Trade*. Montreal and Kingston: McGill-Queen's University Press.

Curran, Rachel. 2016. "The Trudeau Government's Focus on Deliverology Shouldn't Distract It from Building the Public Service's Policy Muscle." *Policy Options*, April 27.

Dupré, J.S. 1987. "The Workability of Executive Federalism in Canada." In *Federalism and the Role of the State*, edited by H. Bakvis and W. Chandler, 236–58. Toronto: University of Toronto Press.

Globe and Mail. 1997. "Spending Limits Irk Cabinet." December 3, A1.

———. 2000. "Penalty Killer PM Plays Rough." December 1, A4.

———. 2006. "Inside Story." November 24, A1, A4.

———. 2007. "All LAV IIIs to Be Replaced within a Year." April 3, A1.

Goldenberg, Eddie. 2006. *The Way It Works: Inside Ottawa*. Toronto: McClelland and Stewart.

Good, David A. 2007. *The Politics of Public Money: Spenders, Guardians, Priority Setters and Financial Watchdogs inside the Canadian Government*. Toronto: IPAC and University of Toronto Press.

Greenspon, Edward, and Anthony Wilson-Smith. 1996. *Double Vision: The Inside Story of the Liberals in Power*. Toronto: Doubleday.

Heeney, A.D.P. 1967. "Mackenzie King and the Cabinet Secretariat." *Canadian Public Administration* 10 (3): 366–75.

Johnston, Richard, André Blais, Henry E. Brady, and Jean Crête. 1992. *Letting the People Decide: The Dynamics of a Canadian Election*. Stanford: Stanford University Press.

Kelly, James B. 2005. *Governing with the Charter: Legislative and Judicial Activism and Framers' Intent*. Vancouver: UBC Press.

Kroeger, Arthur. 1998. "A Retrospective on Policy Development in Ottawa." Ottawa. Mimeo.

MacDougall, Andrew. 2017. "Who in His Cabinet Can Justin Trudeau Actually Trust?" *Ottawa Citizen*, May 12. http://ottawacitizen.com/news/local-news/macdougall-who-in-his-cabinet-can-justin-trudeau-actually-trust.

Murray, Lowell. 2013. "Power, Responsibility and Agency in Canadian Government." In *Governing: Essays in Honour of Donald J. Savoie*, edited by James Bickerton and B. Guy Peters, 25–31. Montreal and Kingston: McGill-Queen's University Press.

Ottawa Citizen. 1997. "Chrétien Set to Remake Top Court." December 14, A7.

Polsby, Nelson W., and Aaron Wildavsky. 1991. *Presidential Elections: Strategies of American Electoral Politics*. New York: Free Press.

Robertson, Gordon. 1971. "The Changing Role of the Privy Council Office." *Canadian Public Administration* 14: 487–508.

Rose, Richard. 1984. *Understanding Big Government*. London: Sage.

Savoie, Donald J. 1990. *The Politics of Public Spending in Canada*. Toronto: University of Toronto Press.

———. 1993. "Introduction." In *Taking Power: Managing Government Transitions*, edited by Donald J. Savoie. Toronto: Institute of Public Administration of Canada.

———. 1995. "Globalization, Nation States, and the Civil Service." In *Governance in a Changing Environment*, edited by B. Guy Peters and Donald J. Savoie. Montreal and Kingston: McGill-Queen's University Press.

———. 1999. *Governing from the Centre: The Concentration of Power in Canadian Politics*. Toronto: University of Toronto Press.

———. 2013. *Whatever Happened to the Music Teacher: How Government Decides and Why*. Montreal and Kingston: McGill-Queen's University Press.

Simpson, Jeffrey. 2005. "From Pariah to Messiah: Send in the Clerk." *Globe and Mail*, March 9, A15.

———. 2008. "After the Storm." *Globe and Mail*, December 5, A17.

Sutherland, Sharon. 1991. "Responsible Government and Ministerial Responsibility: Every Reform Is Its Own Problem." *Canadian Journal of Political Science* 24 (1): 91–120.

———. 1996. "Does Westminster Government Have a Future?" Occasional Paper Series. Ottawa: Institute of Governance.

four
The House of Commons and Responsible Government

LORI TURNBULL

Introduction

The House of Commons has been described by political scientist David E. Smith as "the people's house" (Smith 2007), because it is composed of representatives who are directly elected by the people themselves. Though political party leadership has a major impact on voters' choices at the ballot box, we do not actually vote for our prime minister directly. Instead, we vote for a local representative, a member of Parliament (MP), whose role is to represent a constituency in the House of Commons in Ottawa. At the provincial level, we do the same thing. Normally, candidates for elected positions run under the banner of a political party, though some choose to run as independents.

Collectively, the members of the legislature determine the composition of the government (the prime minister and Cabinet). The prime minister is the member who can hold the confidence of the legislature (more on this later). This is usually, though not necessarily, the leader of the party with the most seats. For example, in the general election of 2015, the Liberal Party of Canada elected members in 184 of Canada's 338 federal constituencies. Not only did the Liberals elect more members than any other party, they also elected enough members to hold a majority of seats in the House. Once the votes were counted, we knew that Liberal leader Justin Trudeau would become the next prime minister because, as leader of the Liberal Party, he would be the MP most likely to hold the confidence of the House.

Political parties play a significant role in the organization, operation, and functioning of the House of Commons, both federally and in provincial legislatures. Parties almost always vote as blocs; in other words, when measures come before the House for a vote, all members of a political party tend to vote the same way. In fact, they are expected to – both by their leadership and by the voters who elected them. This practice is called party discipline. It is common across Westminster parliamentary systems and exists in congressional systems like the United States, though often to a lesser degree. Party discipline gives predictability and stability to a party's actions, and it gives a sense of what the party stands for, but the practice of party discipline also restricts the autonomy of individual MPs while fortifying support around the party leaders. Consider the case of Prime Minister Trudeau: because his party held a majority of seats in the House (until the 2019 election, which reduced the Liberals to a minority government), party discipline virtually inoculated him and his government from a loss of confidence. Even with a minority government a prime minister usually does not lose confidence, though his or her grip on power is less certain.

Once the prime minister and Cabinet are in place, it is the responsibility of the House of Commons to hold the government to account, to scrutinize its spending and policy decisions, and to ask questions of its ministers. The division of labour works roughly like this: the prime minister and Cabinet set the legislative agenda, introduce most of the bills that come before Parliament, and propose a budget for the year. The role of the House of Commons is to either accept or reject the government's plans. Though bills are scrutinized and amended by committees made up of MPs, law-making is not the primary function of the legislature (though this may seem a contradiction in terms). Instead, the role of the House of Commons is best understood as a confidence chamber.

Confidence is the constitutional convention of responsible government that requires that the prime minister and Cabinet continuously demonstrate that they have the support of the majority of MPs in the House of Commons to govern legitimately. This is what makes the parliamentary system democratic: the prime minister and Cabinet are not accountable to voters directly, but instead are accountable to our elected representatives. Some items, like the budget and the Speech from the Throne, are always considered matters of confidence, requiring the support of a majority of MPs. For other matters, it is up to the government to determine whether the vote constitutes a measure of confidence. If a government loses a vote in the House of Commons that is considered a confidence measure, there are two possible courses of action: it must either resign or request the dissolution of Parliament, both of which would normally trigger a new election (more on this later).

In this chapter, we will take a closer look at how members of Parliament are chosen, what their responsibilities are, and how some recent parliamentary reforms have affected the work of MPs. Though the federal jurisdiction is the focus, we consider provincial examples as well, in order to give a balanced perspective on how legislatures operate. The chapter concludes by considering some lessons from the practice of consensus government, in which Westminster parliamentary government operates in the absence of political parties. But first we will consider constitutional conventions that define the practice of parliamentary governance and affect the balance of power between the executive and legislative branches.

Constitutional Conventions in Canada

In Canada, our constitution comprises written and unwritten parts. The written Constitution includes the British North America Act 1867 and the Constitution Act, 1982. The BNA Act is essentially the enabling statute for the House of Commons: it determines the number of MPs per province, it sets the quorum at twenty members, it establishes rules for voting, and it states that the first order of business for MPs in a new Parliament is to choose a Speaker. However, many of the other rules that govern how democracy works in the House of Commons, how MPs select and defeat governments, and how confidence is determined are unwritten conventions. A convention is a rule that is binding in a political but not a legal sense. Even responsible government itself is a constitutional convention. The fact that conventions are uncodified can make it difficult to obtain a consensus on what they mean and how they should be practised (Aucoin, Jarvis, and Turnbull 2011); however, the lack of legal rigidity allows for flexibility and adaptability in the system. There is room for discretion and judgment among the political actors involved so that the decisions can reflect the specific circumstances of the time.

Take, for example, recent events in provincial elections in Canada. In British Columbia, the 2017 provincial election produced what Peter Russell has called a "hung parliament," which means that no single party holds the majority of seats in the legislature (Russell 2008). The results were as follows: the incumbent Liberals won forty-three seats, the New Democratic Party won forty-one, and the Green Party won three. The magic number for a majority was forty-four. By convention, regardless of the results of an election, the incumbent premier has the first right to meet the legislature to determine whether he or she can hold its confidence. Liberal leader and Premier Christy Clark chose to exercise this right, though the process around it was complicated.

The first step for any new legislature, as mentioned above, is to choose a Speaker. The Speaker is responsible for presiding over parliamentary business and maintaining decorum. Though elected as a member of the legislature, normally under the banner of a political party, the Speaker is expected to perform his or her duties in a non-partisan manner in order to be fair to all parties. Speakers do not vote in the legislature unless it is to break a tie and, by convention, the Speaker votes to preserve the status quo and to continue debate on an issue. The Speaker is selected by secret ballot vote of all members of the legislature. Members have to declare that they are *not* interested in becoming the Speaker, otherwise their name will appear on the ballot.

Normally, though not always, the Speaker comes from the government side of the House.

Following the election result in British Columbia, at first it looked as though no one would be willing to stand as a candidate for Speaker. The numbers were just too close. The Liberals were one short of a majority and would need the support of at least one other member of the legislature (MLA) to survive. Together the opposition parties held a majority, and so very quickly after the election they issued a joint statement pledging to work together to defeat the government on the Speech from the Throne. This is normally the first confidence vote after an election and therefore the first opportunity to defeat a government (provided a Speaker is chosen first so that the session can commence). Eventually a Liberal candidate let his name stand for the position of Speaker and the government was defeated on the Throne Speech. In accordance with convention, Premier Clark paid a visit to the lieutenant-governor, the Crown's representative in the province, to request that the legislature be dissolved so that a new election could be held, one that hopefully would produce a clearer result. However, the NDP and the Greens had publicly vowed to work together. Further, they had solidified this partnership with a formal agreement on confidence and supply, one that spelled out the numerous issues on which they planned to cooperate. Given this evidence of a clear alternative to the defeated Liberals, one that constituted a government-in-waiting, the lieutenant-governor denied the premier's request. Clark resigned, and the NDP (with the support of the Greens) formed government.

In New Brunswick in 2018, a similar situation occurred in the sense that the provincial election also produced a hung parliament. This time, though the incumbent Liberals had won a plurality of the vote, they captured only twenty-one of the legislature's forty-nine seats. The Progressive Conservatives won twenty-two, while two smaller parties – the left-leaning Greens and right-leaning People's Alliance – gained three seats apiece. Though Liberal Premier Brian Gallant and his party finished second in seat totals, he exercised his constitutional right to meet the House of Assembly in a bid to remain the government by winning a vote of confidence in the legislature, as Premier Clark did. Similarly, in order to allow the House to conduct its business, a Liberal member of the government caucus came forward to offer himself for the position of Speaker. Not surprisingly, as was the case in BC, the government fell when it lost a confidence vote on its Speech from the Throne. This time, instead of visiting the lieutenant-governor to advise dissolution and a new election as Clark did, Premier Gallant resigned, allowing Progressive Conservative leader Blaine Higgs to form a government. Though the new premier did not create a formal partnership with another party, as was the case in British Columbia, he had obtained a more informal commitment from the People's Alliance to support the government on confidence matters for at least eighteen months.

While the two scenarios overlapped in many ways, the defeated premiers played their cards differently, as did the opposition party leaders – all because unwritten conventions around government transition provided flexibility to allow for the exercise of judgment, discretion, and political calculation. A government leader who is defeated has a choice to make about how to handle it, as does the lieutenant-governor, whose role it is to ensure there is always a government in place. Whereas codified rules would provide certainty, conventions allow political events to play themselves out and to resolve the situation.

While the foregoing examples come from the provincial jurisdiction, they have relevance at the federal level as well, as both use the same Westminster-style parliamentary system wherein political parties organize government and opposition. The examples above discuss how members of the legislature choose governments; in the following section, we will consider how members themselves are chosen to sit in the legislature, federally and provincially.

How Do We Choose MPs and What Do They Do?

The House of Commons is populated by 338 MPs, each representing a geographical constituency or "riding." Each constituency elects one representative using the first-past-the-post (single member plurality) voting system. On election day, voters mark an X next to the name of the candidate they support. If the candidate is affiliated with a registered political party, the party's name appears next to the candidate's name. With all votes counted, the individual with a plurality (the most votes, not necessarily a majority) is declared the winner and awarded the seat.

For decades, there has been debate over whether we should change the rules that elect federal and provincial representatives. Supporters of electoral reform, including the prominent non-profit group Fair Vote Canada, tend to favour a system based on proportional representation, which would create a direct relationship between political parties' share of the popular vote and their share of seats in the legislature. The first-past-the-post system has its benefits: it's easy to vote and to count the votes, and there is a clear line of accountability between the voters and the individual who represents their riding. However, the system can produce significant distortions in how political parties are represented. Further, it almost always over-rewards the party that comes first, as well as any party whose vote is concentrated regionally. For example, in 2015, the Liberal Party elected members in 54 per cent of federal ridings, but won only 39 per cent of the popular vote. A clear majority of people who voted in the election voted for candidates who were not Liberal, but because Liberal candidates came first in most ridings, they claimed a majority of seats in the House of Commons. This allowed them to govern without fear of loss of confidence. In comparison, the New Democratic Party won 19 per cent of the popular vote but elected members in only 13 per cent of ridings. Supporters of proportional representation take exception to this discrepancy and argue for a system that is more fair and balanced in its distribution of seats among the parties (see Brian Tanguay's chapter on democratic reform).

In the 2015 campaign, the Liberals made a commitment to pursue electoral reform. The campaign website included a rather bold pledge: "We are committed to ensuring that 2015 will be the last federal election conducted under the first-past-the-post voting system" (Liberal Party of Canada 2015). In the months following the election, the Special Committee on Electoral Reform (ERRE) "was appointed to identify and conduct a study of viable alternate voting systems to replace the first-past-the-post system, as well as to examine mandatory voting and online voting" (Parliament of Canada 2016). Determining the composition of the committee turned out to be a controversial process. Initially, the government proposed a committee membership that reflected the party's standings in the House, which is normally the way committees are structured. The plan was for the Liberals to have six members, the Conservatives three, and the NDP one, with non-voting positions for the Greens and the Bloc Québécois, because neither had enough members to meet the threshold for official party status. Normally, MPs who are independent or who sit in caucuses that do not have official party status are not entitled to serve as committee members. Opposition leaders quickly criticized the government for attempting to "stack the deck" by giving their own members a majority on the committee, which would allow the government to control the committee and its future recommendations. After some heated exchanges, the government issued a new plan for the committee's design: parties would hold seats based on the popular vote in 2015 rather than their seat share. This would yield only four seats for the Liberals – so not a majority – with the Green and Bloc Québécois members granted full membership, including the right to vote on matters before the committee.

The committee toured the country, as did minister for democratic institutions Maryam Monsef, talking to Canadians, stakeholders, and experts on electoral reform. The committee recommended that the government put together a proposal for a proportional representation system and hold a national referendum to see whether Canadians would support the change (Wherry and Tasker 2017). However, early in 2017, the prime minister announced that, for lack of consensus on the issue, the government would abandon its plans for electoral reform. This decision was met with disappointment from the stakeholder groups and individual Canadians who support electoral reform and saw this as an opportunity for progress. Electoral reform is still on the table in several provinces, including British Columbia, Prince Edward Island, and Quebec, where political leadership has been interested in pursuing the matter.

The first-past-the-post system, as mentioned above, divides the country into geographical ridings, each of which elects one representative to the House of Commons. The parameters of these ridings are determined by independent boundaries commissions established in each province shortly after the completion of each decennial census. The independent commissions, as opposed to politicians, determine the boundaries so that there is no risk of "gerrymandering" (gerrymandering refers to the practice of drawing boundaries strategically to favour a partisan interest). Each commission consists of three people and reports to the chief electoral officer, whose role is to administer elections. Each commission comes up with a new electoral map based on their consideration of several factors: average population numbers, communities of identity or interest, historical patterns of the electoral districts, and the geographical size of electoral districts (Elections Canada 2018). Because these principles are considered in balance, there is significant variation between federal ridings in geographical size and number of people. The Electoral Boundaries Readjustment Act specifies that commissions should ensure that "the population of each electoral district be as close as is reasonably possible to the average population size of a district for that province" (Elections Canada 2018) and no riding should deviate more than 25 per cent above or below the average.

Elected representatives operate on two parallel tracks: one as a constituency representative and one as a member of a legislature. The priorities and lenses in each of these contexts are not necessarily at odds, but they are different. As a constituency representative, an MP is concerned with helping constituents with the matters that affect their daily lives, like applying for passports, finding jobs, and accessing government services. The MP is motivated to be present in the local riding as much as possible in order to be familiar to voters, to understand their needs, and to earn their trust. And, to be frank, MPs (usually) want to be re-elected. Most MPs do not win with a majority of the vote in the constituency and, as the saying goes, "There are no votes in Ottawa." Elections happen at home, so time in the riding is crucial.

Members of Parliament are in Ottawa during "sitting weeks," which generally total eighteen to twenty per year at the federal level. Provincial legislatures differ in how frequently they sit each year, though typically there are fewer sitting days provincially than there are federally. In the legislature, elected members are expected to vote on bills and motions, participate in debates, and serve as members of committees. Every afternoon when the House is sitting, MPs participate in Question Period, which is a roughly one-hour session when backbench MPs (those not in Cabinet) ask questions of Cabinet ministers related to the portfolios that ministers hold. This activity, more than any other on Parliament Hill, gets the attention of the press gallery. Though ministers must respond to questions from MPs, and these exchanges are potentially pivotal to government accountability and transparency, ministers' responses are often rhetorical rather than substantive. Question Period is a highly partisan exercise through which everyone is looking to score political points, embarrass opponents, and land soundbite-style messages that reinforce their party's platform. Even MPs themselves acknowledge that they are performing for the cameras and that things can get out of hand. In fact, in 2014, while the Conservative Party held government under Prime Minister Stephen Harper, the NDP actually put forward a motion in the House requiring ministers to provide "on point" answers to questions. This move was triggered largely by the fact that Parliamentary Secretary Paul Calandra, who had been answering questions in Question Period on behalf the prime minister when he was absent, made a practice of providing responses that were seen to be totally unrelated to the questions posed. For example, he was known to talk about his daughters, his father's pizza shop, and, in response to a question on Iraq, he reacted with a statement about Israel. The NDP's motion did not pass and, even if it had, motions are non-binding statements of the intent of the House and so cannot be used to force MPs or ministers to behave differently. However, Calandra did offer an apology in the House for his controversial approach to Question Period (Huffington Post 2014).

In legislation, MPs have limited opportunities to be proactive. Though most bills come from the government, individual members have the right to introduce "private members' bills" of their own. The House of Commons uses a lottery system to determine which MPs will have the opportunity to introduce their own bills, as there is only enough time in each parliamentary session – devoted primarily to government business – for a limited number of private bills. Usually private members' bills do not pass, but they can spark debate and put pressure on the government to act. For example, in 2016, NDP MP Kennedy Stewart introduced a bill that would financially penalize political parties that failed to incorporate gender balance when they nominated candidates. The government response to the bill, which was made public, largely through a briefing note that was leaked to the media, was that the financial penalties for parties without gender-balanced slates of candidates would be unfair – and perhaps even unconstitutional – because this approach could undermine the accessibility of political office for qualified persons (Raj 2016). Though the bill did not pass, it gained significant attention from the media and from Equal Voice, a prominent non-partisan organization that promotes female representation in legislatures. It also exposed the government on female representation in politics, especially given that the prime minister has frequently styled himself as a feminist.

In order for a bill to become a law, it must go through stages. At first reading, the title of the bill is read and copies of the bill are distributed to members (and usually to the media). At second reading, the appropriate minister speaks to the bill's purpose. At the committee stage, the bill is given close scrutiny by the relevant standing committee of the House of Commons. There are twenty-three standing committees in the House, each of which comprises ten members. As discussed earlier, the composition of each committee reflects the partisan make-up of the House of Commons. For example, during their first mandate, the Liberal government held a majority on every committee of the House. This had a significant effect on the treatment that bills received at committee. Party discipline applies at the committee stage every bit as much as it does on the floor of the House of Commons, and sometimes even more so. The role of an MP on a committee is to pursue and protect the government's agenda, to raise the issues important to the party, and to invite witnesses to speak to the committee about the bill's strengths, weaknesses, and overall implications. At the committee stage individual members are given opportunity to work on issues of particular importance to them (for example, an MP with a keen interest in climate change would likely want to be a member of the Standing Committee on Environment and Sustainable Development). Committees are able to make amendments to a bill, after which point the bill goes back to the House for third reading and a vote. If the House passes the bill, it goes to the Senate, where the bill is studied (and potentially amended) once again. Only after both chambers pass the bill in identical form does it proceed to the governor general for royal assent. Normally a bill is proclaimed as law on the day of assent (proclamation), unless otherwise provided for in the bill itself.

Perhaps the most important role of the legislature is as protector of the public purse. The most anticipated piece of legislation each year is the budget, which is brought forward by the minister of finance and reflects the financial priorities, taxation, and spending plans for the upcoming year. By tradition, finance ministers wear new shoes on "budget day." The shoes can send a message about what kind of budget they are about to "drop." For example, in 1993, when the economy was in trouble and the government decided to cut program spending in order to get the debt under control,

Finance Minister Paul Martin showed up in work boots, indicating that money was tight and that hard work would be necessary to get the country's finances back in order.

It is the job of MPs to scrutinize the government's use of public money. The budget goes to the Standing Committee on Finance for a detailed comb-through before going to the full legislature for debate and a vote. However, the process for budgetary scrutiny has been subject to serious criticism. Experts in parliamentary budgeting, including eminent professor of public administration Donald Savoie, have expressed the concern that MPs cannot provide the oversight necessary to provide accountability and transparency on budgeting (May 2017). This is due to constraints in time, lack of expertise in budget and financial matters, and absence of alignment between the budget – essentially a thematic policy document about how the government plans to raise spend money – and the main estimates, the tome-like "blue books," which are the detailed expenditure plans of government organizations (Environment and Climate Change Canada 2018).

Further to this point, governments have become prone to using an "omnibus" approach to budgets, which means that budgets tend to be very long and multi-thematic, and it is difficult (if not impossible) for the Finance Committee to scrutinize the entire bill in earnest. For example, the Liberal government introduced a budget implementation bill in the fall of 2018 that was 850 pages long; similarly, the budget bill in 2010, introduced by a Conservative government, was 880 pages. Parliamentarians have pushed for years to have omnibus bills broken down into smaller packages for more effective scrutiny. Though both parties have used omnibus budget bills, this does not stop them from criticizing one another for doing so. In fact, as a backbench MP in 1994, Stephen Harper decried the Liberal government's use of the omnibus approach: "The subject matter of the bill is so diverse that a single vote on the content would put members in conflict with their own principles" (Galloway 2018). As prime minister, Harper resorted to the same approach. Finally in 2017, general discontent with this practice led the Trudeau Liberal government to introduce an amendment to the House rules that would allow the Speaker to split up omnibus bills, which Speaker Geoff Regan did that year when he split the budget into five pieces for voting (Wherry 2017).

The health of parliamentary democracy, and, in particular, the ability of the legislative branch to hold the executive to account, is threatened to the extent that the balance of power between the two branches is skewed too heavily in favour of the prime minister and Cabinet. Canada's system of parliamentary government is often accused of concentrating power too heavily in the political executive (the prime minister and closest advisors, elected and unelected) (Savoie 1999). In light of these concerns, there are many proposals on the table to rebalance the relationship between the executive and the legislature by further empowering MPs.

How Could We Make Parliament Better?

It is common for politicians, academics, pressure groups, journalists, and citizens to suggest ways for Parliament to improve, whether from the perspective of efficiency, responsiveness, cost-effectiveness, or democratic legitimacy. Before forming government, Justin Trudeau and the Liberal Party ran a wide-ranging campaign that included a democratic reform component. Some of these promises, like electoral reform and Senate reform, had far-reaching effects on how parliamentary democracy works in Canada. Though the Liberal government decided to shelve its promise to change the electoral system, it did follow through with changes to how senators are chosen. It is the prerogative of the Crown to appoint individuals to the Senate. Though it is the governor general to make the official appointment, the advice of the prime minister on whom to appoint is considered binding. Historically, appointments were made on the basis of political patronage, to reward party loyalists for their work and commitment over the years. This model tends to run counter to modern assumptions about democracy, fairness, and accountability; after all, what would justify the appointment of partisans to positions that are unelected and unaccountable, but protected until age seventy-five and generously compensated? Breaking with tradition, the Trudeau government introduced a process in which Canadians can apply to be senators. An independent advisory board considers applications when senate vacancies become available and make recommendations to the prime minister on whom to appoint. The new model addresses the patronage issue but not the other issues raised here and comes with its own challenges, including the unpredictability of a Senate populated by independents (see Andrew Heard's chapter in this volume).

Notwithstanding the substantial changes made to the Senate with potentially far-reaching consequences, other Liberal promises on democratic reform were relatively straightforward and easy to implement. For example, the platform included a promise to have committee chairs elected by secret ballot of committee members, as opposed to having chairs essentially chosen by the prime minister. This reinforces committees' independence from government and their capacity to scrutinize. Also, the Liberal government followed through on its commitment to introducing a "prime minister's Question Period." Whereas usually the prime minister takes questions only from other party leaders and only during the first few rounds of the Question Period session, every Wednesday he takes every single question that comes from backbench MPs. The prime minister's Question Period gives more MPs the opportunity to pose questions directly to the prime minister. This makes it harder for the prime minister and his advisors to predict questions coming from a cross-section of MPs, as opposed to party leaders, representing a more challenging situation that can enhance accountability to the House. That said, given the limitations of Question Period, despite the increased exposure, criticism and accountability of the prime minister remains superficial.

Some changes that the Liberals intended to bring to Parliament were more controversial than anticipated. For example, in March 2017, Government House Leader Bardish Chagger released a discussion paper to "stimulate discussion" on potential parliamentary reforms. These included reapportioning Friday sitting hours; introduction of the prime minister's Question Period, discussed above; use of electronic voting by MPs; implementation of time limits on MPs' speeches at committee; and implementation of "programming" that would pre-determine time spent on debate and scrutiny of each bill before the House (Government of Canada 2017). These measures did not require legislative change; instead, they were amendments to the Standing Orders of the House of Commons, which govern the internal procedures of the chamber. However, opposition parties strongly opposed the government's attempt to force these changes through without having consulted other parties. They joined to condemn the Liberal proposals as a power-hungry attempt to undermine the ability of parliamentarians to hold the government to account. Subsequently, the government backed down on most proposals after the opposition employed procedural tactics to prevent the proposed reforms from going through. Nonetheless, the following measures were implemented: allowing the Speaker to separate omnibus bills; forcing the government to explain its rationale if it chooses to prorogue the House (in other words, to end a session); taking measures to align the timing of the budget and the main estimates; and devoting one Question Period a week to the prime minister alone (Bryden 2017).

The catalyst for the proposal on prorogation was likely the "prorogation crisis" of 2008, when Governor General Michaëlle Jean prorogued Parliament on the advice of Prime Minister Stephen Harper. To prorogue Parliament is to end a session; neither the House nor its committees meet during prorogation, and any government bill that has not received royal assent dies on the order paper and needs to be reintroduced in a new session. Prorogations are not always controversial. Sometimes a prime minister seeks prorogation simply to "change the channel" in the House once a legislative agenda has been completed. When Parliament returns following a prorogation, it begins with a Speech from the Throne that identifies the government's priorities for the future. This can be a moment of reset and renewal for a government that is midway through its mandate. However, the 2008 prorogation was anything but routine.

In the general election in October 2008, the Conservatives won a minority government. In late November, Finance Minister Jim Flaherty gave a fiscal update in the House of Commons that included a controversial proposal to end the per-vote subsidy to political parties. The opposition parties were caught off guard by the proposal because the Conservatives did not campaign on it. Liberal leader Stéphane Dion and New Democratic Party leader Jack Layton took to the airwaves immediately to announce their intent to defeat the Conservative government at the earliest opportunity and to form a coalition government in its place. Prime Minister Harper reacted to this proposal by dismissing the legitimacy of the proposed coalition, arguing that if the two opposition parties wanted to form government together, they would need the expressed consent of Canadians in the form of an election win. To avoid the pending confidence vote, which his government was sure to lose, Prime Minister Harper announced his intent to seek a prorogation of Parliament.

Academics, journalists, pundits, and constitutional experts across the country debated the constitutional legitimacy of the prime minister's strategy and whether the governor-general had the discretion to deny his request. On December 4, 2008, after keeping the prime minister waiting in Rideau Hall for two hours for an answer, the governor-general prorogued Parliament until January 26, 2009. In the interim, Stéphane Dion was replaced by Michael Ignatieff as the Liberal leader and the Conservatives backed down from their plan to eliminate the per-vote subsidy.

The events of December 2008 created support for restricting prime ministers' access to the power to prorogue, hence the Liberals' idea that governments have to offer justifications if they choose to seek prorogation. Presumably the point is to deter prorogations that are politically motivated. Aucoin, Turnbull, and Jarvis (2011) have argued for a constitutional reform package that would require governments to obtain the support of two-thirds of the House of Commons to prorogue Parliament. This would almost always guarantee a multi-partisan agreement for prorogation, which would limit the prime minister's ability to prorogue for political reasons.

Conclusion

The purpose of this chapter was to expose the reader, through a series of empirical examples, to the main roles and responsibilities of members of Parliament in Canada. The cases and events discussed in the chapter speak to the relationship between the executive and legislative branches, the concentration of power in the Prime Minister's Office, the effect of conventions on government formation and transition, and the ways in which political parties define and shape parliamentary democracy.

As mentioned in the introduction to the chapter, party discipline has the perverse effect of reversing the logic of responsible government. Instead of placing the balance of power in the hands of the legislative branch, the reality of disciplined parties fortifies the government's hold on power. While political parties are integral to parliamentary governance in the federal and provincial context, the legislatures in Nunavut and the Northwest Territories use Westminster parliamentary governance without parties. In this consensus approach to government, all members of the legislature stand for election as independents. Following the election, the members acting together choose the Speaker, the premier and the Cabinet. Premiers can assign and shuffle Cabinet responsibilities but cannot dismiss Cabinet members. In many ways, this is a more pure and true realization of the fundamental principles of Westminster parliamentary democracy. Though institutional and cultural tendencies still concentrate power in the executive, there is significantly more independence of the legislature from the executive branch, primarily because political parties are not present.

Though it is unlikely that federal and provincial jurisdictions will abandon political parties, there are lessons to learn from the consensus model and steps that can be taken to strike a more equitable balance between the legislative and executive branches. For instance, a change in party and media attitudes toward strict party discipline, combined with a narrower definition of which votes need to be treated as confidence measures, would go some way toward more empowered members of Parliament.

References and Suggested Readings

Aucoin, Peter, Mark D. Jarvis, and Lori Turnbull. 2011. *Democratizing the Constitution: Reforming Responsible Government.* Toronto: Emond Montgomery.

Bryden, Joan. 2017. "Trudeau Liberals Drop Most Contentious Proposals for Reforming House Rules." *Globe and Mail*, April 30. https://www.theglobeandmail.com/news/politics/ottawa-drops-contentious-proposals-for-reforming-house-of-commons-rules/article34862021/.

Elections Canada. 2018. "Redistribution of Federal Electoral Boundaries." http://www.elections.ca/content.aspx?section=res&dir=cir/red&document=index&lang=e.

Galloway, Gloria. 2018. "Conservatives Push Through Omnibus Budget Bill in Senate." *Globe and Mail*, June 15. https://www.theglobeandmail.com/news/politics/conservatives-push-through-omnibus-budget-bill-in-senate/article1373176/.

Government of Canada. 2017. "Reforming the Standing Orders of the House of Commons." March. https://www.canada.ca/en/leader-government-house-commons/services/reform-standing-orders-house-commons/2017/march.html.

__________. 2018. "2018–19 Estimates." https://www.canada.ca/content/dam/tbs-sct/documents/planned-government-spending/main-estimates/2018-19/me-bpd-eng.pdf.

Huffington Post. 2014. "Things Tory MP Paul Calandra Has Actually Said in the House of Commons." September 26. https://www.huffingtonpost.ca/2014/09/26/paul-calandra-quotes-tory-conservative_n_5890002.html.

Liberal Party of Canada. 2015. "Electoral Reform." https://www.liberal.ca/realchange/electoral-reform/ (link no longer active).

May, Kathryn. 2017. "Plan to Boost Budget Transparency Will Fail without Culture Change in Bureaucracy, Critics Say." iPOLITICS, July 9. https://ipolitics.ca/2017/07/09/plan-to-boost-budget-transparency-will-fail-without-culture-change-in-bureaucracy-say-critics/.

Parliament of Canada. 2016. "Committees: Special Committee on Electoral Reform." http://www.ourcommons.ca/Committees/en/ERRE (link no longer active).

Raj, Althia. 2016. "NDP MP Kennedy Stewart's Candidate Gender Equity Bill Not Supported by Liberal Government." Huffington Post, October 19. https://www.huffingtonpost.ca/2016/10/19/kennedy-stewart-liberals-candidate-gender-equity_n_12556110.html.

Russell, Peter. 2008. *Two Cheers for Minority Government: The Evolution of Canadian Parliamentary Democracy*. Toronto: Emond Montgomery.

Savoie, Donald. 1999. "The Rise of Court Government in Canada." *Canadian Journal of Political Science* 32 (4): 635–64.

Smith, David E. 2007. *The People's House of Commons: Theories of Democracy in Contention*. Toronto: University of Toronto Press.

Wherry, Aaron. 2017. "Speaker Splits Up Liberal Omnibus Budget Bill, Thanks to New Liberal Rule." CBC News. https://www.cbc.ca/news/politics/omnibus-liberals-speaker-analysis-wherry-1.4393690.

Wherry, Aaron, and John Paul Tasker. 2017. "Minister 'Disappointed' as Electoral Reform Committee Recommends Referendum on Proportional Representation." CBC News, December 1. https://www.cbc.ca/news/politics/wherry-electoral-reform-committee-1.3866879.

five
The Senate: A Late-Blooming Chameleon

ANDREW HEARD

Introduction

The Senate is one of several oddities in the Canadian political system, seemingly left over from a bygone era.[1] Many people have been asking how it makes sense in the modern democratic era to continue with an unelected body that can change or even veto measures already approved by elected MPs in the House of Commons; suggestions and concrete attempts have been made to transform the Senate into an elected body. Some have even questioned the need for a bicameral national parliament at all; for many years, the NDP has made outright abolition of the Senate its preferred option. Opinion among Canadians about the Senate is generally negative, with many believing that it has been too partisan, lacking in legitimacy as an appointed body, wracked by scandal, and not doing enough to justify its existence (Nanos Research 2018, 29–34).

This chapter looks at the role of the Senate in our political process, its history and potential future directions. In coming to understand the value of a bicameral national parliament, one can learn something about the nature of the legislative process, representation in a federation, and, perhaps ironically, the need to counterbalance the shortcomings of modern parliamentary democracy. An exploration of the proposals to reform the Senate help illustrate ways in which Canada's upper house can be restructured. The changes made in 2016 by Prime Minister Trudeau to the appointment process appear to be refashioning the Senate into a more independent body. It has become more active and less prone to scandals than was seen for most of its life as a chamber composed principally of political patronage appointees.

History and Composition

The British Parliament served as the model for the colonial legislatures established under British rule in what is now Canada. In Britain, Parliament divided early in its origins between an "upper house" of noble peers and bishops sitting in the House of Lords, and elected representatives of "commoners" in the House of Commons, which constituted the "lower house" in Britain's bicameral legislature. In its early days, the three elements of Parliament, the monarch, House of Lords, and Commons, held some important powers relative to each other. Indeed, the American notion of checks and balances between the two houses of Congress and the president was heavily influenced by Montesquieu's arguments in *The Spirit of the Laws* (1748), based in part on the potential balancing powers of the three elements of the British Parliament (Resnick 1987). The appeal of a second chamber to act as a check on the impulses of the elected lower house was very much in the mind of the Fathers of Confederation (Ajzenstat 2003, 4–8). Ever since Nova Scotia gained British North America's first legislative assembly in 1758, early colonial legislatures in Canada were set up with an elected lower chamber (the Legislative Assembly) and a smaller, appointed chamber (the Legislative Council) filled with political and business worthies selected by the governor. When legislatures were established for Prince Edward Island in 1773, New Brunswick in 1784, and the provinces of Upper and Lower Canada in 1791, they all followed this same pattern, with an elected assembly and an appointed Legislative Council.

When the Fathers of Confederation gathered in 1864 to debate what national institutions should be created to govern the soon-to-be Dominion of Canada, there was broad support for the British form of parliamentary government that had already shaped Canadian colonial government for over a century.[2] In broad strokes, the general population was to be represented by their elected representatives in the House of Commons, while the wealthy elite would be represented in an appointed Senate. But it is instructive to note that the eventual acceptance of an appointed Senate came only after debates on whether senators should be elected (Smith 2003, 78). The qualifications originally set for membership of the Senate required potential appointees to be at least thirty years old, normally resident in the territory they were to represent, to own real property worth at least $4,000 in that territory, and to have total net assets of at least $4,000. While those seem like small dollar amounts in the modern era, they were very substantial indeed in 1867. The intention in 1867 was to restrict Senate appointments to the successful business and professional men of the day. Only men were appointed to the Senate for many decades after Confederation. Women were appointed only after a court case that became known as "the Persons Case," in which the Judicial Committee of the Privy Council (JCPC) overruled the Canadian Supreme Court and held that section 24 the Constitution Act, 1867, stipulating "qualified persons" may be summoned to the Senate, did in fact encompass both men and women in the meaning of the word *persons* (JCPC 1930). The Constitution Act, 1867 grants the governor general the power to make appointments to the Senate, although by convention the prime minister decides (Heard 2014, 147).

Considerable time was spent on Senate issues during the Confederation debates, with much of the attention on how to divide representation among the provinces. One enduring issue in a bicameral legislature is on what basis seats should be distributed among the regional units of the country. In most bicameral legislatures, seats in the lower house are based roughly on the principle of representation by population (rep by pop), applied to each province or state. And that choice was made in Canada as well, with each province's share of the seats in the House of Commons corresponding to that province's share of the national population.[3] In most federal societies, countries balance "rep by pop" in the lower house with equal or weighted representation of constituent regional units (states or provinces) in the upper house. So, in the United States, for example, each state has two members in the Senate. That equality in upper house representation may be more easily accommodated in a federation with many constituent states, such as the fifty states in the United States, or ones where the national population is fairly evenly distributed. It can become more problematic in a federation such as Canada with far fewer regional units and more skewed population distributions. The difficulty is in providing a meaningful say to the smaller provinces in the upper house without the larger, more populous ones feeling their voice has been unfairly diminished. Right from the beginning, Quebec and Ontario dominated the population of Canada. The compromise struck in 1867 was to grant equal representation of twenty-four seats to each *region* and to categorize Quebec and Ontario as separate regions, with the Maritime provinces constituting a third region. When PEI joined Confederation in 1873, it acquired two seats from each of New Brunswick and Nova Scotia; since then, the two larger provinces in the Maritime region have had ten seats each and PEI four.

As Canada grew with the addition of new provinces and territories, so too did the number of seats in the Senate. Eventually, the four western provinces were grouped as a region with six seats each, an arrangement that continues today. While the western provinces were thinly populated at the time they joined Confederation, modern population shifts have created a difficult situation. British Columbia and Alberta now have populations several times bigger than either Nova Scotia or New Brunswick, and yet they have fewer seats in the Senate. Such a blatant disparity is hard to justify and not surprisingly has led to loud demands by westerners for a redistribution of Senate seats.[4]

The Senate is composed of 105 members, a much smaller chamber than the 338-seat House of Commons. There are twenty-four members divided equally among the four Western provinces, twenty-four each for Ontario and Quebec, twenty-four for the Maritime provinces, six for Newfoundland and Labrador (which joined Canada in 1949), and one each for the northern territories of Yukon, Northwest Territories, and Nunavut. Section 26 of the Constitution Act, 1867 also provides that an extra four or eight senators can be appointed "if … the Queen thinks fit." In practice, the prime minister would make the judgment call and advise the governor general to recommend these extra appointments be made. These "extras" are assigned equally to the four regions (the west, Ontario, Quebec, and the Maritimes). While this initially inflates the Senate in size, no new appointments are made until retirements, resignations, or deaths bring the membership down to its regular number. The one time this process was successfully used came in 1990, when Prime Minister Mulroney decided to appoint eight extra senators to break a deadlock with the Liberal-dominated Senate, which was refusing to pass the government's legislation to create the Goods and Services Tax (GST). Only because the party standings in the Senate were relatively close at the time, could these extra senators give the Conservative government enough votes to pass the GST legislation. Section 26 is widely viewed as a special provision for breaking a deadlock between the Commons and the Senate, a view supported by the British government's 1873 refusal to act on a request for extra senators from Prime Minister Alexander Mackenzie (Dunsmuir 1990). In strict law, however, the extra senators can be appointed for whatever reason the prime minister considers valid.

Roles of the Senate

The Senate has played a number of positive roles in the Canadian political system, encompassing representation, legislation, and policy development. Its representative role gives a platform in Parliament for regional representation, as well as minority or sectional group representation. While the representation of provincial interests has been a central justification for the Senate since Confederation, the Senate has also taken on a meaningful role in recent decades of representing other sectional interests, and offering a forum for the voices of women, Indigenous peoples, and other marginalized groups. A somewhat ironic reality of the Senate is that for several decades it had been more socially diverse than the House of Commons. Of the 101 senators in October 2018, forty-six were women (45.5 per cent) and eleven were Indigenous peoples (10.9 per cent). In contrast, only ninety-one of the 336 MPs in office at that time were women (27.1 per cent) and eleven Indigenous (3.4 per cent).[5] One reason for the higher level of diversity is that the prime minister can deliberately choose to appoint more women and members of minority groups, whereas election to the House of Commons involves many factors that mitigate against increasing the numbers of these groups. For example, over the first two years of his prime ministership, twenty-eight of the forty-three senators chosen by Justin Trudeau were women.[6] Despite this impressive social diversity, however, the Senate has slipped in recent years in its representation of different occupation groups. In early 2018, for example, the Senate did not contain a single farmer, fisher, or military veteran (Huffington Post 2018).[7]

The Senate also provides in-depth policy studies that are often based on a wider cross-party consensus than is usually found in the House of Commons.[8] One factor aiding this policy work is the combination of the professional experience senators have accumulated prior to their appointment and their generally longer terms in office, which permit them to further develop an expertise in particular areas of public policy.

Arguably the most important role of senators is the "sober second thought" they offer in the legislative process. Most bills are introduced and debated in the House of Commons before they are sent to the Senate for a further round of public consultation and debate. The time spent in the Senate offers a chance for government decision-makers to reconsider whether their proposals are well thought-out and properly drafted.

The Senate still retains a potentially influential role in the legislative process because it enjoys almost identical legal powers under the Constitution.[9] Bills must be approved by both the Senate and the House of Commons before they can be presented to the governor general for royal assent. Either house can amend measures already approved by the other. If they do, then the bill cannot be passed into law until the other house agrees to the changes, or the proposed changes are withdrawn. In practice, the majority of amendments made by the Senate are accepted by the House of Commons, many indirectly proposed on behalf of, or with the agreement of, the minister responsible for the bill. And more often than not, the Senate acquiesces when the Commons objects to Senate amendments to a bill that MPs had previously approved. However, there are some occasions when both houses dig in their heels and a bill may be passed back and forth a couple of times over weeks or months. Although in the past some disputes over legislation were settled through representatives of both houses meeting in an ad hoc committee called a "conference," this practice has not been used for many years; indeed, the last conference was held in 1947 (O'Brien and Bosc 2009, 794). In the current era, decisions on how the Commons should respond to Senate amendments to their bills are taken at the Cabinet level, with the minister responsible for the specific bill then tabling a motion in the Commons on how to respond.

Table 5.1 shows how the Senate has varied in its approach over a twenty-year period to amending government legislation already approved by the House of Commons. The Senate had been somewhat active in amending bills, even while the Liberals controlled both houses between 1997 and 2006. However, there was a significant drop-off in Senate amendments once the Conservatives gained control of the Senate. With only one bill amended in the 2011–15 Parliament, when the Conservatives had a majority in both houses, the Senate was increasingly criticized as ineffective

Table 5.1 Treatment in the Senate of Government Bills from the Commons, 1997–2019

Parliament	Bills introduced	3rd reading	No. bills amended	% bills amended	Resolved with Commons	Royal assent
1997–2000	99	97	9	9.3	9	97
2001–4	114	98	11	11.2	9	96
2004–5	46	46	3	6.5	3	46
2006–8	74	65	7	10.8	7	65
2008–11	65	61	3	4.9	1	59
2011–15	106	105	1	1.0	1	105
2015–19	84	83	29	34.9	29	83

Source: Senate 2019

and irrelevant. However, the Senate became far more active after 2016, when Trudeau appointed a large number of independent senators. By the time of dissolution in 2019, the Senate had amended government bills at a rate that is unprecedented in recent decades. However, this increased rate of amending government bills cannot be attributed entirely to the new Independent Senators Group, many of whose members actually supported the government far more frequently than their Conservative and Liberal colleagues in recorded votes (Grenier 2018).

While the Senate has almost co-equal legislative powers with the House of Commons, the House of Commons has a privileged position because it is elected, while the Senate is appointed. Even in the early years of Confederation, it was clear that elected MPs enjoyed a democratic legitimacy senators lacked. For this reason, the principle of responsible government tied the government to the House of Commons in ways that did not apply to the Senate. The prime minister and Cabinet are required to win and maintain the confidence of the House of Commons, not the Senate. The democratic authority of the House of Commons has also resulted in the Senate only rarely exercising its constitutional power to veto Commons legislation. While some senators still insist that the Senate's veto power is legitimate (Joyal 2003, 302), it is rarely exercised. Indeed, an outright defeat of a government bill from the Commons has happened only three times since 1961. In 1991, Bill C-43 on abortion died after a tied vote resulted in the Speaker of the Senate casting the deciding vote to kill the bill. In 1993, Bill C-93, consolidating some national research agencies, was defeated on third reading, as was Bill C-28 in 1996, which would have rescinded contracts to redevelop Toronto's

Pearson Airport. The Senate also killed off two private members' bills previously approved by the Commons, in 1998 and again in 2010.[10] However, the Senate has been less reticent to use its so-called indirect veto, whereby a bill dies because a controlling bloc of senators decides to stall the bill in committee, or otherwise prevent it from coming to a vote on the floor of the Senate. Sometimes this decision is announced publicly and at other times, it is done quietly. The most famous instance of an indirect veto came when the Senate decided not to proceed with a vote on implementing the Canada-US Free Trade Agreement in 1988. The Liberal majority in the Senate believed such a major initiative should not proceed until the matter was placed before voters in a general election. After Brian Mulroney's Progressive Conservatives were returned to power in an election later that year, the Senate dutifully proceeded with its approval of the treaty.

Senate Reform

Given the criticism the Senate has long faced for comprising non-elected partisans granted a plum patronage appointment, and for repeated scandals[11] involving its members, there has been no shortage of proposals for its reform. But, despite being widely discussed for many years, since 1867 only one substantive constitutional reform has been made to the chamber or its members: in 1965, lifetime appointment was changed to mandatory retirement at age seventy-five (grandfathered so as to apply only to senators appointed after the change took effect).[12] Modern debates over reform have centred on several specific issues, producing three primary alternatives: abolition, election, or reform of the appointment process. In recent years, surveys indicate that abolition and election have been roughly tied as the most popular options (Angus Reid 2016; Forum Research 2013; Nanos Research 2018, 39).

A serious challenge is raised by the abolitionist position of the NDP, whether Canada even needs a second parliamentary chamber at all (Mulcair 2015). The NDP introduced a motion in the House of Commons in 2013, trying to kick-start the constitutional process to abolish the Senate (Huffington Post 2013). The party's position builds on widespread views that the Senate lacks legitimacy in the modern democratic era, has been racked by scandal for years, and serves little useful purpose as shown by its minimal impact on legislation. Advocates of abolition point to the fact that every Canadian province that started with a bicameral legislature has since abolished their upper house. However, there is a big difference between the needs of an individual province and those of a large federated country.

In looking around the world at the institutional arrangements of other federations, one sees that every stable democratic federation of any size has a bicameral legislature. Ronald Watts argues bicameralism is not a prerequisite of federalism, since five of the twenty-four federated states in the world have unicameral legislatures (2009, 36). However, each of those five states has very particular circumstances setting it apart from most other federations.[13] The principal argument in favour of bicameralism in federations is to provide additional representation for the regional units to balance out the dominance of the most populous states or provinces in the lower house, where representation is distributed roughly according to population.

Thus, the prime argument against abolition in Canada remains essentially the same as the argument for creating the Senate in the first place. Quebec and Ontario have over 62 per cent of the national population and together can dominate the House of Commons.[14] In order to prevent the other provinces being sidelined from effective governance of the country, counterbalancing representation is provided in the Senate. In the current distribution of seats, Quebec and Ontario control only 45 per cent of the Senate. As a result, broader regional support is required for any bills to be passed into law.

A second argument against abolition, which has gained momentum in recent decades, is that the Senate is needed, even as an appointed body, to counterbalance executive domination of the House of Commons. Modern governments are able to control the legislative process in the House of Commons to such an extent that measures may pass through the lower house with insufficient scrutiny (Aucoin, Jarvis, and Turnbull 2011, 111–51). When the governing party has a majority of MPs, strictly enforced party discipline ensures that measures pass the Commons in the form supported by Cabinet. Any government can use time allocation to limit debate on bills, significantly reducing opposition opportunities to criticize a bill or recommend amendments. Or the government can declare any item to be a confidence measure to limit votes against a government proposal, as a defeat or substantive amendment in the House of Commons would lead to the government either resigning or calling fresh elections (Docherty 2005, 153–65). The increasing tendency to curtail debate was seen with the Harper government invoking time allocation over 100 times between 2011 and 2015 (Maloney 2015). In short, an upper house is needed to help Parliament make independent assessments of legislative proposals that the House of Commons is not always able to provide. Consistent with its potential to counterbalance Cabinet control of the House of Commons, in the period 1997 to 2004 the Senate was almost twice as likely to amend legislation that had been subject to time allocation in the Commons, even though the Liberals controlled both houses.[15]

Proposals for Senate reform have been floated since the early years but gained steam in the rounds of constitutional negotiations in the 1970s. One interesting idea was to reshape the Senate along the lines of the German

Bundesrat, in which the *governments* of the regional units are represented. In the Canadian context, provincial Cabinet ministers would participate in key debates and votes in the Senate, while the day-to-day committee work would be undertaken by provincial civil servants.[16] In essence, this proposal would have seen the Senate develop into a sort of permanent federal-provincial conference. Developments in federal relations during the 1970s had seen increasing use and formalization of these ministerial meetings, so it was not surprising at the time. However, other reform proposals put forward in the 1980s quickly drew attention away from the Bundesrat model.

Two alternate paths to reform came to the fore in the constitutional dynamics of the 1980s. The first was to continue with an appointed Senate, but to involve provincial governments in a joint selection process. During the Meech Lake Accord negotiations in the late 1980s, Prime Minister Mulroney tasked the provincial governments with providing a list of nominees for Senate vacancies, from which the prime minister would select an appointee.[17] Such a change might have at least provided more political legitimacy for senators by breaking the cycle of prime ministers using Senate appointments principally as patronage rewards for their party stalwarts. However, alternative proposals from the western provinces, particularly Alberta, backed the transformation of the Senate into an elected chamber, like the American and Australian senates. Indeed, the Alberta legislature passed the Senatorial Selection Act in 1989, establishing province-wide elections to choose the nominees that the provincial government would forward to the federal government. Soon the rallying cry for many in the west was for a so-called Triple-E Senate: elected, equal, and effective. Very similar to the American model, a Triple-E Senate would have equal representation for each province, popularly elected senators, and effective powers to make the Senate a force to be reckoned with in championing provincial interests. The Charlottetown Accord would have come the closest to accommodating these demands for reform, by giving each province six seats and permitting the provinces to decide whether to allow their voters to elect senators directly or for the MLAs to elect senators indirectly by a vote in the legislature.

One of the debates over the Triple-E proposal is just what powers would make it effective. For example, there are differences of opinion over whether a reformed Senate should continue to have co-equal powers over all areas of legislation, a suspensive veto,[18] or an absolute veto over a subset of issues, such as those touching language rights or federal-provincial relations. Another issue is reconciling an upper house that claims an electoral mandate with the current focus of Cabinet's responsibility to the House of Commons. It has been generally agreed that the Senate should not be a confidence chamber even if it were to be elected. Australia's experience shows, even when conventions limit formal responsibility to the lower house, there is much potential for conflict between two elected houses in a parliamentary system. A constitutional crisis was provoked in 1975 when different parties controlled the two houses of Australia's Parliament, and the Senate refused to approve the government's budget (normally a confidence matter, which by convention the Senate should have passed). In the end Governor General Sir John Kerr intervened and replaced the Labor Party prime minister, Gough Whitlam, with the leader of the Liberal Party controlling the Senate, Malcolm Fraser, on condition that he advise a general election to resolve the impasse; in the end, the new government won the election (Howard 1976; White 1990, 237–9).[19]

During the Meech Lake Accord negotiations, the Alberta government, led by Don Getty, pressed forward with its scheme for consultative elections to select a list of senate nominees.[20] The hope was to pressure the prime minister into drawing from the list of election winners, to fill any Albertan Senate vacancies. General Stanley Waters won the first senatorial nomination election held in 1989 to coincide with the provincial general election. Prime Minister Brian Mulroney bowed to political pressure and appointed Waters in 1990 to fill the existing Alberta vacancy. However, once Jean Chrétien became prime minister in 1993, he refused to consider nominees from Alberta's nomination elections, arguing that the Meech Lake and Charlottetown Accords were dead, and along with them went any right for the provinces to be involved in Senate appointments; his successor Paul Martin also ignored Alberta's Senate elections.

Harper's Attempted Reforms

However, the 2006 election saw Stephen Harper take over as prime minister, and he strongly backed transforming the Senate into an elected chamber. He believed that the way to pressure reluctant provincial governments into adopting an elected Senate was to appoint Alberta's elected nominees to the Senate. And over his almost ten years in office, Harper filled all four Senate vacancies that arose in Alberta with the winners of the provincial nomination elections. So despite Canada having an appointed Senate, one can say there have actually been five elected senators.[21]

Harper not only encouraged other provincial governments to follow Alberta's example and institute nomination elections, his government proposed several bills over its lifetime that would have authorized either provincially or federally organized nomination elections; in addition, the Harper government proposed limiting new senators to a single, non-renewal term of eight years in initial proposals and nine years in his last.[22] It is important to note that Harper argued his measures did not need provincial consent or formal constitutional amendments. His legislation would have left untouched the wording of the Constitution Act, 1867, granting the governor general the power to appoint senators. Instead his legislation was aimed at adding a preliminary process of popular consultative elections, to allow the people of a province to choose whom they would prefer as their senators; the prime minister would be free to use these nominees in his or her recommendations to the governor general, while still not being legally required to do so. There was no doubt, however, that the results of the elections would have been informally binding and followed by the prime minister. The encouragement of provincial measures bore initial but unripened fruit as Saskatchewan's legislature passed a Senate Nominee Election Act in 2009, although never proclaimed into force. Similarly, the New Brunswick premier introduced a bill to provide for senatorial nominations in 2012, but it died on the order paper. And despite the BC government's promise in 2013 to establish enabling legislation for Senate nomination elections, nothing transpired.

The Harper government's attempts to transform the Senate into an elected chamber ground to a halt after Quebec launched a court challenge to the fourth iteration of the Conservatives' Senate reform legislation, Bill C-7 introduced in 2011. After the Quebec Court of Appeal (2013) found Bill C-7 unconstitutional, the Harper government sent its own reference questions to the Supreme Court of Canada to clarify the range of Senate reform that could be achieved through ordinary legislation. In 2014, Canada's top court ruled that any changes to the fundamental role or character of the Senate must involve provincial consent, through a formal constitutional amendment supported by at least seven provinces with 50 per cent of the population. The Court wrote, "The framers of the *Constitution Act, 1867* deliberately chose executive appointment of Senators in order to allow the Senate to play the specific role of a complementary legislative body of 'sober second thought'" (Supreme Court 2014, para 56). The Court went on to say that the original choice of appointed senators was "also intended to ensure that the Senate would be a *complementary* legislative body, rather than a perennial rival of the House of Commons in the legislative process" (para 57).[23] An electoral mandate might empower senators to challenge elected MPs on an equal footing, as senators challenge members of the House of Representatives in the United States. In contrast, constitutional conventions limit the exercise of the appointed Senate's legal powers precisely because its members are appointed and not elected (Heard 2014, 144–53). Effectively, the Senate Reform Reference put paid to any legislative schemes to elect Senate nominees, whether through federal legislation such as the Harper government had proposed, or provincial legislation such as Alberta's.

After the Supreme Court's decision in the Senate Reference, Harper declared that his government would force the provinces to come to the bargaining table and negotiate a constitutional amendment to transform the Senate into an elected chamber. He vowed not to appoint any more senators under the existing provisions of the Constitution. The ultimate goal of this strategy was to reduce the number of senators to the point where it would become difficult for the upper house to conduct its business. His aim was to starve the Senate through attrition to the point where the provinces would have to agree to Senate reform. By the time Harper called the 2015 elections, there were twenty-three vacancies. His strategy was also followed by NDP leader Thomas Mulcair during the 2015 election campaign. In the first weeks of the campaign, the NDP were running ahead in the polls, with the Conservatives second; so it appeared that whether the NDP or Conservatives won office, the process of forcing Senate reform through deliberate attrition would continue. A private citizen launched a court case to seek a declaration from the Federal Court that the governor general is bound by the Constitution Act to fill Senate vacancies in a timely manner, which would in turn require the prime minister to recommend candidates; in 2016, however, the Court ruled the issue was moot as the new prime minister, Justin Trudeau, had moved on election promises to fill the vacancies (Alani 2016).

The Trudeau Reforms

When Justin Trudeau became prime minister in 2015, he radically altered the appointment process without requiring a constitutional amendment. He implemented the Liberal Party's campaign promises to eliminate party patronage in appointments and ultimately to try to eliminate party caucuses in the Senate. Previously in 2014, Trudeau had expelled Liberal senators from the joint House-Senate Liberal caucus. Shortly after becoming prime minister, in January 2016, he set up an arm's-length body, the Independent Advisory Board for Senate Appointments, to provide him with a list of five nominees for any Senate vacancy, from among the applications submitted by Canadians wishing to be appointed to the Senate. A telling requirement for the application process is that prospective candidates should "have the ability to bring a perspective and contribution to the work of the Senate that is independent and non-partisan."[24] The prime minister reviews the short list of potential nominees and picks someone to recommend to the governor general for appointment. With this process, Trudeau claims to have respected the Supreme Court's positions in the 2014 Senate Reform Reference, by maintaining the Senate as an appointed body, even if he aims to remove partisanship from both the appointment process and the future work of the Senate. However, his reforms may be vulnerable to the challenge that he went beyond the Supreme Court's acceptable limits by transforming the Senate away from the partisan body it was created to be in 1867. A more troubling criticism is that many of Trudeau's "independent" Senate appointees have been not free of partisan associations. Over a third of the senators Trudeau appointed by the end of 2019 had a record as either Liberal candidates or financial supporters.[25]

By dissolution in 2019, Justin Trudeau had made fifty appointments under the new appointment process, all of whom sat either as members of the new Independent Senators Group (ISG), or as independents not formally aligned with any group or caucus. While the ISG operates in some senses as a traditional caucus, in receiving a proportionate share of the Senate's support budget and seats on Senate committees, it does not try to adopt a common position on any specific issue or piece of legislation. Rather it seeks to share information among its members with a view to allowing all to make up their own minds how to vote. There is no "whipping" of the votes to ensure a cohesive voting bloc, as with traditional party caucuses. This approach was actually pioneered by Liberal senators after they were expelled from caucus in 2014. At that time they ceased to take official caucus policy positions, allowing individual senators to exercise their independent judgment on issues while still restricting their group membership to senators who personally support the Liberal Party in some way (Cowan 2015, 59).

As a result of these reforms, only the Conservative Party continues to operate as a traditional party in the Senate, with regular, joint meetings of MPs and senators, and party discipline enforced to ensure adherence to Conservative policy positions. Indeed, Conservative Party Leader Andrew Scheer made it known that if he became prime minister he would abandon Trudeau's reform and return to partisan appointments. His senators "would be Conservative senators who would help implement a Conservative vision for Canada that would improve the quality of life for Canadians" (Zimonjic and Barton 2018).

The most important effect of Trudeau's reforms was an increasingly activist Senate, with the independent senators supporting a striking number of amendments to government legislation that had already been approved by the House of Commons. As table 5.1 shows, the period 2015–19 saw a significantly higher portion (34.9 per cent) of government bills amended in the Senate, with an amendment rate three times higher than in previous Parliaments. All the more important to note is that the rate of amendment in this period soared from about 20 to 46 per cent once the independent senators gained control of the upper house in 2018 (Senate 2019). Interestingly, the House of Commons accepted most of the Senate's individual amendments, and the Senate tried only once to insist on its amendments after the Commons had rejected them; senators quickly acquiesced after MPs rejected two Senate amendments to Bill C-49 a second time.

Another aspect of the Senate changed by Trudeau's reforms is its connection to the government of the day. For most of its life, the Senate had at least one senator in Cabinet, the government leader in the Senate; occasionally there were other Cabinet ministers as well. One useful role the Senate has played in the past was to provide a reservoir of potential Cabinet members from provinces where the ruling party had failed to elect enough, or any, members to the House of Commons. For example, Joe Clark in 1979 and Stephen Harper in 2006 both included extra senators in Cabinet in order to increase Quebec representation in Cabinet. Pierre Trudeau appointed senators from BC, Alberta, and Saskatchewan to the Cabinet when his Liberal Party won no seats west of Manitoba in the 1980 election (Heard 2014, 87–90). With at least one senator sitting in Cabinet, senators held formal Question Periods, in which the government leader in the Senate, along with whatever other senators might be in Cabinet at the time, would answer questions about government business. As well, Cabinet ministers in the Senate would be the formal sponsors of government bills introduced in the Senate, and they could discuss the progress of legislation through the Senate with their Cabinet colleagues. The government leader in the Senate also acted as the head of the government party caucus, working with a whip and other caucus officials to distribute committee assignments among caucus members and trying to ensure party cohesion on key votes. However, Stephen Harper abandoned the tradition of Senate appointments to the Cabinet towards the end of his time as prime minister. Justin Trudeau formalized this change after expelling Liberal senators from his caucus, then transforming the character of the Senate with his new appointment process.

Beginning in 2016, the position formerly known as the government leader in the Senate would be given to a senator at arm's length from the Liberal Party. This individual would orchestrate government legislative business in the Senate – but do so without having a government caucus to lead or direct. The new "government representative" would not be a member of Cabinet but would attend Cabinet meetings when necessary to understand government priorities and discuss the progress of matters in the Senate.[26] The first person appointed as government representative, Peter Harder, had previously been a senior civil servant and not a clear Liberal partisan. However, because he is charged with promoting the government's policy agenda and ensuring its passage through the Senate, he soon ran into difficulties with perceptions of his independence. One interesting innovation with the new arrangement was the inauguration of a weekly extended Question Period, in which one or two Cabinet ministers would attend the Senate to answer questions in their policy areas. This experiment has generally been viewed as a success, since it allows for a sustained focus on one or two particular areas of public policy in contrast to the partisan jousting typical of Question Period in the House of Commons.

Because the new Independent Senators Group does not want to be associated with promoting government business, regardless of which party is in power, the ISG decided they could have no formal affiliation with the government representative. It has created its own leadership, beginning with Elaine McCoy, who served as the initial "facilitator" of the ISG, followed by Yuen Pau Woo in 2017. With no caucus to lead, the government representative and assistants have to negotiate with all groups in the Senate in order to manage legislative priorities, time spent on issues, and coordinate proposed amendments.

A positive aspect of the new Senate is that individual senators now have a much more autonomous role to play in policy. They may now use their personal judgment to assess the merits of government proposals, rather than follow the instructions of a party whip. The downside of this new autonomy is that individual senators are more likely to be subjected to pressure tactics from professional lobbyists hoping to sway their votes. For example, a search of the Lobbyists Activity Register showed registered lobbyists filed 6,214 contact reports with senators and Senate officials in 2017, compared with 3,853 in 2014 (Office of the Commissioner of Lobbying of Canada 2018).

Conclusion

Prime Minister Justin Trudeau's reform of the appointment process has resulted in a substantive transformation of the Senate and how it works. The effects of Trudeau's new senatorial selection process will be felt for some time to come; by the time of the next scheduled election in 2023, almost three-quarters of the Senate will comprise his appointees. However, the much more frequent amendment of government bills by a more independent Senate could reshape debate over the continuing usefulness and legitimacy of the upper chamber. It will be interesting to see if the Trudeau reforms can maintain initial popular support; a 2018 Nanos poll found that 71 per cent of Canadians prefer to see senators as independents, while only nineteen thought they should be members of a political party caucus. The alternative of an elected Senate faces major constitutional and logistical challenges; moreover, it is almost inconceivable that there would be Senate elections that did not involve the help of political parties to fund and organize the campaigns. In this scenario, the risk is that elected senators, like their House of Commons counterparts, would become subservient to party leaders. Nevertheless, an enduring trend in Canadian public opinion over several decades has been strong support for electing the Senate rather than simply reforming the appointment process. That said, the required constitutional negotiations to create an elected Senate would almost certainly grow into a much larger package of proposed constitutional changes – a daunting prospect no incoming federal government would relish. Still, despite little to show for decades of debate over Senate reform, there may be a significant transformation of the Senate underway.

For the foreseeable future, Canada's upper house will continue as an integral part of the political process. The potential representational roles played by senators – as a voice for the provinces, for segments of society not well represented in the House of Commons, and for sober *non-partisan* reflection on government legislation – remain a crucial justification for its continuing existence. The constructive role it can play in improving government legislation is evidenced over recent decades by the ready acceptance of most Senate amendments by the government of the day. An enhanced impact in the policy process may also be seen with more policy inquiries and consensus-based proposals that might gain legislative traction when contrasted with the polarized and partisan committee reports often produced by MPs. So long as it remains content to play a complementary role to the House of Commons and does not seek a direct confrontation by either defeating government bills or refusing to acquiesce to the elected Commons after the latter has rejected Senate amendments, it seems likely that the new, partially reformed Senate will avoid the kind of crisis that could lead to its demise.

Notes

1 Another example is seen in the debate over whether Canada should continue with the British Queen as its head of state.

2 An important qualification to this broad support for bicameralism was that the delegates from Upper Canada had had enough negative experience with cronyism and patronage in the Legislative Council that they ensured that the new legislature to be established for Ontario in 1867 would not include an upper house; however, they agreed with delegates from the other provinces that a bicameral national legislature would be needed for the new Dominion of Canada (Boyer 2014, 182–5).

3 For example, in 2018, Ontario was home to 38.8 per cent of Canada's population and had 35.8 per cent of the seats in the House of Commons, while Nova Scotia had 2.6 per cent of the population and

3.0 per cent of the seats; population data calculated from Statistics Canada (2018).

4 The shift in population westward is remarkable. For example, in 1961 Alberta had not quite twice the population of Nova Scotia, but by 2018 it was over four times as populous (Statistics Canada 2009; Statistics Canada 2018). Proposals to increase the representation of both British Columbia and Alberta have been made for many years, as their populations grew dramatically. One example can be found in the motion presented to the Senate by Senators Lowell Murray and Jack Austin and studied by the Senate Special Committee on Senate Reform in 2006. Their suggested constitutional amendment would have seen the Senate raised from 105 to 117 seats, in order to allow for more western representation. The current twenty-four-seat Western Region would have been split, with a new Prairie provinces region of twenty-four seats distributed between Alberta (ten), and Saskatchewan (seven) and Manitoba (seven). British Columbia would have become a half-sized region on its own, with twelve seats (Senate 2006).

5 Calculated from information from Library of Parliament (2018a). An interesting snapshot of the Senate's gender, ethnic, educational, and occupational diversity in 2016 can be found in Griffith (2017).

6 Calculated from information as of October 17, 2018 (Library of Parliament 2018a).

7 A concern is that the new selection process brought in by Prime Minister Trudeau may favour urban activists and professionals, at the expense of some traditional rural occupations.

8 While the Senate has issued many substantive policy reports over the years, one of the most influential was the Kirby Report on health care in Canada (Senate 2002). Links to a range of other Senate committee reports can be found at Library of Parliament (2018b), Senate (2018). For a list of other reports issued between 1961 and 2010, see Senate (2011).

9 Section 53 of the Constitution Act, 1867 provides that "Bills for appropriating any Part of the Public Revenue, or for imposing any Tax or Impost, shall originate in the House of Commons."

10 A vote was taken in 1998 to not proceed with Bill C-220, which was intended to prevent criminals from profiting from their crimes by writing books about themselves. In 2010, the minority government situation allowed the opposition to embarrass the Harper government over non-compliance with climate change accords by combining to pass a private members' bill through the Commons; but this episode came to an end when Conservative senators manoeuvred to defeat Bill C-311.

11 Scandals have involved a senator who lived in Mexico and attended the Senate only once a session, as well as a number of senators who were accused of inappropriate claims for expenses (Boyer 2014; McHugh 2017, 211–27). Another enduring criticism of the Senate is the number of its members who sit on the boards of corporations (Campbell 1978).

12 When the Constitution Act, 1982 came into effect, it brought in a new set of constitutional amendment processes that altered the powers of the Senate. Section 47 stipulates that the agreement of the Senate is not ultimately needed to authorize constitutional amendments in which the federal and provincial governments are required to act in concert. If within 180 days the Senate has not approved an amendment proposal passed by the House of Commons, the House of Commons may reaffirm its support and the measure would proceed to the governor general for proclamation. Since the new amending processes came into effect in 1982, there have been eight formal constitutional amendments requiring joint federal-provincial approval, and in one instance, the Senate did not approve a proposed amendment, and the matter proceeded after the House of Commons passed a second motion after six months. This was the motion to approve what became the Constitution Amendment Proclamation, 1997 (Newfoundland Act) allowing the Province of Newfoundland to create a secular school system to replace the church-based education system. After the Senate proposed changes to the text, the House of Commons re-adopted the original proposal on December 6, 1996, and the matter was later proclaimed into effect by the governor general (Monahan, Shaw, and Ryan 2017, 216). The only type of formal constitutional amendment for which the Senate still retains an absolute veto involves amendments that Parliament may make through ordinary legislation under section 44.

13 The United Arab Emirates is not a democracy, being a federation of emirates ruled by absolute monarchs. Venezuela has degenerated into extreme turmoil in the twenty-first century. And the other three are all very small states: the Comoros, Micronesia, and the federation of St. Kitts and St. Nevis.

14 In 2018, Quebec had 78 seats (23 per cent) and Ontario 121 (36 per cent), totalling about 59 per cent of membership in the Commons.

15 Calculated from House of Commons (2018) and Senate (2018).

16 The Bundesrat model was the basis of the proposal for a new Council of the Federation, proposed by the Pépin-Robarts Commission (Task Force on Canadian Unity 1979, 95–9).

17 The Charlottetown Accord's appointment process reflected one of the earliest proposals for Senate reform, put forward in 1874 by Liberal MP

David Mills to grant provinces the power to select senators (Seidle 1991, 95; Hughson 2015).

18 A suspensive veto would allow for either the automatic approval of bills not disposed of by the Senate within a certain period (six or twelve months) or empower the House of Commons to pass a motion after that time to affirm its support for the bill, after which it could be presented for royal assent (Heard 2015, 51). Proposals for a suspensive veto draw inspiration from the United Kingdom, where the House of Lords has long had only a suspensive veto. For a wide-ranging consideration of the Lords' suspensive veto and the suitability of a suspensive veto for the Canadian Senate, see McHugh (2017, 127–52).

19 The Charlottetown Accord would have resolved this potential problem by stipulating that the Senate could not obstruct money bills; budget and appropriation bills would proceed for royal assent after a month if not disposed of by the Senate. In the event the Senate did amend or defeat a money bill within that month, the House of Commons could simply assert its support for the bill, which could then receive royal assent.

20 British Columbia also enacted a similar law in 1990. The Senatorial Selection Act provided for a nomination election only if there was a vacancy at the time of the next provincial election; as there was none at the time, the law is now moot.

21 The five individuals who have been appointed to the Senate after winning nomination elections in Alberta are Stan Waters (1990), Bert Brown (2007), Betty Unger (2012), Douglas Black (2013), and Scott Tanas (2013).

22 Prime Minister Harper's first round of Senate reforms was contained in two bills introduced in 2006. Bill S-4 would have set terms of no more than eight years for newly appointed senators, and Bill C-43 would have authorized federally organized elections for Senate vacancies at the time of either federal or provincial general elections. After these measures died before prorogation, these proposals resurfaced as Bill C-19 and Bill C-20 in the following session in 2007. Assessments of these two bills are given by various authors in Smith (2009) as well as Hicks and Blais (2008). Following the 2008 elections, the Harper government once again proposed legislation to institute senatorial nomination elections and term limits. In 2010, fresh legislation was introduced that would have authorized provincially organized nomination elections, along with term limits. Following the 2011 election, Harper's final reform proposals were introduced as Bill C-7, providing for provincial elections and a nine-year term for senators. It is worth noting that Harper envisioned senators serving only for one non-renewal term, to preserve their independence in decision-making.

23 Original emphasis. The Supreme Court's findings in this case were not surprising, as the Court built on a previous reference case from 1980, in which it had said that under the old (pre-1982) constitutional framework neither level of government could legislate for direct elections to the Senate (Supreme Court of Canada 1980).

24 The criteria for appointment explicitly state, "Past political activities would not disqualify an applicant." But the clear implication is that any partisan associations must be in candidates' past, and their recent experiences demonstrate they have put that partisanship behind them. A range of information about the criteria for assessment, the selection process, and reports on past selection activities can be found Goverment of Canada (2020).

25 Elections Canada (2019).

26 For more information about the government representative, see the web site of the Senate Government Representative Office, https://senate-gro.ca/.

References and Suggested Readings

Ajzenstat, Janet. 2003. "Bicameralism and Canada's Founders: The Origins of the Canadian Senate." In *Protecting Canadian Democracy: The Senate You Never Knew*, edited by Serge Joyal, 3–30. Montreal and Kingston: McGill-Queen's University Press.

Alani, Aniz. 2016. "Senate Vacancies." http://www.anizalani.com/senatevacancies/.

Angus, Reid. 2016. "Two-in-Three Canadians Say the Senate Is 'Too Damaged' to Ever Earn Their Goodwill." May 3. Vancouver. http://angusreid.org/senate-reform/.

Aucoin, Peter, Mark D. Jarvis, and Lori Turnbull. 2011. *Democratizing the Constitution: Reforming Responsible Government*. Toronto: Emond Montgomery.

Boyer, Patrick. 2014. *Canada's Scandalous Senate*. Toronto: Dundurn.

Campbell, Colin. 1978. *The Senate of Canada: A Lobby from Within*. Toronto: Palgrave Macmillan.

Cowan, James. 2015. "Notes from an Insider: Some Bold Ideas on Senate Reform." *Constitutional Forum* 24 (2): 55–60.

Docherty, David C. 2005. *Legislatures*. Vancouver: UBC Press.

Dunsmuir, Mollie. 1990. "The Senate: Appointments under s.26 of the Constitution Act, 1867." Ottawa: Library of Parliament. http://publications.gc.ca/Collection-R/LoPBdP/BP/bp244-e.htm.

Elections Canada. 2019. "Search for Contributions." n.d. https://elections.ca/wpapps/WPF/EN/CCS/Index?returntype=1.

Forum Research. 2013. "One Half Rate Their Opinion of the Senate as Poor." May 23. http://www.forumresearch.com/forms/News%20Archives/News%20Releases/45953_Senate_%28Forum_Research%29_%2805232013%29.pdf.

Government of Canada. 2020. "Independent Advisory Board for Senate Appointments." https://www.canada.ca/en/campaign/independent-advisory-board-for-senate-appointments.html.

Grenier, Éric. 2018. "Why the Senate Is so Unpredictable – And Its Independents Not so Independent." CBC News, June 19. https://www.cbc.ca/news/politics/grenier-senators-votes-1.4162949.

Griffith, Andrew. 2017. "Diversity in the Senate." *Policy Options*. https://policyoptions.irpp.org/magazines/february-2017/diversity-in-the-senate/.

Harder, Peter. 2018. "Complementarity: The Constitutional Role of the Senate of Canada." https://cdn.senate-gro.ca/wp-content/uploads/2018/04/Complementarity-The-Senates-Constitutional-Role-2018-04-12-Final_E.pdf.

Heard, Andrew. 2014. *Canadian Constitutional Conventions: The Marriage of Law and Politics*. 2nd ed. Toronto: Oxford University Press Canada.

———. 2015. "Tapping the Potential of Senate-Driven Reform: Proposals to Limit the Powers of the Senate." *Constitutional Forum* 24 (2): 47–54.

Hicks, Bruce M., and André Blais. 2008. "Restructuring the Canadian Senate through Elections." *Choices* 14 (5). Montreal: Institute for Research on Public Policy. https://irpp.org/wp-content/uploads/assets/research/strengthening-canadian-democracy/restructuring-the-canadian-senate-through-elections/vol14no15.pdf.

House of Commons. 2018. "LegisInfo." Ottawa. http://www.parl.ca/LegisInfo/Home.aspx.

Howard, Colin. 1976. "The Constitutional Crisis of 1975." *Australian Quarterly* 48: 5–25.

Huffington Post. 2013. "NDP Motion to Abolish Senate Defeated." March 6. https://www.huffingtonpost.ca/2013/03/06/abolish-senate-motion-ndp-defeated_n_2823374.html.

———. 2018. "Senator Irked by How Senate Has No Farmers, Fishers, or Veterans." March 9. https://www.huffingtonpost.ca/2018/03/08/senator-percy-downe-irked-senate-farmers-fishers-veterans_a_23381073/.

Hughson, Heather. 2015. "Senate Reform: The First 125 Years." Policy Options, September. http://policyoptions.irpp.org/magazines/september-2015/the-future-of-the-senate/senate-reform-thefirst-125-years/.

Independent Advisory Board for Senate Appointments. 2018. "Assessment Criteria." https://www.canada.ca/en/campaign/independent-advisory-board-for-senate-appointments/assessment-criteria.html.

Joyal, Serge, ed. 2003. *Protecting Canada's Democracy: The Senate You Never Knew*. Montreal and Kingston: McGill-Queen's University Press.

Judicial Committee of the Privy Council. 1930. *Edwards v Attorney General of Canada* AC 114.

Lawlor, Andrea, and Erin Crandall. 2013. "Committee Performance in the Senate of Canada: Some Sobering Analysis for the Chamber of 'Sober Second Thought.'" *Commonwealth & Comparative Politics* 51: 549–68.

Library of Parliament. 2018a. "Parliamentarians." https://lop.parl.ca/sites/ParlInfo/default/en_CA/People/parliamentarians.

———. 2018b. "Substantive Committee Reports: Senate." https://lop.parl.ca/sites/ParlInfo/default/en_CA/Parliament/procedure/committeeReports/committeeReports Senate (link no longer active).

Macfarlane, Emmett. 2016. "The Uncertain Future of Senate Reform." In *Constitutional Amendment in Canada*, edited by Emmett Macfarlane, 228–47. Toronto: University of Toronto Press.

Mackay, Robert A. 1963. *The Unreformed Senate of Canada*. Rev. ed. Toronto: McClelland and Stewart.

Maloney, Ryan. 2015. "Tories Have Shut Down Debate 100 Times This Parliament: Opposition." Huffington Post, June 10. https://www.huffingtonpost.ca/2015/06/10/time-allocation-tories-brent-rathgeber_n_7556762.html.

McHugh, James T. 2017. *The Senate and the People of Canada: A Counterintuitive Approach to Senate Reform*. Lanham, MD: Lexington Books.

McKenna, Cara. 2015. "NDP Would Not Have Representation in the Senate while Pushing for Abolition." Global News. https://globalnews.ca/news/2130603/ndp-would-not-have-representation-in-senate-while-pushing-for-abolition-mulcair/.

Monahan, Patrick J., Byron Shaw, and Padraic Ryan. 2017 *Constitutional Law*. 5th ed. Toronto: Irwin Law.

Mulcair, Thomas. 2015. "The Future of the Senate: The NDP View." *Policy Options*, September 21. http://policyoptions.irpp.org/magazines/september-2015/the-future-of-the-senate/the-future-of-the-senate-the-ndp-view/.

Nanos Research. 2018. "Majority of Canadians Prefer an Independent Senate." http://www.nanos.co/wp-content/uploads/2018/09/2018-1159-Senate-Populated-Report-FINAL-for-release-with-tabs.pdf.

O'Brien, Audrey, and Marc Bosc. 2009. *House of Commons Procedure and Practice*. 2nd ed. Cowansville: Éditions Yvon Blais.

Office of the Commissioner of Lobbying of Canada. 2018. "Advanced Registry Search." https://lobbycanada.gc.ca/app/secure/ocl/lrs/do/clntSmmrySrch?lang=eng.

Quebec Court of Appeal. 2013. *Reference re Bill C-7 concerning the Reform of the Senate* QCCA 1807.

Resnick, Philip. 1987. "Montesquieu Revisited, or the Mixed Constitution and the Separation of Powers in Canada." *Canadian Journal of Political Science* 20: 97–115.

Russell, Peter H. 1993. *Constitutional Odyssey: Canada Canadians Become a Sovereign People?* 2nd ed. Toronto: University of Toronto Press.

Seidle, Leslie F. 1991. "Senate Reform and the Constitutional Agenda: Conundrum or Solution?" In *Canadian Constitutionalism: 1791–1991*, edited by Janet Ajzenstat, 90–122. Ottawa: Canadian Study of Parliament Group.

Senate of Canada. 2002. "Reforming Health Protection and Promotion in Canada: Time to Act." Standing Senate Committee Social Affairs, Science and Technology. http://www.parl.gc.ca/37/2/parlbus/commbus/senate/com-e/soci-e/rep-e/repfinnov03-e.htm.

———. 2006. "Second Report of the Special Senate Committee on Senate Reform." October 26. https://sencanada.ca/Content/SEN/Committee/391/refo/rep/rep02oct06-e.htm.

———. 2011. "Major Legislative and Special Study Reports by Senate Committees: 1961–2010." http://publications.gc.ca/collections/collection_2011/sen/Y9-15-2010-eng.pdf.

———. 2018. "Committees: Reports." https://sencanada.ca/en/Committees/reports/.

———. 2019. "Progress of Legislation." https://sencanada.ca/en/in-the-chamber/progress /42-1 (link no longer active).

Sharman, Campbell. 2008. "Political Legitimacy for an Appointed Senate." Choices series no. 14–11. Montreal: Institute for Research in Public Policy.

Smith, David E. 2003. *The Canadian Senate in Bicameral Perspective*. Toronto: University of Toronto Press.

Smith, Jennifer, ed. 2009. *The Democratic Dilemma: Reforming the Canadian Senate*. Montreal and Kingston: McGill-Queen's University Press.

Statistics Canada. 2009. "Land Area and Density of Population, by Province, Census Years 1951, 1956 and 1961." https://www65.statcan.gc.ca/acyb02/1967/acyb02_19670186004-eng.htm.

———. 2018. "Population Estimates, Quarterly." https://www150.statcan.gc.ca/t1/tbl1/en/tv.action?pid=1710000901.

Supreme Court of Canada. 1980. *Reference re Authority of Parliament in Relation to the Upper House* 1 SCR 54.

———. 2014. *Reference re Senate Reform* SCC 32.

Task Force on Canadian Unity. 1979. "A Future Together: Observations and Recommendations." Ottawa Supply and Services Canada. http://publications.gc.ca/collections/collection_2014/bcp-pco/CP32-35-1979-eng.pdf.

Watts, Ronald. 2009. "Federal Second Chambers Compared." In *The Democratic Dilemma: Reforming the Canadian Senate*, edited by Jennifer Smith, 35–48. Montreal and Kingston: McGill-Queen's University Press.

White, Randall. 1990. *Voice of Region: The Long Journey to Senate Reform in Canada*. Toronto: Dundurn.

Zimonjic, Peter, and Rosemary Barton. 2018. "Andrew Scheer Says He Will Not Appoint Independent Senators if Elected Prime Minister." CBC News, June 28. https://www.cbc.ca/news/politics/andrew-scheer-interview-barton-1.4182567.

six

The Civil Service

AMANDA CLARKE

Introduction

The election has come to a close, a legislature is formed of newly elected representatives, a government has earned the confidence of the House, and with that, the ability to form a Cabinet of ministers who will implement their policy agenda. Putting this agenda into action and addressing new issues that arise over the course of a government's time in power are no simple tasks. The government must develop new pieces of legislation, adopt policy positions, and design programs and services for the Canadian public across a varied set of complex challenges, including, for instance, the regulation of new pharmaceuticals, navigating international trade negotiations, and tackling homelessness. The government must also "keep the lights on" across a broad spectrum of activities under the state's care – collecting taxes, maintaining roads, schools, and hospitals, and securing the border. Running a modern welfare state demands significant organizational capacity and expertise. Who will provide this capacity and expertise to a government once it takes the reins of power? The civil service.

The civil service, sometimes called the public service or the bureaucracy, is a key player in the day-to-day, practical act of governing. As a result, the civil service is also a central institution within the broader system of Canadian democracy. Through the programs and services it delivers, the civil service acts as a primary interface for citizens in their interactions with the state. To many Canadians, the civil service is the organization that comes to mind when they imagine "the government" writ large. Civil servants also play an intimate role in the workings of Cabinet. They have the ear of the minister, privileged with the opportunity to provide policy advice to support these decision-makers, but also central to the accountable implementation of Cabinet's policy directives; they are tasked, for instance, with ensuring that programs and services are accessible to all Canadians, regardless of ability and language, and that public funds are expended efficiently and transparently.

Focusing its analysis on the federal civil service, this chapter is organized into three parts. Part one details the organizational principles informing the federal civil service and the machinery of government that it comprises. Part two discusses the place of the civil service within Canada's Westminster system of democracy. Turning from founding principles to contemporary life in government, part three identifies three central challenges facing the federal civil service, highlighting how these challenges test the organizational and democratic traditions of Canada's Westminster government. The chapter concludes by tying the health of the civil service to the health of Canadian democracy, underscoring the need for sustained scrutiny of this important institution by students of Canadian politics and citizens alike.

The Organizational Contours of the Federal Civil Service

The federal civil service, as with most civil service institutions today, is a bureaucracy. This is a particular organizational structure, first formally described by German sociologist Max Weber in the late nineteenth century (Weber 1994). Bureaucracy, according to Weber's model, is structured around two organizational principles: hierarchy and silos. Hierarchy is the organizational mechanism that dictates that authority is parcelled out in a government department in a top-down manner, with superiors having greater authority than the subordinates who report to them. Silos, on the other hand, are the organizational structures by which different functions and responsibilities are separated from each other and managed independently within an organization. So, for example, in a given department, individuals responsible for communications might be "siloed off" from those responsible for information technology or program delivery.

In the civil service, hierarchies and silos serve two functions. The first is a *management* function. These structures break down complex activities, such as developing a new government-funded child-care program, for example, into a series of smaller, defined tasks that are then parcelled out to different actors across an organization. Silos split this activity up into defined streams of operations, while hierarchy dictates that management of this activity is governed through top-down directives (e.g., rules, policies, instructions), and upward-reporting mechanisms (e.g., from a lower-level policy analyst reporting on a program's progress to a program manager). As a management tool, hierarchies and silos are employed to ensure orderly, coordinated, and efficient execution of government work (Dunleavy and Hood 1994; Goodsell 2004; Hood 2000; Olsen 2006).

Related to the management function of hierarchies and silos is the *accountability* function they serve. With tasks designated to particular actors (through silos), and superiors having authority over the subordinates they manage (through hierarchy), it becomes easier to identify who is responsible for certain tasks, and to apportion blame or reward for the execution of those tasks. In particular, in civil service institutions, the principle of hierarchy dictates that superiors are accountable for the actions of the subordinates who report to them and whom they manage (Jarvis 2014). In government departments, deputy ministers are the highest-ranking civil servants, sitting atop the bureaucratic hierarchy.

In practice, these hierarchies and silos are given form through the machinery of government, a term that refers to the set of organizations that comprise the civil service, the functions assigned to these organizations, and the structures and processes that link them. In the federal government, the machinery of government consists of a number of different entities, which are for the most part administrative bodies defined by statute in the Financial Administration Act.

Ministerial departments and agencies are led by Cabinet ministers, and can be one of two types. Central agencies sit, as the name implies, at the centre of the machinery of government, and are tasked with coordinating activities across the civil service in order that the government's policy priorities are advanced. These include the Privy Council Office (PCO), the Treasury Board Secretariat, and the Department of Finance. Line departments and agencies, on the other hand, are the departments responsible for particular policy portfolios, such as Environment and Climate Change Canada and Health Canada. In addition, the federal civil service includes a series of departmental corporations, Crown corporations, service agencies and special operating agencies, all governed with various degrees of independence from direct central agency and/or Cabinet control.[1]

While at one point, much of the civil service could be housed in the offices of the East Block of Parliament (Granatstein 1982; Savoie 2003), the federal government has grown considerably in size and complexity over time. To be sure, as noted by Thomas (2014) in the previous edition of *Canadian Politics*, the commonly held assumption that this growth has been unwieldy or excessive – that the civil service is "bloated" – is largely unjustified. The federal civil service has grown at a slower pace than the size of the Canadian population it serves, and at certain times government spending and staffing have been systematically reduced, not expanded (as in the Liberal government's program review exercise of the mid 1990s, and the Conservative government's Deficit Reduction Action Plan of the early 2010s). Even so, it bears noting that while Canada's early civil service once could be characterized as "a small village, where everyone knew everyone else" (Savoie 2003, 65), the organization is now significantly larger and more complex than it was at this early stage. According to the Government of Canada, the federal civil service now comprises 201 departments, agencies, Crown corporations, and special operating agencies, with 262,696 employees.[2]

Growth in the size and complexity of the federal civil service is in part a simple reflection of the expansion of the welfare state following World

War II, expansion that brought more and more policy issues, programs, and services under the federal government's care and that in turn demanded more civil servants and civil service organizations to handle this expanded mandate. The expansion of the federal civil service is also a product of the growing complexity of governance. In addition to managing a diverse group of subject matter experts, working on everything from marine biology research to the minutiae of tax credit changes, governments now require access to a broad range of technical expertise, including statisticians, web developers, translators, lawyers, and those working in communications, information management, stakeholder engagement, and procurement.

The immensity of the machinery of government, and the prominent role that civil servants play in the practical execution of the tasks of governing, presents the question: How are these officials held accountable, and what is their role in the broader system of Canadian Westminster parliamentary democracy?

The Civil Service in the Westminster Tradition

Civil servants sit within the executive branch of government. In contrast with the partisan political actors operating in the executive, including elected officials serving as ministers and their ministerial staff, civil servants in the Westminster tradition are non-partisan. This dictates that civil servants refrain from using government resources to advance the partisan political interests of any given actor or party, whether that party is in power or not. Importantly, civil servants must also be seen to be politically neutral in their public activities, both when acting in their capacity as civil servants and when acting in their capacity as private citizens (though the latter is subject to certain limitations, given Charter-protected rights to political expression) (see Clarke and Piper 2018).

If they are not party loyalists, working for the party in power, then what exactly is the function of civil servants in the day-to-day operations of governing? Under the principle of non-partisanship, civil servants' core function is the provision of "frank advice and loyal implementation" to whichever government is in power, meaning that the advice they provide to ministers should be evidence-informed and neutral (i.e., without bias for particular political agendas or ideologies), and that they dutifully implement whatever directives the government of the day chooses to pursue. Notably, "loyal implementation" dictates that civil servants must equally refrain from actively promoting the partisan strategic gains of the governing party, by, for example, publicly praising the initiatives of the government. In this sense, non-partisanship cuts two ways – civil servants should neither openly critique nor openly applaud the governments they serve (Kernaghan 2010; Savoie 2003; Tait 1996).

Three other characteristics of the Westminster civil service flow from the principle of non-partisanship. The first is that, outside the highest levels of authority (deputy ministers and associate deputy ministers), civil servants are appointed and promoted on a merit basis, that is, for their talents and abilities. This is achieved through a non-political staffing process, administered through the Public Service Commission of Canada and governed by the Financial Administration Act and the Public Service Employment Act (Aucoin, Turnbull, and Jarvis 2011).

Second, civil servants are appointed permanently, meaning that they remain employed by the Government of Canada even when there is a change in political administration. This permanency is made possible by the fact that the civil service does not comprise party loyalists that an incoming government of a different political stripe would rightfully wish to dispense with, but rather subject area experts and technical specialists equipped to support the policy agenda of any government. The principle of permanency means that when a new government comes to power, it inherits the civil service already in place. Even more importantly, because civil servants are permanent, merit-based, non-partisan actors, the incoming government can *trust* them to support its work and implement its policy priorities.

A counterpart to the permanency of the non-partisan civil service is the principle of anonymity, the final characteristic of the Westminster civil service. By this principle, civil servants and the frank advice they provide to ministers are not thrust into the public eye or dragged into partisan political debate. Rather, civil servants properly operate in the background, with their ministers acting as the representative of the government in public matters, and individual civil servants protected from the scrutiny – and potential future sanctions – of opposition parties who at some point may themselves take the reins of power (Grube 2013).

The four principles of non-partisanship, merit, permanency, and anonymity are core to the democratic accountability of the civil service as an unelected body of actors that nonetheless enjoys significant influence over government policies and services. Here it is important to underscore that civil servants are not directly accountable to members of the public, nor are they "servants" of the public (a constitutional reality that has led some to criticize the use of the term *public service* in lieu of *civil service*). Likewise, outside certain exceptions discussed later in this chapter, civil servants are not accountable to Parliament. Rather, civil servants are accountable to their minister, who is individually and collectively (as a member of Cabinet) accountable to Parliament. Members of Parliament are in turn accountable to the Canadian voter. Within this arrangement, it is imperative that civil servants uphold their duty to provide quality, balanced advice to the minister, and to implement that minister's directives loyally; to do otherwise would constitute a significant breach of democratic accountability, with the civil service essentially going "rogue" and using their access to state resources and powers in pursuit of a policy agenda that is not sanctioned through the electoral and legislative processes that justify a minister's power.

At the same time, in managing their portfolios, ministers and their political staff equally have a duty to respect the tenets of the Westminster system. They must allow civil servants to be hired and managed on a merit basis, as opposed to being rewarded or sanctioned for the partisan political support they provide their minister or the minister's party. Ministers and their political staff must also refrain from asking civil servants to employ state resources solely to support their partisan interests, and must equally refrain from publicly "naming and shaming" otherwise anonymous civil servants for the outcomes of the government policies and programs that they are tasked with implementing.

This arrangement has been termed the "public service bargain" (Clarke and Piper 2018; Hood and Lodge 2006; Lodge 2009; Savoie 2003). Under this bargain, civil servants exchange certain political freedoms and public profile for security of employment, and the ability to provide frank, uncensored advice to the government without reprisal. Ministers, in turn, gain access to a corps of experienced administrators and managers – to the organizational capacity of government machinery – while relinquishing their ability to hire and fire at will and to use the civil service for direct partisan gain.[3]

The discussion so far gives a baseline description of the organizational contours and democratic principles that define the federal civil service. This baseline of information does not indicate, however, how accountable and effective the civil service is in practice when navigating the demands of governing today. By one measure, offered in 2017 by the UK think tank Institute for Government, Canada's federal civil service ranks number one in the world as the most effective (Institute for Government 2017). Yet the institution still faces challenges that strain the federal bureaucratic machinery and the Westminster principles that underpin the operations of the civil service. The next section details three central hurdles that the federal civil service is grappling with, and highlights recent efforts to resolve them within the Canadian government.

Three Core Challenges Facing Today's Civil Service

Greater Demands for Open Government

By design, the Westminster civil service is a largely closed institution (Clarke 2019). The principle of anonymity calls for the civil service to operate "behind closed doors," shielding civil servants and their work from public scrutiny, and allowing them in turn to provide frank, uncensored advice to ministers. And as per the principle of hierarchical ministerial accountability, civil servants do not technically share a relationship with the Canadian public. Rather, their relationship to Canadians is mediated through their loyalty to ministers, who are themselves accountable to the public through Parliament. Yet, despite these principles, the activities of government have nonetheless been opened to ever greater public view and scrutiny, with civil servants thrust into direct contact with Canadians in different ways.

Civil service transparency has been fuelled by the introduction of access to information legislation, and the creation in 1983 of a "disclosure watchdog," the Access to Information and Privacy (ATIP) Commissioner. This commissioner reports to Parliament and the public on the state of disclosure within the federal government, evaluating, for instance, the average time it takes for the government to respond to requests for information through the access to information regime, and whether or not these responses represent fulsome disclosure. This would include the number of internal documents released, the number of requests that are denied, and the extent to which the information released is redacted – physically "blacked out" to withhold certain pieces of information in a document.

In some cases, drawing on access to information requests, and in others, relying on direct interviews with civil servants (anonymously or with attribution), government websites, and other publicly available documents, the media have also contributed to an opening up of the machinery of government. It is now common to hear the names of individual civil servants cited in news reports, and for minute details of internal government processes to be the subject of these reports. Alongside media scrutiny, parliamentary scrutiny has also brought the activities of the civil service into the public light, most obviously in the practice of calling deputy ministers and other senior officials before parliamentary committees to testify on departmental matters.

Adding to these trends, the digital age has brought with it expanded and more ambitious standards for open government. In part fuelled by US President Barack Obama's open government initiative, introduced in 2008, and subsequently driven by an international Open Government Partnership, governments' claims to "openness" now not only relate to their adherence to freedom of information and media access, but also to commitments to regularized citizen involvement in policy-making and the release of raw government data for public use ("open data") (Clarke and Francoli 2014; Yu and Robinson 2012).

Prior to the expansion of the global open government movement, the federal civil service already had a tradition of engaging Canadians in policy-making, through, for example, consultations and ministerial roundtables, activities that further eroded the principle of anonymity as civil servants were thrust into public engagement with the citizens and organizations participating in these policy development exercises (Doern 1971; Van Rooy 2012). Under its own open government initiative, first introduced by the Conservative government of Stephen Harper in 2012, the federal civil service committed to expanding upon this tradition with an "Open Dialogue" initiative that would see the federal civil service use digital technologies, such as social media, to engage Canadians in their internal policy processes. The open government initiative also followed international trends in committing the federal civil service to an open data program, by which departments began collecting, cleaning, and releasing their raw data to the public, with an accompanying licence that allowed others to reuse those data to a range of ends, including for commercial applications, but also to hold the government to account (Government of Canada 2012, 2014).

Outside official government initiatives, the civil service has also opened itself to the public through the private online activities of individual civil servants. Today's civil servants, like the rest of the Canadian population, increasingly live their lives online, and in particular, civil servants have taken to platforms such as LinkedIn and Twitter to stay up to date with developments in their policy field, to network with other civil servants and stakeholders, and to discuss their work as civil servants (Clarke and Francoli 2014).[4] In certain instances, managers in the federal government have directly encouraged this activity, such as promoting a government-wide discussion on public service renewal on Twitter (as part of a government-wide reform initiative titled Blueprint 2020, launched in 2013).

In the face of external demands for transparency (from the access to information commissioner, the media, and bodies such as the Open Government Partnership), and given the expectations and realities of a fleet of digital-era civil servants, the federal civil service must now respond to unprecedented demands for openness. How is the institution faring in the face of these demands? The government's success in meeting this challenge is mixed.

Canada was an early global leader in introducing access to information legislation, but has since fallen short on this file. The access to information commissioner regularly criticizes the federal government for failing to meet its obligations to disclose information, arguing that despite promises from the Trudeau government, the government's levels of disclosure have deteriorated, not improved (Stone 2017), and that the government's effort to renew the Access to Information Act with Bill C-58 (passed into law in 2019) is insufficient (Office of the Information Commissioner of Canada 2017).

Turning to its own open government plans, the civil service has been applauded for its advances in releasing its data, and in 2018 topped the World Wide Web Foundation's global open data rankings (World Wide Web Foundation 2018). But alongside successes on open data, the government has been criticized for failing to introduce a more ambitious, digitized model of citizen engagement (Clarke and Piper 2018; Francoli 2014). On the transparency file, the federal civil service still has work to do to meet today's more ambitious standards for open government.

What will it take to meet these standards? In some cases, digital-era open government simply demands more resources – skilled civil servants equipped to design, execute, and interpret the results of large-scale online consultations, information managers to clean and release government data, and access to information officers responding to the multitude of daily requests made through the ATIP regime. Some argue for proactive disclosure – releasing information as it is produced, versus reacting to requests for it – an approach that will demand in the first instance significant improvements to the government's information management practices and systems (work underway through an initiative called GCDocs).[5] The government must also generate new guidelines and training to support civil servants whose digital lives increasingly thrust them into public interactions with service users, journalists, stakeholders, and "everyday Canadians." In particular, the federal government has not yet provided balanced or instructive guidance to help civil servants navigate their duty to political neutrality in their professional and private use of social media (Clarke and Piper 2018), or to support their role as public spokespersons for the government in online consultations.

A thornier issue arises when evaluating the proper balance to be struck between increased demands for transparency and the traditional practice of preserving space for the provision of confidential advice to ministers. This protects civil servants from public scrutiny for the advice they provide (thus encouraging them to speak freely and frankly), preserves ministers' ability to respond to this advice as they wish as per ministerial prerogative, and also ensures that ministers are willing to inform their civil servant advisors about confidential Cabinet discussions relevant to the policy issue at hand (Savoie 2003, 2017). Still, others argue that public exposure of the advice provided to ministers will actually support more robust, evidence-informed decision-making (Jarvis 2016). The degree to which civil service advice provided to ministers should be disclosed remains a live debate hotly contested and unresolved in Canada. Amidst this debate, calls for greater transparency in government roll on. As former president of the Treasury Board Secretariat, Scott Brison, noted in 2016, "The transparency bus has left the station" (Brison 2016). For better or worse, open government is the order of the day, yet there is little evidence that civil servants are sufficiently equipped to deliver on this promise, and unresolved questions remain about the risks that greater openness might invite.

Governing through the Permanent Campaign

The *permanent campaign* is a term now used in Canadian political discussions to refer to the ongoing commitment to election tactics – such as pursuing voters, attacking the opposition, and aggressively promoting a narrow partisan agenda – within the regular course of governing between elections (Marland, Giasson, and Esselment 2017). For the civil service, permanent campaigning dictates that the work of policy design and service delivery is increasingly punctuated by carefully crafted communications and branding strategies. To be sure, the growing prominence of the communications function in the civil service is not a problem per se, and in part simply reflects the expanding role of information and communication technologies in society more generally and in the provision of public services specifically (Clarke 2019; Clarke and Craft 2017; Hood and Margetts 2007). What's more, message management and branding have long been a staple of governing, reaching back to the days of Prime Minister Laurier by one account (Marland 2016). Nonetheless, it is generally accepted that the centrality of communications and marketing to the act of governing warrants greater concern in a context of permanent campaigning, for three reasons.

First, the primacy of centralized communications and marketing strategies can discourage the provision of balanced evidence and analysis to ministers, central to the ideal of the Westminster bargain. According to this argument, permanent campaigning prioritizes communications and branding as the central governance lens (Marland 2016) and competes with robust, evidence-informed decision-making in government, thus undermining the broader policy capacity of the state (Aucoin 2012).

Second, the importance of maintaining a positive public image for the government can compel civil servants to withhold information from the public, especially where that information might point to government shortcomings. This drives the culture of secrecy that the access to information commissioner has criticized, and more generally, threatens the civil service's ability to satisfy growing demands for transparent, participatory government. The primacy of brand management also fuels a sense within the civil service that they must provide "error-free government" that protects their minister from politically costly public exposé (Himelfarb 2005; Jarvis 2016; Lynch 2007, 2008; Savoie 2013).

To this second point, one might respond that it is not unreasonable, and indeed should be expected, that a government strives to avoid errors.

However, this perspective ignores that it is impossible to govern as complex a set of organizations and policy files as the federal civil service does without ever making mistakes (Jarvis 2016). Further – and this is explored later in the chapter – some trial and error is welcome, given that it allows governments to experiment with new and untested ideas, paving the path to policy or service improvements (Bason 2010; Clarke 2016). Instead of prioritizing experimentation and learning, then, civil servants attempting to provide error-free administration become prone to micro-management, and default to excessive layers of rules and oversight to govern daily activities in the civil service. This has led to an oft-decried "web of rules" and a concomitant "reporting burden" in the civil service that diminishes staff morale, creates inefficiencies, and favours a status quo default. which is anathema to innovation (Treasury Board Secretariat 2009).

The third way in which permanent campaigning challenges the civil service is in encouraging its direct politicization. The late Peter Aucoin was particularly critical of this trend in the federal government. Arguing that federal public management can now be characterized as a form of New Political Governance, Aucoin noted that today's civil servants are dragged into partisan communications strategies, and as a perversion of the bargain, expected to publicly promote the partisan agenda of the government through acts of "promiscuous partisanship" (Aucoin 2012). In particular, the Conservative government of Stephen Harper was criticized for politicizing civil service communications. It did this by asking civil servants to use the term *Harper government* in official communications instead of the neutral and accepted *Government of Canada* (Cheadle and Ditchburn 2011), and by using partisan colours and images in government advertising (Marland 2016). In one incident, the government was criticized for recruiting civil servants for a YouTube video that featured the minister of employment and social development Canada, Pierre Poilievre, advancing partisan branding for a new family tax credit (May 2015).

Looking to differentiate itself from the Harper government, the Liberal government of Justin Trudeau began its tenure in government by promising to invest in and restore the civil service's capacity for evidence-informed policy advice. This suggested that the influence of communications and branding considerations in government policy work might be curbed. It also pledged to tighten controls over government advertising, and to support more open dialogue between the civil service and the public. Mandate letters issued to ministers (released publicly for the first time in federal government history) also directly rejected the imperative of "error-free government." Instead, they stated, "It is important that we acknowledge mistakes when we make them. Canadians do not expect us to be perfect – they expect us to be honest, open, and sincere in our efforts to serve the public interest" (Prime Minister's Office 2015a). A near identical set of commitments was included in mandate letters issued by Prime Minister Trudeau following the 2019 federal election (Prime Minister's Office 2019).

At this stage it is difficult to assess the extent to which this change in tone and political leadership will curb the well-entrenched effects of permanent campaigning in the civil service. As long as these effects endure, important facets of the Westminster bargain will be under considerable strain, including the role of the civil service as a source of frank evidence and analysis, and as a properly neutral institution, free from partisan influence. Permanent campaign effects will equally strain the civil service's ability to meet increased expectations for transparency that are now a staple of contemporary democratic societies.

The Imperative of Policy Innovation

Besides growing calls for transparency and the pressures of permanent campaigning, the federal civil service must still tackle a raft of existing and new policy challenges, which are fast-moving and increasingly cross-cutting, demanding expeditious and coordinated responses from across the federal bureaucracy. Acknowledging the need to leverage limited public resources, and in the face of new policy instruments introduced in the digital age (e.g., big data, machine learning, and crowdsourcing), the federal civil service faces new pressures to innovate in its policy and service offerings. However, a number of barriers limit the scope for innovation in the federal civil service, posing serious threats to the institution's effectiveness.

First, innovation often requires that the civil service draw on a range of subject expertise and functions across the bureaucracy. However, despite long-standing recognition that the government must work across its silos to adopt more "systems views" in policy development (Task Force on Horizontal Issues 1996), it remains difficult to mobilize cross-government action in the civil service. This is in part because civil servants still remain primarily accountable to their specific minister, accountability that can become blurred in cases of cross-ministry collaboration (Bakvis and Juillet 2004). In addition, human resources and staffing processes traditionally assign employees to particular departments and units, and in turn are too rigid to facilitate more flexible teamwork and temporary assignments across the bureaucracy (Deputy Minister Committee on Policy Innovation 2015). In this sense, the drive to innovation exposes a mismatch between Weber's silos and the contemporary reality of cross-cutting policy issues, which beg for multidisciplinary problem-solving.

Policy innovation is also hindered by the "web of rules" already discussed, with legislation and corporate guidelines on privacy, procurement, data sharing, grants, and contributions (funding provided to non-government actors to support government objectives) as well as others, creating significant time lags and disincentives for experimentation with new policy options. In some cases, it is not these rules themselves that prevent certain activities, but rather the incorrect assumption made by bureaucrats that they prohibit them, rendering these rules a barrier to innovation even where they technically allow for it (Clarke 2019). At the same time, simply abandoning rules governing the use of public resources and the conduct of civil servants might invite a range of accountability breaches, underscoring the tension between demands for nimble innovation in the civil service and the onerous considerations of equity, fairness, transparency, and consistency that governments must respect.

Alongside these rules, policy innovation can also be hindered by a dearth of appropriate skills and expertise within the civil service, in particular when it comes to wielding new digital policy instruments that require access to technical skills not found in the standard policy-makers' toolkit. Finally, policy innovation can be halted by a culture of risk aversion in the civil service, a product of the drive to "error-free government" that has captured the civil service in recent decades. Ironically, this risk aversion may actually run the risk of producing the very policy and service failures that civil servants seek to avoid, given that it can mean the status quo is favoured even when its shortcomings are apparent. The downside of risk aversion caught the attention of the auditor general in his 2018 assessment of the causes of the Phoenix pay system disaster, which has since 2012 seen the government fail to properly pay tens of thousands of civil servants at a cost of millions in tax dollars. The auditor general argued that adoption of the pay system proceeded despite evidence that it would fail, at least in part because managers in the civil service were not courageous enough to halt its introduction and pursue a different route (Auditor General of Canada 2018).

The need to tackle these barriers to policy innovation earned the attention of a committee of deputy ministers – the Deputy Minister Committee on Policy Innovation – in 2013. It also inspired the creation of a series of dedicated policy innovation labs within the civil service, including in the Privy Council Office. These labs provide defined spaces for civil servants to come together across different units to tackle specific policy challenges in unconventional ways, drawing on the expertise of the lab's staff (Bellafontaine 2013; Tonurist, Kattel, and Lember 2017). In addition to these labs, a series of initiatives have attempted to render it easier to identify and mobilize expertise and skills from across the bureaucracy. The GCTools, for example, have since 2008 served as common digital platforms for producing documents, sharing information, and networking across the civil service (although these tools are set to be retired and replaced as of 2020). Since 2016 a program titled Free Agents has recruited individuals with particular expertise and a track record of innovation to work on a project by project basis across the government, versus being assigned permanently to one specific department or unit (the traditional staffing model). Addressing the skills gap that can limit scope for innovation, the Canada School of Public Service introduced a Digital Academy in 2018, which trains civil servants in a range of areas relevant to digital-era policy work, including design thinking, and use of machine learning. And as part of broader interest in promoting more fluid interchange across government and the private sector (Campbell 2014; Jarvis 2016), the federal civil service has worked with Code for Canada since 2017 to bring private-sector tech talent into the federal government on a short-term basis (Simcoe 2017).

Alongside these worthy initiatives, the Trudeau government prioritized policy innovation through a directive issued following its electoral win in 2015. The mandate letter for then president of the Treasury Board, Scott Brison, called for a fixed percentage of program funds to be dedicated to policy experimentation (Impact and Innovation Unit 2016; Prime Minister's Office 2015b). This experimentation commitment is now managed by the PCO's Impact and Innovation Unit. While the actual impact of this commitment on the civil service's willingness and ability to innovate remains an open question, this directive did satisfy a concern expressed by the Deputy Minister Committee on Policy Innovation in one of its early reports. The committee noted that other jurisdictions had benefited from "positive policies" from political leadership, which provided top-level sanctioning of innovation for civil service leaders who were otherwise inclined toward risk aversion (Deputy Minister Committee on Policy Innovation 2016). In this sense, alongside the prime minister's assurance to ministers that "Canadians do not expect us to be perfect," the experimentation commitment endeavoured to assuage the civil service's long-standing assumption that Cabinet ministers prioritized "error-free government," not trial-and-error experimentation.

Conclusion

Students of Canadian politics may at first blush be inclined to dismiss the civil service as a paper-pushing, bureaucratic organization of little import to the broader functioning of Canadian democracy, and certainly less fascinating than the fast-moving, competitive world of electoral politics and parliamentary affairs. Yet this perspective ignores the significant role that the civil service plays within Canadian democratic institutions, for example by bringing legislative projects to life in government policies and services, and in the indispensable advice it provides to ministers. Accountability in our Westminster system of government also hinges in large part on accountability in the civil service, with recent concerns over the opaqueness and politicization of the civil service underscoring the need for ongoing scrutiny of its operations and implications for the health of Canadian democracy.

At a basic level, the civil service warrants attention, given that its effectiveness – or lack thereof, as the case may be – directly affects the quality of programs and services delivered to the Canadian public. Civil servants are caretakers to some of our most valuable public institutions, including health care, the military, schools, and core infrastructure. Trust in government is mediated by citizens' direct experiences with public services. Where these fall short, so too can citizens' faith in their government. In this sense, the recent focus on innovation within the federal civil service should be applauded, but its progress closely scrutinized, given that a capacity for creative and effective problem solving is essential to tackling the complex challenges facing Canadian society today. In short, the civil service warrants attention not only because it plays a key role in Canadian democratic life, but even more importantly because its capacity to play that role both accountably and effectively is at present far from certain.

Notes

1 For a description of each of these organizations, see Government of Canada (2016).

2 This number includes the Core Public Administration and Separate Agencies, as defined in Schedules I, IV, and V of the Financial Administration Act. Some organizations are not included in this count, including Crown corporations, the RCMP, and the Canadian Forces. Other employees that are included are not generally considered part of the civil service proper, such as staff working for officers of Parliament, and federal judges. See Treasury Board Secretariat (2019).

3 A number of different possible public service bargains might be enacted in a given governing context, and multiple bargains might operate concurrently. The Canadian bargain described in the chapter is often termed the Schafferian bargain, originating in the British Westminster system (Lodge 2009).

4 Many of these civil servants tweet on government matters using the hashtags #goc and #gcdigital.

5 See Statistics Canada (2018).

References and Suggested Readings

Aucoin, P. 2012. "New Political Governance in Westminster Systems: Impartial Public Administration and Management Performance at Risk." *Governance* 25 (2): 177–99.

Aucoin, P., L.B. Turnbull, and M.D. Jarvis. 2011. *Democratizing the Constitution: Reforming Responsible Government*. Toronto: Emond Montgomery Publications.

Auditor General of Canada. 2018. "Message from the Auditor General of Canada," May 29. http://www.oag-bvg.gc.ca/internet/English/parl_oag_201805_00_e_43032.html.

Bakvis, H., and L. Juillet. 2004. *The Horizontal Challenge: Line Departments, Central Agencies and Leadership*. Ottawa: Canada School of Public Service.

Bason, C. 2010. *Leading Public Sector Innovation: Co-Creating for a Better Society*. Bristol, UK: Policy.

Bellafontaine, T. 2013. *Innovation Labs: Bridging Think Tanks and Do Tanks*. Ottawa: Policy Horizons Canada.

Brison, S. 2016. "Speaking Notes for the Honourable Scott Brison, President of the Treasury Board to the Canadian Open Dialogue Forum 2016." Ottawa. https://www.canada.ca/en/treasury-board-secretariat/news/2016/03/speaking-notes-for-the-honourable-scott-brison-president-of-the-treasury-board-to-the-canadian-open-dialogue-forum-2016.html.

Campbell, A. 2014. "Lessons from Cross-Sector Experience." *Public Sector Digest* (Fall).

Cheadle, B., and J. Ditchburn. 2011. "'Harper Government' Not 'Government of Canada': Documents Reveal Working Directive, Contradict PMO." Huffington Post, November 29. http://www.huffingtonpost.ca/2011/11/29/industry-canada-documents-harper-government-communications_n_1118001.html.

Clarke, A. 2016. "The Innovation Challenge: Modernizing the Public Service." Policy Options, May 11. http://policyoptions.irpp.org/magazines/may-2016/the-innovation-challenge-modernizing-the-public-service/.

———. 2019. *Opening the Government of Canada: The Federal Bureaucracy in the Digital Age*. Vancouver: UBC Press.

Clarke, A., and J. Craft. 2017. "The Vestiges and Vanguards of Policy Design in a Digital Context." *Canadian Public Administration* 60 (4): 476–97.

Clarke, A., and M. Francoli. 2014. "What's in a Name? A Comparison of 'Open Government' Definitions across Seven Open Government Partnership Members." *eJournal of eDemocracy and Open Government* 6 (3). https://doi.org/10.29379/jedem.v6i3.227.

Clarke, A., and B. Piper. 2018. "A Legal Framework to Govern Online Political Expression by Public Servants." *Canadian Labour and Employment Law Journal* 21 (1): 1–50.

Deputy Minister Committee on Policy Innovation. 2015. "Advancing Policy Innovation: Conditions, Readiness, and the Path Ahead," April 22.

———. 2016. "A Proposal for a Positive Policy in Support of Experimentation and Innovation ('Pro-Innovation Rule')," February 12.

Doern, G.B. 1971. "Recent Changes in the Philosophy of Policy-making in Canada." *Canadian Journal of Political Science* 4 (2): 243–64.

Dunleavy, P., and C. Hood. 1994. "From Old Public Administration to New Public Management." *Public Money & Management* 14 (3): 9–16.

Francoli, M. 2014. *Canada Progress Report 2012–13*. Open Government Partnership. http://www.opengovpartnership.org/country/canada/progress-report/report.

Goodsell, C.T. 2004. *The Case for Bureaucracy: A Public Administration Polemic*. 4th ed. Washington, DC: CQ.

Government of Canada. 2012. "Canada's Action Plan on Open Government 2012–2014." http://open.canada.ca/en/canadas-action-plan-open-government.

———. 2014, May 2. "Canada's Action Plan on Open Government, 2014–2016." http://data.gc.ca/eng/canadas-action-plan-open-government#toc8.

———. 2016. "Inventory of Federal Organizations and Interests." https://www.canada.ca/en/treasury-board-secretariat/services/reporting-government-spending/inventory-government-organizations/overview-institutional-forms-definitions.html.

Granatstein, J.L. 1982. *The Ottawa Men: The Civil Service Mandarins, 1935–1957*. Toronto: Oxford University Press.

Grube, D. 2013. "Public Voices from Anonymous Corridors: The Public Face of the Public Service in a Westminster System." *Canadian Public Administration* 56 (1): 3–25.

Himelfarb, A. 2005. *Twelfth Annual Report from the Clerk of the Privy Council and Secretary to the Cabinet*. Privy Council Office.

Hood, C.C. 2000. "Paradoxes of Public-Sector Managerialism, Old Public Management and Public Service Bargains." *International Public Management Journal* 3: 1–22.

Hood, C.C., and M. Lodge. 2006. *The Politics of Public Service Bargains: Reward, Competency, and Loyalty – and Blame*. Oxford: Oxford University Press. http://www.oxfordscholarship.com/view/10.1093/019926967X.001.0001/acprof-9780199269679.

Hood, C.C., and H. Margetts. 2007. *The Tools of Government in the Digital Age*. Basingstoke, UK: Palgrave Macmillan.

Impact and Innovation Unit. 2016. "Experimentation Direction for Deputy Heads, December 2016." https://www.canada.ca/en/innovation-hub/services/reports-resources/experimentation-direction-deputy-heads.html.

Institute for Government. 2017. "The International Civil Service Effectiveness (InCiSE) Index 2017." https://www.instituteforgovernment.org.uk/publications/international-civil-service-effectiveness-incise-index-2017.

Jarvis, M.D. 2014. "Hierarchy." In *The Oxford Handbook of Public Accountability*, edited by Mark Bovens, Robert E. Goodin, and Thomas Schillemans, 405. Oxford: Oxford University Press.

———. 2016. *Creating a High-Performing Canadian Civil Service against a Backdrop of Disruptive Change*. Toronto: Mowat Centre.

Kernaghan, K. 2010. "East Block and Westminster: Conventions, Values, and Public Service." In *The Handbook of Canadian Public Administration*, edited by C. Dunn, 289–304. Toronto: Oxford University Press.

Lodge, M. 2009. "Strained or Broken? The Future(s) of the Public Service Bargain." *Policy Quarterly* 5 (1): 53–7.

Lynch, K.G. 2007. *Fourteenth Annual Report to the Prime Minister on the Public Service of Canada. Privy Council Office*. http://www.clerk.gc.ca/eng/feature.asp?mode=preview&pageId=208 (link no longer active).

———. 2008, February. *The Public Service of Canada: Too Many Misperceptions*. Vancouver, BC.

Marland, A.J. 2016. *Brand Command: Canadian Politics and Democracy in the Age of Message Control*. Vancouver: UBC Press.

Marland, A., T. Giasson, and A. Esselment, eds. 2017. *Permanent Campaigning in Canada*. Vancouver: UBC Press.

May, K. 2015. "Boundary between Politics, Public Service Is 'No Man's Land: Expert. *Ottawa Citizen*, May 19. https://ottawacitizen.com/news/national/boundary-between-politics-public-service-is-no-mans-land-expert.

Office of the Information Commissioner of Canada. 2017. "Failing to Strike the Right Balance for Transparency Recommendations to Improve Bill C-58: An Act to Amend the Access to Information Act and the Privacy Act and to Make Consequential Amendments to Other Acts." http://www.oic-ci.gc.ca/eng/rapport-special-c-58_special-report-c-58.aspx (link no longer active).

Olsen, J.P. 2006. "Maybe It Is Time to Rediscover Bureaucracy." *Journal of Public Administration Research & Theory* 16 (1): 1–24.

Prime Minister's Office. 2015a. "Mandate Letters." https://pm.gc.ca/en/mandate-letters.

———. 2015b. "President of the Treasury Board of Canada Mandate Letter." https://pm.gc.ca/en/mandate-letters.

———. 2019. "Mandate Letters." https://pm.gc.ca/en/mandate-letters.

Savoie, D.J. 2003. *Breaking the Bargain: Public Servants, Ministers, and Parliament*. Toronto: University of Toronto Press.

———. 2013. *Whatever Happened to the Music Teacher?: How Government Decides and Why*. Montreal and Kingston: McGill-Queen's University Press.

———. 2017. "Why Keep Cabinet Secrets? Our Democracy Depends on It." *Globe and Mail*, April 27. https://www.theglobeandmail.com/opinion/why-keep-cabinet-secrets-our-democracy-depends-on-it/article34834801/.

Simcoe, L. 2017. "Meet the 2017 Code for Canada Fellows!" Medium, October 3. https://medium.com/code-for-canada/meet-the-2017-code-for-canada-fellows-ac825c6d19b6.

Statistics Canada. 2018. "GCdocs." https://www.statcan.gc.ca/eng/about/pia/GCdocs.

Stone, L. 2017. "Canada's Access-to-Information System Has Worsened under Trudeau Government: Report." *Globe and Mail*, September 27. https://www.theglobeandmail.com/news/politics/canadas-access-to-information-system-has-worsened-under-trudeau-government-report/article36407309/.

Tait, J. 1996. *A Strong Foundation: Report of the Task Force on Public Service Values and Ethics*. Ottawa: Canadian Centre for Management Development.

Task Force on Horizontal Issues. 1996. *Managing Horizontal Policy Issues*. Ottawa: Government of Canada. http://publications.gc.ca/collections/Collection/SC93-8-1996-3E.pdf.

Thomas, P.G. 2014. "Two Cheers for Bureaucracy: Canada's Public Service." In *Canadian Politics*, 6th ed., edited by J. Bickerton and A.-G. Gagnon, 177–98. Toronto: University of Toronto Press.

Tonurist, P., R. Kattel, and V. Lember. 2017. "Innovation Labs in the Public Sector: What They Are and What They Do." *Public Management Review* 19 (10): 1–25.

Treasury Board Secretariat. 2009. *Toward Effective Government: Untangling the Web of Rules*. http://publications.gc.ca/collections/collection_2011/sct-tbs/BT22-120-2009-eng.pdf.

———. 2019. "Population of the Federal Public Service by Department." https://www.canada.ca/en/treasury-board-secretariat/services/innovation/human-resources-statistics/population-federal-public-service-department.html.

Van Rooy, A. 2012. *A History of Public Engagement in the Government of Canada: A Discussion Paper*. Ottawa: Canada School of Public Service.

Weber, M. 1994. *Weber: Political Writings*. Cambridge: Cambridge University Press.

World Wide Web Foundation. 2018. "Open Data Barometer." https://opendatabarometer.org/?_year=2017&indicator=ODB.

Yu, H., and D.G. Robinson. 2012. "The New Ambiguity of 'Open Government.'" SSRN Electronic Journal. https://doi.org/10.2139/ssrn.2012489.

seven

Interest Groups in Canada and in the United States: Evidence of Convergence

ÉRIC MONTPETIT AND GRAHAM WILSON

Introduction

Interest groups exist in all political systems and are a feature of political life in every advanced democracy. How do we think about the similarities and differences among interest groups in different countries? Many people will think instinctively about differences in their power. Do interest groups in one country have more or less important roles in making public policy than interest groups in other countries? Interest groups, however, are not only actors in the policy process but are themselves acted upon. Both individual interest groups and interest group systems are the products of the political systems in which they are embedded. Interest groups are shaped by the institutional and constitutional setting in which they operate. Constitutions and laws define the strategies available to groups and even the likelihood that they will succeed or fail in recruiting members. Tactics regarded as routine in one country may be unavailable, ineffective, or even illegal in another. The political culture of one country might celebrate interest groups as key elements of democracy while in another they are seen as a threat to the national interest.

The North American democracies, Canada and the United States, provide great opportunities for comparing interest groups. The two countries have much in common. They are large, affluent, federal systems with multi-ethnic and multiracial populations. They have, however, very different political institutions and, it has been argued, significantly different political cultures. Canada is a "Westminster model" democracy in which power is held by the leaders of disciplined parties that compete for the majority in the House of Commons that will give them both legislative and executive power. US politics is conducted in three overlapping branches of government in which political parties have been historically less disciplined and unified. US political institutions themselves have also been characterized by limited authority for leaders. Interest groups in Canada operate in an environment that has been associated with strong executive leadership and a weaker legislature. At least since Tocqueville, it has been customary to hail and commend the contribution that interest groups make to the quality of American democracy and even to

American society more generally. For pluralist American thinkers, good policy was simply the result of the competition between interest groups. In Canada, in contrast, it has been common to present the political culture as more deferential and inclined to promote order and good government.

Many of these differences between the two countries rest on practices and institutions that themselves change over time. No one could doubt that the differences between US political parties in the early twenty-first century were real and in consequence party unity in Congress was very high; this had not been the case in the mid-twentieth century. Anyone familiar with the last fifty years of Quebec's history will know how considerably a society and its culture can change. Putnam (2001) expressed very strong concern about the degree to which the United States was ceasing to be a country in which participation in voluntary organizations (including interest groups) was common. Nonetheless, we wrote this chapter with the general expectations that the differences between interest groups in the two countries remain sufficiently entrenched that it is worth subjecting them to critical analysis. We think that the following expectations about the differences between the two countries would be widely held.

1. *Interest groups in Canada recruit a lower proportion of the population and reflect a narrower range of interests than in the United States.*

Almost any textbook on American politics will commonly assert that Americans join and organize voluntary associations more frequently than people in other democracies. In contrast, interest groups are not as important a topic in Canadian politics textbooks, perhaps reflecting the low participation of Canadians in such organizations.

2. *Fewer interest groups representing a narrower range of interests have the opportunity to participate more meaningfully in policy-making in Canada than in the United States.*

The unified government that results from the Westminster model allows policy-makers to control meaningful opportunities to shape policy on favoured groups. It is unlikely that Parliament will defeat or significantly amend recommendations by the government (or the prime minister). Interest groups therefore need access to policy while it is still in flux in discussions within and between government departments. Policy-makers have important incentives to seek the views of groups that possess technical expertise or that can help implement policy. In practice, these groups are likely to be representatives of economic interests and not so much of the values and concerns of broader social movements. Fragmented between the executive and legislative branches, as well as within the legislative branch, American policy-makers cannot select the groups with which they interact to the same extent. As a consequence, a wider range of interests and values is likely to access the American government.

As much as these two hypotheses make sense, we found some evidence that the Canadian interest group system has been converging toward the American one. In fact, Canadian interest groups mobilize a larger share of the Canadian population than one would expect from these system differences; and those accessing government represent a wider diversity of interests than expected. Before presenting the evidence, we say a few words on the influence of political culture and institutions on interest groups.

Political Culture and Institutions

Political scientists use the concept of culture in various ways, sometimes to designate individual values (e.g., Kahan and Braman 2006), sometimes referring to broad characteristics that make a society distinct from other societies (e.g., Hartz 1969). Here we use the concept of culture in this latter sense, referring to generalizations about the distinctive traits of the American and Canadian societies. As stated above, numerous observers since Tocqueville have suggested that American political culture combines the strands of participation and individualism to an unusual degree. Tocqueville famously suggested that Americans have a high propensity to form and join voluntary associations, including interest groups. In contrast, Canadian scholars argue that their country has preserved fragments of the conservative culture of the British colonizers that were rejected south of the border during the American Revolution (Horowitz 1978). Canadian political culture is thus seen to be more deferential toward elite accommodation and less supportive of participation in interest groups in particular (Presthus 1973). We can also expect to see differences in culture result in a different type of interest group system in Canada. The lesser emphasis on individual participation and greater emphasis on functional representation in Canadian culture are expected to result in fewer Canadians joining interest groups and a larger role for those interest groups defined by occupation or economic role rather than for groups representing the values and commitments of large segments of the population.

Cultures can change over time and there is some evidence that both the Canadian and American political cultures have done so. Writing about American society, Putnam (2001) argues that participation in associations, including interest groups, has declined in the United States. Nevitte (1996) wrote in the 1990s that younger generations of Canadians do not value deference to authority as much as older generations, possibly affecting their attitude toward interest groups. Therefore, it is possible that the political cultures of the United States and Canada have less effect than in the past on sustaining distinctive interest group systems between the two countries.

In addition to culture, political institutions can be expected to influence interest groups. Canada's executive-dominated parliamentary system has been predicted to limit the access of interest groups to political decision-makers. Scholars have insisted frequently on the incompatibility of Canada's Cabinet system of government with interest group power, questioning whether policy-makers had much interest in consulting with groups. In Canada, the executive branch of the federal government negotiates with the executive branch of provincial governments, not interest groups (Smiley 1987). Unsurprisingly, the literature on Canadian politics has accorded far less space to interest groups than the literature on American politics. As Haddow (1999, 503) observes, textbooks on Canadian politics failed to include any discussion of interest groups prior to the 1970s. The first major books on interest groups in Canada were published in the mid-1980s (Pross 1986; Thorburn 1985).

Coleman and Skogstad's (1990) work on policy networks is particularly effective at capturing the particularities of the interactions between government and interest groups in the Canadian context, highlighting differences with the United States. Sensitive to political institutions, the policy network approach has shown that in Cabinet systems, with strong bureaucracies, interest groups have access to policy-makers to the extent that they can provide expertise in policy formulation and implementation, as opposed to being sources of political pressure on policy-makers, notably in the electoral context. Canadian institutions allow policy-makers and bureaucrats to provide access preferentially to interest groups with the most to offer in technical advice or help in executing policy, resulting in an interest group system with fewer, more resourceful groups accessing government than in the United States (Montpetit 2005). These groups with access have been designated in the study of British politics as groups with "insider" status (Grant 1989; Page 1999). Likewise, Canadian policy-makers and bureaucrats provide insider status to a limited set of interest groups that have useful policy suggestions and that can help implement policy once adopted (Atkinson and Coleman 1989).

The sharing of power between branches of government and extensive fragmentation of power within them (notably in Congress) prevents government in the United States from granting insider status to the select groups that possess sufficient resources to contribute to policy formulation and implementation. American bureaucracies, like their Canadian counterparts, possibly prefer interacting with groups that have technocratic expertise, but in the United States groups that do not have such expertise can still approach Congress and hope to exert influence. Fragmented political institutions facilitate and even encourage the emergence of a fragmented interest group system in the United States. American policy-makers do not enjoy the same control over access as their Canadian counterparts and as a result more groups gain access to government in the United States. In fact, the pluralist tradition in the United States has long emphasized the sheer number and diversity of interest groups. As the early work on American politics has established, interest group competition is a key characteristic of the country's political system (Bentley 1908; Truman 1971).

Moreover, Canadian institutions can be expected to promote a focus on technocratic expertise and discourage the overt involvement of groups in electoral campaigns, which risks offending the party that actually wins. In contrast, in the United States, power is much less concentrated institutionally and so the risks of offending the winner of a particular election are reduced. US interest groups are therefore much freer to enter the electoral arena. The costs of playing electoral politics for interest groups in the United States are lessened by the fact that unsuccessful intervention in one sphere (for example, a presidential election) might be offset by a victory in a different sphere (such as a congressional race). The risks of electoral failure are also lessened by the requirement (most notably in the US Senate) for supermajorities to achieve significant policy change. In the Canadian system, while the parliamentary system might make the rewards of actively campaigning for a winning party very high, the costs of campaigning and losing could be very considerable.

The contribution of interest groups to electoral campaigns thus is a prominent issue in American politics. Newly elected members of Congress have been advised by their parties to spend more time on raising money than on their legislative responsibilities (Grimm and Saddiqui 2013). There is a $5,000 limit on group contributions to campaigns, but the Supreme Court in its 2010 decision in *Citizens United v Federal Election Commission* made this nominal limit meaningless. The majority on the Court held that campaign expenditures by organizations independent of the candidate's campaign could not be restricted because they were protected as free speech under the First Amendment. While *Citizens United* did not declare contribution limits to candidates unconstitutional, it opened a way for unrestricted quantities of money to be spent by "super PACs": political action committees, which are organizations working to support (or oppose) candidates that in theory – though often not in practice – are independent of political parties or candidates.

As *Citizens United* shows, institutions, just like culture, can change. While it is not clear that *Citizens United* has favoured business corporations as was anticipated, it has signalled to the American public that access to government is easier for the resourceful few. That the decision was made in a context of growing wealth inequality has fed into the perception that large corporations and wealthy elites control policy-making in the United States (Hacker and Pierson 2010, 2016). In contrast, institutional change in Canada might have had the opposite effect on interest group systems. It is accepted that the inclusion of a Charter of Rights and Freedoms in the Canadian Constitution in 1982 is the single most important institutional change that has occurred since 1867, and scholars noted that this constitutional change was likely to transform Canadian politics significantly, notably with regard to the role of interest groups. The Charter in fact formally recognizes some minority groups, notably linguistic minorities (Cairns 1992), and it provides a venue to a wide array of groups that make rights-based claims, which allegedly had less influence on policy-making in the past (Morton and Knopff 2000). As in the case of *Citizens United*, empirical evidence does not clearly tie the Canadian Charter to its anticipated effect (Epp 1998), but the Charter certainly has created the impression that the Canadian interest group system was converging toward that of the United States. Canadian policy-makers might no longer have the capacity they once had to selectively choose some groups for insider status while excluding others (Montpetit 2016). We now turn to some evidence indicating that some convergence in Canadian and American interest group systems has indeed occurred.

Is Group Density Higher in the United States Than in Canada?

Interest group density can be understood as referring to the number of groups in relation to the size of a country's economy (as measured by GDP) (Gray and Lowery 1998). There is general agreement that group density in the United States has increased since the early 1980s. Schlozman, Verba, and Brady (2012) argue that this increase is attributable to new organizations in the areas of education, health, and state and local governments. Berry (1999) emphasizes the growth of public interest groups representing interests such as consumers and environmentalists. While more limited, studies show similar trends in Canada. Concerned by the difficulty minority interests experienced in mobilizing members and resources, the federal government began funding interest groups in the 1970s. Citing data from Pal (1993), Young and Everitt (2004, 77) write that "by the mid-1980s, the Secretary of State was funding 3,500 organizations, mainly official language-minority groups, multicultural organizations and women's groups." By the early 1990s, this funding was reduced and partly redirected toward service-oriented community organizations (Jenson and Phillips 1996), but federal funding has nonetheless encouraged the growth of public interest groups.

The legal framework within which Canadian groups operate enable us to track these patterns. Following growth in group activities in Ottawa in the 1980s, the federal government introduced the country's first lobbying regulations in 1989. Inspired by the American regulation of lobbying, the Lobbyist Registration Act went further than what was in place in the United States at the time, requiring the disclosure of all lobbying activities. For its part, the United States, where disclosure was initially voluntary, moved toward compulsory disclosure in 1995 (Chari, Murphy, and Hogan 2007).[1] Disclosure of lobbying activities by Canadian groups reveals that 30 per cent received federal funds in 1996–2009. Likewise, American interest groups often obtain government grants, although restricted to the carrying out of non-political activities. The charitable status of some groups in Canada prevents them from receiving funds for political activities. However, unlike American policy, the Government of Canada has consciously and deliberately funded interest groups (Boatright 2009, 25). Comparison of the proportion of interest groups that receive federal funds in the two countries is complicated by differences in regulations restricting what the funds can be spent on, as well as differences in disclosure requirements. We nonetheless estimate that the percentage of government-funded groups is lower in the United States than the 30 per cent we calculated for Canada.

Still, whether intentionally or accidentally, the United States uses the tax system to support interest group activities. Tax allowances are in effect subsidies. While contributions to a PAC such as one supporting candidates who favour the repeal of environmental protection laws are not tax deductible, contributions to an organization that seeks to promote knowledge of the economic costs of environmental regulation are. This remains the case even if the organization's commercials end with a call that is implicitly a message of opposition to one of the major candidates, such as "contact Senator Shaheen and tell her New Hampshire cannot afford the burdensome regulations she's been promoting." The Internal Revenue Service has been very reluctant to punish organizations that receive tax deductible contributions (for example, churches) when they stray into electoral politics. Its few attempts to do so have produced a sharp political backlash against the agency.

Canadian policy, as well as the cultural and institutional changes discussed above, might have helped the country catch up with US group density. According to the Canadian lobbyist registry, there were 4,274 registered lobbyists in the country in 2007. With a GDP of US$1,270 billion in 2007 (OECD data), Canadian group density was 3.37 lobbyists per US$ billion of

GDP. Note that this figure is high, which is not entirely surprising. Comparative studies have found that the relationship between the number of groups and GDP is parabolic; that is, up to a certain point the number of groups increases with the total size of the GDP, then declines (Gray and Lowery 1994). Canada has a small economy in comparison to the United States and by that logic might have a higher group density. In fact, Open Secrets claims that 15,276 lobbyists were active in the United States in 2007. With a GDP of US$13,741 billion (OECD data), American group density was 1.11 lobbyists per US$ billion of GDP. We should be careful with these data since the information on the number of lobbyists comes from two distinct lobbying disclosure procedures, constituted under different legislation. Despite these limitations, we are confident in stating that Canada does not lag significantly behind the United States for group density.

Are Groups in the United States More Diverse Than in Canada?

The relatively large number of groups in Canada does not necessarily mean that the diversity of the interest group system is equally high. Diversity refers to the range of issues interest groups cover in their relationship to governments. Issue diversity can be related to group density, as a low density normally translates into a low diversity (Gray and Lowery 1994). However, high group density does not as automatically mean high issue diversity; a large number of groups can have similar preoccupations. Therefore, the fairly high group density found in Canada cannot be taken as an indication that Canadian policy-makers have as broad a policy agenda as American policy-makers. It might still be possible that policy-makers and bureaucrats in Canada select a limited set of resourceful groups with which they collaborate for policy-making. The high density that we found might simply reflect a proliferation of service-oriented groups that have sporadic interactions with the federal government, which the law requires them to report.

The diversity of interest groups in the United States is large and well documented. Interest groups cover topics ranging from abortion rights to discrimination against Zen Buddhists. Some are relatively narrow in focus, as when a corporation engages in interest group activity to obtain a government contract or a tax concession. Other groups claim to speak on behalf of huge swaths of the population, such as women. During the latter decades of the twentieth century, many of the apparent gaps in the range of concerns addressed by interest groups were filled. One of the most influential arguments on interest groups has been from Olson, who wrote that securing the representation of widely diffused interests such as consumers would be difficult. In his highly influential book, *The Logic of Collective Action,* Olson (1965) suggested that without selective incentives it was not rational for people to join organizations that produced public goods such as cleaner air, since if the group was successful, it would be available to all and not just group members. Soon after Olson's book was published, however, there was an "advocacy explosion" characterized chiefly by a rapid increase in the number, size, and strength of groups focused on public goods, the very type whose failure Olson had predicted (Berry 1999).

Although the range of issues covered by interest groups attracted much attention, partly because it seemed to move the American interest group system closer to the pluralist ideal of having all interests represented and taken into account, the more dramatic growth in group activity was in the representation of business interests. Today the vast majority of large corporations have their own lobbyists in Washington; this was far from the case fifty years ago. Meanwhile trade associations and umbrella groups speaking on behalf of business as a whole have also grown in strength. As Baumgartner et al. (2009) show, a clear majority of lobbyists working in Washington represent either individual businesses or trade associations that represent businesses in a particular industry. Baumgartner et al. also show that important gaps remain in who is represented and who is not in the interest group system. Not surprisingly, as interest group politics require resources, the poor and low-income people do not have their own representation in Washington, but are dependent on unions (which themselves tend to represent better-paid workers) or sympathetic organizations such as churches to advance their cause. Schattschneider's (1960) famous criticisms of the interest groups system as being biased towards the economically advantaged are still true today, at least in the distribution of resources (see also Schlozman, Verba, and Brady 2012).

However, Baumgartner et al. (2009) argue that the distribution of resources is not decisive. In fact, most policy debates in Washington set one diverse coalition including both well-resourced and under-resourced groups against another coalition that is similarly diverse. Likewise, although business dominates Washington numerically, this does not mean that business always wins. There are forces in politics other than interest groups. Careful studies by Smith (2000) and by Baumgartner et al. (2009) have demonstrated that for all its advantages, business often fails to secure policy changes it favours or to prevent those it does not. In fact, groups supporting the policy status quo often win, whether they are business groups or others. We should also note that business has many reasons to be represented in Washington other than engaging in combat with public interest groups or unions. Corporations use political influence to seek government contracts. Trade relations with other countries matter intensely to a growing proportion of businesses. Government regulations on issues such as the distribution of waveband to cell phone companies or connection rights make all the difference between profit and loss for many businesses. Business lobbyists can therefore often be engaged in fighting each other, often seeking allies from outside their ranks.

There are fewer studies on group diversity in Canada and on the dominance of business in particular. Coleman (1988) conducted one such study in the 1980s and concluded that trade associations provide key expertise and advice in policy-making. Using data from the Canadian lobbying commissioner, Boucher (2015) has shown that business groups are particularly present in Ottawa, and they do not content themselves with access to the executive branch; they also target Parliament. However, the words of caution that we applied to the United States also apply here. That is, the presence of a large number of business groups in Ottawa should not be taken as evidence of their power. As in Washington, businesses often compete among themselves in Ottawa rather than competing with labour or environmental interests for policy influence. When a business interest wins, it often does so at the expense of another business interest. Moreover, business groups have a wider array of reasons to be present in Ottawa than just to exert policy influence (e.g., to seek government contracts), while the presence of most other groups in the capital is mostly to present their views on government policy. More importantly, the size of the business representation – the number of groups – does not say anything about its capacity to restrict the government agenda to issues of its concern. Interests with fewer representatives in Ottawa may be particularly effective at pushing issues that business interests would prefer seeing unattended by the federal government.

When they register a lobbying file, American and Canadian groups are invited to specify the issues covered by their lobbying. We use this information to assess the diversity of the issues pushed on government by interest groups. Specifically, we have extracted large random samples of recent lobbying files in the two countries and created two lists of disclosed issues.[2] The random samples were of 19,662 lobbying files in the United States and of 9,642 in Canada, and they were collapsed by topic to produce table 7.1. Note that American lobbyists are more than twice more likely to leave blank the space to disclose issues than Canadian lobbyists and therefore we adjusted sample sizes between the two countries to obtain comparable frequencies. Moreover, we did not code the topic, and therefore the topics listed in table 7.1 are as reported by the lobbyists. Thanks to these samples, we discovered that group activities in the two countries cover several hundred issues, ranging from sewer conversion projects to improved nutrition. Naming just a few issues in the hundreds included in the two countries'

Table 7.1 Issues on Which Groups Lobby Most Frequently

United States		Canada	
Issues	**# of files**	**Issues**	**# of files**
Budget/appropriations	695	Taxation and finance	729
Defence	399	Industry	580
Health	317	International trade	488
Taxation/internal revenue code	281	Government procurement	398
Energy/nuclear	201	Health	327
Transportation	179	Transportation	325
Medicare/Medicaid	172	Environment	265
Education	164	Defence	265
Environment/superfund	159	Science and technology	243
Agriculture	141	Regional development	197
Trade (domestic/foreign)	116	Consumer issues	196
Homeland security	98	Energy	190
Natural resources	94	Financial institutions	182
Government issues	86	Telecommunications	168
Telecommunications	81	Employment and training	160
Clean air and water	73	Intellectual property	141
Labour/workplace	72	International relations	134
Science/technology	66	Indigenous affairs	131
Aviation/airlines/airports	59	Internal trade	128
Indian/Native American affairs	59	Infrastructure	127
Foreign relations	55	Arts and culture	118
Law enforcement/crime	51	Small business	115
Financial institutions	50	Agriculture	115
Copyrights/patents	47	Education	89
Banking	46	Broadcasting	87
Communications/broadcasting	45	Fisheries	82
Marine/fisheries	44	Tourism	70
Economics/economic development	43	Forestry	67
Medical/disease research	42	Labour	64
Insurance	42	Justice and law enforcement	61

lists will not do justice to the impressive diversity of the issues they disclose. However, narrowing our examination of issues to those most frequently disclosed by groups in the two countries provides an appreciation of the importance of business issues over all other kinds of issues. Table 7.1 thus presents the thirty most frequently disclosed issues in each country's random sample. The country lists are side-by-side, presenting the issues in descending order, starting with the issue most frequently disclosed in the lobbying files of each country.

Unsurprisingly, business interests, including those related to taxation, trade, defence, transportation, and financial institutions are frequently disclosed in both countries. Judging by the table, however, it would be unfair to characterize Canada and the United States only as "corporate states" in which issues unwelcome to business are kept off the political agenda. Issues such as the environment, Indigenous affairs, labour, and education are frequently subjects of lobbying in both countries. Health is particularly interesting. It will come as no surprise that health policy has prompted a great deal of lobbying in the United States and that much of that lobbying comes from business. In the United States, corporations play a major role in the health care system through purchasing health insurance for employees and families or providing it if they are insurance companies.[3] In comparison, the private sector plays a modest role in Canada. However, health is among the most frequently disclosed issues in the two countries. This similarity suggests that the growing attention policy-makers have paid to health since the 1990s has encouraged overall group activity in this sector. Had business driven the issue, health would not be as important in Canada as it is in the United States. In fact, the Canadian Medical Association, the Canadian Cancer Society, and the Canadian Cancer Institute of Canada have registered more health-related files than any Canadian business group. In short, the range of issues disclosed by American and Canadian groups is strikingly similar in diversity and in the place accorded to business issues in comparison with other issues.

If our data on group density should be used with caution, they nonetheless indicate that Canada is not below the United States in the numerical presence of groups, after controlling for the size of the two economies. Groups representing business and economic interests surely account for a large share of the groups found in the two countries. However, groups representing diffuse interests in marginalized sectors of society are also active in the two countries, contributing to the expansion and the diversity of issues to which governments pay attention. Several of these issues would certainly not have been pushed by business had business groups controlled the agenda. In other words, Canada and the United States are similar in group density and diversity.

Do Interest Groups Influence Elections More in the United States Than in Canada?

Elections presumably matter to American interest groups, while Canadian interest groups refrain from intervening too much. The outcomes of presidential elections such as those of 2000 or 2008 changed the balance of power between groups considerably; the fact that Bush won the 2000 election resulted in a surge in the power of business interests in policy-making. It is not surprising, therefore, that interest groups intervene or use the threat of intervening in elections to exert influence. In Canada, federal elections do not have a comparable impact on interest groups, if only because government turnovers are not as frequent as they are in the United States. Since 1970, only the 1984 and the 2006 elections removed the Liberal Party of Canada from the government for a significant period of time. Moreover, the Liberal and Conservative parties are similarly close to business groups, although the Conservative Party is often seen as closer to the oil industry of Alberta and the Liberal Party to the manufacturing industry of Ontario.

Interest group participation in elections can be arrayed along a spectrum. At the lower end, interest groups simply give money to those they wish to see win. The United States has complex laws on how and when this money can be raised and distributed to politicians by interest groups. Generally, financial contributions have to be funnelled through a special arm of the interest group, a PAC, and contributions are limited to low levels ($5,000 per election). Contributions must be recorded and published; it is hoped this in itself will restrain the influence of PAC contributions on politicians. However, interest groups are adept at finding ways around limits on contributions, such as making contributions through the coordinated giving (bundling) of contributions from high-level officials in the business or group; if, hypothetically, 100 high-level executives give the maximum individual contribution of $2,700, the total is far higher than the maximum from their PAC ($270,000 versus $5,000). As noted earlier, the 2010 Supreme Court decision in *Citizens United v Federal Election Commission* allowed corporations to spend money from their general accounts rather than merely from their PACs on advertising and supporting candidates as long as the expenditure was not formally coordinated with the candidate's campaign. However, perhaps because corporations have been reluctant to become closely associated with individual politicians for commercial reasons (offending customers), the main impact of the decision has been to strengthen the role of individual billionaires in US politics. In many cases of course, such billionaires own businesses; the Koch brothers, major funders, are owners of Koch Industries, producers of carbon-rich coal and oil.

Canadian law regulates groups' contributions to political parties more strictly. Since 2004, the law has limited group contributions to local candidates and capped their amount at $1,100. Following the so-called sponsorship scandal, in which public money for a publicity campaign was illegally diverted to the Liberal Party, the law was amended in 2006 to prohibit all group contributions to parties outright. Only individuals can donate to political parties and candidates, and the maximum total donation was $1,550 in 2017. As we will see below, these severe restrictions might have unintended consequences in the longer term, encouraging groups to adopt practices that are commonly used in the United States.

Some groups not only make donations, they also work to influence how their members vote. Labour unions, for example, have been important supporters of the Democratic Party, not only because they provide major campaign contributions, but also because they work strenuously to persuade members and their families to support favoured candidates. Money spent by unions on mobilizing their membership is not defined as a campaign contribution and so unions spend far more on elections than their PAC reports suggest. Some of the interest groups most feared by US politicians, such as the American Israel Political Action Committee (AIPAC) or the National Rifle Association (NRA), are able to exert influence not only because of their campaign contributions but also because of their supposed or actual ability to deliver a bloc of votes large enough to change the outcome of elections. While political scientists tend to be skeptical of these claims, most Washington politicians think that some of those who have been targeted by AIPAC or the NRA have been defeated.

Unions in Canada have also encouraged their members to vote for a party, the New Democratic Party. However, the failure of unions to deliver a block vote is even more evident than in the United States. In fact, the NDP has never formed a government at the federal level and became the official opposition in Ottawa only once during its entire existence. However, it has been more successful in some provinces. Beside unions, Canada does not have groups comparable to the NRA that openly seek to deliver block votes. In a comparison of campaign finance reform in the United States and Canada, Boatright (2009) argues that Canada has been more effective at removing group involvement in elections. And a significant part of the effectiveness of campaign finance reform in Canada is attributable to the electoral system that, as explained above, discourages group involvement in elections.

Finally, some groups in the United States undertake campaigns targeted not only on their members, but on the general public. So long as interest groups run these campaigns separately from the candidate's own campaign and avoid calling explicitly for the election or defeat of a particular candidate, these expenditures were also not counted, but rather were regarded as constitutionally protected speech. Anti-abortion groups and teachers' unions had been particularly active in these "independent" campaigns. The 2010 *Citizens United* ruling eliminated the restriction against direct electioneering (and the "magic words," vote for ______") in unregulated, independent advertising. Severe restrictions on campaign donations have encouraged similar practices in Canada. "Third parties" are authorized to produce and disseminate advertisements promoting a political party or a candidate during an electoral campaign. They do so, however, under strict conditions. An initial ban on third-party advertising was successfully challenged before the Supreme Court of Canada and was replaced by new legislative restrictions in 2000, upheld by the Court in 2004. These restrictions include a broad definition of third-party advertising, which encompasses publicity about issues associated with parties and candidates and not just the parties and candidates themselves. They also include strict spending limits. Understandably, third-party advertising is thus more limited in Canada than it is in the United States. It nonetheless offers interest groups, prohibited from donating directly to political parties, a way to spend money to promote their preferred parties, candidates, or issues during electoral campaigns.

Do interest groups decide elections? Certainly not in Canada. In the United States, the number of groups whose members feel so intensely on an issue that they will follow a group's lead is quite small; AIPAC and the NRA are among the few plausible examples. Unions struggled especially during the Reagan years to limit their members' support for Republican candidates. PAC and other contributions tend to cancel each other out, and decades of systematic research by political scientists have cast doubt on whether they change votes in Congress (Wright 2003; Baumgartner et al. 2009; Asher, Heberlig, and Ripley 2001). In other words, American and Canadian interest groups might adopt different strategies during electoral campaigns, but it is not at all clear that these differences matter much for electoral outcomes.

Are Groups More Oriented toward the Provision of Expertise in Canada Than in the United States?

Given that Canadian institutions concentrate power with the members of the executive, we expect groups in Canada to be more oriented toward the provision of expertise than those in the United States. Career civil servants in executive agencies have different expectations toward groups than legislators. While legislators might expect campaign contributions and electoral support, administrators will be more interested in groups' capacity to help them solve policy problems. They expect groups to provide technocratic analysis, based on staff research and information collected from members. As the result of contacts with their members, some groups have access to considerable expertise and data to which no one else does. These groups can therefore make unique contributions to policy development. Groups can also make important contributions to policy implementation, a primary concern of civil servants. Given that the members of the executive control access to the Canadian government, it is likely that groups capable of providing expertise are preferred. Pross (1993) argues that federal funding for interest groups was motivated partly by a desire of the federal government to increase the capacity of groups that have fewer resources to contribute effectively to policy-making. Consequently, we might expect Canadian groups to invest more than American groups in the development of expertise, analysis, and the collection of information.

Data from lobbying registries collected prior to 2009 confirm that Canadian groups target the bureaucracy while American groups target Congress. When Canadian and American lobbyists were disclosing their activities before 2009, they were required to identify the government institutions with which they make contacts (American groups still do). Among the active lobbying files in Canada in May 2009, the House of Commons and the Senate were mentioned only 6 per cent of the time. In the United States, the figure for the House of Representatives and the Senate was 61.7 per cent. American groups mention government bureaucracies frequently as well, but they clearly spend more time interacting with legislative institutions, while Canadian groups spend more time interacting with the civil service. While confirming that Canadian groups interact less with Parliament than American groups with Congress, a study finds that in 2013 40 per cent of the contacts that interest groups have with government are in fact with parliamentarians, compared with 60 per cent in the United States with Congress (Boucher 2015, 849). What appears as a huge increase in contact between interest groups and the Canadian Parliament between 2009 and 2013 might simply reflect a change in the Canadian lobbying registration act. In fact, since 2008, a communication report must be sent to the lobbying commissioner each time a lobbyist contacts a public office holder, whether elected or appointed, and whatever the purpose of the contact. Lobbying files, upon which we relied to produce our own data, reveal only the more substantive interactions of lobbyists with government. Whatever the source of information used to make the assessment, it is clear that interest groups in Canada target the executive branch more than they target Parliament.

While the reverse is true in the United States, Boucher's (2015) analysis nevertheless shows that 41 per cent of the American lobbying reports indicated contacts with the bureaucracy in 2013. Just like the 40 per cent figure for contact between Canadian groups and legislators appears high, the 41 per cent figure for contacts between American groups and bureaucrats is also unexpected, perhaps indicating that the difference in expertise between Canadian and American interest groups is not very large. Baumgartner et al. (2009, 56) report that US lobbyists are experts with enough knowledge to "write a book" on the policy issues that they work on. Several groups in Washington produce analysis of the kind that bureaucrats will appreciate for their contribution to policy-making.

It is not easy to provide a quantitative measure of the expertise of groups. The Canadian registration of lobbyists requires the disclosure of the number of individuals employed by each interest group, which might be used as a proxy for expertise. The larger the number of individuals an interest group employs, the larger its capacity to collect information and conduct analysis. Not all groups will employ the same share of its staff for expertise-related tasks, but the number of employees is as close to a measure of expertise as we can have. Unfortunately, the American registration does not require interest groups to disclosure their size in terms of personnel, depriving us of comparative data.

We nonetheless examined the Canadian data to see whether the groups with the largest number of employees represent a narrow set of interests, presumably related to business. Using the large sample of lobbying files presented above, we found that well-staffed groups represent a diversity of interests. For example, the Canadian Federation of Independent Businesses employs around fifty individuals, depending on the year. Meanwhile, the Canadian Labour Congress employs sixty individuals. With about fifty-three employees, the Canadian Cancer Society is larger than the Canadian Association of Petroleum Producers, which has thirty-five employees. Several farm groups have about twenty employees, just like several professional groups, including the Canadian Association of University Teachers. Environmental groups, including Greenpeace and the Canadian Environmental Law Association, disclose about ten employees each, as do several industry representatives such as the Canadian Gas Association. We have to be careful when drawing conclusions from these data; some groups might contract out expertise and others might use their staff mostly to provide group members with services rather than to produce expert knowledge about policy. To the extent that our data are valid, we conclude that interest groups provide government with a wide range of expertise. Following Baumgartner et al. (2009), we believe that the provision of expertise by interest groups in the United States is not very different from what it is in Canada (see also Holyoke 2011; Mansbridge 1992).

Conclusion

The Canadian political system has changed dramatically over the past forty years, sometimes in ways that make it increasingly similar to that of the United States. We have argued here that such convergence is occurring for interest group systems. Group density in Canada is comparable to what it is in the United States, after accounting for the size of the two economies. In both Canada and the United States, interest groups interact on a wide range of issues, contributing to the diversity of government agendas in both countries. Group strategies during electoral campaigns differ between the two countries, but it is not clear that these differences significantly affect group influence. It has been argued that groups in Canada must build significant policy expertise if they want access to policy-makers. In fact, it seems that American groups have equal capacity to provide government with policy expertise. In short, we have come across more evidence of similarities between the interest group systems of the two countries than we have seen evidence of differences.

We would suggest that this convergence is not merely the result of Canada emulating the United States, but it is a reflection of complex changes in society and policy dynamics common to both countries – and indeed to other economically advanced democracies more generally. Even corporatist European countries known for their highly coordinated interests group systems and their controlled access to policy-making venues are becoming more and more pluralist (Öberg et al. 2011; Lundberg 2013). Like governments in these countries, Canadian policy-makers no longer have the legitimacy – if not the institutional capacity – to grant insider status to a limited number of narrow interests. Like American policy-makers, Canadian policy-makers interact with a dense and diverse set of interest groups capable of contributing information and analytical expertise in policy-making processes.

Notes

1 In this chapter, we draw much of our empirical evidence from the Canadian and American lobbying registries. Compiled data from the American registry were made publically available recently (United States Senate 2020). Canadian data were extracted by computer analysts from the Office of the Commissioner of Lobbying of Canada.
2 The number of lobbying files in each country is too large to analyze them all, hence the necessity of sampling.
3 Note that the random sample was collected before Obamacare, which generated significant lobbying by business.

References and Suggested Readings

Asher, Herbert B., Eric S. Heberlig, and Randall Ripley. 2001. *American Labor Unions in the Electoral Arena: People Passion and Power.* Lanham, MD: Rowan and Littlefield.

Atkinson, Michael M., and William D. Coleman. 1989. *The State, Business, and Industrial Change in Canada.* Toronto: University of Toronto Press.

Baumgartner, Frank, Jeffrey M. Berry, Marie Hojnacki, David C. Kimball, and Beth L. Leech. 2009. *Lobbying and Policy Change.* Chicago: University of Chicago Press.

Bentley, A.F. 1908. *The Process of Government: A Study of Social Pressures.* Chicago: University of Chicago Press.

Berry, Jeffrey. 1999. *The New Liberalism: The Rising Power of Citizen Groups.* Washington, DC: Brookings Institution.

Boatright, Robert G. 2009. "Interest Group Adaptations to Campaign Finance Reform in Canada and the United States." *Canadian Journal of Political Science* 42 (1): 17–44.

Boucher, Maxime. 2015. "L'effet Westminster: Les cibles et les stratégies de lobbying dans le système parlementaire canadien." *Canadian Journal of Political Science* 48 (4): 839–61.

Cairns, Alan C. 1992. *Charter versus Federalism: The Dilemmas of Constitutional Reform.* Montreal and Kingston: McGill-Queen's University Press.

Chari, Raj, Gary Murphy, and John Hogan. 2007. "Regulating Lobbyists: A Comparative Analysis of the United States, Canada, Germany and the European Union." *Political Quarterly* 78 (3): 422–38.

Coleman, William D. 1988. *Business and Politics: A Study of Collective Action.* Toronto: University of Toronto Press.

Coleman, William D., and Grace Skogstad, eds. 1990. *Policy Communities and Public Policy in Canada: A Structural Approach.* Mississauga, ON: Copp Clark Pitman.

Epp, Charles R. 1998. *The Rights Revolution: Lawyers, Activists, and Supreme Courts in Comparative Perspective.* Chicago: University of Chicago Press.

Grant, Wyn. 1989. *Pressure Groups, Politics and Democracy in Britain.* London: Philip Allan.

Gray, Virginia, and David Lowery. 1994. "Interest Group System Density and Diversity: A Research Update." *International Political Science Review* 15 (5): 5–14.

———. 1998. "The Density of Interest-Communities: Do Regional Variables Matter?" *Publius* 28 (2): 61–79.

Grimm, Ryan, and Sabrina Saddiqui. 2013. "Call Time for Congress Shows How Fundraising Dominates Bleak Workweek." Huffington Post, January 9.

Hacker, Jacob S., and Paul Pierson. 2010. *Winner-Take-All Politics: How Washington Made the Rich Richer – and Turned Its Back on the Middle Class.* New York: Simon & Schuster.

———. 2016. *American Amnesia: How the War on Government Led Us to Forget What Made America Prosper.* New York: Simon & Schuster.

Haddow, Rodney. 1999. "Interest Representation and the Canadian State: From Group Politics to Policy Communities and Beyond." In *Canadian Politics*, edited by James Bickerton and Alain-G. Gagnon, 3rd ed., 501–22. Peterborough, ON: Broadview.

Hartz, Louis. 1969. *The Founding of New Societies: Studies in the History of the United States, Latin America, South Africa, Canada, and Australia.* New York: Houghton Mifflin Harcourt.

Hibbing, John R., and Elizabeth Theiss-Morse. 2002. *Stealth Democracy: Americans' Beliefs about How Government Should Work.* Cambridge: Cambridge University Press.

Holyoke, Thomas T. 2011. *Competitive Interests: Competition and Compromise in American Interest Group Politics.* Washington, DC: Georgetown University Press.

Horowitz, Gad. 1978. "Notes on 'Conservatism, Liberalism and Socialism in Canada.'" *Canadian Journal of Political Science* 11 (2): 383–400.

Jenkin, Michael. 1983. *The Challenge of Diversity: Industrial Policy in the Canadian Federation*. Ottawa: Science Council of Canada.

Jenson, Jane, and Susan D. Phillips. 1996. "Regime Shift: New Citizenship Practices in Canada." *International Journal of Canadian Studies* 14: 111–35.

Kahan, Dan M., and Donald Braman. 2006. "Cultural Cognition and Public Policy." *Yale Law & Policy Review* 24 (1): 149–72.

Lundberg, Erik. 2013. "Does the Government Selection Process Promote or Hinder Pluralism? Exploring the Characteristics of Voluntary Organizations Invited to Public Consultations." *Journal of Civil Society* March, 1–20.

Mansbridge, Jane J. 1992. "A Deliberative Theory of Interest Representation." In *The Politics of Interest: Interest Groups Transformed*, edited by Mark P. Petracca, 32–57. Boulder, CO: Westview.

Montpetit, Éric. 2005. "Westminster Parliamentarism, Policy Networks and the Behaviour of Political Actors." In *New Institutionalism: Theory and Analysis*, edited by André Lecours, 225–44. Toronto: University of Toronto Press.

———. 2016. *In Defense of Pluralism: Policy Disagreement and Its Media Coverage*. Cambridge: Cambridge University Press.

Morton, Fredrick Lee, and Rainer Knopff. 2000. *The Charter Revolution and the Court Party*. Peterborough, ON: Broadview.

Nevitte, Neil. 1996. *The Decline of Deference*. Peterborough, ON: Broadview.

Öberg, PerOla, Torsten Svensson, Peter Munk Christiansen, Asbjørn Sonne Nørgaard, Hilmar Rommetvedt, and Gunnar Thesen. 2011. "Disrupted Exchange and Declining Corporatism: Government Authority and Interest Group Capability in Scandinavia." *Government and Opposition* 46 (3): 365–91.

Olson, Mancur. 1965. *The Logic of Collective Action: Public Goods and the Theory of Groups*. Cambridge, MA: Harvard University Press.

Page, Edward C. 1999. "The Insider/Outsider Distinction: An Empirical Investigation." *British Journal of Politics and International Relations* 1 (2): 205–14.

Pal, Leslie A. 1993. *Interests of State: The Politics of Language, Multiculturalism and Feminism in Canada*. Montreal and Kingston: McGill-Queen's University Press.

Presthus, Robert V. 1973. *Elite Accommodation in Canadian Politics*. Cambridge: Cambridge University Press.

Pross, Paul A. 1986. *Group Politics and Public Policy*. 2nd ed. Toronto: Oxford University Press.

———. 1993. "The Mirror of the Sate: Canada's Interest Group System." In *First World Interest Groups: A Comparative Perspective*, edited by Clive S. Thomas, 67–80. Westport, CT: Greenwood.

———. 1995. "Pressure Groups: Talking Chameleons." In *Canadian Politics in the 1990s*, edited by Michael S. Whittington and Glen Williams, 252–75. Toronto: Nelson Canada.

Putnam, Robert D. 2001. *Bowling Alone: The Collapse and Revival of American Community*. New York: Simon & Schuster.

Savoie, Donald J. 1999. *Governing from the Centre: The Concentration of Political Power in Canada*. Toronto: University of Toronto Press.

Schattschneider, E.E. 1960. *The Semisovereign People: A Realist's View of Democracy in America*. New York: Holt, Rinehart and Winston.

Schlozman, Kay Lehman, Sidney Verba, and Henry E. Brady. 2012. *The Unheavenly Chorus: Unequal Political Voice and the Broken Promise of American Democracy*. Princeton, NJ: Princeton University Press.

Smiley, D.V. 1987. *The Federal Condition in Canada.* Toronto: McGraw-Hill Ryerson.

Smith, Mark A. 2000. *American Business and Public Power.* Chicago: University of Chicago Press.

Thorburn, Hugh G., ed. 1985. *Interest Groups in the Canadian Federal System.* Toronto: University of Toronto Press.

Truman, David B. 1971. *The Governmental Process: Political Interests and Public Opinion.* New York: Alfred A. Knopf.

United States Senate. 2020. "Downloadable Lobbying Databases." http://www.senate.gov/legislative/Public_Disclosure/database_download.htm/ (link no longer active).

Wilson, Graham K. 1990. *Interest Groups.* Oxford: Basil Blackwell.

———. 2005. "Farmers, Interests and the American State." In *Surviving Global Change? Agricultural Interest Groups in Comparative Perspective*, edited by Darren Halpin. Aldershot: Ashgate.

Wright, John R. 2003. *Interest Groups and Congress: Lobbying, Contributions, and Influence.* New York: Longman.

Young, Lisa, and Joanna Everitt. 2004. *Advocacy Groups.* Vancouver: UBC Press.

PART THREE

Federalism and the Charter

eight
Practices of Federalism in Canada

JENNIFER WALLNER

> Prime Minister Justin Trudeau and most of the premiers signed a historic pan-Canadian framework Friday to fight climate....
>
> Saskatchewan and Manitoba both said they would not be able to sign the agreement Friday.
>
> Premier Brad Wall has steadfastly opposed any sort of carbon pricing....
>
> Premier Brian Pallister ... pivoted to talk of more health care funding when asked about his willingness to sign the climate deal.
>
> The Prime Minister's Office told CBC News that the two sides are unlikely to reach a consensus on that file at this point....
>
> Before Friday's meeting even began, Wall blasted the federal government's approach, which he said "unilaterally" laid down a carbon price scheme....
>
> "We'll probably see them in court," he told reporters on his way into the talks.
>
> – John Paul Tasker, CBC News, December 9, 2016

Introduction

The signing of the Pan-Canadian Framework on Clean Growth and Climate Change captures many of the patterns and conflicts swirling throughout federalism in this country. Knowledge of the formal division of powers expressed in Canada's Constitution offers a partial glimpse into the multifaceted institutional ecosystem within which authoritative decisions are made. Decoding this account of the major intergovernmental agreement on climate change requires a robust understanding of the components that constitute this institutional pillar of Canada's political world.

Institutions, comprising formal and informal rules, provide supports that "undergird, enable, and regulate the interaction of individuals and organizations in particular areas of life" (Rueschemeyer 2009, 204). These rules establish opportunities and constraints that shape behaviour. Institutions are neither benign nor unbiased. They can lock in particular asymmetries of power and entrench differences in status that may be challenging to overcome. Such aspects of institutions, however, are rarely intrinsic; instead they emerge through the ways in which the formal and informal rules of an institution are used, interpreted, adjusted, replaced, and discarded. The effects of institutions can be understood through observing the human use of those institutions in *practice*.

The metaphor of practice draws our attention to unpacking dynamic processes rather than fixating on the seeming stasis of an institution. It is intended to help us reconceive of an institution from a fixed structure into a breathing, living, and ever-changing entity. *Practice* further enables the recognition that actors working within an institutional framework are themselves fumbling to find strategies to fit within the framework. Effective strategies are not given and must be rehearsed through repeated exercise. Also, "effective" strategies are themselves contested; what is effective to some may be anathema to others. The choices actors make and the ways in which the rules of an institution are used establish the actual application of that institution – the customs, habits, and expected procedures that give life to the structure itself.

Focusing on the dynamics at work between the two orders of government in Canada, three modes of practice become apparent: colonial, classical, and interdependent federalism.[1] The manifestation of each *mode of practice* emerges from the ways in which actors use the formal and informal features of federalism in Canada: constitutional provisions, the federal spending power, and dynamics in intergovernmental relations. What is more, while a certain mode may have dominated in particular periods, features and elements of each mode appear concurrently and persist today. This exploration of federalism in Canada thus reveals the extent to which one mode of practice never fully gives way or is completely replaced over time.

Federalism (in Canada) Is:

Federalism is not easily defined. The standard reference point of a federal state as one with different levels – or orders – of government only scratches the surface of its rich set of ideational and institutional elements.[2] This section provides an overview of these components of federalism in Canada, outlining in turn: the principle of federalism and its justifications, the constitutional division of powers, the role of the courts, intergovernmental relations, and the fiscal arrangements among the constituent members. This information provides the backbone to appreciating the manifestation of the alternative practices of federalism in Canada.

... Divided Sovereignty ...

Federalism rests on the *idea* that sovereignty can be "shared and powers divided between two or more levels of government, each of which enjoys a direct relationship with the people" (Hueglin and Fenna 2006, 33). Most critical is that one order of government cannot unilaterally alter or revoke the powers of another. Those living within a federation have the task of reconciling such seemingly contradictory principles as unity and diversity, shared rule and self-rule, and integration and autonomy, all within a collective, yet individually independent, space (Théret 2005; Elazar 1987; Fafard, Rocher, and Côté 2010, 21). Consequently, federal systems often witness considerable tension as individuals and communities endeavour to find effective and legitimate arrangements to reconcile these somewhat incongruous principles.

The justifications for dividing sovereignty in a country are varied, both across and within federations. Two prominent ones voiced in Canada centre on either the preservation of self-determination or the advancement of efficiency (see also Laforest and Gagnon, this volume). While not necessarily antithetical – political leaders at times use both simultaneously – the interplay of these alternative justifications for federalism has encouraged marked transformations in the way divided sovereignty is practised in Canada.

For some, the federal idea enables the coexistence of diverse peoples nested within a shared territorial space. Federalism, in this way, counters the notion of a singular national identity and accepts that individuals can belong to several communities simultaneously (Elazar 1987). Such a rationale is particularly salient in multinational federations like Canada, where more than one nation inhabits the territory. Former Quebec minister responsible for Canadian Relations and the Canadian Francophonie Jean-Marc Fournier neatly summed this up when he wrote, "Allegiance to Québec and a sense of belonging to Canada are the foundations for the identity expressed by a large majority of Quebecers" (2017, ii). Pooling sovereignty while maintaining a division of powers thus offers a way to ensure that governments closer to the people are able to protect local culture and identity. In the Canadian context, federalism thus offers an opportunity for discrete political communities to coexist and gather strength through shared rule in certain areas while allowing these communities the opportunity to maintain self-rule in others.

Additionally, federalism is advanced as a means to achieve greater efficiency and improve the quality of life for a territory (Hueglin and Fenna 2006, 40). On the one hand, smaller communities may lack the resources to meet the needs of their people. Furthermore, without common standards on key initiatives, the coherence required for collective action may not be achievable. On the other hand, representatives and bureaucratic officials based in areas that are remote from these smaller communities are unlikely to have the appreciation for local conditions to govern effectively. By coming together under shared rule, individual communities likely increase their relative capacities; by retaining autonomy over certain fields through self-rule, these communities will continue to be led by representatives who can make more informed policy choices. Canada's first prime minister, Sir John A. Macdonald (1865), captured such arguments when he declared,

> Having come to the conclusion that a legislative union, pure and simple, was impracticable, our next attempt was to form a government upon federal principles, which would give to the General Government the strength of a legislative and administrative union, while at the same time it preserved that liberty of action for the different sections which is allowed by a Federal Union. And I am strong in the belief that we have hit upon the happy medium in those resolutions, and that we have formed a scheme of government which unites the advantages of both, giving us the strength of a legislative union and the sectional freedom of a federal union, with protection to local interests.

This rationale thus pivots on a more utilitarian understanding of governance and accents federalism as a means to foster the realization of efficiency, rather than prioritizing other values oriented to self-determination.

... A Constitutional Division of Powers ...

The idea for dividing sovereignty in a federation is imperfectly captured in its set of governing *institutions*. Emphasis must be placed on the imperfect quality of these institutions, because rules are written at specific moments in time, crafted and influenced by distinct constellations of actors, informed by their own interests and perspectives. The negotiations that preceded Canada's formation and the Constitution Act, 1867, for example, advanced without the engagement of the Indigenous peoples of the territory, were undertaken with only the direct involvement of men of British and French descent, the subsequent constitutional document produced only in English, with no mention of many items that have evolved into critical issues. Not only did this fail to represent the diversity of the population at the time, it does not reflect the composition of the Canadian polity today or provide jurisdictional clarity for key areas of government activity. Therefore, as Pierre Elliott Trudeau wrote (1968, 121), "The compromise of federalism is generally reached under a very particular set of circumstances. As time goes by these circumstances change.... To meet these changes, the terms of the federative pact must be altered."

A constitution sets out the formal division of powers between at least two orders of government in a federation. In Canada, the distribution of legislative authority between the federal and provincial governments is captured in sections 91, 92 and 92A, 93, 94(A) and 95 of the Constitution Act, 1867 and Constitution Act, 1982. The exclusive powers of the federal Parliament include the regulation of trade and commerce, direct and indirect taxation, citizenship, currency, banking, and criminal law. Exclusive powers of provincial legislatures concern such matters as direct taxation within the provinces, hospitals, municipalities, property and civil rights, education, and natural resources. Concurrent – or shared powers – are specified in sections 94A and 95. They are immigration, agriculture, and old age pensions (added in 1951). This distribution of power sought to allocate matters of a shared interest to the federal government and matters of a local nature to the provinces.

... Interpreted through Judicial Review ...

Despite the constitutionalized division of powers, jurisdictional conflicts between the orders of government are unavoidable. As Gerald Baier writes, "Canada's federal system features a rather large gap between the jurisdictional map of the written constitution and the actual activities of its governments" (2012, 79). When questions arise as to whether a law enacted by one order falls within its constitutionally allocated authority, the courts act as an umpire. Between 1867 and 1949, the Judicial Committee of the Privy Council (JCPC), based in London, performed this function until it was replaced by the Supreme Court of Canada as the final court of appeal (see Bazowski's chapter in the volume). Decisions of the JCPC tended to elevate or prioritize provincial jurisdiction, curbing the scope of federal authority and limiting overlaps between the two orders of government. This is where the metaphor of "watertight compartments" finds its origin, when Lord Atkin used it "to illustrate the need to protect the autonomy of each order of government and balance its powers" (Brouillet 2017, 141).

Rather than adhering to this seemingly more literal – or what can be termed "classical" – interpretation of a division of powers and divided sovereignty, the Supreme Court of Canada pursued an alternative route. In some of its early rulings, the Court declared that the notion of exclusive powers was not imperative, and that cooperation – or perhaps better stated, interdependence[3] – between the orders of government was the "dominant tide" of modern federalism.[4] According to Brouillet (2017, 142), "The Supreme Court has affirmed the ability of each order of government to incidentally affect matters under the jurisdiction of the other order when both are legislating in their own areas of jurisdiction." While accepting interdependence, the Court nevertheless also appears to preserve and protect divided sovereignty. For instance, the recent ruling in *Comeau* (2018), that centred on the scope of free trade among the provinces of Canada,[5] declared, "In this case, the federalism principle is vital. It recognizes the autonomy of provincial governments to develop their societies within their respective spheres of jurisdiction and requires a court interpreting constitutional texts to consider how different interpretations impact the balance between federal and provincial interests." Judicial review of the constitution has thus undeniably shaped the practice of federalism in Canada.

... Enacted through Intergovernmental Relations ...

At the time of Confederation, the framers appeared confident that their division of powers had established two orders of government that were free to act unimpeded from the other. "These powers were so arranged," declared "founding father" and Nova Scotia Premier (1864–7) Charles Tupper, "as to prevent any conflict or struggle which might lead to any difficulty between the several sections."[6] So assured was Sir John A. Macdonald that he concluded, "We have avoided all conflict of jurisdiction and authority."[7] Perhaps this is why the Constitution Act, 1867 was entirely silent on the matter of intergovernmental relations (Gibbins 2014, 50). The absence of formal rules, however, did not prevent the gradual emergence of an informal set of arrangements for intergovernmental relations in the country.

It was the provincial premiers who took the first steps toward formalizing intergovernmental relations. The first gatherings of the premiers were held in 1887 and 1902, respectively. Regular meetings of the premiers thereafter gradually transformed into the Annual Premiers' Conferences (APC) in 1960. In 2003, the premiers created the Council of the Federation (CoF), which now meets at least twice a year. According to its founding agreement, the CoF will "abide by a rotating chair schedule, respect the rules of consensus decision-making and share the costs of CoF operations on a per capita basis" (Wesley 2018, 3). Supported by a Steering Committee of Deputy Ministers and a small permanent secretariat, the council is intended to enable the premiers to "play a leadership role in revitalizing the Canadian federation and building a more constructive and cooperative federal system" (Council of the Federation 2003).

It was not until 1906, at the request of the provinces to discuss the issue of financial subsidies, that Prime Minister Sir Wilfrid Laurier convened the first meeting of the prime minister with all the premiers, what are now known as First Ministers' Conferences (FMCs). Called at the pleasure of the prime minister of Canada, FMCs are perhaps the most publicly familiar of the intergovernmental arrangements. Despite this standing, FMCs remain only weakly institutionalized, operate with minimally fixed procedures, and generally convene only when it suits the prime minister's interest and idea of federalism.

To demonstrate, between 2006 and 2015, when the federal government was led by Prime Minister Stephen Harper, only two FMCs were called (Simeon, Robinson, and Wallner 2014).

In addition to FMCs, a series of intergovernmental tables operate sectorally, bringing together ministers and officials across all the jurisdictions (Inwood, Johns, and O'Reilly 2011). From finance to infrastructure, immigration to justice, intergovernmental tables may be long-lasting or created and disassembled as required. Typically chaired alone by the federal government or co-chaired with a province or territory, tables may meet up to four times annually to foster coordination, collaboration, and learning in key policy areas. All of these tables nevertheless operate behind closed doors with only minimal information released publicly on the discussions (Simmons 2012).

... Supported by a Fiscal Architecture ...

Fiscal arrangements redistribute and decentralize economic and financial matters. Data from 2014, compiled by the Organisation for Economic Co-operation and Development (OECD), indicate that fully 78 per cent of all government spending in Canada happens at the subnational levels of government; by comparison, in the United States it is only 48 per cent, while across the OECD, the average is a mere 32 per cent. Furthermore, Canadian provinces secure more than 50 per cent of their total revenues from their own taxes as opposed to grants and transfers from the federal government, which is the case in the overwhelming majority of OECD countries (Chatry 2017). Both orders of government may impose taxes and borrow money. The main distinction is that provincial (and territorial) governments are restricted to direct taxes while the federal government can use both direct and indirect taxation. In contrast to other federations, section 92A of the Constitution Act, 1867 (which was an amendment added in 1982) allocates exclusive rights over natural resources to the provinces, translating into an additional source of revenues for resource-rich provinces. Together, this means that Canada is arguably the most fiscally decentralized federation in the world (Milligan 2017).

Ideally, to ensure that each order of government can discharge its constitutionally mandated responsibilities, "the division of financial resources should correspond to the division of powers" (Noël 2009a, 276). Finding such a balance is notoriously difficult to achieve. Long-standing conflicts across multiple federations reveal the pervasiveness of *vertical* and *horizontal* fiscal imbalances between and among governments; Canada is no exception.

Vertical imbalance refers to the potential mismatch or gap between the fiscal capacities of the different orders of government and their spending responsibilities (Noël 2009b, 129). Grants, transfers, and tax points are typically used to help manage this vertical imbalance. Grants tend to be one-off allocations from one government to another for specific purposes with conditions. Transfers, which may be conditional or unconditional, are usually allocated on a multi-year basis, set according to an accepted formula, and used for a more diffuse range of issues. The Canada Health Transfer (CHT), for example, is the largest transfer to the provinces and territories. As a multi-year allocation, the transfer provides long-term predictable funding for health care and supports the five principles of the Canada Health Act: universality, comprehensiveness, portability, accessibility, and public administration (Department of Finance Canada 2011). Tax points, finally, involve transferring a portion of one government's "tax room" to another order of government. To illustrate, in 1977, under the terms of Established Programs Financing (EPF), "the federal government reduced its tax rates and all provincial and territorial governments simultaneously raised their tax rates by an equivalent amount, such that the changes in federal and provincial/territorial tax rates offset one another" (Gauthier 2012, 1).

The horizontal imbalance focuses on the relative capabilities of individual provinces and territories to raise revenues and provide quality programs for their residents. Jurisdictions with a smaller tax base may be incapable of generating sufficient revenues to act in their areas of constitutionally afforded sovereignty. Excessive horizontal imbalances thus compromise the principle of divided sovereignty. To remedy this situation in Canada, the federal government uses its spending power to support a fiscal equalization program (Béland et al. 2017). Officially launched in 1957, and later entrenched in the Constitution Act, 1982, equalization payments are calculated on the basis of a complicated formula with the intention of raising fiscal capacities of qualifying provinces to a national average. Equalization payments are sourced directly from federal revenues and transferred unconditionally to receiving provinces. The program thus works to ensure all provinces have the financial means to discharge their constitutional responsibilities.

The principle of divided sovereignty and its justification(s), the formal constitution, the judicial rulings, the mechanisms for intergovernmental relations, and the fiscal arrangements between the two orders of government, together constitute the building blocks for a federation. While the formal and informal rules of an institution may have intrinsic features that encourage certain trajectories and outcomes, these are not foregone conclusions. Rather, it is through the use, misuse, adjustment, replacement, and even discarding of rules that the actual effects of institutions can be observed. Moreover, the same feature may have different consequences, depending how it is used. In the context of Canadian federalism, the same institutional element may encourage the autonomy of some constituent members, while privileging the federal government at the expense of the others. The clouds of ambiguity dissipate somewhat only when we detail the *practices* of the institution itself in a specific federation.

The Practices of Federalism in Canada

Canada is one of the oldest federations in the world. Over time, it has witnessed considerable transformations with shifts in the balance and execution of political authority. In general, three modes of practice are distinguishable: colonial, classical, and interdependent. While a certain mode prevailed or dominated during a particular period, elements of all three have coexisted simultaneously and can be observed today.

Colonial Federalism

As a concept, and a mode of practice, colonial federalism refers to situations wherein the central government is able to dominate the other partners. Often used as a means of geographic expansion by incorporating new territory, colonial practices have been retained by the federal government to exert political and economic control over the other jurisdictions, thus at times prioritizing the principle of unity over diversity, shared rule over self-rule, and integration over autonomy.

Following the enactment of the Constitution Act 1867, most knowledgeable observers predicted Canada would evolve into a federation that privileged the principle of shared rule over self-rule. Sir John A. Macdonald and other like-minded constitutional framers sought to formalize dividing sovereignty, with Ottawa firmly at the helm of the ship of state. The provinces would be responsible for sixteen itemized powers while the federal government retained control over residual powers. Ottawa was granted unlimited taxation powers and the authority to regulate trade and commerce. Most tellingly, Ottawa was given the power to disallow provincial legislation deemed in conflict with federal priorities and to declare unilaterally any work or undertaking regarded in the dominion's general advantage to fall under federal authority. Capitalizing on these constitutional advantages in the years following Confederation to realize the vision of a transcontinental economy, the federal government implemented strong national policies to integrate the Maritimes and expand into the resource-rich western territory. Colonialist dynamics were thus the norm throughout these early years.

The creation of Canada's Prairie provinces was achieved through colonialist practice. Where Canada's original provinces were former colonies of

British North America, with their own semi-autonomous governing councils within the British Empire, three of Canada's provinces were carved from land that was originally part of the Northwest Territories, albeit through markedly different processes. In 1868, the Government of Canada purchased the North-Western Territory and Rupert's Land from the Hudson's Bay Company. The federal government then passed An Act for the temporary Government of Rupert's Land and the North-Western Territory when united with Canada, establishing an advisory council made up of members chosen by Ottawa. The first lieutenant-governor of Rupert's Land and the North-Western Territory was William McDougall, a founding father and supporter of Macdonald's drive to expand and consolidate Canada's authority over the territory. The land transfer sparked the 1869–70 uprising in the Red River Colony led by Métis leader Louis Riel. That year, the Métis declared their own provisional government and announced it would negotiate the terms of entry into Confederation. Resistance ceased in 1870 with the Manitoba Act, which gave the Government of Canada the lands it wanted and created a version of what would become the Province of Manitoba.

By 1888, the Northwest Territories was administered by a legislative assembly entrusted with such powers as taxation, issuing of permits, establishment of municipal institutions and courts, provision of schools, and public works. But these powers were certainly not comparable with those retained by the other members of Canada's federation. Most significantly, the territories could not borrow money, obtain revenues from public lands, or tax the railway. Then, on September 1, 1905, the Saskatchewan Act and the Alberta Act were passed by Ottawa, carving out two new provinces from the existing territory. However, unlike other provinces, ownership of natural resources was retained by the dominion government in Ottawa, ostensibly to support the infrastructure costs associated with western settlement. It was not until 1930, after protracted battles between federal and provincial leaders from Alberta and Saskatchewan, that natural resource rights were transferred, placing them on the same constitutional footing as the other provinces.

The unilateral and controlling aspects associated with colonial federalism are at times apparent in the deployment of the federal spending power. Defined as "the power of parliament to make payments to people or institutions or governments for purposes on which it (parliament) does not necessarily have the power to legislate" (Trudeau 1969, 4), the legitimacy of this power remains contested (Telford 2003). Uncertainty has not stopped the federal government from using it, with at times decidedly negative effects on provincial budgets. On the positive side of the ledger, it was to expand social programs in areas of provincial jurisdiction in the 1940s, 1950s and 1960s. Starting as 50/50 shared cost-programs, Ottawa later unilaterally decided to slow increases in spending, leaving the provinces to fill the resulting gaps. More dramatically, and now on the negative side of the ledger, to "restore the fiscal health that is essential for a strong and growing economy" (Department of Finance Canada 1995), in 1995 the Government of Canada cut more than $29 billion of program spending spread over three years. Once again, this decision was made without consulting the provinces, who bore the burden of federal austerity measures (Bickerton 2010, 59). Finally, aside from rare exceptions, the federal government continues to guard its decision-making autonomy over critical financial agreements such as equalization. Most recently, the 2018 federal budget renewed and extended the existing equalization formula until 2024. According to many provincial politicians, and contrary to traditional practice, this decision was taken "without negotiating with the provinces" (Ward 2018). While federal officials claim that consultation occurred, intergovernmental relations are shrouded in secrecy, complicating our ability to determine whether jurisdictions were meaningfully engaged or simply unilaterally informed of this major policy pronouncement.[8]

Evidence of colonialist dynamics is most visible when we consider the three northern territories (in this connection, on Indigenous peoples, see Papillon, this volume). Since their creation in the late nineteenth century, territorial governments were essentially an arm of the federal bureaucracy governed by political appointees under Ottawa's direct control (Sabin 2014, 375). Starting in the 1960s, the federal government turned its attention to offering greater autonomy to the two northern territories and engaged in a process of devolving powers (Alcantara 2013). As devolution advanced, the territories introduced responsible government and elected territorial councils. By 1992, the prime minister and the premiers included the territorial leaders as full participants in FMCs (Alcantara 2013, 28). Then, in 1999, Nunavut was created. Made possible by a comprehensive land claims agreement signed in 1993 by the Inuit of the eastern Arctic region, the federal government, and the Government of the Northwest Territories, the new territory of Nunavut adopted a public government structure and for the most part now exercises the same powers as the other two territories, including participation in intergovernmental relations. While devolution transfer agreements were finalized with Yukon in 2001 and the Government of the Northwest Territories in 2014, Nunavut is still negotiating the terms of a comparable agreement with the federal government.

Despite enjoying powers similar to those of the provinces, the territories are not formally entrenched in Canada's constitutional order. The federal government could unilaterally decide to alter or reclaim the devolved authority, compromising the realization of divided sovereignty.[9] What is more, the territories are significantly more reliant on federal funds to support operations. In 2018–19, for example, Prince Edward Island received $638 million through major transfers from the federal government. This translates into $4,131 per capita, the highest among all the provinces. The same year, Yukon received $1 billion in transfers with a per capita allocation of $25,836, Northwest Territories received $1.3 billion at $29,666 per capita, and Nunavut received $1.6 billion translating into $42,204 per capita (Department of Finance Canada 2018). This high degree of fiscal dependence leaves territorial autonomy rather precarious, compared to provincial counterparts. For example, in 2017, in reaction to a series of unilateral federal government decisions affecting the Northwest Territories, Premier Bob McLeod issued a "red alert," saying, "The promise of the North is fading and the dreams of northerners are dying as we see a re-emergence of colonialism" (Canadian Press 2017). In some ways, then, the contemporary practice of federalism retains colonial elements.

Classical Federalism

In his effort to describe American federalism, Lord Bryce provided an image of what is known as "classical federalism." According to Bryce, the system should operate "like a great factory wherein two sets of machinery are at work, their revolving wheels apparently intermixed, their bands crossing one another, yet each set doing its own work without touching or hampering the other" (quoted in Grodzins 1967, 261). Such a "watertight" arrangement has certain advantages, including better citizen awareness of government responsibilities, minimization of overlap and duplication, and potentially reducing the need for intergovernmental entanglements (Norrie, Simeon, and Krasnick 1986, 43). The classical mode may thus provide a greater balance between shared rule and self-rule, unity and diversity, and integration and autonomy. It is supported in Canada by advocates of federalism as a means to both achieve efficiency and to ensure the preservation of distinct internal communities.

For many of the provinces, the colonialist practices exerted by the federal government in the years following Confederation were unwelcome. Macdonald's assertions of a federal authority to build a single Canadian nation contradicted alternative images of federalism in the country. For such leaders as George-Étienne Cartier, federalism was not an instrument to advance efficiency but rather a means to assure self-determination for the two founding nations – English and French – of the Canadian state. Quebec jurist T.J.J. Loranger, in the meantime, further advocated for Quebec's rights as a province and pressed back against federal incursions (Romney 1999, 23). Finally, countering the image of Canada as a federation with subservient provinces under the control of the central government, at the first intergovernmental meeting of the premiers, Ontario Premier Oliver Mowat described Canada as a "compact" among the provinces. Beyond political posturing and arguments, the concrete realities of economic development and industrialization advanced in ways that took place primarily under provincial jurisdiction, and provinces were decreasingly reliant on federal grants and subsidies.

Provinces also began to experiment and engage in creative policy-making, launching such things as the first income taxes, minimum wages, highway construction, expanding the provision of schooling, and mothers' allowances, while seeing their constitutional areas of authority strengthened by decisions rendered by the JCPC (Creamer 1984, 20). Whereas the federal government had been willing to use its power of disallowance early in the country's history when it asserted a colonialist mode of federalism, the last case of disallowance occurred in 1943. While formally this provision remains in the Constitution, constitutional convention prescribes that it remain dormant, inaccessible for federal use. Finally, in fiscal affairs, starting in 1959, the federal government introduced the idea of "opting out" (Bélanger 2000). This innovative measure enables provinces to assume primary responsibility for financing and administering a program being implemented under standard federal-provincial cost-sharing arrangements, with the corollary – so as not to be financially penalized for opting out – that it be fiscally compensated by the federal government. While used only by Quebec, opting out affords a greater opportunity to pursue a classical interpretation of the division of powers. Together, these developments shifted the practice of federalism in Canada from a colonial mode to a classical one, which reduced provincial subservience to federal decision-makers.

Looking at the country as a whole, one sector where the classical mode is most apparent is elementary and secondary education. Canada is one of the only federations in the world without a "national" department of education. Instead, thirteen systems operate concurrently from coast to coast to coast, each led by a provincial or territorial government. An intergovernmental body, the Council of Ministers of Education Canada, is the most institutionalized of all intergovernmental tables and operates without the federal government. Initiatives among jurisdictions, such as pan-Canadian assessments, are voluntary, as opposed to hierarchically or coercively enforced. To be sure, the federal government plays an important role in preserving the educational rights of minority-language speakers through a substantial funding contribution. Its role is nevertheless indirect, and all thirteen jurisdictions maintain clear, independent authority.

Focusing more on the relations between the orders of government, the classical mode is arguably most visible in multiple aspects of Quebec's relations with other federal partners. The province's commitment to divided sovereignty for self-determination within the federation has been a constant theme throughout Canada's history. Two examples are presented here. In 1936, when the Rowell-Sirois Commission sat in Quebec, Mr. Emery Beaulieu issued a statement in the name of the Government of Quebec: "Confederation is a pact voluntarily agreed upon and which can be modified only by the consent of all parties.... It is at the same time a form of government freely chosen in preference to legislative union, because it is better designed to ensure protection for minorities and the peaceful and harmonious development of a country" (quoted in the Kwavnick 1973, 137–8).

This perspective on the purpose of federalism was firmly restated on June 20, 1991, when the Québec National Assembly adopted An Act Respecting the Process for Determining the Political and Constitutional Future of Québec ("Bill 150"). The preamble reads: "Whereas Quebecers are free to assume their own destiny, to determine their political status and to assure their economic, social and cultural development" (Government of Quebec 1991). There can be no misinterpretation of the justification for the federal principle as stated here.

Evidence of the classical mode at work in Quebec-Canada relations can be found across an array of policy fields. Whereas the other provinces entered into agreements with Ottawa for tax collection services and pensions over time, Quebec retains its own separate systems.[10] With pensions, an agreement between Quebec and Ottawa in 1964 allowed the province to create its own pension plan, simultaneously securing the right to opt out from joint federal-provincial programs with compensation. When the Government of Canada entered into the Social Union Framework Agreement with the other provinces and territories in 1999, Quebec refused to sign. The rationale in the province was clear and principled: Quebec could not recognize the federal spending power in areas of provincial jurisdiction (Noël 2000). In addition, Quebec has a long tradition of introducing unique social programs in Canada, including universal child care and extended parental leave benefits. Such programs have moved social policy in the province to more closely resemble regimes at work in social democratic Nordic countries than their more liberal Canadian counterparts (Noël 2017). Multiple governments led by different political parties in Quebec have expressed disagreements with broader Canadian initiatives and intergovernmental agreements by adding a footnote or asterisk noting that the province shares objectives with the program in question but chooses to opt out of it (Gauvin 2017, 52). Such activities expose the extent to which Quebec seeks and adheres to a more classical practice of federalism in relations with the rest of Canada.

Interdependent Federalism

In biology, interdependence refers to situations when two or more organisms rely on each other for survival. In the context of a federation, interdependence draws attention to the ways in which partners of a federation rely on each other to achieve respective goals and discharge their constitutional obligations. Interdependence does not mean uniformity and unanimity; rather, variation in practices and asymmetries in relations among the partners prevail. While managed and approached in different ways over time in Canada (*cooperatively, competitively, collaboratively* are adjectives employed to describe these dynamics), interdependence between the orders of government is a pervasive and unavoidable reality.

The Great Depression of the 1930s exposed the degree to which both orders of government needed to find ways to work together to respond to challenges of the twentieth century. The economic collapse of 1929 led to mass unemployment throughout the country. In the 1930s, the federal government attempted to introduce remedies to address these challenges: the Weekly Day of Rest and Industrial Undertakings Act, the Minimum Wage Act, and the Legitimation of Hours of Work Act. In addition, Ottawa also entered into the realm of employment insurance with the Employment and Social Insurance Act. The Law Lords of the JCPC, however, determined these initiatives fell outside federal jurisdiction and rendered them invalid. Subsequently, both orders of government had to work together to craft the arrangements of what would become the welfare state.

Here the ambiguous nature of federalism's institutional features becomes readily apparent. Rather than pursuing change through major constitutional amendments to formally adjust the division of sovereignty, interdependence has been generally managed through two informal means: the federal spending power and intergovernmental relations. Whereas we have seen the ways in which the federal spending power can be deployed in a manner that fosters a colonialist mode in the practice of federalism, it is also one of the critical features that enables an interdependent mode as well.

Between the 1940s and 1960s, the federal government offered conditional grants to provinces to encourage the dissemination of social programs. From hospital insurance to post-secondary assistance, aid for disadvantaged groups and mothers' allowances, intergovernmental negotiations led to agreements that saw the federal government committing to share costs with the provinces on a 50:50 basis to build the welfare state. According to Hogg (2006, 6), "Shared-cost programs have assured Canadians a high minimum level of some important social services. Without the federal initiative, and the federal sharing of the costs, it is certain that some at least of these services would have come later, at standards which varied from province to province, and not at all in some provinces."

The parameters of shared-cost programs were hammered out through intergovernmental negotiations and federal-provincial conferences. During these negotiations, Quebec objected strongly to what it regarded as federal intrusion into provincial jurisdiction, at times even refusing to accept federal funds. At the Federal-Provincial Premiers' Conference in 1960, Premier Lesage denounced the shared-cost programs model, arguing that "joint programmes do not permit the provinces to use their own revenues as they wish nor to take local conditions sufficiently into account." Herein the former premier articulated the value of the division of sovereignty in a manner that prioritized efficiency more than emphasizing the protection of self-determination. What is more, equity within the federation was itself at risk as residents within a province that was refusing federal funds for programs without compensation would miss out on the accompanying benefits;[11] citizens in such a province would continue to pay taxes to the federal government, while being shorn of the reciprocating gains. Left unchecked, this kind of arrangement would be intolerable and undermine the legitimacy of the state.

Through subsequent intergovernmental negotiations, the federal government proposed an opt-out formula allowing provinces to withdraw from an "established" shared-cost program and receive compensation in the form of an abatement of tax points and financial payments. Accepted by Quebec in 1965, the opt-out provision has been used by the province for a variety of federal initiatives. Some within Quebec regard the opt-out provision as a powerful tool. According to René Lévesque (1985, 325–6, quoted in Graham 2011, 110), in comparison with a constitutional veto, "the right to opt out, which we had learned to use in the sixties – the best example being the creation of the Caisse de dépôt – is in my view a much superior weapon, at one and the same time more flexible and more dynamic." While affording flexibility, the federal government nevertheless continues to oblige Quebec to develop and maintain alternative programs that comply with certain standards to remain eligible for the opt-out provision. This aspect of minimal conditionality thus reinforces the interdependent mode.

Evidence of interdependence can be found in unexpected places. The legalization of cannabis and the handling of Canada's international trade policy provide two fruitful examples.

At first glance, the legalization of cannabis would appear to fall firmly under the jurisdiction of the federal government's authority under the Criminal Code. As an illegal substance (with the exception of authorized medical use) under the federal Controlled Drug and Substances Act, changes to the legal status of cannabis is up to the federal Parliament. However, maintaining the provisions to ensure a safe market and regulate public safety fall under either shared or provincial (and territorial) jurisdiction.

The arrangements for impaired driving, public health, education, and taxation see both orders of government engaged. In the meantime, workplace safety, distribution and wholesaling, the retail model, and public consumption engage the provincial and territorial orders primarily. When developing a strategy for the federal government to pursue legalization, the federal Task Force on Cannabis Legalization and Regulation was clear in its recommendation: "The wholesale distribution of cannabis be regulated by provinces and territories and that retail sales be regulated by the provinces and territories in close collaboration with municipalities" (Health Canada 2016, 4). Moreover, as Hartmann (2018) observes, many of the associated health care and policing costs will be borne by provincial and municipal governments. This is why the federal, provincial, and territorial governments reached an agreement to divide the tax with 75 per cent of revenues going to the provinces and territories and the federal government receiving 25 per cent. To quote the backgrounder for the Federal-Provincial-Territorial Agreement on Cannabis (Department of Finance Canada 2017), "The Government of Canada is committed to legalizing, regulating and restricting access to cannabis to keep it out of the hands of youth, profits out of the hands of criminals.... Furthermore, Finance Ministers recognize that meeting the objectives of the legalization of cannabis will entail sustained cooperation between both orders of government and municipalities."

International trade is perhaps the most surprising area of interdependence. Under the terms of the Constitution, the power to conclude treaties and manage international trade falls to the federal government. In practice, however, the provinces (and now, in some instances, the territories) are increasingly significant in trade negotiations. Documenting patterns in trade policy, Skogstad concludes (2012, 203), "The two orders of government are working collaboratively and closely ... a model described here as de facto shared jurisdiction." Interdependence in this field was clearly apparent during the negotiation of the Comprehensive Economic and Trade Agreement with the European Union. This process marked the first time that provincial and territorial representatives were formally at the table with EU negotiators (Kukucha 2016). During the most recent round of negotiations with the United States and Mexico that led to the ratification of USMCA, moreover, the federal government remained in constant contact with the premiers and relied on them to provide a unified front pressing Canadian interests with their trading partners abroad. The critical reality is that in many areas neither order of government can achieve objectives without the constructive engagement of others.

Conclusion

Institutional effects can be understood only by watching an institution in practice. With this seemingly simple launchpad, I endeavoured to make three contributions: theoretical, metaphorical, and empirical.

Theoretically, the chapter identified the ways institutional features create opportunities for change and adaptation, depending upon the ways in which authoritative actors choose to use them. Take the alternative means to address the vertical imbalance: grants (both conditional and unconditional), transfers, and tax points. Each remedy carries different implications for the preservation of the division of powers and the achievement of divided sovereignty; they vary according to the extent of autonomy gained by or retained for the constituent jurisdictions. With short-term conditional grants, the central government retains the upper hand. Alternatively, the longer-time horizons of transfers foster greater predictability and stability for the receiving government, somewhat levelling the field between the orders. Finally, as a reallocation of access to tax revenue (or "tax room"), the transfer of tax points affords the greatest autonomy for the receiving jurisdictions when they have a sufficient tax base to reap the expected benefits. Each strategy influences the degree to which shared rule or self-rule may be preserved and protected; each strategy informs and shapes the practice of federalism in a country potentially enabling a colonial mode, a classical mode, or an interdependent mode.

Using the metaphor of practice, I revealed the ways in which federalism is a living, breathing institution, with actors constantly using and adapting customs, procedures, and habits activated through formal and informal rules. Keeping the focus on the fiscal arrangements, while channelling certain behaviours, the arrangements do not themselves *determine* outcomes. It is the choices made by authoritative actors that matter. This is where the ambiguity of institutions becomes clear. Federal decisions on the deployment of its spending power promoted all three modes of practice. The rules of an institution are thus not intrinsically one way or another. Rather, the effects of an institution manifest through the choices of authoritative actors. Far from being static, institutions are constantly moving and adapted as actors make choices.

Finally, my exploration of three modes to the practice of federalism suggests that the dynamics in the relations between the orders of government should not be conceived in terms of waves, with one practice giving way to another. Instead, by tracking decisions in the use of constitutional provisions, intergovernmental affairs, and fiscal arrangements, we see that aspects of colonial, classical, and interdependent modes of practice have occurred simultaneously and can be detected in action today. Let's return to the Pan-Canadian Framework on Clean Growth and Climate Change. In the high-profile intergovernmental forum of a First Ministers' Conference, the use of the fiscal architecture was questioned and challenged by two premiers – one calling for more funding in health care, the other opposing the potential unilateral imposition of a new federal tax. The jurisdictional conflict between the two orders of government is likely to go before the courts, who will act as an arbitrator of the activity in an area of constitutional ambiguity. Addressing climate change requires action from both orders, reflecting an interdependent mode. One premier is nevertheless accusing Ottawa of using the somewhat colonialist tactic of unilateralism while defending a classical interpretation of the division of powers to avoid the imposition of a certain outcome. Federalism, as an institution, is far from a static structure; it is a living, evolving, and adapting entity that is shaped by and shapes human behaviour.

Notes

1 Here in this chapter I am using the term *colonial* in the context of the relationship between the federal government, as a settler colonial entity, and other settlers in the provinces and territories. Consequently, I do not grapple with the historical and ongoing settler–colonial relationship between Canada and Indigenous peoples across the country.

2 In the 1990s, Canadian scholars began abandoning the term *levels* of government in favour of the somewhat less hierarchically oriented term of *orders* of government, to capture better the nature of the federal union.

3 Interdependence is the state of being, whereas cooperation is a mode of managing that state of being. Similarly, competition and collaboration are modes of managing interdependence.

4 *Ontario (AG) v OPSEU*, [1987] 2 SCR 2, para 27.

5 Referred to colloquially as the "free the beer case," *Comeau* involved a resident of New Brunswick being apprehended in a sting operation for purchasing beer in Quebec at a lower price and bringing it back home with him. At issue was whether provinces have the right to impose non-tariff barriers on trade within Canada.

6 House of Assembly, April 10, 1865. Referenced in Ajzenstat et al. (1999, 69).

7 House of Assembly, April 10, 1865.

8 For instance, in a review of all the official communiqués from the meetings of the federal-provincial-territorial finance ministers between 2015 and 2018, the word *equalization* never appears. It is thus possible to infer that this critical fiscal arrangement was never on the official agenda during the formal meetings of the respective ministers.

9 Unilateral interventions into the affairs of governments are not uncommon in Canada, particularly in the context of provincial governments into municipal affairs. The Conservative Government of Ontario recently decided unilaterally and without consultation to reduce the size of Toronto's City Council during the 2018 municipal election campaign. While municipalities are conventionally known as "creatures of the provinces," for many, the recent actions of the provincial government lack the necessary legitimacy in the context of a democracy.

10 The Government of Alberta is the only other province that still administers its own provincial corporate income taxes, collected by the Alberta Tax and Revenue Administration (TRA). According to the TRA, administering corporate taxes offers greater flexibility to the province and seemingly reduce costs for individual businesses. See Canadian Tax Foundation (2016).

11 During the Duplessis administration, Quebec refused conditional grants in multiple areas. According to Bélanger (2000), "In 1959, it was estimated that Quebec received $46 million in conditional grants while it refused a further $82 million."

References and Suggested Readings

Ajzenstat, Janet, Paul Romney, Ian Gentles, and William D. Gairdner, eds. *Canada's Founding Debates*. Toronto: University of Toronto Press, 1999.

Alcantara, Christopher. 2013. "Ideas, Executive Federalism and Institutional Change: Explaining Territorial Inclusion in Canadian Fist Ministers' Conferences." *Canadian Journal of Political Science* 46 (1): 27–48.

Baier, Gerald. 2012. "The Courts, the Constitution, and Dispute Resolution." In *Canadian Federalism: Performance, Effectiveness, and Legitimacy*, edited by Herman Bakvis and Grace Skogstad, 3rd ed., 79–95. Don Mills, ON: Oxford University Press.

Bakvis, Herman, and Grace Skogstad, eds. 2012. *Canadian Federalism: Performance, Effectiveness, and Legitimacy*. 3rd ed. Don Mills, ON: Oxford University Press.

Banting, Keith. 1987. *The Welfare State and Canadian Federalism*. 2nd ed. Montreal and Kingston: McGill-Queen's University Press.

Béland, Daniel, André Lecours, Gregory P. Marchildon, Haizhen Mous, and M. Rose Olfert. 2017. *Fiscal Federalism and Equalization Policy in Canada*. Toronto: University of Toronto Press.

Bélanger, Claude. 2000. "Opting Out." Readings in Quebec History. http://faculty.marianopolis.edu/c.belanger/quebechistory/readings/opting.htm.

Bickerton, James. 2010. "Deconstructing the New Federalism." *Canadian Political Science Review* 4 (2–3): 56–72.

Brouillet, Eugénie. 2017. "The Supreme Court of Canada: The Concept of Cooperative Federalism and Its Effect on the Balance of Power." In *Courts and Federal Countries: Federalists or Unitarists?* edited by Nicholas Aroney and John Kincaid, 135–64. Toronto: University of Toronto Press.

Canadian Press. 2017. "N.W.T. Premier Issues 'Red Alert' on 'Colonial' Attack on Territory's Oil and Gas Future." CBC, November 1. https://www.cbc.ca/news/canada/north/nwt-premier-bob-cleod-drilling-arctic-1.4381837.

Canadian Tax Foundation. 2016. "Alberta to Continue to Run Its Own Corporate Income Tax." *Canadian Tax Focus* 6 (1). https://www.ctf.ca/ctfweb/EN/Newsletters/Canadian_Tax_Focus/2016/1/160102.aspx.

Chatry, Isabelle. 2017. "Fiscal Decentralisation and Subnational Finance: Strengthening Local Level Capacity." https://www.oecd.org/regional/regional-policy/Fiscal-decentralisation-and-subnational-finance-ENG.pdf (link no longer active).

Council of the Federation. 2003. "Founding Agreement." http://www.canadaspremiers.ca/founding-agreement/.

Creamer, Brian. 1984. *Canadian Federalism: Its Changing Nature.* November. Backgrounder Research Branch. Library of Parliament.

Department of Finance Canada. 1995. "Overview of the 1995 Budget."

———. 2011. "Canada Health Transfer." https://www.fin.gc.ca/fedprov/cht-eng.asp (link no longer active).

———. 2017. "Federal Support to Provinces and Territories." https://www.fin.gc.ca/fedprov/mtp-eng.asp (link no longer active).

———. 2018. "Backgrounder: Federal-Provincial-Territorial Agreement on Cannabis Taxation." https://www.fin.gc.ca/n17/data/17-122_1-eng.asp (link no longer active).

Elazar, Daniel. 1987. *Exploring Federalism.* Tuscaloosa, AL: University of Alabama Press.

Energy, Mines, and Resources Canada. 1980. *The National Energy Program.* Ottawa: Ministry of Supply and Services. http://publications.gc.ca/collections/collection_2016/rncan-nrcan/M23-12-80-4-eng.pdf.

Fafard, Patrick, François Rocher, and Catherine Côté. 2010. "The Presence (or Lack Thereof) of a Federal Culture in Canada: The Views of Canadians." *Regional & Federal Studies* 20 (1): 19–43.

Fournier, Jean-Marc. 2017. "A Word from the Minister." In *Quebecers, Our Way of Being Canadian: Policy on Québec Affirmation and Canadian Relations.* Quebec City: Gouvernement du Québec. https://www.saic.gouv.qc.ca/documents/relations-canadiennes/politique-affirmation-en.pdf.

Gauthier, James. 2012. *The Canada Social Transfer: Past, Present and Future Considerations.* Publication no. 212-48-E. Ottawa. https://lop.parl.ca/staticfiles/PublicWebsite/Home/ResearchPublications/BackgroundPapers/PDF/2012-48-e.pdf.

Gauvin, Jean-Philippe. 2017. "Les relations intergouvernementales et la coordination des politiques publiques au Canada: Entre relations formelles et informelles." PhD diss., l'Université de Montréal. https://papyrus.bib.umontreal.ca/xmlui/bitstream/handle/1866/19309/Gauvin_Jean-Philippe_2017_these.pdf?sequence=2.

Gibbins, Roger. 2014. "Constitutional Politics." In *Canadian Politics*, edited by James Bickerton and Alain-G. Gagnon, 6th ed., 47–64. Toronto: University of Toronto Press.

Government of Quebec. 1991. "An Act Respecting the Process for Determining the Political and Constitutional Future of Québec."

———. 1997. "Guidelines from the Government of Québec Regarding Canadian Intergovernmental Relations, December 4, 1997." Document 37. https://www.sqrc.gouv.qc.ca/documents/positions-historiques/positions-du-qc/part3/Document37_en.pdf.

———. 2007. "Strong Leadership: A Better Canada." Speech from the Throne, October 16. http://publications.gc.ca/collections/collection_2007/gg/SO1-1-2007E.pdf.

Graham, Ron. 2011. *The Last Act: Pierre Trudeau, the Gang of Eight, and the Fight for Canada.* Toronto: Allen Lane Canada.

Grodzins, Morton. 1967. "The Federal System." In *American Federalism in Perspective*, edited by Aaron Wildavsky. Boston: Little, Brown.

Hartmann, Erich. 2018. "Sharing the Costs of Cannabis in Canada: Key Takeaways." Mowat Centre. August 29. https://munkschool.utoronto.ca/mowatcentre/sharing-the-costs-of-cannabis-in-canada/.

Health Canada. 2016. *A Framework for the Legalization and Regulations of Cannabis in Canada: The Final Report of the Task Force on Cannabis Legalization and Regulation.* Ottawa: Her Majesty the Queen in Right of Canada, as represented by the Minister of Health.

Hogg, Peter W. 2006. *Constitutional Law of Canada.* Toronto: Carswell.

Hueglin, Thomas O., and Alan Fenna. 2006. *Comparative Federalism: A Systematic Inquiry.* Peterborough, ON: Broadview.

Inwood, Gregory J., Carolyn M. Johns, and Patricia L. O'Reilly. 2011. *Intergovernmental Policy Capacity in Canada: Inside the Worlds of Finance, Environment, Trade, and Health.* Montreal and Kingston: McGill-Queen's University Press.

Kukucha, Christopher J. 2016. "Provincial/Territorial Governments and the Negotiation of International Trade Agreements." *IRPP Insight*, October, 1–16. http://irpp.org/wp-content/uploads/2016/10/insight-no10.pdf.

Kwavnick, David, ed. 1973. *The Tremblay Report.* Toronto: McClelland and Stewart.

Macdonald, John A. 1865. "John A. Macdonald on the Federal System." In *Parliamentary Debates on the Subject of the Confederation of the British North American Provinces, 3rd Session, 8th Provincial Parliament of Canada.* Quebec: Hunter, Rose, Parliamentary Printers.

Milligan, Kevin. 2017. "Canada's Radical Fiscal Federation: The Next 50 Years." November. Paper presented at Canada and Its Centennial and Sesquicentennial. Toronto, University of Toronto. http://faculty.arts.ubc.ca/kmilligan/research/papers/Milligan-Radical-Federation.pdf.

Noël, Alain. 2000. "Without Quebec: Collaborative Federalism with a Footnote? Policy Matters." Montreal: Institute for Research on Public Policy. http://irpp.org/wp-content/uploads/2014/09/pmvol1no2.pdf.

———. 2009a. "Balance and Imbalance in the Division of Financial Resources." In *Contemporary Canadian Federalism: Foundations, Traditions, Institutions*, edited by Alain-G. Gagnon, 273–302. Toronto: University of Toronto Press.

———. 2009b. "A Report That Almost No One Has Discussed: Early Responses to Quebec's Commission on Fiscal Imbalance." In *Canadian Fiscal Arrangements: What Works, What Might Work Better*, edited by Harvey Lazar, 127–53. Montreal and Kingston: McGill-Queen's University Press.

———. 2017. "Social Investment in a Federal Welfare State: The Quebec Experience." In *The Uses of Social Investment*, edited by Aton Hemerijck, 254–65. Oxford: Oxford University Press.

Norrie, Kenneth, Richard Simeon, and Mark Krasnick. 1986. *Federalism and the Economic Union in Canada.* Toronto: University of Toronto Press.

R v Comeau, 2018 SCC 15. https://scc-csc.lexum.com/scc-csc/scc-csc/en/item/17059/index.do.

Romney, Paul. 1999. "Provincial Equality, Special Status and the Compact Theory of Canadian Confederation." *Canadian Journal of Political Science* 32 (1): 21–39.

Rueschemeyer, Dietrich. 2009. *Usable Theory: Analytic Tools for Social and Political Research.* Princeton: Princeton University Press.

Sabin, Jerald. 2014. "Contested Colonialism: Responsible Government and Political Development in Yukon." *Canadian Journal of Political Science* 47 (2): 375–96.

Simeon, Richard, Ian Robinson, and Jennifer Wallner. 2014. "The Dynamics of Canadian Federalism." In *Canadian Politics*, edited by James Bickerton and Alain-G. Gagnon, 6th ed., 65–92. Toronto: University of Toronto Press.

Simmons, Julie. 2012. "Democratizing Executive Federalism: The Role of Non-Governmental Actors in Intergovernmental Agreements." In *Canadian Federalism: Performance, Effectiveness, and Legitimacy*, edited by Herman Bakvis and Grace Skogstad, 3rd ed., 320–39. Don Mills, ON: Oxford University Press.

Skogstad, Grace. 2012. "International Trade Policy and the Evolution of Canadian Federalism." In *Canadian Federalism: Performance, Effectiveness, and Legitimacy*, edited by Herman Bakvis and Grace Skogstad, 3rd ed. 203–22. Don Mills, ON: Oxford University Press.

Stoney, Christopher, and Katherine A.H. Graham. 2009. "Federal-Municipal Relations in Canada: The Changing Organizational Landscape." *Canadian Public Administration* 52 (3): 371–94.

Tasker, John Paul. 2016. "Trudeau Announces 'Pan-Canadian Framework' on Climate – but Sask., Manitoba Hold Off." CBC News, December 9. https://www.cbc.ca/news/politics/trudeau-premiers-climate-deal-1.3888244.

Telford, Hamish. 2003. "The Federal Spending Power in Canada: Nation-Building or Nation-Destroying." *Publius* 33 (1): 23–44.

Théret, Bruno. 2005. "Du principe fédéral à une typologie des fédérations: Quelques Propositions." In *Le Fédéralisme dans tous ses états: Gouvernance, Identité et Méthodologie*, edited by J.-F. Gaudreault-Desbiens and F. Gélinas, 99–133. Cowansville, QC: Les Éditions Yvon Blais.

Trudeau, Pierre Elliott. [1968] 1998. *The Essential Trudeau*, edited by Ron Graham. Toronto: McClelland and Stewart.

———. 1969. *Federal-Provincial Grants and the Spending Power of Parliament*. Ottawa: Government of Canada.

Ward, Rachel. 2018. "Alberta Finance Minister Will Raise 'Problems' with Equalization Formula Extension at Ottawa Meeting." CBC News, June 22. https://www.cbc.ca/news/canada/calgary/jason-kenney-equalization-decision-1.4717962.

Wesley, Jared J. 2018. "Coordinating Federalism: Intergovernmental Agenda-Setting in Canada and the United States." *IRPP Insight* 21. http://irpp.org/wp-content/uploads/2018/05/Coordinating-Federalism-Intergovernmental-Agenda-Setting-in-Canada-and-the-United-States.pdf.

nine
Politics and the Charter of Rights and Freedoms

RAYMOND BAZOWSKI

Introduction

In what is still a relatively rare practice, Chief Justice Richard Wagner held a news conference barely six months into his tenure as the head of the Canadian Supreme Court where he claimed the Canadian judicial system was an exemplary defender of democracy and the rule of law in a time when these values "are seriously attacked by other countries or leaders of other countries who pretend to be democratic" (C.J. Wagner quoted in MacCharles 2018). By suggesting that Canadian courts have much to teach the rest of the world about how to resist authoritarian populism, the chief justice implied that judges, when performing their roles judiciously, are above the fray of politics. But is it realistic to say that judges are non-political actors dispassionately guarding a pristine legal order that is said to underpin liberal democracy? This chapter will address the question by looking at the political role played by the Canadian judiciary in the age of the Charter of Rights and Freedoms. Specifically, the chapter will focus on two issues that directly engage the subject of politics and the courts. First is the ongoing debate over the "judicialization of politics," that is, the conversion of political into legal disputes to be decided in the courtroom. Second is the now largely overlooked question of the way in which the Charter of Rights was originally conceived as a nationalizing instrument intended as a counterweight to centrifugal tendencies in Canadian federalism, and especially those caused by Quebec nationalism.

The Judicialization of Politics

The term *judicialization of politics* has at least two interrelated meanings. Most directly it implies that courts have intruded into the policy-making arena to an extent not contemplated by the classic doctrine of the separation of powers. This doctrine holds that well-ordered government consists of distinct functional branches best kept within their own spheres of competence. Elegant in its simplicity, the idea that governmental powers should be housed in separate institutions is beset by some elementary problems, not least of which is who gets to decide whether the walls meant to sequester these powers have been breached by office-holders. One solution to this latter question presented itself in the United States. The Americans had constitutionalized the doctrine in the eighteenth century, but it was politics that was responsible for the resolution of the boundary maintenance problem when the US Supreme Court artfully asserted its authority as final constitutional arbiter in *Marbury v Madison* [1803].

It pays to remember, however, that there are a number of possible solutions to the boundary problem contained in the doctrine of the separation of powers. Britain, for example, has a constitutional court with only a limited power of judicial review. Observing the principle of parliamentary sovereignty (the idea that Parliament is the supreme law-making body), Britain's version of constitutionalism presently accords its constitutional court the power only to invalidate secondary legislation (i.e., regulations made by subordinate bodies), and to make a declaration of incompatibility in those instances where it believes a law passed by Parliament breaches one of the rights contained in the European Convention on Human Rights. Such a declaration of incompatibility does not, however, nullify the offending law, for in Britain parliamentary sovereignty trumps judicial review, which means that only Parliament can decide whether to alter or rescind a law of its own making.

Given Canada's political heritage, it should come as no surprise that devotion to the principle of parliamentary supremacy has long been a commonplace in this country's democratic discourse. Reconciling that principle with the power of judicial review was relatively uncontroversial in the pre-Charter era, because constitutional jurisprudence in Canada prior to 1982 was confined largely to questions of which level of government, federal or provincial, was entitled under the 1867 BNA Act to legislate on some contested subject matter. A metaphor frequently used to describe what many deemed to be the court's unassuming constitutional role was that of an umpire impartially administering the rules defining the Canadian game of federalism. While umpires might be essential to the successful conduct of any game, they are hardly expected to displace the players themselves, but rather are intended to remain in the background, rulebook always at the ready. Of course this benign image of the unbiased referee hardly captures the complex story of adjudication and Canadian federalism. In truth, the JCPC, the British tribunal that till 1949 was the final court of appeal in constitutional matters, and subsequently the Supreme Court of Canada, made their own revisions to the rulebook, effectively altering the federal division of powers in a number of key rulings spanning the centuries.

That courts have an impact on politics through their rulings is an unremarkable observation. That these rulings might be informed by the political beliefs of judges, on the other hand, strike some as an illegitimate mixing of law and politics. Yet it is hard to imagine any court giving substance to the letter of constitutional law without drawing upon conceptions of justice, political ideals, theories of government, administrative assumptions, and a host of other considerations that can only be characterized as political. If adjudication can never be free of politics in this latter sense, why the present-day concern with the judicialization of politics? The customary answer is that the addition of a bill of rights to a federal constitution changes the political calculus involved in judicial decision-making. No longer restricted to ruling on which level of government has authority to legislate on some subject matter,[1] the incorporation of the Charter has meant judges now have the ability to invalidate laws enacted by any level of government on the basis that the substance of those laws infringes upon enumerated rights whose meaning the courts ultimately decide. It is because they have been armed with this enlarged power of judicial review that courts have acquired a much more contentious image in some quarters as self-appointed and self-important oracles of the constitution with their own legislative ambitions.

In addition to concerns about an imperial judiciary exceeding what is seen as its traditional adjudicative responsibilities, critics of the judicialization of politics often raise a second related objection by claiming that conflicts that are at root political are increasingly being transformed into legal issues to be resolved through a categorical judicial language in an impenetrable institutional setting by an appointed and largely unaccountable body. In this alternate depiction of the phenomenon of the judicialization of politics, what is presented as particularly worrisome is the notion that the vocabulary by which we come to identify issues requiring public action has become infected by a *rights-based* language, which prioritizes the individual over the collective. Not only does this mean that efforts to imagine what constitutes a public good have been made more difficult, but that the arena in which contested claims about individual rights and public goods has, for all intents and purposes, become the courts (whose decisions typically create winners and losers). As a well-known authority on the courts had warned at the onset of the Charter era, this development could only accelerate the "flight from politics" by contributing to a "deepening disillusionment with the procedures of representative government and government by discussion as a means of resolving fundamental questions of political justice" (Russell 1982, 32).

While reproaches offered by critics like Russell focus on the effects of judicialized politics on parliamentary democracy, an opposite case can be made that the Charter has contributed to the politicization of the judiciary. On this view, an illicit boundary crossing has been *forced* on judges by parliamentarians who are only too willing to shun their own legislative responsibilities and thrust onto courts politically sensitive issues they would prefer to avoid. Retired Justice Marie Deschamps complained of this tendency when she spoke of the avoidance behaviour of politicians who pass on "hot potato" issues to the courts: "The clear message is: Let the judges do it ... We are caught in these situations. We see those cases coming and we cannot say no" (Deschamps quoted in Makin 2013c, 1).

These various concerns have given rise to some rather elementary debates about the proper reach of judicial review. On the one side are those who believe courts should limit themselves to interpretations that respect the intentions of the original framers of the constitution or that are restricted to the plain meaning of the words contained in it, or that can be reasonably derived from the text.[2] On the other side are those who advocate a "living tree" approach to legal interpretation in which jurists are encouraged to take into account contemporary social facts when devising the meaning of specific provisions in the constitution.[3] While these opposing positions are not exhaustive of the variety of interpretative strategies prescribed or in use in actual courtrooms, their salience has often been marked by the way they have been assimilated into an even broader distinction between judicial restraint and judicial activism, the former signifying an attitude of deference to legislatures while the latter a willingness to substitute the court's understanding of the law for that of legislatures. It must be noted that this distinction between restraint and activism is less edifying than it might seem on the face of it, for so-called restrained judges have been known to defy conventional constitutional understandings (and therefore legislative intent) for political purposes, while nominally activist judges have done the opposite.[4]

Given the vagaries surrounding the terms used in the debates over the appropriate role of the courts in a liberal democracy, are critics correct in deploring a trend towards the judicialization of politics? Or are these so-called problems wrongly posed insofar as they presuppose a departure from an idealized picture of courts supplying narrow technical interpretations of the law that is itself a fiction? In what follows it will be argued that reservations about the political role of the modern judiciary are in part overstated, and otherwise are offered up in a way that usually is too decontextualized to afford us a truly useful perspective on the relationship between law and politics.

Judicial Review and the Charter

A conventional argument has it that revulsion at the atrocities of World War II coupled with the widespread popularity of the 1948 UN Declaration of Human Rights helped launch a rights revolution wherein civil and human rights became a dominant political idiom, and efforts to make such rights enforceable in courtrooms a mark of progressive politics (Ignatieff 2008). As it happened, Canada was somewhat late in joining the revolution. While the Diefenbaker government did adopt a bill of rights in 1960, the fact that it was an ordinary piece of legislation and applicable only to actions of the federal government lent it so uncertain a constitutional status that in the main, the courts ignored its provisions.[5]

The Court's reluctance to use its legal resources to vigorously defend civil rights prior to the introduction of the Charter of Rights and Freedoms in 1982 is in one sense not that surprising. In his comparative study of judicial activism, Charles Epp has suggested that courts are much more likely to be emphatic champions of civil liberties if there already exist within society institutional and cultural support structures that can reinforce an emboldened judiciary (Epp 1998). The relative absence in Canada in the early postwar years of such a foundation for judicial activism goes some way in explaining the Supreme Court's disappointingly intermittent concern for protecting civil liberties. By the same token, the subsequent decades-long campaign for a constitutionally entrenched Charter of Rights, the multiplication of public interest groups prepared to include legal action in their repertoire of political tactics (helped along by government programs designed for just such a purpose), the demonstration effect of successful civil rights undertakings in the United States under the Warren Court, changes in professional legal education as well as assorted efforts to make legal knowledge more widely available to the general public – they all acted to produce an environment more conducive to judicial activism.

Still, considering its reluctance to seize upon a civil rights agenda when provided the opportunity with the earlier Bill of Rights, it remained to be seen whether the Court would be more favourably disposed to wield its enhanced power under the Charter of Rights. In the event, the Supreme Court initially proved a Charter enthusiast, awarding victories in decisions that were almost always unanimous to more than half of all Charter claimants in the first twenty-five cases (1984–6). Thereafter, however, the success rate for Charter challenges declined, ranging from a third to as little as a fifth, as was the case in 2012 and again in 2017.[6]

At the same time, disagreements in the Court have become more commonplace. While the latter might be taken as a sign that ideological camps are solidifying in a manner comparable to what has occurred in the United States, students of the attitudinal characteristics of Canadian Supreme Court justices have concluded that for the most part liberal/conservative ideological distinctions are inadequate in accounting for the incidence of concurrences and dissents in the Court (Alarie and Green 2009; Ostberg and

Wetstein 2007; McCormick 2004). If anything, as Monahan suggests, the emergence of different voting blocs in recent years might be best explained by the degree of deference different groups of judges are prepared to show to elected governments, particularly in disputes that have fiscal consequences (Monahan cited in Makin 2008). It should be said, however, that such conclusions about the lack of clear ideological divisions among justices on the Supreme Court may be historically bounded, as more recent controversies over judicial appointments, particularly in the latter years of the Harper Conservative government, have raised doubts that overt partisanship is absent in the staffing of Canadian courts.

Success rates for Charter challenges and the frequency of dissents in the end do not tell us all that much about the ideological and practical impact of Charter jurisprudence on public policy. More revealing are the patterns discernible amongst the hundreds of Charter cases heard by the Supreme Court since 1982, and the interpretative strategies the Court has developed over this period. The Charter, it should be recalled, has some unique features which were meant to guide courts in their interpretation of its enumerated rights. For example, the general legal right contained in section 7 guaranteeing the right to life, liberty, and security of person is qualified by the phrase "in accordance with the principles of fundamental justice" to indicate broadly the circumstances where governments may be justified in depriving citizens of this right. Or again, section 15, guaranteeing equal treatment before and under the law and equal protection and benefit of the laws, has an additional phrase implying that its purpose is to protect against specific types of discrimination – for instance, that based on race or religion or sex. Moreover, section 15 is followed by a clause exempting from Charter challenge affirmative action programs, thereby reinforcing the notion that it should be seen primarily as a remedial right aimed at those historically disadvantaged by prejudices and intolerance.

The internal limitations and interpretative clues contained in these and other rights in the Charter are further qualified by three pivotal application clauses, sections 1, 24, and 33. Section 1 instructs courts to treat the rights and freedoms of the Charter as only conditionally guaranteed, as they are subject to "such reasonable limits prescribed by law as can be demonstrably justified in a free and democratic society." This latter phrase permits governments to defend a prima facie Charter breach by arguing that it is a reasonable limitation on the infringed right. Should a Charter violation be found to exist and not be justified under section 1, courts are charged under section 24 with devising a remedy they consider "appropriate and just in the circumstances." This enforcement section confers on the courts discretionary power in deciding just how to respond to a Charter violation, which means that when totalling Charter victories, one should always pay heed to the remedy ordered up, because a Charter "win" does not automatically mean that the victor obtains the sought-after result.

Finally, section 33 acts to bracket almost all the fundamental rights of the Charter by allowing the federal Parliament or provincial legislatures to override sections 2 and 7 through 15 through simple statutory declarations for repeatable periods of five years. This controversial notwithstanding clause was a concession that the federal government made during constitutional negotiations leading up to the Charter to those provincial premiers who were hesitant to relinquish the principle of parliamentary supremacy, though it should be noted that this same provision had also been a part of the 1960 Bill of Rights.[7] While section 33 seems to impose a considerable restriction on the Charter, and hence on the court's power of judicial review, in practice this has not been the case. Except for a period in the 1980s when the government of Saskatchewan used the notwithstanding clause to try to pre-empt a constitutional challenge to back-to-work legislation, and governments in Quebec for symbolic political reasons used it to insulate as much of that province's legislation as possible from Charter challenge (and later, to override an adverse court ruling on its language laws), section 33 increasingly became a less credible option for governments as its public legitimacy declined in the intervening years. That legitimacy has been called into question again with the CAQ (Coalition Avenir Québec) government of Quebec invoking section 33 when passing its controversial Bill 21 (An Act Respecting the Laicity of the State, 2019) prohibiting selected public officials, including teachers, from wearing religious symbols while at work. Interestingly, Premier Legault alluded to his party's democratic mandate to reflect the will of the majority as a justification for using the notwithstanding clause, an argument suggestive of the illiberal populist challenges to the rule of law that Chief Justice Wagner had warned against in his remarks to the press (Lowrie 2019).

While the fate of the notwithstanding clause remains an open-ended question, Canadian courts have not shied away from affirming their power to interpret Charter rights in an expansive fashion. This can be seen in the way the Supreme Court has developed a number of interpretative strategies to give substance to Charter rights. One such strategy has been to interpret the purpose of the rights contained in the Charter – that is, the values they are designed to protect or advance – by canvassing their historical, political, or philosophical sources. This "purposive approach" to Charter interpretation, first articulated by Chief Justice Dickson in his ruling in *Hunter v Southam* [1984], ensured that the Court would not confine itself to legally narrow representations of the newly entrenched constitutional rights, nor be bound by a studied deference to legislative intent. Another interpretative approach favoured by the Court has been called "contextualism." The contextual approach, first elaborated by Justice Wilson in *Edmonton Journal v AG Alta* [1989], invites courts to be more sensitive to the complexities of individual rights claims by acknowledging that "a particular right or freedom might have a different value depending on the context" (1355–6). By endorsing a contextual approach, the Court has signified that it is indisposed to rely on a simple formula to decide upon the validity of a rights claim, preferring instead to examine the underlying circumstances and competing values that might clarify what actually is at stake in the claim.

Understandably, some are uncomfortable with the interpretative latitude the Court seemingly enjoys when it uses a purposive approach to define the meaning of Charter rights, and a contextual approach to decide upon their relative weight in concrete legal disputes. Likewise there are those who are disconcerted by how the courts have come to interpret the limitations clause of section 1. In an early Charter case, *R v Oakes* [1986], Chief Justice Dickson outlined a test to determine when a government might be justified in infringing a Charter right. The so-called *Oakes* test, originally devised to be quite rigorous but subsequently relaxed in practice, requires governments found in violation of a Charter right to satisfy the Court on four points: (1) that a pressing and substantial public purpose is being served by the controverted measure, (2) that it is rationally connected to that purpose, (3) that the affected right has been impaired in a minimal fashion, and (4) that the public benefits of the measure outweigh the costs of this impairment. Significantly, the way the *Oakes* test has been construed invariably involves the Court in policy assessments, for there is no other practical way for it to conclude whether a disputed law or government action is rationally connected to the public purpose it is meant to serve – or, even more acutely, whether a right has been minimally impaired – except to compare policy alternatives. Predictably, it is at the section 1 stage of a Charter hearing that courts are most vulnerable to the charge of subverting the democratic process by substituting their own policy preferences for those of elected legislatures.

Whether these several structural features of the Charter, along with the interpretative doctrines the Supreme Court has settled upon, have led judges to illicitly inject their political values into the field of democratic policy-making is something that can be determined only by examining the kinds of Charter-based nullifications the courts have dispensed. Before embarking on such a review, however, it is worthwhile briefly considering the effects of the Charter on federalism, an issue that in the past had caused a number of provincial premiers, including successive premiers from Quebec, to resist the inclusion of such a document in the Constitution.

The Charter as Tool of National Integration

The once lively question regarding the capacity of the Charter to assist in the cause of national integration is now largely neglected outside of Quebec. Yet it pays to remember, as a number of commentators insisted at the time of its adoption, the Charter's primary political purpose was the consolidation of a pan-Canadian identity in a period when Quebec nationalism, as well as conflicts arising from province-building initiatives elsewhere in the country, challenged the foundations of Canadian federalism.[8] This nationalizing assignment can be understood from three different perspectives. The first is the most straightforward. Provisions in the Charter such as section 6 guaranteeing citizens the right to move and take up a livelihood in any province, section 23 guaranteeing English and French minority education rights, as well as the bilingualism clauses in sections 16–22, were uniquely Canadian additions to what typically are found in conventional bills of rights. Their political function was to counter the territorial bilingualism then being promoted by the Quebec government with an alternative vision of national bilingualism endorsed by the Trudeau government. This aim was most vividly expressed in the minority education rights clause crafted to directly challenge the education clause contained in the Quebec's Bill 101, the latter designed by the governing Parti Québécois to maintain Quebec's *visage linguistique*.

The second way in which the Charter purportedly played a nationalizing role has to do with the allegiances it was meant to generate. In the turbulent nation-defining political battles in the decades following the Quiet Revolution in Quebec, supporters of the Charter hoped its language of common citizen rights would displace or at least offset the territorial political loyalties characteristic of federalism. This symbolic value pointed to a third and most far-reaching nationalizing prospect of the Charter, its potential to lead to a nation-wide standardization of public policy because a judicial invalidation of a provincial law based on individual rights establishes a precedent applicable to all provinces.

Has the Charter fulfilled the nationalizing project ascribed to it? The evidence is mixed. By its very design, the minority language rights clause did what it was intended to, though predictably court rulings that compelled the Quebec government to change its education laws reinforced the view amongst many Quebecers about the illegitimacy of the repatriated Constitution with its Charter of Rights. That sentiment became stronger still when the Supreme Court ruled that the sign law authorized under Bill 101 violated the Charter guarantee of freedom of expression, leading the provincial government to utilize the notwithstanding clause to pass that same law again. These events in Quebec in turn had an effect on the symbolic appeal of the Charter in the rest of Canada that further complicated federal relations, mostly dramatically in two failed constitutional accords (Meech Lake and Charlottetown). These attempts to amend the Constitution in a way that would acknowledge Quebec's distinct society status in Canadian federalism proved unsuccessful, in part because such recognition was seen by many outside of Quebec as undermining the ideal of equal citizenship. Posed as a conflict between universalizing Charter values and the particularistic accommodations regarded as indispensable to a multinational federation, this episode in Canadian constitutional history suggests that the objective of creating a shared citizen identity based on Charter rights may have been a guileless if not altogether misguided ambition. Oddly, however, attitudinal studies have repeatedly shown the Charter enjoys consistently high levels of support throughout the country, including in Quebec (Fletcher and Howe 2000; CRIC 2002; Parkin 2002).

The apparent anomaly between reports of the Charter's popularity in Quebec and the reproofs of its critics who regard it as an impediment to an accommodative asymmetrical federalism could be accounted for by the fact that it is a constitutional document with two distinct faces. On the one hand, it contains the familiar negative liberties that are supposed to protect citizens from an overbearing state. Opinion surveys tend to show that it is this liberal feature of the Charter that is most valued by respondents. If liberal populism – that is to say, a generalized distrust of the powers of government – is indeed a principal motivating factor in the Charter's seeming wide acceptance in Canada, this helps explain not only its approval in Quebec but also the counterintuitive finding of one recent study that reported the strongest regional support for judicial supremacy came from Quebec (Nanos 2007). Liberal constitutionalism in its populist form reinforces an individualist ethos that portrays government as an ever-present threat to liberty, and encourages the belief that courts are a bulwark against tyranny.

On the other hand, the second face of the Charter attempts to give constitutional force to a particular *political* arrangement reflective of the time of its passage, such as in its provisions for national as opposed to territorial bilingualism, its sections signalling that the Charter should not be used to overturn existing or prospective political settlements (such as the rights of denominational schools), or unspecified Indigenous rights; and even its soft interpretative clause instructing courts to be mindful of multiculturalism. Whether intended or not, including details like these in the Charter ensured that some of the political divisions that have characterized Canadian federalism would end up in courts in the guise of individual or group rights, effectively reframing older intergovernmental battles. Those schooled in these long-standing federalism conflicts understandably are troubled by the Charter's potential to obscure if not upend the pragmatic political adaptations that have tended toward a functional asymmetrical federalism in the decades following the Meech Lake and the Charlottetown Accords.

If Quebecers, like Canadians more generally, are attracted to the liberal face of the Charter, a simultaneous attachment of that province's political class to the Quebec *nation* also leads many to be suspicious of its other, overtly political face. This is not to say that Quebec nationalists are inexorably opposed to the Charter. One of the most eloquent critics of the Trudeau vision of Canadian constitutionalism, Guy Laforest, has proposed a way of reconciling the Charter and aspirations for a multinational federal state (Laforest 2009). Laforest's suggestion is to amend section 1 of the Charter to acknowledge that Canada is first and foremost a federation, and that within that federation Quebec constitutes a distinct society. Furthermore, he proposes a change to the multiculturalism clause, section 27, acknowledging that this country's multicultural heritage is embedded in the institutional networks of two host societies. Interestingly, if such proposals were ever to be put into effect, the result would still be a transposition of federalism conflicts into rights conflicts ultimately decided by courts, albeit conflicts that at least would give Quebec governments constitutional grounds for arguing for the reasonableness of measures to protect or strengthen that province's distinct society.

Having constitutional grounds to advance a particular legal argument does not guarantee that such arguments will prevail in court. It all depends on how judges interpret and weigh arguments for rights and corresponding arguments for their limitation. This leads to a consideration of the third perspective on the nationalizing power of the Charter – its alleged propensity to lead to uniform public policies through judicial review. Arguments to this effect usually refer to structural features of the Charter and common law rules of precedent as evidence that federal uniformity flows naturally from Charter jurisprudence.[9] Yet closer analysis of the actual disposition of Charter cases suggests that such a national alignment amongst provincial laws has not taken place to any significant degree. Thus constitutional commentators such as Yves De Montigny have reported that the "Charter has not had the devastating impact on the legislative authority of Quebec (and the other provinces) that some may have feared" (Montigny 1997, 21). Likewise, his statistical analysis of Charter cases has caused James Kelly to conclude that the Charter has had "a minimal impact on federal diversity" (Kelly 1999, 685). In fact, on more than one occasion the Supreme Court has shown a willingness to countenance considerable flexibility in its interpretation of rights in a federal context, as evidenced by the ruling in *Quebec (AG) v A (2013)* where a divided court upheld the constitutionality of a provision in the Quebec Civil Code treating common-law spouses differently from married couples or those in civil unions. Significantly, the deciding vote from then Chief Justice McLachlin referred to a government's latitude under section 1 to realize the underlying goals of the Charter, in effect giving voice to something like Laforest's suggested reconciliation of the Charter with federalism.

Political Impact of the Charter

The history of Charter cases reveals patterns in judicial decision-making that illustrate the temper and tempo of judicialized politics in Canada. For example, between 1982 and 2017 the Supreme Court ruled that 113 federal or provincial statutes or regulations contravened the Charter or section 35 of the Constitution Act, 1982, the latter containing guarantees of Aboriginal and treaty rights, which are not a part of the Charter (but approached by the Court in a manner analogous to its Charter jurisprudence).[10] Of these 113 constitutional breaches, sixty-three involved federal and fifty provincial statutes or regulations. Roughly half of federal laws or regulations found to be unconstitutional (thirty-six of sixty-three) were faulted for procedural rather than substantive matters, which has meant in principle that Parliament could remedy the problem with amended legislation or new regulations with relative ease. In the case of impugned provincial statutes and regulations, the majority (thirty-six of fifty) have been judged unconstitutional on substantive grounds, which means that it has been comparatively harder, though again not impossible, for these governments to repair the legislation or regulation. Significantly, the tendency in recent years has been for courts to suspend declarations of constitutional invalidity for a period in cases where the policy implications of such declarations are consequential or the subject matter contentious, thus giving legislators time to consider alternatives to impugned laws.[11] Another noteworthy tendency throughout the Charter era has been for courts to sever or read down legislative provisions or regulations rather than invalidate entire laws, arguably a less intrusive judicial practice in the policy-setting arena.[12] Finally, it should be observed that the decline in Charter cases reaching the Supreme Court in recent years – a decline made more notable by the smaller overall caseload of the Court during this period – supports the contention of long-time court watcher Peter McCormick that "the time of really big change is over, and that the Supreme Court has gone 'steady state'" (McCormick 2015, 171).

If the Charter has indeed become a less prominent feature in recent Canadian jurisprudence, this is not to say that the Court's political impact through its Charter rulings over the past decades has been negligible. But that impact cannot be comprehended by an ambiguous term like *judicial activism*. Rather, it is the patterns in Charter rulings that are more instructive, for among other things, they reveal that the Supreme Court has appreciated both the perils and possibilities of its enhanced political role. The most conspicuous of these patterns has been the extent to which legal rights dominate Charter jurisprudence. Most frequently at issue in Charter litigation, claims based on legal rights (7–14) also have tended to be the most successful. Not surprisingly, the Supreme Court, just as it had done in a much more modest fashion with the Bill of Rights, has proved most receptive to Charter arguments in a realm of the criminal justice system, for which it feels it possesses a special competence.

While in general it might be said that the Court has favoured a due process model of law enforcement in its legal rights rulings, that commitment has never been unalloyed.[13] For instance, in several recent section 8 decisions, the Supreme Court broadened the legal concept of a reasonable expectation of privacy while also ruling that illegally obtained evidence in the cases under review could still be admitted into court, because to do otherwise would be to bring the administration of justice into disrepute.[14] Even in the Court's most unequivocal policy-making gesture in the area of legal rights, the decision in *Jordan* (2016) to set numerical limits for unreasonable delay in completing criminal trials, the sought-after effect of more speedy trials may well remain illusory. For as Justice Cromwell noted in his assessment of the majority decision, because the limits established in *Jordan* could still be challenged by the Crown on a case-by-case basis, "there is little reason to think these presumptive ceilings would avoid the complexities inherent in deciding whether a particular delay is unreasonable in all circumstances … it simply moves the complexities of the analysis to a new location" (*Jordan* 2016, para 294–96).

However one estimates the effectiveness of those Supreme Court's rulings upholding the rights of the accused and the incarcerated, its reputation as a champion of due process has been amplified as a result of its treatment of the Truth in Sentencing Act (2009), Abolition of Early Parole Act (2011), and Safe Streets and Communities Act (2013). These pieces of legislation were among a number of measures undertaken by the Harper Conservative government in its tough-on-crime approach to the criminal justice system. In a series of contested rulings, the Supreme Court nullified or attenuated the reach of these acts in what many regarded as a repudiation of the government's criminal law agenda. But as with many of its section 8 rulings, some of these decisions had an equivocal message. For example, while the Court referred to the Charter to affirm its discretionary authority to impose sentences appropriate to the cases at hand, the actual sentences challenged by the appellants were still upheld as justifiable.[15]

If the Supreme Court's due process approach to legal rights is overstated, its handling of fundamental freedoms – freedom of expression, religion, association, and assembly – shows that it has favoured a balanced approach, though that very approach has made it vulnerable to the charge of constitutional capriciousness. For instance, in *R v Big M Drug Mart Ltd* [1985], the Court struck down the Federal Lord's Day Act on grounds that it infringed the guarantee of freedom of religion, but subsequently in *Edwards Book and Art Ltd v the Queen* [1986] upheld the validity of Ontario's Retail Holiday Act, ruling that the latter was a justifiable limitation on the same right. Freedom of expression cases have also come in for some rather variable treatment. In *R v Keegstra* [1990], for example, the Court upheld a federal law on hate speech under section 1, but in *R v Zundel* [1992] declared another federal hate speech law unconstitutional because it was deemed to be overly broad and for this reason an objectionable encroachment on freedom of speech. And while upholding the constitutionality of hate speech provisions in provincial human rights codes, the Court has insisted on a "reasonable person test" to guide assessments of harm sufficiently serious enough to warrant a charge (*Saskatchewan Human Rights Commission v Whatcott* [2013]). In obscenity cases, the Supreme Court upheld the federal obscenity law in *R v Butler* [1992], although it also effectively read that law down to narrow its application. Likewise, in *R v Sharpe* [2001] the Supreme Court upheld the federal law on the possession of child pornography, but at the same time read in exceptions to that law to cover situations it believed posed no risk of harm to children. In these cases the Court countenanced restrictions on free speech using as justification the notoriously vague "community standards test," only to abandon it in *R v Labaye* [2005] in favour of a more straightforward evidentiary harm test, though this latter retains many of the ambiguities of the legal analysis it replaced.[16]

The Court's equality jurisprudence has been especially notable for its doctrinal difficulties, and, as in other Charter cases, has entailed contrasting rulings.[17] After setting out an interpretative framework to help decide what constitutes an infringement of equality rights in *Andrews v Law Society of British Columbia* [1989], the Supreme Court's subsequent section 15 rulings were remarkable for their variability. For example, the Court refused arguments that provisions in the Income Tax Act discriminated against women in *Symes v Canada* [1993] and *Thibaudeau v the Queen* [1995], but allowed the argument that failure to provide translation services for deaf patients in BC hospitals constituted a violation of section 15 in *Eldridge v BC* [1997]. If the *Eldridge* ruling signalled the advent of a substantive interpretation of the equality section of the Charter, it was a short-lived episode, as evidenced by the ruling in *Auton v British Columbia* [2004], where the Court decided not to order the provincial government to fund costly, specialized treatment for autistic children. Part of the problem with engendering consistent equality rulings was that the Court moved away from its *Andrews* framework in *Law v Canada (Minister of Employment and Immigration)* [1999], where it devised what proved to be an unwieldy dignity test to determine when discriminatory treatment has occurred. A return to the *Andrews* framework, signalled in *R v Kapp* [2008] and *Ermineskin Indian Band and Nation v Canada* [2009] has not alleviated the problem, as evidenced in the stark divisions among the justices in *Quebec (AG) v A* [2013].

The vacillations exhibited in these and other rulings seem to illustrate not so much a Court seized with Charter hubris but one that has been rather gingerly muddling through with its enhanced power of judicial review, usually choosing to nullify laws for procedural defects or for being overly broad, rather than reproving them in their entirety. This is not to say that courts have not produced controversial Charter judgments. Whether extending to corporations the same legal rights available to individuals in *Hunter v Southam* [1984], or invalidating the federal abortion law in *R v Morgentaler* [1988], or nullifying Quebec's sign law in *Ford v Quebec* [1988], or declaring the common-law definition of marriage unconstitutional, thereby opening the door to gay marriage in *Halpern et al v Canada (AG) et al* [2003], or upending their own precedent by declaring unconstitutional the Criminal Code proscription of assisted suicide in *Carter v Canada (AG)* [2015], Canadian courts have periodically handed down highly contentious decisions that arguably have encroached upon the policy prerogative of legislatures.

How can one possibly justify permitting unrepresentative and unaccountable judges to replace the policy preferences of elected officials with their own? It is instructive to observe that both left- and right-wing analysts of the Court refer to this counter-majoritarian dilemma when sounding the alarm about the judicialization of politics.[18] But there are significant differences between left and right appraisals of judicial politics that are worth recounting. Left critics have generally been concerned that judges, by virtue of their class background and training, will invariably tend to be conservative in outlook. A principal fear is that this conservative judiciary will use the Charter, in particular its ostensibly libertarian components such as section 7, to reinforce the already powerful position business interests possess at common law.[19] A related concern is that the Charter conveys a beguiling message to progressives by suggesting that genuine social reform is possible through courtroom forensics, something that not only is unlikely but also debilitating for truly effective political action (Petter 1987; Mandel 1994; Hutchinson 1995; Bakan 1997).

Some of the force of this left critique has dissipated over the years as the Supreme Court repeatedly refused to employ section 7 to fortify economic rights (but by the same token it has also declined to use this section to help those who have sought a constitutional guarantee for welfare and other social rights). But in the event, it has been the right-wing critics of the Court who have become more influential in the debate about the judicialization of politics, a fact that perhaps should not be surprising, given the contemporary growth of political conservatism (Morton and Knopff 2000; Manfredi 2001; Martin 2003; Leishman 2006). For right-leaning critics, the overriding trepidation is that the Court will exploit the egalitarian section of the Charter to advance a radical redistributive agenda.[20] Given the prominence that the writings of F.L. Morton and Rainer Knopff have gained in both academic and political circles, their arguments on this score deserve close attention. Morton and Knopff's main contention is that self-serving special interest groups such as feminists, LGBTQ+ people, and ethnic and other identity-based groups, which they deem "the court party," have allied themselves with the jurocracy (a shorthand for Charter enthusiasts who are legal professionals and advocates within law schools, the bureaucracy, and the judiciary) to get through the courts what they haven't been able to secure through the ordinary legislative process. This court party, they protest, typically inflate their claims when employing the vocabulary of rights in a way that is inhospitable to the spirit of compromise and conciliation supposedly characteristic of the legislative arena. Morton and Knopff have frequently been criticized for assimilating a deliberately selective cast of characters into what amount to ideological categories of court party and jurocracy, and for using a disingenuous conception of democracy as a normative foundation for their critique of the courts (Smith 2002). Nonetheless, the impression of a furtive style of politics conducted in courtrooms remains powerful enough to have summoned a variety of justificatory arguments for the power of judicial review.

The most straightforward defence of the court's constitutionally enhanced role under the Charter is that the capacity to strike down legislation in order to protect vulnerable minorities from the depredations of legislative majorities is precisely what is intended by a bill of rights in the first place (Bayefsky 1987). A more refined version of this proposition relies on a process-based conception of democracy. According to this argument, judicial review based on a bill of rights actually promotes democracy by giving the courts the power to ensure that the mechanisms of political representation operate fairly, with special consideration given to the plight of minorities who might otherwise be effectively excluded from the political process (Monahan 1987). On either view, an activist court is ordinarily regarded a success rather than a problem. Needless to say, judicial adversaries are hardly persuaded by such arguments, countering that the very fact that courts are unaccountable hardly qualifies them for presuming to act as guardians of democracy.

Because courts are forever susceptible to this latter charge, their supporters have lately fastened on another justificatory strategy in which it is asserted that judges do not have the final word on the disposition of individual rights and freedoms but rather are engaged in a dialogue with elected legislatures over their interpretation. Proponents of the *dialogue thesis* contend that so long as a judicial decision is capable of being reversed, modified, or avoided by ordinary legislative means, then the relationship between courts and legislatures should be regarded as a conversation rather than one of subordination and super-ordination (Hogg and Bushell 1997; Roach 2001). The Charter supposedly facilitates this dialogue because it features such clauses as sections 1 and 33, which offer legislatures room to contribute their own interpretations of contested constitutional values, and in some instances ignore entirely their judicial explication.

Evidence of a genuine dialogue, it should be pointed out, has been disputed.[21] Even proponents of the thesis disagree over whether courts, legislatures, or executives guide the process (Hiebert 2002; Kelly 2005). These reservations notwithstanding, courts are for obvious reasons attracted to the dialogue thesis because it makes judicial review appear a benign exercise in value discovery. It is not surprising, therefore, that shortly after the pioneering Hogg and Bushell dialogue article was published, Justice Iacobucci, writing for the majority of the Supreme Court, cited it approvingly in the *Vriend* case, remarking that "dynamic interaction among branches of government … has aptly been described as a 'dialogue'" (para 139). Even more telling, Chief Justice McLachlin and Justice Iacobucci, again writing for the majority in *R v Mills* [1999], referred to the dialogue thesis in support of their decision not to overrule the federal government's amended "rape-shield" law, even though that law departed from what the Court had previously announced would be constitutionally acceptable (para 57). Governments also have gravitated to this portrayal of judicial power. For instance, after courts in British Columbia, Ontario, and Quebec ruled separately that marriage must be open to same-sex couples, the federal government decided not to appeal, electing instead to recruit the Supreme Court as a political advisor by submitting to it a set of reference questions related to the constitutionality of same-sex marriage. The Department of Justice declared that in "taking this course of action, the Government of Canada is ensuring, through a dynamic dialogue between the Courts and Parliament, that our laws reflect the fundamental values of the Charter" (Canada, Department of Justice 2003).

This marked concern for public acceptance by both the Supreme Court and the federal government of the power of judicial review suggests that there is a much more fundamental process underlying the judicialization of politics than its critics are prepared to grant. This more fundamental process is nothing less than the recurrent legitimation crises experienced by executive-centred governments in the post-war period. Legitimation crisis is routinely described in social scientific literature as a situation where government fails to elicit sufficient allegiance to its authority. The roots of these crises are typically complex and multi-faceted. In Canada, for example, legitimacy crises of varying intensity emerged as the post-war pattern of elite accommodation, predicated on the creation of a regulatory and welfare state, began to decompose in face of accelerated social change. Among these changes was a breakdown in the political compromise between French and English Canada at a time when other identities demanded acknowledgment in something other than a narrowly construed binational state. This period also witnessed a growing economic enfranchisement of women, with accompanying demands for equal treatment. At the same time, the ideal of the nuclear family increasingly became contested and the presumptive norms of heterosexuality more openly defied. Added to these bids for recognition and equitable treatment, struggles between capital and labour, never entirely displaced during the formation of the welfare state, gained a new salience as neo-liberalism emerged as a dominant economic and political paradigm. And that paradigm itself, no less than its welfarist predecessor, encountered escalated attacks by opponents of immoderate economic growth, a consumerist culture, and widening inequalities.

While these diverse political currents presented challenges to settled democratic norms and practices, they were also opposed by the very interests and institutions most closely associated with the post-war regulatory and welfare state. In these circumstances, where many of the new movements found their claims marginalized and their political ventures effectively organized out of established democratic pathways, it is not surprising that some would seek to influence public policy through the courts. Nor should it be surprising that the judiciary might sometimes be solicitous of these otherwise disempowered groups. After all, one of the by-products of the post-war political settlement was the relative decline of the Supreme Court's constitutional purpose, as witnessed in its dwindling number of federalism cases. The Charter made it possible for the Court to redefine its constitutional role as defender of "discrete and insular" minorities[22] just at the time that the legitimacy of existing democratic practices, and the distribution of goods and services they have underwritten, increasingly came to be assailed, and politics-as-usual more difficult to pursue.[23]

It is in the confluence of these events that the judicialization of politics gains its significance, both as an emerging political reality and as an object of normative critique. While this phenomenon has provoked a great deal of concern and demands for reform ranging from a more transparent appointments procedure to an outright curbing of the courts, rather less attention has been paid to the underlying circumstances that have sustained the judiciary's growing political prominence and the counter-tendencies that have worked to moderate it. Of the latter, suffice it to say that as courts become more of a focal point in public policy debates that polarize Canadians, they too risk having their legitimacy undermined, particularly when they are involved in fundamental questions about entitlements, both public and private. Perhaps it has been a recognition of just such a risk that has led to the marked decrease in Charter cases reaching the Supreme Court. This waning of Charter jurisprudence is matched by another noteworthy development – the growing inclination of the Court to construe Charter violations more narrowly, either as instances of misconduct by state officials (for example, police officers) or procedural defects in impugned legislation, thereby averting direct quarrels with legislatures over substantive issues in law.

This is not to say that the Court has been entirely absent from politics in recent years, as has been so amply demonstrated in its rulings on the Harper government's crime control laws, or even more vividly, in its judgment declaring ineligible that government's Supreme Court nominee, Justice Marc Nadon.[24] Given the way the Charter has come to inspire litigation strategies involving public law, the Court will never be able to withdraw from politically charged cases. Nor can its members, as divided as the rest of the population over fundamental political values, convincingly maintain that they are unmoved by political considerations in their judgments. Opponents of judicial politics too often imagine a judiciary somehow limited to a world of legal principles safely distanced from the contests over power that obtain in democratic arena. If, however, political power and legal principles are not so easily separable, then the vision of a sequestered court may be illusory. It may also distract us from more fruitful lines of empirical inquiry concerning the process of democratic demand-setting and the periodic eruption of judicial policy-making. As for the aptitude of Canadian courts to resist authoritarian populism remarked upon at the beginning of this chapter, that too is politically contingent, in no small part determined by the process by which judges are elevated to superior courts, as history continues to show.

Notes

1 Among some legal commentators there is an assumption that division of powers rulings are politically less consequential because the logical implication of such a ruling is that if one level of government in a federal state does not have the authority over a particular matter, the other does, and hence courts cannot impede public policy but merely

redirect its source. The problem with this position is that legal equivalence doesn't imply equal political capacity, a point driven home when both the Supreme Court and the JCPC ruled in the midst of the Great Depression in re Employment Social Insurance Act, 1937 that the subject matter of unemployment insurance remained within the jurisdiction of the provinces, notwithstanding the fiscal incapacity of provinces to offer such a program.

2 These positions, known respectively as originalism, textualism, and strict constructionism, are most commonly used in American jurisprudential debates and have been associated with the views of conservative judges such as Robert Bork, Antonin Scalia, and the recently appointed Brett Kavanaugh.

3 While it is widely assumed that the living tree approach is more characteristic of Canadian jurisprudence, some legal scholars and jurists advocate interpretative strategies that resemble the doctrines of originalism and textualism. See, for example, the contributions in Huscroft and Brodie (2004) and Huscroft and Miller (2011). For an argument that originalism is not absent in Canadian Supreme Court rulings, see Oliphant (2015).

4 A classic illustration was *Bush v Gore* (2000), where the ostensibly restrained conservative judges on the US Supreme Court devised a novel constitutional principle to stop the recount of the vote in Florida as prescribed by state law, thus ensuring the election of George W. Bush as president.

5 The Supreme Court upheld rights claims under the Bill of Rights cases only five times, four of which involved reading into federal criminal law due process requirements. The lone federal law that the Court invalidated under the Bill of Rights was a provision of the Indian Act in *R v Drybones* [1970] (Morton 1986, 5).

6 Success rates in Charter cases are not always a reliable measure of judicial activism. For example, in 2013–17, the average success rate has been almost 50 per cent (thirty-six out of seventy-five cases in which Charter arguments had been made). But when these figures are analyzed further, that rate seems less imposing. To start with, two-fifths of the successful Charter claims involved acts of public officials, such as police officers overstepping their power of search and seizure, or indefensible protracted proceedings in criminal trials. While these results may have some broad public policy implications, they are generally rendered in ways that are case specific. As for the cases involving statutes or regulations, roughly half have involved easily repairable procedural issues.

7 For opposing views on the wisdom of including section 33 in the Charter, see Whyte (1990) and Russell (1991).

8 See, for example, Russell (1983) and Cairns (1992).

9 See, for example, Woehrling (2009) and Brouillet (2005).

10 These data are taken from Kelly (1999), Monahan (2002), and a statistical analysis of Supreme Court cases 2002–17 undertaken by the author.

11 For example, in 2013–17, of the eleven federal and provincial laws or regulations found to be unconstitutional for substantive reasons, there were five such suspended declarations. Three involved federal laws on prostitution (*Bedford*, 2013), assisted suicide (*Carter*, 2015), and associational rights of the RCMP (*Mounted Police Association of Ontario,* 2015), and two involved provincial laws on protection of privacy (*Alberta v UFCW, Local 40,* 2013) and the right to collective bargaining (*Saskatchewan Federation of Labour*, 2015).

12 For example, during the same period, 2013–17, the Supreme Court read down or severed eight of the twenty-two federal or provincial laws or regulations it found to be in breach of the charter.

13 For an overview of the effects of Charter rulings on the Canadian criminal justice system, see Stuart (2017).

14 See *R v Grant,* 2009; *R v Cole,* 2012; *R v Aucoin,* 2012; *R v Spencer,* 2014.

15 See *R v Nur* (2015).

16 On this point see Jochelson (2009).

17 Former Chief Justice Beverley McLachlin, for instance, had protested that the Charter right to equality is the "most difficult right" (McLachlin 2001). The Supreme Court's jurisprudence certainly bears out this observation, as evidenced by the often sharp disagreements amongst the justices over how to understand this constitutional guarantee.

18 The term *counter-majoritarian* was coined by the American legal scholar Alexander Bickel (1986) when writing about the civil rights jurisprudence of the Warren Court.

19 The cautionary tale left critics of the court most frequently invoke when warning of the reactionary potential of a bill of rights is the regrettable *Lochner* era in US constitutional history. For most of the first three decades of the twentieth century a very conservative US Supreme Court elevated the reference to property rights in the fourteenth amendment into nothing short of a constitutional warrant for laissez-faire capitalism, in the process continually striking down progressive legislation passed by state and federal governments.

20 For right-leaning critics it is also a US judicial episode – the vigorous civil rights program and due process decisions of the Warren Court – that stands as the embodiment of all that can go wrong with an unbridled judiciary.

21 See Manfredi and Kelly (1999) and the reply furnished by Hogg and Thornton (1999). See also Choudhry and Hunter (2003), whose study

of judicial activism casts doubt on the claim that the Supreme Court frequently strikes down majoritarian legislation.

22 The phrase "discrete and insular minorities" was introduced by Justice Stone of the United States Supreme Court in his oft-cited footnote in *United States v Carolene Products Co.* [1938], where he proposes that the Court defer to the legislatures in economic policy but subject to "more exacting judicial scrutiny" legislation that relies on prejudices against minorities. The same phrase appeared in Canadian jurisprudence as the Court attempted to devise a credible test for applying the section 15 equality right (Hogg 2002, 52.7.g).

23 Doubtless it was this sense of political paralysis that led a chagrined Chief Justice Lamar to complain that the reason the Supreme Court has become involved in policy issues in the era of the Charter is because "too often timid politicians have been afraid to confront them directly." Lamar cited in Greene et al. (1998, 194).

24 Justice Marc Nadon of the Federal Court of Canada had been appointed to the Supreme Court by the Harper government in 2013 to a vacancy that under the Supreme Court Act could be filled only by a superior or appeal court judge from Quebec, or by a lawyer with at least ten years' standing at the Quebec Bar. After his appointment was challenged in court, the government referred the question of Justice Nadon's eligibility to the Supreme Court. In a majority decision, the Court ruled that Justice Nadon was ineligible because he was not a member of the Quebec Bar at the time of his appointment. Reference re Supreme Court Act, ss 5 and 6, SCC 21, [2014] 1 SCR 433.

References and Suggested Readings

Alarie, Benjamin, and Andrew Green. 2009. "Charter Decisions in the McLachlin Era: Consensus and Ideology at the Supreme Court of Canada." *Supreme Court Law Review* 47 (2d): 475–511.

Bakan, Joel. 1997. *Just Words: Constitutional Rights and Social Wrongs.* Toronto: University of Toronto Press.

Bayefsky, Ann. 1987. "The Judicial Function under the Canadian *Charter of Rights and Freedoms.*" *McGill Law Journal* 32: 791–833.

Bickel, Alexander. 1986. *The Least Dangerous Branch: The Supreme Court at the Bar of Politics.* 2nd ed. New Haven, CT: Yale University Press.

Brouillet, Eugénie. 2005. *La négation de la nation: l'identité québécoise et le fédéralisme canadien.* Quebec: Septrentrion.

Bushnell, Ian. 1992. *The Captive Court: A Study of the Supreme Court of Canada.* Montreal and Kingston: McGill-Queen's University Press.

Cairns, Alan C. 1971. "The Judicial Committee and Its Critics." *Canadian Journal of Political Science* 4: 301–45.

———. 1992. *Charter versus Federalism*. Montreal and Kingston: McGill-Queen's University Press.

Canada, Department of Justice. 2003. "Backgrounder: Reference to the Supreme Court." http://canada.justice.gc.ca/en/news/nr/2003/doc30946.html (link no longer active).

Choudhry, Sujit, and Claire E. Hunter. 2003. "Measuring Judicial Activism on the Supreme Court of Canada: A Comment on Newfoundland (Treasury Board v NAPE." *McGill Law Journal* 48: 525–62.

CRIC. 2002. "The Charter: Dividing or Uniting Canadians?" The CRIC Papers 5. Montreal: Centre for Research and Information on Canada.

Epp, Charles R. 1998. *The Rights Revolution: Lawyers, Activists, and Supreme Courts in Comparative Perspective*. Chicago: University of Chicago Press.

Fletcher, Joseph, and Paul Howe. 2000. "Public Opinion and the Courts." *Choices* 6: 4–56.

Greene, Ian, Carl Baar, Peter McCormick, George Szablowski, and Martin Thomas. 1998. *Final Appeal: Decision-Making in Canadian Courts of Appeal*. Toronto: James Lorimer.

Hein, Gregory. 2000. "Interest Group Litigation and Canadian Democracy." *Choices* 6: 3–30.

Hiebert, Janet L. 2002. *Charter Conflicts: What Is Parliament's Role?* Montreal and Kingston: McGill-Queen's University Press.

Hogg, Peter W. 2002. *Constitutional Law in Canada*. Student ed. Toronto: Carswell.

Hogg, Peter W., and Allison Bushell. 1997. "The Charter Dialogue between Courts and Legislatures (Or Perhaps the Charter of Rights Isn't Such a Bad Thing after All)." *Osgoode Hall Law Journal* 35: 75–124.

Hogg, Peter W., and Allison Thornton. 1999. "Reply to 'Six Degrees of Dialogue.'" *Osgoode Hall Law Journal* 37: 529–36.

Huscroft, Grant, and Ian Brodie, eds. 2004. *Constitutionalism in the Charter Era*. Markham, ON: LexisNexis Butterworths.

Huscroft, Grant, and Bradley W. Miller, eds. 2011. *The Challenge of Originalism: Theories of Constitutional Interpretation*. New York: Cambridge University Press.

Hutchinson, Alan C. 1995. *Waiting for CORAF: A Critique of Law and Rights*. Toronto: University of Toronto Press.

Ignatieff, Michael. 2008. *The Rights Revolution*. Toronto: House of Anansi.

Jochelson, Richard. 2009. "After *Labaye*: The Harm Test of Obscenity, the New Judicial Vacuum, and the Relevance of Familiar Voices." *Alberta Law Review* 46 (3): 741–67.

Kelly, James B. 1999. "The Charter of Rights and Freedoms and the Rebalancing of Liberal Constitutionalism in Canada, 1982–1997." *Osgoode Hall Law Journal* 37: 625–95.

———. 2005. *Governing with the Charter: Legislative and Judicial Activism and Framers' Intent*. Vancouver: UBC Press.

Laforest, Guy. 1992. "La *Charte* canadienne des droits et liberté au Québec: nationaliste, injuste et illégitimate." In *Bilan québécois du fédéralisme canadien*, edited by François Rocher, 124–51. Montreal: VLB.

———. 2009. "The Internal Exile of Quebecers in the Canada of the Charter." In *Contested Constitutionalism: Reflections of the Canadian Charter of Rights and Freedoms*, edited by C.P. Manfredi and James Kelly. Vancouver: UBC Press.

Leclair, Jean. 2003. "Réflexions critiques au sujet de la métaphore du dialogue en droit constitutionnel canadien." *Revue du Barreau* (numéro spécial) 379: 402–12.

Leishman, Rory. 2006. *Against Judicial Activism: The Decline of Freedom and Democracy in Canada*. Montreal and Kingston: McGill-Queen's University Press.

Lowrie, Morgan. 2019. "Legault Defends Quebec's Religious-Symbols Bill, Calls Notwithstanding Clause 'Legitimate Tool.'" *Globe and Mail*, March 31. https://www.theglobeandmail.com/canada/article-legault-defends-quebecs-religious-symbols-bill-calls-notwithstanding/.

MacCharles, Tonda. 2018. "Canada's Top Judge Says Supreme Court Should Provide Leadership at a Time When Fundamental Values Are Being Undermined in the World." *Toronto Star*, June 22. https://www.thestar.com/news/canada/2018/06/22/canadas-top-judge-says-supreme-court-should-provide-leadership-at-a-time-when-fundamental-values-are-being-undermined-in-the-world.html.

MacFarlane, Emmett. 2013. "Supreme Confusion." *Policy Options*, March, 45–8.

Makin, Kirk. 2008. "Top Court Takes More Time on Fewer Decisions." *Globe and Mail*, April 18, A4.

———. 2013a. "Justice Department Whistleblower on a Crusade to Sustain the Rule of Law." *Globe and Mail*, February 23. http://www.theglobeandmail.com/news/national/justice-department-whistleblower-on-a-crusade-to-sustain-the-rule-of-law/article9001991/.

———. 2013b. "Supreme Court Becoming 'Charter-Averse,' Expert Says." *Globe and Mail*, April 12. http://www.theglobeandmail.com/news/national/supreme-court-becoming-charter-averse-expert-says/article11177678/.

———. 2013c. "Supreme Court Needs More Women, Departing Judge Says." *Globe and Mail*, February 2. http://www.theglobeandmail.com/news/national/supreme-court-needs-more-women-departing-judge-says/article8149711/.

Mandel, Michael. 1994. *The Charter of Rights and the Legalization of Politics in Canada*. Rev. ed. Toronto: Thompson Educational Publishing.

Manfredi, Christopher P. 2001. *Judicial Power and the Charter: Canada and the Paradox of Liberal Constitutionalism*. 2nd ed. Don Mills, ON: Oxford University Press.

———. 2007. "The Day the Dialogue Died: A Comment on Sauvé v. Canada." *Osgoode Hall Law Journal* 45 (1): 105–23.

Manfredi, Christopher P., and James Kelly. 1999. "Six Degrees of Dialogue: A Response to Hogg and Bushell." *Osgoode Hall Law Journal* 37: 513–27.

Martin, Robert I. 2003. *The Most Dangerous Branch: How the Supreme Court Has Undermined Our Law and Our Democracy*. Montreal and Kingston: McGill-Queen's University Press.

McCormick, Peter. 2000. *Supreme at Last: The Evolution of the Supreme Court of Canada*. Toronto: James Lorimer.

———. 2004. "Blocs, Swarms and Outliers: Conceptualizing Disagreement on the Modern Supreme Court." *Osgoode Hall Law Journal* 42: 99–138.

———. 2015. *The End of the Charter Revolution: Looking Back from the New Normal*. Toronto: University of Toronto Press.

McLachlin, Beverley C.J. 2001. "Equality: The Most Difficult Right." *Supreme Court Law Review* 14: 17–27.

Monahan, Patrick. 1987. *Politics and the Constitution: The Charter, Federalism and the Supreme Court of Canada*. Toronto: Carswell/Methuen.

———. 2002. "The Charter at Twenty." April 13. Paper delivered at the Charter at Twenty Conference, Professional Development Programme Centre, Osgoode Hall, Toronto.

Montigny, Yves De. 1997. "The Impact (Real or Apprehended) of the Canadian Charter of Rights and Freedoms on the Legislative Authority of Quebec." In *Charting the Consequences: The Impact of the Charter of Rights and Freedoms on Canadian Law and Politics*, edited by David Schneiderman and Kate Sutherland, 3–33. Toronto: University of Toronto Press.

Morton, F.L. 1986. "The Political Impact of the Charter of Rights." Occasional Papers Series, Research Study 2.2. Research Unit for Socio-Legal Studies, University of Calgary, Calgary.

Morton, F.L., and Rainer Knopff. 2000. *The Charter Revolution and the Court Party*. Peterborough, ON: Broadview.

Morton, F.L., Peter H. Russell, and Troy Riddell. 1994. "The Canadian Charter of Rights and Freedoms: A Descriptive Analysis of the First Decade, 1982–1992." *National Journal of Constitutional Law* 5: 1–69.

Nanos, Nik. 2007. "Charter Values Don't Equal Canadian Values: Strong Support for Same-Sex and Property Rights." *Policy Options*, February, 50–5.

Oliphant, Benjamin. 2015. "Originalism in Canadian Constitutional Law." *Policy Options*, June 25.

Ostberg, C.L., and Matthew E. Wetstein. 2007. *Attitudinal Decision-Making in the Supreme Court of Canada*. Vancouver: UBC Press.

Parkin, Andrew. 2002. "The Charter and Judicial Activism: An Analysis of Public Opinion." *Windsor Yearbook of Access to Justice* 21: 361–84.

Petter, Andrew. 1987. "The Immaculate Deception: The Charter's Hidden Agenda." *Advocate* 45: 857–66.

Roach, Kent. 2001. *The Supreme Court on Trial: Judicial Activism or Democratic Dialogue*. Toronto: Irwin Law.

Russell, Peter H. 1982. "The Effect of a Charter of Rights on the Policy-Making Role of Canadian Courts." *Canadian Public Administration* 25: 1–33.

———. 1983. "The Political Purposes of the Canadian *Charter of Rights and Freedoms*." *Canadian Bar Review* 61: 30–54.

———. 1987. *The Judiciary in Canada: The Third Branch of Government*. Toronto: McGraw-Hill Ryerson.

———. 1991. "Standing Up for Notwithstanding." *Alberta Law Review* 29: 293–309.

Smith, Jennifer. 1983. "The Origins of Judicial Review in Canada." *Canadian Journal of Political Science* 16: 115–34.

Smith, Miriam C. 2002. "Ghosts of the JCPC: Group Politics and Charter Litigation in Canadian Political Science." *Canadian Journal of Political Science* 35: 13–29.

Snell, James G., and Frederick Vaughn. 1985. *The Supreme Court of Canada: History of the Institution*. Toronto: University of Toronto Press.

Stuart, Don. 2017. "The Charter and Criminal Justice." In *The Oxford Handbook of the Canadian Constitution*, edited by Peter Oliver et al., 795–814. New York: Oxford University Press.

Trudeau, Pierre E. 1968. *Federalism and the French-Canadians*. Toronto: Macmillan of Canada.

Valiante, Giuseppe. 2018. "Quebec Ready to Reform Family Law to Protect Children of Common-Law Spouses." Canadian Press, November 21. https://globalnews.ca/news/4687415/quebec-ready-to-reform-family-law-to-protect-children-of-common-law-spouses/.

Whyte, John D. 1990. "On Not Standing for Notwithstanding." *Alberta Law Review* 28: 347–57.

Woehrling, José. 2009. "The Charter of Rights and Freedoms and Its Consequences for Political and Democratic Life and the Federal System." In *Contemporary Canadian Federalism: Foundations, Traditions, Institutions*, edited by Alain-G. Gagnon, 224–49. Toronto: University of Toronto Press.

ten

Five Faces of Quebec: Shifting Small Worlds and Evolving Political Dynamics[1]

ALAIN-G. GAGNON

Introduction

The choice of concepts and narratives in the world of politics is not a question of details but rather it is a way to establish a world view, to order priorities, or – stated more simply – to advance a political posture. So it is not insignificant when political leaders in a federal system speak of *levels* of government rather than *orders* of government; or utilize the notion of subnational units to discuss multinational states; or substitute region for founding member of a federation. Similarly, in the Canadian context it matters when scholars of federalism and politicians alike use the notions of federal government, central government, or the Government of Canada interchangeably. This confuses lines of authority and power relations in the mindset of citizens by subtly suggesting that it does not matter where, how, or by whom decisions are being made.[2]

Richard Simeon made an important point when he stated more than forty years ago that the concept of "regions [and other concepts for this matter] are simply containers ... and how we draw the boundaries around them depends entirely on what our purposes are: it is an *a priori* question, determined by theoretical needs or political purposes" (Simeon 1977, 293). Consequently, when discussing Quebec, it is important to come to terms with the objectives being pursued by individuals, groups, and communities as well as political parties and political entrepreneurs in positions of influence and authority. Various uses of key concepts such as political nationality, nation, distinct society, province state, and multinational democracy have a significant impact on the way one imagines constituent units in federal states. My intention in this chapter is to introduce the main faces or images of Quebec and the political narratives that have surfaced and resurfaced since the beginning of the Quiet Revolution in Quebec (Gagnon and Montcalm 1990) and to assess their impact on the mindset of Canadians and Quebecers. I want to make clear at the outset that I have chosen not to include the notion of a *stateless nation* to depict Quebec, as this political community has developed for itself major state apparatuses; whether in para-diplomacy, education, culture, economy, or intergovernmental matters, Quebec's activity in these areas would make many countries envious of its accomplishments. Nor will I make use of the concepts of *minority nation* or *global society* to discuss Quebec-Canada dynamics, since Quebecers generally conceive of themselves as forming one of the two principal political communities in the country (see Brouillet, Gagnon, and Laforest 2018).

Accordingly, in this chapter I will focus on five political faces[3] of Quebec: Quebec as a key partner in the formation of a new political nationality; Quebec as a founding nation in a dualist (binational) Canada, supporting the principle of co-sovereignty; Quebec as a province state that has led the battle for provincial rights and provincial autonomy; Quebec as a distinct society within Canada; and, finally, Quebec as a multinational democracy in its own right.

Face 1: Political Nationality

In the construction of narratives, the place of history matters a great deal (Bouchard 2013), as we will see with the first image of Quebec to be discussed. Canada's beginning is characterized by a series of political events that have had a major impact on how Canadians see themselves. For instance: were French Canadians conquered by the British or did France simply cede its territory north of what is now the United States to its archrival? Was Confederation a compact between the French and the English cohabiting on Canadian soil, or was it a political arrangement between the four original provinces and the British imperial government? Who was the depository of sovereignty in 1867, or, stated differently, who formed the constituent power(s) in the new federation? Contradictory answers have been provided to these questions based on either people's vision of the original compact or the influence exercised by one's dominant identity. George-Étienne Cartier remains a key political figure for Canada, not only at the time of Confederation but throughout the last century and a half. Cartier wanted the new federation, of which he was a founding father, to be built on political allegiance and loyalty to the country as a whole. This loyalty, however, was not to be based on linguistic or cultural belonging. Cartier promoted a political unity that would be respectful of cultural diversity. His understanding of the Canadian experiment, to borrow from Donald Smiley, was that it was a "noble vision" (Smiley 1967, 128) that repudiated parochialism, majority nationalism, and imperialism; that it did not seek to "impose a single way of life on its citizens" (LaSelva 1996, 24). "Confederation would be unacceptable if French and English had come together merely to war with each other; it would be equally unacceptable if it created an all-inclusive Canadian nationalism. If Confederation was to succeed, it had to create a new kind of nationality, which Cartier called a political nationality" (25). A noble vision, perhaps, but it should be pointed out that this vision failed to provide the core values and claims that would give substance and meaning to being Canadian, while at the same time respecting other political identities.

Cartier made it clear that French Canadians would not renounce their distinct culture and identity because of Confederation. They would form a national community of their own, respectful of different value systems with which "neither the national origin, nor religion of any individual would interfere" (LaSelva 1996, 25). That being said, in the years after Confederation the advent of a political community such as the one imagined by Cartier failed to materialize. Instead, the first seven decades of Canadian history can be depicted as a political tug-of-war between the central government in Ottawa and determined, assertive provincial governments such as Ontario under Mitchell Hepburn (1934–42) and Quebec under Maurice Duplessis (1936–9, 1944–59) (Gagnon and Iacovino 2007). This is why historians such as J.M.S. Careless have depicted this condition of intergovernmental friction as being the expression of "limited identities," further arguing that Canada was not reducible to a single identity under which all other identities could be subsumed (Careless 1969).

A point worth mentioning here is the role played by the Judicial Committee of the Privy Council (JCPC), which was Canada's final court of appeal until the Supreme Court took on this role in 1949. The JCPC was instrumental in defending the rights and powers of member states of the Canadian federation and thereby protecting their "limited identities." This contributed to making Quebecers strong defenders of British parliamentary traditions and practices, while encouraging them to continue their support for the Canadian federation.

It is important to recognize the growing capacity of the central government, along with the nine predominantly anglophone provinces, to replace Cartier's original notion of political nationality with their preferred concept of Canada as a single, all-encompassing nation (Gagnon 2010). This sidelining of Cartier's vision has contributed to the alienation of many Quebecers from the Canadian state, and from the version of Canadian federalism that became predominant. This point is well made in the Quebec government's 2017 constitutional position paper, which states that while the federal compromise was initially consistent with the French-Canadian national reality, "the failure to take into account Québec's national reality in contemporary constitutional developments has been the main source of the difficulties experienced by Quebec in fully adhering to Canada" (Quebec 2017, 96).

Face 2: The Two-Nations View

The second image of Quebec imagines it as one of two founding nations at the origin of Canada's federal pact. Again, it was George-Étienne Cartier who best expressed this two-nations view, without contradicting his more subsuming concept of Canada as a new political nationality. In 1867, Cartier made a statement that would become familiar to Quebecers as it was repeated throughout the decades. In Cartier's own words, "Such is … the significance that we must attach to this constitution, which recognizes the French-Canadian nationality. As a distinct, separate nationality, we form a State within a State with the full use of our rights and the formal recognition of our national independence."[4] For Quebec, what mattered most about the constitutional deal embodied in the 1867 BNA Act, as we shall see, was that Quebec's civil law tradition was formally recognized, that provincial autonomy was guaranteed in matters dealing with education and culture, and further that social policies and language would fall under the jurisdiction of Quebec. Those terms of union were central in the eyes of French Canadians who saw them as emblematic of the principle of equality between two founding peoples.

The image of a dualist Canada has been consistently used, although mostly by French Canadians, to depict Quebec-Canada dynamics. It portrays Canada as the constitutional expression of a compact that brought together two nations or, stated differently, two equal peoples with minority linguistic and religious guarantees secured throughout the country as a matter of respect and as a matter of right. Historian Ramsay Cook, at the time of the Laurendeau-Dunton commission on bilingualism and biculturalism in the 1960s, depicted this view: "In the attempt to protect and extend the rights of the religious and linguistic minorities, the theory of Confederation as a compact between cultures, an Anglo-French entente, was developed. According to this theory, Confederation was a partnership of equal cultures whose rights were guaranteed mutually throughout the whole Confederation. It can be said that by 1921 the doctrine of provincial rights and its compact underpinnings had gained the ascendant among Canadian politicians, and was at least partly accepted by legal scholars" (Cook 1969, 65).

While the two-nation view gained some prominence from 1867 to the end of the 1920s, it remains that some prominent English-Canadian historians (Frank Underhill and, more recently, Jack Granatstein and Michael Bliss) refer to Canada as a single nation, showing a lack of sensitivity toward the original constitutive components of the federation (Gagnon and Dionne 2009, 10–50).

In contrast, the young Pierre Trudeau, in reference to Canada's early history, remarked in 1962 that "British Canadians gave themselves the illusion of it [equating the Canadian state with the British Canadian nation] by walling in, as far as possible, the French fact in the Quebec ghetto – whose powers were often clipped by centralizing measures – and by fighting with astonishing ferocity against all symbols which could have destroyed this illusion outside Quebec" (Trudeau 1962, 52–3).

This two-nations interpretation gives credit to the view that "Canada" came into being through the voluntary consent of the two main political communities. However, there has been debate on this issue, as English-Canadian politicians and Ottawa bureaucrats at different junctures have attempted to reinterpret Canada's key formative moment and have tried to impose the view that "Canada" predated the creation of the four original provinces (Lower Canada, Upper Canada, Nova Scotia, and New Brunswick).

In contrast, the two-nations view of Confederation argues that, upon entering the Canadian federation in 1867, Quebec possessed its own political identity and maintained some of its original powers and institutions; this had been formalized by the British Crown almost a century before in the Quebec Act of 1774. With Confederation, Quebec consented to share some of its powers while relinquishing others to the newly formed federal government. Political philosopher James Tully has argued in connection with this point that "the acts of confederation did not discontinue the long-standing legal and political cultures of the former colonies and impose a uniform legal and political culture, but, rather, recognized and continued their constitutional cultures in a diverse federation in which the consent of each province was given" (Tully 1994, 84–5).

Tully's position has been profoundly influenced by a school of thought rooted in legal pluralism that was clearly influenced by legal experts such as Judge Thomas-Jean-Jacques Loranger and Judge P.B. Mignault. Loranger summarized his interpretation in his famous 1883 Letters on the Constitution.[5] That interpretation was later consolidated and further developed by Mignault, who elaborated on the concepts of shared, divided, and common sovereignties.

We said that the contracting parties (the federal and the provincial governments) divide their sovereignty and create through common and reciprocal concessions a new power that contains them without absorbing them. We must draw one essential result from this. Each state or province maintains its own existence and the powers it has not yielded to the central government. The province is not subordinate to the central government, nor is the latter subordinate to the province. There is absolute equality and a common sovereignty;

each government is supreme within its own jurisdiction and within the scope of its power (P.-B. Mignault quoted in Ramsay Cook 1969, 66).

Michael Burgess and I have updated some of those well-anchored federal ideals in *Federal Democracies* (Burgess and Gagnon 2010). Burgess continued this line of inquiry in more detail in another book, *In Search of the Federal Spirit* (Burgess 2012).

It should be noted that this understanding of legal pluralism has been frequently restated and updated by Quebec representatives at government commissions throughout the years. Some examples are the Tremblay Commission (1953–6) and the Bélanger-Campeau Commission (1990–2), as well as during constitutional negotiations between Ottawa and the provinces.

So the image of Canada as a compact between two founding peoples has continued to be used by representatives of the Quebec government consistently since Confederation. In more recent times, however, and especially after the 1982 patriation of the Constitution from Britain, the two-nations view seems to have lost ground in the rest of Canada (ROC). This can be attributed in good part to the fact that the federal government has sought to speak as the national government of all Canadians and to impose its political authority accordingly. The receding of the two-nations view is also due to the fact that starting in the late 1960s there has been a growing schism between francophone communities evolving in a minority context in ROC and the Quebec government and people.[6] This is a matter that political scientists and historians alike have for too long neglected to research and understand.

To sum up, over time and especially between the beginning of the Quiet Revolution in 1960 and the 1982 Constitution Act, Canadians and Quebecers alike have tended to use the notion of dualism to depict the Canadian experiment (Wade and Falardeau 1960). However, in proceeding with the patriation of the Constitution from Britain and the adoption of the Charter of Rights, Ottawa imposed its view that Quebec ought to be considered as a province like any other. This constituted a major setback for defenders of the notion of Canada as a binational political community.

Let's turn our attention now to a third way of conceiving Quebec.

Face 3: Province State

For many decades, it has been acknowledged that Quebec is not a province like the others, as most students of Quebec politics quickly discover. This said, it remains clear that Quebec has always been at the forefront of political battles to uphold provincial rights. In fairness to other provinces, Quebec was never alone in doing so. It has been joined in the fight by provincial partners at different times, though over the past several decades Alberta and Newfoundland most often joined Quebec in defending provincial rights and autonomy in the Canadian federation.

Keith Brownsey and Michael Howlett have introduced the notion of a *provincial state* to depict provinces in Canada since "they qualify as states. Not only are they constitutionally empowered to make binding decisions on their residents, they are shaped and defined by the very constitutional arrangements that give them their authority as much as they are by their internal class structures and external economic relations" (Brownsey and Howlett 2009, 14). To be clear, Canadian provinces and territories share significant institutional features that amount to state power. However, Brownsey and Howlett fail to recognize that Quebec is the only member of the federation that can truly be depicted as a *province state*, since the unique criterion of statehood resides in the international realm. In this connection, Quebec alone among Canadian provinces aspires to play such a role, not only within the Francophonie (the francophone nations) but as a leader among minority nations in the world seeking to obtain a larger political status for themselves (Gagnon 2014).

There is an important stream of political science literature in Canada that insists on the central role of Quebec as a historic champion of provincial rights. While that story is generally understood by all Canadians, it needs to be underlined here, considering its influence in the defence of provincial autonomy and the non-subordination of government powers – two central features of federalism.

The Confederation of 1867 embodies a strong defence of provincial rights, since the Constitution confirmed that powers were to be shared between a central state and provincial states, all of which were to be responsible for their own spheres of jurisdiction. A convention developed that the British North America (BNA) Act provided both the central and provincial governments with exclusive jurisdictions in those domains that were essential to their particular responsibilities and interests. This interpretation emerges clearly from the Quebec resolutions (known also as the Confederation proposal, Brouillet, Gagnon, and Laforest 2018). Quebecers cling to this interpretation of Confederation and have been consistent in asking that the spirit of 1867 be translated into appropriate political institutions and reflected in power relations.

The most refined depiction of Canada as a compact of provinces was provided by the previously mentioned Judge Loranger, one of Quebec's most influential jurists, who published a series of constitutional texts in 1883 that have had a long-lasting effect on Canadian jurisprudence. The most recent echoes can be found in the 1993 and 1995 reports tabled by the

Royal Commission on Aboriginal Peoples. The basic premises of Loranger's account of provincial rights are threefold:

- The confederation made up of the British provinces was the result of a compact entered into by the provinces and the United Kingdom.
- The provinces entered into the federal union with their corporate identity, former constitutions, and all their legislative powers intact. A portion of these powers was ceded to the federal Parliament, to exercise in the common interest of the provinces. The powers not ceded were retained by the provinces' legislatures, which continued to act within their own sphere according to their former constitutions, under certain modifications or established by the federal compact.
- The powers of the provinces were not conferred on them by the federal government; rather, they are the residue of their former colonial powers. The federal government is therefore the creation of the provinces, the result of their association and of their compact. (Canada, Royal Commission on Aboriginal Peoples 1993, 22–3)

This interpretation laid the foundation for a school of thought that supported provincial rights and provincial autonomy, exerting much influence within Quebec and some other provinces over the years. It is particularly noteworthy that Loranger's account has gone virtually unchallenged in Quebec. In contrast, many political leaders and federalist thinkers in ROC have usually rejected this view and argued instead that provinces are simply the creation of the central government and therefore subservient to it. At times, this fundamental disagreement created an uneasy relationship between certain provinces and the central government, as illustrated by intense conflicts between Ontario and Ottawa from the 1870s to the 1940s.

Before World War II, Liberal party leaders such as Wilfrid Laurier and Mackenzie King were inclined to support provincial rights as long as they did not weaken Ottawa's political leadership and authority. However, this defence of provincial rights at the federal level declined after World War II as a succession of prime ministers (mostly Liberal) sought to invest the central government in Ottawa with a dominant power position within the federation, especially under the leadership of Pierre Trudeau and Jean Chrétien.

The 1956 report of the Quebec Royal Commission of Inquiry on Constitutional Problems (the Tremblay Commission) was inspired by the Loranger doctrine. In that report, emphasis was given to the concepts of provincial autonomy and coordination between orders of government (Rocher 2009). Both autonomy and coordination were to operate in tandem; otherwise the federal spirit would not be fully expressed. On the basis of this understanding, it was possible (and perhaps even a duty) for a member state of the federation to refuse central government assistance to fully exercise its responsibilities as agreed to in the original compact. Building on the principle of subsidiarity and influenced by the social doctrine of the Catholic Church, the Tremblay Report argued that higher levels of authority should not seek to exercise powers that can be employed more effectively at lower levels: "Only federalism as a political system permits two cultures to live and develop side by side within a single state: that was the real reason for the Canadian state's federative form.... So, therefore, there can be no federalism without autonomy of the state's constituent parts, and no sovereignty of the various governments without fiscal and financial autonomy" (cited in Kwavnick 1973, 209, 215).

The Tremblay Report provided additional philosophical support to Loranger's earlier arguments. This historical and philosophical grounding has made Quebec's constitutional position both powerful and persistent, to the point that the First Nations have built their arguments upon it to advance their self-government claims, as have provinces such as Alberta and Newfoundland, from time to time, when seeking to defend provincial autonomy.

The Quiet Revolution pursued similar autonomist ambitions for Quebec and pushed them much further than at any time before (Gagnon and Montcalm 1990). This approach, known as the Gérin-Lajoie doctrine, argued for the extension of provincial jurisdictions beyond the borders of Canada: any provincial competence could be exercised vis-à-vis other provinces or nation-states as long as Quebec (or any provincial state) was willing to assume its sovereign powers in areas of exclusive provincial jurisdiction (Paquin 2006).

The Gérin-Lajoie doctrine attempted to shore up the role of Quebec as a province state by giving substance and meaning to Quebec's special status within Confederation. This doctrine was elaborated toward the end of the second Lesage government in the mid-1960s and has been revamped at critical moments under successive Quebec governments, whether liberal in orientation under Premiers Robert Bourassa and Jean Charest or inclined toward social democracy under governments led by René Lévesque and Pauline Marois. The Gérin-Lajoie doctrine remains a constitutional position universally agreed to by key provincial actors in Quebec, and it supports Quebec's intention to play a central role in Confederation. Brian Mulroney's decision to grant Quebec the status of a participating government in the Francophonie starting in 1985 was inspired by the respect he had for the Gérin-Lajoie doctrine. One can make a similar remark about Stephen Harper's decision to allow Quebec to play a significant role within the Canadian delegation at UNESCO starting in 2006.

Quebec has been (and continues to be) at the forefront of battles to defend provincial rights, to prevent Ottawa from intruding into provincial domains of competence, and to roll back such intrusion where it has already occurred. The best example is provided by the leadership played by Quebec in the establishment of the Council of the Federation in 2003, in large part due to the determination of Quebec's former minister of intergovernmental affairs, Benoît Pelletier. During his tenure, Pelletier continued to push for the notion of provincial autonomy and made it palatable to government leaders in many other provinces. He spoke at dozens of meetings across the country during the years that followed the election of the first Charest government in 2003, making the following important statement at each:

> In its universal aspect, the federal formula implies the existence of two orders of government, each being sovereign in the exercise of their constitutional jurisdictions. However, certain conditions must be met in order for any federation to be able to function and evolve in a healthy manner:
>
> 1. There must be a balanced distribution of powers between the two orders of government.
> 2. Each order of government must have the capacity, in tax resources, to fully and adequately assume its responsibilities. No order of government should find itself in a position of financial dependence vis-à-vis the other.
> 3. The provinces must have the possibility to express their views on the governance of the federation and have a certain influence on the federal legislative process. As an example, this could be accomplished through a truly effective second house of the federal Parliament, or other equivalent body, where the provinces could assert their points of view and, in so doing, have a real and positive influence on the future of our federation.
> 4. Effective mechanisms must be put in place to foster intergovernmental dialogue in sectors where convergence is required between a priori divergent interests. (Pelletier 2004)

Quebec has advanced the cause of provincial rights through different means since the end of World War II. In this regard, let's mention a few constitutional and political battles that have taken place since then: on taxation, Quebec has fought to regain control over its tax regime and to expand its fiscal powers; on the constitutional front, Quebec has supported the idea of granting all provinces a right of veto over constitutional changes; on the question of social programs, Quebec has insisted that each province could exercise its right to withdraw from a national program that fell within provincial jurisdiction, with full compensation.

Face 4: Distinct Society

In the early 1980s, constitutionalist Gil Rémillard (who later became Quebec minister of intergovernmental affairs) portrayed the BNA Act as a "constitutional treaty that would permit [French Canadians] to assert themselves as a distinct people on an equal footing with the Anglophone majority" (Rémillard 1980, 112; also cited in O'Neal 1995, 3). Politicians and intellectuals alike have used the phrase "distinct society" (and "distinct people") to convey the idea that Quebec possesses a specific culture in North America: a culture that has been shaped by its French language, its Catholic heritage, its civilist tradition, and its British parliamentary institutions. Over the years, the notion of distinct society has been transformed to mean a deep commitment to public policies based on a pronounced social solidarity in education, culture, child care, and the third sector or non-profit segment of the economy, as well as regional development and a more activist and corporatist approach to economic development.

Notions such as *special status* for Quebec or Quebec as forming a *distinct society* have often been viewed with suspicion, as they could constitute a slippery slope pointing toward Quebec's secession. Pierre Trudeau was very keen to undermine the distinct society concept during his tenure as Canada's prime minister (1968–79, 1980–4). However, historian Ramsay Cook reminds us that the idea of Quebec as a distinct society has been present in Canada since the very beginning of Confederation, although we should stress that the use of the notion has been popularized only during the last half of the twentieth century. For example, Cook writes, "Section 94 recognized the civil law of Quebec as distinct and, if the intent expressed in that provision had been fulfilled ('uniformity of all and any laws relative to Property and Civil' in all provinces except Quebec), Quebec would have had a 'special status' in that area. In addition the special character of Quebec was recognized in Section 133 which not only made French, for the first time, an official language of Canada, but also made Quebec alone among the original provinces, bilingual" (Cook 1989, 149–50).

In other words, Quebec's distinct identity was a pillar of the BNA Act of 1867 and, as we are reminded by the Erasmus-Dussault Commission on Aboriginal Peoples, "The distinct character of the Quebec civil law system was reflected in a clause that allowed the Parliament of Canada to make provision for uniformity of laws in all federating provinces except for Quebec, thus recognizing an asymmetrical element in Confederation" (Canada, Royal Commission on Aboriginal Peoples 1993, 25).

The notion of distinct society forcefully entered the political milieu in the late 1950s in the wake of the Tremblay Commission (discussed above), as Quebec's provincial political parties tried to identify the best ways to assert Quebec's place within the Canadian federation. Public intellectuals and politicians rallied to make clear to other partners in the Canadian federation that Quebec needed special instruments to protect the institutions, values, and culture that made Quebec so unique in North America (see Laforest with Mesa 2014).

Over the years, the distinct society notion has been interpreted by competing political forces in several ways: as a dangerous concept that could lead to Canada's dismantling, as the way to an expanded set of privileges for Quebec, or as a political "sleight of hand" that proffered only cosmetic changes that would never satisfy Quebec's political claims and ambitions. In other words, the concept has been disqualified by both Canadian and Quebec nationalists, for opposite reasons, in the process largely discrediting the idea within the two main language communities.

Certainly some efforts have been made over the years to sensitize Canadians to the presence of Quebec as a distinct society. It is worth pointing out two of Ottawa's initiatives: the 1972 Special Joint Committee of the Senate and the House of Commons on the Constitution (see below) and the 1979 Task Force on Canadian Unity, known as the Pépin-Robarts Commission.

When the report of the Royal Commission on Bilingualism and Biculturalism was tabled in 1968, Ottawa decided to convene a federal-provincial conference to revamp the Constitution. Ottawa also struck a Special Joint Committee of the Senate and of the House of Commons on the Constitution to appraise potential changes. What matters here is not so much the committee's main report as the minority report signed by Martial Asselin and Pierre De Bané. Both opposed the main report because it did not mention that Quebec constitutes a distinct society in Canada: "Nevertheless … Quebec's society forms a distinct entity … which is gradually realizing that it cannot achieve its fullest development without a freedom for action and the presence of certain psychological conditions which it lacks at the present time" (De Bané and Asselin 1972, 8).[7] The two authors also heavily criticized the main report (and the Canadian Constitution) because "nowhere does it recognize the existence of a distinct Quebec society, a shortcoming which has real consequences" (10). This minority report was not well received in Ottawa and indeed most MPs chose to ignore it. Nevertheless, in hindsight, Asselin and De Bané had clearly identified a fundamental shortcoming of the Canadian Constitution.

Following the election of René Lévesque's Parti Québécois government in November 1976, the federal government in Ottawa launched its Task Force on Canadian Unity that would bring to the fore the concepts of regionalism and dualism. Members of the task force wrote extensively on the fact that Quebec forms a distinct society, stressing that "Quebec is distinctive and should, within a viable Canada, have the powers necessary to protect and develop its distinctive character[;] any political solution short of this would lead to the rupture of Canada" (Task Force on Canadian Unity 1979, 87). Language politics were specifically targeted by the task force, which endorsed key policies of the Quebec government, namely Law 101, backing "efforts of the Quebec provincial government and the people of Quebec to ensure the predominance of the French language and culture in that province" (51). Notably, this position was in direct opposition to the one adopted by the Liberal Party of Canada after Pierre Trudeau's election as party leader in 1968.

Members of the task force were concerned that their report might be viewed as encouragement for the development of asymmetrical federalism (whereby Quebec could exercise powers not available to other provinces); to avoid this – and the inevitable opposition it would generate in other parts of Canada – they recommended giving all provinces the chance to act within the same sphere of jurisdictions. They suggested granting "to all the provinces powers in the areas needed by Quebec to maintain its distinctive culture and heritage" (Task Force on Canadian Unity 1979, 87). Quebec's status as a distinct society would effectively be granted to all provinces (Gagnon 2002, 105–20). This approach – in effect, extending distinct society status to all provinces – rendered it much less significant politically. The idea that every province constituted a distinct society might have been a political framework that would gain acceptance in the rest of Canada, but it conflicted with Quebec's own vision of its place within Canada.

Nonetheless, the distinct society notion gained prominence within the federalist camp in Quebec, as it was viewed as the "bottom line" needed to preserve Canadian unity and respond to Quebec's claim to self-determination. The concept is present throughout the Quebec Liberal Party's *Beige Paper* (1980) to advance the federalist cause in Quebec at the time of the first Quebec referendum, scheduled to take place on May 20, 1980. Federal Liberals, though never at ease with the notion, strategically agreed not to air their disagreement with their provincial allies in view of the need to maintain a common front in the referendum. Subsequently, "distinct society" would become a rallying cry to convince Quebecers to support the 1987 Meech Lake Accord negotiated with the provinces by Prime Minister Brian Mulroney and designed to bring Quebec back into the federal fold following its rejection of the 1982 constitutional settlement. Though the federal Liberals (then under the leadership of John Turner) were divided over the wisdom of the Accord, in the end all the parties in Parliament voted in favour of it. On the other hand, former Prime Minister Pierre Trudeau catalyzed opposition by arguing that recognition of Quebec as a distinct society would encourage secessionist aspirations and provide Quebec with special privileges that would undermine the principle of equality of the provinces.

Though the failure of the Meech Lake Accord ensured that the distinct society concept would never be entrenched in the Constitution, it was used by the Mulroney government to revamp an intergovernmental accord on immigration between Quebec and Ottawa, and later, following the second referendum in Quebec in 1995, by Jean Chrétien's Liberals when passing a motion in the House of Commons stating that Quebec formed a distinct society within Canada.[8] Since then, the once hotly contested notion of distinct society has received surprisingly little attention, especially in Quebec, where other ideas or visions have superseded it, including the political image of Quebec as a multinational democracy.

Face 5: Multinational Democracy

To complete our political sketches of Quebec, let's examine the image of Quebec as a multinational democracy. With the 2017 publication of the Quebec government's policy of political affirmation and Canadian relations, a policy firmly rooted in the spirit of plurinational and asymmetrical federalism, it seems fair to advance that this image is the one most in tune with Quebec citizenry at this historical moment. At least four elements give shape and substance to this emerging form of political association. (Here I am particularly influenced by the pioneering work that James Tully has done on the topic.)[9] First, a multinational democracy contains more than one nation.

Minimally, members of these nations have the right to exercise internal self-determination and to engage in continuous deliberations and negotiations with a view to developing relations between partners based on mutual trust. Representatives of these constituent nations are free to seek recognition in international forums. Michael Keating has noted that self-determination of this sort does not necessarily lead to political secession. For Keating, there is "no logical reason why self-determination should be linked to statehood, apart from the entrenched dogmas of sovereignty discourse.... Another way of looking at self-determination is to see it as the right to negotiate one's position within the state and supranational order, without necessarily setting up a separate state" (Keating 2001, 10). I will come back to this second point shortly.

We are very far from the classic Westphalian model that conceives of states as forming a single *demos* within which "internal, subnational 'minorities' seek group rights" rather than "societies of two or more, often overlapping nations that are more or less equal in status" (Tully 2001, 3).

Second, multinational federal democracies are characterized by the fact that each nation within the federation forms a plural society. Such is the case in Quebec. A concrete expression of it was given in 1985 when the Québec National Assembly adopted a resolution recognizing the existence of the Arenac, Algonquin, Atikamekw, Cree, Huron, Micmac, Mohawk, Montagnais, Naskapi, and Inuit nations.[10] (An eleventh nation, the Malécite, was recognized in 1989.) In connection with this interpretation of Quebec as constituting a plural society, Tully goes as far as saying that in such contexts "the jurisdictions, modes of participation and representation, and the national and multinational identities of citizens overlap and are subject to negotiation" (Tully 2001, 3).

Third, multinational democracies adopt the principles of constitutional democracy, which challenge the norm of a democratic setting founded on a single nation. As such, this "multinational association rests on their [each nation's] adherence to the legal and political values, principles and rights of constitutional democracy and international law" (Tully 2001, 3).

Fourth, multinational democracies need to develop institutions that bring members and representatives of the various nations into permanent contact while encouraging political exchanges. In the case of Quebec, one can view the policy and politics of "interculturalism" – the Quebec version of cultural pluralism (see the Bouchard-Taylor Commission 2007) – as a clear expression of the desire to erect a polity founded on interconnectedness between societal partners. In this connection, the adoption of Bill 21, An Act Respecting the Laicity of the [Quebec] State, was at the centre of political debate during the 2019 federal election in Canada. The law contains provisions on the wearing of religious symbols by certain public servants. However, its application is fairly narrow: it applies only to officials who must interact with the public, only while exercising their official duties, and only to people newly hired in these positions. It is worth remembering that the Quiet Revolution was in large part about secularization of the public sphere (education, health, law enforcement, etc.) to escape the pervasive influence of religion on Quebec society (in the form of the Catholic Church). As one former advisor to prime ministers and Quebec premiers noted, the law provoked anger amongst Canadians for its apparent intolerance of cultural diversity, which then created anger inside Quebec at the rest of Canada's "virtue signalling and self-righteous condemnation" of a widely supported, legitimate law within the National Assembly's constitutional authority. The controversy reopened old wounds by becoming yet another "dialogue of the deaf" over acceptance of the distinct character of Quebec society versus interference in Quebec's internal affairs on matters about which the rest of Canada is largely ignorant (White 2019).

With regard to the province's Inuit and First Nations, Quebec's main political parties, so far, have been slow to support their further empowerment. Arguably, Quebec's National Assembly has led in identifying avenues for the economic and social development of the north of Quebec, the traditional territory of many First Nations. However, much more needs to be done to eradicate the colonial heritage that long dominated relations between Quebec and its original peoples. Denys Delâge aptly reminds us that "current Aboriginal leaders are more involved in fighting for their rights than in engaging in an overall questioning of the colonial system that constrains them.... The goal would be for aboriginal people to escape the colonial heritage of wardship and the denial of access to full citizenship" (Delâge 2001, 135). The dedicated pursuit of such objectives would contribute to the engagement of all Quebecers, whatever their origins, in the shared project of building a better and fairer society.

Finally, it is important to point out that if at some time Quebec should secede from Canada, it would have yet another nation to recognize: anglophone Quebecers. For the time being, however, this community identifies strongly with the Canadian majority, and as such does not perceive itself – and is not being perceived by others – as constituting a separate minority nation within Quebec.

Conclusion

In this chapter, I have analyzed five faces used to depict Quebec: political nationality, founding nation, province state, distinct society, and multinational democracy. Each of these faces tends to propose and promote different characteristics and suggests a unique world view with particular meaning systems. These portrayals of Quebec also suggest different takes on relations of power. The use of these images is not insignificant, as we are reminded by E.E. Schattschneider, who argued that "the definition of alternatives [read 'faces'] is the supreme instrument of power; the antagonists can rarely agree on what the issues are because power is involved in the definition. He who determines what politics is about runs the country, because the definition of the alternatives is the choice of conflicts and the choice of conflicts allocates power" (Schattschneider 1960). So the prevailing face of politics – the shared vision of the political community – gives overall direction to policy preferences and appropriate arrangements for power sharing.

To return to the point made by Richard Simeon in the introduction, it is clear that defining key concepts has consequences that go to the core of societal arrangements and that can suddenly tilt the political balance in ways that have long-term consequences, as we were reminded in 1982[11] at the time of the patriation and the establishment of a new constitutional order in Canada.

Notes

1 The first version of this text was discussed at the international workshop organized by Michael Burgess on the theme of "Small Worlds: The Character, Role and Significance of Constituent Units in Federations and Federal Political Systems" under the auspices of the Centre international de formation européenne and Canterbury Christ Church University, Canterbury, April 21–6, 2013. My thanks go to all participants for their input. Special thanks go to Dan Pfeffer, post-doctoral researcher with the Canada Research Chair in Quebec and Canadian Studies at the Université du Québec à Montréal, and to Jim Bickerton for their valuable suggestions.

2 This will remind the reader of Lasswell (1936).

3 The idea of "faces" was suggested by an article published by James Mallory in 1965 in which he referred to the "five faces of federalism" to depict phases experienced by the country's federal system between 1867 and the early 1960s: quasi, classical, emergency, cooperative, and double-image federalism. Mallory's way of categorizing Canada's transformation was highly accurate at the time. See Mallory (1965, 3–15). It is Michael Burgess, though, who suggested that I set some time aside to write on the images to depict Quebec as an evolving small universe/world.

4 Quoted in Gagnon and Iacovino (2007, 78–9). Originally published in *La Minerve,* Montreal, July 1, 1867.

5 For a solid discussion of those letters by Loranger, refer to Canada, Royal Commission on Aboriginal Peoples (1993).

6 On the *rupture thesis,* see Marcel Martel (2003, 129–45), and Anne-Andrée Deneault (2013).

7 The House of Commons refused to accept the official tabling of the minority report.

8 Most political commentators and jurists felt that such recognition fell short, as it was not entrenched in the Constitution Act, 1982. For such an account, see Gérald Beaudoin (1996).

9 In addition, one can consult an important collection of essays edited by Michael C. van Walt van Praag and Onno Seroo (1999).

10 For a solid discussion of Quebec's evolving policy in autochtonous matters, refer to Éric Gourdeau (1993, 349–71).

11 For a critical account of the patriation of the Constitution Act in 1982, see François Rocher and Benoît Pelletier (2013).

References and Suggested Readings

Beaudoin, Gérald. 1996. "Constitution: Ne travailler que sur un plan B serait admettre que la sécession est inévitable." *La Presse*, February 16.

Bickerton, James, and Alain-G. Gagnon. 2017. "Regions." In *Comparative Politics*, edited by Daniele Caramani, 4th ed., 260–73. Oxford: Oxford University Press.

Bouchard, Gérard, ed. 2013. *National Myths: Constructed Pasts, Contested Presents*. London: Routledge.

Bouchard-Taylor Commission. 2007. *Building the Future: A Time for Reconciliation*. Quebec: Bibliothèque et Archives nationales du Québec.

Brouillet, Eugénie, Alain-G. Gagnon, and Guy Laforest, eds. 2018. *The Quebec Conference of 1864: Understanding the Emergence of the Canadian Federation*. Montreal and Kingston: McGill-Queen's University Press.

Brownsey, Keith, and Michael Howlett, eds. 2009. *The Provincial State in Canada: Politics in the Provinces and Territories*. Toronto: University of Toronto Press.

Burgess, Michael. 2006. *Comparative Federalism: Theory and Practice*. Abingdon, UK: Routledge.

———. 2012. *In Search of the Federal Spirit: New Theoretical and Empirical Perspectives in Comparative Federalism*. Oxford: Oxford University Press. http://dx.doi.org/10.1093/acprof:oso/9780199606238.001.0001.

Burgess, Michael, and Alain-G. Gagnon. 2010. *Federal Democracies*. London: Routledge.

Careless, J.M.S. 1969. "'Limited Identities' in Canada." *Canadian Historical Review* 50: 1–10.

Cook, Ramsay. 1969. *Provincial Autonomy, Minority Rights and the Compact Theory, 1867–1921*. Studies of the Royal Commission on Bilingualism and Biculturalism. Ottawa: Queen's Printer for Canada.

———. 1989. "Alice in Meechland or the Concept of Quebec as a 'Distinct Society.'" In *The Meech Lake Primer*, edited by Michael Behiels, 285–94. Ottawa: University of Ottawa Press.

De Bané, Pierre, and Martial Asselin. 1972. Special Joint Committee of the Senate and of the House of Commons on the Constitution, *A Minority Report*. March 7. Ottawa.

Delâge, Denys. 2001. "Quebec and the Aboriginal People." In *Vive Quebec: New Thinking and New Approaches to the Quebec Nation*, edited by Michel Venne, 127–36. Toronto: James Lorimer.

Deneault, Anne-Andrée. 2013. "Divergences et solidarité: Une étude sociologique des rapports entre le Québec et les francophones d'Amérique." PhD diss., University of Ottawa.

Gagnon, Alain-G. 2002. "La condition canadienne et les montées du nationalisme et du régionalisme." In *Le débat qui n'a pas eu lieu. La Commission Pepin-Robarts quelque vingt ans après*, edited by Jean-Pierre Wallot, 105–20. Ottawa: Les Presses de l'Université d'Ottawa.

———. 2010. *The Case for Multinational Federalism: Beyond the All-Encompassing Nation*. Abingdon, UK: Routledge.

———. 2014. *Minority Nations in the Age of Uncertainty: New Paths to National Emancipation and Empowerment.* Toronto: University of Toronto Press.

Gagnon, Alain-G., and Xavier Dionne. 2009. "Historiographie et fédéralisme au Canada." *Revista d'Estudis Autonòmics i Federals* 9 (October): 10–50.

Gagnon, Alain-G., and Raffaele Iacovino. 2007. *Federalism, Citizenship and Quebec: Debating Multinationalism.* Toronto: University of Toronto Press.

Gagnon, Alain-G., and Mary Beth Montcalm. 1990. *Quebec: Beyond the Quiet Revolution.* Scarborough, ON: Nelson Canada.

Gourdeau, Éric. 1993. "Quebec and the Aboriginal Question." In *Quebec: State and Society*, edited by Alain-G. Gagnon, 2nd ed., 349–71. Scarborough, ON: Nelson Canada.

Guibernau, Montserrat. 1999. *Nations without States: Political Communities in a Global Age.* Cambridge: Polity.

Keating, Michael. 1996. *Nations against the State: The New Politics of Nationalism in Quebec, Catalonia and Scotland.* London: Palgrave Macmillan. http://dx.doi.org/10.1057/9780230374348.

———. 1998. *The New Regionalism in Western Europe: Territorial Restructuring and Political Change.* Cheltenham, UK: Edward Elgar.

———. 2001. *Plurinational Democracy: Stateless Nations in a Post-Sovereignty Era.* Oxford: Oxford University Press. http://dx.doi.org/10.1093/0199240760.001.0001.

Kwavnick, David. 1973. *The Tremblay Report: Report of the Royal Commission of Inquiry on Constitutional Problems.* Toronto: McClelland and Stewart.

Laforest, Guy, with the collaboration of Oscar Mejia Mesa. 2014. *Interpreting Quebec's Exile within the Canadian Federation: Selected Political Essays.* Brussels: Peter Lang.

Lajoie, Andrée. 2009. "Federalism in Canada: Provinces and Minorities – Same Fight." In *Contemporary Canadian Federalism: Foundations, Traditions, Institutions*, edited by Alain-G. Gagnon, 163–86. Institutions. Toronto: University of Toronto Press.

LaSelva, Samuel V. 1996. *The Moral Foundations of Canadian Federalism: Paradoxes, Achievements, and Tragedies.* Montreal and Kingston: McGill-Queen's University Press.

Lasswell, Harold Dwight. 1936. *Who Gets What, When, How?* New York: McGraw-Hill.

Mallory, James. 1965. "Five Faces of Canadian Federalism." In *The Future of Canadian Federalism*, edited by P.-A. Crépeau and C.B. Macpherson, 3–15. Toronto: University of Toronto Press.

Martel, Marcel. 2003. "Le débat de l'existence et de la disparition du Canada français: état des lieux." In *Aspects de la nouvelle francophonie canadienne*, edited by Simon Langlois and Jocelyn Létourneau, 129–45. Quebec City: Les Presses de l'Université Laval.

National Assembly of Québec. 2019. *Bill no 2: An Act Respecting the Laicity of the State.* Quebec: Quebec Official Publisher.

O'Neal, Brian. 1995. *Distinct Society: Origins, Interpretations, Implications.* December. Ottawa: Library of Parliament, BP-408 E.

Paquin, Stéphane, ed. 2006. *Les relations internationales du Québec depuis la Doctrine Gérin-Lajoie (1965–2005). Le prolongement externe des compétences internes.* Quebec City: Les Presses de l'Université Laval.

Pelletier, Benoît. 2004. "The State of Our Federation: A Québec Perspective." Speech given by Mr. Benoît Pelletier, Minister for Canadian Intergovernmental Affairs and Aboriginal Affairs during a luncheon organized by the Canada West Foundation, March 24.

Quebec. 2017. *Quebecers, Our Way of Being Canadian: Policy of Québec Affirmation and Canadian Relations.* Quebec City: Ministère du Conseil exécutif.

Royal Commission on Aboriginal Peoples. 1993. *Partners in Confederation: Aboriginal Peoples, Self-Government, and the Constitution.* Ottawa: Canadian Government Publishing.

Rémillard, Gil. 1980. *Le fédéralisme canadien*. Montreal: Québec Amérique.

Rioux Ouimet, Hubert. 2012. "Le 'Lion celtique': néolibéralisme, régionalisme et nationalisme économique en Écosse, 1979–2012." MA thesis, UQAM.

Rocher, François. 2009. "The Quebec-Canada Dynamic or the Negation of the Ideal of Federalism." In *Contemporary Canadian Federalism: Foundations, Traditions, Institutions*, edited by Alain-G. Gagnon, 81–131. Toronto: University of Toronto Press.

Rocher, François, and Benoît Pelletier, eds. 2013. *Le nouvel ordre constitutionnel canadien. Du rapatriement de 1982 à nos jours*. Coll. Politeia. Quebec City: Les Presses de l'Université du Québec.

Ryan, Claude. 1980. "Une Nouvelle Fédération Canadienne." Report of the Constitutional Commission of the Quebec Liberal Party, Quebec City.

Schattschneider, E.E. 1960. *The Semisovereign People: A Realist's View of Democracy in America*. Chicago: Holt, Rinehart and Winston.

Simeon, Richard. 1977. "Regionalism and Canadian Political Institutions." In *Canadian Federalism: Myth or Reality?* edited by J. Peter Meekison, 292–303. Toronto: Methuen.

Smiley, Donald V. 1967. *The Canadian Political Community*. Toronto: Methuen.

Task Force on Canadian Unity. 1979. *A Future Together: Observations and Recommendations*. Ottawa: Government of Canada.

Trudeau, Pierre Elliott. 1962. "The Multi-National State in Canada: The Interaction of Nationalism in Canada." *Canadian Forum* 42: 52–4.

Tully, James. 1994. "The Crisis of Identification: The Case of Canada." *Political Studies* 42: 77–96.

———. 2001. "Introduction." In *Multinational Democracies*, edited by Alain-G. Gagnon and James Tully, 1–33. Cambridge: Cambridge University Press. http://dx.doi.org/10.1017/CBO9780511521577.003.

Wade, Mason, in collaboration with Jean-Charles Falardeau. 1960. *La dualité canadienne: essais sur les relations entre Canadiens français et Canadiens anglais/Canadian Dualism: Studies of French-English Relations*. Laval/Toronto: Les Presses de l'Université Laval/University of Toronto Press.

Walt van Praag, Michael C. van, and Onno Seroo. 1999. *The Implementation of the Right to Self-Determination as a Contribution to Conflict Prevention*. Barcelona: UNESCO Catalunya.

White, Peter. 2019. "A Memo for Canada: Back Off Quebec's Bill 21." *Globe and Mail*, November 7.

eleven
The Two Faces of Treaty Federalism

MARTIN PAPILLON

It is important for all Canadians to understand that without Treaties, Canada would have no legitimacy as a nation.
– Truth and Reconciliation Commission (2015)

Modern treaties have great potential. They can provide a framework for mutually beneficial relationships between the Crown and Aboriginal peoples.… Unfortunately, if they are not properly implemented, modern treaties also have the potential to perpetuate great harm. They can become a tool of dispossession. They can be used to disenfranchise and marginalize us.
– Matthew Coon Come (2015)

Introduction

In its 2015 final report on the legacy of residential schools, the Truth and Reconciliation Commission (TRC) reminded Canadians of the historical importance of treaties with Indigenous peoples. The revitalization and renewal of treaty relationships, it argued, is an essential component of a lasting reconciliation between Canada's Indigenous and settler societies. Twenty years earlier, the Royal Commission on Aboriginal Peoples similarly focused on treaties as the cornerstone of a renewed nation-to-nation relationship between Indigenous peoples and Canada (RCAP 1996). Treaty-based arrangements, under various forms, also occupy a central place in an ever-growing number of essays on Indigenous-settler reconciliation (Asch 2014; Borrows and Coyle 2017; Poelzer and Coates 2015).

As Peter Russell (2017) argues in his historical account of Canada's constitutional odyssey, if treaties are seen as fundamental to our common future, it is largely because they were key to our past. Early relations between Indigenous peoples and French and British imperial powers were established and conducted through treaties and political covenants. Later, as British imperial and Canadian settler authorities sought to ascertain their jurisdiction on the land, they again negotiated treaties with Indigenous peoples. However deceitful the subsequent interpretation of these land cession treaties was, they remain fundamental to a great number of Indigenous nations, who see them as the foundation of their relationship with Canada (Miller 2009).

After a long hiatus, during which federal and provincial authorities simply assumed that treaties were no longer necessary in light of the weakening of Indigenous nations and their expected assimilation to the Canadian polity, treaty-making returned to Canada in the 1970s. The James Bay and Northern Quebec Agreement, signed in 1975, was the first in a series of negotiated settlements formally known as comprehensive land claims agreements (CLCAs). At the time of writing, twenty-five such modern treaties had been ratified, most notably in the northern territories, British Columbia, and Quebec.[1]

Unlike their historic predecessors, modern treaties are detailed legal documents that, among other things, establish new land tenure regimes as well as co-governance and self-governance arrangements for their Indigenous signatories. Significantly, the rights defined in treaties, including modern ones, are now protected under section 35(1) of the Constitution Act, 1982. In theory, this means the institutions established through modern treaties are shielded against unilateral federal, provincial, and territorial actions, creating what some argue are quasi-federal regimes of self-rule and shared rule in significant parts of the country (Sabin 2017; White 2002; Wilson, Alcantara, and Rodon 2020).

Yet modern treaties remain controversial. Negotiations leading to CLCAs can drag on over decades, and once agreements are reached, they are regularly rejected in community referenda.[2] Some Indigenous nations with unsettled claims refuse to engage in the negotiation of modern treaties, preferring to have the courts settle their claims. Others prefer to negotiate more limited agreements with governments or private corporations rather than commit to long-term comprehensive treaties. Those who have agreed to a modern treaty are also often struggling to have their agreement properly implemented (Fenge 2015; LCAC 2008). Many treaty signatories end up in court defending their treaty rights against government agencies unwilling to fulfil their part of the deal.

To what extent, then, do modern treaties contribute to the transformation of the relationship between their Indigenous signatories and the settler state? Following former Cree Grand Chief Matthew Coon Come, cited in the second epigraph above, this chapter suggests modern treaties are in fact Janus-faced institutions. On the positive side, treaties have had a profound impact on the governance regime of vast areas of the country, especially in Northern Canada. They have also enhanced Indigenous identities as distinct polities, boosted their institutional capacity, and established their position as central actors in the governance of their traditional lands. Yet modern treaties can also be institutional straitjackets confining Indigenous self-determination within the strict boundaries of the Canadian federal regime, reproducing many of the patterns and assumptions of colonial governance and limiting their transformative potential.

To understand the two faces of modern treaties, it is important to underscore the motivations and underlying narratives that inform Indigenous peoples and governments when negotiating and implementing such agreements. While there is no single uniform view among Indigenous peoples, treaties are generally understood as political compacts designed to rebalance their relationship with the state, based on the recognition of their rights on the land and their status as inherently self-governing nations. However, these expectations are rarely met (LCAC 2008). Federal, provincial, and territorial authorities see modern treaties more pragmatically, as legal transactions with the purpose of clarifying the land tenure regime and facilitating economic development. While treaties can be a way to prevent repeating historical wrongs, they do not aim to radically transform the structure of the Canadian federation. These diverging views of treaties, as *relational* versus *transactional* agreements, explain much of the institutional resistance Indigenous peoples face when negotiating and implementing their treaty.

After a look back at the fundamental role of treaty-making in Canada, this chapter briefly discusses the concept of treaty federalism as an organizing principle for rethinking the relationship between Indigenous peoples and the settler society in Canada. It then provides an overview of modern treaties and underscores the institutional resistance to change faced by Indigenous peoples when negotiating and implementing these agreements. It concludes with a brief discussion of the future of treaty-making in the age of reconciliation.

A Long Tradition of Treaty-Making

Indigenous societies were well versed in the art of treaty-making long before the arrival of Europeans in what is now known as North America. Treaties established the conditions of peaceful relations and forged durable alliances between Indigenous nations (Williams 1997). Pre-colonial treaties relied on oral traditions and were formalized through ceremonies, gift exchanges, and other conventions. French and British authorities recognized these Indigenous practices when they developed military and commercial alliances with the original inhabitants of the land (Miller 2009; Russell 2017).

The Great Peace of Montreal is an early example of a treaty-like agreement that built on Indigenous traditions. After years of negotiations, more than 1300 delegates from thirty-nine Indigenous nations met in Montreal in August 1701 in a ceremonial setting to establish the conditions of a general peace with the French. The treaty put an end, for a time, to decades of conflicts between the Haudenosaunee Confederacy, the French fur traders, and their Indigenous allies (Havard 2001).

The British followed a similar pattern in the eighteenth century when they negotiated peace treaties, notably with the Mi'kmaq and Maliseet in what are now Canada's Maritime provinces (Miller 2009). Then, under the Royal Proclamation of 1763, the British Crown committed to negotiate with Indigenous nations before authorizing settlement on their lands (Slattery 2015). Less than a year after that, representatives of the Crown and more than two hundred Indigenous leaders met at Niagara to establish, through a treaty, what the latter thought were the foundations of a peaceful relationship of coexistence. In exchange for their consent to European settlements, Indigenous peoples received guarantees from the Crown that their own autonomy and access to the land would be protected (Borrows 2017).

Those early diplomatic relations were never egalitarian. Europeans were convinced of their moral, cultural, and technological superiority and used treaties to circumvent the military threat posed by Indigenous nations, who at the time were numerically superior. But these agreements were nonetheless negotiated between nations. European powers recognized the political status and authority structures of the Indigenous peoples with whom they were negotiating (Russell 2017).

As the British confirmed their dominant status in North America, the practice of negotiating treaties continued. However, the land cession and numbered treaties negotiated in the nineteenth and twentieth centuries – mainly in Ontario and the Prairies – were concluded under conditions radically different from those of the early "peace and friendship" alliances. For British and later Canadian authorities, the purpose of treaty-making was still to secure access to the territory for permanent settlement, but the notion of peaceful coexistence gave way to a different logic, as Indigenous peoples came to be viewed as wards of the Crown. Indigenous peoples were now convinced (or, as was often the case, deceived) to "cede" their title to the land in exchange for financial compensations and promises concerning the benevolent protection of the Crown (Miller 2009; Russell 2017). Treaties, in other words, became instruments of land dispossession and political subjugation.

Crown sovereignty was further entrenched with the creation of the Canadian federation. Under section 91(24) of the Constitution Act, 1867, the responsibility for "Indians and Lands reserved for the Indians" was transferred from the imperial government in London to Canada's dominion government in Ottawa. While Indigenous peoples were never consulted or invited to participate in its creation, relations with Indigenous peoples became an internal affair of the new federation.

The adoption of the consolidated Indian Act in 1876, under which the federal government established a tight regime of control to facilitate assimilation of the Indigenous population to the dominant settler society, reinforced this shift. From partners in a treaty-based association, Indigenous peoples became subjects in a federation of provinces that they never consented to.

With their authority firmly established and the federation extended from eastern Canada all the way to the Pacific, federal and provincial authorities eventually abandoned the practice of treaty-making. The last land cession treaty was signed in 1923. Treaties were not negotiated in most of British Columbia, the northern territories, Quebec, and parts of Atlantic Canada. Treaties, it was thought at the time, were a thing of the past.

Reaffirming the Original Treaty Relationship

Land-cession treaties were instrumental to the affirmation of Crown sovereignty on Indigenous lands and communities. However, Indigenous signatories and their descendants continue to see their treaties not as acts of subjection but as acts of mutual recognition, constitutive of lasting relationships between distinctive but interrelated and interdependent peoples (Borrows 2017). It is this vision of treaties, as covenants amongst equal partners, that is being revived today under theories of treaty federalism.

In its broadest sense, federalism suggests a constitutionally protected system of self-rule and shared rule between two or more co-equal partners. Federations like Canada, where sovereignty is divided between two orders of independent governments, are the most common model of federalism. However, there are other ways to combine the federal principles of self-rule and shared rule (Elazar 1987; Watts 2008).

In the context of Indigenous-settler relations, treaty federalism (Henderson 1994), or treaty constitutionalism as some prefer to call this approach (Tully 2008; Borrows 2017; Ladner 2009), starts from the premise that Indigenous peoples were and continue to be self-determining polities with their own distinctive legal and political orders. It is through treaties, the argument goes, that Indigenous and Crown authorities have historically established mechanisms to coordinate their respective spheres of jurisdiction and established mutually agreed upon boundaries of self-rule and shared rule. A similar approach should inform contemporary attempts to reconcile settler and Indigenous claims on the land.

The revitalization of the original treaty relationship can take different forms. For the Royal Commission on Aboriginal Peoples, which embraced the notion of a treaty-based nation-to-nation relationship in its final report in 1996, the reactivation of the treaty relationship should result in the negotiation of a new division of powers between federal, provincial, and Indigenous governments, the last forming a third order of governments within the Canadian federation (RCAP 1996, 215).

This vision of treaty federalism as an extension of the federal regime through recognition of a third order of Indigenous governments is not endorsed by all advocates of treaty federalism. The RCAP model, Kiera Ladner (2009) argues, accepts the supremacy of the Canadian Constitution and places treaties under its overarching framework, despite the fact that Indigenous peoples never consented to this constitutional regime. Ladner instead argues for a confederal model that echoes James Tully's vision of deep constitutional pluralism (Tully 2008).

From this perspective, Indigenous governing institutions and rules should be fully recognized for what they are: the expression of distinctive constitutional orders that today continue to exist in parallel to Canada's own Constitution (Borrows 2017; Ladner 2009; Russell 2017). While there are nuances in their respective positions, advocates of this stronger model of constitutional pluralism invite us to rethink Canada as a double federation, governed simultaneously through the 1867 division of powers and a distinctive constitutional regime established progressively through treaties between the Crown and the original inhabitants of the land. Far from being subordinated to the former, the latter constitutes the founding pillar on which the legitimacy of the Canadian state rests (Tully 2008; Borrows 2017; Russell 2017; Slattery 2015).

Despite some differences, theories of treaty federalism or constitutional pluralism share a common starting point in the fundamental value of treaties as covenant between distinct and autonomous nations. Treaties are seen as essential to the revitalization of Indigenous inherent jurisdictions on the land and to their repositioning as partners, rather than subalterns, in a relationship of self-rule and shared rule based on mutual consent. This decolonizing vision of treaties is echoed in the Truth and Reconciliation Commission's final report when it argues the revitalization of treaties is essential to any lasting reconciliation between settler and Indigenous societies.[3]

Treaty federalism offers an enticing theoretical model for recasting settler-Indigenous relations from a model characterized by land dispossession and political subjugation to one of mutual consent and coexistence. Of course, moving from theoretical constructs to more concrete institutional reforms is, not surprisingly, a challenging endeavour. The resistance Indigenous peoples face when negotiating and implementing modern treaties illustrates the persistence of the colonial narrative.

Modern Treaties and the Real World of Treaty Federalism[4]

Treaties returned to the forefront of Canadian politics almost by accident. In its 1969 White Paper on Indian policy, the federal government promoted full integration of all Indigenous peoples, no matter their status, into the Canadian citizenship regime. Among other measures, it announced its intention to offer signatories of historic treaties a final compensation package in exchange for their abolition. For Prime Minister Pierre E. Trudeau, a liberal in the classic sense, it was inconceivable that the citizens of a nation make treaties with one another (Trudeau 1969). The reaction of Indigenous peoples whose ancestors had signed treaties with the Crown was clear and unequivocal. According to the chiefs of Alberta's response to the 1969 white paper, "To us, to us who are Treaty Indians, there is nothing more important than our Treaties for our lands and the well-being of our future generation.... The Government must admit its mistakes and recognize that treaties are historic, moral and legal solemn agreements that carry obligations" (Chiefs of Alberta 1970, 189).

Ironically, the white paper contributed to the revitalization of the treaty narrative. While signatories of historic treaties mobilized to defend their treaty rights, those without a treaty sought some form of recognition of their status and rights. Among them were the Nisga'a in British Columbia, who were engaged in a long legal battle to have the title to their ancestral lands recognized in Canadian law (Aldridge 2015). In 1973, the Supreme Court released its landmark *Calder* decision, in which it divided over the claim of the Nisga'a, but nonetheless recognized for the first time the possibility that an Aboriginal title may have survived the assertion of Crown sovereignty where no treaty was negotiated.[5]

The *Calder* case is arguably one of the most important court decisions on Indigenous rights in Canada's history. It altered the rules of the game in significant parts of the country where the land remained "unceded" through historic treaties. From the settlers' perspective, the possibility that Indigenous nations could still have some form of ownership rights to vast tracts of lands infused a new degree of legal uncertainty on economic activities and capital investments in those areas. And this at a time when governments were promoting the expansion of the natural resource extraction sector in light of the energy crisis of the 1970s.

A few months later, when Justice Malouf of the Quebec Superior Court issued an interlocutory injunction putting a stop to the construction of the James Bay hydroelectric complex until Indigenous rights in the area were clarified, federal and provincial authorities had little choice but to negotiate an agreement. This resulted in the 1975 James Bay and Northern Quebec Agreement (JBNQA), the first of what would come to be known as modern treaties.

At the time of writing, twenty-five modern treaties – or comprehensive land claims agreements (CLCAs), as they are formally titled – have been negotiated and ratified in Canada (CIRNAC 2018a). Each has its own specificities and its own context and history. A distinctive negotiation process was also established in British Columbia in the 1990s.[6] All this being said, the overall logic governing modern treaties is broadly similar from one agreement to another.

Quasi-Federal Regimes

Depending on the formula adopted at the time, the Indigenous signatories agree to "cede," "release," "suspend," or "modify" their Aboriginal rights and titles in the claimed area. In exchange, they receive monetary compensations and some form of legal ownership (generally under fee simple title) on parcels of their traditional territories. For example, the Nisga'a Final Agreement provides for Nisga'a control of approximately 2,000 square kilometres of land in the Nass Valley in British Columbia, including surface and subsurface resources. The Nunavut Land Claims Agreement recognizes Inuit ownership of 350,000 square kilometres of land, of which 35,257 square kilometres include mineral rights. While significant, it is important to keep in mind that these represent only a small fraction of the traditional territories originally claimed by the Nisga'a and the Inuit.

In the rest of the settled area, Indigenous signatories are generally recognized as having hunting, fishing, and trapping rights, as well as a role in regional governance and land-use planning through co-management boards. Few of these shared-rule instruments have decision-making authority, but their role in shaping environmental policy in the area can be significant nonetheless (White 2002). Some modern treaties also include commitments to socio-economic development goals, while others (more recent) often include revenue-sharing formulas for resource extraction on claimed lands (Eyford 2015).

For many Indigenous nations engaged in treaty negotiations, the key feature of their agreement remains recognition of some level of local and regional autonomy. Before 1995, the federal government refused to include self-government provisions directly under treaties. The conditions of self-rule were instead negotiated under distinct agreements outside constitutionally protected treaties. In Yukon, eleven self-government agreements were negotiated since the ratification of the Yukon Umbrella Agreement in 1994.

In some cases, land rights were negotiated on a regional basis, while self-government rights negotiated on a community basis. This is notably the case for the Sahtu Land Claim, under which each community is negotiating its own self-government agreement.

Since 1995, CLCAs generally contain self-government provisions, including a division of powers and more or less detailed provisions for the creation (or recognition) of Indigenous legislative and executive bodies with jurisdiction on a set territory. For example, the Nisga'a Final Agreement establishes law-making authority for the Nisga'a Lisims (regional) Government and four Village Governments. These governments operate according to the Nisga'a Constitution and have primary jurisdiction over Nisga'a lands in several areas, including the management of community lands, environmental regulation, citizenship, and local matters (Aldridge 2015). The Tlicho Agreement provides for a constitutionally protected Tlicho Government at the regional level, but it also establishes Tlicho municipalities created under legislation of the Government of the Northwest Territories.

The Nunavut Land Claims Agreement follows a somewhat different model. The agreement does not contain self-government provisions for Inuit lands, but it provides for the creation of a public government over a much larger area, the Territory of Nunavut, where Inuit form the majority population. The Government of Nunavut was created in 1999, with powers similar to those of other territorial governments in northern Canada. Like the other two territories, Nunavut does not have the constitutional status of a province. In practice, however, its role is equivalent to that of a province, with the important exception of natural resources on Crown lands, which remain under federal control. While it is formally a public government, the Nunavut government has a mandate to promote the interests, language, culture, and traditions of the Inuit majority (Hicks and White 2015).

Modern treaties have changed the governance landscape for their Indigenous signatories. The Supreme Court of Canada qualifies modern treaties as "quantum leaps" compared to their historical counterparts.[7] The combination of land-ownership regimes, shared rule through co-management boards for lands and resources, and forms of self-government have created complex systems of multilevel governance under which federal, provincial/territorial, and Indigenous authorities have areas of overlapping jurisdiction. This complex structure makes multilevel coordination an essential part of treaty implementation (Papillon 2015). This is especially striking in in the northern territories, where Indigenous governments and management boards now have a key role in most aspects of local and regional governance, resulting in what some have called a form of "nested" federalism (Sabin 2017; Wilson, Alcantara, and Rodon 2020). Since the rights defined in modern treaties are explicitly included under section 35(1) of the Constitution Act, 1982, these regimes of multilevel governance arguably benefit from an indirect constitutional protection that adds to their federal or quasi-federal nature.

Change or Continuity?

While modern treaties are certainly transformative, they fall short of the ideal models envisaged by treaty federalism. In fact, a number of Indigenous nations with unsettled claims simply refuse to engage in the negotiation of modern treaties, while others continue to negotiate unsuccessfully for decades. In a 2015 report for the federal government on the state of land claims negotiations, Douglas Eyford noted that at the time of writing, "75 claims are at various stages of negotiation. More than 80 per cent of those tables have been in the treaty process for longer than ten years, some for more than two decades" (Eyford 2015, 5).

While "institutional barriers and procedural obstacles" (Eyford 2015) may explain some of the delays in negotiating modern treaties, there are deeper problems that explain Indigenous peoples' reluctance to settle their land claims through a modern treaty. Indigenous peoples who engage in modern treaty negotiations do so for various reasons. Many are pressured into settling their claims in light of advancing resource extraction activities on their lands, as were the James Bay Cree and Inuit in the early 1970s (Papillon and Lord 2013). Others see economic opportunities in treaties and a concrete avenue for regaining some leverage in the governance of their lands and communities (Fenge 2015). Yet in general, Indigenous peoples tend to see modern treaties in much the same way as their predecessors. They see treaties as political covenants that reset their relationship with the settler state on more equal footing. After hearing testimonies from Indigenous elders and leaders, the Senate Committee on Aboriginal Peoples concludes in a 2008 report, "Modern treaties are the basic building blocks of their relationship with Canada. They serve to establish stable, peaceful and beneficial partnerships … that provide the basis for rebuilding their nations, regain their autonomy and work toward a better future within the country" (Senate of Canada 2008, vii).

Federal, provincial, and territorial authorities approach modern treaties from a somewhat different standpoint. While they generally agree with the regenerative function of treaties for Indigenous communities, the main rationale for entering into treaty negotiation is less relational than transactional. The goal is to ensure a legal and political context favourable to economic development, notably for extractive industries who seek access to the territory. Like earlier land cession treaties, modern ones are in essence legal transactions, under which undefined rights are traded for specific rules and procedures in order to achieve legal "certainty" regarding the property regime governing the land. While the language to that effect has evolved since 1973, the most recent federal interim policy on land claims rests on that very same premise. The primary goal of modern treaties, it states, is to establish a "mutually agreed-upon and enduring framework for reconciliation … that provides lasting certainty regarding the parties' respective rights to ownership, use and management of lands and resources in order to promote a secure climate for economic and resource development that can benefit all Canadians" (CIRNAC 2018b).

The inherent tension between Indigenous approaches to treaties as political-relational compacts and the federal government's vision of treaties as legal transactions to enable economic development reverberates in the negotiation process. Treaty negotiations have little to do with rebuilding nation-to-nation relations. The federal negotiation policy sets a series of preconditions that the Indigenous party must accept even before entering into negotiation. Such preconditions include, for example, limits on the amount of Crown lands that are "up for discussion" and a set list of powers the government is willing to transfer for self-government. As a result, what begins for Indigenous peoples as a process for reconciling their interests and world views with those of the settler state often ends up looking more like an exercise in collective bargaining, where lawyers and consultants acting on behalf of Indigenous communities seek to extract the best possible deal out of government negotiators (Irlbacher-Fox 2009).

The most controversial aspect of the federal land claims settlement policy is arguably the requirement that the Indigenous party surrenders or trades its unsettled rights and titles to the land in exchange for those defined in the treaty. The purpose, again, is to maximize legal certainty for economic development. The JBNQA of 1975 sets a standard in this respect. In exchange for the benefits defined in the agreement, the Indigenous parties agreed to "cede, release, surrender and convey … all their claims, rights, titles and interests" to federal and provincial authorities" (JBNQA 1975, s. 2.1).

Indigenous groups engaged in treaty negotiations have been vocal in opposing this "surrender" requirement, which they rightly see as a continuation of the land dispossession practices associated with historic treaties (Fenge 2015). Treaties, they argue, should implement rights, not curtail them. The federal government has acknowledged the problematic nature of the surrender clause and in some of the more recent agreements, the Indigenous party is invited to "suspend" or "modify" the exercise of its inherent rights in light of the principles set out in the treaty (for examples, see Eyford 2015, 72). In its most recent interim policy on land claims, the federal government still insists that the exercise of Indigenous rights must be harmonized with the objectives of certainty and stability, but it acknowledges this may be achieved through other "legal reconciliation techniques" (CIRNAC 2018b). The underlying message remains that Indigenous peoples' rights will be recognized only to the extent that they can be reconciled with other (primarily economic) interests in the negotiation of treaties.

This asymmetry between transactional and relational visions of treaties is clearly displayed as well in the process of implementing comprehensive land claims agreements. Because they see treaties from a transactional standpoint, federal, provincial, and territorial authorities tend to define their role in the implementation of treaties in programmatic terms. Government bureaucrats are called upon to implement the quantifiable aspects of treaties that require a specific measure or action, but they are rarely invited to take a holistic approach to their role, beyond the strict letter of the agreement. Even more problematically, treaty implementation was expected, until very recently, to take place within the structures and operational mandates of public administration. Modern treaties, in other words, must fit into existing programs, many of them designed under the Indian Act.

In a series of reports on modern treaty implementation, the auditor general of Canada (2003, 2007) noted the consequences of this administrative approach. Among other things, the reports underlined the lack of coordination across departments, the lack of clear responsibilities for overseeing the overall implementation of treaties, as well as the inadequacy of the formulas to fund treaty implementation obligations. The Senate Committee on Aboriginal Affairs reached similar conclusions in its 2008 report on modern treaties. Implementation, the Senate Committee argues, is not only about fulfilling specific transactional obligations. It is also about honouring and fulfilling the "spirit and intent" of modern treaties (Senate of Canada 2008).

In 2015, the federal government adopted a new Cabinet directive on modern treaty implementation that addresses some of these issues. Among others, it creates a "one stop shop" for modern treaty signatories to engage with the federal government and promotes a "whole of government" approach to implementation, under which the departments concerned with treaty implementation are expected to act in coordinated fashion (CIRNAC 2015). It was too early to assess the impact of these measures at the time of writing, but it is worth noting that it resulted in the co-development, with self-governing Indigenous governments, of a new fiscal policy for funding programs under self-government agreements (Nicol et al. 2020).

In light of these structural limitations and despite some recent positive developments, some critics of modern treaties argue they do little more than reproduce the core features of colonialism (Manuel 2015). Indigenous peoples who enter the modern treaty process are forced to accept the rules, norms, and practices unilaterally set by the settler state. As with historic numbered treaties, the legitimacy of federal institutions, and the sovereignty of the Crown more broadly, is simply assumed, rather than problematized as the starting point of negotiations. The fact that Indigenous peoples are invited to "surrender" or "suspend" the exercise of their inherent rights on most of their traditional territories also suggests continuity with the logic of land surrender and appropriation that characterized colonial treaties (Samson 2016). The essentially administrative approach to treaty implementation adopted by the federal government further confirms its view of land claims settlements as political matters internal to the Canadian state rather than as instruments to regulate relations between coexisting sovereign polities.

Why, then, do Indigenous peoples who have signed modern treaties insist on their importance? A more nuanced view suggests treaties are instruments of both change and continuity. Modern treaties profoundly transform Indigenous societies, identities, economies, and political structures, let alone their relationships to the Canadian state (Davidson 2018). This is especially striking in northern regions, where the presence of the state was, until recently, rather sparse and sporadic. As Paul Nadasdy (2017) argues in an insightful study of modern treaties and self-government in Yukon, through their treaties, Indigenous signatories are effectively invited to participate in institution-building in northern Canada. This is a major advance over Indian Act governance. Yet – and this is the paradox according to Nadasdy – self-rule and shared rule institutions designed through treaties and other agreements must operate in a manner that is consistent with the logic and expectations of Canadian federalism. Land management regimes are designed with the explicit purpose of stabilizing the property regime to facilitate capitalist investments. By entering into a modern treaty relationship, Indigenous peoples, willingly or not, are accepting what Nadasdy defines as the entailments of modern liberal democracy and capitalist development.

To paraphrase James C. Scott (1998), Indigenous peoples are invited through treaties to see and act like the state. This model of relative autonomy is empowering at some levels, but it is not clear whether it leaves much room for the revitalization of Indigenous world views, norms, and legal traditions, let alone for a form of treaty federalism based on constitutional pluralism.

Conclusion: Reconciliation beyond Treaties

Despite their contradictions, modern treaties will continue to play a structuring role in Indigenous-settler relations. Treaties, after all, are part of Canada's constitutional DNA (Russell 2017). Some of the modern treaty signatories have made significant advances in developing federal-like relations with Canadian governments. Many are exercising a deciding influence on the pace and nature of economic development on their traditional lands. But the initial enthusiasm for treaty federalism is dwindling in parts of the country.

Part of the reason for this decline in interest has to do with the challenges inherent to treaty negotiations and the strong institutional resistance in government circles to a relational approach to treaties, as discussed in this chapter. Alternative routes to self-determination have also emerged in recent years, arguably making treaties and their entailments less attractive.

In its 2014 *Tsilhqot'in* decision, the Supreme Court of Canada took the step that it didn't take in the *Calder* case forty years earlier. It recognized the title (proprietary right) of the Tsilhqot'in Nation on 1,750 square kilometres of land in central British Columbia.[8] Despite some criticisms, this decision created a small tsunami in Indigenous law circles (McIvor 2016). Suddenly, treaties were no longer the sole avenue for Indigenous peoples seeking to have their authority on the land recognized in Canadian law. A number of Indigenous nations in British Columbia – and to a lesser extent elsewhere in the country – have since diverted their energies and resources away from treaty negotiations and towards title recognition through the court system. Building their legal case is no panacea and there is no guarantee of success. The criteria defined by the Supreme Court in *Tsilhqot'in* are quite stringent and the Court has set limits on the exercise of Indigenous jurisdiction on title lands. Yet, the obvious advantage of the title recognition route is that it does not come with all the limitations and, arguably, political co-optation, of a negotiated settlement.

In parallel to their title claims, a number of Indigenous nations are also unilaterally revitalizing their own traditional laws and governance systems, in order to exercise what they consider their inherent jurisdiction. Instead of waiting for the state to recognize their authority, they simply begin to exercise it. The revitalization of Indigenous law can take various forms, from the development of child welfare and family law to the regeneration of traditional land tenure regimes as well as Indigenous constitutions (Borrows 2016). Some Indigenous nations have mobilized their traditional governance systems and laws to challenge government policies or regulatory decisions. Traditional Indigenous law is notably mobilized to challenge state-driven environmental impact assessments and regain control over the decision-making process in mining or pipeline projects.[9]

Unlike self-government under modern treaties, this revitalization of Indigenous laws and governance institutions is taking place outside of any formal state-sponsored channels. It therefore doesn't face the same restriction and curtailment as treaty-based agreements. Of course, to have a broader impact on state laws, policies, and actions, these Indigenous-led processes will have to be recognized by Canadian governments. Indigenous peoples are very much aware of this. Formal processes are now underway both in British Columbia and at the federal level to establish a legislative framework to recognize Indigenous inherent rights and jurisdictions in Canadian law.[10] There are still many hurdles to cross before a so-called recognition framework becomes law, but the fact of the process itself indicates a fundamental shift in perspective among Canadian authorities. The revitalization of Indigenous laws also resonates with Canada's commitments under the United Nations Declaration on the Rights of Indigenous Peoples, which protects and promotes the right of Indigenous peoples to self-determination and the related right to define their own governance rules and practices.

Cleary, treaties are not the only pathway to reconciliation. Yet, a relationship that is based on respect, trust, and a spirit of coexistence, as the TRC advocates, can be achieved only through one form or another of mutual agreement. Whether it is under a treaty or through a different framework, it is becoming increasingly clear that reconciliation cannot be a one-way process under which Indigenous peoples are expected to accept settler-colonial institutions in exchange for some form of limited autonomy and land rights. To paraphrase John Borrows (2017), whether it is through treaties or other means, the route to reconciliation with Indigenous peoples requires Canada to recognize its inherently plurinational and pluri-constitutional character.

Notes

1 For an overview of modern treaties negotiated so far and of those under negotiation, see Eyford (2015).

2 The Lheidli T'enneh First Nation is the most recent example of an Indigenous community voting down a comprehensive land claims agreement under the British Columbia treaty process. See https://www.cbc.ca/news/canada/british-columbia/lheidli-t-enneh-first-nation-votes-no-to-government-treaty-1.4720082

3 To reconcile can be interpreted as a meeting of the minds or a compromise. The Truth and Reconciliation Commission warns us against this approach. For the TRC, reconciliation entails "repairing damaged trust" through a profound transformation of existing relationships, based on respect for Indigenous world views, legal traditions and existence as distinct polities (TRC 2015, 6–7).

4 The concept of reconciliation is itself controversial. To reconcile can be interpreted as a meeting of the minds or a compromise. The Truth and Reconciliation Commission warns us against this approach. For the

TRC, reconciliation rests first and foremost on a transformation of the settler society. It entails "repairing damaged trust" through the development of relationships based on respect for Indigenous world views, legal traditions and existence as distinct polities (TRC 2015, 6–7).

5 *Calder v British Columbia (AG)* [1973] SCR 313.

6 For an overview, see BC Treaty Commission at: http://www.bctreaty.ca/negotiations.

7 *Beckman v. Little Salmon/Carmacks*, [2010] 3 SCR 103, para. 12.

8 *Tsilhqot'in Nation v. British Columbia*, 2014 SCC 44.

9 An interesting example is the Stk'emlupsemc Te Secwepemc Nation (SSN) process for opposing the Ajax Mine in their traditional territory. See https://stkemlups.ca/process/. The Tsleil-Waututh Nation mobilized a similar strategy in its opposition to the Trans Mountain pipeline. See https://twnsacredtrust.ca.

10 At the time of writing, the Indigenous groups involved in the federal process expressed serious doubts about the value of the proposed model and negotiations were suspended. See CIRNAC (2018c) and Barrera (2018).

References and Suggested Readings

Aldridge, J. 2015. "The 1998 Nisga'a Treaty." In *Keeping Promises: The Royal Proclamation of 1763, Aboriginal Rights, and Treaties in Canada*, edited by T. Fenge and J. Aldridge, 138–52. Montreal and Kingston: McGill-Queen's University Press.

Anaya, J. 2014. *Report of the Special Rapporteur on the Rights of Indigenous Peoples: The Situation of Indigenous Peoples in Canada*. New York: United Nations Human Rights Council. A/HRC/27/52/Add.2.

Asch, M. 2014. *On Being Here to Stay: Treaties and Aboriginal Rights in Canada*. Toronto: University of Toronto Press.

Auditor General of Canada. *2003 Report of the Auditor General of Canada to the House of Commons*. Chapter 8, "Indian and Northern Affairs Canada, Transferring Federal Responsibilities to the North." http://www.oag-bvg.gc.ca/internet/docs/20031108ce.pdf.

———. *2007 Report of the Auditor General of Canada to the House of Commons*. Chapter 3, "Inuvialuit Final Agreement," http://www.oag-bvg.gc.ca/internet/docs/20071003c_e.pdf.

Barrera, J. 2018. "Battle Brewing over Indigenous Rights Recognition Framework." CBC News, September 11. https://www.cbc.ca/news/indigenous/indigenous-rights-framework-bennett-1.4819510.

Borrows, J. 2016. *Freedom and Indigenous Constitutionalism*. Toronto: University of Toronto Press.

———. 2017. "Canada's Colonial Constitution." In *The Right Relationship: Reimagining the Implementation of Historical Treaties*, edited by J. Borrows and M. Coyle, 17–38. Toronto: University of Toronto Press.

Borrows, J., and M. Coyle. 2017. "Introduction." In *The Right Relationship: Reimagining the Implementation of Historical Treaties*, edited by J. Borrows and M. Coyle, 4–16. Toronto: University of Toronto Press.

Chiefs of Alberta. [1970] 2011. "Citizens Plus." Reproduced in *Aboriginal Policy Studies* 1 (2): 188–281. http://dx.doi.org/10.5663/aps.v1i2.11690.

Coon Come, M. 2015. "Cree Experience with Treaty Implementation." In *Keeping Promises: The Royal Proclamation of 1763, Aboriginal Rights, and Treaties in Canada*, edited by T. Fenge and J. Aldridge, 153–72. Montreal and Kingston: McGill-Queen's University Press.

Crown-Indigenous Relations and Northern Affairs Canada (CIRNAC). 2015. "Cabinet Directive on the Federal Approach to Modern Treaty Implementation." https://www.rcaanc-cirnac.gc.ca/eng/1436450503766/1544714947616.

———. 2018a. "Treaties and Agreements." https://www.rcaanc-cirnac.gc.ca/eng/1100100028574/1529354437231#chp4.

———. 2018b. "Renewing the Comprehensive Land Claims Policy: Towards a Framework for Addressing Section 35 Aboriginal Rights." https://www.rcaanc-cirnac.gc.ca/eng/1408631807053/1544123449934.

———. 2018c. "Government of Canada to Create Recognition and Implementation of Rights Framework." Press release, February 14. https://pm.gc.ca/eng/news/2018/02/14/government-canada-create-recognition-and-implementation-rights-framework.

Davidson, A. 2018. "Flexibility in the Federal System? Institutional Innovation and Indigenous Nations' Self-Determination in the US and Canadian Far North." PhD diss., University of Toronto.

Elazar, D. 1987. *Exploring Federalism*. Tuscaloosa: University of Alabama Press.

Eyford, D. 2015. *A New Direction: Advancing Aboriginal and Treaty Rights*. Ottawa: AANDC.

Fenge, T. 2015. "Negotiating and Implementing Modern Treaties between Aboriginal Peoples and the Crown." In *Keeping Promises: The Royal Proclamation of 1763, Aboriginal Rights, and Treaties in Canada*, edited by T. Fenge and J. Aldridge, 105–37. Montreal and Kingston: McGill-Queen's University Press.

Havard, Gilles. 2001. *The Great Peace of Montreal of 1701: French-Native Diplomacy in the Seventeenth Century*. Montreal and Kingston: McGill-Queen's University Press.

Henderson, J.Y. 1994. "Empowering Treaty Federalism." *Saskatchewan Law Review* 58: 241–330.

Hicks, J., and G. White. 2015. *Made in Nunavut: An Experiment in Decentralized Government*. Vancouver: UBC Press.

Irlbacher-Fox, S. 2009. *Finding Dahshaa: Self-Government, Social Suffering and Aboriginal Policy in Canada*. Vancouver: UBC Press.

James Bay and Northern Quebec Agreement (JBNQA). 1975. Quebec: Éditeur Officile du Québec.

Ladner, K. 2009. "Take 35: Reconciling Constitutional Orders." In *First Nations, First Thoughts: The Impact of Indigenous Thought in Canada*, edited by Annis May Timpson, 279–300. Vancouver: UBC Press.

Land Claims Agreement Coalition (LCAC). 2008. *Honour, Spirit and Intent: A Model Canadian Policy on the Implementation of Modern Treaties between Aboriginal Peoples and the Crown*. http://www.tunngavik.com/documents/publications/LCAC%20Model%20Policy.pdf.

Manuel, A. 2015. *Unsettling Canada: A National Wake-Up Call*. Toronto: Between the Lines.

McIvor, B. 2016. "The Downside of the Tsilhqot'in Decision." First Peoples Law. https://www.firstpeopleslaw.com/index/articles/286.php.

Miller, J.R. 2009. *Compact, Contract, Covenant: Aboriginal Treaty-Making in Canada*. Toronto: University of Toronto Press.

———. 2015. "Canada's Historic Treaties." In *Keeping Promises: The Royal Proclamation of 1763, Aboriginal Rights, and Treaties in Canada*, edited by T. Fenge and J. Aldridge, 153–72. Montreal and Kingston: McGill-Queen's University Press.

Nadasdy, P. 2002. *Hunters and Bureaucrats: Power, Knowledge, and Aboriginal-State Relations in the Southwest Yukon*. Vancouver: UBC Press.

———. 2017. *Sovereignty's Entailments: First Nation State Formation in the Yukon*. Toronto: University of Toronto Press.

Nicol, R., A. Perry, B. Clark, and M. Papillon. 2020. "A New Relationship? Reflections on the Collaborative Federal Fiscal Policy Development Process." *Northern Public Affairs* 6: 34–40. https://www.northernpublicaffairs.ca/index/volume-6-special-issue-2-special-issue-on-modern-treaty-implementation-research/a-new-relationship-reflections-on-the-collaborative-federal-fiscal-policy-development-process/.

Papillon, M. 2015. "The Promises and Pitfalls of Aboriginal Multilevel Governance." In *The State of the Federation: Aboriginal Multilevel Governance*, edited by M. Papillon and A. Juneau, 3–15. Montreal and Kingston: IIGR and McGill-Queen's University Press.

Papillon, M., and A. Lord. 2013. "Les traités modernes: vers une nouvelle relation?" In *Les Autochtones et le Québec. Des premiers contacts au Plan Nord*, edited by A. Beaulieu, S. Gervais, and M. Papillon, 334–48. Montreal: Presses de l'Université de Montréal.

Poelzer, G., and K. Coates. 2015. *From Treaty Peoples to Treaty Nation: A Road Map for All Canadians*. Vancouver: University of British Columbia Press.

Royal Commission on Aboriginal Peoples (RCAP). 1996. *Final Report*. Ottawa: Canada Communications Group.

Russell, P. 2017. *Canada's Odyssey: A Country Based on Incomplete Conquests*. Toronto: University of Toronto Press.

Sabin, J. 2017. *A Federation within a Federation? Devolution and Indigenous Government in the Northwest Territories*. IRPP Study 66. Montreal: Institute for Research on Public Policy.

Samson, C. 2016. "Canada's Strategy of Dispossession: Aboriginal Land and Rights Cessions in Comprehensive Land Claims." *Canadian Journal of Law and Society* 31 (1): 87–102.

Scott, James C. 1998. *Seeing Like a State: How Certain Schemes to Improve the Human Condition Have Failed*. New Haven, CT: Yale University Press.

Senate of Canada. 2008. *Honouring the Spirit of Modern Treaties: Closing the Loopholes. Special Study on the Implementation of Comprehensive Land Claims Agreements in Canada.* Standing Senate Committee on Aboriginal Peoples. Ottawa: Senate of Canada.

Slattery, B. 2015. "The Royal Proclamation of 1763 and the Aboriginal Constitution." In *Keeping Promises: The Royal Proclamation of 1763, Aboriginal Rights, and Treaties in Canada*, edited by T. Fenge and J. Aldridge, 14–32. Montreal and Kingston: McGill-Queen's University Press.

Trudeau, P.E. 1969. *Speech on Aboriginal and Treaty Rights*. August 8. Vancouver: UBC Press.

Truth and Reconciliation Commission of Canada. 2015. *Final Report Vol. 6, Reconciliation*. Montreal and Kingston: McGill-Queen's University Press.

Tully, J. 2008. *Public Philosophy in a New Key (Ideas in Context)*. Cambridge: Cambridge University Press.

Watts, R. 2008. *Comparing Federal Systems*. 3rd ed. Montreal and Kingston: McGill-Queen's University Press.

White, G. 2002. "Treaty Federalism in Northern Canada: Aboriginal-Government Land Claims Boards." *Publius* 32 (3): 89–114.

Williams, R.A. 1997. *Linking Arms Together: American Indian Treaty Visions of Law and Peace, 1600–1800*. New York: Oxford University Press.

Wilson, G., C. Alcantara, and T. Rodon. 2020. *Nested Federalism and Inuit Governance in the Canadian Arctic*. Vancouver: UBC Press.

PART FOUR

Electoral Politics and Political Communication

twelve
Public Opinion and Political Cleavages in Canada

ALLISON HARELL, LAURA STEPHENSON,
AND LYNE DESCHATELÊTS

Introduction

Canadian public opinion is structured around important social, political, and regional divides that shape how Canadians think about and engage in politics. Divisions by class, ethnicity, language, religion, and region have helped to shape the nature of partisan competition in Canada. Indeed, these are fundamental components of how we understand political culture in Canada. Some of these cleavages continue to structure Canadians' political preferences today. Political cleavages, or the relatively stable differences in political preferences across salient groups of voters, are the focus of this chapter. How do we understand political cleavages, which ones are salient, and how do they play out in contemporary electoral politics in Canada? In this chapter, we explore how scholars have thought about and studied the nature of political cleavages in Canada over time, drawing on approaches from both political culture and political behaviour research. We then turn to analyzing the level and stability of political cleavages in the current party system, drawing on data from the Canadian Election Study (CES) from 2004 to 2015.

The Structure of Canadian Public Opinion

Public opinion simply refers to the ways in which individual political attitudes aggregate within a given society, or subgroup of the population. If Canadians, on average, want to spend more on education or health care, we might expect that this reflects (a) the current spending levels in these areas, as well as (b) their social identities (e.g., whether "people like me" benefit from these policies), and (c) their political ideology (e.g., support for versus opposition to more redistribution). In turn, politicians should respond to the public's expressed wishes by adjusting spending levels (Soroka and Wlezien 2004). This is, in fact, at the heart of the concept of representation in electoral democracies. Elected officials seek to gain office, and stay in office, by responding to their constituents (Stimson, Mackuen, and Erikson 1995). As we will see in this chapter, what citizens want from the government varies across salient social and political cleavages that are relatively stable over time. In this section, we explore how we understand the underlying nature of Canadians' attitudes toward the state and politics from a political culture perspective and from a political behaviour perspective.

Underlying Structure of Political Attitudes in Canada: A Political Culture Perspective[1]

Historically, the structure of Canadian public opinion has been understood through the lens of political culture, which "refers to the shared values, orientations, and attitudes that define various social groups (such as nations, regions, and groups of people that share ethnic or religious backgrounds)" (Harell and Deschatelêts 2014, 229). Political culture as a concept assumes far more stability in values and attitudes than public opinion, and focuses on a collectivity's "fundamental orientations and assumptions about politics" (Stewart 2002, 24).

One recurring finding in the literature is that Canadian society is less individualistic than American society and more deferential toward state institutions and intervention in society (Lipset 1986, 1990). Canadians tend to believe that the state can and should play an active role and in turn they are more willing to support egalitarian public policies such as public health care and state-owned enterprises such as public broadcasting (Brooks 2009). One classic argument explaining this difference comes from Lipset (1986, 1990) and his theory of formative events. For Lipset, the driving differences between these two societies stems from how they experienced the American Revolution. In the United States, Lipset argues, the Revolution led to the endorsement of liberal individualism and a rejection of hierarchical and centralized state power. Canada, in contrast, remained tied to Britain, which bred a more conservative liberalism that was reinforced by an influx of Loyalists fleeing the United States. As a result, Canadians became more deferential to authority, more willing for the state to intervene in society in both economic development and social policy, and more concerned about maintaining social order than maximizing individual freedom. In Lipset's 1990 study, he argues that there are durable differences along these dimensions, and others have found (some) supporting evidence (e.g., Perlin 1997; Cole, Kincaid, and Rodriguez 2004; Brooks 2009). We should be cautious, however, because on many dimensions the similarities between Canadians and Americans stand out more than their differences (Perlin 1997; Brooks 2009; although see Adams 2003 for a counter-argument). In fact, within certain sectors of the population, there is more ideological similarity between Canadians and Americans than among Canadians (Farney 2012).

Political culture research in Canada tends to focus on specific subcultures within Canada and the variation across distinct groups. In particular, the difference between English Canada and French Canada is of enduring interest. Perhaps the most well-known approach to Canadian political culture is the fragment theory. American historian Louis Hartz (1964) argued that New World colonies were settled by groups representing only ideological fragments of the European societies from whence they came. That is to say, whereas European societies tended to contain the full spectrum of political and social thought (including feudal/conservative, liberal, and socialist ideologies), immigrant waves from these societies were not fully representative of this diversity. Settler societies, shaped by who was emigrating and at what point in history, tended to be biased toward a specific ideological orientation, creating in the New World what Hartz viewed as homogeneous societies in cultural terms. Kenneth McRae (1964, 1978) and others applied this approach to Canada and argued that English Canada's political culture congealed around a liberal fragment, while French Canada (New France and Acadia) were settled by a feudal – or conservative – fragment (see also Bouchard 2008).

As in the United States, liberalism in English Canada was imported by British immigrants – but unlike in the United States, those immigrants came not only from England, but also from Loyalists fleeing the American Revolution south of the border (see especially Horowitz 1966). As a result, some fragment theorists claim that English Canada's liberalism is "tory-touched." In other words, whereas American liberalism is defined heavily in terms of individualism and personal freedom, the more conservative elements in Canada resulted in more acceptance of social hierarchy (society comprising interdependent social classes) and recognition of the key role of the state in the pursuit of the public good. The result was a dialectic between the dominant liberalism and more conservative elements in Canadian society, allowing for greater recognition and acceptance of collective concerns, expressed through a variant of mild socialism.

French Canada, in contrast, was settled (according to fragment theorists) by a purely pre-revolutionary fragment from France. These conservative elements "congealed" before French Canada could be affected by the liberalizing effects of the French Revolution and were further reinforced by the dominance of conservative institutions, such as the Catholic Church, following the ceding of French Canada to Britain. Characterized as an anti-liberal and collectivist ideology, this quasi-feudal conservatism, often referred to as the idea of *La Survivance* in French Canada (and especially in Quebec), was the dominant form of political culture until the Quiet Revolution. Unlike in English Canada, where the dominant liberalism was "touched" by conservative toryism, in Quebec the opposite was true: the dominant conservative culture was "touched" by liberal elements, creating a dialectic that allowed for the creation of Quebec's own version of socialism, which combines active state intervention and liberal elements with collective concerns about national identity.

Nationalism and its different manifestations in Quebec came full circle, as Hartz suggested it could. A feudal past when combined with a sudden influx of liberal ideas in the mid-twentieth century produced a political environment where the seeds of socialism could sprout. Quebec socialists since the 1960s have drawn on both the collectivist and organic principles of French Canada's feudal past and the egalitarian and rationalist components of its liberal Quiet Revolution. Today, then, Quebec is no more traditional or socially conservative than English Canada, but it does have a distinct political culture that is arguably more collectivist, more pacifistic, and more open to non-traditional lifestyles than other Canadians (Brooks 2009).

While the distinction between English and French Canada's political cultures is clearly a key component of understanding politics in Canada, many authors argue that this view is too simplistic, especially with respect to English Canada (Horowitz 1966; Wiseman 2007). Canadian politics has long been characterized by its regional nature (Meisel 1964, 1974; Blake 1972; Elkins and Simeon 1974; Schwartz 1974; Young and Archer 2002). Indeed, some authors have gone so far as to argue that "Canadian politics is regional politics; regionalism is one of the pre-eminent facts of Canadian life" (Elkins and Simeon 1974, 397). This regionalism has also played a role in political behaviour perspectives for understanding Canadian public opinion.

Underlying Structure of Political Attitudes in Canada: A Political Behaviour Perspective

A political behaviour perspective takes a very different approach to the study of public opinion. While political culture focuses on history and events, political behaviour focuses on individuals. This has been possible only since the development of large-scale, individual-level surveys of populations. In Canada, the CES was the first large-scale academic study of Canadian electors, and it remains a key longitudinal resource. Beginning in 1965, the study has continued in every federal election with the exception of 1972 and provides a wealth of information about the structure of citizen attitudes toward politics and political actors (for a review, see Kanji, Bilodeau, and Scotto 2012). The use of individual-level surveys to study citizen behaviour in Canada was part of a larger trend of survey research dominated by two schools of thought developed in the American context. The Columbia school (named after the university where the research took place) focused primarily on social demographic variables, finding that the social group to which you belong largely determine the party you eventually vote for (Lazarsfeld, Berelson, and Gaudet 1944). The idea, essentially, is that people think politically as they are socially (27). The Michigan school, in contrast to this sociological model, focuses primarily on the importance of party identification as the major determinant of vote choice (Campbell et al. 1960). Party identity is a long-term, social-psychological connection to a political party. While party identification often is related to socio-demographics, it can assume a life of its own and become a major force in political opinions and vote choice.

Much of the early work on voting behaviour in Canada stressed two key features of Canadian politics that challenge the appropriateness of the Columbia and Michigan models. First, Clarke et al. (1984, 1991, 1996) maintain that Canadian political parties are *brokerage* parties; they seek to bring together a diverse set of voters not linked by a shared ideology. Issue positions are chosen in order to court votes, and parties are seen primarily as vote-getting machines. Thus, Clarke et al. maintain that in the Canadian case there are not many stabilizing forces, such as partisan identification or the underlying social demographics, that structure vote choice. Instead, vote choices are best understood as a combination of attitudes about issues and leaders. Kanji and Archer (2001) also adopt this view. They argue that sociological models do not explain Canadian vote choice very well because Canadians are fragmented and their social groups are not clearly associated with a particular party position.

A second key feature, related to the brokerage party image of Canadian politics, is the contention that partisan identification is meaningless in the Canadian context (Meisel 1974) or at least functions differently here (LeDuc et al. 1984; Clarke et al. 1984, 1991, 1996). Clarke and colleagues have shown that many Canadians identify with a party but not in the same way as was assumed in the Michigan social-psychological model. In fact, Clarke and his colleagues argue that because Canada has brokerage parties, most Canadians are *flexible partisans*, defined by less stability over time, less intensity, and inconsistency across federal and provincial levels of government (compared to *durable partisans*, who more closely fit the Michigan definition). Durable partisans act more like their American partisan counterparts, and flexible partisans are less attached to parties and prone to much greater instability in choice.

The image of a volatile electorate with little stable attachment to parties, combined with parties that are not anchored in long-term ideological orientations, is prevalent in the literature. This suggests that political cleavages in Canada will be minimal, or at least of short duration. In effect, the lack of ideological thinking within the electorate removes the restraint in the United States in how parties construct their issues in order to maximize their votes.

While this interpretation has compelling features, it has been challenged. Beginning in the 1990s, Canadian Election Study teams have contended that the Canadian electorate does exhibit some stable characteristics. Johnston et al. (1992) argued that partisan ties are present in the Canadian electorate and the instability that Clarke and colleagues observed was primarily the result of problems with how partisan identification was measured (which did not give non-identifiers an option). They argue instead that Canadians do have stable, meaningful party identifications. More recently, Blais and his colleagues (2002) have argued that partisan identification does constitute a meaningful attachment that structures the vote choice of Canadians. This, they argue, is part of the reason why Liberals have historically had so much electoral success. Simply, they have a larger share of party identifiers who are predisposed to vote for them. (For a more direct comparison of American and Canadian party identification effects, see Bélanger and Stephenson 2014.)

Furthermore, these scholars also argue that political cleavages in Canada are structured by social characteristics. Using the "funnel of causation" model developed for studies of American voting behaviour (Campbell et al. 1960; Miller and Shanks 1996), Blais and his colleagues show that stable social demographic variables and partisan identification are both important explanatory variables in vote choice, along with values and attitudes and the election campaign (Blais et al. 2002). In particular, ethnicity, religion, gender, urban/rural residence, and regional differences in the electorate were strong predictors of vote choice in the 2000 election. Ethnic minorities and Catholic voters were more likely to vote for the Liberals, women were more likely to vote for the NDP, and people residing in the rural west were more likely to vote for the Canadian Alliance (see also Blais 2005). In the 1997 election, region of residence was actually the most powerful social demographic variable explaining vote choice (Gidengil et al. 1999).

What is more, these authors find that Canadian voters do think ideologically. In particular, they find that voters have consistent values structured largely around attitudes about the free market (Nevitte et al. 1999; Blais et al. 2002). Voters are capable of associating particular parties with particular issues (Bélanger 2003). While voters are not highly sophisticated in their understandings of the political system (Fournier 2002), this more recent research agenda demonstrates convincingly that there are longer-term determinants of vote choice. While the campaign and the leaders of the parties are always important (Johnston et al. 1992; Blais et al. 2002), socio-demographic and partisan characteristics of voters are also relevant factors in how individuals vote in Canadian elections. While some cleavages, such as class (Brodie and Jenson 1990, though see Johnston 2017) have been less salient, others such as region, religion, and ethnicity have proven important in explaining vote choice (see Blais 2005).

How, then, does one explain large swings in the electoral fortunes of Canadian political parties? One explanation is the electoral system. With a first-past-the-post system, the candidate who receives the plurality of votes in a riding wins the seat. This means that relatively small swings in overall support for parties can lead to big shifts in the number of seats they win. As a result, Canadian politics often appears more volatile than the underlying distribution of voter preferences, which tends to remain fairly stable.

Political Cleavages in Contemporary Canadian Politics

One defining feature of partisan politics today is the new federal party system, which has its roots in the shocking outcome of the 1993 election. That contest saw the emergence of two new federal parties (the Bloc Québécois, a sovereigntist party based in Quebec, and the Reform Party, a right-wing party with a stronghold in the west) and the decimation of a classic brokerage party, the Progressive Conservatives, as well as the smaller social democratic option, the New Democrats (NDP). So cataclysmic was this "electoral earthquake" that the official opposition in Canada's Parliament after the 1993 election was a party committed to Quebec separation. Over the next decade (during which the Liberals held onto power), a movement to unite the two right-wing parties (the Progressive Conservatives and Reform Party's successor, the Canadian Alliance) finally resulted in a 2003 merger that created the new Conservative Party of Canada (CPC) (see Bélanger and Godbout 2010 for details). In 2011, the NDP also made history when it became the official opposition for the first time, relegating the Liberal Party (traditionally considered "the Government Party") to third-party status. Furthermore, despite its key role in politics in the 1990s, the BQ has slowly lost its grip on Quebec's French-speaking voters. Since 2004, then, Canada has moved away from the brokerage party system of an earlier era when the two main parties crowded the political centre. It now has a multi-party system in which there is a clear right- and left-wing option. In this next section, we explore how citizens relate to this new party system through an examination of how their social characteristics and partisan attachments are structured.

First, we focus on the key socio-demographic cleavages – language, education, gender, immigrant status, religion, and region. As we discussed in the previous section, immigration, religion, and region have been important in Canadian politics from both a political culture and political behaviour perspective. To these we add language, education, and gender, which have been found to be important in other work. Language obviously is a marker that corresponds with region and religion (e.g., Quebec), but also is a key dividing line in Quebec politics (Bélanger and Nadeau 2009). Education is a marker of social class, a key cleavage in many industrialized democracies, but it has been less prominent in Canada (though see Johnston 2017). Finally, there is important work showing the emergence of a gender gap in voter preferences, with women more likely to vote for parties on the left and men for more conservative, right-wing alternatives (Gidengil et al. 2005).

Figure 12.1 reports the marginal effects of each variable upon vote choice outside of Quebec, for Liberal, Conservative, and NDP votes for all elections combined between 2004 and 2015.[2] If social demographic cleavages structure vote choice, we should observe a clear distinction in the effect of a variable on support for each party, such that the marginal effect for some parties is positive (greater than 0) and for another party it is negative (less than 0). Significant differences can be distinguished by observing that the confidence intervals do not overlap.[3]

Figure 12.1 reveals some very striking results. Most interestingly, religion has the strongest effect on vote choice.[4] Non-Catholic Christians are much

Figure 12.1 Marginal Effects on Vote Choice outside Quebec

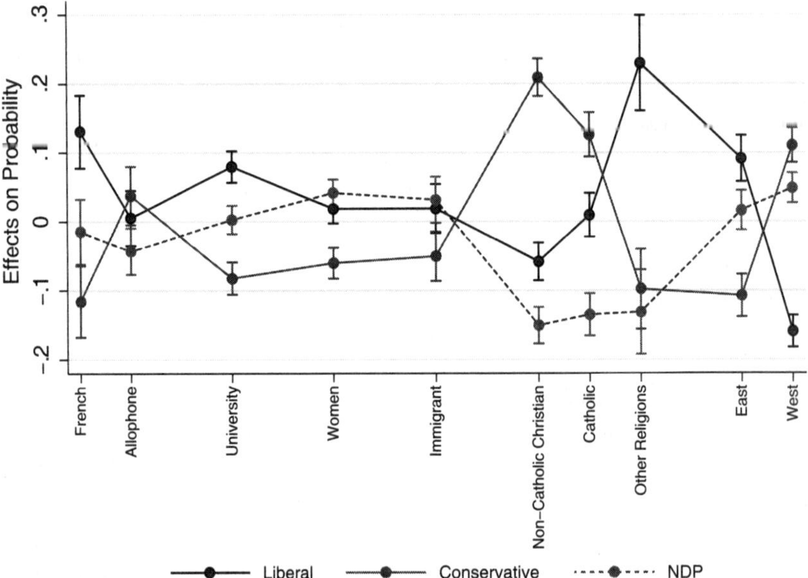

Source: Canadian Election Study, 2004–15.
Note: Graph shows the marginal effects of each socio-demographic variable for voting for each party (outside Quebec). The estimations are based on a multinomial regression model that includes all socio-demographic variables, as well as election year. Results are weighted.

more likely than the non-religious to support the Conservative Party, rather than either the Liberals or NDP. This effect is similar for Catholics, although the effect for Liberal voting is not significantly different from zero. On the other hand, other non-Christian religions are much more supportive of the Liberals than either the NDP or Conservatives. What is particularly interesting about this finding is that religious people in general are less supportive of the NDP, regardless of denomination; however, there are denominational differences in support for the Conservatives and Liberals.

Other social demographic cleavages that distinguish between Canadian political parties are language, education, gender and region. French speakers outside of Quebec are more supportive of the Liberals than they are other parties. And women are less supportive of the Conservatives than men, which is consistent with earlier research (Gidengil et al. 2005). While these two cleavages define support for one party, they do not define opposition to a single, specific other party. Education, however, clearly divides the Conservatives and Liberals, with people having university education more likely to vote for the Liberals and less likely to vote Conservative.

Finally, we look at the effect of region outside Quebec by distinguishing voters to the east (Newfoundland and Labrador, Prince Edward Island, Nova Scotia, and New Brunswick) and west (Manitoba, Saskatchewan, Alberta, and British Columbia) of Ontario. We examine Quebec separately (see figure 12.2). Eastern Canadians are more likely to vote Liberal and less likely to vote Conservative than those in Ontario. In the west, the reverse is the case. Westerners are more likely to vote Conservative. Interestingly, people living in the west are also more supportive of the NDP, although to a lesser extent than the Conservatives.

Figure 12.2 shows the results for voters in Quebec. Here we see only two cleavages are important – French language and religion (in particular, having a non-Christian religion). The partisan divide here is between the Liberals and Bloc Québécois. French speakers support the Bloc and not the Liberals, compared to anglophones. Allophones (first language neither French nor English) are also slightly more likely to vote for the Bloc compared to anglophones. For religion, those identifying with a non-Christian religion support the Liberals and not the Bloc, compared to the non-religious.

Thus, if we simply consider the socio-demographic bases of party support in Canada, we see important differences in what parties Canadians prefer. These differences partly work through how they structure more proximate variables to vote choice, such as partisanship and campaign specific variables. Partisanship, in particular, is a concept that is grounded in people's social backgrounds. As noted above, many have shown that party identification is a significant and important factor in Canadian vote choice; however, this does not

Figure 12.2 Marginal Effects on Vote Choice in Quebec

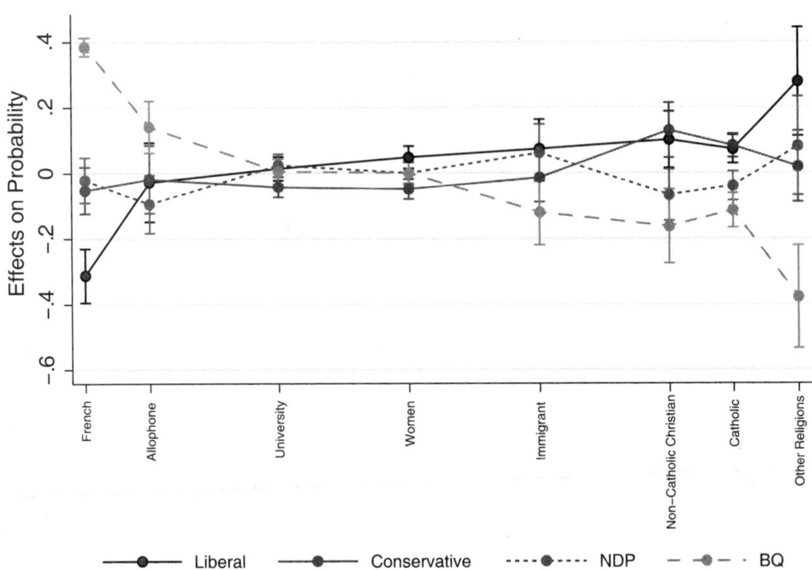

Source: Canadian Election Study, 2004–15.
Note: Graph shows the marginal effects of each socio-demographic variable for voting for each party (in Quebec). The estimations are based on a multinomial regression model that includes all socio-demographic variables, as well as election year. Results are weighted.

mean social demographic cleavages are irrelevant. When we conduct the same analyses controlling for party identification, the general patterns observed in figures 12.1 and 12.2 remain, though the size of these differences shrinks and in some cases disappears. Outside of Quebec, the gender difference in vote choice disappears completely, while the other effects get smaller. Within Quebec, the picture remains largely unchanged. In other words, social demographic cleavages are important considerations in understanding Canadian voters and their preferences, not only because they likely structure partisanship, but also because they continue to be important *even after* accounting for party identification.

Partisanship clearly matters, though, especially outside of Quebec. Figure 12.3 shows the percentage of the population who indicate they identify "fairly strongly" or "very strongly" with each party. Several points stand out. The overall number of partisans in the population is telling. There has been an increase in partisanship since 2004 in conjunction with the increased ideological polarization of the party system that has given voters clearer right- and left-wing options. Partisanship reached its high point in 2011, when the Conservative Party finally won a majority government.

Figure 12.3 Partisanship in the Contemporary Era

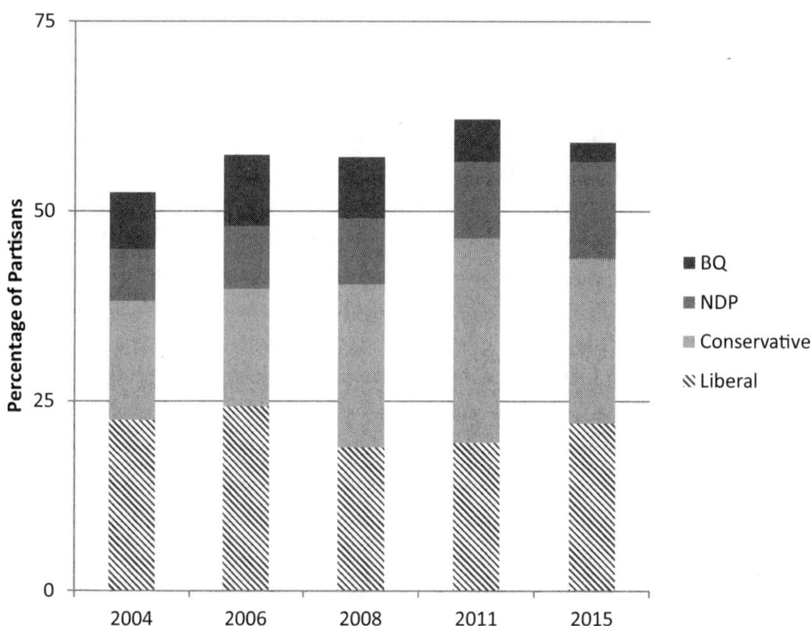

Source: Canadian Election Study, 2004–15.
Note: Graph shows percentage of those with partisan identity by party, where partisanship is defined by strong or fairly strong attachment to a party. Results are weighted.

Also important is the relative size of partisan groups in the public. Despite its weakness prior to 2015, the Liberal Party of Canada (LPC) maintained the firm support of a large segment of the population (approximately 21 per cent). This finding is interesting, considering that the Liberal Party is more centrist than the NDP and thus a less clear alternative to the Conservative Party, the other major party in Canada (supported by about 20 per cent of the population). This suggests that the Liberal Party still benefits from a partisan advantage, as Blais and his colleagues (2002) noted in earlier research. Together, loyalty toward the LPC and CPC covers approximately 40 per cent of the Canadian population. The NDP, despite its 2011 success at becoming the official opposition, lays claim to significantly less partisan support in the population (less than 10 per cent on average). The decline of the Bloc Québécois is also clear from the figure, falling to less than 3 per cent in 2015.

This is important because partisans are obviously more likely to vote for the party they are attached to, but also because they are more likely to vote in general. Partisanship captures, in part, social cleavages in society. It influences how and if people vote, thus serving as a key dividing line in Canadian public opinion.

Conclusions

We care about political and social cleavages because we want to know not only what causes them, but also their consequences for Canadian democracy. In this chapter, we have seen how Canadian public opinion is structured around social divides, especially language, religion, and region, and to a lesser extent education, immigrant status, and gender, as well as partisan attachment. The Liberal Party has a stronger base of support among francophones outside Quebec (and anglophones in Quebec) and those with university education, and it is particularly popular in the Atlantic provinces. The new Conservative Party of Canada is built in part on the traditional base of the Progressive Conservatives and Alliance/Reform, with stronger support among Christians, Western Canadians, those with English as their first language, and men. The NDP, the party of the left in Canada, does better among the non-religious, and in the west (though not to the same extent as the CPC). In Quebec, the main social divide is by language and the difference between minority religions versus both Christians and the non-religious.

These differences are important because they constrain what parties are willing to offer during election campaigns, and what they do when they are in office. A party with a strong base in the west is unlikely to promote or adopt policies that are clearly counter to their base of support. While voters are rarely attentive watchdogs to their party's behaviour, parties are strategic. They want to win elections, and they win elections by ensuring that their bases turn out to vote for them while at the same time trying to attract new voters. This is why elections are fundamental to the process of representation. The party that does this best, in theory, wins the election and is given the opportunity to govern. However, if these cleavages are too stable – if a party can count on a base of support, regardless of what they do – then parties are no longer constrained in their behaviour.

The cleavages that have defined the contemporary era in Canadian politics are not new. One question moving forward will be the extent to which this stability may strengthen, and in particular whether partisanship is becoming a more defining characteristic of the electorate. As we have seen, there is some evidence that partisanship is increasing, and the comparative context south of the border certainly has become more polarized in recent elections. In Canada, we have seen increased partisan sorting, defined as when "partisans correctly identify and align themselves with the party that best matches their preferences, thereby creating more uniform preference sets among a given party's supporters" (Kevins and Soroka 2018, 5). At least for some policy domains (such as those relating to redistribution), there is evidence that partisan sorting has increased (5). As partisans become more aligned with their parties, this can reduce the likelihood and ability of electorates to react to what parties are actually doing. True representation in an electoral democracy like Canada requires that parties constantly seek to respond to the preferences of their bases, but also the potential is there for them to reach beyond their bases in order to attract other voters. Without this possibility, public opinion can become more rigidly polarized, something that is counter to Canada's history of brokerage politics.

Notes

1 This section draws heavily on Harell and Deschatelêts (2014). In this chapter, we have essentially added another author and expanded our perspective to include public opinion.

2 These results, and those in figure 12.1, are based upon multinomial logistic regressions. The dependent variable was vote choice (Liberals, Conservative or NDP) and the independent variables the various social cleavages and election year. In other words, figure 12.1 shows the probability of various social characteristics on the vote for each party, controlling for the effects of the other social demographic variables as well as the election year (full model not shown).

3 Confidence intervals indicate the range within which the real effect of the variable is likely to fall. When confidence intervals between two variables do not overlap, it indicates that there is little chance for the two variables to share the same value.

4 There is a long tradition of studying the role of religion in Canadian elections (see Laponce 1969, 1972; Meisel 1956, 1973; Irvine 1974; Johnston 1985, 1991; Blais 2005; Stephenson 2010). Traditionally, it was Catholics who supported the Liberal Party and the causes behind this connection constitute an unsolved mystery. The relationship, however, seems to have dissipated in recent elections.

References and Suggested Readings

Adams, Michael. 2003. *Fire and Ice: The United States, Canada, and the Myth of Converging Values.* Toronto: Penguin.

Bélanger, Éric. 2003. "Issue Ownership by Canadian Political Parties 1953–2001." *Canadian Journal of Political Science* 36 (3): 539–58.

Bélanger, Éric, and Jean-François Godbout. 2010. "Why Do Parties Merge? The Case of the Conservative Party of Canada." *Parliamentary Affairs* 63 (1): 41–65.

Bélanger, Éric, and Richard Nadeau. 2009. *Le comportement électoral des Québécois*. Montreal: Presses de l'Université de Montréal.

Bélanger, Éric, and Laura B. Stephenson. 2014. "The Comparative Study of Canadian Voting Behaviour." In *Comparing Canada: Citizens, Government, and Policy*, edited by Luc Turgeon, Martin Papillon, Jennifer Wallner, and Stephen White, 97–122. Vancouver: UBC Press.

Blais, André. 2005. "Accounting for the Electoral Success of the Liberal Party in Canada." *Canadian Journal of Political Science* 38 (4): 821–40.

Blais, André, Elisabeth Gidengil, Richard Nadeau, and Neil Nevitte. 2002. *Anatomy of a Liberal Victory*. Peterborough, ON: Broadview.

Blake, Donald E. 1972. "The Measurement of Regionalism in Canadian Voting Patterns." *Canadian Journal of Political Science* 5 (1): 55–79.

Bouchard, Gérard. 2008. *The Making of the Nations and Cultures of the New World: An Essay in Comparative History*. Montreal and Kingston: McGill-Queen's University Press.

Brodie, Janine, and Jane Jenson. 1990. "The Party System." In *Canadian Politics in the 1990s*, edited by M.S. Whittington and G. Williams, 249–67. Toronto: Nelson.

Brooks, Stephen. 2009. "Canadian Political Cultures." In *Canadian Politics*, edited by James Bickerton and Alain-G. Gagnon, 5th ed., 45–70. North York: University of Toronto Press.

Campbell, Angus, Philip E. Converse, Warren E. Miller, and Donald E. Stokes. 1960. *The American Voter*. Chicago: Chicago University Press.

Clarke, Harold D., Jane Jenson, Lawrence LeDuc, and Jon H. Pammet. 1984. *Absent Mandate: The Politics of Discontent in Canada*. Toronto: Gage.

———. 1991. *Absent Mandate: Interpreting Change in Canadian Elections*. Toronto: Gage.

———. 1996. *Absent Mandate: Canadian Electoral Politics in an Era of Restructuring*. Toronto: Gage.

Cole, Richard L., John Kincaid, and Alejandro Rodriguez. 2004. "Public Opinion on Federalism and Federal Political Culture in Canada, Mexico, and the United States." *Publius* 34 (3): 201–21.

Elkins, David J., and Richard E.B. Simeon. 1974. "Regional Political Cultures in Canada." *Canadian Journal of Political Science* 7 (3): 397–437.

Farney, James. 2012. *Social Conservatives and Party Politics, Canada and the United States*. Toronto: University of Toronto Press.

Fournier, Patrick. 2002. "The Uninformed Canada Voter." In *Citizen Politics: Research and Theory in Canadian Political Behaviour*, edited by Joanna Everitt and Brenda O'Neill. Don Mills, ON: Oxford University Press.

Gidengil, Elisabeth, André Blais, Neil Nevitte, and Richard Nadeau. 1999. "Making Sense of Regional Voting in the 1997 Federal Election: Liberal and Reform Support Outside Quebec." *Canadian Journal of Political Science* 32 (2): 247–72.

Gidengil, Elisabeth, Matthew Hennigar, André Blais, and Neil Nevitte. 2005. "Explaining the Gender Gap in Support for the New Right: The Case of Canada." *Comparative Political Studies* 38 (10): 1171–95.

Harell, Allison, and Lyne Deschatelêts. 2014. "Political Culture(s) in Canada: Orientations to Politics in a Pluralist, Multicultural Federation." In *Canadian Politics*, edited by J. Bickerton and A-G. Gagnon, 6th ed. Toronto: University of Toronto Press.

Hartz, Louis, ed. 1964. *The Founding of New Societies: Studies in the History of the United States, Latin America, South Africa, Canada, and Australia*. New York: Harcourt, Brace and World.

Horowitz, Gad. 1966. "Conservatism, Liberalism, and Socialism in Canada: An Interpretation." *Canadian Journal of Economics and Political Science* 32: 143–71.

Irvine, William P. 1974. "Explaining the Religious Basis of the Canadian Partisan Identity: Success on the Third Try." *Canadian Journal of Political Science* 7 (3): 560–3.

Johnston, Richard G. 1985. "The Reproduction of the Religion Cleavage in Canadian Elections." *Canadian Journal of Political Science* 18 (1): 99–113.

———. 1991. "The Geography of Class and Religion in Canadian Elections." In *The Ballot and Its Message*, edited by Joseph Wearing, 108–35. Toronto: Copp Clarke Pitman.

———. 2017. *The Canadian Party System: An Analytic History*. Vancouver: UBC Press.

Johnston, Richard G., André Blais, Henry E. Brady, and Jean Crête. 1992. *Letting the People Decide*. Montreal and Kingston: McGill-Queen's University Press.

Kanji, Mebs, and Keith Archer. 2001. "The Theories of Voting and Their Applicability in Canada." In *Citizen Politics: Research and Theory in Canadian Political Behaviour*, edited by Joanna Everitt and Brenda O'Neill, 160–83. Don Mills, ON: Oxford University Press.

Kanji, Mebs, Antoine Bilodeau, and Thomas Scotto, eds. 2012. *The Canadian Election Studies, Assessing Four Decades of Influence*. Vancouver: UBC Press.

Kevins, Anthony, and Stuart Soroka. 2018. "Growing Apart? Partisan Sorting in Canada, 1992–2015." *Canadian Journal of Political Science* 51 (1): 103–33.

Laponce, J.A. 1969. "Ethnicity, Religion, and Politics, in Canada: A Comparative Analysis of Survey and Census Data." In *Quantitative Ecological Analysis in the Social Sciences*, edited by Mattei Dogan and Stein Rokkan, 187–216. Cambridge, MA: MIT Press.

———. 1972. "Post-Dicting Electoral Cleavages in Canadian Federal Elections, 1959–68: Material for a Footnote." *Canadian Journal of Political Science* 5 (2): 270–86.

Lazarsfeld, Paul F., Bernard Berelson, and Hazel Gaudet. 1944. *The People's Choice: How the Voter Makes Up His Mind in a Presidential Campaign*. Oxford: Duell, Sloan and Pearce.

LeDuc, Lawrence, Harold D. Clarke, Jane Jenson, and Jon H. Pammett. 1984. "Partisan Instability in Canada: Evidence from a New Panel Study." *American Political Science Review* 78 (2): 470–84.

Lipset, Seymour Martin. 1986. "Historical Traditions and National Characteristics: A Comparative Analysis of Canada and the United States." *Canadian Journal of Sociology* 11: 113–55.

———. 1990. *Continental Divide: The Values and Institutions of the United States and Canada*. New York: Routledge.

McRae, Kenneth D. 1964. "The Structure of Canadian Society." In *The Founding of New Societies: Studies in the History of the United States, Latin America, South Africa, Canada, and Australia*, edited by Louis Hartz, 219–74. New York: Harcourt, Brace and World.

———. 1978. "Louis Hartz's Concept of the Fragment Society and Its Application to Canada." *Études canadiennes* 5: 17–30.

Meisel, John. 1956. "Religious Affiliation and Electoral Behaviour: A Case Study." *Canadian Journal of Economics and Political Science* 22 (4): 481–96.

———, ed. 1964. *Papers on the 1962 Election: Fifteen Papers on the Canadian General Election of 1962*. Toronto: University of Toronto Press.

———. 1973. *Working Papers on Canadian Politics*, enlarged ed. Montreal and Kingston: McGill-Queen's University Press.

———. 1974. *Cleavages, Parties and Values in Canada*. London: Sage.

Miller, Warren E., and J. Merrill Shanks. 1996. *The New American Voter*. Cambridge, MA: Harvard University Press.

Nevitte, Neil, André Blais, Elisabeth Gidengil, and Richard Nadeau. 1999. *Unsteady State: The 1997 Federal Election*. Don Mills, ON: Oxford University Press.

Perlin, George. 1997. "The Constraints of Public Opinion: Diverging and Converging Paths." In *Degrees of Freedom: Canada and the United States in a Changing World*, edited by Keith Banting and George Hoberg, 71–149. Montreal and Kingston: McGill-Queen's University Press.

Schwartz, Mildred A. 1974. *Politics and Territory*. Montreal and Kingston: McGill-Queen's University Press.

Soroka, Stuart N., and Christopher Wlezien. 2004. *Degrees of Democracy: Public Opinion and Policy in Comparative Perspective*. Center for Advanced Study in the Social Sciences Working Paper Series. Madrid: Juan March Institute.

Stephenson, Laura. 2010. "The Catholic-Liberal Connection: A Test of Strength." In *Voting Behaviour in Canada*, edited by Cameron D. Anderson and Laura B. Stephenson, 86–106. Vancouver: UBC Press.

Stewart, Ian. 2002. "Vanishing Points: Three Paradoxes of Political Culture Research." In *Citizen Politics: Research and Theory in Canadian Political Behaviour*, edited by Joanna Everitt and Brenda O'Neill, 21–39. Don Mills, ON: Oxford University Press.

Stimson, James A., Michael B. Mackuen, and Robert S. Erikson. 1995. "Dynamic Representation." *American Political Science Review* 89 (3): 543–65.

Wiseman, Nelson. 1988. "A Note on 'Hartz-Horowitz at Twenty': The Case of French Canada." *Canadian Journal of Political Science* 21 (4): 795–806.

———. 2007. *In Search of Canadian Political Culture*. Vancouver: UBC Press.

Young, Lisa, and Keith Archer, eds. 2002. *Regionalism and Party Politics*. Don Mills, ON: Oxford University Press.

thirteen

Parties and Elections: An End to Canadian Exceptionalism?

JAMES BICKERTON

Introduction

This chapter will divide its discussion of parties and elections into four parts. The first provides an overview of electoral politics in the first and second party systems, while noting certain distinctive and persistent features of party politics in Canada. Historically, there have been several reorderings of the party system triggered by a major realignment of partisan loyalties within the electorate, along with the rise and demise of one or more political parties. The second section will examine the third party system that followed one of these reorderings and lasted from the 1960s to the 1990s.

While cultural and regional diversity and major social changes each played a role in these dramatic disruptions, so too did other institutional features of the political system that have shaped the party system, such as an executive-dominated parliamentary system and the first-past-the-post electoral system. The contribution of cultural and institutional factors to the rise of insurgent "third" parties – and the regionalization of the party system this occasioned – constitutes the third section of the chapter.

In the last section, our attention will turn to theories of vote choice and their application to elections in the current party system, which dates back to the system-shattering election of 1993. Consideration will be given to the perennial balancing act that parties must perform: to sustain themselves they must build and maintain a stable foundation of voter support within a changing electorate; but to be truly successful they must find ways to reach beyond their core supporters to gather sufficient votes to contest for power. Finally, there will be a discussion of the long-term factors that have combined in the past to produce the unique character of the party system, and whether this "Canadian exceptionalism" will persist.

Canada's First Two-Party Systems

Of first importance to note is that Canada's party system has not always been as it is today in the number of political parties, the kind of appeals they make to voters, and their bases of support in the electorate. At the same time, certain elements of continuity helped to structure and shape party politics in each era of party competition. If a party system is defined as the pattern of competition and cooperation among all political parties within a given political system, then Canada can be said to have had several party systems since its creation in 1867 (Carty 1993; Carty, Cross, and Young 2000).

The first period of Canadian party politics spanned the half century from the country's origins until 1921, the year of the first general election following World War I. Party competition during this period took the form of a classic two-party system. Political scientists consider this a normal feature of political systems that use the simple plurality or "first-past-the-post" (FPTP) electoral system. The Liberal and Conservative parties operated as broad-based national parties, alternating in power and building electoral coalitions that comprised different regions, classes, religions, and language groups. Politics was primarily a battle over the spoils of power between the "Ins" and "Outs," unsullied by ideological principle and focused mainly on parochial concerns at the local level (Siegfried 1966). This combination of two-party competition and highly personalized politics, with its focus on the use of patronage, policies, and patriotic appeals to build and maintain national party organizations and winning electoral coalitions, had the additional effect over time of integrating a diverse Canadian polity and constructing the framework of a viable nation-state.

While the first party system served Canada reasonably well during the crucial early phase of state-building and national development, it did not survive the nationalist-imperialist cross-pressures generated by Canada's participation in World War I, and the growth of class and regional antagonisms thereafter. The issue that proved particularly vexing was wartime conscription, which had the support of English-speaking Canadians still closely tied to Britain, but strongly opposed by French Canada. It was at this time that the Liberal Party was able to consolidate its electoral advantage among Catholic and French-Canadian voters, which would prove crucial to Liberal Party success for the remainder of the century and provide a foundation for "Canadian exceptionalism": a party system dominated by a party of the centre, rather than one that alternates between left and right-wing alternatives.

The system-changing election of 1921, which effectively marked the beginning of Canada's second party system, signified the failure of the traditional parties to contain the rising political tensions and social conflicts within the country (Brodie and Jenson 1980). Over the next two decades, several protest parties with populist ideologies and significant voter support in western Canada would permanently alter the old pattern of partisan allegiances. Most prominent were the Progressives, spawned by a farmers' movement sweeping the country in the post–First World War period, and later, during the Depression years, the socialist Cooperative Commonwealth Federation (CCF) and conservative Social Credit party. The Liberals during this "second party system" became Canada's dominant party based primarily on their continuing hold over Quebec's parliamentary seats and their superior ability, in classic brokerage party style, to accommodate the interests of different regions, classes, and language groups. Mackenzie King, who would become Canada's longest-serving prime minister (1921–30, 1935–48), was particularly adept at this process. His cautious approach was effective for managing threatening social tensions and maintaining political stability, but it was not a recipe for inspirational leadership; King did not frame the task of Canadian governance in terms of lofty ideals and goals.[1]

As an unbroken string of Liberal governments under King and his successor, Louis St-Laurent, stretched into the mid-1950s, Cabinet ministers grew old in office, and critics began to raise concerns about perceived Liberal arrogance spawned by uninterrupted decades in power and the ever-closer relationship among political, bureaucratic, and corporate elites (Whitaker 1977). Canadian nationalists, for their part, disliked policies that they argued were encouraging the economic and cultural integration of Canada with the United States, producing a growing unease about the future of Canadian sovereignty, culture, and identity, as well as the country's long-term economic development prospects (Bashevkin 1991; Russell 1966; Grant 1970). These concerns became key issues in the government's eventual political defeat in 1957, when the Progressive Conservatives, under their new leader John Diefenbaker, scored an unexpected minority victory, to be quickly followed by a massive majority win in 1958.

"Dief the Chief," as he came to be known, was an impressive speechmaker and political campaigner, an ardent defender of Canada's ties to the British Commonwealth, and wary of the embrace of the United States. It did not take long, however, for his governing style to alienate voters in Canada's burgeoning urban areas, as well as French Canadians at odds with Diefenbaker's "One Canada, One Nation" views on Canadian national identity. Although the PCs remained the popular choice in rural and small-town English-speaking Canada, Diefenbaker's majority government was pruned back to a minority in 1962 and then defeated in 1963. This rapid sequence of elections (four in six years) effectively ushered in Canada's third party system (Newman 1963).

Party Politics in the Modern Era

In 1963, the Liberals returned to power under the leadership of Lester B. Pearson, a former diplomat and Nobel Peace Prize winner. The party would resume the dominance it enjoyed during the second party system, not relinquishing control of the government for twenty-one years (absent a brief stint in opposition in 1979). The prime minister for most of this time was Pierre Elliott Trudeau, a prominent Quebec intellectual recruited by Pearson to help the federal government in Ottawa meet the rising challenge of Quebec nationalism and separatism (English 2009). The third party system would be primarily a three-party affair (though the Social Credit and its Quebec variant, the Creditistes, were able to win a handful of seats as late as 1980), with the Liberals and Progressive Conservatives locked in a contest for power and the smaller New Democratic Party (NDP) – founded in 1961 as a successor to the CCF – occasionally acting as the spoiler or gaining political leverage during periods of minority government (Johnston 1992).

The profound changes taking place in Canadian society during this period – expansion of a well-educated and affluent middle class, increasing multiculturalism, and the changing status of women as they made advances toward gender equality – profoundly affected the dynamics of party competition and placed new demands on all political parties. While in opposition, the Liberals renovated their party organization and leadership, shifted to the left in their party program and ideological appeal, and became more urban-oriented in their policies and voter base (Bickerton 1990, 163–7). By adopting the mantle of moderate social democracy, which was the dominant leitmotiv of Western industrialized societies at that time, they were able to limit the electoral gains of their NDP rivals on the left (Smith 1973; Wearing 1981). Just as important, by developing a national unity/national identity strategy under Trudeau based on the promotion of bilingualism and multiculturalism, they were able to reinforce the party's traditional support base among French Canadians, Catholics, and ethnic minorities. It was their strong positioning in this key cultural dimension of politics that forestalled the political fate of centrist parties elsewhere in the Western world, who tended to be sidelined by the polarization between a business-oriented, conservative alternative on the right and a socialist or social democratic one on the left (Johnston 2010).

With an impregnable Quebec base but only a weak presence in western Canada, Pierre Trudeau's Liberal Party pursued electoral victories in urban Ontario, a strategy sometimes thwarted by the NDP's oscillating appeal to left-of-centre voters there. The Progressive Conservatives, whether under Diefenbaker or subsequent leaders Robert Stanfield (1967–76) and Joe Clark (1976–83), often won the most seats in English Canada but suffered from a chronic inability to win seats in Quebec. As table 13.1 illustrates, the overall result was continued Liberal dominance but no party that was competitive in all regions of the country, with the ever-present possibility of minority governments (Johnston et al. 1992).

Table 13.1 Valid Votes Cast (%) and Candidates Elected by Political Party at Canadian General Elections, 1963–1988

Party	1963	1965	1968	1972	1974	1979	1980	1984	1988
Liberal	41.7% **128**	40.2% **131**	45.5% **155**	38.5% **109**	43.2% **141**	40.1% 114	44.3% **147**	28.0% 40	31.9% 83
PC	32.8% 95	32.4% 97	31.4% 72	34.9% 107	35.4% 95	35.9% **136**	32.5% 103	50.0% **211**	43.0% **169**
NDP	13.1% 17	17.9% 21	17.0% 22	17.7% 31	15.4% 16	17.9% 26	19.8% 32	18.8% 30	20.4% 43
Ralliement des creditistes	—	4.6% 9	4.4% 14	—	—	—	—	—	—
Social Credit	11.9% 24	3.7% 5	0.8% 0	7.6% 15	5.0% 11	4.6% 6	1.7% 0	0.1% 0	* 0
Reform	—	—	—	—	—	—	—	—	2.1%–
Others	0.4% 1	1.2% 2	0.9% 1	1.2% 2	0.9% 1	1.5% 0	1.7% 0	3.0% 1	2.6% 0
Total valid votes	7,894,076	7,713,316	8,125,996	9,667,489	9,505,908	11,455,702	10,947,914	12,548,721	13,175,599
Voter turnout	79.2%	74.8%	75.7%	76.7%	71.0%	75.7%	69.3%	75.3%	75.3%
Total seats	265	265	264	264	264	282	282	282	295

Note: Columns may not add up to 100% as the result of rounding.
* Less than 0.1%
Source: T.J. Coulson, revised by S. Geobey (2007); Elections Canada, "Voter Turnouts" (www.elections.ca). The figures in bold indicate the seat total of the winning party.

Pierre Trudeau's departure from politics in 1984 would also mark the beginning of the end of the third party system. The Liberal government, along with the Liberal stranglehold over voters in Quebec, was washed away in a landslide victory for the Progressive Conservatives under the leadership of Brian Mulroney. In Quebec, Mulroney's strategy was to target the "soft" nationalists who constituted a solid majority of the province's voters. Besides the competitive advantage Mulroney enjoyed, conferred by his fluency in French, his native Quebecer credentials, and his intimate knowledge of Quebec politics, the long-sought breakthrough in Quebec can be attributed to his professed openness to renewed constitutional negotiations that would revise the 1982 constitutional settlement that had been vehemently opposed by Quebec. Of course, this strategy had its risks as well as rewards, relying as it did on a rather unstable coalition of francophones and francophobes (Johnston 2017). In Mulroney's case, cementing this alliance involved promising a constitutional deal that would be acceptable to both Quebecers and the party's traditional voter base elsewhere in Canada. Though an awkward political marriage, it was temporarily accomplished by Mulroney with the signing of the Meech Lake constitutional accord in 1987 and the Canada-US Free Trade Agreement (favoured by both Quebec and Alberta) in 1988. This laid the foundation for a second consecutive Progressive Conservative majority government, thereby confirming the Quebec-West alliance that was at the core of Mulroney's political success (Johnston et al. 1992).

Mulroney's dream was to displace the Liberals as Canada's "natural governing party." Instead, subsequent years were marked by sustained constitutional conflict, mounting economic difficulties, and ultimately a spectacular collapse of voter support for his Progressive Conservative Party. Contributing mightily to this outcome was the rapid rise of two new regional parties – the Bloc Québécois and the Reform Party (later to become the Canadian Alliance) – spurred into creation by fundamental disagreement within the party base over key government policies. After the crushing 1993 defeat of the Progressive Conservatives (by then led by Kim Campbell), each of these new parties would serve as official opposition to the governing Liberals, who were once again returned to power under the leadership of Jean Chrétien.

Brokerage Politics and Regionalization

The issues that triggered the "electoral earthquake" of 1993 were constitutional, cultural, and economic: two failed constitutional accords that polarized the debate between Quebec and English-speaking Canada, a hotly contested free trade agreement with the United States, and a deteriorating fiscal and economic situation. In the process, many Canadians became alienated not only from the Progressive Conservative Party, but also more generally from brokerage-style politics (Tanguay 1994; Bickerton 1997; Carty, Cross, and Young 2000). To some extent, the easy hegemony of the Chrétien Liberals after 1993 – they went on to win three consecutive majorities – can be attributed to the fact that they were the last brokerage party left standing. However, the resumption of their familiar role as the government party concealed somewhat fragile foundations: a narrowed regional base (with the loss of both Quebec and the west) and fragmentation of conservative votes between the Reform Party and the fatally weakened Progressive Conservatives (Bickerton, Gagnon, and Smith 1999).

Liberal victories during these years (1993, 1997, 2000, 2004) were aided by their traditional social base among Catholic voters – a much-queried anomaly of Canadian politics (Blais 2005) – and the continued support of visible minority communities. In truth, however, their electoral success was due primarily to the implosion of the electoral coalition constructed by Brian Mulroney. Its sudden demise ushered in Canada's fourth party system, which has been more fragmented, regionalized, and ideologically polarized than its predecessor. The more populist and ideological conservatism of Preston Manning's Reform Party took over the large base of Progressive Conservative seats in western Canada, while pushing the party system's ideological spectrum in a more radically conservative direction. Simultaneously, a second third-party insurgency was occurring in Quebec, fuelled by anger over failed constitutional negotiations. The beneficiary was the Bloc Québécois (BQ), a new nationalist party vowing to defend Quebec's interests in Ottawa while supporting the sovereignty agenda of the provincial Parti Québécois. Led by former Mulroney confidante and Cabinet minister Lucien Bouchard, the BQ effectively took over the PC voter base in francophone Quebec. Reduced from 169 to two seats (on 16 per cent of the popular vote), the election result was a disaster for the Progressive Conservatives. Things didn't go much better for the NDP. With its representation in Parliament reduced to eight seats (on 7 per cent of the vote), it too was being pushed to the fringe of Canadian politics, if not the edge of political oblivion (Bickerton, Gagnon, and Smith 1999).

Clearly, as indicated by these election results, many Canadians were alienated from and angry with the mainstream political parties. While transforming the party system, it also confirmed that party politics remained the primary means of registering political protest and that voting for a radical alternative was still perceived as an available outlet for the expression of regional discontent. New political formations could arise to challenge the political status quo; traditional parties could be severely chastised and even disappear if they failed to respond adequately to voter concerns and demands.

More than bringing an end to the third party system, the 1993 election has been interpreted too as the "beginning of the end" for the traditional brokerage approach to Canadian electoral politics. This mode of politics – for more than a century the presumed key to winning and retaining power at the federal level in Canada – stood in contrast to what students of comparative politics have considered a "normal" pattern of political competition whereby parties "reflect and perpetuate the salience of particular lines of social cleavage and provide a mechanism for reconciling differences and balancing interests." In contrast, brokerage parties succeeded by obscuring and muffling differences (such as social class divisions) in favour of regional accommodation and the promotion of national unity (Carty 2013, 11). They did this by eschewing ideological agendas in order to pursue a pragmatic "middle-ground" consensus position, one that could win support from all groups and classes of voters. Party leaders were central to this process; they had to be free from ideological constraints or firm policy commitments in order to be unfettered in the primary task of brokering competing interests in order to assemble a winning coalition of voters (16).

In the opinion of at least one notable brokerage party theorist, throughout the twentieth century the Liberals were the only true brokerage party in Canada. Only they were able to accommodate Canada's ethno-linguistic and religious cleavages, thereby giving them an unassailable advantage on the national unity issue. The Conservatives and NDP – though drawn toward the brokerage model – represented a narrower, more ideological conception of Canadian identity and interests (Carty 2013, 18–19). The fourth party system would change this, however, with politics becoming more regionally fragmented and ideological, "confounding the possibilities for creating and sustaining genuine national coalitions" (21).

Not all experts on electoral politics and voter behaviour agree with this conclusion about the altered character of Canadian politics in the fourth party system. Clarke et al. argue that "the new parties [ushered in by the 1993 election] continued to operate in the mould of brokerage politics inherited from their predecessors … the voters' behavior was also in this mould" (2019, 169). For Clarke et al., brokerage parties display three elements: they rebuild their coalitions at each election, organize their identities around their leaders more than ideologies, and sustain within their program a wide variety of conflicting policy stances. For their part, voters tend to be flexible partisans with only lukewarm attachment and little loyalty to parties, leading to high levels of volatility (dramatic shifts in support for various parties) in voter behaviour (20–1). Indeed, for Clarke et al., volatility continues to be "the hallmark of Canadian electoral politics" (44).

From a different perspective, Richard Johnston's broad historical analysis of Canadian elections suggests that the dramatic rise of two new parties and virtual collapse of the Progressive Conservatives in 1993 is simply part of an electoral cycle that has repeated itself at regular intervals. Johnston argues that the rise of *insurgent parties* (such as Reform and the BQ) that fragments the vote along regional lines is a recurring event, though this fragmentation always has been followed by a period of reconsolidation and renationalization of the party system. The "kicker," according to Johnston, is that each time this happens, the party system remains at a higher level of party system fragmentation than previously, with the major parties winning a smaller overall share of the popular vote. This might suggest the diminishing capacity over time of brokerage parties to "shoulder the burden" of national political integration imposed by Canada's regional, ethnic, and linguistic diversity (Johnston 2005).

Canada has long been an exceptional case among comparable political systems in its propensity to support insurgent "third parties" (Lipset 1990; Gagnon and Tanguay 1996; Bélanger 2007). Although only two parties have ever formed government at the federal level, the party system since 1921 has included three to five parties with elected members of Parliament. Most of the smaller parties have relied on distinct regional bases of support, even those presenting themselves as national alternatives. Others have had no such pretensions beyond their narrow regional appeal.[2]

There have been a variety of explanations for this distinctive characteristic of the party system, which, along with the electoral dominance of a centrist party, accounts for Canada's "exceptionalism." Some of these explanations have been situation-specific, such as C.B. Macpherson's interpretation of Alberta's unusual "quasi-party" tradition, the origins of which, he argued in the 1950s, lay in its neocolonial relationship with eastern Canada and homogeneous (at that time) agrarian class structure (Macpherson 1962). Other perspectives have been more generally applicable, such as Maurice Pinard's one-party dominance theory that identifies two factors conducive to third-party formation: regional one-party dominance conjoined with conditions of societal strain, the combination of which discredits the dominant party as well as the traditional political alternative (Pinard 1975). For their part, Gagnon and Tanguay (1996) cite a more general composite factor at work in third-party formation and success: the "non-responsiveness" of the national party system to particular regional interests and concerns.

The concept of "non-responsiveness" in this context suggests a systemic failure of the national brokerage parties model. At least one scholar has directly faulted the behaviour of these parties for this shortcoming

(Smith 1985). Others have targeted the interaction of the party system with other political institutions: the executive dominance and strict party discipline typical of Westminster-style parliamentary democracy, the inadequacies of the Canadian Senate as a venue for effective regional representation, and the perverse workings of the "first-past-the-post" electoral system.

Canada's parliamentary system has been widely criticized for its democratic failings. The biggest knock against it is the concentration of power with the political executive and, more particularly, the prime minister. To some critics, the concentration of power in the hands of the prime minister, the doctrine of Cabinet and caucus secrecy, and the strict enforcement of party discipline effectively turn elected members of the House of Commons into "trained seals" rather than true representatives of their constituents (Simpson 2001). Relatively powerless and rigidly bound by party discipline, MPs are ill-suited to the task of effective regional representation. Further, the federal Cabinet, once an important venue for regional accommodation (and still constructed to give every region a share of ministerial posts), is now a shadow of its former self, as ministerial autonomy and power has faded relative to the prime minister and the central agencies that provide the head of government with information and advice (Bakvis 2000–1; Savoie 1999).

The inadequacy of the House of Commons for the task of regional representation is not rectified by the role of the other chamber of Parliament. Almost alone among comparable federal states – witness the substantive role of senates in the United States, Australia, and Germany – the Canadian Senate has never performed this role (Sayers 2002). As prime ministerial appointees, its members have lacked both the legitimacy and the inclination to act as defenders of regional interests, contributing to popular and scholarly opinion that the institution is dysfunctional and irrelevant (Smiley and Watts 1986; Sayers 2002; Bickerton 2007).

Another long-standing vein of criticism applies to the electoral system, which distorts regional interests and identities by systematically misrepresenting voter preferences within Parliament. It does this by overrepresenting the strongest parties in regions (the "winners") and under-representing weaker ones (the "losers"), often out of proportion to the actual levels of voter support enjoyed by each party. While parties with regional bases of support are rewarded for their geographically narrow appeal, smaller parties with diffuse national support are severely punished. The overall result is that after each election, parties often find themselves bereft of seats in some regions and oversupplied in others. Not surprisingly, this creates a self-perpetuating cycle of regionalized party politics (Cairns 1968; Gibbins 2005). The electoral system is also an identified culprit in explanations for the sustained downturn in voter participation. The high degree of regionalization it facilitates – where parties dominate whole regions – reduces political competitiveness and suppresses voter turnout (see Tanguay's chapter for further discussion of this topic).

Although the regionalized character of the party system has exacerbated regional conflict and widened regional divisions, insurgent third parties have been key sources of policy innovation. The mainstream parties have been poor performers in policy development and innovation, traditionally relying on government-appointed royal commissions to advise them (Bradford 1999). Third parties, on the other hand, have brought radical proposals for change to the table and when able to gain power at the provincial level have often have been innovators of new policies and programs (Thorburn 1991).[3]

Finally, new parties have given voters an institutional outlet for their frustration, anger, or disillusionment with government policies, with the mainstream parties or more broadly with the political system in general. By channelling dissent into the electoral arena, new parties provide the traditional parties with clear evidence of their failings and the need to craft policy or institutional remedies in response. And by becoming part of the "national conversation" in the electoral arena and Parliament, protest parties gradually become institutionalized, containing and moderating the more radical or extreme elements within their own support base. In this way, the challenge they pose stimulates the party system as a whole to moderate and absorb political dissent (Gagnon and Tanguay 1996).

Parties and Voters in the Fourth Party System

The exceptionalism of the Canadian party system has been described in terms of periodic system-changing realignments, one-party dominance by a centrist party, the relative absence of class-based politics, and a propensity to third-party formation or "multipartism." There can be no clear explanation for these persistent features, however, without some greater understanding of party–voter relations. Broadly speaking, there are three general models that offer competing explanations for electoral outcomes in Canada over the past few decades. One model portrays voters as political consumers choosing between parties that offer them competing packages of benefits (often in the form of campaign promises) and making their vote choice strictly on the basis of their own narrow self-interest, unhindered by other factors or considerations.[4] While this *rational choice* model of voter behaviour captures an important dimension of electoral politics and voter behaviour, it greatly underestimates other considerations in people's evaluations and perceptions of the political realm. As a result, it has been widely critiqued and shown to be difficult to sustain in the face of contrary evidence.

The second model sees voting as primarily a response to psychological factors, with vote choice heavily dependent upon two short-term influences: voters' evaluations of the candidates (and especially party leaders) and voters' issue attitudes. In this model, both tend to be linked to a third factor: emotional attachment to a political party (referred to as party identification or partisanship).[5] Clarke et al. (1984, 2019) and others have applied this approach to Canadian elections to argue that Canada can best be understood as a case of "permanent dealignment" (Clarke et al. 2019, 171). This describes a situation where partisanship is weak, which translates into a high level of electoral volatility. Using data from successive Canadian Election Study (CES), Leduc suggests that the percentage of Canadians who are only weakly partisan or do not identify with any federal political party has risen steadily, eroding any solid basis of partisan support within the Canadian electorate. His conclusion is that Canadians have the weakest political-party affinity in the Western world (Valpy 2008). One corollary of this is weak ideological commitments and general ideological confusion. Approximately 40 per cent of respondents to one national survey place themselves in the ideological centre, while a further 30 per cent reject the notion of ideological placement entirely or fail to locate themselves on a simple left-right continuum (Leduc 2007, 170). This ideological "no man's land" (Valpy 2008), whatever its ultimate causes, creates a situation in which parties are discouraged from offering ideological appeals, thereby reinforcing the already prevailing tendencies and trends within the electorate. As a consequence, centrist politics and ideological inconsistency is the most likely winning electoral strategy for Canadian parties. Almost by default, leaders are placed front and centre in crafting an appeal to voters and "making the party" (Clarke et al. 2019, 20), defining it in terms of policy and personality.

This portrait of the Canadian voter does not go uncontested. Other scholars reject it for being too dismissive of the continuing influence on vote choice of stable, long-term factors. These include the social background characteristics of voters and their fundamental values and beliefs (akin to ideological orientation), as well as their party attachment (Gidengil et al. 2012). This third model of party and voter behaviour sees parties as reliant on a core bloc of voters who tend to be overrepresented within certain identifiable social groups.[6] It has also been argued that these core party supporters tend to hold certain basic values and beliefs that in broad terms are in sync with the philosophy or ideological orientation expounded by the party to which they become attached (14–18). It disputes the characterization of voters as permanently "dealigned" from parties and divorced from ideological world views.

Gidengil et al. (2012), Nevitte et al. (2000), Johnston (2005, 2017), and others have reinterpreted the results of voter surveys to argue that it is difficult to make sense of voting behaviour in Canada unless the effects of certain key social background characteristics are taken into account. As for party identification or attachment, they argue that this is influenced by both social background characteristics and basic values and beliefs, and that "this anchoring in social identities and in values and beliefs is what limits the flexibility of people's party ties" (Gidengil et al. 2012, 16). In short, even when voters who have a partisan tie defect to a rival party (as they sometimes do), they usually do not stray very far (in ideological terms) and they often later return to their original party. In effect, though they may not be tightly bound to a particular party, they do tend to be "tethered" by durable, if flexible, partisan ties.

How do these models of voter behaviour, and particularly the third model cited above, help us to make sense of voter–party relations in Canada's fourth party system? In 2012, researchers engaged with the Canadian Election Study (CES) published *Dominance and Decline: Making Sense of Recent Canadian Elections* (Gidengil et al. 2012). They purport to explain the inter-party dynamics of voter support and the dramatic shift in the electoral fortunes of political parties during the first decade of the twenty-first century.[7] The following overview, except where otherwise indicated, represents a selective synopsis of their findings and analysis.

In the social bases of party support, the Liberals continued to be favoured by Catholics and visible minority voters, as well as anglophones within Quebec and francophones outside Quebec. However, their lack of appeal in western Canada and with francophone Quebecers continued to drag on their overall support in the fourth party system prior to 2015. The Reform/Canadian Alliance (CA) Party (1993–2003) attracted strong support from western and rural voters, as well as fundamentalist Christians, married people, and male voters. Their merger with the Progressive Conservatives to form the Conservative Party of Canada (CPC) transferred their distinctive social base to the new party, though under Stephen Harper's leadership this was expanded to become less western and rural. To the extent that the NDP had an identifiable social base, the party did better with voters from unionized households, those with no religious affiliation, and women voters. As for the BQ, language has clearly been the defining cleavage for its support base, with other socio-demographic factors exerting only a mild effect on vote choice in Quebec (Gidengil et al. 2012, chap. 2).

In the realm of basic values and beliefs, the Conservatives have had the most ideologically distinct and coherent voter base, rooted in support for market liberalism (pro-market, anti-state) and moral traditionalism (socially conservative views). They also have benefited from the long-standing sense of alienation felt by voters in the west. Liberals and New Democrats compete for the same voters in values and beliefs: socially liberal, with a more positive view of the role of government and more skeptical about the benefits of a free-market economy. This is also the ideological terrain worked by the BQ and the Green Party, creating the potential for a severe fragmentation on the centre-left of Canada's political spectrum. While moral traditionalism and religiosity have been declining, and the number of Canadians professing views consistent with support for market liberalism has been stagnant at best, the CPC between 2004 and 2011 was helped by vote-splitting on the centre-left, just as the Liberals had previously benefited from the same process on the centre-right (see table 13.2). But importantly, there has been no growth in the Conservative Party's core constituency in Canadians' ideological orientation, which suggests a ceiling on the CPC's *potential* electorate (Gidengil et al. 2012, chap. 3).[8]

After three consecutive elections that returned minority Parliaments (2004, 2006, 2008), with the Conservatives forming the government following Paul Martin's brief period as prime minister, Stephen Harper finally won a majority victory in 2011 (see table 13.2). This sequence of four elections in seven years transformed the dynamics of party competition in Canada, first by gradually shaking loose Liberal voters to the benefit of the Conservatives and second by transferring the votes of francophone Quebecers from the BQ to the NDP. This left a political landscape that would have been unimaginable a decade previously: a majority Conservative government, the NDP as official opposition on the strength of its popularity in Quebec, the Liberals struggling with their relegation to third place, and the BQ – the party of choice for francophone Quebecers for almost two decades – reduced to a mere handful of seats.

These changes in electoral outcomes can be explained by gradual shifts in the size and composition of each party's core support base, especially the shrinking Liberal base and the loss of its historically privileged position with Catholic voters (Gidengil et al. 2012, 175). Short-term factors played a role, particularly the sponsorship scandal in Quebec, which was a key factor in the decline of Liberal fortunes in the 2004 and 2006 elections (94–6, 173–4). Though Conservative attack ads on the capability of Liberal leaders Stéphane Dion (2008) and Michael Ignatieff (2011) were generally viewed as highly effective, leader evaluations were much less determinant than portrayed in media coverage (114), while another media trope – the notion that Canadians opted to give a majority to the Conservatives in 2011 because of their growing aversion to minority governments – also lacked evidence to support it (chap. 8). Nevertheless, the 2011 results were dramatic enough that they led some observers to judge the outcome – especially the Liberal collapse and NDP ascendency – as confirmation of the onset of yet another new party system, and that majority Liberal governments could now be considered a thing of the past (Koop and Bittner 2013, 311, 329).

Table 13.2 Valid Votes Cast (%) and Candidates Elected by Political Party at Canadian General Elections, 1993–2019

Party	1993	1997	2000	2004	2006	2008	2011	2015	2019
Liberal	41.3% **177**	38.5% **155**	40.8% **172**	36.7% **135**	30.2% 103	26.2% 77	18.9% 34	39.5% 187	33.1% 157
PC	16.0% 2	18.8% 20	12.2% 12	—	—	—	—	—	—
Reform Party/ Canadian Alliance★	18.7% 52	19.4% 60	25.5% 66	—	—	—	—	—	—
Conservative†	—	—	—	29.6% 99	36.3% **124**	37.6% B	39.6% **166**	31.9% 99	34.4% 121
NDP	6.9% 9	11.0% 21	8.5% 13	15.7% 19	17.5% 29	18.2% 37	30.6% 103	19.7% 44	15.9% 24
BQ	13.5% 54	10.7% 44	10.7% 38	12.4% 54	10.5% 51	10% 49	6.0% 4	4.7% 10	7.7% 32
Green	—	—	—	4.3% 0	4.5% 0	6.8% 0	3.9% 1	3.4% 1	6.5% 3
Others	3.6% 1	1.6% 1	2.3% 0	1.3% 1	1.0% 1	1.2% 2	0.9% 0	0.8% 0	2.4% 1
Total valid votes	13,863,135	13,174,698	12,997,185	13,683,570	14,908,703	13,929,093	14,823,408	17,592,778	17,890,264
Voter turnout‡	69.6%	67.0%	64.1%★★	60.9%	64.7%	58.8%	61.1%	68.3%	65.95%
Total seats	295	301	301	308	308	308	308	338	338

★ The Canadian Reform Conservative Alliance replaced the Reform Party of Canada in the 2000 election.
★★ Official figure was 61.2% but Elections Canada later corrected this when they realized the voters list was artificially inflated by almost a million duplicate names.
† The Conservative Party of Canada was formed from the merger of the Progressive Conservatives and Canadian Alliance parties in December 2003.
‡ For earlier figures on voter turnout, see Heard (n.d.).
Source: T.J. Coulson, revised by S. Geobey (2007); Elections Canada, "Past Elections" (www.elections.ca)

The 2015 and 2019 Elections

The 2015 federal election reversed the direction of the previous four elections and produced yet another surprising result: a Liberal majority government, with the NDP pushed back into its traditional third-party role. As with the Conservatives in 2011, the Liberals earned less than 40 per cent of the vote, though thanks to the electoral system this proved sufficient to claim a strong majority of parliamentary seats. As well, predictions of a party system realignment (noted above) were not borne out, as the 2015 result re-established a pattern of party support reminiscent of the third party system. Thus, though the Conservatives were able to retain their core voter base in western Canada and rural Ontario, the electorate's appetite for change was palpable, an impression confirmed by the surge in voter turnout to its highest level in two decades. This meant most of the "action" during the campaign took place on the left of the political spectrum, with a significant movement of voter support between the two main parties vying for the "change vote": the Liberals and NDP. When mid-campaign polls began showing voter intentions shifting to the Liberals, beginning in Quebec, NDP support began to collapse, suggesting (yet again) the importance of strategic considerations as voters coalesced behind the party that presented itself as the most viable alternative to the government (Marland and Giasson 2015; Johnston 2017).

What factors contributed to this turn back to the Liberals? The 2015 election outcome reinstated a geographic and social base of support similar to Liberal Party victories during the third party system: Atlantic Canada, Quebec, and large urban centres (in Ontario and elsewhere), along with immigrant communities. Especially significant was the party's comeback in Quebec, where it had not won a majority of seats since 1980. In general, the party was also able to avoid being "squeezed out" by the ideological competition between left- and right-wing alternatives by closing the ideological gap with the NDP, even outflanking them on the left with a progressive platform that promised to raise taxes for the wealthiest Canadians, add to the deficit to create jobs and expand social infrastructure, and reform an outdated electoral system (Marland and Giasson 2015). This replicated the competitive dynamic in the 1988 election, when Liberals responded to the threat of displacement as the primary opponent to the Conservatives by adopting a left nationalist platform in opposition to the Canada-US Free Trade Agreement (Johnston et al. 1992).

In leadership appeal, the choice of Justin Trudeau in 2013 immediately improved the Liberal party's prospects, especially with younger voters and traditional Liberal identifiers. In fact, some observers claimed the CPC's well-practised attack ad strategy – which on this occasion questioned Trudeau's leadership "readiness" – backfired by lowering expectations that Trudeau was then able to exceed during the election campaign. Finally, and perhaps most crucially, the 2015 election demonstrated that the Liberal brand amongst Canadians remained strong. Even at its low ebb, the party continued to hold a clear advantage over the NDP in partisan identification – the number of voters who identified as Liberals. This well of latent support, linked to the party's long history of political success and its close association with key institutions and policies, provided it with a degree of brand resilience that, in retrospect, increased the likelihood of what was otherwise an improbable 2015 comeback (Marland and Giasson 2015).

In the election's aftermath, both the Conservatives and the NDP made leadership changes, with Andrew Scheer replacing Stephen Harper and Jagmeet Singh replacing NDP leader Thomas Mulcair (who was summarily ousted at a party convention). Both were young and untested, as concerned with consolidating support for their leadership as challenging the Liberal government. The former quickly became an issue for Scheer when his primary leadership rival, Maxime Bernier, quit to start his own hard right alternative: the People's Party of Canada (PPC).[9]

In the general election of 2019, the 184-seat Liberal majority was reduced to a 157-seat minority. At 46 per cent of the 338 available seats, this was enough to secure a "strong minority" position for the Liberals in Canada's Forty-Third Parliament. Due to the wondrous working of the first-past-the-post (FPTP) electoral system, this result was accomplished with just 33 per cent of the popular vote, the smallest winning vote percentage for any party forming government in Canadian history (Brean 2019). While the Conservatives actually won the popular vote by a slight margin, they finished a distant second with 121 seats. In FPTP parlance, the CPC vote was much less "efficient" than the Liberal, chiefly because it clustered large majorities in the Prairie provinces. Voter turnout in the election slid to 66 per cent, in line with average turnout in the fourth party system. Also consistent with past election outcomes, setting aside the 2011 election, was the 65/35 division of voter support between left-of-centre progressive and right-of-centre conservative voters. One more element of continuity in 2019 is that the new minority government was the thirteenth in Canada since 1921, representing 43 per cent of all Canadian governments formed over the past century. This proclivity to elect minority governments has no parallel in any other country using the FPTP electoral system, again reinforcing Canada's exceptional status in comparative terms.

Besides the two major parties, three other parties won seats in the 2019 election. In Lazarus-like fashion, the BQ rebounded to win thirty-two Quebec seats, enough to make them the third largest parliamentary contingent.

While the NDP collected more than double the 7 per cent vote share of the BQ, it finished fourth in seats with twenty-four. The few remaining parliamentary seats were divided between the Greens (three seats on roughly 7 per cent of the vote) and one notable independent (former Liberal justice minister Jody Wilson-Raybould). Bernier's PPC took a mere 1.6 per cent of the vote, yielding no seats, including the loss of Bernier's seat.

Liberal strength in 2019 was concentrated in eastern Canada and the country's multicultural urban regions, particularly Montreal, Toronto, and Vancouver. They won twenty-seven of thirty-two seats in Atlantic Canada, the largest number of seats in Quebec (thirty-four), and the bulk of seats in the greater Toronto region (including all twenty-five in the city itself). In a mirror image, the CPC did poorly in Atlantic Canada and Quebec, and it was unable to erode the Liberal stranglehold on Toronto and its seat-rich suburbs. However, it continued to be the dominant party in the west, especially Saskatchewan and Alberta, as well as rural Manitoba and the BC Interior (Fife and Walsh 2019).

During the campaign, the two major parties remained in a virtual deadlock in the polls at around one-third of voter support each, with neither able to garner the additional five points that historically is needed to produce a majority. Both Justin Trudeau and Andrew Scheer suffered negative media coverage during the campaign, including the long-simmering controversy over accusations of prime ministerial interference with the independence of the attorney general in the SNC-Lavalin affair and then during the campaign the appearance of embarrassing pictures of a younger Trudeau in blackface-brownface costuming. For Scheer, it was revelations about his unrevealed US citizenship and an erroneous claim on his resumé; more problematic was his difficulty repelling charges that in deference to his social conservative base he would allow long-settled issues such as abortion and same-sex marriage back onto the political agenda. As a result, questions about leadership character, judgment, and ethics dominated the campaign, to the exclusion of more substantive policy-related discussion (Shaheen 2019).

The BQ benefited from an effective performance by new party leader Yves-Francois Blanchet and rose steadily in the polls after the midway point in the campaign. Many Quebecers, it seems, were comfortable with a well-known "Quebec-first" party that had foresworn (for the time being) any pursuit of sovereignty if elected. Similarly, NDP support recovered from a pre-election low point as a result of a strong showing by Singh, though ultimately the party suffered a sharp decline in seats (retaining only one of its fourteen seats in Quebec, leaving party strength concentrated in BC) and a diminished share of the popular vote (down from 19.7 to 15.9 per cent). Finally, despite the Green Party claiming their first seat in eastern Canada and increasing their vote share, disappointment that the long hoped-for breakthrough did not materialize was a factor in Elizabeth May's quick post-election announcement that after thirteen years as party leader she was stepping down (though staying on as an MP) (Walsh 2019).

A number of key policy commitments in 2019 separated the Conservatives on the right and the several progressive parties on the left of the political spectrum. The consensus on fiscal policy (deficit reduction and balanced budgets) was no longer in evidence, with only the Conservatives (and Bernier's PPC) continuing to target the deficit as a problem. Two other long-standing issues also gained more salience in the 2019 campaign: (1) proposals from the Liberals, NDP, and Greens to create a national pharmacare program and (2) plans of action by every left-of-centre party to dramatically reduce Canada's greenhouse gas emissions. The latter contributed to the unpopularity of the Liberals in Alberta and Saskatchewan, where the government's carbon tax and its more stringent environmental regulations (Bill C-69) proved highly unpopular (Hunter 2019; Wall 2019). At the same time, the Conservative Party's failure to put forward a credible environmental policy proved a major liability with voters who were not already part of the party's core support base and who considered the need for climate action to be imperative – in effect, a deal-breaker in choosing how to cast their ballot (Radwanski 2019).

Finally, there were familiar competitive dynamics at work during the election campaign, with each major party asking voters to cast their ballot in order to prevent its main competitor from winning. The introduction of this strategic calculus into party appeals – warning that vote-splitting might determine the outcome – has traditionally been most useful to the Liberals in their effort to corral the support of progressive-minded voters. In 2019, this appeared to have worked again, at least to some extent. In an Angus Reid survey conducted shortly after the election, 45 per cent of those who voted Liberal claimed to have cast their vote primarily to prevent another party from winning power. This likely hurt the NDP in particular, since that party's supporters have typically been more willing to switch their allegiance in order to forestall a Conservative victory (Campbell 2019).

In the aftermath of the election, Justin Trudeau vowed to win support in Parliament for his minority government on a vote-by-vote basis rather than any formal or informal coalition agreement. While a less secure way of ensuring his government's survival, this would give him more flexibility to seek support from different parties on different measures. As well, with many areas of basic agreement in Liberal and NDP platforms, there was no shortage of "low-hanging fruit" for cooperation (Explainer 2019). A more vexing problem was the return of western alienation and what measures it could introduce to address regional grievances and discontent. In this connection, a familiar representation problem created by the continued failure to reform key political institutions was made obvious by the election result. While the electoral system again over-rewarded the Liberals with seats despite a weak national vote share, it left the government without any caucus members (or potential Cabinet representatives) from two western provinces. A serious political legitimacy issue naturally ensues from such a situation. To make matters worse, the past government practice – though always inadequate and undemocratic – of reaching into the appointed Senate for a regional representative has been removed as an option after Justin Trudeau's "termination" of the Liberal caucus in the Senate in favour of independently appointed, non-partisan senators (see Andrew Heard's chapter). In effect, a gaping hole has been opened up in the regional minister system at the centre of government, one that cannot easily be patched.

Conclusion

The collapse of Canada's third party system revealed the rewards but also the perils for parties involved in brokerage politics. As regional and ideological fault-lines widened amidst unresolved fiscal, economic, and constitutional problems, the grand coalition underlying the electoral success of Mulroney's Progressive Conservative Party broke apart, to be only partially reassembled a decade later with the merger that created the new Conservative Party. The national patchwork of parties created by the 1993 election result constituted the most regionalized and ideologically polarized party system in Canadian history.

During the third and fourth party systems, Liberal party competition and voter exchange with the NDP has been mirrored by Conservative competition with insurgent parties. Historically, Conservative majorities have required a large swing of voters in Quebec, enticing the Conservatives to adopt an "ends-against-the-middle" strategy – building an electoral coalition embracing both pro-Quebec and anti-Quebec elements. This proved unsustainable, leading to a long-term pattern of electoral booms and busts. Insurgent parties were the result of the frustrations prompted by this cycle, often as vehicles for debate over the meaning of conservatism. This has created a dynamic of electoral competition on the political right in Canada that is disconnected from the competition between the Liberal Party and NDP on the left. In combination, these political forces have produced the one-party dominance, weak class-based voting, multipartism, and episodic electoral volatility that are the calling cards of Canadian exceptionalism (Johnston 2017, 250).

There is some indication that this party system and pattern of voter behaviour may be changing. Most significant is a trend toward more "partisan sorting" along ideological lines. Already in 2011, the relationship between how the electorate votes, their partisan identification and support for welfare state (an indicator of ideological positioning) was higher than any previous year going back to 1992. In the 2015 election, the same relationship held true for other measures of redistributive preferences: increased party polarization (policy positions) was giving rise to more consistent ideological voting in the electorate and more sharply defined partisan sorting (ideologically like-minded citizens clustering into parties) (Kevins and Soroka 2018, 116). What this portends for the future of party politics, however, is not yet clear.

Perhaps Canadian voters do exhibit weak attachment to political parties while lacking any consistent ideological outlook, as argued by some analysts. On the other hand, in its own way Canada may now represent the characteristics of a European-style multi-party system, with each party cultivating its own relatively stable voter base, more reliant than in the past on core supporters who are predisposed to their ideological appeals. Electoral volatility and voter shifting happens within "ideological families" of like-minded parties, rather than across the wider ideological gap that now separates the left from the right (Nevitte et al. 2000). Issues and leadership have made and will continue to make a significant difference in party fortunes. Of greater continuous import, however, is the persistence of core electorates "tethered" to particular parties or party types, with voter behaviour anchored in social and regional characteristics, fundamental values and beliefs (ideological orientation), and established partisan allegiances (Gidengil et al 2012; Kevins and Soroka 2018).

What does the future hold for parties and elections in Canada? One possibility is that the trend toward partisan sorting and ideological divergence will be an important and enduring feature, with party consolidation on both the left and the right bringing an end to "Canadian exceptionalism." A second possibility, however, is that the centrist Liberal party will continue to dominate on the basis of its unusual resilience and ability to "re-tool its cultural appeal" (Johnston 2017, 258). In a country of diverse cultures and identities, with ingrained national cohesion issues that must be skilfully managed, a party positioned to succeed at this task better than its competitors will always have a decisive advantage.

Notes

1 In the words of poet Frank Scott, King retained power by "doing nothing by halves that could be done by quarters ... and never taking sides, because he never allowed sides to take shape" (Scott 1967, 36).
2 Examples of the former include the CCF-NDP and the Reform Party; of the latter, Social Credit and the Bloc Québécois.

3 Such was the case, for instance, in Canada's system of public health care, which was first instituted by an NDP government in Saskatchewan. Family policy innovations were pioneered by the Parti Québécois. And the western-based Reform Party was the first to fully embrace the neo-liberal critique of big government, prescribing lower taxes, spending cuts, deregulation, and decentralization as the cure for Canada's ills.

4 The political economy work of Anthony Downs is usually credited with providing the intellectual foundations for this approach to party and voter behaviour (Downs 1957).

5 This approach to voting studies is closely associated with the social-psychological model of voter behaviour developed by researchers at the University of Michigan, who were motivated to do so by perceived shortcomings of the established Columbia model, which relied heavily on the distribution of social background characteristics of voters to explain election outcomes (Gidengil et al. 2012, 8). Campbell et al. (1960) were pioneers of this social-psychological approach.

6 This sociological approach is often referred to as the Columbia school and is associated with the work of Lazarsfeld, Berelson, and Gaudet (1944).

7 Using data from a series of Canadian Election Studies, and employing a multi-stage model of statistical analysis, the researchers – Elizabeth Gidengil, Neil Nevitte, André Blais, Joanna Everitt, and Patrick Fournier – constructed a composite model of vote choice that seeks to incorporate all major explanatory factors associated with the three models introduced to the reader in the preceding paragraphs (Gidengil et al. 2012, chap. 1).

8 This finding, which confirms previous studies that shed a similar light on Canadian values and beliefs (Adams 2009), casts doubt on recent assertions by some commentators that the national constituency for a more conservative Canada has grown significantly and will continue to do so (Bricker and Ibbitson 2013).

9 Another development in the election's aftermath was the collapsing voter support and organizational chaos that beset the BQ; the party suffered a serious bout of in-fighting and a number of MP defections (seven of ten sitting MPs) in protest against new leader Martine Ouellet, who had replaced former leader Gilles Duceppe, who had failed to win his own seat in 2015. Only a year into her leadership, Ouellet lost a leadership review referendum and was forced to resign. Subsequently, the BQ parliamentary contingent regrouped under interim leader, Mario Beaulieu.

References and Suggested Readings

Adams, Michael. 2009. *Fire and Ice: The United States, Canada and the Myth of Converging Values*. Toronto: Penguin Canada.

Bakvis, Herman. 2000–1. "Prime Minister and Cabinet in Canada: An Autocracy in Need of Reform?" *Journal of Canadian Studies* 35 (4): 60–79.

Bashevkin, Sylvia. 1991. *True Patriot Love: The Politics of Canadian Nationalism*. Toronto: Oxford University Press.

Bélanger, Éric. 2007. "Third Party Success in Canada." In *Canadian Parties in Transition*, edited by A.B. Tanguay and A.-G. Gagnon, 3rd ed., 83–109. Peterborough, ON: Broadview.

Bickerton, James. 1990. *Nova Scotia, Ottawa and the Politics of Regional Development*. Toronto: University of Toronto Press.

———. 1997. "Crime et Châtiment: Le Parti progressiste-conservateur du Canada entre 1984 et 1993." *Politique et Sociétés* 16 (2): 117–44. http://dx.doi.org/10.7202/040069ar.

———. 2007. "Between Integration and Fragmentation: Political Parties and the Representation of Regions." In *Canadian Parties in Transition*, edited by A.B. Tanguay and A.-G. Gagnon, 3rd ed., 411–35. Peterborough, ON: Broadview.

Bickerton, James, Alain-G. Gagnon, and Patrick Smith. 1999. *Ties That Bind: Parties and Voters in Canada*. Toronto: Oxford University Press.

Blais, André. 2005. "Accounting for the Electoral Success of the Liberal Party in Canada." *Canadian Journal of Political Science* 38 (December): 821–40.

Bradford, Neil. 1999. "Innovation by Commission: Policy Paradigms and the Canadian Political System." In *Canadian Politics*, edited by J. Bickerton and A.G. Gagnon, 3rd ed., 541–64. Peterborough, ON: Broadview.

Brean, Joseph. 2019. "All-Time Low Share of Popular Vote Is Enough for Liberals to Win Power." *National Post*, October 22.

Bricker, Darrell, and John Ibbitson. 2013. *The Big Shift: The Seismic Change in Canadian Politics, Business and Culture and What It Means for Our Future*. New York: Harper Collins.

Brodie, Janine, and Jane Jenson. 1980. *Crisis, Challenge and Change: Party and Class in Canada*. Toronto: Methuen.

Cairns, Alan C. 1968. "The Electoral System and the Party System in Canada, 1921–1965." *Canadian Journal of Political Science* 1 (1): 55–80. http://dx.doi.org/10.1017/S0008423900035228.

Campbell, Angus, Philip Converse, Warren Miller, and Donald Stokes. 1960. *The American Voter*. New York: John Wiley.

Campbell, Meaghan. 2019. "Liberals Benefitted Most from Strategic Voting, Poll of Late Deciding Voters Finds." *National Post*, October 25.

Carty, R.K. 1993. "Three Canadian Party Systems: An Interpretation of the Development of National Politics." In *Canadian Political Party Systems*, edited by R.K. Carty, 563–86. Peterborough, ON: Broadview.

———. 2013. "Has Brokerage Politics Ended?" In *Parties, Elections and the Future of Canadian Politics*, edited by A. Bittner and R. Koop, 10–23. Vancouver: UBC Press.

Carty, R.K., William Cross, and Lisa Young. 2000. *Rebuilding Canadian Party Politics*. Vancouver: UBC Press.

Clarke, H.D., J. Jenson, L. Leduc, and J. Pammett. 1984. *Absent Mandate: The Politics of Discontent in Canada*. Toronto: Gage.

———. 2019. *Absent Mandate: Strategies and Choices in Canadian Elections*. Toronto: University of Toronto Press.

Coulson, T.J. 2007. "Statistical Appendices: Canadian Federal Election Results, 1925–2006." In *Canadian Parties in Transition*, edited by A. G. Gagnon and A.B. Tanguay, 3rd ed., 518–48. Peterborough, ON: Broadview.

Downs, Anthony. 1957. *An Economic Theory of Democracy*. New York: Harper Collins.

English, John. 2009. *Just Watch Me: The Life of Pierre Elliot Trudeau: 1968–2000*. Toronto: Knopf Canada.

Explainer. 2019. "Federal Election 2019: The Definitive Guide to the Issues and Party Platforms." *Globe and Mail*, October 21.

Fife, Robert, and Marieke Walsh. 2019. "Federal Election 2019: Liberals Win Strong Minority but Lose Popular Vote to Conservatives." *Globe and Mail*, October 22.

Gagnon, A.G., and A.B. Tanguay. 1996. "Minor Parties in the Canadian Political System: Origins, Functions, Impact." In *Canadian Parties in Transition*, edited by A.G. Gagnon and A.B. Tanguay, 2nd ed., 106–35. Toronto: Nelson.

Gibbins, Roger. 2005. "Early Warning, No Response: Alan Cairns and Electoral Reform." In *Insiders and Outsiders: Alan Cairns and the Reshaping of Canadian Citizenship*, edited by Gerald Kernerman and Philip Resnick, 39–50. Vancouver: UBC Press.

Gidengil, E., N. Nevitte, A. Blais, J. Everitt, and P. Fournier. 2012. *Dominance and Decline: Making Sense of Recent Canadian Elections*. Toronto: University of Toronto Press.

Grant, George. 1970. *Lament for a Nation*. Toronto: McClelland and Stewart.

Heard, Andrew. n.d. "Elections Canada Voter Turnout, 1867–2015." www.sfu.ca/~aheard/elections/historical-turnout.html.

Hunter, Adam. 2019. "Conservative Sweep in Saskatchewan Shows Rejection of Liberal Policies and Increased Tensions." CBC News, October 22.

Johnston, R., A. Blais, H.E. Brady, and J. Crête. 1992. *Letting the People Decide: Dynamics of a Canadian Election*. Montreal and Kingston: McGill-Queen's University Press.

Johnston, Richard. 1992. "The Electoral Basis of Canadian Party Systems, 1878–1984." In *Canadian Political Party Systems*, edited by R. Kenneth Carty, 587–623. Peterborough, ON: Broadview.

———. 2005. "The Electoral System and the Party System Revisited." In *Insiders and Outsiders: Alan Cairns and the Reshaping of Canadian Citizenship*, edited by Gerald Kernerman and Philip Resnick, 51–64. Vancouver: UBC Press.

———. 2010. "Political Parties and the Electoral System." In *The Oxford Handbook of Canadian Politics*, edited by J.C. Courtney and D.E. Smith, 91–207. New York: Oxford University Press. http://dx.doi.org/10.1093/oxfordhb/9780195335354.003.0012.

———. 2017. *The Canadian Party System: An Analytic History*. Vancouver: UBC Press.

Kevins, Anthony, and Stuart Soroka. 2018. "Growing Apart? Partisan Sorting in Canada, 1992–2015." *Canadian Journal of Political Science* 51 (1): 103–33.

Koop, Royce, and Amanda Bittner. 2013. "Parties and Elections after 2011." In *Parties, Elections and the Future of Canadian Politics*, edited by A. Bittner and R. Koop, 308–31. Vancouver: UBC Press.

Lazarsfeld, Paul F., Bernard Berelson, and Hazel Gaudet. 1944. *The People's Choice: How the Voter Makes Up His Mind in a Presidential Campaign*. New York: Duell, Sloan & Pearce.

Leduc, Lawrence. 2007. "Realignment and Dealignment in Canadian Federal Politics." In *Canadian Parties in Transition*, edited by A.G. Gagnon and A.B. Tanguay, 3rd ed., 163–78. Peterborough, ON: Broadview.

Lipset, Seymour Martin. 1990. *Continental Divide: The Values and Institutions of the United States and Canada*. London: Routledge.

MacPherson, C.B. 1962. *Democracy in Alberta*. 2nd ed. Toronto: University of Toronto Press.

Marland, Alex, and Thierry Giasson, eds. 2015. *Canadian Election Analysis: Communication, Strategy, and Democracy*. Vancouver: UBC Press.

Nevitte, Neil, André Blais, Elisabeth Gidengil, and Richard Nadeau. 2000. *Unsteady State: The 1997 Canadian Federal Election*. Don Mills, ON: Oxford University Press.

Newman, Peter C. 1963. *Renegade in Power: The Diefenbaker Years*. Toronto: McClelland and Stewart.

Pinard, Maurice. 1975. *The Rise of a Third Party*, enlarged ed. Montreal and Kingston: McGill-Queen's University Press.

Russell, Peter. 1966. *Nationalism in Canada*. Toronto: McGraw Hill.

Radwanski, Adam. 2019. "Federal Election 2019: The Vote Was Scheer's to Win, but He Failed to Expand Support beyond the Conservative Base." *Globe and Mail*, October 22.

Savoie, Donald. 1999. *Governing from the Centre: The Concentration of Power in Canadian Politics*. Toronto: University of Toronto Press.

Sayers, Anthony. 2002. "Regionalism, Political Parties, and Parliamentary Politics in Canada and Australia." In *Regionalism and Party Politics in Canada*, edited by Lisa Young and Keith Archer, 209–21. Don Mills, ON: Oxford University Press.

Scott, F.R. 1967. "WLMK." In *The Blasted Pine: An Anthology of Satire, Invective and Disrespectful Verse*, edited by F.R. Scott and A.J.M. Smith. Toronto: Palgrave Macmillan.

Shaheen, Kareem. 2019. "Scandal on All Sides as Canada Heads for 'Election of Discontent.'" *Guardian*, October 13.

Siegfried, André. [1907] 1966. *The Race Question in Canada*. Toronto: McClelland and Stewart.

Simpson, Jeffrey. 2001. *The Friendly Dictatorship*. Toronto: McClelland and Stewart.

Smiley, Donald, and Ronald L. Watts. 1986. *Intrastate Federalism in Canada, Research Studies: Royal Commission on the Economic Union and Development Prospects for Canada*, vol. 39. Toronto: University of Toronto Press.

Smith, David E. 1985. "Party Government, Representation and National Integration in Canada." In *Party Government and Representation in Canada*, Peter Aucoin, research coordinator, *Research Studies: Royal Commission on the Economic Union and Development Prospects for Canada*, vol. 36, 1–68. Toronto: University of Toronto Press.

Smith, Denis. 1973. *Gentle Patriot: A Political Biography of Walter Gordon*. Edmonton: Hurtig.

Tanguay, A.B. 1994. "The Transformation of Canada's Party System in the 1990s." In *Canadian Politics*, edited by J. Bickerton and A.G. Gagnon, 2nd ed., 113–40. Peterborough, ON: Broadview.

Thorburn, Hugh. 1991. "Interpretations of the Canadian Party System." In *Party Politics in Canada*, edited by H. Thorburn, 6th ed., 114–24. Scarborough, ON: Prentice-Hall.

Valpy, Michael. 2008. "The Growing Ideological No Man's Land." *Globe and Mail*, September 21.

Wall, Brad. 2019. "Want a Unity Crisis? Pass Bill C-69 and C-48 into Law." *National Post*, May 30.

Walsh, Marieke. 2019. "Elizabeth May Resigns as Green Party Leader after 13 Years, Plans to Remain MP." *Globe and Mail*, November 4.

Wearing, Joseph. 1981. *The L-Shaped Party: The Liberal Party in Canada 1958–1980*. Toronto: McGraw-Hill Ryerson.

Whitaker, Reginald. 1977. *The Government Party: Organizing and Financing the Liberal Party of Canada, 1930–1958*. Toronto: University of Toronto Press.

fourteen
Democratic Reform and the Vagaries of Partisan Politics in Canada

A. BRIAN TANGUAY

Introduction[1]

Canadians, for the most part, appear to be quite happy with the overall health of their political system. Ask them whether they are satisfied with the way democracy works in their country, and a solid majority will answer yes. This has been the case in a wide variety of public opinion surveys conducted since the late 1990s, although the size of the majority has fluctuated from the mid-fifties to the low-seventies over this period. Canadians are, moreover, inordinately proud of their polity and much more likely than their counterparts in the United States to believe that the basic rights of citizens are well protected by their political system. Many scholars share this exuberance about Canadian democracy: in his assessment of the work of the Democratic Audit project,[2] R. Kenneth Carty boldly declared that "most comparative measures suggest that Canada and Canadians have built one of the most successful societies and polities anywhere" (Carty 2010, 244).

Canadian voters' sanguine outlook on the health of their democratic system stands in stark contrast to the increasingly gloomy prognostications about the fate of democracy in the rest of the world. The cover of the October 2018 issue of the *Atlantic Monthly* screamed out the question, in gigantic font, "Is Democracy Dying?" A recent documentary film directed by Astra Taylor, *What Is Democracy?*, provides insight into the role played by "oligarch-led global capitalism" in placing a straightjacket on ordinary citizens' ability to govern themselves (Phillips 2018). Recent scholarly publications such as *How Democracies Die,*[3] *The People vs. Democracy: Why Our Freedom Is in Danger and How to Save It,*[4] *Democracy in America? What Has Gone Wrong and What We Can Do About It,*[5] and *How Democracy Ends*[6] have raised the alarm that democracy in parts of Europe and North America risks being suffocated by a rising coterie of demagogic leaders and their increasingly fanatical and desperate followers.

There is very little evidence to suggest that Canada is imminently vulnerable to such a slide into authoritarianism. There are, however, more than a few disquieting signs of what one group of researchers refer to as "weakness in Canada's democratic fabric" (Gidengil et al. 2010, 95) and others simply label a "democratic malaise" (Law Commission of Canada 2004, 3) or a "democratic deficit" (Axworthy 2003–4; Martin 2002–3; Norris 2012). Voter turnout at the federal level, despite a modest increase in the 2015 general election, remains low by international standards. The situation at the provincial level, where turnouts under 60 per cent of registered voters are becoming the norm, is even more alarming. Young voters in particular are often uninterested in or disengaged from the traditional mechanisms of representative democracy. And Canadians of all ages combine an immoderate pride in their democratic system with a corrosive distrust of the institutional actors that work within it – political parties, most obviously, but also the media, Parliament, and the prime minister. Perhaps most worrisome is the fact that Canadians' apparent lack of interest in the niceties of institutional reform has created something of a democratic reform void, allowing the mainstream parties to manipulate this dossier for their own nakedly partisan purposes. This has resulted in an unhealthy policy lurch, where successive governments of different partisan complexion seek to undo the reforms introduced by their predecessors.

The following analysis comprises three sections. In the first, we will examine three indicators of democratic health in Canada – trust in the major political institutions, voter turnout, and political engagement among young voters. In the second and third we will provide overviews of recent provincial and federal initiatives to address the perceived democratic deficit, before concluding the chapter with a brief discussion of the prospects for meaningful democratic reform in the country.

Democratic Malaise in Canada? Good News ... Bad News

In a twenty-nine-nation survey of attitudes towards democracy and governance in the Americas, conducted in 2016–17, Canadians show themselves "to be among the most positive in the hemisphere about their democratic system of government" (Environics Institute 2017b).[7] This is true across a variety of indicators, including the belief that their leaders pay attention to the views of ordinary citizens and the conviction that the political system protects basic rights. "Canadians also continue to have the highest level of social trust in others" among all the nations included in the survey (Environics Institute 2017b).

Data from the Canadian Election Study (CES) over the past two decades reinforce the findings of the AmericasBarometer. Figure 14.1 shows that levels of satisfaction with the way democracy works in the country have been fairly stable since the early 1990s, typically ranging from the low to the mid-sixties (in 2000, 2006, 2011, and 2015). Satisfaction peaked at 71 per cent in 2008, at the conclusion of Stephen Harper's first minority Conservative

Figure 14.1 Satisfaction with Democracy in Canada, 1997–2015

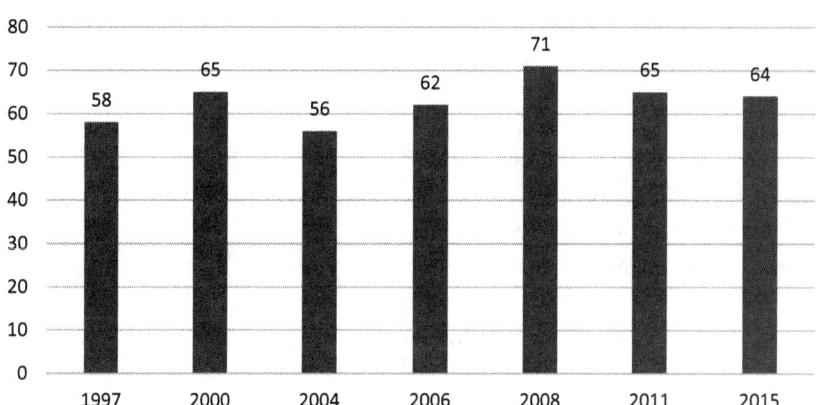

government, which had brought an end to the Liberals' thirteen-year hold on power (1993–2006). Satisfaction with democracy in Canada was at its lowest in 1997 (58 per cent of voters) and 2004 (56 per cent). Neither of the latter two results should be surprising: the 1997 survey was conducted in the immediate aftermath of the rancorous debate over Quebec's place in Confederation, which had culminated in a nerve-rackingly close referendum result in 1995,[8] while in 2004, the effects of the so-called sponsorship scandal, which tarnished the reputations of many prominent federal Liberals in Quebec, were still being felt at the time the election was held.[9]

There are some interesting provincial variations in satisfaction with democracy, as the data in tables 14.1 and 14.2 demonstrate. Provinces to the west of Quebec all had higher than average levels of satisfaction with democracy in 2015, with Albertans being the most satisfied in the country (75 per cent). Voters in the provinces to the east of Quebec were generally less satisfied than average, with the exception of those in Newfoundland and Labrador (68 per cent). It is Quebec, however, that displays the most idiosyncratic distribution of opinions on this indicator: only 54 per cent of Quebec's voters in 2015 were happy with the way democracy was working in the country, the lowest figure in the country – although Prince Edward Island was not far behind, at 61 per cent. This low level of satisfaction among Quebecers was almost entirely due to the unhappiness of the province's francophones: only 52 per cent of those with French as their mother tongue were satisfied with the state of democracy, as opposed to 71 per cent of anglophones and 70 per cent of allophones (those with neither French nor English as their mother tongue).[10] Whether the grievances of Quebec's francophones are primarily economic, political, or constitutional – a subject beyond the scope of this

Table 14.1 Satisfaction with Democracy in Canada, 2015

	Total	BC	AB	SK	MB	ON	QC	NB	NS	PEI	NL
% Satisfied	664	667	775	773	669	770	554	662	664	661	668
*N**	10,785	1241	730	313	443	3762	3337	299	347	199	204

* Total for both satisfied and not satisfied
Source: Patrick Fournier, Fred Cutler, Stuart Soroka, and Dietlind Stolle. 2015. *The 2015 Canadian Election Study* (dataset).

Table 14.2 Satisfaction with Democracy by Mother Tongue* in Quebec, 2015

	Total	Anglophone	Francophone	Allophone
% Satisfied	54	71	52	70
*N***	3175	228	2768	179

* Defined in the census as the language the respondent first learned and still understands. Allophone designates those whose mother tongue is neither French nor English.
** Total for both satisfied and not satisfied.
Source: Patrick Fournier, Fred Cutler, Stuart Soroka and Dietlind Stolle. 2015. *The 2015 Canadian Election Study* (dataset).

chapter – these data point to a fundamental, still unresolved problem in the Canadian polity (see Gagnon, chapter 10 in this volume).

In stark contrast to their generally positive evaluations of the overall health of their democratic system, Canadians reveal a deep distrust of specific political institutions in their country, which the data in table 14.3 reveal, as shown by the AmericasBarometer surveys of 2012 and 2016–17. Political parties, the mass media, and Parliament are particularly distrusted, with only 10, 16, and 19 per cent of Canadians respectively – in 2016–17 – indicating that they have "a lot" of trust in these institutions. These figures were up marginally from those in 2012. Only 16 per cent of Canadian voters expressed a lot of trust in the prime minister in 2012. This figure shot up by 10 points, to 26 per cent, in 2016–17. As the authors of the Environics report on the AmericasBarometer survey note, "The change in government in Ottawa since 2014 (and its change in 'tone') appears to have had a positive effect in terms of improving public confidence in the Prime Minister and in how elections are run" (Environics 2017b: "Overall Trends"). In both surveys, voters' trust was highest in the coercive and judicial branches of the state – the armed forces (53 per cent), the RCMP (43 per cent), and the Supreme Court (37 per cent).

Public mistrust of politicians and government has been growing stronger over the past three decades or so, not only in Canada but in most established

Table 14.3 Political Trust in Canada, 2012–2017*

To what extent do you trust:	2012	2017
Justice system	26	27
Armed forces	53	53
RCMP	37	43
Parliament	17	19
Prime minister	16	26
Supreme Court	34	37
Political parties	6	10
Mass media	10	16

Note: Figures in each cell represent the percentage of respondents in the two highest categories (6 and 7).
* Responses are on a seven-point scale, where 1 = "not at all" and 7 = "a lot."
Source: Environics Institute (2012, tables 29f, 29g, 29h, 29i, 29j, 29k, 29l, and 29p); Environics Institute (2017a, tables 30g, 30h, 30i, 30j, 30k, 30l, 30m, and 30p). These data were supplied by the Latin American Public Opinion Project at Vanderbilt University, which bears no responsibility for any interpretation of the data.

democracies. An analysis of survey data from about twenty of the so-called trilateral democracies[11] concluded that between the mid-1970s and the turn of the century there was a steady decline in public confidence in politicians in twelve out of thirteen countries for which data were available. A similar decline in confidence in legislatures occurred in eleven out of the fourteen countries. Over the same period, membership in political parties in most of these countries plummeted and the percentage of citizens expressing a partisan attachment (party identification) also declined significantly (Putnam, Pharr, and Dalton 2000, 14, 17, 19). Membership in Canada's political parties continues to be extremely low, even by these already low international standards (Carty 2010, 227). Cross and Young (2004, 428) contend that "Canadian parties are generally in a less than healthy state. Few Canadians belong to political parties. Those who do belong are not representative of the general electorate, and for the most part their commitment to their parties – as demonstrated by contribution of volunteer labour – is relatively weak."

Politicians and political parties have become a lightning rod for voter discontent in Canada, as they have elsewhere in the industrialized democracies. Pammett and LeDuc (2003, 7), in their study of non-voters in the Canadian federal election of 2000, remark that there "is a widespread perception that politicians are untrustworthy, selfish, unaccountable, lack credibility, are not true to their word, etc." Or, to use the pithy formulation of the German essayist and social critic Hans Magnus Enzensberger, parties in the industrialized world "have degenerated into corrupt self-service stores" – at least in the view of large swathes of the electorates in these countries (1987, 81).

This deep-seated distrust of political parties and politicians is one factor among several contributing to increasing political disengagement generally and rapidly declining voter turnout in particular – the second major indicator of democratic malaise in Canada and most of the industrialized nations today. Peter Mair (2013, 1–44), in a brilliant dissection of what he calls the "hollowing of western democracy," argues that as the failings of political parties become more and more evident, citizens are abandoning the arenas of traditional politics, like elections and party activism, in growing numbers. Parties, he contends, "are failing because the zone of engagement – the traditional world of party democracy where citizens interacted with and felt a sense of attachment to their leaders – is being evacuated" (16).

In the Canadian case, Pammett and LeDuc (2003, 7) point out that an overwhelming majority of voters in this country – almost 70 per cent – cite "negative public attitudes toward the performance of ... politicians and political institutions" as the principal factor underlying declining voter turnout in the country. Paul Martin, in a speech on parliamentary reform and public ethics that he delivered at Osgoode Hall in 2002 when he was still minister of finance, noted that in the general elections of 1997 and 2000, non-voters outnumbered those who supported the winning party by a considerable margin. Martin acknowledged that particular circumstances in each election might account for some of the drop in political interest among voters, but he nonetheless argued that "at some stage we have to face up to the fact: *something is going wrong here, and in a fundamental way*. Casting a ballot is the most basic function of our democratic system. That so many Canadians choose not to do so is the political equivalent of the canary in the coalmine ... far too many Canadians cannot be bothered to vote because they don't think their vote matters" (Martin 2002–3, 11; emphasis added).

Figure 14.2 displays data for turnout in federal elections in Canada from 1945 to 2019, expressed as a percentage of registered voters. Through the first four decades of the postwar period, voter turnout averaged in the mid- to high 70s; the sole exceptions were the elections of 1953 (68 per cent), 1974 (71 per cent), and 1980 (69 per cent). Pammett and LeDuc note that these three "exceptional" elections were held either at the height of the summer (August 1953 and July 1974) or the middle of winter (February 1980). Each took place in an exceptional political situation as well: "The 1953 election came during a long period of one-party dominance. The 1974 and 1980 elections were occasioned by the fall of minority governments and held in a climate of relative public dissatisfaction with politics in general" (2003, 4).

Figure 14.2 Voter Turnout (% of Registered Voters) in Federal Elections in Canada, 1945–2015

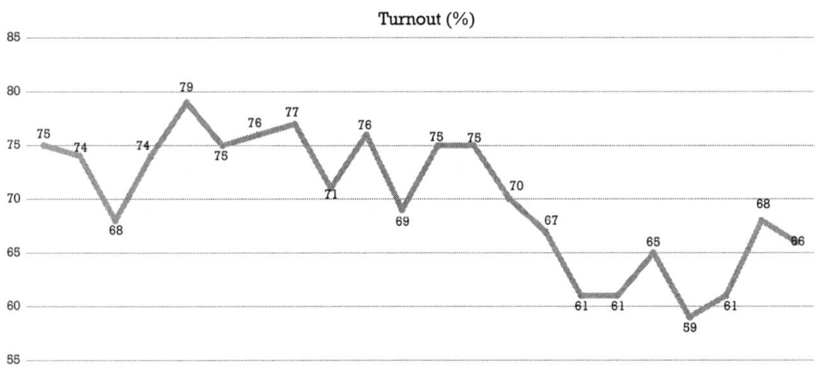

Source: Elections Canada (n.d.).

Turnout declined in each successive election from 1993 to 2004: from 70 per cent in 1993, to 67 per cent in 1997, to 61 per cent in 2000 and 2004. The 2006 election, in which the Conservative Party under Stephen Harper ousted the Liberals after a thirteen-year tenure in power, witnessed a small uptick in turnout, to 65 per cent. The competitiveness of this particular election, with the two major parties so evenly matched and the stakes of the outcome so high, contributed to this increase. In 2008, however, a number of factors – confusing rules regarding voter identification, along with the existence of a contingent of demoralized Liberal supporters who could not bring themselves to vote for Stéphane Dion and his Green Shift program (Heard 2008) – led to a precipitous drop in turnout, to a historic low of 59 per cent. Turnout recovered modestly in the 2011 federal election, reaching 61 per cent in a contest that yielded Harper's long-sought majority government. In 2015, voter turnout reached its highest level – 68 per cent – since the 1993 election, in part because of the "Justin effect." The hip, telegenic new leader of the Liberal Party seemed to energize youth in particular; indeed, the Huffington Post credited the Liberal majority to the disproportionate support the party received from young voters (Raj 2016). More than the youthful vigour of Justin Trudeau was at play here, too: the Liberal Party of Canada's message of change – embodied in its pledge to legalize recreational use of marijuana – was very successfully marketed to young voters. According to Harell and Gosselin (2015, 119), "Polling data suggests that Justin Trudeau and the Liberal Party 'brand' were both most appreciated by those under 30."[12]

In the 2019 federal election, turnout declined but only slightly, to 66 per cent of registered voters.

Nine of the provinces have also experienced drops in voter turnout since the early 1990s (see table 14.4). Most of these declines are quite substantial: a full 25 points in Saskatchewan, 23 percentage points in Newfoundland and Labrador, and 22 in Nova Scotia. British Columbia (-14), Manitoba (-14), and New Brunswick (-13) have also witnessed dramatic drops in voter turnout over this period. In four of the ten provinces, turnout in the most recent elections has been less than 60 per cent of registered voters. By contrast, at the turn of the twenty-first century, only two provinces – Alberta and Ontario – had turnouts in the 50 per cent range. The only province that has been able to resist this trend is Prince Edward Island, which in most elections held since the early 1990s witnessed turnouts over 80 per cent of registered voters. In this case, too, however, there has been a dip in turnout in recent elections; only 76 per cent of registered voters in the province cast their ballots in the 2019 general election.

Canada is not unique in experiencing a drop in voter turnout since the end of World War II. Wattenberg has asserted that declining turnout is a "nearly universal" trend in the industrialized OECD countries, and that "it is rare within comparative politics to find a trend that is so widely generalizable" (2000, 71). A study undertaken by the International Institute for Democracy and Electoral Assistance (IDEA) confirms that voter turnout, measured as a percentage of registered voters, has declined in every region of the globe since the early 1990s, but the sharpest drop has occurred in Europe (Solijonov 2016, 24–5).[13] Plummeting turnouts in Europe are attributable mainly to the declines experienced in the post-communist nations, whose first free elections were held in the late 1980s. Solijonov notes, however, that "a consistent decline in turnout of about 10 per cent [occurred] in the established European democracies during the same period, albeit from a higher base" (25). In his preface to this study, Yves Leterme, the secretary-general of International IDEA, contends that declining voter turnout is a symptom of the "deep problems democracies are facing today." He draws an explicit link between turnout and political parties, echoing in certain respects Peter Mair's analysis in *Ruling the Void*: "Lower turnout suggests that fewer citizens consider elections the main instrument for legitimizing political parties' control over political decision-making. It may even show that citizens are less interested in political parties as the main bodies of democratic representation as such" (2013, 9).

Widespread disengagement of young voters constitutes the third indicator of democratic malaise in Canada. As Thomas Axworthy puts it, "Turnout has not declined in the electorate as a whole but it has fallen like a stone among

Table 14.4 Voter Turnout (% of Registered Voters) in Provincial Elections since the Early 1990s

Province	Early 1990s	Early 2000s	Early 2010s	Most recent election	Decline 1990–present
BC	75 (1991)	71 (2001)	57 (2013)	61 (2017)	-14
AB	60 (1993)	53 (2001)	54 (2012)	64* (2019)	+4
SK	83 (1991)	71 (2003)	67 (2011)	58 (2016)	-25
MB	69 (1990)	54 (2003)	56 (2011)	55 (2019)	-14
ON	64 (1990)	57 (2003)	48 (2011)	57 (2018)	-7
QC	82 (1994)	70 (2003)	75 (2012)	66 (2018)	-16
NB	80 (1991)	69 (2003)	70 (2010)	67 (2018)	-13
NS	75 (1993)	66 (2003)	58 (2009)	53 (2017)	-22
PEI	81 (1993)	85 (2000)	77 (2011)	76 (2019)	-5
NL	84 (1993)	72 (2003)	58 (2011)	61* (2019)	-23

* Unofficial figures
Sources: All data have been compiled from the websites of the chief electoral officer of each of the provinces. Additional information available upon request.

Canadians born after 1970" (2003–4, 16). Pammett and LeDuc's study (2003) of non-voters in the 2000 federal election showed that Canadians born after 1975 were far less likely to vote than their elders. Only 22 per cent of voters between the ages of eighteen and twenty, and 28 per cent of those aged twenty-one to twenty-four, bothered to vote. Voter turnout increased with each successive age cohort, to a high of 83 per cent among those aged sixty-eight years or older. A more recent review of the empirical evidence suggests that while Pammett and LeDuc may have underestimated turnout among young voters in the 2000 federal election, the basic trend they identified holds true in subsequent elections: turnout among the group of voters most likely to go to the polls – those aged sixty-five to seventy-four – "has been more or less double that of young adults under twenty-five in each of the … three federal elections" held between 2004 and 2008 (Howe 2010, 7).

An important study published in 2016 reinforces the earlier findings of Howe and Pammett and LeDuc: from 1980 to 2011, the turnout rate for young voters in Canadian federal elections was "well below" that of "all other demographic groups" (Canada, Library of Parliament 2016, 1). In the four general elections that were held between 2004 and 2011, estimated turnout among the youngest voters (those aged eighteen to twenty-four) was roughly 19 to 21 percentage points lower than the overall average turnout (3). As noted above, all of this changed dramatically in the 2015 general election, when turnout increased among all age groups, but most markedly among the eighteen to twenty-four cohort, an estimated 57 per cent of whom cast their ballots. This represented an increase of 18 percentage points from the 2011 election, although young voters still turned out in fewer numbers than their older counterparts (4).

Young voters are not necessarily more cynical about politics than their older counterparts – in fact they are slightly less so (Blais et al. 2002, 54) – but they are markedly less interested in or informed about politics than any previous generation. They are, in the words of Gidengil et al., a "tuned out" generation rather than a "turned off" one (2003, 11; see Blais et al. 2002, 57, 61). In addition to their lack of interest in politics generally and in the nuances of particular election campaigns, young voters are more likely to experience problems with the registration process (getting their names on the permanent voters' list) than any other group of voters, apart from those over sixty-five years of age. Young voters are also most likely to report that they were simply too busy with work or family or school to get out to the polling station (Pammett and LeDuc 2003, table 12). This suggests that a combination of administrative reasons and lack of interest in and knowledge about politics prevents young Canadians from voting in higher numbers. The former, at least, might be rectified through the use of new technologies – like the internet – for registration and voting itself. The latter, however, constitutes a much more intractable problem: strategies for increasing young voters' awareness of and interest in politics include more intensive instruction of civics and government at the high school level, but there is no guarantee that this will make a dent in the turnout rates among youth (see the discussion in Pammett and LeDuc 2003, 52–9).

There are some disquieting signs that young people in Canada, as in most other industrialized democracies, now place less importance on democracy as an ideal than do older citizens. In his recent book, *The People vs. Democracy*, Yascha Mounk (2018, 107) affirms that "even young people in countries that are often portrayed as especially resistant to the current crisis of liberal democracy – like Canada, Germany, and Sweden – are much more critical of democracy than their parents or grandparents." Evidence from the most recent AmericasBarometer survey supports this claim: in 2016–17, only 52 per cent of voters aged eighteen to twenty-nine, and 51 per cent of those aged thirty to forty-four, agreed that "democracy is preferable to any other form of government." In stark contrast, 71 per cent of voters aged forty-five to fifty-nine, and 81 per cent of those sixty and older thought that democracy was the most preferred form of government (Environics 2017a, 94 [Q37]). Even more disturbing is the fact that in the same survey, 50 per cent of Canadian voters under the age of forty-five answered yes to the question, "In your opinion would a military coup be justified when there is a lot of corruption/crime?" Only 38 per cent of those aged forty-five to fifty-nine, and a mere 25 per cent of those aged sixty and over, felt the same way (Environics 2017a, 100 [Q41]). As the authors of the Canadian portion of the AmericasBarometer note, young voters in Canada – defined expansively as those under the age of forty-five – became "more positive in their views about democracy and the country's institutions" between 2012 and 2017. Paradoxically, "this young cohort is the least committed to democracy as the best or only form of government" (Environics 2017b: "Group Trends"). Again, it is important to note that these data do not in any way foreshadow an imminent collapse of the Canadian polity into authoritarianism. They do, however, demonstrate that Canada is by no means immune to the growing disenchantment with democracy identified by Mounk and other researchers.

Rampant distrust of the major political institutions in the country, declining voter turnout at both the federal and provincial levels, and high levels of political disengagement among the young in Canada: these three trends, documented above, were obvious in the early 2000s to political decision-makers at all levels of government in the country. Growing concern over the democratic malaise prompted a number of provincial governments to investigate ways of improving the responsiveness of representative institutions in their jurisdictions, and the outcome of these inquiries will be briefly examined in the next section, before we move on to a discussion of recent federal democratic reform efforts.

Democratic Reform Initiatives in the Provinces, 2000–2019

The provinces have often served as incubators of important policy and institutional innovations in the Canadian polity, and this was certainly the case when it came to dealing with the democratic deficit in the early 2000s. One province in particular, British Columbia, took the lead in democratic reform, thanks to a serendipitous convergence between the "perceived self-interest" of the newly elected Liberal government of Gordon Campbell in 2001 (Pilon 2010a, 104), on the one hand, and the reformist impulses of civil society actors, especially those on the populist right of the ideological spectrum, on the other. Elected with a crushing majority of seventy-seven seats in a seventy-nine-seat legislature, the BC Liberals might have appeared at first glance to be unlikely reformers, but they had already been victimized by the occasionally perverse mechanics of the single-member plurality[14] electoral system in the 1996 election. In that contest, the NDP were "wrong winners," forming a majority government despite trailing the Liberals by almost three percentage points in the popular vote (Pilon 2015, 296). As a result of that election debacle, and spurred on by a variety of activist groups such as Fair Voting BC, along with well-known public intellectuals of a populist bent, the Liberals fought the 2001 election campaign in part on a democratic reform platform, pledging to adopt fixed dates for elections, allow for the greater use of referendums to decide issues of public policy, and change the electoral system (Pilon 2010a, 99–101; Pilon 2015, 299–301). Despite their massive majority, and contradicting many pundits' firm conviction that no government would ever seek to change the rules of the game under which it had come to power, the Campbell government adopted a law in 2001 setting a fixed date for future provincial elections. More substantively, it created an independent citizens' assembly consisting of individuals drawn randomly from the BC voters' list (two from each of the seventy-nine constituencies) and charged it with reviewing the strengths and weaknesses of the existing first-past-the-post electoral system (Gibson 2002; Ruff 2003).

Four other provinces soon followed British Columbia's lead. In March 2003, the Quebec government's Estates-General on the Reform of Democratic Institutions (better known as the Béland Commission) issued a report in which the democratic deficit was highlighted as a prominent theme (Quebec, Comité directeur des États généraux sur la réforme des institutions démocratiques 2003). At the same time, the Liberal government of Dalton McGuinty in Ontario established a Democratic Renewal Secretariat and announced plans "to reach out to Ontarians and engage them in the most ambitious democratic renewal process in Ontario history, including fixed election dates, new ways to engage young people and innovative tools that could include Internet and telephone voting" (Ontario, Ministry of the Attorney General/Democratic Renewal Secretariat 2003). In New Brunswick, Progressive Conservative Premier Bernard Lord fulfilled one of his key promises during the 2003 election campaign by establishing a Commission on Legislative Democracy whose mandate was to "examine and make recommendations on strengthening and modernizing New Brunswick's electoral system and democratic institutions and practices to make them more fair, open, accountable and accessible to New Brunswickers" (New Brunswick 2003). Finally, the Progressive Conservative government of Pat Binns in Prince Edward Island set up a one-man Electoral Reform Commission under Norman Carruthers, which issued its final report in December 2003 (Prince Edward Island, Commissioner of Electoral Reform 2003, chap. 9).

What did this brief flurry of democratic reform initiatives yield in concrete policies? One popular innovation, first adopted by British Columbia in 2001, was fixed election dates, in an effort to remove or minimize the presumed electoral advantage that redounds to the governing party when it can determine the timing of an election by itself. In a notable illustration of the process of policy diffusion,[15] eight other provinces and two territories soon followed BC's lead: Newfoundland and Labrador (2004), Ontario (2005), New Brunswick (2007), Saskatchewan (2008), Prince Edward Island (2008), Manitoba (2008), Alberta (2011) and Quebec (2013) – along with the Northwest Territories (2006) and Nunavut (2014) – have all enacted legislation establishing fixed election dates (Canada, Parliament, n.d.; Canadian Press 2013).[16] The federal government followed suit in 2007, when Stephen Harper's Conservatives were in power. As a number of critics have pointed out, Harper was able to circumvent his own law when trying to manufacture a dissolution of Parliament in 2008 – so that his party could profit from favourable public opinion at the time – a tactical manoeuvre that "makes it apparent that even such a limited reform may be of uncertain value" (White 2010, 59).

Milner (2005, 28) has argued that one principal benefit of establishing fixed election dates is that it would create a "political season, a period in the year when paying special attention to public affairs and politics is the norm. This would make attentiveness to politics and voting more a matter of habit than it is now. And recent work has shown that voting is, to a not insignificant extent, a matter of forming the habit while still young." Evidence thus far to support this claim is weak; in fact, Dodek (2010, 217) argues with some justification that "proponents of fixed election date legislation overpromised and underdelivered."

The second and far more significant initiative to respond to the democratic malaise is a concerted effort at electoral reform. Five provincial governments – those of British Columbia, Prince Edward Island, Ontario, New Brunswick, and Quebec – have explored the possibility of replacing their existing first-past-the-post (FPTP) systems with a more proportional alternative.[17] Three of these provinces have held referendums or plebiscites on the question of replacing FPTP; in fact, BC and PEI have each conducted three such consultations over the past fifteen years (see table 14.5). Electoral reform has also become the focal point for civil society organizations – groups such as Democracy Watch, Fair Vote Canada, and the Mouvement pour une démocratie nouvelle – that have sought to revitalize representative democracy in Canada.

For the advocates of electoral reform, the results of these initiatives have been crushing disappointments, with just two exceptions. One occurred in PEI in 2016, when an online plebiscite yielded majority support (52.4 per cent) for mixed-member proportional representation (MMP) in a ranked-ballot vote on five different electoral systems, including first-past-the-post. Barely one-third (36.5 per cent) of registered voters turned out to cast their ballots on the issue, however, despite the fact

Table 14.5 Electoral Reform Referenda in the Provinces, 2005–2018

Province	Date of referendum	Turnout(%)	% in favour of new system	Majority in favour of new system in how many ridings?
BC	May 17, 2005	61.5	57.7	77 out of 79
PEI	November 28, 2005	33.2*	36.4	2 out of 27
ON	October 10, 2007	50.2	36.9	5 out of 107
BC	May 12, 2009	55.1	39.1	8 out of 85
PEI	October 29– November 7, 2016[§]	36.5	52.4[¶]	N/A
BC	October 22– December 7, 2018[†]	42.6	38.7	16 out of 87
PEI	April 23, 2019	76.5[‡]	48.3	15 out of 27

* This is an estimate, since no separate enumeration was done for the plebiscite. Elections PEI, in its report on the plebiscite, indicates that this turnout figure is based on the enumeration for the preceding provincial election, held in 2003.

§ "A provincial plebiscite on electoral reform was held utilizing online voting methods paired with two days of in-person paper ballot voting. The plebiscite offered five choices to Islanders on the preferential ballot":
First-past-the-post (FPTP)
First-past-the-post plus leaders
Mixed-member proportional representation (MMP)
Dual-member proportional representation
Preferential ballot (ranked ballot)

¶ MMP won on the fourth ballot, after FPTP+leaders, preferential voting (ranked ballot), and dual member PR had been successively excluded. The final round of voting pitted the existing system, first-past-the-post, against MMP.

† A mail-in referendum was conducted, posing two questions: first, whether BC "should keep the current First Past the Post voting system or move to a system of proportional representation"; and second, voters were asked "to rank three proportional systems: Dual Member Proportional (DMP), Mixed Member Proportional (MMP), and Rural-Urban Proportional (RUP)." MMP received the most support among the minority of voters in favour of a PR system.

‡ There were 107,109 registered voters in PEI for the 2019 general election. Whereas 83,185 of them cast ballots for candidates in the election, for a turnout of 77.6 per cent, only 81,888 voted in the concurrently held referendum on electoral reform, for an implied turnout rate of 76.5 per cent.

that for the first time in Canadian electoral history, sixteen- and seventeen-year-olds were allowed to vote in the referendum (Desserud and Collins 2017). Liberal Premier Wade MacLauchlan, citing the low turnout, questioned whether the endorsement of MMP could be "considered a clear expression of the will of Islanders" (MacDonald 2016). In the third referendum on electoral reform in the province, held concurrently with the general election on April 23, 2019, slightly fewer than half of the voters – 48.3 per cent – cast their ballots in favour of a mixed-member proportional system.

Another exception occurred in BC in May 2005. In that referendum, nearly 58 per cent of registered voters endorsed the citizens' assembly's recommended alternative to the existing first-past-the-post electoral system, which it had dubbed BC-STV. This result failed to meet both supermajority thresholds established by the Liberal government, however – at least 60 per cent of valid votes in 60 per cent of the province's seventy-nine ridings – and was therefore not binding.

Researchers have cited different factors to explain the disappointing (for advocates of reform) referendum outcomes. Pilon (2010b, 74) emphasizes elite manipulation of the referendum process: each time an electoral reform proposal was put to the citizens of a province, political elites devised "numerous innovative … barriers against change" – such as the unprecedented supermajorities required to make the results binding. According to Pilon, this partially accounts for the near success of the first referendum in BC: established elites were insufficiently prepared to counter the spasm of populist outrage that nearly led to the adoption of STV. The hostility of mainstream political parties to any deviation from the status quo, or in some cases, the confused signals sent out by party elites on the desirability of electoral reform, also militated against successful electoral reform (Stephenson and Tanguay 2009, 20–1; Fournier et al. 2011, 139–41). In all three provinces where referendums were held, widespread ignorance among voters about the basic features of the proposed alternatives to the first-past-the-post system was a primary contributor to the outcome (McKenna 2006, 58–9; Pilon 2010b, 82).

Despite the demoralizing defeats suffered by advocates of PR over the past decade and a half, the window for significant electoral reform in the country has not closed entirely, for a variety of reasons. Chief among them is that the biggest beneficiaries of the existing system, historically, have been the Liberal and Conservative parties (Tanguay 2020). Other parties, especially the NDP and the Greens, have not fared as well under FPTP and have long maintained a commitment to proportional representation as a key value, even if the NDP has sometimes contrived ways of avoiding this commitment when it has come to power. We can expect, however, that in a province where the NDP manages to win a future election, especially if it forms a minority government (particularly with the support of the Greens), it will explore the possibility of electoral reform in some manner, whether through creation of another citizens' assembly, a legislative task force, or a referendum. The latest province to entertain the idea of substantive electoral reform is

Quebec, where the recently elected Coalition Avenir Québec government of Premier François Legault has pledged to hold a referendum concurrently with the next general election, scheduled for 2022, on whether to adopt a mixed-member proportional system (Authier 2019).

Prospects for meaningful electoral reform in the provinces are dim, however, for three reasons. First, the mainstream parties will continue to act overtly or covertly against reform because they view their chances of winning power as being maximized under the existing rules of the game. The closer a party gets to power, the more likely it is to backpedal on previous commitments to electoral reform. Second, if reform proposals are put to a referendum, the decision will ultimately be made by a majority of voters who lack sufficient knowledge of or interest in electoral system design and who are therefore most likely to opt for the status quo. This is the pessimistic conclusion drawn by Fournier et al. (2011, chap. 9) in their examination of the work of the citizen assemblies in BC, Ontario, and the Netherlands. Third, as Johnston, Krahn, and Harrison (2006, 175, 178) have pointed out, electoral reform proposals seem to many voters to be too "formal and abstract"; for most ordinary citizens, "concerns over the health of democracy are much more immediately rooted in a widespread general distrust in government as being too powerful and secretive than in concerns about the inadequacy of political institutions."

Democratic Reform at the Federal Level, 2000–2019

The first systematic effort to confront the perceived democratic deficit at the federal level was made by the government of Paul Martin, who succeeded Jean Chrétien as leader of the Liberal Party of Canada and prime minister in late 2003. His first Cabinet included a minister responsible for democratic reform, and his "Action Plan for Democratic Reform" was released in early February 2004, before the sponsorship scandal engulfed his government. Contending that "democracy is an active process – one that requires ongoing engagement between citizens and their elected representatives," the action plan proposed "a fundamental change in parliamentary culture, a rebalancing of the relationship between the Cabinet and the House" (Canada, Privy Council Office 2004, 1, vi). Some of the main objectives of this democratic reform action plan included allowing greater freedom for MPs to voice their opinions by loosening party discipline in routine votes in the House of Commons and to allow for greater parliamentary review of government appointments to key state agencies. Before Martin could establish himself as the "democratic deficit slayer," however, his minority government fell, in part as a result of political fallout from the sponsorship scandal.

With the election of Stephen Harper's Conservatives in 2006, democratic reform initiatives became focused on party finance, the role of interest groups in election campaigns – labelled as *third parties* in election law – and the powers of the chief electoral officer. Efforts to deal with these problems have sparked intense and often bitter partisan debate. In order to make sense of this most recent phase of democratic reform initiatives, we need to examine the actions of Paul Martin's predecessor, Jean Chrétien.

During his ten years as prime minister, Jean Chrétien gave few indications that he thought the modernization and revitalization of the structures of representative democracy were urgent priorities. Chrétien was a reactive rather than an innovative leader, content to work within the institutions and mores of political life as he had found them when he assumed office. It was only when Martin's accession to the leadership of the Liberal Party became inevitable that Chrétien began to think about his legacy as prime minister and focus on restoring public confidence in representative government. Chrétien's hand was also forced by Auditor General Sheila Fraser's report in the spring of 2002, which first raised concern about questionable spending under the sponsorship program, and by other comparatively minor scandals at this time.

On June 11, 2002, Chrétien outlined an eight-point action plan on ethics in government in a speech in the House of Commons. A key item in this plan was a proposed overhaul of the Canada Elections Act in order to ban contributions by corporations and trade unions to political parties. Chrétien's intention was to restore the public's faith in the democratic system, which was being eroded by the perception that large contributions to political parties by their friends in the corporate sector were buying access to government decision-makers and favourable policies.

Bill C-24, An Act to Amend the Canada Elections Act and the Income Tax Act (Political Financing), received royal assent on June 19, 2003. The bill represented the most significant reform of Canada's election finance laws since the 1974 Election Expenses Act established the existing regime of party finance, one based on spending limits for candidates and parties, disclosure of campaign expenses and contributions, and partial public reimbursement of election expenditures (Canada, Library of Parliament, Parliamentary Research Branch 2003, 1–2).

In addition to severely restricting corporate and union contributions to parties and candidates and establishing limits on individual donations (initially set at $5,000 annually, since reduced to $1,000), Bill C-24 provided for annual public subsidies of registered political parties, intended to compensate them for foregone revenue from the now drastically reduced corporate and trade union donations. The law initially set the subsidy at $1.75 per vote (subsequently raised to $2) received by the party in the previous election, for any registered party winning more than 2 per cent of the popular vote, or 5 per cent of the vote in those ridings where it ran candidates.

This provision of the legislation quickly became its most controversial feature. The Conservative Party, which emerged as the most successful fund-raiser – by far – under the new dispensation, was unalterably opposed to any form of state "allowance," arguing that existing tax credits and other financial inducements were more than sufficient to subsidize party activities. Shortly after being returned to power with a second consecutive minority government in October 2008, the Harper administration unveiled a fiscal update that was supposedly intended to outline Canada's response to the accelerating meltdown in the world economy and included several nakedly partisan provisions. Among the latter was the elimination of the annual per-vote subsidy to qualifying registered political parties. This fiscal update precipitated the parliamentary crisis that ultimately led to the nascent Liberal-NDP coalition that threatened to bring down the government, as well as Harper's tactical (and controversial) prorogation of Parliament in response (Valpy 2009, 8–17). In the midst of this crisis, the Conservative government backed away from its pledge to abolish the per-vote subsidy.

Once he had achieved his long-coveted majority government in 2011, however, Stephen Harper homed in on the party allowance provision yet again. In the massive budget implementation bill introduced into the House in December 2011, the Harper government indicated that it would gradually phase out the party subsidy over a period of four fiscal years, completely eliminating it by April 2015. "Funding for political activities," the minister of state for democratic reform, Tim Uppal, claimed, "should come from ordinary Canadians who choose to contribute – not from corporations, not from unions, and not from government" (Canada, Minister of State [Democratic Reform] 2012).

State funding of political parties can help to strengthen the quality of democracy, but it involves intrinsic risks as well. On the positive side of the ledger, state financing can, in theory, help divert some of a party's focus away from the accumulation of the money needed to harvest votes and direct it toward policy innovation and similar activities. In Canada, where the educational dimension of party life has particularly atrophied, this might improve the quality of democracy (see Cross 2010b, 158–9). However, a 2007 study concluded that the presumed benefits of state funding of parties – augmenting their policy and educational functions – never did materialize in Canada: "There is little evidence to suggest state funding has liberated the parties to engage in more meaningful ways with the electorate. Parties have not taken on a more prominent role in policy development, mobilization of citizens, or public education with their new funds" (Young, Sayers, and Jansen 2007, 352). Canada's parties continue in the main to be vote-harvesting machines.

The Conservative government's second major democratic reform initiative was the Fair Elections Act, passed in June 2014. Introduced by the minister of democratic reform, Pierre Poilievre, the first draft of the legislation aimed, among other things, to rein in the powers of the chief electoral officer quite drastically, prohibiting him or her from encouraging voter turnout either through civic engagement programs or the publication of pertinent research studies. Critics of the bill decried this as a brazen attempt to muzzle the chief electoral officer, while some of its defenders, like Conservative Senator Linda Frum, argued that the CEO was in a conflict of interest when attempting to encourage higher voter turnout, since this might lead him or her to overlook or downplay voter fraud.[18] Other provisions in the draft bill would have prohibited the use of the voter information card as proof of identity or residence and outlawed the practice of vouching.[19] According to the draft bill's many critics – over 460 academics signed an open letter calling on the Harper government to withdraw the legislation (Centre for the Study of Democratic Institutions n.d.) – these two provisions would have made it more difficult for certain categories of voters, like Indigenous peoples living on reserves or highly mobile youth, to actually cast their ballots. This would have been tantamount, in the eyes of the critics, to voter suppression.

As it turned out, in the face of intense pressure from civil society organizations and the opposition parties, Minister Poilievre performed a "major climbdown" on vouching and on restricting the chief electoral officer's educational powers in the final version of the legislation. Nonetheless, we can detect in this episode the echoes of the highly polarized and partisan debate over who has the right to vote that has roiled the United States in the past few years.

The last major phase of democratic reform at the federal level was initiated by Justin Trudeau and the Liberals after they assumed power in October 2015. Having fought the election partly on the high-profile promise to make that campaign the last one conducted under the "unfair" first-past-the-post system, Trudeau and his government beat a hasty and embarrassing retreat once the Special Committee on Electoral Reform[20] recommended in its final report that a referendum be held on whether to replace the existing first-past-the-post system with "a proportional electoral system that achieves a Gallagher Index score of 5 or less."[21] In parliamentary debate after the Special Committee's final report was delivered, the minister of democratic institutions, Maryam Monsef, held up a sheet on which the mathematical formula for the Gallagher Index was displayed and remarked that instead of outlining a concrete alternative to FPTP, the committee had become obsessed with technicalities: "'They did not complete the hard work we had expected them to.... On the hard choices that we asked the committee to make, Mr. Speaker, they took a pass'" (cited in Wherry and Tasker 2016).

Having no appetite for a referendum on electoral reform, Prime Minister Trudeau shelved the Special Committee's report, lamely justifying his actions in an interview with *Le Devoir* by claiming that there was no longer an urgent need for substantial institutional change now that Stephen Harper and his unpopular government had been defeated: "'Now, with the current system, voters have a government with which they are more satisfied. And the desire to change the electoral system is less pressing [or glaring],' Trudeau claimed"[22] (Vastel 2016). The subordination of democratic reform to the imperatives of partisan politics is virtually complete here.

Monsef was quickly shuffled out of the democratic institutions portfolio and replaced by Karina Gould, who shepherded Bill C-76, An Act to amend the Canada Elections Act and other Acts and to make certain consequential amendments, through Parliament. The legislation received royal assent on December 13, 2018. Among its main provisions, the law established limits on election spending by third parties, sought to protect the privacy of individual voters and, for the first time, to rein in the spread of "fake news." It also "aimed at undoing some of what the Conservatives introduced through their Fair Elections Act – including restoring the use of the voter identification card as a valid piece of ID" (Smith 2018).

Conclusion

This chapter has reviewed the evidence that Canada is in the grip of a democratic malaise, despite the fact that large numbers of voters continue to express their overall satisfaction with the way their polity works. Widespread distrust of key political institutions such as political parties, the media, and Parliament; sharply declining rates of voter turnout at both the federal and provincial level over the past twenty-five years; and the rise of a disengaged cohort of young voters: these are all indicators that former prime minister Paul Martin was not far off the mark when he claimed that there is something fundamentally wrong with our political system. Even if it is true that Canadian democracy is not in as bad shape as that in the United States or certain European states, we are certainly not immune to the trends being exhibited elsewhere.

Political elites in the country were certainly not unaware of these indicators of democratic malaise, and in the early part of the twenty-first century concerted efforts were made at both the provincial and federal level to improve the quality of democratic governance. As we have seen, however, relatively minor reforms such as the adoption of fixed election dates have had little impact in lessening voter cynicism. Stephen Harper himself demonstrated in 2008 that this legislation could be circumvented if partisan interests dictate it. A more substantive reform, such as the ban on corporate and union donations to political parties, along with implementation of state subsidies for registered parties, has also had limited beneficial effect on political trust among voters. Some of the putative benefits of the legislation, such as strengthening the educational function of political parties and bolstering the ties between party elites and the organizational grassroots, were simply never realized. Finally, efforts to replace the existing first-past-the-post electoral system at both the provincial and federal levels have failed in the face of elite intransigence and voter ignorance. Established elites within the mainstream political parties are wedded to the existing system and, as argued by Dennis Pilon, they have worked diligently in each referendum to throw up obstacles to reform. Moreover, a majority of voters have tended to see electoral reform as an abstract issue championed by wonkish intellectuals. Advocates of PR have not been able to convince sufficient numbers of voters that a new electoral system would provide them with the kind of political change they seek: to make government more transparent and trustworthy.

Some will argue that the limited success of democratic reform efforts in the first decade of the twenty-first century is of little consequence. What does it matter if electoral reform or attempts to clean up the realm of party finance fail, or take a back seat to partisan tactical considerations, when a solid majority of voters continue to express their satisfaction with the state of democracy in the country? On this view, distrust of political institutions and the political class will always exist as the background noise of Canadian political life. Advocates of democratic reform counter that poorly designed institutions create perverse incentives and thus have a way of inducing public servants to behave in ways contrary to the public interest. For this reason, proposals for democratic reform should remain at the core of political debate in this country.

Notes

1 The author is indebted to Bianca Jamal of Wilfrid Laurier University for her research assistance in compiling the data for tables 14.1 and 14.2. Any errors or idiosyncrasies of interpretation are, of course, the author's responsibility alone.

2 The Democratic Audit project brought together a team of social scientists to evaluate components of Canada's political system according to the criteria of inclusiveness, participation, and responsiveness. See Cross (2010b) for a summary of the Democratic Audit project.

3 Levitsky and Ziblatt (2018).
4 Mounk (2018).
5 Page and Gilens (2017).
6 Runciman (2018).
7 Details of the survey methodology, sample sizes, and countries surveyed for the AmericasBarometer can be found in Cohen, Lupu, and Zechmeister (2017).
8 Slightly more than a percentage point separated the Yes and No sides in the referendum result: 50.6 per cent of voters cast their ballots against the proposal to make Quebec a sovereign nation, while 49.4 per cent were in favour. Turnout was a remarkable 93.5 per cent of registered voters.
9 In the wake of the close 1995 referendum result, the government of Jean Chrétien established a secret program to award advertising contracts to select firms – most of them based in Quebec and many with close ties to the Liberal Party – to boost the visibility of the federal government and thereby strengthen national unity. Many of these contracts were for little or no actual work and some of the money made its way back to prominent Liberals in the form of kickbacks. A full-scale judicial inquiry under Justice John Gomery was established in 2004; it exposed widespread corruption in the awarding of these contracts and ultimately led to the criminal convictions of key players in the affair. See CBC News Online (2006) and Bakvis and Tanguay (2012, 108) for discussions of the political consequences of the sponsorship scandal.
10 The sample sizes of Quebec anglophones and allophones in the CES are small, and for this reason we should be cautious about the interpretation of the data.
11 The trilateral countries include those of North America, Western Europe, and Japan. The Trilateral Commission, an influential private think tank founded in 1973 to foster cooperation among the three major democratic industrialized areas of the world on common problems facing them, issued a report on "governability" entitled *The Crisis of Democracy* (Crozier, Huntington and Watanuki 1975). The volume of essays edited by Pharr and Putnam was published to commemorate the twenty-fifth anniversary of the publication of this earlier Trilateral Commission study.
12 We will return below to the role played by young voters in propelling Justin Trudeau and the Liberals to a majority government.
13 The five regions included in the study are Africa, the Americas, Asia, Europe, and Oceania.
14 Popularly known as the first-past-the-post electoral system (FPTP).

15 Alcantara and Roy (2014, 266) sketch an interesting theoretical explanation for the timing of fixed election date legislation in the Canadian provinces, one that focuses primarily on "an opposition party that adopts fixed election dates in its party platform prior to" taking power from an incumbent government that had often had a lengthy stay in office.

16 Nova Scotia is the lone provincial holdout.

17 In PEI (2005) and Ontario (2007), the alternative to first-past-the-post was a mixed-member proportional (MMP) system, similar to the one employed in Germany and Scotland, among other countries. In BC (in both 2005 and 2009) the alternative was single transferable vote (STV), a proportional, ranked ballot system used in the Republic of Ireland and in Australia for Senate elections. In two of the most recent public consultations, in PEI (2016) and BC (2018), a wider variety of alternatives have been presented to voters. Detailed discussion of the impressive array of proportional and semi-proportional electoral systems that could replace FPTP is beyond the scope of this chapter. Interested readers are encouraged to consult the Law Commission of Canada report (2004) as well as Reynolds, Reilly, and Ellis (2005).

18 Senator Frum made this claim on the CBC radio program *As It Happens*, on November 29, 2014 (CBC Radio 2014). Readers interested in the Fair Elections Act and the divergent responses to it may consult a very useful website, curated by the Centre for the Study of Democratic Institutions at the University of British Columbia (n.d.).

19 According to the chief electoral officer (Canada, Chief Electoral Officer 2014), "Currently, an elector who does not have the necessary proof of identity or residence may prove that identity and residence by taking an oath if he or she is accompanied by an elector of the same polling division who provides the poll official his or her own proof of identity and residence and vouches for the elector under oath. Vouching or taking an oath is permitted in all Canadian provinces where proof of identity and residence is required. Removing the possibility of vouching at the federal level takes away the last safety net for those electors who do not have the necessary documents to prove identity and residence."

20 Created pursuant to Standing Order 81(16) on June 7, 2016, and charged with "identify[ing] and conduct[ing] a study of viable alternate voting systems to replace the first-past-the-post system, as well as … examin[ing] mandatory voting and online voting" (Canada, House of Commons, Special Committee on Electoral Reform 2016, 169). The committee was given only six months to conduct public hearings and town halls and issue its report, a very tight timeline.

21 Canada, House of Commons, Special Committee on Electoral Reform (2016, 164). There is a lot to unpack in this recommendation and in the activities of the Special Committee. This could legitimately form the subject of a chapter by itself. Suffice it to say that on the Gallagher Index, the Special Committee observes (69), "One tool that has been developed to measure an electoral system's relative disproportionality between votes received and seats allotted in a legislature is the Gallagher Index, developed by Michael Gallagher (who appeared before the Committee). As noted by Byron Weber Becker, the Gallagher Index 'combines both over and under-representation for each party into a single number.' According to Professor Becker, a Gallagher Index of less than 5 is considered 'excellent.'"

22 My translation of "'Or, sous le système actuel, ils ont maintenant un gouvernement avec lequel ils sont plus satisfaits. Et la motivation de vouloir changer le système électoral est moins percutante [ou moins criante],' a plaidé M. Trudeau."

References and Suggested Readings

Alcantara, Christopher, and Jason Roy. 2014. "Reforming Election Dates in Canada: Towards an Explanatory Framework." *Canadian Public Administration* 57 (2): 256–74.

Aucoin, Peter, Mark D. Jarvis, and Lori Turnbull. 2011. *Democratizing the Constitution: Reforming Responsible Government*. Toronto: Emond Montgomery Publications.

Authier, Philip. 2019. "Quebecers Will Vote on Electoral Reform in a Referendum in 2022." *Montreal Gazette*, September 25. https://montrealgazette.com/news/quebec/quebecers-will-vote-on-electoral-reform-in-a-referendum-in-2022.

Axworthy, Thomas S. 2003–4. "The Democratic Deficit: Should This Be Paul Martin's Next Big Idea?" *Policy Options* 25 (1): 15–19.

Bakvis, Herman, and A. Brian Tanguay. 2012. "Federalism, Political Parties, and the Burden of National Unity: Still Making Federalism Do the Heavy Lifting." In *Canadian Federalism*, edited by Herman Bakvis and Grace Skogstad, 3rd ed., 96–115. Toronto: Oxford University Press.

Blais, André, Elisabeth Gidengil, Richard Nadeau, and Neil Nevitte. 2002. *Anatomy of a Liberal Victory: Making Sense of the Vote in the 2000 Canadian Federal Election*. Peterborough, ON: Broadview.

Canada. Chief Electoral Officer. 2014. "Proposed Amendments to Bill C-23 Presented by the Chief Electoral Officer to the Standing Committee on Procedure and House Affairs," March 6. https://democracy2017.sites.olt.ubc.ca/files/2014/03/Mayrand-Chart.2014-Mar-06.pdf.

———. House of Commons. Special Committee on Electoral Reform [referred to by Parliament as ERRE, short form for Electoral Reform/Réforme électorale]. 2016. *Strengthening Democracy in Canada: Principles, Process and Public Engagement for Electoral Reform*, 42nd Parliament, 1st Session, December.

———. Library of Parliament. 2016. *Youth Voter Turnout in Canada*. Ottawa. Publication no. 2016-104-E.

———. Library of Parliament. Parliamentary Research Branch. 2003. "Bill C-24: An Act to Amend the Canada Elections Act and the Income Tax Act (Political Financing) – Legislative Summary." LS-448E, February 5, revised February 11.

———. Minister of State (Democratic Reform). 2012. "Harper Government Highlights Taxpayer Savings through Diminished Subsidies for Political Parties." News release, May 17. http://www.democraticreform.gc.ca/eng/content/harper-government-highlights-taxpayer-savings-through-diminished-subsidies-poltical-parties (link no longer active).

———. Parliament. 2003. *Debates.* 37th Parliament, 2nd Session. January–June.

———. Parliament. n.d. "Fixed-Date Elections in Canada." http://www.parl.gc.ca/ParlInfo/Compilations/ProvinceTerritory/ProvincialFixedElections.aspx (link no longer active).

———. Privy Council Office. 2004. *Ethics, Responsibility, Accountability: An Action Plan for Democratic Reform.* Ottawa. http://publications.gc.ca/collections/Collection/CP22-74-2004E.pdf.

Canadian Press. 2013. "Nine Provinces Now Have Fixed Election Dates, after Quebec Adopts Measure." *Winnipeg Free Press*, June 14. http://www.winnipegfreepress.com/canada/nine-provinces-now-have-fixed-election-dates-after-quebec-adopts-measure-211632341.html link no longer active.

———. 2018. "PEI Poised for Battle over Electoral Reform." *Toronto Star*, June 13. https://www.thestar.com/news/canada/2018/06/13/pei-poised-for-battle-over-electoral-reform.html.

Carty, R. Kenneth. 2010. "Canadian Democracy: An Assessment and an Agenda." In *Auditing Canadian Democracy*, edited by William Cross, 223–46. Vancouver: UBC Press.

CBC News Online. 2006. "In Depth: Federal Sponsorship Scandal," October 26. https://www.cbc.ca/news2/background/groupaction/.

CBC Radio. 2014. "Fair Elections Act: Frum." *As It Happens*, November 29. https://www.cbc.ca/radio/asithappens/fair-elections-act-frum-1.2612070.

Centre for the Study of Democratic Institutions. University of British Columbia. n.d. "Resources on the Fair Elections Act (Bill C-23)." https://democracy.arts.ubc.ca/fairelectionsact/.

Cohen, Mollie J., Noam Lupu, and Elizabeth J. Zechmeister. 2017. *The Political Culture of Democracy in the Americas, 2016/17: A Comparative Study of Democracy and Governance.* Latin American Public Opinion Project, Vanderbilt University, Nashville, TN. In Association with the United States Agency for International Development. August.

Cross, William. 2010a. "Constructing the Canadian Democratic Audit." In *Auditing Canadian Democracy*, edited by William Cross, 1–17. Vancouver: UBC Press.

———. 2010b. "Political Parties." In *Auditing Canadian Democracy*, edited by William Cross, 143–67. Vancouver: UBC Press.

Cross, William, and Lisa Young. 2004. "The Contours of Political Party Membership in Canada." *Party Politics* 10 (4): 427–44.

Crozier, Michel, Samuel P. Huntington, and Joji Watanuki. 1975. *The Crisis of Democracy.* Report on the Governability of Democracies to the Trilateral Commission. New York: New York University Press.

Desserud, Don, and Jeffrey F. Collins. 2017. "The Ongoing Saga of Electoral Reform in PEI." Policy Options, April 11. http://policyoptions.irpp.org/magazines/april-2017/the-ongoing-saga-of-electoral-reform-in-pei/.

Dodek, Adam. 2010. "The Past, Present and Future of Fixed Election Dates in Canada." *Journal of Parliamentary and Political Law* 4: 215–38.

Elections Alberta. 2015. "Provincial Results." http://officialresults.elections.ab.ca/orResultsPGE.cfm?EventId=31.

Elections BC. 2005. "Statement of Votes: Referendum on Electoral Reform." http://www3.elections.bc.ca/docs/rpt/SOV-2005-ReferendumOnElectoralReform.pdf.

———. 2009. "Statement of Votes: Referendum on Electoral Reform." https://www3.elections.bc.ca/docs/rpt/2009Ref/2009-Ref-SOV.pdf.

———. 2018. "May 9, 2017, General Election." https://elections.bc.ca/docs/rpt/2017-General-Election-Report.pdf.

Elections Canada. n.d. "Voter Turnout at Federal Elections and Referendums." http://www.elections.ca/content.aspx?section=ele&dir=turn&document=index&lang=e.

Environics Institute. 2012. *AmericasBarometer: The Public Speaks on Democracy and Governance across the Americas. Canada 2012. Final Report.* https://www.environicsinstitute.org/projects/project-details/americasbarometer-2012.

———. 2017a. "AmericasBarometer – Canada 2017." Detailed Data Tables. https://www.environicsinstitute.org/docs/default-source/project-documents/americasbarometer-2017/americasbarometer---canada-2017---data-tables---canada.pdf?sfvrsn=e3f34459_2.

———. 2017b. "AmericasBarometer – Canada 2017." Final Report. https://www.environicsinstitute.org/docs/default-source/project-documents/americasbarometer-2017/americasbarometer---canada-2017---final-report.pdf?sfvrsn=5f8edadf_2.

Enzensberger, Hans Magnus. 1987. *Europe, Europe*. Translated by Martin Chalmers. New York: Pantheon Books.

Fournier, Patrick, Henk van der Kolk, R. Kenneth Carty, André Blais, and Jonathan Rose. 2011. *When Citizens Decide: Lessons from Citizen Assemblies on Electoral Reform*. Oxford: Oxford University Press.

Gibson, Gordon. 2002. *Report on the Constitution of the Citizens' Assembly on Electoral Reform*. Vancouver: UBC Press, December 23.

Gidengil, Elisabeth, André Blais, Neil Nevitte, and Richard Nadeau. 2003. "Turned Off or Tuned Out? Youth Participation in Politics." *Electoral Insight* 5 (2): 9–14.

Gidengil, Elisabeth, Richard Nadeau, Neil Nevitte, and André Blais. 2010. "Citizens." In *Auditing Canadian Democracy*, edited by William Cross, 93–117. Vancouver: UBC Press.

Harrel, Allison, and Tania Gosselin. 2015. "The Youth Vote in the 2015 Election." In *Canadian Election Analysis 2015: Communication, Strategy, and Democracy*, edited by Alex Marland and Thierry Giasson, 118–19. Vancouver: UBC Press. http://www.ubcpress.ca/CanadianElectionAnalysis2015.

Heard, Andrew. 2008. "Historical Voter Turnout in Canadian Federal Elections and Referenda, 1867–2008." http://www.sfu.ca/~aheard/elections/historical-turnout.html.

Howe, Paul. 2010. *Citizens Adrift: The Democratic Disengagement of Young Canadians*. Vancouver: UBC Press.

Huffington Post Canada. 2013. "Voter Turnout: B.C. Election Results 2013 by Numbers," May 15. http://www.huffingtonpost.ca/2013/05/15/voter-turnout-bc-election-results_n_3282380.html.

Johnston, W.A., Harvey Krahn, and Trevor Harrison. 2006. "Democracy, Political Institutions and Trust: The Limits of Current Electoral Reform Proposals." *Canadian Journal of Sociology* 31 (2): 165–82.

Law Commission of Canada. 2004. "Voting Counts: Electoral Reform in Canada." Report submitted to the Minister of Justice, March.

Levitsky, Steven, and Daniel Ziblatt. 2018. *How Democracies Die*. New York: Crown.

MacDonald, Michael. 2016. "P.E.I. Plebiscite Results Don't Reflect Will of the People, Says Premier." *Toronto Star*, November 8. https://www.thestar.com/news/canada

/2016/11/08/pei-voters-support-switch-to-proportional-representation-in-non-binding-plebiscite.html.
Mair, Peter. 2013. *Ruling the Void: The Hollowing of Western Democracy.* London: Verso.
Martin, Paul. 2002–3. "The Democratic Deficit." *Policy Options* 24 (1): 10–12.
McKenna, Peter. 2006. "Opting Out of Electoral Reform: Why PEI Chose the Status Quo." *Policy Options* (June): 58–61.
Milner, Henry. 2005. "Fixing Canada's Unfixed Election Dates: A Political Season to Reduce the Democratic Deficit." *IRPP Policy Matters* 6 (6).
Mounk, Yascha. 2018. *The People vs. Democracy: Why Our Freedom Is in Danger and How to Save It.* Cambridge, MA: Harvard University Press.
New Brunswick. 2003. "Premier Bernard Lord Creates Commission on Legislative Democracy." News release, December 19. http://www.gnb.ca/cnb/news/ld/2003e1208ld.htm.
Norris, Pippa. 2012. "The Democratic Deficit: Canada and the United States in Comparative Perspective." In *Imperfect Democracies: The Democratic Deficit in Canada and the United States,* edited by Patti Tamara Lenard and Richard Simeon, 23–50. Vancouver: UBC Press.
Ontario. Ministry of the Attorney General/Democratic Renewal Secretariat. 2003. "McGuinty Government to Strengthen Our Democracy and Improve the Way Government Serves People." News release, December 8. http://www.attorneygeneral.jus.gov.on.ca/english/news/2003/20031208-dr1.asp.
Page, Benjamin I., and Martin Gilens. 2017. *Democracy in America? What Has Gone Wrong and What We Can Do About It.* Chicago: University of Chicago Press.
Pammett, Jon H., and Lawrence LeDuc. 2003. "Explaining the Turnout Decline in Canadian Federal Elections: A New Survey of Non-Voters." *Elections Canada,* March. https://www.elections.ca/content.aspx?section=res&dir=rec/part/tud&document=index&lang=e.
Phillips, Charlie. 2018. "What Is Democracy? Review – Searing Analysis of Who's Really in Control." *Guardian,* June 11. https://www.theguardian.com/film/2018/jun/11/what-is-democracy-review-astra-taylor-documentary.
Pilon, Dennis. 2010a. "Democracy BC-Style." In *British Columbia Politics and Government,* edited by Michael Howlett, Dennis Pilon, and Tracy Summerville, 87–108. Toronto: Emond Montgomery Publications.
———. 2010b. "The 2005 and 2009 Referenda on Voting System Change in British Columbia." *Canadian Political Science Review* 4 (2–3): 73–89.
———. 2015. "British Columbia: Right-Wing Coalition Politics and Neoliberalism." In *Transforming Provincial Politics,* edited by Bryan M. Evans and Charles W. Smith, 284–312. Toronto: University of Toronto Press.
———. 2017. "Assessing Gordon Campbell's Uneven Democratic Legacy in British Columbia." In *The Campbell Revolution? Power, Politics and Policy in British Columbia,* edited by J.R. Lacharite and Tracy Summerville, 37–60. Montreal and Kingston: McGill-Queen's University Press.
Prince Edward Island. Commissioner of Electoral Reform. 2003. "Report," December 18. http://www.gov.pe.ca/photos/original/er_premier2003.pdf.
Putnam, Robert D., Susan J. Pharr, and Russell J. Dalton. 2000. "Introduction: What's Troubling the Trilateral Democracies?" In *Disaffected Democracies,* edited by Susan J. Pharr and Robert D. Putnam, 3–27. Princeton, NJ: Princeton University Press.
Quebec. Comité directeur des États généraux sur la réforme des institutions démocratiques [Béland Commission]. 2003. "Prenez votre place! La participation citoyenne au coeur des institutions démocratiques québécoises."

Raj, Althea. 2016. "Liberals Won Majority Thanks to Young Voters, Poll Suggests." Huffington Post, April 19. https://www.huffingtonpost.ca/2016/04/19/liberals-young-voters-trudeau-canada-election-2015_n_9727026.html.

Reynolds, Andrew, Ben Reilly, and Andrew Ellis. 2005. *Electoral System Design: The New International IDEA Handbook*. Stockholm: International Institute for Democracy and Electoral Assistance.

Ruff, Norman. 2003. "BC Deliberative Democracy: The Citizens' Assembly and Electoral Reform 2003–2005." Paper presented to the annual conference of the Canadian Political Science Association, Halifax, NS, June 1.

Runciman, David. 2018. *How Democracy Ends*. New York: Basic Books.

Smith, Joanna. 2018. "Liberal Elections Bill Looks to Make Voting Easier, Tighten Rules on Privacy, Spending." *National Post*, April 30. https://nationalpost.com/news/politics/big-new-liberal-bill-to-reveal-long-promised-changes-to-elections-law.

Solijonov, Abdurashid. 2016. *Voter Turnout Trends around the World*. Stockholm: International Institute for Democracy and Electoral Assistance.

Stephenson, Laura, and A. Brian Tanguay. 2009. "Ontario's Referendum on Proportional Representation: Why Citizens Said No." *IRPP Choices* 15 (10).

Tanguay, A. Brian. 2020. "Parties, Elections and Canadian Federalism in the 21st Century: Cairns Revisited – Again." In *Canadian Federalism and Its Future: Actors and Institutions*, edited by Alain-G. Gagnon and Johanne Poirier. Montreal and Kingston: McGill-Queen's University Press.

Valpy, Michael. 2009. "The 'Crisis': A Narrative." In *Parliamentary Democracy in Crisis*, edited by Peter H. Russell and Lorne Sossin, 3–18. Toronto: University of Toronto Press.

Vastel, Marie. 2016. "Trudeau ne garantit plus une réforme électorale majeure." *Le Devoir*, October 19. http://www.ledevoir.com/politique/canada/482514/la-reforme-electorale-n-est-plus-garantie.

Wattenberg, Martin P. 2000. "The Decline of Party Mobilization." In *Parties without Partisans: Political Change in Advanced Industrial Democracies*, edited by Russell J. Dalton and Martin P. Wattenberg, 64–76. Oxford: Oxford University Press.

Wherry, Aaron, and John Paul Tasker. 2016. "Minister 'Disappointed' as Electoral Reform Committee Recommends Referendum on Proportional Representation." CBC News, December 1. https://www.cbc.ca/news/politics/wherry-electoral-reform-committee-1.3866879.

White, Graham. 2010. "Cabinets and First Ministers." In *Auditing Canadian Democracy*, edited by William Cross, 40–64. Vancouver: UBC Press.

Young, Lisa, Anthony Sayers, and Harold Jansen. 2007. "Altering the Political Landscape: State Funding and Party Finance." In *Canadian Parties in Transition*, edited by Alain-G. Gagnon and A. Brian Tanguay, 3rd ed., 335–54. Peterborough, ON: Broadview.

fifteen
Media and Strategic Communication in Canadian Politics

ALEX MARLAND

Introduction

This chapter introduces readers to broad concepts in media studies and some of the strategic devices employed in political communication in Canada. It begins with an overview of mediated communications and traces the historical development of technological changes. The chapter then sketches the media landscape in Canada and some of the biases found in media coverage. It touches on the ways that political actors attempt to manipulate the information that audiences receive. Woven throughout is an enduring theme of journalists and political communicators jostling for control.

The chapter illustrates that political actors are interested in pinpointing targeted messages to narrow segments of the electorate through channels that bypass media filters. They seek to control their messaging as they leverage whatever public resources are at their disposal. While this is a more efficient way of communicating with Canadians, it comes at a cost: reduced objectivity of political information and centralized message control at the top of an organizational hierarchy.

Mediated Communication in Canada

Citizens receive political information from politicians, political parties, governments, and non-governmental organizations in many ways. Politicians are the main intermediary with government institutions. Their methods of communicating with citizens combine in-person interactions with mediated communication and, increasingly, social media.

Communicating without mediating technology requires a personal presence. Years ago, candidates addressed crowds from tree stumps, by standing on overturned soap crates, and by bellowing from temporary election structures known as hustings. They attended campaign picnics, which were literally outdoor lunches where electors munched on cold meats while listening to candidates and a brass band (Nolan 1981, 33). They participated in debates and attended political rallies. Leaders covered large distances by train to deliver speeches to waiting supporters and local notables at community stops along the way. These tactics of yesteryear have given rise to idioms in news coverage of Canadian elections such as a politician who is "stumping for votes," an activist expressing views from a "political soapbox," and a travelling party leader who is "on the hustings" or on a "whistle-stop" tour. More modern ways of personally mixing with groups of electors include mingling at Tim Hortons, hosting barbeque events, chatting in sports arenas, stopping into corner shops, visiting retirement homes, and attending funerals. As election day approaches, vote-hungry candidates engage in one-on-one communication by talking to electors on their doorsteps. Once the elected government is in office, in-person interactions with constituents are limited.

Politicians cannot possibly speak with each constituent individually. They must use communications technology to reach the masses and to learn about issues of concern to the general public. In this sense, Canada is a mediated democracy, meaning that most Canadians obtain information about their elected representatives through the mass media rather than through personal interactions. Print, broadcast, and internet communication reaches hundreds, thousands, or even millions of citizens.

Several works explore the evolution of Canadian political news media (e.g., Levine 1993; Taras 1990, 2015; Sauvageau 2012). In the nineteenth century Canadian newspapers were organs of political parties and blatantly promoted propaganda. The biased interpretation of parliamentary proceedings by the party-affiliated press prompted the commissioning of official Hansard transcriptions beginning in 1875. By World War I, the party press and its reliance on government advertising and partisan benefactors gave way to more independent operations that generated revenues from commercial advertising. The emergence of radio in the 1920s ended the print media's monopoly on mass communication. Elites could use their own voices to connect with the masses, and the later emergence of political talk radio gave a voice to the concerns of average Canadians. During this period, some citizens obtained information about public affairs through newsreels that were presented at movie theatres and, beginning in 1939, through National Film Board of Canada features about government policy (Druick 2007). It was when Canadians began buying TV sets in the 1950s that mass communication experienced its most dramatic change. Television increased the importance of images, emotion, personalities, soundbites, and symbols. Coverage of politics evolved with the introduction of cameras into the House of Commons in 1977; the emergence of all-news programming on what are now known as the CBC News Network in 1989 and CTV News Channel in 1997; and the raw footage provided by the Canadian Public Affairs Channel (CPAC) in 1992. By then the political news cycle had become a 24/7 operation.

A distinguishing feature of Canadian media is the prevalence of two official languages. Official bilingualism means that all federal government communication is expected, if not required, to be available in both English and French. The tone of media coverage varies depending on language; for instance, French political journalists often report on topics different from those of their English counterparts and they tend to be more analytical (Taras 1990, 76). The political clout of so-called ethnic media is increasing. There are now more allophones – Canadians whose mother tongue is neither English nor French – than there are francophones, and the population of the former is growing faster than the latter (Canada 2018b). Ethnic minority groups can obtain information from small multicultural news outlets such as the *Indo-Canadian Times* and OMNI in addition to English and French media. Yet regardless of language, media organizations are confronted with economic challenges wrought by digital technology.

A broader concern with the way that Canadians receive news is that the same information is received through multiple platforms owned by the same corporations, a phenomenon known as media convergence. For instance, Québecor Media is a conglomerate that in 2018 operated TVA broadcasting channels, including twenty-four-hour news, entertainment programming, sports, children's programs, pay-per-view movies, and real estate content. Québecor owns TVA magazines such as *Elle*, *Canadian Living*, *Style at Home*, and *7Jours*; Vidéotron telephone, cable TV, internet access, and mobile phone services; the Canoe online news portal; as well as a book publishing business, a music chain, a video distributor, transit advertising, and even YouTube content creation (Québecor 2018). Across such operations or "media platforms" there is a tendency to share editorial perspectives and to repurpose content. An excellent example occurs in Ottawa where the *Ottawa Citizen* and the *Ottawa Sun* used to be competitors; they now share and repackage otherwise identical stories.

The Canadian Radio-television and Telecommunications Commission (CRTC), which regulates Canadian communications systems, believes that the concentration of ownership of wireless and internet networks is a potential problem. The CRTC is mindful that content sharing is likely to increase as Canadians receive digital information on laptops, smartphones, tablets, and smart TVs (Theckedath and Thomas 2012). The regulator monitors such changes in consumer media consumption. At the forefront of these shifts in behaviour are the evolution of information and communication technologies (ICTs).

ICTs permit the rapid, inexpensive, and targeted transmission of text, audio, and video through computers. While television remains Canadians' preferred source of news, increasing numbers obtain political information online and are cancelling their cable TV. Campaign websites, political blogs, email blasts, and social networking are just some of the ways that information and opinions circulate in cyberspace. Rapidly, Canadians have turned to online video and audio streaming, ranging from domestic sources such as CTV and Global, to American-based Netflix and YouTube. Citizens are customizing what they consume, searching for online information and entertainment that suits their interests and moods (CRTC 2018). Facebook is a social media behemoth that is so successful at aggregating online news that it is achieving the company founder's desire for Facebook to become users' "personal newspaper" (Canadian Press 2018). This personalized nature of online content consumption is attractive to advertisers who can more precisely reach target audiences at a fraction of the cost of traditional ads on mainstream media. Traditional media may still dominate, but they are losing market share and advertising revenues and are on the wrong side of trends showing consumers gravitating towards accessing specialized content on demand.

The disruptive nature of internet communication has implications for media companies. Print media are in crisis because a "freebie culture" of news consumption exacerbates the industry's difficulty in adapting to technological innovations (Sauvageau 2012, 33). Newspapers are struggling to compete for advertising dollars. Many have thinned out their content, laid off local reporters, and introduced online paywalls. A number have closed operations. This is problematic when we consider that newspapers and news magazines offer more in-depth coverage and analysis than other forms of media tend to do. Radio and traditional TV programming, while popular, are grappling with similar economic pressures as people turn to online streaming, social media, and other forms of digital content.

The growing use of social media for news brings into question the very credibility of information. Facebook is thought to suppress conservative viewpoints in favour of promoting liberal ideas (Canadian Press 2018). More ominously, the deliberate spread of misinformation online including hoaxes and propaganda is a significant problem with no obvious solution. "Fake news" is a scourge of democratic debate that threatens to influence how Canadians think about their political leaders. Some have urged the government to step in with funding for established news organizations to ensure the civic function of journalism (Public Policy Forum 2017). There is no obvious solution: the Trudeau government's allocation of nearly $600 million to subsidize eligible news media outlets has raised concerns about media independence from the state.

The democratization of media is having profound consequences for the public sphere. The speeding up of information transfer means that complex policy or political matters are reduced to short, sometimes superficial messages. ICTs make it easier to coordinate petitions, to organize political events, to mobilize protests, and to draw attention to a call for action. People tend to huddle in online communities that act as echo chambers reinforcing a particular view, rather than exposing themselves to a pluralistic range of opinions. Citizens are uploading newsworthy digital content and are part of a new social media elite that operates on the margins of professional politics (McKelvey, Côté, and Raynauld 2018). Whether all this is good or bad for Canadian democracy is a matter of opinion. Through it all, the relationship between political and media elites is "like a chess game" where players seek to exploit their symbiotic relationship and never truly trusts the others' motives or agenda (Taras 1990, 47).

Political Communication Practices

This communications backdrop sets the stage for discussing ways that journalists and political actors try to shape and control what information Canadians are exposed to. Even as their exclusivity over information wanes, the mainstream media and political elites remain locked in a struggle of public persuasion as they jockey for power to frame events and control the public agenda. Members of the Canadian Parliamentary Press Gallery (CPPG) are defenders of the fourth estate's institutional role in Canadian democracy. These journalists and their provincial-territorial counterparts fancy themselves as watchdogs with the capacity to filter political messages, integrate a variety of perspectives, and report on matters that would otherwise not be disclosed or exposed. However, the evolving nature of news gathering in the digital media environment has some wondering whether the press gallery is a relic of the past (Paré and Delacourt 2014). Before examining how ICTs are changing journalism and ways that public relations personnel attempt to exploit norms of communication, we must recognize why politicians try to curtail the ability of journalists to gather and produce news.

News production involves a mixture of media economics and practices. Journalism is market-oriented, which is to say that news is conditioned by intense competition to attract audiences, and consequently information is rarely impartial. Public affairs journalism does not discuss government or political parties in a strictly factual way. Rather, political information is packaged to make it dramatic, presenting a story arc with heroes and villains. The media piles onto controversies and events, portraying political elites as self-interested, and exuding idealistic concern for the downtrodden. Interest in horse-race coverage of who is up or down has broadened from who is leading public opinion polls to who is ahead in quarterly party fundraising reports and opining about who won a skirmish on social media. Routine and episodic topics are presented in a superficial and sensationalistic manner, resulting in infotainment. Political talk shows such as *Power and Politics* (CBC), *Question Period* (CTV), and *The West Block* (Global) feature informed commentary among politicians and partisan spinners. To make debate exciting the guests are pitted as combatants. The popular *Tout le monde en parle* talk show on ICI Radio-Canada Télé weaves discussion about political events with human interest conversation. Political satire such as *This Hour Has 22 Minutes* (CBC) ruthlessly mocks politicians while creating homegrown celebrities who project the state's own sense of political and cultural identity (Cormack and Cosgrave 2014). Yet rather than signal a decline in journalism, infotainment attracts audiences who otherwise do not pay attention to politics (Bastien 2018, 9).

Of greater concern is that there are political slants in news production. Some journalists have their own political agenda and their reporting does not always treat their interviewees fairly (Miljan and Cooper 2003). They may be skilled and experienced, but they use loaded language that prompts an emotional reaction, bringing the quality of their reporting into question. News outlets such as the *Toronto Star* tend to be sympathetic to progressive politics and Liberal and/or New Democratic parties. Others such as the *National Post* favour economic liberalism and Conservative parties. The state-funded CBC is bemoaned by conservatives for exuding a left of centre bias (e.g., Uechi 2014), while those on the political left extol alarm about the existence of right-wing *Rebel Media*. Outlets such as the Canadian Public Affairs Channel (CPAC) and the wire service Canadian Press have audiences across the political spectrum and so are motivated to be more concerned about minimizing bias.

Nevertheless, all forms of mediated communication exhibit prejudices. Women, the working class, the poor, youth, the elderly, queer people, and religious groups are depicted by the mainstream media in an "erratic, shallow and tokenistic" way (Fleras 2011, 3). The media sexualize women and assign gendered norms of expected behaviours, such as constructing ideal forms of leadership based on masculine traits (Trimble 2017). Racialized coverage draws attention to the race of visible minority politicians rather than to their qualifications, marginalizes them, and ultimately influences whether some choose to seek office (Tolley 2015, 42–6). As well, although there are increasing numbers of LGBT candidates, they tend to be most successful if they do not publicly disclose their sexual orientation until after they are elected (Everitt and Camp 2014). Specialized media seek to counterbalance mainstream media by delivering news through different perspectives, such as Indigenous voices (Burrows 2018). In many ways, the media's biases reflect those of society itself.

A surreptitious form of bias concerns the relationship between journalists and politicians. Ideally, journalists will collect a variety of unfettered information from diverse sources. Citizens should be able to receive facts that are free from partisanship and sensationalism. However, in addition to the economic incentive to respond to consumer preferences, it is difficult to strip away slants because information gathering requires the complicity of others. Political insiders feed the media stories to cultivate a relationship with a reporter, leak details of a policy, destabilize opponents, and correct false information (Taras 1990, 83). Politicians who develop friendly relations with select reporters are willing to divulge government news with a quid pro quo understanding that they will receive positive coverage in return. They grant exclusive interviews or delegate staff to appear in the news as unnamed sources. Conversely, they freeze out journalists who they believe are antagonistic and even scold them when they disapprove of their reports (Levine 1993, 218; Taras 1990, 44, 125). The culture of distrust between politicians and the media is likened to a downward spiral, whereby subversive political tactics breed negative reporting about politics, which contributes to public cynicism and civic disengagement (Cappella and Jamieson 1997).

Heads of government, regardless of party stripe or era, tend to develop tense relations with journalists and devise tactics for managing their relationship with the media. At one point during his tenure as prime minister, Louis St-Laurent went eight months between press conferences, which broadcast media were not permitted to record because the CPPG denied them membership until 1959 (Levine 1993, 186, 214; Taras 1990, 72). During the 1974 election campaign, Pierre Trudeau answered a total of six questions during a four-day train tour. After he returned to power with a majority government, Trudeau stopped participating in scrums in favour of press conferences where his staff selected which reporters could ask questions (Levine 1993, 287–90; see also Taras 1990, 140). Stephen Harper was criticized for not participating in media scrums, for refusing to disclose when his Cabinet met (thereby denying the media the opportunity to pounce on ministers), and for restricting the CPPG's ability to set the terms for their questioning. Furthermore, in successive election campaigns journalists were required to stand ten metres away from Harper, who accepted a maximum of five questions per day. Justin Trudeau promised a more amicable relationship with the press, and yet his government retains many of the communications management functions of its predecessors (Marland 2017).

The battle to control how information reaches journalists and their audiences is intentional. Political spinmeisters are acutely aware that the packaging of information changes how it is presented to, and interpreted by audiences, a process known as *framing* (e.g., DeCillia 2018). This motivates them to think strategically about how a leader, an issue, or an opponent is presented, based on the belief that the frame they construct will in turn influence citizens' perceptions. For instance, suppose a government announces spending reductions or tax increases. Its communications personnel will position this as a responsible decision made by strong stewards. Opponents will attempt to frame it as an irresponsible decision with dire consequences for vulnerable populations. When journalists filter these conflicting positions, they must choose what frame to apply in their news treatment. Controlling the frame can be necessary for politicians to implement a political platform for which they claim to have obtained a mandate in the previous election.

The competition to control how political information is framed and what deserves the public's attention is known as *agenda setting* (e.g., Soroka 2002). An agenda-setting mentality assumes that the greater the prominence that the mass media give a topic, the more importance audiences will attach to the issue. People involved in politics are thus in a constant state of attempting to ensure that the issues they want citizens to think about are receiving media coverage. Likewise, they try to limit attention to what they deem to be an undesirable topic, or else to stir negativity about it. Reporters, editors, and producers must sift through political spin, their own investigative work, and other sources of information as they decide what deserves to be on the public agenda, what does not, and how it should be communicated to citizens. The lead story in a national news broadcast understandably receives more political attention than an issue buried in a local print publication or that receives no media coverage at all.

Attracting attention is easier when political personalities are part of the story. Politics and popular culture are converging in a world drawn to celebrity. The celebritization of leaders grew with television. John Diefenbaker defeated St-Laurent in the 1957 election in part because of how they appeared on the new medium of TV; in the 1960s, television coverage of Lester Pearson emphasized his lack of charisma even though he was charming in person; and in the 1970s reporters sometimes paid more attention to Pierre Trudeau's personal life than to his politics (Levine 1993, 248, 278). Under Harper, government resources were used by the Prime Minister's Office (PMO) to issue photos, sometimes of his family. Startling at the time, the PMO's digital information services are now normal, even expected. Justin Trudeau's photographer routinely uploads professional-style photos and video to online platforms so that the images will be repurposed and shared. The visuals frame the prime minister with desired traits and values, fuel his celebrity status, and provide journalists with free content (Lalancette and Raynald 2017). In contrast, digital videos created by the offices of Canadian premiers are more likely to project accessibility, although these are likewise staged and one-sided (Lewis and Yates 2018).

Journalists are not the only ones who benefit from easily available digital content. Why would citizens struggle to locate a relevant government number in a phone book (if one even exists) and call a switchboard during business hours if the information they are seeking can be easily found online via information gateways such as canada.ca? Technology is chipping away at a long-standing culture of government secrecy. Information that was previously hidden is now publicly available, including policy documents and details of politicians' expenses; ministerial mandate letters from the prime minister or premier; accountability reports that did not previously exist; and the thousands of datasets released as part of "open government" (Clarke 2019).

Among the data available online are responses to access to information requests that are no longer exclusive to the requester. Citizens in a democracy have a right to obtain information about their government. Access to information legislation was introduced in 1983 and thereafter in all provinces and territories, as well as many municipalities (Larsen and Walby 2012, 1). For a nominal fee, or sometimes none at all, citizens can request copies of government records easily found with a brief internal search. Those records can be posted online for others' benefit. Nonetheless, secrecy persists. Cabinet confidences and other private details are exempt, which means that some records are not released or the content is heavily redacted. The time that it takes for public servants to process requests is a common frustration. Growing expectations of transparency are pitted against a governmental culture that seeks to limit and shape the release of information.

Strategic Communication

Strategic communication activities such as media relations, advertising, permanent campaigning, branding, and micro-targeting are practised by governments, political parties, politicians, public relations personnel, non-governmental actors, and many others. They jockey with each other and the media to control frames and what is in the news, with an objective of getting key messages to audiences, and conveying a desired image. The withering of the fourth estate facilitates the delivery of partisan content, reducing journalistic filters, and polarizing citizens into opposing sides. These trends show no signs of abatement in a digital marketplace.

All political organizations interact with the media. Given the stakes, there is every incentive to practise media management. Political communications personnel exploit media economics by providing ready-made content suitable for reproduction in the form of news releases, opinion pieces, written quotes instead of interviews, and posts on social media. They attempt to spin a topic with their preferred slant, authorizing which of their members are allowed to communicate publicly and instructing these representatives in what to say. They stage news conferences, speeches, protests, and photo-ops. These events are so obviously designed to attract and shape media publicity that they are collectively known as "pseudo-events" (Boorstin 1992). Moreover, political parties exploit opportunities in real time, such as by texting suggested questions to journalists while an event is in progress (McLean 2012, 7). During election campaigns, making available evidence of an opposing candidate saying something unpalatable – such as a remark on Facebook or Twitter posted years ago – is a common tactic that detracts from more meaningful policy discourse. Journalists must navigate these manipulation attempts as they assess what is truly newsworthy.

The news media's response to such contrived communication varies. Media lapdogs are prone to repeat political messages for any number of reasons: because they share the same point of view, or lack the resources to support proper investigative journalism, or face the time pressures of the twenty-four-hour news cycle, or simply have no other way to obtain the information that is given to them. Canadian media that are the most resistant to manipulation tactics are well-resourced organizations with large audiences, such as the *Globe and Mail*, CBC, and CTV. Nevertheless, as newsroom budgets shrink, and as the availability of timely information expands, all media organizations are under competitive pressure to avail themselves of freely available information.

Using media relations tactics to earn free publicity is a gamble. By comparison, advertising allows the sponsor to control the message delivery, but this is expensive. When the Government of Canada advertises, it tends to promote a nationalist myth and political identity (Rose 2003); this elicits criticism for using public resources for quasi-partisan purposes. For their part, political parties deploy negative advertising that seeks to shock audiences and communicate unsettling facts about an opponent's policies or behaviour. The focus tends to be on leaders rather than parties, especially if a leader is already unpopular (Pruysers and Cross 2016). Political advertising brings the added incentive of stretching communications resources because the news media often runs "adwatches" where the latest partisan volleys are discussed. Increasingly the mainstream media dissect social media advertisements that are otherwise visible only to select audiences.

Constant political communication seeks to influence how citizens feel and think about political issues and leaders. The origins of non-stop campaigning are in American politics, where it initially meant that a governing party should unabashedly avail itself of government resources to gain public support for its agenda (Marland, Esselment, and Giasson 2017). Permanent campaigning describes the persistence of partisan electioneering by political parties and elected officials, even during governance periods between elections. Advertising, fundraising, grassroots mobilization, polling, and a rapid response mentality are a normal component of everyday politicking. During elections, political parties maintain war rooms that are hubs of information management, media monitoring, opposition research, and message dissemination. After the election, a 24/7 war-room mentality persists in caucus research bureaus located around Parliament Hill: the Liberal Research Bureau, the Conservative Resource Group, and NDP Caucus Services. Contemporary political communication operates with an urgency, intensity, and centralization that was previously identified only with election periods.

Political marketers use simple messages to cut through the communications clutter and reach voters who pay little attention. Citizens are exposed to so much information that, in the words of one journalism professor, "strategic political communicators must compete with extraordinary intensity to make their messages resonate above the din of the daily glut" (McLean 2012, 20). A consistent underlying message is needed in order to harmonize all types of communication. In my own line of research, I have argued that Canadian political parties and governments use the same branding principles that are practised in commercial marketing (Marland 2016). Political parties pay close attention to logos, colour schemes, visual backdrops, and the overall image of their leader as part of their effort to shape a political brand. The Government of Canada's branding is formalized through the Federal Identity Program, which outlines how public servants should attempt to communicate a clear corporate identity. In party politics the image of the leader, its sloganeering, and the party's predominant colour are promoted. As the permanent campaign intersects with the Canadian public service, there is conflict when the government's brand begins to assume partisan characteristics. For instance, it is common for the colour palettes of government advertising, websites, and communications products to be synchronized with the governing party's colours and sloganeering.

Branding works in conjunction with direct marketing. Communicators exploit many technological methods to bypass editorial filters and provide exact information to targeted recipients. Direct marketing uses technology to facilitate personal interactions with a large universe of citizens and attempts to cultivate a relationship with this audience. The same script is easily customized for thousands of electors, each of whom can be reached in a controlled manner, without the knowledge of political opponents. Direct mail gives the illusion of personalized correspondence if the recipient's name is inserted in the salutation of a form letter, while telemarketing follows the same principle but by telephone, often in a completely automated nature known as robocalling. Even more cost-effective precision is possible through emailing, social media campaigns, and texting. Anchoring messaging in core brand principles and values eliminates the potential for conflicting information and controversy.

Direct marketing has evolved into database marketing – drawing upon a growing dataset of names and contact details to issue customized electronic messages. Data-driven communications are cost and time efficient for both the sender and recipient because more exact information is circulated. Audiences benefit from less sifting through uninteresting content and become more informed about matters they care about. However, political parties maintain massive databases filled with information about citizens. There is a relentless search for voter data that enable partisan narrowcasting and wedge politics that polarize audiences (Patten 2017). This evokes privacy concerns about who has access to party databases and how people's information will be used.

In Canada, the advent of sophisticated database management coincided with the transition from door-to-door enumeration of electors to the creation of a permanent National Register of Electors in 1997. The register maintains contact data for over 93 per cent of Canadian electors, which are provided to Elections Canada by the Canada Revenue Agency, Citizenship and Immigration Canada, National Defence, driver's licence agencies, vital statistics agencies, and other political jurisdictions' lists, as well as by electors themselves (Canada 2018a). For each registered elector, Elections Canada maintains the name, mailing address, and a unique code for record management. These data are available in an electronic file to election candidates to assist them with identifying the vote. More significantly, the list is provided annually to political parties and members of Parliament, thereby facilitating a permanent campaign that includes direct communication, fundraising appeals, and membership recruitment. Political actors supplement the list with additional data provided by electors, such as information supplied to a party website or provided at a political event; by scrutinizing public records that identify the names of people who donated over $200 to a party or candidate; and voter identification results from the last election. The cost efficiencies and speed of electronic media are incentives for parties to build lists of elector email addresses, Facebook accounts, and Twitter handles. Canada's political parties manage databases known as Liberalist, NDP Populus, and the Conservatives' constituent information management system (CIMS) to issue robocalls and emails to potential supporters to advise them of a local party event, to invite them to participate in a live group phone or video discussion, to remind them to vote, or to encourage them to donate, volunteer, or post a sign.

Database marketing goes even further in the name of precision. Data analysts divide electors into groups with shared characteristics. The segmentation of electors into clusters, such as "hockey moms," identifies existing supporters who need reinforcement, potential supporters who need persuasion, and opponents who can be ignored. Political parties slice the electoral marketplace by examining socio- and geo-demographic data. This micro-targeting results in targeted public policy, where a series of minor policy commitments are tailored to narrow segments of the electorate. The design of micro policies is dependent on what will appeal to targeted market segments in a manner that is consistent with the party's overall ideology. Data analytics also improves the ability for political parties to engage in seats triage. Just as medical emergency personnel make quick decisions to prioritize the allocation of resources (triage), political parties use data to identify which electoral districts to focus their attention on, and which ones to ignore. With the increasing precision of political communication, it is possible to prioritize resources for the air and ground war that will reach narrow segments of the electorate who reside in key seats.

Analysis of an array of available data, including audience metrics, enables narrowcasting. The fracturing of broadcast media allows strategists to contact slivers of the electorate through regional and specialist media. Narrowcasting extends beyond advertising on specialist cable programming such as the Sports Network or OMNI. It encompasses digital communications that reaches sub-segments of the electorate. This includes customized advertising that appears on internet searches, personalized advertising on websites, and micro-targeting of ads on social media platforms (Small 2017, 401). What Karim (2012, 179) calls "diasporic cybercommunities" includes the multitude of online news sites, blogs, social media, and listservs accessed by ethnic minorities, including recent immigrants. Appeals to narrow audiences can draw attention to specialized political causes.

It is within this context that political consultants and staff engage in data mining to help them identify what people think and what they want. The ability to understand public opinion polling, detailed election results, and Statistics Canada data improves with computing software and skilled analytics. Internet cookies are used to profile voters on the basis of their web viewing history and online purchasing behaviour. These insights into the electorate's mindset enable smarter, though not necessarily more palatable, use of finite communications resources. This gives rise to treating electors as consumers. An idealistic view of political marketing holds that democracy is enriched and improved when opinion research is used to scientifically uncover citizens' needs and desires. Survey data and other forms of market intelligence theoretically can inform decisions about public policy and political communication in a manner that prioritizes the electorate's preferences. However, this benign view overlooks the fact that political leadership must make unpopular decisions, and that the public lacks sufficient information or expertise to appraise the implications of most policies. Moreover, the reality of politics is that strategists use marketing mostly for their own partisan purposes rather than for the benefit of electors, and for their own ideological reasons, irrespective of democratic purposes or ideals. Of particular concern is that digital marketing avoids the filtering undertaken by mainstream news media and provides information directly to exclusive audiences. This diminishes the importance that politicians attach to accommodating journalists. A result is that they are less accessible during election campaigns, feel free to skip debates, and can ignore journalists' questions while the party machine rallies the base with provocative messages sent electronically to select groups. This is a problem because the loss of journalistic scrutiny increases the control that political actors have over the information that citizens receive (Small 2017, 393).

Conclusion

This chapter illustrates that many aspects of political communication in Canada are evolving with technology while others seem impervious to change. Social media and digital communication have profound implications for how political parties, interest groups, election candidates, and journalists engage with the public. Political actors employ strategies and tactics in a contest to control the public agenda, to frame the debate, to shape their leader's image, and to target particular segments of the electorate using partisan political messaging.

The activities described in this chapter have several implications for Canadian democracy. On the one hand, computing and communications technology assists political parties with understanding what citizens want and improves their ability to respond to public preferences. New ways of communicating enable them to spread information in the most efficient and direct manner possible. The availability of email, websites, and social media allows political actors and electors to avoid the gatekeeping filters of the mainstream media. More information than ever before about government is available to anyone with internet access. This democratization of media and information reduces the power, influence, and bias of news editors and members of the press gallery, and counters the trend of diverse journalistic perspectives being absorbed into media conglomerates. As well, the relentless permanent campaigning by political parties increases their outreach and accountability.

On the other hand, trends in political communication threaten the quality of Canadian democracy. Political parties can more easily communicate by stealth in an attempt to reach only selected narrow segments of the electorate, to avoid the scrutiny of media watchdogs, and to thwart critical reaction from detractors. They scrub their opponents' digital footprints to unearth controversial content that can be released at an opportune time. Government officials risk becoming consumed with the short-term implications of policy decisions and what is released under access to information legislation. Public servants are prevented from answering journalists' questions while designated government spokespersons, if they can be reached, may insulate themselves from scrutiny by emailing a statement instead of having a conversation. Citizens' elected representatives are losing their independence and individuality as branded communications requires message consistency. This increases the clout of the party centre and the scope and strength of party discipline. Journalists, who are increasingly chasing whatever is new and trending, are unable to explore important matters that deserve scrutiny. Moreover, they are susceptible to free information provided by political actors and seem endlessly fascinated by the horse race aspect of party politics.

There is no definitive answer about whether all of this is a net positive or negative for Canadian democracy. For instance, when looking at internet politicking in Canada, there is debate about whether communications technology is innovating democratic dialogue or simply used to reinforce existing practices (Small 2017). It is clear, however, that as the techniques, tactics, and strategy of political communication evolve, there are some enduring themes and practices – such as framing, agenda setting, pseudo-events, political marketing, and infotainment – that will continue to shape this crucial aspect of Canadian government and politics.

References and Suggested Readings

Bastien, Frédérick. 2018. *Breaking News? Politics, Journalism, and Infotainment on Quebec Television*. Vancouver: UBC Press.

Boorstin, Daniel J. 1992. *The Image: A Guide to Pseudo-Events in America*. New York: Vintage Books.

Burrows, Elizabeth. 2018. "Indigenous Media Producers' Perspectives on Objectivity, Balancing Community Responsibilities and Journalistic Obligations." *Media, Culture & Society* 40 (8): 1117–34.

Canada. 2018a. "Description of the National Register of Electors." Elections Canada. https://www.elections.ca/content.aspx?section=vot&dir=reg/des&document=index&lang=e.

Canada. 2018b. "The Evolution of Language Populations in Canada, by Mother Tongue, from 1901 to 2016." Statistics Canada. https://www150.statcan.gc.ca/n1/pub/11-630-x/11-630-x2018001-eng.htm.

Canadian Press. 2018. "Facebook Axing 'Trending Section,' Testing Breaking News Labels." Huffington Post, June 1. https://www.huffingtonpost.ca/2018/06/01/facebook-axing-trending-section-testing-breaking-news-labels_a_23448990/.

Canadian Radio-television Commission (CRTC). 2018. "Harnessing Change: The Future of Programming Distribution in Canada." https://crtc.gc.ca/eng/publications/s15/.

Cappella, Joseph N., and Kathleen Hall Jamieson. 1997. *Spiral of Cynicism: The Press and the Public Good.* Oxford: Oxford University Press.

Clarke, Amanda. 2019. *Opening the Government of Canada: The Federal Bureaucracy in the Digital Age.* Vancouver: UBC Press.

Cormack, Patricia, and James F. Cosgrave. 2014. "Theorising the State Celebrity: A Case Study of the Canadian Broadcasting Corporation." *Celebrity Studies* 5 (3): 321–39.

DeCillia, Brooks. 2018. "'But It Is Not Getting Any Safer!': The Contested Dynamic of Framing Canada's Military Mission in Afghanistan." *Canadian Journal of Political Science* 51 (1): 155–77.

Druick, Zoë. 2007. *Projecting Canada: Government Policy and Documentary Film at the National Film Board*, vol. 1. Montreal and Kingston: McGill-Queen's University Press.

Everitt, Joanna, and Michael Camp. 2014. "In Versus Out: LGBT Politicians in Canada." *Journal of Canadian Studies* 48 (1): 226–51.

Fleras, Augie. 2011. *The Media Gaze: Representations of Diversities in Canada.* Vancouver: UBC Press.

Karim, Karim H. 2012. "Are Ethnic Media Alternative?" In *Alternative Media in Canada*, edited by Kirstin Kozolanka, Patricia Mazepa, and David Skinner, 165–83. Vancouver: UBC Press.

Lalancette, Mireille, and Vincent Raynald. 2017. "The Power of Political Image: Justin Trudeau, Instagram, and Celebrity Politics." *American Behavioral Scientist.* https://doi.org/10.1177/0002764217744838.

Larsen, Mike, and Kevin Walby. 2012. "Introduction: On the Politics of Access to Information." In *Brokering Access: Power, Politics, and Freedom of Information Process in Canada*, edited by Mike Larsen and Kevin Walby, 1–32. Vancouver: UBC Press.

Levine, Allan. 1993. *Scrum Wars: The Prime Ministers and the Media.* Toronto: Dundurn.

Lewis, J.P., and Stéphanie Yates. 2018. "From Elitism to Idealization: The Representation of Premiers in Social Media Videos." In *Political Elites in Canada: Power and Influence in Instantaneous Times*, edited by Alex Marland, Thierry Giasson, and Andrea Lawlor, 109–27. Vancouver: UBC Press.

Marland, Alex. 2016. *Brand Command: Canadian Politics and Democracy in the Age of Message Control.* Vancouver: UBC Press.

———. 2017. "Strategic Management of Media Relations: Communications Centralization and Spin in the Government of Canada." *Canadian Public Policy* 43 (1): 36–49.

Marland, Alex, Anna Lennox Esselment, and Thierry Giasson. 2017. "Welcome to Non-Stop Campaigning." In *Permanent Campaigning in Canada*, edited by Alex Marland, Thierry Giasson, and Anna Lennox Esselment, 3–27. Vancouver: UBC Press.

McKelvey, Fenwick, Marianne Côté, and Vincent Raynauld. 2018. "Scandals and Screenshots: Social Media Elites in Canadian Politics." In *Political Elites in Canada: Power and Influence in Instantaneous Times*, edited by Alex Marland, Thierry Giasson, and Andrea Lawlor, 204–22. Vancouver: UBC Press.

McLean, James S. 2012. *Inside the NDP War Room.* Montreal and Kingston: McGill-Queen's University Press.

Miljan, Lydia, and Barry Cooper. 2003. *Hidden Agendas: How Journalists Influence the News.* Vancouver: UBC Press.

Nolan, Michael. 1981. "Political Communication Methods in Canadian Federal Election Campaigns." *Canadian Journal of Communication* 7 (4): 28–46.

Paré, Daniel, and Susan Delacourt. 2014. "The Canadian Parliamentary Press Gallery: Still Relevant or Relic of Another Time?" In *Political Communication in Canada:*

Meet the Press and Tweet the Rest, edited by Alex Marland, Thierry Giasson, and Tamara A. Small, 111–26. Vancouver: UBC Press.

Patten, Steve. 2017. "Databases, Microtargeting, and the Permanent Campaign: A Threat to Democracy?" In *Political Elites in Canada: Power and Influence in Instantaneous Times*, edited by Alex Marland, Thierry Giasson, and Andrea Lawlor, 47–64. Vancouver: UBC Press.

Pruysers, Scott, and William Cross. 2016. "'Negative' Personalization: Party Leaders and Party Stragegy." *Canadian Journal of Political Science* 49 (3): 539–58.

Public Policy Forum. 2017. "The Shattered Mirror: News, Democracy and Trust in the Digital Age." Ottawa. https://shatteredmirror.ca/.

Québecor. 2018. "Our Activities." https://www.quebecor.com/en/our-activities.

Rose, Jonathan. 2003. "Government Advertising and the Creation of National Myths: The Canadian Case." *International Journal of Nonprofit and Voluntary Sector Marketing* 8 (2): 153–65.

Sauvageau, Florian. 2012. "The Uncertain Future of the News." In *How Canadians Communicate IV: Media and Politics*, edited by David Taras and Christopher Waddell, 29–44. Edmonton: Athabasca University Press.

Small, Tamara A. 2017. "Two Decades of Digital Party Politics in Canada: An Assessment." In *Canadian Parties in Transition*, edited by Alain-G. Gagnon and A. Brian Tanguay, 4th ed., 338–408. Toronto: University of Toronto Press.

Soroka, Stuart N. 2002. "Issue Attributes and Agenda-Setting by Media, the Public, and Policymakers in Canada." *International Journal of Public Opinion Research* 14 (3): 264–85.

Taras, David. 1990. *The Newsmakers: The Media's Influence on Canadian Politics*. Scarborough, ON: Nelson Canada.

———. 2015. *Digital Mosaic: Media, Power and Identity in Canada*. Toronto: University of Toronto Press.

Theckedath, Dillan, and Terrence J. Thomas. 2012. "Media Ownership and Convergence in Canada." Parliamentary Information and Research Service, Library of Parliament, April 10. https://central.bac-lac.gc.ca/.item?id=2012-17-eng&op=pdf&app=Library.

Tolley, Erin. 2015. *Framed: Media and the Coverage of Race in Canadian Politics*. Vancouver: UBC Press.

Trimble, Linda. 2017. *Ms. Prime Minister: Gender, Media, and Leadership*. Toronto: University of Toronto Press.

Uechi, Jenny. 2014. "Conservative Party Email Complains about CBC 'Bias.'" *Vancouver Observer*, May 30. https://www.vancouverobserver.com/news/conservative-party-email-complains-about-cbc-bias.

PART FIVE

Citizenship and Diversity

sixteen
Citizenship, Communities, and Identity in Canada

WILL KYMLICKA

Introduction

Much of the Canadian political system is founded on the premise that, in the words of the Supreme Court, the "accommodation of difference is the essence of true equality." While Canadian history contains its share of intolerance, prejudice, and oppression, it also contains many attempts to find new and creative mechanisms for accommodating difference. As a result, Canada has developed a distinctive conception of the relationship between citizenship and identity.

As in all other liberal democracies, one of the major mechanisms for accommodating difference in Canada is the protection of the civil and political rights of individuals, such as those listed in sections 2–15 of the Canadian Charter of Rights and Freedoms. Freedom of association, religion, speech, mobility, and political organization enable individuals to form and maintain the groups and associations that constitute civil society, to adapt these groups to changing circumstances, and to promote their views and interests to the wider population. The protection afforded by these common rights of citizenship is sufficient for many of the legitimate forms of diversity in society.

However, it is widely accepted in Canada that some forms of difference can be accommodated only through special legal measures, above and beyond the common rights of citizenship. Some forms of group difference can be accommodated only if their members have what Iris Marion Young calls "differentiated citizenship" (Young 1989). These special measures for accommodating difference are the most distinctive, and also the most controversial, aspect of the Canadian conception of citizenship identity.

Forms of Group Difference in Canada

Historically, the major challenge in Canada has been the accommodation of ethnocultural difference. There are three forms of ethnocultural pluralism in Canada that need to be distinguished.

First, Canada is a New World settler state – that is, it was constructed through the European colonization and settlement of territories historically occupied by Indigenous peoples. In this respect, it is like the other British settler states – Australia, New Zealand, and the United States – or the Spanish settler states of Latin America. Although the nature of European colonization and settlement varies enormously in these different countries, the rights of Indigenous peoples (and their relationship to the settler society built on their traditional territories) remains an issue in all of them, including questions about their land rights, treaty rights, customary law, and rights to self-government.

Canada differs from these other European settler states, however, in that it was colonized and settled by two different European powers – Britain and France – who fought for supremacy over the territory of what is now Canada. While the British eventually won this struggle, and thereby incorporated "New France" into "British North America," the reality was that there were two distinct settler societies within Canada – one French, located primarily in Quebec, and one British – each with its own languages, laws, and institutions. As a result, when Canada became an independent state in 1867, it recognized "the French fact" through official bilingualism and through provincial autonomy for Quebec. In this respect, unlike other New World settler states, Canada is sometimes said to be a "bi-national" settler state, constructed through the joining together of its "two founding peoples" – the French and British settler societies.

Of course, to say that the French and British were "founding peoples" ignores the role of Indigenous peoples, on whose territory this new country was built, and whose activities and agreements were vital to the building of Canada. They clearly are the "first peoples" of the country. As a result, it is more common today, and more accurate, to say that Canada is a multination state rather than a bi-national state. Its historical development has involved the federation of three distinct peoples or nations (British, French, and Indigenous). These groups are "nations" in the sociological sense of being historical communities, institutionally complete, occupying a given territory or homeland, and sharing a distinct language and history. Because Canada contains more than one nation, it is not a nation-state but a multination state, and the Québécois and Indigenous communities form "substate nations" or "national minorities." The desire of these groups to be seen as "nations" is reflected in the names they have adopted. For example, the provincial legislature in Quebec is called the "National Assembly"; the major organization of status Indians is known as the "Assembly of First Nations."

The original incorporation of these national groups into the Canadian political community was largely involuntary. Indigenous homelands were colonized by French settlers, who were then conquered by the English. If a different balance of power had existed, it is possible that Aboriginals and French-Canadians would have thwarted any attempt to incorporate them into the larger Canadian federation. And it is still possible that Quebec will leave the federation. However, the historical preference of these national groups has not been to secede, but to renegotiate the terms of federation, so as to increase their autonomy within it.

Many of the pivotal moments in Canadian political history have centred on these attempts to renegotiate the terms of federation between English, French, and Indigenous peoples. One such effort at renegotiation ended in October 1992, when the Charlottetown Accord was defeated in both a pan-Canadian referendum and a separate Quebec referendum. This Accord (discussed below) would have entrenched an "inherent right of self-government" for Indigenous peoples and would have accorded Quebec a special status as "the only society with a majority French language and culture in Canada and in North America."

In addition to being a multination state, Canada is also a multi-ethnic or polyethnic state. Canada, like the United States, accepts large numbers of individuals and families from other cultures as immigrants. They are expected to integrate into the public institutions of either the francophone or anglophone societies – for example, they must learn either French or English (Canada's two official languages) to acquire citizenship. Prior to the 1960s, they were also expected to shed their distinctive heritage and assimilate almost entirely to the dominant cultural norms. The ideal was that immigrants would become generally indistinguishable from native-born Canadians in their speech, dress, and lifestyle. However, in the early 1970s, under pressure from immigrant groups, the Canadian government rejected this assimilationist model, and instead adopted a more tolerant policy (known as the policy of "multiculturalism"), which allows and supports immigrants to maintain aspects of their ethnic heritage. Immigrants are free to maintain some of their old customs regarding food, dress, recreation, and religion and to associate with each other to maintain these practices. This is no longer seen to be (as it once was) unpatriotic or "unCanadian."

But such groups are not "nations" and do not occupy homelands within Canada. Their ethnocultural distinctiveness is manifested primarily in their private and social lives, and does not preclude their institutional integration. They still participate within either anglophone or francophone public institutions, and speak one or the other of the official languages in public life. Because of extensive immigration of this sort, Canada has a large number of "ethnic groups" who form loosely aggregated subcultures within both the English- and French-speaking societies.

So Canada is both multinational (as a result of colonization, conquest, and confederation) and multi-ethnic (as a result of immigration). Those labels are less popular than the term "multicultural," which can be confusing, precisely because it is ambiguous between multinational and multi-ethnic. Indeed, this ambiguity has led to unwarranted criticism of Canada's "multiculturalism policy," the term the federal government uses for its post-1971 policy of promoting accommodation rather than assimilation for immigrants. Some Québécois have opposed the "multiculturalism" policy because they think it reduces their historic claims of nationhood to the level of immigrant ethnicity. Other people had the opposite fear, that the policy was intended to treat immigrant groups as nations within Canada, and hence support the development of institutionally complete cultures alongside the francophone and anglophone societies. In fact, neither fear was justified, since "multiculturalism" is best understood as a policy of supporting the recognition and accommodation of immigrant ethnicity within the national institutions of the anglophone and francophone societies. This is indeed explicit in the phrase "multiculturalism within a bilingual framework" that the government used when introducing the policy.

Three Forms of Group-Differentiated Citizenship

There are at least three forms of differentiated citizenship in Canada intended to accommodate these ethnic and national differences: (1) self-government rights; (2) accommodation rights; and (3) special representation rights. I will say a few words about each.

(1) *Self-government rights*: As I noted, Indigenous peoples and the Québécois view themselves as "peoples" or "nations," and, as such, as having the inherent right of self-determination. Both groups demand certain powers of self-government that they say were not relinquished by their (initially involuntary) incorporation into the larger Canadian state. They want to govern themselves in certain key matters, to ensure the full and free development of their cultures and the best interests of their people.

This quest for self-government is not unique to Canada. National minorities in many other Western democracies make similar demands. Consider Puerto Rico in the United States, Catalonia and the Basque Country in Spain, Scotland and Wales in Great Britain; Flanders in Belgium; Corsica in France. These are just a few of the many national minorities seeking greater self-government within Western democracies. Similarly, Indigenous peoples around the world are seeking greater autonomy, including the American Indians, the Maori in New Zealand, the Inuit in Greenland, and the Sami in Scandinavia.

One mechanism for recognizing claims to self-government is federalism. Where national minorities are regionally concentrated, the boundaries of federal subunits can be drawn so that the national minority forms a majority in one of the subunits. Under these circumstances, federalism can provide extensive self-government for a national minority, guaranteeing its ability to make decisions in certain areas without being outvoted by the larger society.

Federalism was adopted in Canada precisely for this reason. Under the federal division of powers, the province of Quebec has extensive jurisdiction over issues that are crucial to the survival of the francophone society, including control over education, language, and culture, as well as significant input into immigration policy. The other nine provinces also have these powers, but the major impetus behind the existing division of powers, and indeed behind the entire federal system, is the need to accommodate the Québécois. When Canada was created in 1867, most English-Canadian leaders were in favour of a unitary state, like England, and agreed to a federal system primarily to accommodate French Canadians. Had Quebec not been guaranteed these substantial powers – and hence protected from the possibility of being outvoted on key issues by the larger anglophone population – it is certain that Quebec either would not have joined Canada in 1867 or would have seceded sometime thereafter.

While federalism has satisfied the desire for self-government to a certain extent, it is not a magic formula for resolving the claims of national minorities. Indeed, federalism has itself become a source of division in Canada. The problem is that French- and English-speaking Canadians have adopted two very different conceptions of federalism, which we can call "multination" federalism and "territorial" federalism (Resnick 1994). Whereas the former conception emphasizes the link between federalism and self-government for national minorities, the latter ignores or downplays this link. The public debates over the Meech Lake and Charlottetown Accords revealed that many of our constitutional dilemmas stem from these competing conceptions of federalism.

Purely "territorial" forms of federalism are not designed or adopted to enable a national minority to exercise self-government; they are simply intended to diffuse power within a single nation on a regional basis. The original and best-known example of such a "territorial" federalism is the United States; other examples include Germany, Australia, and Brazil. None of these federations have any federal subunits dominated by a national minority. As a result, they have no reason to give any of their subunits distinctive rights of national self-government.

In "multination" federations, by contrast, one or more subunits have been designed with the specific intention of enabling a national minority to form a local majority and to thereby exercise meaningful self-government. Historically, the most prominent examples of federalism being used in this way to accommodate national minorities are Canada and Switzerland. Since World War II, however, there has been a flood of new multination federations, including India, Belgium, Spain, Nigeria, Ethiopia, Iraq, Nepal, and Russia.

The Canadian federation has many of the hallmarks of a genuinely multination federation. This is reflected in the fact that the 1867 Constitution not only united four separate provinces into one country, it also divided the largest province into two separate political units – English-speaking Ontario and French-speaking Quebec – to accommodate ethnocultural divisions. This decision to create (or, more accurately, to re-establish) a separate Quebec province within which the French formed a clear majority was the crucial first step toward accommodating national self-government within Canadian federalism.

However, many English-speaking Canadians have not fully accepted a multination model of federalism. Instead, they tend to view American-style territorial federalism as the appropriate model for Canada. This is reflected in demands for an American-style "Triple-E" Senate. It is also reflected in opposition to any form of "special status" for Quebec, whether in the form of an asymmetrical division of powers, or in the form of a "distinct society" clause. From the point of view of multination federalism, the special status of Quebec is undeniable. It is the only province that is a vehicle for a self-governing national minority, while the nine other provinces reflect regional divisions within English-speaking Canada. Quebec, in other words, is a "nationality-based unit" – it embodies the desire of a national minority to remain a culturally distinct and politically self-governing society – while the other provinces are "region-based units," which reflect the decision and desire of a single national community to diffuse some of the powers of government on a regional basis.

In a multination conception of federalism, because nation-based units and region-based units serve different functions, there is no reason to assume that they should have the same powers or forms of recognition. Indeed, there is good reason to think that they will require some degree of differential treatment. Nation-based units are likely to seek different and more extensive powers than region-based units, both because they may need greater powers to protect a vulnerable national language and culture, and as a symbolic affirmation that they (unlike regional subdivisions within the majority) are "distinct nations." We see demands for asymmetry in most multination federations, including Spain, the United Kingdom, India, and Russia, as well as in Canada.

How we evaluate these demands for asymmetrical powers will depend on our conception of the nature and aims of political federation. For national minorities like the Québécois, federalism is, first and foremost, a federation of peoples, and decisions regarding the powers of federal subunits should recognize and affirm the equal status of the founding peoples. On this view, to grant the same powers to region-based units and nation-based units is in fact to deny equality to the minority nation, by reducing its status to that of a regional division within the majority nation. By contrast, for most English-speaking Canadians, federalism is, first and foremost, a federation of territorial units, and decisions regarding the division of powers should affirm and reflect the equality of the constituent units. On this view, to grant unequal powers to nation-based units is to treat some of the federated units as less important than others.

One of the fundamental questions facing Canada is whether we can reconcile these two competing conceptions of federalism. In the past, there was a sort of implicit compromise: English-speaking Canadians accepted a significant degree of de facto asymmetry in powers for Quebec, but rejected attempts to formally recognize asymmetry in the Constitution (Gagnon and Garcea 1988). For much of the 1980s and 1990s, this compromise position seemed to be coming unstuck: the Québécois were becoming more insistent on explicit recognition, and English-speaking Canadians were becoming more hostile to even informal forms of de facto asymmetry. The Charlottetown Accord was an attempt to paper over the differences between these two conceptions. It contained some provisions that seemed to endorse the multination model (e.g., the "distinct society" clause) while other provisions seemed to endorse the territorial model (e.g., the equality of provinces clause). The failure of the Accord in the 1992 referendum suggests that there is no easy way to reconcile these two conceptions.

When the failure of the Accord was followed by the near-success of the 1995 referendum on secession in Quebec, many commentators argued that the opposing dynamics of public opinion within Quebec and the rest of Canada were inevitably pulling the country apart. Since 1995, however, there has been a noticeable retreat from the precipice. One could argue, indeed, that the old historic compromise of de facto asymmetry without formal constitutional recognition has been successfully revived. This is reflected, for example, in House of Commons resolutions recognizing Quebec as a "distinct society" (1995) and as a "nation" (2006), in new intergovernmental agreements to expand Quebec's autonomy (e.g., the 2004 health care agreement), and in the Supreme Court's 1998 ruling that Quebec's distinctness must be taken into account when interpreting the Constitution. Many people on both sides have come to recognize that this historic compromise was actually quite an accomplishment. It enabled both sides to work together to create a peaceful and prosperous country, without insisting that either side renounce its fundamental beliefs about the nature of nationhood and statehood. The historic compromise allows the Québécois to think and act like a nation, while allowing English-speaking Canadians to think and act as if they live in a territorial rather than a multination federation. The result may seem unsatisfactory for those who believe that states require a single, unifying ideology or mythology, and of course the persistence of these opposing views makes federal-provincial relations an ongoing source of tension. But experience shows that these tensions can be managed, and potential conflicts sidestepped, so long as people put pragmatism over ideological purity.

The demands of Indigenous peoples for recognition of their inherent right of self-government raise some of the same issues as Quebec's demand for asymmetry. In both cases, there is an insistence on national recognition, collective autonomy, distinctive rights and powers, and equality of peoples. However, unlike the Québécois, Indigenous peoples find traditional forms of federalism to be unsuitable, as there is no way to redraw provincial boundaries to create a province with an Indigenous majority.

Instead, Indigenous self-government has been tied primarily to the system of reserves and the devolution of power from the federal government to the band councils that govern each reserve. First Nations bands have been acquiring increasing control over health, education, policing, criminal justice, and resource development. In some provinces, they have also negotiated self-government agreements with the provinces (e.g., James Bay and Northern Agreement as well as Nunavik in Quebec). In the future, it is widely expected that they will become a constitutionally recognized third order of government within or alongside the federal system, with a collection of powers that is carved out of both federal and provincial jurisdictions, as was proposed in the Charlottetown Accord (RCAP 1996; Cairns 2000). This is often seen as a cornerstone of a larger process of "reconciliation" between Indigenous peoples and the Canadian state.

However, the administrative difficulties are forbidding – First Nations bands differ enormously in the sorts of powers they desire and are capable of exercising. Moreover, they are territorially located within the provinces and must therefore coordinate their self-government with provincial agencies. And just as many Canadians reject "special status" for Quebec, so too are they reluctant to provide any explicit recognition of national rights for Indigenous peoples. In short, as with the Québécois, there is considerable de facto self-government for Indigenous peoples, yet no explicit constitutional recognition of rights of self-government.

(2) *Accommodation rights*: Many immigrant groups and religious minorities have demanded public support and legal recognition of their cultural practices. These demands take a variety of forms, including recognition of Jewish

religious holidays in school schedules; exemptions from official dress codes so that Sikh men can wear turbans; revisions to the history and literature curricula in public schools to give greater recognition to the historical and cultural contribution of immigrant groups; greater representation of immigrant groups in the police; CRTC guidelines to avoid ethnic stereotyping in the media; anti-racism educational campaigns; cultural diversity training for police, social workers, and health care professionals; workplace and school harassment codes prohibiting racist comments; funding of ethnic festivals and ethnic studies programs; and so on.

Most of these demands have been accepted as part of the policy of "multiculturalism," and a general commitment to such measures is reflected in section 27 of the Canadian Charter of Rights and Freedoms, which says, "This Charter shall be interpreted in a manner consistent with the preservation and enhancement of the multicultural heritage of Canadians."

Unlike self-government rights, these accommodation rights are usually intended to promote integration into the larger society, not self-government. None of the demands mentioned above involves the desire to establish a separate and self-governing society. On the contrary, they typically aim to reform mainstream institutions so as to make immigrant groups feel more at home within them. These measures are consistent with, and intended to promote, the integration of immigrants into the public institutions of the mainstream society. They seek to help ethnic groups and religious minorities express their cultural particularity and pride without it hampering their success in the economic and political institutions of the dominant society.

Here again, Canada is not unique. We find similar developments in the other major immigration countries. While Canada was the first country to explicitly adopt an official "multiculturalism" policy, other countries quickly followed, including Australia, New Zealand, Britain, the Netherlands, Sweden, and South Korea. We see many of the same developments occurring informally in the United States, even though it does not have any official "multiculturalism" policy.

To be sure, these ideas are controversial, and some countries firmly resist any talk of multiculturalism (e.g., France). As well, some countries that initially embraced multiculturalism have since witnessed a clear backlash and retreat (e.g., the Netherlands). Other countries such as Britain appear to have abandoned the word "multiculturalism" even as they maintain the policies that used to be justified in the name of multiculturalism, preferring now to use some other term such as "interculturalism" or "community cohesion" policies. The extent to which there has been a genuine (as opposed to merely rhetorical) retreat from multiculturalism in Europe is a matter of ongoing debate (Vertovec and Wessendorf 2010; Banting and Kymlicka 2013; Joppke 2014).

In Canada, however, popular and elite support for multiculturalism remains high, in part because of evidence that it has indeed facilitated the integration of immigrants (Adams 2007; Bloemraad 2006, 2012; Kymlicka 2012) and has helped insulate Canada from the waves of far-right anti-immigrant politics that have roiled other Western societies (Ambrose and Mudde 2015; McCoy 2018). There was a lively debate in Quebec in 2007 about whether the "reasonable accommodation" of immigrants and religious minorities had "gone too far," and some people viewed this debate as a first sign that Canada might witness the sort of backlash against multiculturalism found in Western Europe. A provincial government commission, co-chaired by Gérard Bouchard and Charles Taylor, found that the existing policy of accommodation (known in Quebec as "interculturalism" rather than "multiculturalism") was in fact working well and that there was no basis for a U-turn in policy (Bouchard and Taylor 2008). Nonetheless, the issue remains divisive in Quebec, and the provincial government adopted legislation (Bill 21) in 2019 to restrict certain religious accommodations.

(3) *Special representation rights*: While the traditional concern of national minorities and immigrant ethnic groups has been with either self-government or accommodation rights, there has been interest by these groups, as well as other non-ethnic social groups, in the idea of special representation rights.

Many Canadians believe the political process is "unrepresentative," in the sense that it fails to reflect the diversity of the population. This was illustrated most vividly during the constitutional negotiations leading up to the Charlottetown Accord, in which the fundamental terms of Canadian political life were said to have been negotiated by eleven middle-class, able-bodied white men in suits (the prime minister and the premiers of the ten provinces). A more representative process, it was said, would have included women, members of ethnic and racial minorities, and people who are poor or disabled.

This has led to increasing interest in the idea that a certain number of seats in the Senate should be reserved for the members of disadvantaged or marginalized groups. During the debate over the Charlottetown Accord, for example, the National Action Committee on the Status of Women recommended that 50 per cent of Senate seats should be reserved for women, and that proportionate representation of ethnic minorities also be guaranteed; others recommended that seats be reserved for the members of official language minorities or for Indigenous peoples.

The recent demands for special representation by women and other disadvantaged groups are largely an extension of long-standing demands for effective Senate representation by smaller provinces. Canada currently has an unelected Senate, which is widely viewed as illegitimate and ineffective.

Many Canadians would like to simply abolish the Senate. But the less populated regions of English-speaking Canada – that is, the Atlantic provinces and the western provinces – want to reform the Senate and use it as a forum for increased regional representation within the federal Parliament. Some have demanded an American-style Senate, in which each province would elect an equal number of senators, regardless of its population. This is intended to ensure "effective representation" for smaller provinces that hold little sway in the House of Commons, where the majority of members of Parliament come from the two most populated provinces (Ontario and Quebec).

Some Canadians have begun to believe that if small, disadvantaged, or marginalized regions need special representation, then so surely do disadvantaged or marginalized groups, such as women or the poor. Historical evidence suggests that these groups, even more than smaller provinces, are likely to be under-represented in Parliament and ignored in political decision-making. Here again, demands for group representation are not unique to Canada. We find very similar debates occurring in Great Britain, Scandinavia, France, the United States, and Latin America (Phillips 1995; Mansbridge 2000; Williams 1998; Htun 2004, 2016; Rubio-Marin 2012).

In the end, the Charlottetown Accord rejected most proposals for the guaranteed representation of social groups, and instead focused on increased regional representation. The one exception was a proposal for guaranteed seats for Indigenous peoples. However, the Accord allowed each province to decide how its senators would be elected, and three of the ten provincial premiers said that they would pass provincial legislation requiring that 50 per cent of the Senate seats from their province be reserved for women (Ontario, British Columbia, and Nova Scotia). While the Accord was defeated, it is possible that any future proposal for Senate reform will have to address the issue of group representation as well as regional representation.

Group representation rights are often defended as a response to some systemic barrier in the political process that makes it impossible for the group's views and interests to be effectively represented. For example, Iris Young, writing in the American context, argues that special representation rights should be extended to "oppressed groups" because they are at a disadvantage in the political process, and "the solution lies at least in part in providing institutionalized means for the explicit recognition and representation of oppressed groups" (Young 1989, 259).

Insofar as these rights are seen as a response to oppression or systemic disadvantage, they are most plausibly seen as a temporary measure on the way to a society where the need for special representation no longer exists – a form of political "affirmative action." Over time, society should remove the oppression and disadvantage, thereby eliminating the need for these rights.

However, the issue of special representation rights is complicated in Canada, because special representation is sometimes defended, not on grounds of oppression, but as a corollary of self-government for national minorities. The right to self-government in certain areas seems to entail the right to guaranteed representation on any bodies that can intrude on those areas. Hence, it is argued, a corollary of self-government is that the national minority be guaranteed representation on any body that can interpret or modify its powers of self-government (e.g., the Supreme Court), or that can make decisions in areas of concurrent or conflicting jurisdiction.

On the other hand, insofar as self-government reduces the jurisdiction of the federal government over the national minority, self-government may imply that the group should have reduced influence (at least on certain issues) at the federal level. For example, if self-government for the Québécois leads to the asymmetrical transfer of powers from Ottawa to Quebec so that the federal government would be passing laws that would not apply to Quebec, some commentators argue that Quebecers should not have a vote on such legislation (particularly if they could cast the deciding vote). In this context, it is worth noting that although Quebec has its own pension plan, separate from the Canada Pension Plan, federal ministers from Quebec have often been in charge of the latter.

***

These are the three major forms of differentiated citizenship in Canada. As we've seen, they are not unique to Canada, but are found in most Western democracies. Insofar as differentiated citizenship involves the adoption of one or more of these group-differentiated rights, then virtually every modern democracy recognizes some form of it. While these forms of differentiated citizenship are common, they remain controversial. Many liberals have opposed these policies as inconsistent with liberal democratic principles of freedom and equality. I will discuss two standard liberal objections: the conflict between group rights and individual rights, and the bases of social unity.

Individual and Group Rights

Recognizing groups in the Constitution is often perceived as an issue of "collective rights," and many liberals fear that collective rights are, by definition, inimical to individual rights. This view was popularized in Canada by former Prime Minister Pierre Trudeau, who explained his rejection of collective rights for Quebec by saying that he believed in "the primacy of the individual" (Trudeau 1990).

However, we need to distinguish two kinds of collective rights that a group might claim. The first involves the right of a group against its own members; the second involves the right of a group against the larger society. Both kinds of collective rights can be seen as protecting the stability of national, ethnic, or religious groups, but they respond to different sources of instability. The first kind is intended to protect the group from the destabilizing impact of internal dissent (e.g., the decision of individual members not to follow traditional practices or customs), whereas the second protects the group from the impact of external pressures (e.g., the economic or political decisions of the larger society). To distinguish these two kinds of collective rights, I will call the first "internal restrictions" and the second "external protections." Internal restrictions involve intra-group relations; external protections regulate inter-group relations.

Internal restrictions are arguably inconsistent with liberal-democratic values. Such collective rights are found in many parts of the world where groups seek the right to legally restrict the freedom of their own members in the name of group solidarity or cultural purity; this is especially common in theocratic and patriarchal cultures where women are oppressed and religious orthodoxy enforced. This type of collective right, then, raises the danger of individual oppression.

External protections, by contrast, do not raise problems of individual oppression. Here the aim is to protect a group's distinct identity not by restricting the freedom of individual members but by limiting the group's vulnerability to the political decisions and economic power of the larger society. For example, guaranteeing representation for a minority on advisory or legislative bodies can reduce the chance that the group will be outvoted on decisions that affect the community; financial subsidies can help provide goods and services to a minority that they could not afford in a market dominated by majority preferences; and revising dress codes and work schedules can help ensure that decisions originally made by and for the dominant group are sufficiently flexible to accommodate new ethnic groups.

These sorts of external protections are not inconsistent with liberal democratic principles and may indeed promote justice. They may help put the different groups in a society on a more equal footing, by reducing the extent to which minorities are vulnerable to the larger society.

Do the three kinds of differentiated citizenship in Canada involve internal restrictions or external protections? Primarily the latter. The Québécois, Indigenous peoples, and ethnic minorities are concerned primarily with ensuring that the larger society does not deprive them of the conditions necessary for their survival. They are less concerned with controlling the extent to which their own members engage in untraditional or unorthodox practices. Special representation within the political institutions of the larger society, the devolution of self-government powers from the federal government to the minority, and the protection of cultural practices through accommodation rights all reduce the vulnerability of minority communities to the economic and political decisions of the larger society.

These various forms of external protections are, I believe, compatible with liberal values. One can imagine cases where external protections go too far in protecting a minority from a majority, to the point where the minority in fact is able rule over the majority – apartheid in South Africa is a clear example where "minority rights" for whites were invoked to dispossess the majority. However, this does not seem to be a real danger for the particular external protections currently being claimed in Canada. The special veto powers demanded by the Québécois, or the land rights demanded by Indigenous peoples, or the heritage language funding demanded by ethnic minorities will hardly put them in a position to dominate English Canadians. On the contrary, they can be seen as putting the various groups on a more equal footing, in terms of their relative power vis-à-vis each other.

Moreover, none of these external protections need conflict with individual rights, since they do not, by themselves, tell us anything about whether or how the ethnic or national group exercises power over its own members.

There are also some internal restrictions in Canada, although their scope is less clear. Both self-government rights and accommodation rights can, under some circumstances, be used to oppress certain members of the minority group. For example, some Québécois and Indigenous leaders have sought qualification of, or exemption from, the Canadian Charter of Rights and Freedoms in the name of self-government. These limits on the Charter create the possibility that individuals or groups within Quebec or Aboriginal communities could be oppressed in the name of group solidarity or cultural authenticity.

Whether there is a real danger of intra-group oppression in Canada is a matter of debate. The most commonly discussed example concerns the potential for sexual discrimination in minority cultures. Some women's groups (mostly from outside Quebec) worried that the Quebec government might use the "distinct society" clause to impose oppressive family policies on women (e.g., restricting access to birth control or abortion to maintain a high birth rate). Whether this was a realistic worry is dubious. Women's groups within Quebec were quick to reject the idea that enhanced or asymmetric autonomy for Quebec was a threat to their equality, and indeed Quebec has some of the most progressive policies on gender equality in the country.

The concern has also been expressed that Indigenous women might be discriminated against under certain systems of Aboriginal self-government if these are exempt from the Charter. This concern has been voiced by women's organizations both inside and outside Indigenous communities. Indeed, the Native Women's Association of Canada has demanded that the decisions of Indigenous governments be subject to the Canadian Charter (or a future Indigenous Charter, if it also effectively protects sexual equality).

On the other hand, many Indigenous leaders insist that this fear of sexual oppression reflects misinformed or prejudiced stereotypes about Indigenous cultures. They argue that Indigenous self-government needs to be exempt from the Charter of Rights – not to restrict the liberty of women within Indigenous communities, but to defend the external protections of Indigenous peoples vis-à-vis larger society. Their special rights to land or to guaranteed representation, which help reduce their vulnerability to the economic and political pressure of the larger society, could be struck down as discriminatory under the Charter (e.g., guaranteed representation for Indigenous peoples could be seen as violating the equality rights of the Charter, as could restrictions on the mobility of non-Indigenous people on Indigenous lands). Also, Indigenous leaders fear that white judges may interpret certain rights (e.g., democratic rights) in ways that are culturally biased. Hence, many Indigenous leaders seek exemption from the Charter but affirm their commitment to the basic human rights and freedoms that underlie the Charter.

Similar debates have occurred over accommodation rights. There are fears that some immigrant groups and religious minorities may use "multiculturalism" as a pretext for imposing traditional patriarchal practices on women and children. There are concerns that some groups will demand the right to stop their children (particularly girls) from receiving a proper education, so as to reduce the chances that the child will leave the community, or the right to continue traditional customs such as clitoridectomy or forced arranged marriages. Such fears were often expressed in Quebec's recent debate about whether reasonable accommodation had gone too far.

Such internal restrictions clearly do have the potential to deny individual freedom. But Canada's current multiculturalism policy does not endorse such practices, and there is little public support for allowing them, even within minority communities. Instead, most collective rights for ethnic and national groups are defended in terms of, and take the form of, external protections against the larger community. To be sure, there are always some conservative members within any given ethnic or religious group who try to encourage or pressure other members to follow what they believe to be the "authentic" practices of the community, and who oppose reformers who wish to revise or adapt these practices. But such internal debates existed long before the adoption of multiculturalism policies, and continue in countries that have rejected multiculturalism. Some commentators have worried that multiculturalism policies strengthen the hand of conservative members of groups, giving them greater power to impose particular "scripts" on other members about what it means to be a Jew, say, or to be Chinese. But here again, there is no evidence that multiculturalism favours conservatives over reformers within ethnic and religious groups, and indeed some evidence suggests that multiculturalism policies have helped to ensure the greater representation of women and youth within such communities, in part because norms of gender equality and human rights are themselves explicitly built into the goals of the federal multiculturalism policy.

More generally, there is no enthusiasm for the idea that ethnic or national groups should be able to protect their historical customs by limiting the basic civil liberties of their members. For example, there is no public support for restricting freedom of religion in the name of protecting the religious customs of a community.

Social Unity and Differentiated Citizenship

Liberals are also concerned that differentiated citizenship will be a source of disunity and will inhibit the development of a sense of shared Canadian identity. They believe it could lead to the dissolution of the country, or, less drastically, to a reduced willingness to make the mutual sacrifices and accommodations necessary for a functioning democracy and effective welfare state. If groups are encouraged by the very terms of citizenship to turn inward and focus on their "difference" (whether racial, ethnic, religious, sexual, etc.), then citizenship cannot perform its vital integrative function. Nothing will bind the various groups in society together or prevent the spread of mutual mistrust or conflict.

This is a serious concern, reinforced by evidence from other countries, that there may be a negative correlation between diversity and solidarity. Indeed, this is now sometimes called the new "progressive's dilemma": progressives today want to be more open to diversity, yet this may erode the traditional progressive goal of a robust welfare state (Pearce 2004).

In evaluating this concern, however, we need to keep in mind the distinctions between the three forms of differentiated citizenship. Generally speaking, demands for both representation rights and accommodation rights are demands for inclusion. Groups that feel excluded want to be included in the larger society, and the recognition and accommodation of their "difference" is intended to facilitate this.

As I noted, the right to special representation can be seen as an extension of the familiar idea of guaranteeing special representation for underrepresented regions (e.g., an equal number of Senate seats for all states or provinces, whatever their population). This practice is widely seen as promoting both participation and fairness, and hence integration. Proponents of special representation simply extend this logic to non-territorial groups, who may equally be in need of better representation (e.g., ethnic and racial minorities, women, the disabled). There are practical obstacles to such a proposal (Phillips 1995). For example, how do we decide which groups are entitled to such representation, and how do we ensure that their "representatives" are in fact accountable to the group? Nevertheless, the basic impulse underlying representation rights is integration, not separation.

Similarly, most demands for accommodation rights reflect a desire by members of ethnic minority groups to participate within the mainstream of society. Consider the case of male Sikhs who wanted to join the Royal Canadian Mounted Police, but, because of their religious requirement to wear a turban, could not do so unless they were exempted from the usual requirements regarding ceremonial headgear. Such an exemption was opposed by many Canadians, who viewed it as a sign of disrespect for one of Canada's "national symbols." But the fact that these men wanted to be a part of the RCMP, and participate in one of Canada's national institutions, is evidence of their desire to participate in and contribute to the larger community.

Indeed, the evidence suggests that the adoption of the multiculturalism policy in 1971 has helped, rather than hindered, integration in Canada. Immigrants today are more likely to take out Canadian citizenship than immigrants who arrived before 1971. They are also more likely to vote, to learn an official language, to have friends (or spouses) from another ethnic group, to participate in mainstream social organizations, and so on. On all of these criteria, ethnic groups in Canada are more integrated today than they were before the multiculturalism policy was adopted in 1971. Moreover, Canada does a better job of integrating immigrants on these criteria than countries that have rejected the idea of multiculturalism, like the United States or France. Multiculturalism has been criticized for promoting ethnic segregation in Canada (Bissoondath 1994), but in fact there is no evidence to suggest that multiculturalism has decreased the rate of integration of immigrants, or increased the separatism or mutual hostility of ethnic groups. On the contrary, it seems that multiculturalism has succeeded in its basic aim: making immigrants and their children feel more at home within mainstream Canadian institutions.

Self-government rights, however, do raise problems for the integrative function of citizenship. While both representation and accommodation rights take the larger political community for granted and seek greater inclusion in it, demands for self-government may reflect a desire to weaken the bonds with the larger community, and may indeed question its very nature, authority, and permanence. If democracy is the rule of the people, group self-government raises the question of who "the people" really are. National minorities claim that they are distinct peoples, with inherent rights of self-determination that were not relinquished by their (often involuntary) inclusion within a larger country. Indeed, the retention of certain powers is often explicitly spelled out in the treaties or federal agreements that specified the terms of their inclusion. Self-government rights, therefore, are the most complete case of differentiated citizenship, since they divide the people into separate "peoples," each with its own historic rights, territories, and powers of self-government, and each, therefore, with its own political community.

Can differentiated citizenship serve an integrative function in this context? If citizenship is primarily membership in a political community, then self-government rights seem to give rise to a sort of dual citizenship, and to conflicts about which community citizens identify with most deeply. Moreover, there seems to be no natural stopping point to the demands for increasing self-government. If limited autonomy is granted, this may simply fuel the ambitions of nationalist leaders who will be satisfied with nothing short of their own nation-state. Indeed, one of the defining features of nationalism, historically, has been the quest for an independent state. Even if not explicitly secessionist, nationalists typically insist that the nation is the primary locus of political loyalty and allegiance, so that participation in any supra-national political community is conditional, assessed on the basis of how well such participation serves the interest of the primary national community. Once the Québécois or Crees define themselves as a nation, therefore, it seems that their allegiance to Canada can only be derivative and conditional. Democratic multination states are, it would seem, inherently unstable for this reason.

It might seem tempting, therefore, to ignore the demands of national minorities, avoid any reference to such groups in the Constitution, and insist that citizenship is a common identity shared by all individuals, without regard to group membership. This is often described as the American strategy for dealing with cultural pluralism. But with a few small-in-number exceptions – such as the American Indian, Inuit, Puerto Rican, and Native Hawaiian populations – the United States is not a multination state. It has faced the problem of assimilating voluntary immigrants and involuntary slaves, who arrived in America as individuals or families, rather than incorporating historically self-governing communities whose homeland has become part of the larger community. And where the "ethnicity-blind" strategy was applied to national minorities (e.g., American Indians), it has often been a spectacular failure. Hence many of these national groups are now accorded self-government rights within the United States. Indeed, there are very few democratic multination states that follow the strict "common citizenship" strategy. This is not surprising, because refusing demands for self-government rights may simply aggravate alienation among these groups, and increase the desire for secession.

It might seem that we are caught between Scylla and Charybdis: granting self-government rights seems to encourage a nationalist project whose end-point is independence; denying self-government seems to encourage alienation and withdrawal. It is not surprising, therefore, that many commentators have concluded that multination states are unlikely to be successful or stable.

And yet many multination federations have survived, and indeed flourished. Countries such as Switzerland, Belgium, Great Britain, and Canada have not only managed these conflicts in a peaceful and democratic way, but also have secured prosperity and individual freedom for their citizens. Indeed, it is a striking fact that no multination federation in the West has yet fallen apart. This is truly remarkable when one considers the immense power that nationalism has shown in this century. Nationalism has torn apart colonial empires and Communist dictatorships, and redefined boundaries all over the world. Yet democratic multination federations have tamed the force of nationalism. No other form of political structure can make this claim.

This suggests that multination federations combine a rather weak sense of unity with surprising levels of resilience and stability. Weak bonds of social unity may nonetheless be enduring, and conditional allegiances may nonetheless be powerful. What "glue" provides this sort of resilience remains a matter of debate (Webber 1994; Tully 1995; Norman 2006; Taylor 1993; Gagnon and Tully 2001; Gagnon, Rocher, and Guibernau 2003). But the ideal of a stable and prosperous multination state – which recognizes the self-government rights of its national minorities while simultaneously promoting a common identity among all citizens – is neither a conceptual contradiction nor a practical impossibility. We do not yet have a theory about how such states are possible: we have no clear account of the basis of social unity in such a multination state. But we shouldn't let the lack of a theory blind us to the reality that such states exist and prosper in the modern world.

Conclusion

Canada has a long history of accommodating group difference, particularly national and ethnic difference. It is difficult to say whether this history is a successful one. On the one hand, the continued existence of the country has often been in question, and remains so today. On the other hand, Canada has enjoyed 150 years of peaceful coexistence between three national groups and innumerable ethnic groups, with an almost total absence of political violence. While many groups continue to feel excluded, the political system has proven flexible enough to accommodate many demands for self-government, multicultural accommodations, and special representation. It is difficult to find a scale that allows us to add up these successes and disappointments to arrive at some overall judgments of the Canadian experiment in accommodating group difference. Indeed, perhaps the major lesson to be drawn from the Canadian experience is the sheer heterogeneity of group differences, and of the mechanisms for accommodating them. The sorts of demands made by national, ethnic, and social groups differ greatly in their content and in their relation to traditional liberal democratic principles of equality, freedom, and democracy.

References and Suggested Readings

Adams, Michael. 2007. *Unlikely Utopia: The Surprising Triumph of Canadian Pluralism*. Toronto: Viking.

Adelman, Howard, and Pierre Anctil, eds. 2011. *Religion, Culture, and the State: Reflections on the Bouchard-Taylor Report*. Toronto: University of Toronto Press.

Alesina, Alberto, Reza Baqir, and William Easterly. 2001. *Public Goods and Ethnic Diversity*. NBER Working Paper No. 6069. Cambridge: National Bureau of Economic Research.

Ambrose, Emma, and Cas Mudde. 2015. "Canadian Multiculturalism and the Absence of the Far Right." *Nationalism and Ethnic Politics* 21 (2): 213–36.

Anderson, Liam. 2012. *Federal Solutions to Ethnic Problems: Accommodating Diversity*. London: Routledge.

Banting, Keith, and Will Kymlicka, eds. 2006. *Multiculturalism and the Welfare State: Recognition and Redistribution in Contemporary Democracies*. Oxford: Oxford University Press. http://dx.doi.org/10.1093/acprof:oso/9780199289172.001.0001.

———. 2013. "Is There Really a Retreat from Multiculturalism Policies? New Evidence from the Multiculturalism Policy Index." *Comparative European Politics* 11 (5): 577–98. http://dx.doi.org/10.1057/cep.2013.12.

———, eds. 2017. *The Strains of Commitment: The Political Sources of Solidarity in Diverse Societies*. Oxford: Oxford University Press.

Bissoondath, Neil. 1994. *Selling Illusions: The Cult of Multiculturalism in Canada*. Toronto: Penguin.

Bloemraad, Irene. 2006. *Becoming a Citizen: Incorporating Immigrants and Refugees in the United States and Canada*. Berkeley: University of California Press.

———. 2012. "Understanding 'Canadian Exceptionalism' in Immigration and Pluralism Policy." In *Rethinking National Identity in the Age of Migration*, edited by Migration Policy Institute, 145–70. Berlin: Verlag Bertelsmann Stiftung.

Bouchard, Gérard, and Charles Taylor. 2008. *Building the Future: A Time for Reconciliation: Report of the Consultation Commission on Accommodation Practices Related to Cultural Differences* (Gouvernement du Québec).

Cairns, Alan. 2000. *Citizens Plus: Aboriginal Peoples and the Canadian State*. Vancouver: UBC Press.

Cornell, Stephen. 2015. "Processes of Native Nationhood: The Indigenous Politics of Self-Government." *International Indigenous Policy Journal* 6 (4): 1–27.

Deveaux, Monique. 2006. *Gender and Justice in Multicultural Liberal States*. New York: Oxford University Press. http://dx.doi.org/10.1093/acprof:oso/9780199289790.001.0001.

Dick, Caroline. 2012. *The Perils of Identity: Group Rights and the Politics of Intragroup Difference*. Vancouver: UBC Press.

Eisenberg, Avigail. 2009. *Reasons of Identity: A Normative Guide to the Political and Legal Assessment of Identity Claims*. Oxford: Oxford University Press.

Eisenberg, Avigail, and Jeff Spinner-Halev, eds. 2005. *Minorities within Minorities*. Cambridge: Cambridge University Press. http://dx.doi.org/10.1017/CBO9780511490224.

Fraser, Nancy. 1997. "From Redistribution to Recognition? Dilemmas of Justice in a 'Postsocialist' Age." In *Justice Interruptus: Critical Reflections on the 'Postsocialist' Condition*, 11–40. New York: Routledge.

Gagnon, Alain-G., and Joseph Garcea. 1988. "Quebec and the Pursuit of Special Status." In *Perspectives on Canadian Federalism*, edited by R.D. Olling and M. Westmacott, 304–25. Scarborough, ON: Prentice-Hall.

Gagnon, Alain-G., François Rocher, and M. Montserrat Guibernau, eds. 2003. *The Conditions of Diversity in Multinational Democracies*. Montreal: Institute for Research on Public Policy.

Gagnon, Alain-G., and James Tully, eds. 2001. *Multinational Democracies*. Cambridge: Cambridge University Press. http://dx.doi.org/10.1017/CBO9780511521577.

Havemann, Paul, ed. 1999. *Indigenous Peoples' Rights in Australia, Canada and New Zealand*. Oxford: Oxford University Press.

Htun, Mala. 2004. "Is Gender Like Ethnicity? The Political Representation of Identity Groups." *Perspectives on Politics* 2 (3): 439–58.

———. 2016. *Inclusion without Representation in Latin America: Gender Quotas and Ethnic Reservations*. Cambridge: Cambridge University Press.

Jenson, Jane. 1993. "Naming Nations: Making Nationalist Claims in Canadian Public Discourse." *Canadian Review of Sociology and Anthropology / La Revue Canadienne de Sociologie et d'Anthropologie* 30 (3): 337–58.

Joppke, Christian. 2014. "The Retreat Is Real – But What Is the Alternative? Multiculturalism, Muscular Liberalism, and Islam." *Constellations* 21 (2): 286–95.

Kymlicka, Will. 1995. *Multicultural Citizenship*. Oxford: Oxford University Press.

———. 2007. *Multicultural Odysseys: Navigating the New International Politics of Diversity*. Oxford: Oxford University Press.

———. 2012. "Multiculturalism: Success, Failure, and the Future." In *Rethinking National Identity in the Age of Migration*, edited by Migration Policy Institute, 33–78. Berlin: Verlag Bertelsmann Stiftung.

———. 2015. "The Essentialist Critique of Multiculturalism: Theory, Policies and Ethos." In *Multiculturalism Rethought: Interpretations, Dilemmas and New Directions*, edited by Varun Uberoi and Tariq Modood, 209–49. Edinburgh: Edinburgh University Press.

Lefebvre, Solange, and Patrice Brodeur, eds. 2017. *Public Commissions on Cultural and Religious Diversity: Analysis, Reception and Challenges*. London: Routledge.

Levy, Jacob. 1997. "Classifying Cultural Rights." In *Ethnicity and Group Rights*, edited by Ian Shapiro and Will Kymlicka, 22–66. New York: New York University Press.

Maloney, Ryan. 2015. "Maxime Bernier Doubles Down on Tweets about 'Extreme' Multiculturalism." Huffington Post, August 18, 2018. https://www.huffingtonpost.ca/2018/08/15/maxime-bernier-tweets_a_23502758/.

Mansbridge, Jane. 2000. "What Does a Representative Do?" In *Citizenship in Diverse Societies*, edited by Will Kymlicka and Wayne Norman, 99–123. Oxford: Oxford University Press. http://dx.doi.org/10.1093/019829770X.003.0004.

McCoy, John. 2016. *Protecting Multiculturalism: Muslims, Security, and Integration in Canada*. Montreal and Kingston: McGill-Queen's University Press.

McRoberts, Kenneth. 1997. *Misconceiving Canada: The Struggle for National Unity*. Toronto: Oxford University Press.

Newman, Dwight. 2011. *Community and Collective Rights: A Theoretical Framework for Rights Held by Groups*. Oxford: Hart.

Norman, Wayne. 2006. *Negotiating Nationalism: Nation-Building, Federalism and Secession in the Multinational State*. Oxford: Oxford University Press. http://dx.doi.org/10.1093/0198293356.001.0001.

Okin, Susan. 1999. *Is Multiculturalism Bad for Women?* Princeton, NJ: Princeton University Press.

Pearce, Nick. 2004. "Diversity versus Solidarity: A New Progressive Dilemma." *Renewal: A Journal of Labour Politics* 12 (3): 79–87.

Pearson, David. 2001. *The Politics of Ethnicity in Settler Societies: States of Unease*. London: Palgrave Macmillan. http://dx.doi.org/10.1057/9780333977903.

Phillips, Anne. 1995. *The Politics of Presence*. Oxford: Oxford University Press.

Putnam, Robert. 2007. "*E Pluribus Unum*: Diversity and Community in the 21st Century." *Scandinavian Political Studies* 30 (2): 137–74. http://dx.doi.org/10.1111/j.1467-9477.2007.00176.x.

Resnick, Philip. 1994. "Toward a Multination Federalism." In *Seeking a New Canadian Partnership: Asymmetrical and Confederal Options*, edited by Leslie Seidle, 71–90. Montreal: Institute for Research on Public Policy.

Royal Commission on Aboriginal Peoples (RCAP). 1996. *Report of the Royal Commission on Aboriginal Peoples*. Ottawa: Royal Commission on Aboriginal Peoples.

Rubio-Marin, Ruth. 2012. "A New European Parity-Democracy Sex Equality Model and Why It Won't Fly in the United States." *American Journal of Comparative Law* 60 (1): 99–126.

Rubio-Marin, Ruth, and Will Kymlicka, eds. 2018. *Gender Parity and Multicultural Feminism: Towards a New Synthesis*. Oxford: Oxford University Press.

Shachar, Ayelet. 2001. *Multicultural Jurisdictions: Preserving Cultural Differences and Women's Rights in a Liberal State*. Cambridge: Cambridge University Press. http://dx.doi.org/10.1017/CBO9780511490330.

Taylor, Charles. 1993. *Reconciling the Solitudes: Essays on Canadian Federalism and Nationalism*. Montreal and Kingston: McGill-Queen's University Press.

Trudeau, Pierre Elliott. 1990. "The Values of a Just Society." In *Towards a Just Society*, edited by Thomas Axworthy, 357–404. Toronto: Viking.

Tully, James. 1995. *Strange Multiplicity: Constitutionalism in an Age of Diversity*. Cambridge: Cambridge University Press. http://dx.doi.org/10.1017/CBO9781139170888.

Vertovec, Steven, and Susanne Wessendorf, eds. 2010. *The Multiculturalism Backlash: European Discourses, Policies and Practices*. London: Routledge.

Walters, Mark. 2008. "The Jurisprudence of Reconciliation: Aboriginal Rights in Canada." In *The Politics of Reconciliation in Multicultural Societies*, edited by Will Kymlicka and Bashir Bashir, 165–91. Oxford: Oxford University Press.

Webber, Jeremy. 1994. *Reimagining Canada: Language, Culture, Community and the Canadian Constitution*. Montreal and Kingston: McGill-Queen's University Press.

Williams, Melissa. 1998. *Voice, Trust and Memory: Marginalized Groups and the Failings of Liberal Representation*. Princeton, NJ: Princeton University Press.

Young, Iris Marion. 1989. "Polity and Group Difference: A Critique of the Ideal of Universal Citizenship." *Ethics* 99 (2): 250–74. http://dx.doi.org/10.1086/293065.

seventeen
Diversity in Canadian Politics

YASMEEN ABU-LABAN

> In Canada, we see diversity as a source of strength, not weakness. Our country is strong not in spite of our differences, but because of them.
> – Justin Trudeau (2016)

Introduction

Liberal Prime Minister Justin Trudeau has frequently forwarded the idea that "diversity is our strength," particularly on issues pertaining to citizenship, immigration, and multiculturalism in Canada. The regularity with which the idea has been repeated by Trudeau and members of his Cabinet since coming to power with a strong majority in 2015, and re-elected as a minority in 2019, has ensured that it is not merely a feature, but rather a mantra of his government. As such, the 2018 decision of opposition Quebec Member of Parliament Maxime Bernier to forge a new People's Party of Canada committed primarily to rejecting the idea that diversity is a strength might seem natural in a context of partisan and electoral politics (CBC Radio 2018). As Bernier was a former Conservative Party leadership hopeful, Cabinet minister under Prime Minister Stephen Harper, and a seasoned veteran of party politics and the rough-and-tumble of campaign strategizing and vote-getting, from the vantage point of electoral politics it was significant when he failed to win his own seat in the 2019 federal election. While the People's Party of Canada faced an uncertain future in elections, Bernier launched a weekly web broadcast called *The Max Bernier Show* on the party's YouTube channel (Grenier 2020). As such it remains important to consider the underlying ideas that Bernier articulated that continue to be brought into Canadian political discourse. In particular, whereas some twenty-five or thirty years ago debates over multiculturalism and immigration levels were generally expressed by reference to Canada's "national unity" (Cardozo and Musto 1997), Bernier, like many others today, is expressing discomfort in relation to preserving "Western values," especially gender equality and LGBTQ rights, and preventing "distrust, social conflict, potentially violence" (as cited in CBC News 2018). The tools of political science, with its focus on power and the state, are needed to make sense of this shift and why such varied discussions pertaining to diversity matter.

At a demographic level, Canada is diverse and becoming more so. Many governments as well as business and civil society groups have expressed interest in retaining a tradition of having a census that includes a mandatory questionnaire with in-depth questions, a tradition that had been dropped during the 2011 Census when it became voluntary to fill out (Fekete 2010; Siddiqui 2010). The 2016 Census reverted to this practice of a mandatory long-form survey, allowing for better-quality data about Canada's population of just over 35 million. The findings show that at present more than one in five Canadians (21.9 per cent) is foreign-born (Statistics Canada 2017c), and Canadians are now more ethnically diverse than ever. For instance, while the 1871 Census recorded about twenty ethnic origins, the 2016 Census enumerated over 250, with 41.1 per cent claiming more than one ethnicity (Statistics Canada 2017a, 1). Additionally, there is ever-increasing racial diversity, with 19.1 per cent of the population comprising visible minorities, who are defined by the Canadian government as "persons other than Aboriginal persons who are non-Caucasian in race or non-white in colour" (Statistics Canada 2017c). Linguistic diversity is also an evident feature in Canada's population, with 58.1 per cent claiming English as their mother tongue, 21.4 per cent claiming French as their mother tongue, 0.6 per cent claiming an Indigenous language as their mother tongue, and 22.3 per cent claiming another language as their mother tongue (with Mandarin, Cantonese, Punjabi, Tagalog, and Spanish being the most common) (Statistics Canada 2017b). Because many Canadians regularly encounter "diversity" among friends, neighbours, colleagues, and even within their own families, such demographic realities underscore why "diversity" — particularly when it comes to place of birth, language, ethnicity, or race — is a compelling consideration for so many in Canada.

This chapter focuses primarily on cultural, ethnic, and racial diversity and its relevance, both historically and currently, in Canadian politics. It examines how these forms of diversity have been addressed both by the Canadian state through its policies and by the contemporary Canadian political science tradition. It argues that diversity is significant for political analyses in both areas because it is relevant to power, a central disciplinary concern. Put differently, whether historic or contemporary, inequalities between identifiable groups are important to political scientists because such inequalities may affect the extent to which all groups feel their voices are heard and their interests are represented in Canadian institutions. This is closely related to what political scientists refer to as "legitimacy," or the popular acceptance of a governing authority or regime. More broadly, inequities can tell us about the character of Canadian liberal democracy.

In order to address this argument, this chapter takes a threefold approach. In the first section, major state policies and practices pertaining to diversity are reviewed in relation to Canada's history and evolution. In the second, three different emphases in Canadian political science approaches are highlighted: culture, race, and colonialism. To illustrate how each approach may inform us, the third section offers a close examination of religious diversity, especially as it pertains to both Indigenous peoples historically and Muslim-Canadians today.

Diversity and the Evolving Canadian State

Canada's history as a settler colony, characterized by pre-existing and distinct Indigenous societies, European settler colonization, and repeated waves of immigration, is a testament to the fact that "diversity" is not new. Historically, both the British-origin and French-origin groups attempted to assert dominance over the Indigenous population, although the patterns of colonization of each were distinct (Dickason 1992). It is, however, Canada's foundation as a so-called white settler colony of Britain that fostered a legacy of group-based inequalities that forms the basis of many grievances and ongoing political struggles. This is because the historic project of modelling Canada after Britain (in political, economic, cultural, and demographic terms) often led to assimilative and discriminatory measures.

The Royal Proclamation of 1763 established the framework by which British administration of the North American territories would take place and served to enforce British sovereignty while at the same time acknowledging Aboriginal tribes and land title rights. In particular, the proclamation outlawed the expropriation of Aboriginal lands by colonies or by settlers unless treaties with the Crown were completed. This was the beginning of the imperial government's contradictory policy of assimilation and recognition, which was later replicated by Canada (Stasiulis and Jhappan 1995, 107).

Assimilation and recognition also characterized relations with the French, and these tensions were further woven into the development of liberal democracy and eventually federalism in Canada. The 1774 Quebec Act allowed the freedom to practise the Catholic faith and retained French civil law and seigneurial landholding systems. While it did not say anything about the use of the French language, the appointed council (overseen by a colonial governor) allowed for Roman Catholics to hold office. The 1791 Constitutional Act created Upper Canada (the present-day province of Ontario) and Lower Canada (the southern part of present-day Quebec), governed by bicameral legislatures consisting of elected assemblies with limited powers and more powerful appointed legislative councils that worked on behalf of the colonial governors and the Crown. In both Upper and Lower Canada, reformers fought for responsible government. The response to these struggles, which took the form of armed uprisings in 1837–8, was the 1840 Act of Union that united Upper and Lower Canada into a single colony (Canada) with one Parliament and, notably, English as the only official government language. As well, in the 1840s and 1850s, thousands of immigrants, among them a significant number of Irish, were discriminated against by the British authorities (Cardin and Couture 1996, 208).

In light of pre-Confederation practices, it is unsurprising that after 1867 the Canadian state also reflected linguistic, ethnic, and racial hierarchies in practices, policies, and laws (Stasiulis and Jhappan 1995, 96), as exemplified, for instance, in the growing state security functions and intense surveillance directed at Irish Catholics for purported Fenian associations following the assassination in 1868 of one of the Fathers of Confederation, Thomas D'Arcy McGee (Whitaker, Kealey, and Parnaby 2012, 31). The founding of the modern Canadian state stemmed from a number of factors, not least of which were fears of an American invasion and the distinctly privileged position of "white settler colonies" to enjoy relative political autonomy within the British Empire. With Confederation in 1867, the colonies of British North America — Canada, Nova Scotia, and New Brunswick — were united into a dominion with British-style political institutions. Unlike Britain, however, and as outlined in the Constitution Act, 1867, Canada adopted a federal system of government. The province of Quebec gained control over education and culture (see Wallner, chapter 8 for a discussion of federalism), and both French and English were to be the languages used in federal (and Quebec) legislative debates and records. The adoption of a federal system was the result of intense struggle by French Canadians, as many British-origin politicians (such as the first prime minister, Sir John A. Macdonald) would have preferred a unitary state (Abu-Laban and Nieguth 2000, 478). Confederation ushered in a new discourse upholding the British and the French as Canada's "two founding peoples" or "two founding races" (Stasiulis and Jhappan 1995, 110). This discourse held out the promise that the collective aspirations of two collectivities (the British and the French) could be simultaneously accommodated. Yet despite the discourse and the stated provisions of the Constitution Act, 1867, the promise was never met. As summed succinctly by Richard Day (2000, 180), "the Canadian state … lived, worked, and most importantly, *dreamed* in English."

As a by-product, the discourse on "two founding peoples" helped legitimize the federal government's assuming jurisdiction over Indigenous affairs and lands reserved for Indigenous peoples, paving the way for the seizure of Indigenous lands by provinces both with and without the use of treaties (see Green 1995; Green and Peach 2007). Similarly, except in periods when the pool of labour was insufficient to fuel agricultural or industrial expansion, Canada's immigration policy favoured white, English-speaking, British-origin Protestants (Abu-Laban and Gabriel 2002, 37–55). Even after World War II, Prime Minister Mackenzie King emphasized that Canada did not want immigration from "the orient," since this would negatively alter "the character" of the population (King 1947). By referencing the "orient," King meant to exclude all areas in the eastern hemisphere beyond Europe; this policy position guided Canada's immigration intake until 1967.

In 1967 a new immigration policy explicitly banned discrimination on the basis of race or ethnicity and introduced a "point system" of selection, giving points to immigrants arriving for economic purposes to such areas as education and skills. (Elements of the point system are still in effect in the revamped system introduced in 2015 known as Express Entry, which ranks economic immigrants, whereas those coming as family members of immigrants, or as refugees, are considered under different systems.) In addition to immigration, the 1960s marks a turning point for policies in a number of areas. Combined, such changes may be related in part to the international realm, where the saliency of the idea of human rights (emphasizing the equal worth and dignity of all persons) coincided with the growing success of many anti-colonial struggles and movements; the growth of the Keynesian-style welfare state, which opened new possibilities of social spending; and the re-mobilization of segments of the Canadian population into identity-based political movements and organizations demanding inclusion in the existing system and, in some cases, self-rule. This was clearly a period in which the inclusiveness of Canada's democracy, inequities in the distribution of power, and the legitimacy of its institutions were put in question.

In response, federal policies were shaped by the resurrection of older discourses and understandings in a new context. For example, in Quebec, the Quiet Revolution was symbolized by the election of the provincial Liberal government of Jean Lesage in 1960. Commitment to a philosophy of *maîtres chez nous* (masters in our own house) led successive Quebec governments to assume greater jurisdictional and fiscal powers for the province as well as to seek federal recognition of the distinct constitutional status of Quebec because the French were a "founding people" at Confederation. Indigenous peoples drew on the Royal Proclamation of 1763 that gave them status as "nations within" (or "first nations"); the proclamation also provided a legal basis for their contemporary and ongoing land and rights claims, including self-government.

In other cases, new federal discourses aiming to foster legitimacy also emerged. The rise in the 1960s of widespread political contestation across

Canada of French-speaking Canadians, especially in Quebec and New Brunswick (where many young people identified with anti-colonial struggles in Algeria and South America), led the federal Liberals of Prime Minister Lester B. Pearson to form the Royal Commission on Bilingualism and Biculturalism. As a consequence of the findings of this commission, which demonstrated that the principle of equality between French and English had been systematically violated in the Canadian federation, the federal Liberal government of Pierre Elliott Trudeau passed the Official Languages Act in 1969. Emerging from its English dream, the Canadian state made clear through this act that English and French were the official languages of Canada, that public servants could use these languages at work (at least in many cases), and that most federal services were to be made available to Canadians in both languages. At the same time, the word *multiculturalism* was introduced as a way for the "third force" (i.e., non-French, non-British, and non-Indigenous immigrants and their descendants) to be symbolically recognized by the Canadian state. It too was the outcome of a struggle by these groups, especially Ukrainian-origin Canadians in the western provinces, for representation. By 1971, the Trudeau government announced a policy of "multiculturalism within a bilingual framework," which continues to the present day.

Although the province of Quebec has never received the constitutional recognition (or veto power) its leaders have continually sought, the 1982 Canadian Charter of Rights and Freedoms did give recognition to English and French as the two official languages (sections 16–22), official language minority education rights for French-speakers outside Quebec and English-speakers in Quebec (section 23), Aboriginal rights as recognized in the Royal Proclamation of 1763 (section 25), and the multicultural heritage of Canada (section 27).

The Charter, reflecting the value of human rights, also prohibited discrimination on the basis of race, ethnicity, gender, and mental or physical disability, among other grounds (section 15). Nonetheless, section 15 also allowed for the possibility of government programs designed to ameliorate disadvantage experienced by specific groups. This gave constitutional legitimacy to new programs, developed from the mid-1980s, dealing with employment equity for groups deemed to have been historically disadvantaged in the labour market. The specific focus of employment equity is on women, Indigenous peoples, visible minorities, and persons with a disability. Employment equity seeks to increase the numeric representation of these four groups in federally regulated corporations (such as banks, broadcasting, and airlines). Similar employment equity policies were also adopted in the mid-1980s to increase the numerical representation of the same groups in the public service itself and in companies doing business with the government (so-called federal contractors).

The federal government's prioritizing of certain groups for employment was not entirely new – for instance, in 1918 the Canadian government favoured the recruitment of male World War I veterans for jobs in the civil service. However, the consequences of employment equity for the four target groups have been uneven, depending on the group and the work sector. For example, in the federal public service visible minorities in particular have faced slow progress in achieving increased representation that corresponds to their numbers available for participation in the workforce (Abu-Laban 2006, 72–3; Block and Galabuzi 2011, 9–11; Treasury Board 2017). More broadly, the 1990s brought new challenges with the rise of neo-liberal ideology. Neo-liberalism emphasizes balanced budgets through cuts to social spending, asserts the necessity for individual self-sufficiency, and assumes markets are fair and efficient allocators of public goods. In this context, many identity-based groups (women, minorities, Indigenous peoples, etc.) were vilified for being "special interests" out of tune with "ordinary Canadians," and programs faced cuts and re-workings of their terms (Abu-Laban and Gabriel 2002). As one example, under these new terms it has been impossible to get funding for certain kinds of activities previously funded through multiculturalism, and it has been cumbersome for community groups, many relying on underpaid workers or overworked volunteers, to apply for money. As such, the 1980s-style human rights and equality agenda for ethnic minorities may be seen to have weakened, even though the Liberal government of Justin Trudeau has put more stress on combatting racism and inequality than the previous Conservative government of Stephen Harper (Abu-Laban and Gabriel 2002; Kobayashi 2008; Abu-Laban 2013).

However, the weakening of the human rights agenda does not mean that real inequality has disappeared. Consider the case of visible minorities. Census data from 2016 show that visible minorities earned only 81.2 per cent of what non-visible minorities earned in 2015, and this gap has actually grown by 2.5 percentage points since 2000 (Mahboubi 2017). This finding finds corroboration in other studies. For example, the Canadian Centre for Policy Alternatives showed that visible minorities have slightly higher rates of labour force participation than others (suggesting a desire to work) but they also experience much higher rates of unemployment, earn less income, are more likely to be in insecure and poorly paid jobs, and are much more likely to experience poverty than non-racialized minorities (Block and Galabuzi 2011, 3–5). Another earlier study found that while visible minorities in Canada were more likely than others to have university degrees and other post-secondary training, they nonetheless experienced higher unemployment and poverty rates, irrespective of whether they were foreign or Canadian-born (NVMCLFD 2004). Such findings in different surveys raise profound questions about racism and discrimination (NVMCLFD 2004) that are all the more pressing as the number of visible minorities projected to be part of the working population by 2036 is between 34.7 and 39.9 per cent (Statistics Canada, Demosim Team 2017).

Notwithstanding the focus of employment equity on so-called visible minorities, or shifts in the federal multiculturalism policy in the 1980s away from folkloric "song and dance" towards fighting racism (and more recently since the election of Justin Trudeau), for the most part ethnocultural and linguistic diversity are central to how the modern Canadian state has conceptualized "diversity" in its policies (Bloemraad 2006, 237–8; Abu-Laban 2018). In other words, "race" (or "racism") is not a primary focus but is secondary to "culture." Just as critically, the two (race and culture) are not automatically linked in policies or policy-making. This creates a situation whereby certain groups who cross traditionally conceived divides may fall outside the policy radar – for example, French-speaking visible minorities outside Quebec face compounded disadvantages that have yet to be adequately addressed through federal policy, as well as those of other levels of government (see M'pindou 2002; Abu-Laban and Couture 2010; Gallant 2010/11).

Likewise, redress for historic injustices and past policies has proven difficult to adequately address, even when there is acknowledgment of claims. For example, in recent years the Canadian state has engaged with redress claims (James 1999, 2004, 2013). This would include the 1988 federal apology and compensation for Japanese-Canadians who experienced internment during World War II; the 1996 apology by the federal government for the physical and sexual abuse often suffered by Indigenous children at residential schools that were run through the partnership of state and church; and the 2006 apology and compensation for Chinese-Canadians who experienced the "head tax." Moreover, in 2008 the federal government announced a Truth and Reconciliation Commission (TRC) on residential schools. Its purpose was to offer a space to acknowledge individual experiences and to foster reconciliation between Indigenous peoples and non-Indigenous Canadians, thus suggesting the potential value of South Africa's post-apartheid Truth and Reconciliation model for redressing Canada's settler-colonial legacies (Abu-Laban 2001). In 2015 the Truth and Reconciliation Commission of Canada, headed by (now Senator) Murray Sinclair, reported its findings and issued ninety-four Calls to Action touching on a wide range of Canadian institutions. As significant as the TRC may prove to be, the federal government has not dealt with Canadian history in a way that views colonial oppression as an overarching system that persists even in the present (Henderson and

Wakeham 2009, 2). Moreover, the federal government has yet to deal with all of the ninety-four Calls, including Call 53 to monitor progress on reconciliation. It is telling that in launching a website to monitor responses, CBC reported in March 2018 that in the nearly three years since the TRC Calls had been issued, a mere ten had been completed (Carreiro 2018), a situation that had not changed by January 2020 (CBC News 2020).

Despite these lingering challenges, in comparison with much of Canadian history, policies implemented since the 1960s have a much less overt and blunt assimilative edge. "Angloconformity" as an ideal has given way to human rights and pluralism. In light of shifting federal policy, it is clear that the politics of diversity are not static but dynamic, subject to change and ongoing contestation. This is also because the population of Canada itself is changing, as the 2016 Census reveals. Such complexities, along with the fact that despite its cultural emphasis, federal policy has had to deal with racism and historical redress, may help attune us as to how best to approach the study of diversity.

Diversity and the Evolving Canadian Political Science Tradition

For much of the post–World War II period, Canadian political scientists paid uneven attention to diversity, particularly on questions of race, immigrants, and Indigenous peoples. However, reflecting shifts since the late 1980s, in 2008 the Canadian Political Science Association (CPSA), the main national body representing political scientists across Canada, created a new conference section entitled "Race, Ethnicity, Indigenous Peoples, and Politics/Race, Ethnicité, Peuples Autochtones et Politique" (CPSA 2008). The presence of this section symbolizes the growing interest and scholarship of political scientists in themes such as diversity, multiculturalism, immigration, and Indigeneity (Harell and Stolle 2010; Banting 2010; Bird 2015; Paquet 2014; White et al. 2015; Ladner 2017).

Indeed, since the late 1980s, both political philosophers and empirical political scientists have developed distinct approaches to understanding and studying diversity. Perhaps reflecting the dominant emphasis of the Canadian state on themes of culture, "culture" is undoubtedly the central lens through which diversity has been viewed. Less prominent, but equally worthy of consideration, are two other approaches, one emphasizing "race" and the other emphasizing "colonialism." Each approach alerts us to different dimensions of power inequalities experienced by different groups, and as such it may be useful, and indeed desirable, to use them in combination to better understand diversity in Canada.

Turning first to the *lens of culture*, it is notable that in addition to reflecting the dominant organizing unit of the Canadian state, the cultural approach is central to a larger international debate generated by a "Canadian" contribution to political philosophy. In *The Rights Revolution* (2000, 11), Michael Ignatieff talks about how Canadians have been at the forefront both politically and intellectually in dealing with group rights. This intellectual expression of rights philosophy Ignatieff attributes specifically to, among others, Will Kymlicka, Charles Taylor, and James Tully, who defend group-based recognition for cultural minorities. The contribution of such Canadian thinkers to a global debate on multiculturalism is clear and evident (see, for example, Mansouri and De B'béri 2014).

This body of work is sensitive to power inequalities based on cultural difference – especially that of groups who fall outside the dominant culture and may utilize the language of nationalism (e.g., in Canada this would include the Québécois as well as Indigenous peoples). James Tully, for instance, has noted that demands for recognition by distinct cultural groups are based on a shared sense of longing for self-rule and a belief that the status quo is unjust (Tully 1997, 4–5). At the heart of the defence of recognition given by philosophers like Taylor and Kymlicka is the view that culture is centrally important to the quality of individual human existence. For example, Kymlicka argues that culture, stemming from a shared language and way of life, "provides people with meaningful options, and with a sense of belonging and identity that helps them negotiate the modern world" (1998, 96). Taylor also suggests that "we become full human agents capable of understanding ourselves, and hence of defining our identity, through our acquisition of rich human languages of expression" (1992, 32). Because belonging to a culture is seen to be so central, it forms the justification for recognizing difference and providing differentiated rights and citizenship.

The emphasis on culture as the basis for rights and difference has generated a particular criticism for opponents of multiculturalism working within the liberal paradigm: the official recognition of group rights on the basis of cultural identity might allow grounds to violate the rights of the individual, and in this respect it is an affront to liberalism (Fierlbeck 1996, 21). Others have added that the focus on cultural collectivities can strengthen the power of some members within the collectivity over others (e.g., men over women) and as such may be undemocratic. Canadian theorists like Avigail Eisenberg (2006) and Monique Deveaux (2006) have taken the lead in exploring and attempting to reconcile such potential tensions as those between gender justice and multiculturalism.

As a totality, the Canadian tradition has created greater space for political science scholarship on diversity than compared to the 1960s and 1970s. For example, the Royal Commission on Bilingualism and Biculturalism set the stage for what would eventually become Canada's bilingualism and multiculturalism policies, and through the 1960s and 1970s the multidisciplinary field of ethnic studies gained momentum. Yet in comparison with other disciplines, political scientists were not heavily involved (Palmer 1977, 173). Even in 1989, Gilbert H. Scott observed that "thus far, the study of multiculturalism has been pursued mainly by sociologists, anthropologists and historians. Other social scientists such as political scientists have largely ignored the area" (Scott 1989, 228).

Given this, the period since Scott's 1989 observation is somewhat remarkable, as multiculturalism and diversity moved on to the agenda of Canadian political science because of constitutional politics and the evident demands from ethnic minorities and Indigenous peoples (Cairns 1992; Abu-Laban and Nieguth 2000). After the failure of the Charlottetown Accord in 1992, when constitutional politics shifted to the back burner, issues surrounding diversity did not recede in the discipline's study of Canada. This may be seen to be related to the salience of these issues, underscored by the intellectual contribution of the political theorists discussed above.

On a less positive note, however, there are ways in which the work represented by the Canadian political theory tradition has tended to conflate – under the rubric of culture – race, ethnicity, language, and religion. As such, this work has not directly challenged a larger tendency in the discipline to take "ethnic" or "racial" groups as somehow a natural given. Indeed, in Rupert Taylor's (1999) scathing assessment of political science as an international discipline whose epicentre lies in the United States, he critiques both the limited extent that ethnicity and race have been studied in the discipline overall, and the manner in which race and ethnicity have been approached in that country. What concerns him are typical election studies that categorize in a very un-nuanced way "ethnic" or "racial" groups (e.g., the "Hispanic vote," the "ethnic vote," the "African-American vote"). For Rupert Taylor, political science cannot advance thinking without a different vision – the vision that has inspired the sociological study of race and ethnicity.

The sociological tradition emphasizes the socially constructed character of ethnic groups, racial groups, and other identity groups, and their contextual and historical variability. In particular, British sociologist Robert Miles (2000) has advanced the argument that race should not be treated as a "thing." To this end, Miles favours abandoning the use of the term *race* in favour of looking at the experience of racism and processes of racialization. Racialization is understood as a socially created and historically specific process whereby members (or perceived members) of certain groups are viewed by the majority as inferior by reason of their supposed biology. More recently, culture (and cultural difference or cultural inferiority) has been seen by scholars of race as playing a prominent role in contemporary expressions of racism and processes of racialization. For example, the idea of a "clash of civilizations" between the West and the Rest – or, more bluntly, Christianity and Islam (Huntington 1996) – has helped fuel some contemporary examples and discourses used by the far right (Betz 2002). British political theorist Tariq Modood, who is concerned specifically with the experiences of British Muslims, usefully distinguishes "colour" and "cultural" forms of racism. As he puts it, "There are of course colour or phenotype racisms but there are also cultural racisms which build on 'colour' a set of antagonistic or demeaning stereotypes based on alleged or real cultural traits" (Modood 2007, 44–5).

Drawing from these international currents, *the lens of "race"* and processes of racialization may be viewed as a second approach taken by Canadian political scientists. For many analysts concerned with racism and racialization, there is a sense that the Canadian policy emphasis on multiculturalism detracts from a focus on the reality of racism (Fernando 2006; Smith 2003). Moreover, an emphasis on cultural groups – insofar as this typically implies ethnicity, language, and nation – may be seen to detract from race or its intersection with other forms of diversity that generate inequality (Abu-Laban 2007; Thompson 2008; Dhamoon 2009; Nath 2011; Nath, Tungohan, and Gaucher 2018). For example, there are powerful ways in which "whiteness" has structured intellectual thought and power, as Bruce Baum (2006) shows in his genealogy of the meaning of *Caucasian*, a classification still used by the Canadian state. As well, an uncritical emphasis on cultural difference may fuel forms of racialization and differential treatment, especially in the post-9/11 climate (Abu-Laban 2002, 2004; Abu-Laban and Abu-Laban 2007; Abu-Laban 2017).

Political scientists working with race as a central concept have drawn attention to how race has played an important role in Canadian mythology, which ignores Canada's own history with slavery in favour of narratives stressing the role of Canadians in "rescuing" enslaved African-Americans (Bakan 2008). Likewise, analysts working with the lens of race have underscored its significance in socio-economic differences both in Quebec (Salée 2007) and Canada as a whole – what Grace Edward Galabuzi (2006) refers to as economic apartheid. A distinct aspect of the focus on race (as opposed to simply culture) is that analysts working in this tradition typically also are expressly concerned with identifying popular forms of combating racism (what is also referred to as anti-racism) rather than just taking existing power relations as a given (see, for example, Bakan and Kobayashi 2007; Abu-Laban 2007; Bakan and Dua 2014).

While "race" has emerged as an alternative lens to culture, yet another approach to consider would be one that uses the *lens of colonialism* and its legacies. The distinct characteristic of this approach is that it expressly draws attention to how inequalities emerged in the first place and links the past, and narratives of the past, to the present (Abu-Laban 2001, 2007; Ladner 2017; Nath, Tungohan, and Gaucher 2018). Although the themes of colonialism and post-colonialism permeate the work of many scholars dealing with contemporary Quebec and French Canada (Lamoureux, Maillé, and de Sève 1999; Maclure 2003; Desroches 2003; Gagnon 2004), in recent years it has been Indigenous scholars in particular who have explicitly insisted on the salience of colonialism as the lens for understanding Indigenous peoples and politics in Canada. Thus, for Taiaiake Alfred (1999, 2005), Canada remains a colonial state exerting power over the lives of Indigenous peoples in ways that are obvious (the Indian Act) and less obvious (from self-government arrangements to how the consumption of food today differs from traditional practices). This emphasis on colonialism as a lens through which to view both history and the present is also to be found in the writings of Joyce Green (1995), Kiera Ladner (2008) and Glen Coulthard (2010, 2014). The value of this perspective is that it automatically draws a clear connection between the history leading up to and emanating from the founding of Canada as a settler colony, as well as informing the ongoing current inequalities between settlers (whenever and however they came to Canada) and the Indigenous population (Snelgrove, Dhamoon, and Corntassel 2014; Battell Lowman and Barker 2015).

While anti-racist scholars have cautioned that the specific struggle of Indigenous peoples in Canada against colonialism is distinct from that of racialized immigrants and their descendants against racism (Dua 2008), it is arguable that the scholarly study of diversity needs to consider colonialism and racialization along with culture. Attending to the dominant foci of all three of these approaches can aid in understanding real and ongoing struggles that reflect power differentials. Such a multidimensional approach may also be consistent with approaches attuned to feminist intersectional understandings of identity and power (where it is understood that the experiences of women vary, depending on race, class, and other markers of difference) as well as anti-oppressive frameworks attuned to the ways people's lives may be marked by domination and disempowerment. In the next section, religion will be used to illustrate how a multidimensional approach considering culture, racialization, and colonialism may capture the complexity of power relations and policy-making in "diversity."

Religion, Power, and Complexity

Since September 11, 2001, *religion*, especially Islam, has emerged as a political flashpoint in international relations because of the American-led "war on terror." Canadian politics has not been immune. Although the presence of Muslims in Canada dates back to the latter half of the nineteenth century, since 9/11 their presence has been securitized through the reworking of state border and security policies (Abu-Laban 2004, 2005, 2017; Dobrowolsky, Rollings-Magnussen, and Doucet 2009). Media and popular representations of Muslim men tend to stereotype them as both dangerous and sexist, and Muslim women are stereotyped as passive and subjugated by Muslim men (Razack 2008). Additionally, after 9/11, media coverage of religion and Muslim-Canadians increased during elections, and specific surveys came to be devoted to the question of their voting preferences (Abu-Laban and Trimble 2006; Grenier 2016). Popular and partisan debates over "reasonable accommodation" of religious minorities in Quebec (especially heated in 2007–8) and over faith-based arbitration using shari'a law in Ontario (in 2005) offer just two examples of the politicization of religious difference. However, for well over a decade the niqab (a head and face covering worn by a very small minority of Muslim women) has emerged as a consistent theme across levels and branches of governance. The right to wear the niqab in voting was questioned by the former federal Conservative government of Stephen Harper in 2007 (CBC News 2007) and the right to wear the niqab in giving or receiving public services was a theme in legislation passed by the Liberal government of Philippe Couillard in Quebec in 2017, though legally halted for lack of clarity (Paperny 2017). Immediately following the 2018 election of a majority Coalition Avenir Québec government, Premier François Legault promised to use the notwithstanding clause to restrict the display of religious symbols in giving or receiving public services, and in June 2019 he passed Bill 21, aimed at eradicating religious symbols in the public sector including by banning the wearing of religious symbols by professionals like teachers, police officers, or judges. The right of a sexual assault victim to wear a niqab in testifying was denied even by the Supreme Court of Canada in a controversial 2012 decision (Chambers and Roth 2014).

Not least, the issue of wearing the niqab at citizenship ceremonies made its way into the 2015 national election, and is therefore worth exploring further in considering a multidimensional approach to diversity. In 2011 the government of Conservative Prime Minister Stephen Harper banned the extension of citizenship to any would-be Canadians not showing their face at a citizenship ceremony. That this ban was directed largely at immigrant women wearing the niqab was made clear in subsequent pronouncements regarding the ban, including by Prime Minister Harper who argued the niqab was "rooted in a culture that is anti-women" (cited in Kestler-D'Amours 2015). A 2015 federal court ruling that this ban violated religious freedom was one that the Conservative government vowed to appeal during the federal election campaign; however, following their defeat the new Trudeau Liberal government dropped any appeal and, as noted at the start of this chapter, has broadly emphasized the value of "diversity" to Canada.

What should we make of this? As this chapter has shown in the preceding historical discussion, religion has been one of many points of difference recognized through policies even prior to Confederation, and thus the twenty-first-century emphasis on religion (or religious difference) is not new. Religion, on the face of it, may seem to have everything to do with cultural difference rather than racism and how that structures material inequalities between groups or the impact of colonialism on historic relations between groups. However, a discussion framed primarily or only in relation to differences in values, beliefs, or culture may have limitations.

Consider, for example, the settler colony of Canada and Indigenous spirituality. Indigenous spirituality is tied to life-ways on the land and, as such, might be explored from the vantage point of culture and cultural difference in relation to Christianity or secularism. However, an exploration grounded only in relation to culture may miss some key realities. As religious studies professor David Seljak notes, in the Canadian context, "no community has suffered more from Christian hegemony than Canada's Aboriginal peoples" (Seljak 2007, 91). Residential schools epitomized the abuses of church and state, and were fuelled by both colonial practices and racism. The federal apology and compensation for residential schools, and even the Truth and Reconciliation Commission, may only go so far, because the Canadian state has yet to deal with a deeper issue that any recognition of traditional Aboriginal spirituality (tied to the land) inevitably involves recognition of land claims. The failure to address land claims is complex, involving power, colonialism, and racism. As such, "the conflict between Aboriginal peoples' definition of land, property and rights and that of mainstream Canadian society illustrates in the starkest terms the thorny issue of structural discrimination and the connection of the right to religious freedom to a host of broader public policy issues" (Seljak 2007, 91).

In the case of the niqab and citizenship ceremonies, discussions of the views and perspectives of Muslims, and specifically Muslim women who wear the niqab, were starkly absent from much of the public debate, as well as policy development. As such, it is hard to view the niqab citizenship ban only through the lens of culture, at least as it concerns the idea of cohesive groups making demands for differentiated rights and citizenship in the way described by many Canadian political theorists. Indeed, scholarly analysis by religious studies professor Lynda Clarke of the tiny fraction of Muslim women who do wear the niqab found that none felt forced to wear it. They did so out of individual religious conviction and exhibited a willingness to be flexible in relation to reasonable identification requirements (Kestler-D'Amours 2015). In this way, while the debate over the niqab and citizenship may at first glance seem to epitomize the demands for cultural recognition acknowledged by Canadian political theorists, it has peculiar features that do not neatly correspond to how analysts might envision group-based claims-making.

This then points to the relevance of extending beyond culture to think about power and racism in the post-9/11 period when national security concerns have been fuelled by arguments that there is an inevitable civilizational clash between the West and Islam (Abu-Laban 2017). In this particular climate, where Islam and terrorism have been so fused in the minds of many policy-makers and Canadians, culture offers a viable explanation only when it is linked with racialization and colonial discourses. While the presence of Muslims in Canada spans three centuries, the most recent available figures show that more than two-thirds (68 per cent) of Canadian Muslims are immigrants, and the vast majority (almost 90 per cent) are visible minorities under the federal government's definition (Environics 2016, 13). Given Modood's idea of the linkage of colour and cultural racism, it is notable that Peter Beyer's study of religion, education, and income finds that Muslim Canadians who immigrated since the 1970s and their Canadian-born children have among the lowest income levels of all religious groups, even though they have the second-highest rate of educational attainment (Beyer 2005). Muslim Canadians also suffer from one of the highest rates of unemployment, despite this high educational attainment (Government of Canada, Policy Research Initiative 2009, 83). They have been frequent targets of discrimination (Environics 2016, 3) as well as hate crimes, with the 2017 shooting deaths in the Islamic Cultural Centre in Quebec City being a graphic example. Therefore, to frame the question of Muslims and Canadian citizenship on the niqab debate as one of culture (or religious freedom) risks being silent on power as reflected in socio-economic status (their immigrant and visible minority status, their employment earnings, and their high unemployment rates) as well as racism.

It is equally relevant to consider contemporary power and anti-Muslim racism in relation to history and colonialism, and in particular the long-standing colonial discourses associated with "Orientalism." Orientalism is the term coined by Edward Said to explain the formation of Europe and its colonial expansion through stories, policies, and analyses that view the peoples and cultures of "the Orient" as exotic, dangerous, barbaric, irrational, and inferior to those of Europe (Said 1979). Sherene Razack has drawn attention to the relevance of racism and these older discourses of colonialism and empire in her attempt to understand why visible religious differences as concerns Islam and women have been such a flashpoint in the twenty-first century when they were not prior to 9/11 (2008, 174).

Given that the niqab debates have arisen largely in the absence of Muslim Canadians making any demand, analysts would do well to consider the insights drawn from discussions of culture alongside race and colonialism and, in the case of Muslim Canadians, the lingering relevance of Orientalism and the way it has been appropriated today into discourses purportedly supporting gender equality and LGBTQ rights. It is precisely these dimensions that help explain why diversity has increasingly been constructed as a threat to "Western values" in the twenty-first century. Such a focus might also invite consideration into how, at the popular level, resistance to these problematic and stereotyped understandings of Islam and Muslims is expressed by both state and non-state actors (see, for example, Abu-Laban 2002).

Conclusion

This chapter has addressed different policy responses of the Canadian state to diversity, as well as different approaches used by Canadian political scientists to understand diversity. As argued here, both the study of diversity and the responses to it say much about issues of power and the ongoing struggles of collectivities to overturn (or in some cases to reinforce) group-based differences. The responses to such inequalities have much to do with the nature of Canadian democracy and the inclusivity of the practices, policies, and institutions that underpin liberal democracy.

As this chapter has noted, culture has been a dominant frame of reference both for the Canadian state and for Canadian analysts. While culture is important for helping to identify existing inequalities, as this chapter has also pointed out, the demands of some groups also draw attention to racism, racialization, and anti-racism as a means of resistance. Additionally, other approaches draw attention to colonialism as a means for understanding the relationship between history and the present. This would suggest that as political scientists consider ways to best understand the politics of diversity, attention should be given to themes of culture along with race/racialization/anti-racism and colonialism. The value of such a multidimensional approach will help deal with the shifting terrain of state policies and of understandings of the ways in which people identify and make demands – some of which may have deep resonance in Canadian history. Such a multidimensional approach may also foster better and more inclusive dialogues across Canadian politics as well as in the sphere of policy-making. As well, a multidimensional approach may help deal with new perspectives and demands, as well as the new and hybrid forms of identity that Canadians may increasingly exhibit as their colleagues, friends, family, and acquaintances reflect both historic and new forms of diversity that characterize twenty-first-century Canada in a globalizing world. Not least, such a multidimensional approach may also alert us to distinguish between actual demands and attributed demands, as in the case of the ballot box and the niqab.

As it stands, and returning to where this chapter began, the ongoing politicization of the presence and value of diversity shows no signs of abating in national elections and Canadian politics. As this chapter has suggested, the study of diversity has become increasingly prominent within scholarship in Canadian political science. As a result, Canadian political scientists now confront new questions that involve consideration of the impact of historic and contemporary state policies, as well as the analytical approach (or approaches) that may best yield understanding of power and group-based inequities in studying diversity in Canadian politics.

References and Suggested Readings

Abu-Laban, Yasmeen. 2001. "The Future and the Legacy: Globalization and the Canadian Settler State." *Journal of Canadian Studies* 35 (4) (2000–1): 262–76.

———. 2002. "Liberalism, Multiculturalism, and the Problem of Essentialism." *Citizenship Studies* 6 (4): 459–82.

———. 2004. "The New North America and the Segmentation of Canadian Citizenship." *International Review of Canadian Studies* 29:17–40.

———. 2005. "Regionalism, Migration, and Fortress North America." *Review of Constitutional Studies* 10 (1–2): 135–62.

———. 2006. "Stalemate at Work: Visible Minorities and Employment Equity." In *New Citizens, New Policies: Developments in Diversity Policy in Canada and Flanders*, edited by Leen d'Haenenks, Marc Hooghe, Dirk Vanheule, and Hasibe Gezduci, 71–87. Ghent: Academia.

———. 2007. "Political Science, Race, Ethnicity, and Public Policy." In *Critical Policy Studies*, edited by Michael Orsini and Miriam Smith, 137–57. Vancouver: UBC Press.

———. 2013. "On the Borderlines of Human and Citizen: The Liminal State of Arab Canadians." In *Targeted Transnationals: The State, the Media and Arab Canadians*, edited by Bessma Momani and Jenna Hennebry, 68–88. Vancouver: UBC Press.

———. 2017. "Civic Virtue and Cultural Pluralism from the Standpoint of the Other: Debating Multiculturalism in the Age of Security and Surveillance." In *Citizenship and Multiculturalism in Western Liberal Democracies*, edited by David Edward Tabachnick and Leah Bradshaw, 119–36. Lanham, MA: Lexington.

———. 2018. "Recognition, Re-distribution and Solidarity: The Case for Multicultural Canada." In *Diversity and Contestations over Nationalism in Europe and Canada*, edited by John Erik Fossum, Riva Kastoryano, and Birte Siim, 237–62. London: Palgrave Macmillan.

Abu-Laban, Yasmeen, and Baha Abu-Laban. 2007. "Reasonable Accommodation in a Global Village." *Policy Options* (September): 28–33.

Abu-Laban, Yasmeen, and Claude Couture. 2010. "Multiple Minorities and Deceptive Dichotomies: The Theoretical and Political Implications of the Struggle for a Public French Education System in Alberta." *Canadian Journal of Political Science* 43 (2): 433–56.

Abu-Laban, Yasmeen, and Christina Gabriel. 2002. *Selling Diversity: Immigration, Multiculturalism, Employment Equity, and Globalization.* Peterborough, ON: Broadview.

Abu-Laban, Yasmeen, and Tim Nieguth. 2000. "Reconsidering the Constitution, Minorities and Politics in Canada." *Canadian Journal of Political Science* 33 (3): 465–97.

Abu-Laban, Yasmeen, and Linda Trimble. 2006. "Print Media Coverage of Muslim-Canadians at Recent Federal Elections." *Electoral Insight* 8 (2): 35–42.

Alfred, Taiaiake. 1999. *Peace, Power, Righteousness: An Indigenous Manifesto.* Don Mills, ON: Oxford University Press.

———. 2005. *Wasasé: Indigenous Pathways of Action and Freedom.* Peterborough, ON: Broadview.

Bakan, Abigail B. 2008. "Reconsidering the Underground Railway: Slavery and Racialization in the Making of the Canadian State." *Socialist Studies* 4 (1): 3–29.

Bakan, Abigail B., and Enakshi Dua, eds. 2014. *Theorizing Anti-Racism: Linkages in Marxism and Critical Race Theory.* Toronto: University of Toronto Press.

Bakan, Abigail B., and Audrey Kobayashi. 2007. "'The Sky Didn't Fall': Organizing to Combat Racism in the Workplace: The Case of the Alliance for Employment Equity." In *Race, Racialization, and Antiracism in Canada and Beyond,* edited by Genevieve Fuji Johnson and Randy Enomoto, 51–78. Toronto: University of Toronto Press.

Banting, Keith. 2010. "Is There a Progressive's Dilemma in Canada? Immigration, Multiculturalism and the Welfare State (Presidential Address to the Canadian Political Science Association). *Canadian Journal of Political Science* 43 (4): 797–820.

Battell Lowman, Emma, and Adam J. Barker. 2015. *Settler Identity and Colonialism in 21st Century Canada.* Halifax: Fernwood.

Baum, Bruce. 2006. *The Rise and Fall of the Caucasian Race.* New York: New York University Press.

Betz, Hans Georg. 2002. "Xenophobia, Identity Politics, and Exclusionary Populism in Western Europe." In *Fighting Identities: Race, Religion, and Ethno-Nationalism: Socialist Register 2003,* edited by Leo Panitch and Colin Leys, 193–210. London: Merlin.

Beyer, Peter. 2005. "Religious Identity and Educational Attainment among Recent Immigrants to Canada: Gender, Age, and 2nd Generation." *Journal of International Migration and Integration* 6 (2): 177–99.

Bird, Karen. 2015. "'We are Not an Ethnic Vote!' Representational Perspectives of Minorities in the Greater Toronto Area." *Canadian Journal of Political Science* 48 (2): 249–79.

Block, Sheila, and Grace-Edward Galabuzi. 2011. *Canada's Colour Coded Labour Market: The Gap for Racialized Workers.* Ottawa: Canadian Centre for Policy Alternatives.

Bloemraad, I. 2006. *Becoming a Citizen: Incorporating Immigrants and Refugees in the United States and Canada.* Berkeley: University of California Press.

Cairns, Alan C. 1992. *Charter versus Federalism: The Dilemmas of Constitutional Reform.* Montreal and Kingston: McGill-Queen's University Press.

Canadian Political Science Association. 2008. "CPSA 2009 Conference Section: Race, Ethnicity, Indigenous Peoples, and Politics." POLCAN email communiqué, April 16.

Cardin, Jean-François, and Claude Couture. 1996. *Histoire du Canada: Espace et Différences.* Québec: Les Presses de l'Université Laval.

Cardozo, Andrew, and Louis Musto, eds. 1997. *The Battle over Multiculturalism: Does It Help or Hinder Canadian Unity?* Ottawa: Pearson-Shoyama Institute.

Carreiro, Donna. 2018. "Beyond 94: Where Is Canada at with Reconciliation?" CBC.ca, March 19. https://www.cbc.ca/news/indigenous/beyond-94-truth-and-reconciliation-1.4574765.

CBC News. 2007. "Harper Slams Elections Canada Ruling on Veils." CBC News, September 9. https://www.cbc.ca/news/canada/harper-slams-elections-canada-ruling-on-veils-1.648173.

———. 2018. "Maxime Bernier Explains What He Means by 'Extreme Multiculturalism,'" September 21. https://www.cbc.ca/radio/asithappens/as-it-happens-friday-edition-1.4833110/maxime-bernier-explains-what-he-means-by-extreme-multiculturalism-1.4833113.

———. 2020. "Beyond 94," January 22. https://newsinteractives.cbc.ca/longform-single/beyond-94?&cta=1.

Chambers, Lori, and Jen Roth. 2014. "Prejudice Unveiled: The Niqab in Court." *Canadian Journal of Law and Society* 29 (3): 381–95.

Coulthard, Glen. 2010. "Place against Empire: Understanding Indigenous Anti-Colonialism." *Affinities: A Journal of Radical Theory, Culture and Action* 2 (Fall): 79–83.

———. 2014. *Red Skins, White Masks: Rejecting the Colonial Politics of Recognition.* Minneapolis: University of Minnesota Press.

Day, Richard J.F. 2000. *Multiculturalism and the History of Canadian Diversity.* Toronto: University of Toronto Press.

Desroches, Vincent. 2003. "Présentation: En quoi la littérature québécoise est-elle postcoloniale?" *Quebec Studies* 30 (Spring/Summer): 3–14.

Deveaux, Monique. 2006. *Gender and Justice in Multicultural Liberal States.* Oxford: Oxford University Press.

Dhamoon, Rita. 2009. *Identity/Difference Politics: How Difference Is Produced and Why It Matters.* Vancouver: UBC Press.

Dickason, Olive P. 1992. *Canada's First Nations: A History of Founding Peoples from Earliest Times.* Toronto: McClelland and Stewart.

Dobrowolsky, Alexandra, Sandra Rollings-Magnussen, and Marc G. Doucet. 2009. "Security, Insecurity and Human Rights: Contextualizing Post 9/11." In *Anti-Terrorism: Security and Insecurity after 9/11*, 13–31. Halifax: Fernwood Publishing.

Dua, Enakshi. 2008. "Thinking Through Anti-Racism and Indigeneity in Canada." *Ardent* 1 (1): 31–5.

Eisenberg, Avigail, ed. 2006. *Diversity and Equality: The Changing Framework of Freedom in Canada.* Vancouver: UBC Press.

Environics Institute for Survey Research. 2016. *Survey of Muslims in Canada, 2016: Final Report* (April).

Fekete, Jason. 2010. "Census Consensus Eludes Premiers: Several Scold Harper." *Gazette*, August 6. http://www.montrealgazette.com/news/Census+consensus+eludes+premiers+Several+scold+Harper/3369649/story.html.

Fernando, Shanti. 2006. *Race and the City: Chinese Canadian and Chinese American Political Mobilization.* Vancouver: UBC Press.

Fierlbeck, Katherine. 1996. "The Ambivalent Potential of Cultural Identity." *Canadian Journal of Political Science* 29: 3–22.

Gagnon, Alain-G., ed. 2004. *Québec: State and Society.* 3rd ed. Toronto: University of Toronto Press.

Galabuzi, Grace-Edward. 2006. *Canada's Economic Apartheid: The Social Exclusion of Racialized Groups in the New Century.* Toronto: Canadian Scholars' Press.

Gallant, Nicole. 2010/2011. "Communautés francophones en milieu minoritaire et immigrants: entre ouverture et inclusion." *Revue du Nouvel-Ontario* 35–6: 69–105.

Government of Canada, Policy Research Initiative. 2009. "Religious Diversity in Canada." *Horizons* 10 (2) (March).

Green, Joyce A. 1995. "Towards a Détente with History: Confronting Canada's Colonial Legacy." *International Journal of Canadian Studies* 12 (Fall): 85–105.

Green, Joyce A., and Ian Peach. 2007. "Beyond 'Us' and 'Them': Prescribing Postcolonial Politics and Policy in Saskatchewan." In *Belonging? Diversity, Recognition, and Shared Citizenship in Canada*, edited by Keith Banting, Thomas J. Courchene, and F. Leslie Seidle, 263–84. Montreal: Institute for Research on Public Policy.

Grenier, Éric. 2020. "Dozens of People's Party Riding Associations Deregistered." CBC.ca, Feburary 24. https://www.cbc.ca/news/politics/ppc-eda-deregistration-1.5473896.

Grenier, Éric. 2016. "Liberals Won Over Muslims by a Huge Margin in 2015, Poll Suggests." CBC.ca, April 29. https://www.cbc.ca/news/politics/grenier-environics-muslims-politics-1.3555216.

Harell, Allison, and Dietlind Stolle. 2010. "Diversity and Democratic Politics: An Introduction." *Canadian Journal of Political Science* 43 (2): 235–56.

Henderson, Jennifer, and Pauline Wakeham. 2009. "Colonial Reckoning, National Reconciliation? Aboriginal Peoples and the Culture of Redress in Canada." *English Studies in Canada* 35 (1): 1–26.

Huntington, Samuel. 1996. *The Clash of Civilizations: Remaking of World Order*. New York: Simon and Shuster.

Ignatieff, Michael. 2000. *The Rights Revolution*. Toronto: Anansi.

James, Matt. 1999. "Redress Politics and Canadian Citizenship." In *The State of the Federation 1998/99: How Canadians Connect*, edited by Harvey Lazar and Tom McIntosh, 247–81. Montreal and Kingston: McGill-Queen's University Press.

———. 2004. "Recognition, Redistribution, and Redress: The Case of the 'Chinese Head Tax.'" *Canadian Journal of Political Science* 37 (4): 883–902.

———. 2013. "Neoliberal Heritage Redress." In *Reconciling Canada: Critical Perspectives on the Culture of Redress*, edited by Jennifer Henderson and Pauline Wakeham, 31–46. Toronto: University of Toronto Press.

Kestler-D'Amours, Jillian. 2015. "Muslim Women in Canada Explain Why They Wear a Niqab." *Toronto Star*, March 13. https://www.thestar.com/news/canada/2015/03/13/muslim-women-in-canada-explain-why-they-wear-a-niqab.html.

Kobayashi, Audrey. 2008. "Ethnocultural Political Mobilization, Multiculturalism, and Human Rights in Canada." In *Group Politics and Social Movements in Canada*, edited by Miriam Smith, 131–57. Peterborough, ON: Broadview.

Kymlicka, Will. 1998. *Finding Our Way: Rethinking Ethnocultural Relations in Canada*. Toronto: Oxford University Press.

———. 2007. "Ethnocultural Diversity in a Liberal State: Making Sense of the Canadian Models." In *Belonging? Diversity, Recognition, and Shared Citizenship in Canada*, edited by Keith Banting, Thomas J. Courchene, and F. Leslie Seidle, 39–104. Montreal: Institute for Research on Public Policy.

Ladner, Kiera L. 2008. "*Aysaka'paykinit*: Contesting the Rope around the Nations' Neck." In *Group Politics and Social Movements in Canada*, edited by Miriam Smith, 227–49. Peterborough, ON: Broadview.

———. 2017. "Taking the Field: 50 Years of Indigenous Politics in *CJPS*." *Canadian Journal of Political Science* 50 (1): 163–79.

Lamoureux, Diane, Chantal Maillé, and Micheline de Sève. 1999. *Malaises identitaires: Échanges féministes autour d'un Québec incertain*. Montreal: Remue-ménage.

Mackenzie King, William Lyon. 1947. "Hansard (Thursday, 1 May)." In *A Report of the Canadian Immigration and Population Study*. Vol. 2, *The Immigration Program*, edited by Canada, Manpower and Immigration, 201–7. Ottawa: Information Canada, 1974.

Maclure, Jocelyn. 2003. *Quebec Identity*. Montreal and Kingston: McGill-Queen's University Press.

Mahboubi, Parisa. 2017. "What Is to Blame for the Widening Racial Earnings Gap?" *Globe and Mail*, November 13. https://www.theglobeandmail.com/report-on-business/rob-commentary/what-is-to-blame-for-the-widening-racial-earnings-gap/article36945869/.

Mansouri, Fehti, and Boulou Ebanda De B'béri, eds. 2014. *Global Perspectives on the Politics of Multiculturalism in the 21st Century: A Case Study Analysis*. New York: Milton Park.

Miles, Robert. 2000. "Apropos the Idea of 'Race' Again." In *Theories of Race and Racism: A Reader*, edited by Les Back and John Solomos, 125–43. London: Routledge.

Modood, Tariq. 2007. *Multiculturalism: A Civic Idea*. Cambridge: Polity.

M'pindou, Jacques Luketa. 2002. "La Jeunesse congolaise dans la société canadienne." In *L'Alberta et le multiculturalisme francophone: témoignages et problématiques*, edited by Claude Couture and Josée Bergeron, 33–6. Edmonton: Canadian Studies Institute.

Nath, Nisha. 2011. "Defining Narratives of Identity in Canadian Political Science: Accounting for the Absence of Race." *Canadian Journal of Political Science* 44 (1): 161–93.

Nath, Nisha, Ethel Tungohan, and Megan Gaucher. 2018. "The Future of Canadian Political Science: Boundary Transgressions, Gender and Anti-Oppression Frameworks." *Canadian Journal of Political Science* 51 (3): 610–42.

National Visible Minority Council on Labour Force Development (NVMCLFD). 2004. *Building Our Future Workforce: A Background Paper on Visible Minority Labour Force Development*. Ottawa: NVMCLFD.

Palmer, Howard. 1977. "History and Present State of Ethnic Studies in Canada." In *Identities: The Impact of Ethnicity on Canadian Society*, edited by Wsevolod Isajiw, 167–83. Canadian Ethnic Studies Association. Toronto: Peter Martin.

Paperny, Anna Mehler. 2017. "Canadian Judge Suspends Quebec Niqab Ban." Reuters, December 2. https://www.reuters.com/article/us-canada-religion-quebec-lawsuit/canadian-judge-suspends-quebec-niqab-ban-idUSKBN1DW01B (link no longer active).

Paquet, Mireille. 2014. "The Federalization of Immigration and Integration in Canada." *Canadian Journal of Political Science* 47 (3): 519–48.

Razack, Sherene. 2008. *Casting Out: The Eviction of Muslims from Western Law and Politics*. Toronto: University of Toronto Press.

Said, Edward. 1979. *Orientalism*. New York: Vintage Books.

Salée, Daniel. 2007. "The Quebec State and the Management of Ethnocultural Diversity: Perspectives on an Ambiguous Record." In *Belonging? Diversity, Recognition, and Shared Citizenship in Canada*, edited by Keith Banting, Thomas J. Courchene, and F. Leslie Seidle, 105–42. Montreal: Institute for Research on Public Policy.

Scott, Gilbert H. 1989. "Race Relations and Public Policy: Uncharted Course." In *Canada 2000: Race Relations and Public Policy*, edited by O.P. Dwivedi, Ronald D'Costa, C. Lloyd Stanford, and Elliot Tepper, 227–32. Guelph, ON: Department of Political Studies, University of Guelph.

Seljak, David. 2007. "Religion and Multiculturalism in Canada: The Challenge of Religious Intolerance and Discrimination." Report prepared for the Department of Canadian Heritage. Strategic Policy, Research and Planning Directorate, Multiculturalism and Human Rights Program. Ottawa: Department of Canadian Heritage.

Siddiqui, Haroon. 2010. "Gutting of Census Stirs Opposition to Stephen Harper." *Toronto Star*, July 10. http://www.thestar.com/news/canada/2010/07/10/siddiqui_gutting_of_census_stirs_opposition_to_stephen_harper.html.

Smith, Malinda. 2003. "'Race Matters' and 'Race Manners.'" In *Reinventing Canada*, edited by Janine Brodie and Linda Trimble, 108–29. Toronto: Prentice Hall.

Snelgrove, Corey, Rita Dhamoon, and Jeff Corntassel. 2014. "Unsettling Settler-Colonialism: The Discourse and Politics of Settlers, and Solidarity with Indigenous Nations." *Decolonization: Indigeneity, Education and Society* 3 (2): 1–32.

Stasiulis, Daiva, and Radha Jhappan. 1995. "The Fractious Politics of a Settler Society: Canada." In *Unsettling Settler Societies: Articulations of Gender, Race, Ethnicity, and Class*, edited by Daiva Stasiulis and Nira Yuval-Davis, 95–131. London: Sage.

Statistics Canada. 2017a. *Ethnic and Cultural Origins of Canadians: Portrait of a Rich Heritage*. Ottawa: Minister of Industry.

———. 2017b. *Focus on Geography Series, 2016 Census*. Statistics Canada catalogue no. 98-404-X2016001. Ottawa: Data Products, 2016 Census.

———. 2017c. "Immigration and Ethnocultural Diversity: Key Results from the 2016 Census." *Daily*, October 25.

Statistics Canada, Demosim Team. 2017. *Immigration and Diversity: Population Projections for Canada and Its Regions, 2011 to 2036*. Catalogue no. 91-551-X. Ottawa: Minister of Industry.

Taylor, Charles. 1992. "The Politics of Recognition." In *Multiculturalism and the Politics of Recognition*, edited by Amy Gutmann, 25–73. Princeton, NJ: Princeton University Press.

Taylor, Rupert. 1999. "Political Science Encounters 'Race' and 'Ethnicity.'" In *Ethnic and Racial Studies Today*, edited by Martin Bulmer and John Solomos, 115–23. London: Routledge.

Thompson, Debra. 2008. "Is Race Political?" *Canadian Journal of Political Science* 41 (3): 525–47.

Treasury Board of Canada Secretariat. 2017. *Building a Diverse and Inclusive Public Service: Final Report (Joint Union/Management Task Force on Diversity and Inclusion)*. Ottawa: Treasury Board of Canada Secretariat.

Trudeau, Justin. 2016. Address to the 71st Session of the United Nations General Assembly, September 20.

Truth and Reconciliation Commission of Canada. 2015. *Truth and Reconciliation Commission of Canada: Calls to Action*.

Tully, James. 1997. *Strange Multiplicity: Constitutionalism in an Age of Diversity*. Cambridge: Cambridge University Press.

Whitaker, Reg, Gregory S. Kealey, and Andrew Parnaby. 2012. *Secret Service: Political Policing in Canada from the Fenians to Fortress America*. Toronto: University of Toronto Press.

Whittington, Les. 2012. "Visible Minorities Increasing in Canada." *Toronto Star*, May 17. http://www.thestar.com/news/canada/2012/05/17/visible_minorities_increasing_in_canada.html.

White, Stephen, Michael M. Atkinson, Loleen Berdahl, and David McGrane. 2015. "Public Policies toward Aboriginal Peoples: Attitudinal Obstacles and Uphill Battles." *Canadian Journal of Political Science* 48 (2): 281–304.

eighteen
Of Pots and Pans and Radical Handmaids: Social Movements and Civil Society[1]

MICHAEL ORSINI

If you're in costume, even 10 people is a visible demonstration.
– Julie Lalonde of the Radical Handmaids

Knowing a lot of social movement theory does not make a good activist.
– J. Pickerill and J. Krinsky

Introduction

Social movement activism comes in many shapes and sizes. From the tent communities inspired by the Occupy movement's efforts to expose corporate greed to the pot-clanging student protests in 2012 that paralyzed Quebec during the Printemps érable, to the theatrical antics of the Ottawa-based feminist collective the Radical Handmaids, it has been a busy time for social movement actors vying for public and media attention in Canada. How should we interpret these seemingly increasing episodes of protest activity, especially in light of concerns that social movements are "past their apex" (Phillips 1999)? Are these simply isolated pockets of protest that, like other movements, come and go? Is neo-liberalism and the attendant retreat of the welfare state to blame for the emergence of many of these movements?

While critics are quick to point out that movements tend to attract an assortment of generally disgruntled people, there are also signs that citizens who might be less accustomed to protest are swelling the ranks of some movements, as was argued in a CBC Fifth Estate documentary, "You Should Have Stayed at Home," which focused on the controversial arrests of several anti-G20 demonstrators in 2010 in Toronto (CBC 2011). It is common – almost fashionable – to criticize movements for being unclear or confused regarding what they seek in concrete goals. And while it is appropriate to ask what movements are demanding, it is equally critical to recognize that movements, by their very nature, reflect competing and nascent demands, employ a "diversity of tactics" (Conway 2003), and expend a great deal of their activist energy figuring out exactly what they want. Viewing movements in a narrow, instrumental sense as focused solely on scoring policy victories or on transforming, broad-scale value change, as political scientists often do, misses a crucial feature of social movement activism: movements are as much concerned with *how* they do things as with *why* they engage in activism. The Occupy movement, discussed later in the chapter, is an excellent example.

This chapter introduces the reader to the changing landscape of social movement activism in Canada and examines whether we need new tools and concepts to grapple with a rapidly evolving social movement field. Drawing on Staggenborg (2008), I discuss the Canadian social movement by distinguishing three levels of analysis: macro (large-scale), meso (organizational), and micro (individual). While there are important connections between these three levels of analysis, each level asks specific questions that can help us to unpack the dynamic and evolving world of social movement activism. The macro level, which is of particular interest to political scientists, focuses on how large-scale structures influence movements. The meso (or organizational) level allows us to appreciate the role of internal factors in explaining movement strategies and outcomes, as well as interactions among and between social movement organizations, while the micro level informs, among other issues, the subjective experience of activism on individuals themselves. The goal here is not to privilege one level of analysis but to group some of the issues and challenges faced by social movements in terms of these levels of analysis.

Drawing on contemporary and historical examples, including the Black Lives Matter movement, Idle No More Indigenous organizing, feminist activism, and the Quebec student movement, I explore whether we need to employ new theoretical and analytical tools to understand this dynamic social movement arena. Specifically, I suggest that the study of social movements can benefit from greater engagement with how emotions shape collective action and movement actors themselves, which corresponds primarily with the micro level of analysis identified above. While there is general agreement that citizens and elected officials alike are "moved" by emotional appeals, there has been a general reluctance to bring emotions into our analytical toolkits. It is perhaps not surprising that scholars have been slow to integrate emotions, given that social movement theory itself emerged in response to approaches that sought to explain the rise of movements as little more than irrational outbursts of time and place (see Flam and King 2005; Gould 2009; Jasper 1998, 2011; Orsini and Wiebe 2014).

Political scientists have long lamented the "decline of deference" (Nevitte 2000) and the ensuing drift from participation in traditional democratic institutions (e.g., voting and membership in political parties) toward increased engagement with social movements and organized interest groups. This explanation fails to appreciate, however, what exactly is going on in this crowded social movement field, not to mention the important links or disjunctures between and among social movements, and between social movements and democratic institutions. Many movement actors challenge state authority, but others seek to bypass the state altogether, which is itself a political act. Moreover, in addition to looking at the more familiar movements that provoke a strong police presence and media attention, I examine forms of protest that often escape the mass media glare but provide equally dramatic expressions of new forms of solidarity and organizing that might be adopted later by other movements. One example is a feminist collective, the Radical Handmaids. Furthermore, there are important tensions between and among progressive social movements, as was clearly demonstrated when activists associated with the Black Lives Matter (BLM) movement clashed with Pride Parade organizers in Toronto. BLM (Toronto) demanded a ban on police officers marching in uniform or carrying guns, to underscore the effects of police violence on Black and other racialized populations (Walcott 2017). They were also highlighting how many LGBTQ+ people in racialized communities do not enjoy the same rights afforded to white queers.

Before moving on to the three fields of analysis outlined above (macro, meso, and micro), I begin by identifying some key concepts discussed in the social movement literature.

Clarifying Terms

Pinning down a solid definition of a social movement is challenging, given the competing interpretations jockeying for position. For the purposes of this chapter, I use della Porta and Diani's definition, as it best captures the dynamic nature of movements. Social movements, they note, are "informal networks, based on shared beliefs and solidarity, which mobilize about conflictual issues, through the frequent use of various forms of protest" (della Porta and Diani 1999, 16).[2] Social movements include formal social movement organizations (SMOs) as well as loose networks of activists connected to a movement's broad goals but perhaps not linked to a formal organizational structure. Social movements often rely on these networks, which they can mobilize at a moment's notice. Empirically, however, we cannot isolate a social movement in the same way that we can study a social movement organization. Indeed, we must be careful not to view a social movement as the unit of analysis, treating action as though there are no actors: "Every empirical phenomenon offers us a cross-section of a social structure, rather like a split in a rock reveals its inner composition and strata. Just as a photograph of a rock as a whole cannot be confused with the minerals and strata that compose it, so collective phenomena do not disclose their meaning to us if we only consider them in their totality" (Melucci 1994, 106).[3] Therefore, the study of social movements should encompass a careful understanding of the organizations that populate the movement, the subjective interpretations of movement participants themselves, and the interactions among movement participants and between movement participants and authorities.

Another important distinction is between interest groups and social movements.[4] Sometimes, for instance, the two terms are folded into a broader notion of civil society and used interchangeably to emphasize their similarities (Smith 2005a; see Laforest 2011 for a discussion of the "voluntary sector" in Canada). It is nonetheless useful to provide at least some conceptual clarity on potential differences in the use of the two terms, recognizing that each represents a form of collective action outside the formal political party system. Schwartz and Paul (1992, 221–2) identify two key factors that help to distinguish interest groups from movements:

> Interest groups always work with institutionally mandated authorities and follow prescribed institutional procedures for accomplishing their goal. Social movements may do this, but they may also break rules and disrupt normal processes in an effort to achieve this end.
>
> Interest groups may call upon their constituency for active support, but their predominant and perhaps exclusive modus operandi is interaction between group leaders and responsible officials. Social movements rely in some way on mass mobilization of their constituency to accomplish their goals, though membership action may be as moderate as petition signing.

Finally, there are various ways to classify movements. McCarthy and Wolfson distinguish conflict and consensus movements. Within the social movement literature, there is a bias for conflict-oriented movements, which are "typically supported by minorities or slim majorities of populations and confront fundamental, organized opposition in attempting to bring about social change" (McCarthy and Wolfson 1992, 273). Examples include the feminist, civil rights, and labour movements. Consensus movements, on the other hand, are defined as "those organized movements for change that find widespread support for their goals and little or no organized opposition from the population of a geographic community" (273).

A second distinction is between identity-oriented and strategy-oriented movements (see Cohen 1985). Identity-oriented movements, often termed new social movements (NSMs), are described as relating "to other political actors and opponents not in terms of negotiations, compromise, reform, improvement or gradual progress to be brought about by organizational pressures and tactics, but, rather, in terms of sharp antinomies such as yes/no, them/us, the desirable and the tolerable, victory or defeat, now or never, etc." (Offe 1985, 829). NSMs are presumed to be disinterested in the economy or the state, display post-material values and a concern with quality-of-life issues. Strategy-oriented movements, on the other hand, have been associated with more instrumental action centred on the economy and the state. In reality, movements employ elements of both strategy and identity in their repertoires of contention, rather than being reducible to one or the other.

Macro Level: Seeing the Big Picture

A focus on a movement's external environment helped scholars to appreciate that it was insufficient to isolate the resources internal to a movement to explain its success or failure, as early proponents of resource mobilization theory had done (Eisinger 1973; Tarrow 1994, 1998; Orsini 2002). The key term employed by advocates of a broader approach is *political opportunity structure*. As Tarrow explains (1994, 18), the concept of political opportunity emphasizes resources external to the group – unlike money or power – that can be taken advantage of by weak or disorganized challengers. Social movements form when ordinary citizens, sometimes encouraged by leaders, respond to changes in opportunities that lower the cost of collective action, reveal potential allies, and show where elites and authorities are vulnerable.

To speak of a structure of political opportunity is a misnomer, since opportunities are always "situational" or context-dependent. Nonetheless, the concept is useful because it helps us to understand how mobilization can move from actors with deep-seated grievances and an abundance of resources to those with fewer grievances and less-than-adequate resources.

Movements, of course, operate in a context not entirely of their own making. As Jenson correctly described, actors are "simultaneously subjects of structures and acting subjects carrying in their practices and meaning systems the possibilities of both social stability and change" (Jenson 1989, 236). The structure of federalism in Canada, for instance, is a permanent feature of the institutional context in which movements must operate. But it is not static or fixed. While there are differing views on whether federal systems offer more institutional openings for movements, or muddy the waters for movement actors who must decide whether to focus on the provincial or federal scale, or ignore this altogether in favour of transnational action (Jenson and Papillon 2000), federalism is a structural feature of the political environment that is part of the furniture, so to speak. Movements might try to exploit opportunities afforded by the federal system, but they would be hard pressed to ignore it.

Meso Level: Finding the Middle Ground

A focus on the meso level brings sustained attention to the internal organizational dynamics at work in the social movement field. First, movement actors typically identify goals and desired outcomes. Gamson (1975), for instance, distinguishes two general types of movement goals: simple versus multiple, and displacing versus non-displacing. The dilemma for many movements is choosing between a single issue or addressing a wide range of grievances (in the Quebec student movement, seeking cancellation of a tuition hike or contesting the form of governance in the province). Each strategy has its strengths and weaknesses. Single-issue organizations that achieve their goal may have greater difficulty in attracting a broad base of support than they would if they were addressing multiple issues. On the other hand, an organization pursuing a single issue can more successfully stave off dissension and factionalism within its ranks. A multiple-issue approach allows an organization that has achieved a particular goal to shift its energies to other goals, thus providing some organizational longevity. Alternatively, multiple-issue organizations may spread their resources and energies too thin (Marx and McAdam 1994, 109). Of the second type of goal, displacing versus non-displacing, Gamson is referring to a movement's attitude toward its opponents. Displacing goals seek to remove or replace the group's opponents.

Movement actors must also choose from three types of action: institutionalized versus non-institutionalized action, legal versus illegal, and non-violent versus violent. According to Marx and McAdam (1994), if a social movement organization chooses to advance its interests through the "proper channels," it does not qualify as a social movement. Such an approach, however, freezes out the possibility that movements may blend the institutional with the non-institutional. In a study of activism by individuals infected with tainted blood in the 1980s, I found that movement actors were quite willing to use what they called "back room" and "front room" strategies: "My answer (to government negotiators) always was, 'you can deal with them (the demonstrators outside) or you can deal with me.' We can sit here and deal at the table and hopefully we will come up with a rational solution or you can go out and deal with them. And the more outrageous people became out there, the easier it was for us to say, 'deal with us.' It made a great deal of sense" (quoted in Orsini 2002, 487).

The second choice, between legal and illegal means, is admittedly difficult. On the one hand, law-breaking may help the movement by eliminating normative and symbolic controls as an effective response to the movement. Law-breaking or rule-breaking, if used wisely, can be strategically advantageous, since it not only demonstrates to their opponents that fear of arrest will not faze protesters, but it also limits the options available to their opponents to control the group, providing, of course, that movement activists are careful enough not to cross over from rule-breaking into outright or wanton violence. On the other hand, such a tactic may hurt the movement in the court of public opinion, by reversing its previously favourable image in the media or solidifying previously held negative views. The third choice, violence versus non-violence, is particularly tricky because any movement that opts for violence must recognize the possible repercussions of such action, both internally and externally. Internally, the use of violence poses the real threat of litigation, which may place undue financial strain on the movement and its resources. The issue of violence can be especially challenging when movements are seeking to broaden their support, while ensuring that some of the movement actors who join the fold do not discredit the movement. This was the case with Black Bloc anarchists, who were criticized for being "credibility-sapping parasites" who attached themselves to a range of protest movements, such as Occupy and the Quebec student movement (Hamilton 2012).

A focus on the meso level also calls our attention to the role of framing, and how it interacts with the macro level of "political opportunity structure." Since an "opportunity unrecognized is no opportunity at all," it is crucial to determine "the shared meanings and definitions that people bring to their situation" (McAdam, McCarthy, and Zald 1996, 5). Framing involves "the conscious strategic efforts by groups of people to fashion shared understandings of the world and of themselves that legitimate and motivate collective action" (cited in McAdam, McCarthy, and Zald 1996, 6). As Goffman wrote of framing, "There is a sense in which what is play for the golfer is work for the caddy" (Goffman cited in Gusfield 1997, 202). Movement actors frame the problems/issues they seek to address, and the nature/substance of their claims. These "framing processes" constitute the critical work that movement actors perform to present issues and ideas to other actors in ways that motivate them to pursue collective action. It is insufficient, therefore, to chart the opportunities available solely to movement actors; rather, one must examine why, given the opportunity, they choose to mobilize or not.

As noted, framing processes refer to the shared meanings and definitions that people bring to their situation. Collective action frames "underscore and embellish the seriousness and injustice of a particular social condition or redefine as unjust and immoral what was previously seen as unfortunate but perhaps tolerable" (Benford 1997, 416). One main component of collective action frames is a sense of injustice. It "arises from moral indignation related to grievances," and may also refer to a feeling that authorities are not dealing adequately with a social problem. As Gamson notes, "When we see impersonal, abstract forces as responsible for our suffering, we are taught to accept what cannot be changed and make the best of it.... At the other extreme, if one attributes undeserved suffering to malicious or selfish acts by clearly identifiable groups, the emotional component of an injustice frame will almost certainly be there" (Gamson, in della Porta and Diani 1999, 70).

Micro Level: Actors in Movement

As noted earlier, the micro level can often be the most volatile since it is shaped by individual interactions. As Staggenborg (2008) explains, this is the arena in which individuals come to decide that collective action is worthwhile. This decision can be affected by a host of factors, including a sense that there is nothing to lose or a feeling that one has a personal responsibility to express a grievance in solidarity with others. Either way, what occurs at this micro level can provide us with important insights into movement success and outcomes, especially if we consider the underlying emotional features of movement activity. As outlined, scholars have begun to explore how emotions figure in the individual decision-making of movement actors. Bringing emotions into the study of social movements represents an effort to destabilize the separation of emotion and reason in the study of social movements (Gould 2009; Flam and King 2005; Goodwin, Jasper, and Polletta 2001). Once we accept that emotions interfere with reason, we can begin to appreciate how emotions – hope, fear, rage, guilt, pride, shame, despair – are fundamental to politics and necessitate a place in our analytical toolkits. Applying an emotions lens to the study of social movements helps us to think about how activists and policy discourses themselves contain emotional scripts that can normalize and legitimize certain modes of behaviour and belonging. While "rational" openings in political opportunities matter, they do so "only to the extent that an emotional charge attaches to these openings" (Gould 2009, 18). The turn to emotions challenges us to think about the ways in which seemingly rational behaviours and actions might operate within emotional scripts. It also connects with an interest in the macro level of analysis discussed earlier. Institutional opportunity structures may present "openings" for movements, but they tell us little about the ways in which different groups and actors attach feelings and emotions to these vectors (18). In this vein, the types of emotions that are privileged or discouraged in political discourse matter greatly. For instance, Mothers against Drunk Driving, which was largely credited with helping to overturn prevailing views about the social acceptability of drinking and driving, succeeded by shaping our individual and collective emotional responses to this emerging social problem (Jasper 1998). While efforts to influence policy came later, the first line of attack was to appeal to our compassion for victims of drunk driving and to provoke our collective revulsion toward individuals who choose to drive while under the influence of alcohol.

A conventional focus on social movements as involving rational, strategic actors who are always "mobilizing resources" or fashioning collective identities has provided little room to explore how feelings and emotions can be organizing sites of political agency in their own right.

If we start from the assumption that institutions encompass formal and informal rules, the ways in which emotions are ordered and expressed in political environments, and the impact they have on social movement actors and their claims-making, could complement more conventional approaches. The concept of feeling rules, first used by Hochschild (1979) to talk about the emotional work performed by flight attendants, has begun to be applied to the social movement context (Gould 2009; Broer and Duyvendak 2009). Unlike other rules, feeling rules "do not apply to action but to what is often taken as a precursor to action" (Hochschild 1979, 566). What might be appropriately felt in one context may not be in another. If one shifts this to the social movement context, one can imagine that activists might expect to feel something that is at odds with what they understand to be appropriate, given their understanding of the dominant feeling rules. Moreover, movement actors communicate with one another and with authorities, and might reproduce feelings that defy conventions because they deem it necessary to express themselves in ways that depart from what is expected of them. The feminist movement, for instance, expended significant effort over several decades to convince women that it was acceptable – and indeed vital – to express outrage about gender discrimination. In a similar manner, the AIDS movement was able to channel anger over the reluctance of governments to take seriously the devastating toll of the virus into productive challenges to the scientific and medical establishment (see Gould 2009). The slogan "Silence = Death," with its inverted pink triangle symbol, was adopted by the radical AIDS organization ACT UP to urge lesbians and gay men "to turn anger, fear, grief into action" (129).

Situating Social Movements in Neo-liberal Canada: Continuity or Rupture?

Movements operate in an increasingly neo-liberal, globalized environment that can be enabling or constraining in direct and indirect ways. The ability of movement actors to connect with like-minded individuals in faraway places can enable productive forms of organizing that might yield concrete results and allow supporters to become engaged without leaving the comfort of their computer keyboard. Directly, neo-liberalism and the shrinking role of the welfare state means some of the social movement organizations that previously were supported by the state find themselves struggling to survive or defunded out of existence.[5] Indirectly, but perhaps more profoundly, the paradigm shift ushered in by neo-liberalism and globalization places greater emphasis on values such as individualism, commodification, and marketization. These values can stand in direct opposition to the goals and tactics of social movements, which often emphasize solidarity, community, and opposition to the increasing "colonization" of the public sphere by market forces (Larner in Smith 2005a, 15).

While movements may be influenced by a broader neo-liberal discourse that has transformed the ways in which citizens interact with the state, movement actors also borrow from the scripts of their predecessors, adjust those messages, adapt forms of protest that have been successful in the past, or adopt new methods and strategies to reflect the context in which they are operating.[6] In Canada, it is difficult to ignore the trail-blazing efforts of equality-seeking movements, including the feminist, disability, and LGBTQ+ (lesbian, gay, bisexual, transgender, and queer) movements. Each of these has been influenced by key institutional features of our political system such as the adoption of the Charter in 1982, as well as the advent of a progressive "citizenship regime" (Jenson and Phillips 1996) that supported the rights of marginalized people. This rights-based discourse, which was cemented by the arrival of the Charter, meant that movements that focused in their early years on collective identity building and consciousness raising could now turn to legal strategies to make rights-based claims against the state. But we should be careful about overstating institutional arguments to explain movement successes and failures in this regard. The Charter did not somehow magically transform these movements; a rich tradition of activism and contestation had preceded the arrival of the Charter, notwithstanding the criticisms of well-known critics such as Morton and Knopff, who lament the arrival of the so-called Charter-created "Court Party" (Morton and Knopff 2000; also see Smith 2005b).[7]

In addition to these equality-seeking movements, the Canadian social movement landscape has been characterized by a diverse range of movement activity, including an older labour movement, a strong environmental movement, and anti-poverty organizing, among others (see Smith 2005a for a good historical overview of key social movements). Tracing movements historically reveals that they are influenced by the resources they can mobilize internally as well as by a larger political environment over which they have little control. Normally, this environment can be daunting, forcing some to ask what compels individuals to opt for this type of activity in the first place when there are significant obstacles to participation, including the commitment of time in exchange for little or nothing in the way of tangible outcomes. One argument advanced to explain why individuals join movements has centred on issues of collective identity. Movements are said to provide a sense of "we-ness" to individuals, a sense of kinship or community. While some of these identities may be pre-existing, such as in the LGBTQ+ communities or the feminist movements, they can be transformed in the context of movement struggle. For groups with a history of being marginalized or stigmatized, this coming together can itself be a potent outcome if it means they are able to overcome an otherwise "spoiled identity" (Goffman 1963). Building and constructing a narrative is a critical component of such collective identity formation: "In telling the story of our becoming – as an individual, a nation, a people – we establish who we are. Narratives may be employed strategically to strengthen a collective identity but they may also precede and make possible the development of a coherent community, or nation, or collective actor.... Stories thus explain what is going on in a way that makes an evolving identity part of the explanation" (Polletta 1998, 141). The #MeToo movement is, in some respects, a powerful reminder of the potential of collective identity building, albeit through the painful experience of sexual violence. Although the movement came to public attention through the outing of high-profile celebrities such as Hollywood mogul Harvey Weinstein, actor Bill Cosby, and several other media personalities, one should not overlook its radical potential as a grassroots movement. As Donegan reminds us, "By saying 'me too,' an individual woman makes herself a part of a broader group, and chooses to stand with others who have been harassed, assaulted or raped. This solidarity is powerful. It is still rare to see such a large group of women identifying their suffering as women's suffering, claiming that they have all been harmed by the same forces of sexism, and together demanding that those forces be defeated" (2018).

Economist Mancur Olson (1971), drawing on a rational choice approach, was less interested in subjective measures of collective identity building. Rather, he famously argued that the natural tendency is not to organize collectively. Groups must work hard to overcome the "free-rider problem," which emerges because individuals can reap the rewards of collective action regardless of their involvement. Groups, therefore, must find ways in which to confer benefits (selective incentives or inducements) to discourage individuals from free riding.

The tactics and strategies that movements employ may be familiar, such as marches or demonstrations or legal mobilization via courts, or they may be unconventional – the way that the North American AIDS movement employed "die-ins" in the 1980s in which activists dropped to the ground and others drew police-like chalk outlines around their "dead" bodies to symbolize the deaths from the AIDS epidemic. Engaging in forms of protest that might stand outside the norms of conventional protest suggests that the "tried and true" might work in some environments, but not necessarily in others. Moreover, some critics suggest that demonstrations have become a more palatable form of protest that "succeeds" (somewhat ironically) precisely because it sits well with moderates (see Samuel 2012). The anti-G20 protests in Toronto and the Quebec student protests provoked a strong media backlash as well as internal infighting on whether to support violence and damage to property, which were linked to anarchists affiliated with the Black Bloc. In the G20 case, People First, a movement led by Ontario unions, clashed with other G20 activists, such as the Black Bloc, who supported more violent tactics. The focus on protester-led violence, however, tends to neglect the violence committed by the police against protesters, which is recounted in the powerful CBC documentary featuring interviews with activists who were injured in scuffles with police (CBC 2011).

In addition to mobilizing others to join forces collectively on issues of common concern, social movements often challenge the very meaning of what is political. As Jenson has described, "the universe of political discourse" is constituted through interaction, when actors work to overturn or challenge problems that are not seen as "public" problems worthy of state or societal intervention (1989). In Ottawa, for instance, a feminist collective calling itself the Radical Handmaids (after the dystopian Margaret Atwood novel, *The Handmaid's Tale*) took to the streets in the fall of 2012 to repoliticize the issue of women's reproductive freedoms. They were protesting against attempts by federal Conservative MP Stephen Woodworth to reopen the debate on abortion and the legal definition of when a fetus becomes a human (Cruikshank 2012).

Donning red robes and large white cardboard hats, the women blended humour and satirical performance to dramatize their concerns about attempts to introduce Motion 312, which would have supported the creation of a twelve-member committee to study the legal definition of a fetus. The Handmaids also urged women to participate in the "Wall of Wombs," in which supporters crocheted, knitted, or sewed uteruses and vaginas, mailing them to several MPs who were known to be anti-choice (Cruikshank 2012). The action was notable for its effort to reposition reproductive justice in the public consciousness, to challenge the assumption that women no longer had to worry about access to a safe abortion, and that this was no longer a public problem worthy of political action. As one activist explained, "The idea that 'we shouldn't be protesting this anymore' is something that is felt among many feminists and many women across Canada."[8] The Radical Handmaids were "successful" in the sense that the bill to protect the rights of the fetus was eventually defeated. While it is difficult to discern whether the policy defeat could be attributed solely to their actions, the activist added, "We would like to say that our rallying and organizing – making people aware that these bills are being discussed in the House (of Commons) – had something to do with it. However, it was only defeated marginally. And there were still many people who wanted the Bill to pass."[9]

While some movement organizations such as the Radical Handmaids are roused to action in direct response to proposed policy change, others have a more complex genealogy. For instance, the contemporary indigenous movement Idle No More began, innocuously enough, with a tweet in November 2012 by movement co-founder Jessica Gordon:

> @shawnatleo wuts being done w #billc45 evry1 wasting time talking about Gwen stefani wth!? #indianact #wheresthedemocracy #IdleNoMore

Idle No More supporters targeted Indigenous leaders such as Shawn Atleo, head of the Assembly of First Nations, claiming that they had "sold out" First Nations and not done enough to protect treaty rights. Movement activists expressed strong opposition to the omnibus legislation associated with Bill C-45, which they claimed trampled on treaty rights, but it became clear that Bill C-45 was neither the sole nor primary target of their intervention. Instead, Idle No More might be more appropriately read as a form of Indigenous political resurgence, one that is connected to previous struggles, such as the "Oka Crisis" of 1990, which resulted in a seventy-eight-day standoff between Quebec provincial police and Mohawk protesters, including members of the Warrior Society. While perhaps less dramatic than the armed standoff during that summer, Idle No More surprised many by gaining steam quickly through coordinated actions across the country in a range of venues, including a much-publicized hunger strike by Attawapiskat Chief Theresa Spence that attracted international media attention and became synonymous with the movement (Galloway 2013; Simpson 2013; Loewen and Matthews 2013). As evidence of an interest in attracting and retaining the curiosity of Indigenous youth, activists communicated their stories and perspectives using a variety of media – including film, video, song, spoken word, and visual art – broadcast primarily via social media. Moreover, they took direct aim at the media's portrayal of the movement through online commentary (see Divided No More, website) and blogs, as well as numerous teach-ins at colleges and universities across Canada.

Most recently, Indigenous resistance to the expansion of the Trans Mountain Pipeline brought a halt to the project (at least temporarily), even though

Prime Minister Justin Trudeau had approved the plan in 2016. The Federal Court of Appeal's decision in 2018 effectively rescinded this government approval on the grounds that the parties involved did not properly consult with those most affected, namely First Nations communities (Barrera 2018). In a surprising reversal, however, a recent Supreme Court decision (7–2) called into question this duty to consult, ruling against the Mikisew Cree First Nation in Alberta, "which had argued that two omnibus budget bills introduced by the former Conservative federal government in 2012 affected its constitutionally protected treaty rights" (Tasker 2018).

New Movements, New Concerns, New Tools?

We now turn to one of the main issues raised at the start of the chapter. Do we need new theoretical tools to capture emergent forms of protest that sometimes bypass the state, utilize a range of unconventional tactics that recall the importance of symbols, slogans, and emotions, and engage new actors using different forms of media, including do-it-yourself (DIY) media interventions?

If we accept Alberto Melucci's assertion that "movements no longer operate as characters but as signs" (1988, 249), then we need to train our analytical lens on examining how movements "translate their action into symbolic challenges that upset the dominant cultural codes and reveal their irrationality and partiality by acting at the levels (of information and communication) at which the new forms of technocratic power also operate" (249). This will require a more sophisticated treatment of the framing role media actors play in articulating, countering, or reinforcing movement messages, not to mention the increasingly common practice of movement actors to create their own media that bypasses more conventional forms of engagement with mainstream media. Of course, the media will continue to be an important target for movements that lack resources. As Gusfield notes, "Mass media do more than monitor: they dramatize. They create vivid images, impute leadership, and heighten the sense of conflict between movements and the institutions of society" (Gusfield 1994, 71).

Movements need the news media for three major purposes: mobilization, validation, and scope enlargement. While the media often rely on social movements to provide "good copy," Gamson and Wolfsfeld argue that movements need the media far more than the media need them. As a result of this unequal power relationship, movements must "deal with a potential contradiction between gaining standing [in the media] and getting their message across" (Gamson and Wolfsfeld 1993, 121). Sometimes, for instance, movement actors must resort to flashy or noisy tactics to attract attention. Getting in, however, is only half of the battle, as this affects how the movement actors are portrayed in the media: "The framing of the group may obscure any message it carries. Those who dress up in costume to be admitted to the media's party will not be allowed to change before being photographed" (122). Interestingly, however, the activists associated with Radical Handmaids sought precisely to draw attention to themselves as a result of what they were wearing, and categorically reject the idea that "dressing up" necessarily implies that their interventions are any less serious.

Returning to the Idle No More and the Quebec student movements, both of which sustained intense (and sometimes negative) media attention, what kinds of lessons can we learn from their forays into the social movement arena? First, as students of social movements, we need to pay closer attention to the language and symbols that movements employ to communicate their messages, and the things or objects that sometimes become synonymous with movements. In the case of the student movement, the red square pinned to the lapels of many supporters of the student strike symbolizes "being squarely in the red" in terms of student debt (Messer 2012).

As one activist explained, "I think most students don't know the history.... We chose a sign, a symbol for [the many] students in the chain. The chain of student debt. It's a very strong and powerful statement" (Messer 2012). The red square also links the student struggle to the broader Quebec fight against poverty, which predates the student movement and is strongly associated with the province's progressive social policy. The Collectif pour un Québec sans pauvreté (Collective for a poverty-free Quebec) claims that it first used the red square in October 2004 when it appeared before the Committee on Social Affairs in the Quebec National Assembly to oppose Bill 57, a law to regulate social welfare and assistance.

For the Occupy movement, the slogan "We are the 99 per cent," whatever the critiques of the accuracy of that statement, was used successfully by the Occupy movement to communicate a sense of "we-ness" among potential supporters. Turning again to language, the use of the term *occupy* "turned politics on its head" and had a "stronger and more controversial implication than simply to set up a camp or hold a sit-in" (Pickerill and Krinsky 2012, 281). Similarly, the use of the phrase "Idle No More" by First Nations protesters communicates as a call to action, as well as being a mobilizing expression for a range of political interventions to bring together generations of Indigenous peoples from all walks of life. While Chief Spence attracted some particularly negative media coverage as a result of her attachment to the movement, for better or worse, her plight became a potent symbol of the broader Indigenous struggle, and communicated a sense of urgency to the demands being made by leaders of the movement.

In addition to paying closer attention to the emotional components of language and symbols used by movement actors, we need to ask new questions about movements that do not target the state directly. What happens when a social movement seeks to bypass the state, partially or entirely? What does it mean to study social movements without the state? The Occupy movement, and to a lesser extent Idle No More, refuses to recognize the "legitimacy of the state as an agent capable of or willing to implement policy" (Pickerill and Krinsky 2012, 283). In the case of Occupy, for instance, "By establishing temporary tent communities with kitchens, bathrooms, libraries, first-aid posts, information centres, sleeping areas and educational space, they recreated new spaces of provision: prefigurative alternative communities with very few resources" (283). Thinking about the role of the state in the study of social movements does not mean assuming that the state has lost its relevance, however. Is it best, for instance, to "institutionally disaggregate the state into agencies with which movements are likely to make headway (at least at times) and ones they are not?" (283).

Just as we need to challenge the ways in which we think about social movements, it might be wise to apply the same critical lens to the study of the state, recognizing that state power is diffuse, complex, and, at times, contradictory. In a different sense, Ladner's (2008) discussion of Indigenous social movement contention raises some similar issues with regard to the refusal of Indigenous activists to take the state as given, or at least to accept a particular vision of state power that fails to recognize a colonial history of subjugation. In other cases, however, state power is synonymous with more traditional Weberian notions of the state as retaining the monopoly over the legitimate use of physical force (violence).

As Samuel argues (2012, 12) in an article on the G20 protests in Toronto, while many debate whether violent protesters tarnish otherwise legitimate forms of protest, "debates about the relationship among divergent protest tactics risk neglecting a central feature of domination: the impossibility of adopting a 'right' form of protest in a 'wrong' political field." A wrong political field is one in which it is "impossible for dominated actors to gain sufficient position within that field to alter its basic structures and therefore the relations of domination that are structured by the field and ultimately to alter the social construction according to which the field is reproduced" (12).

Conclusion

This chapter has sought to chart the shifting terrain of social movement protest in Canada, with a focus on how these movements challenge or disrupt conventional ways of understanding the goals, outcomes, and meanings of protest. While some movements are only peripherally engaged in challenging particular policies and have difficulties articulating their specific demands, others, such as the Radical Handmaids, emerged directly in the wake of proposed legislation. While movements may "succeed" in the initial goal they set out for themselves – for instance, defeating a bill or reversing a policy stand – their actions do not end there. In other cases, movement actors might seek change, but they encounter difficulties in trying to organize the sources of their mobilization into easily digestible media sound bites. In still other cases, the purpose of the movement itself might be centred on wider cultural changes associated with creating alternative, self-sustaining communities that might be distinguished from the capitalist system against which the movement has railed. As the Occupy movement demonstrates, a critique of the capitalist system of accumulation does not always lend itself to a series of pithy, media-friendly demands.

While there are important questions to ask about why certain movements emerge or not during particular historical periods, it is equally crucial to ask what difference social movements make. How should we assess what they do or achieve? What, for instance, has changed as a result of the critiques of Pride and white queer organizing advanced by Black Lives Matter activists? While the "Queer Civil War" still rages, there is also evidence of important moments for solidarity and coalition building, especially among BLM activists and Indigenous organizing around common concerns about policy brutality. Do they simply provide us with a glimpse into the growing well of discontent in society that has hardened or solidified into social movement protest? Do they remind us that the only way to initiate change is to refuse to play by the institutional rules of the game, to disrupt or challenge the boundaries of acceptable political expression or dissent? The Black Lives Matter activists in Toronto who refused to register a float in the Pride parade but instead held up the parade to communicate their demands is another example of disrupting assumptions about acceptable forms of activism (Walcott 2017).

The student movement in Quebec, which morphed into a broader movement of citizens displeased with the Liberal provincial government, gained media attention, some of it especially negative in anglophone Quebec because it chose to openly disrupt business as usual, shutting down many universities and colleges in the province and inciting others to communicate their anger through the simple gesture of making noise with pots and pans. Perhaps unbeknownst to the protesters, the government's decision to impose Bill 78 – which restricted the right to picket and protest on college and university campuses and throughout the province – gave a further boost to the movement, as supporters united in opposition to what they saw as an excessively draconian bill (National Assembly [Québec] 2012). Characterized as one of the worst laws for civil liberties since the 1970 War Measures Act, the bill was later repealed by the newly elected Parti Québécois government.

Social movements are intriguing subjects of analysis precisely because they combine the unpredictable with the unconventional, because their actions are not always easy to interpret. While they may prove frustrating to journalists (and academics) who are eager to label them, movements' ability to disrupt what we understand as "politics as usual" makes them worthy of the interest of social scientists. Many of the issues and themes that have moved into the mainstream of Canadian politics – LGBTQ+ issues, feminist concerns, Indigenous peoples' grievances – owe much to the trailblazing of social movement activists who struggled to position them when few people were paying any attention. The movements of today are not, however, simply a direct outgrowth of their forerunners. The Indigenous movement that mobilized in the early 1970s in opposition to the 1969 White Paper that threatened to abolish the Indian Act (and with it the legal status and treaty rights of Indians) is qualitatively different from the media-savvy Idle No More movement, including the catalytic role played by Indigenous women in its founding. While Indigenous peoples have been resisting state authority and colonialism for several centuries (Simpson 2013), they are using different methods and tactics today to confront colonial power and authority.

Collective actors in society will continue to interact with the state and with conventional institutions such as courts to make their demands heard and to transform their grievances into political issues. However, we need to cast our net wider to think more closely about how groups and movements respond to and try to shape the political landscape itself, which contains and reflects shifting values and beliefs about the legitimate expression of dissent and collective action.

Notes

1 The author thanks the editors for helpful comments on this chapter. Some of the material presented here draws on ideas developed in Orsini (2008) and Orsini and Wiebe (2014).

2 In *The Power of Identity*, Castells (1997, 3) defines social movements as "purposive collective action whose outcome, in victory as in defeat, transforms the values and institutions of society." This definition can be problematic because the criteria used to judge a movement – actual effects on societal institutions and values – are difficult to satisfy, especially within such a limited time frame. Tarrow uses the term to describe "collective challenges by people with common purposes and solidarity in sustained

interaction with elites, opponents, and authorities" (Tarrow 1994, 4). In the second edition of *Power in Movement*, he revises this definition somewhat, referring to movements "as those sequences of contentious politics that are based on underlying social networks and resonant collective action frames, and which develop the capacity to maintain sustained challenges against powerful opponents" (Tarrow 1998, 2).

3 Benford refers to this as the reification problem, or the tendency among social movement scholars to speak "about socially constructed ideas as though they are real, as though they exist independent of the collective interpretations and constructions of the actors involved" (Benford 1997, 418). Benford has identified three problems related to reification. First, when we speak about movements, identities, ideologies, and frames, we tend to "anthropomorphize" them. That is, we speak of movements as if they are doing the "framing," "interpreting," and "acting," when in fact it is movement participants who engage in these activities. As he remarks: "Social movements do not frame issues; their activists or other participants do the framing" (Benford 1997, 418). Second, there is a paradoxical tendency to neglect human agency. Social movements are not monolithic and rarely "speak" with one voice; rather, they comprise actors who interact, co-act, and react. Finally, the third problem relates to the neglect of emotions, which is discussed in the chapter. Movement actors are not "Spock-like beings, devoid of passion and other human emotions" (Benford 1997, 418).

4 Burstein suggests that the traditional distinction between interest groups and social movement organizations is deeply flawed. The key distinction – that SMOs are almost always operating at the margins with little or no direct link to the power holders in society, while interest groups enjoy relatively easy access – rests on a false dividing line. Instead, he counsels, the only useful distinction between non-governmental political organizations is a legal one. Political parties, which enjoy a special legal status as "political organizations that have a place on the ballot and a formal role in organizing legislatures" (Burstein 1999, 9), occupy one end of the continuum, while "interest organizations," the term he uses to group interest groups and social movement organizations, occupy the other end.

5 On the recent cuts to key Aboriginal organizations, see Orsini and Papillon (2012).

6 See Meyer and Whittier's (1994) discussion of the concept of "social movement spillover."

7 In the case of the disability movement, despite some important advances in the recognition of their claims, there are persistent concerns about the invisibility of disabled people more generally in Canadian political life (see Prince 2009; Vanhala 2011).

8 Personal communication with activist Polly Leonard, Ottawa, March 2013.

9 Personal communication with activist Polly Leonard, Ottawa, March 2013.

References and Suggested Readings

Barrera, Jorge. 2018. "First Nations Express Doubts, Hopes for Ottawa's New Trans Mountain Consultation Effort." CBC News, October 3. https://www.cbc.ca/news/indigenous/first-nations-trans-mountain-pipeline-consultations-1.4848977.

Benford, Robert. 1997. "An Insider's Critique of the Social Movement Framing Perspective." *Sociological Inquiry* 67 (4): 409–30. http://dx.doi.org/10.1111/j.1475-682X.1997.tb00445.x.

Broer, Christian, and Jan Willem Duyvendak. 2009. "Discursive Opportunities, Feeling Rules, and the Rise of Protests against Aircraft Noise." *Mobilization: An International Journal* 14 (3): 337–56.

Burstein, Paul. 1999. "Social Movements and Public Policy." In *How Social Movements Matter*, edited by Marco Giugni, Doug McAdam, and Charles Tilly, 3–21. Minneapolis: University of Minnesota Press.

Castells, Manuel. 1997. *The Power of Identity*. London: Blackwell Publishers.

CBC. 2011. "The Fifth Estate, You Should Have Stayed at Home." https://www.cbc.ca/player/play/1818705754.

Cohen, Jean L. 1985. "Strategy or Identity: New Theoretical Paradigms and Contemporary Social Movements." *Social Research* 52 (4): 663–716.

Conway, Janet. 2003. "Civil Resistance and the 'Diversity of Tactics' in the Anti-Globalization Movement: Problems of Violence, Silence, and Solidarity in Activist Politics." *Osgoode Hall Law Journal* 41 (2–3): 505–29.

Cruikshank, Julie. 2012. "Getting Radical: Handmaids Take Pro-Choice Message to Parliament." *Xtra*, October 12. https://www.dailyxtra.com/getting-radical-2422.

della Porta, Donatella, and Mario Diani. 1999. *Social Movements: An Introduction*. London: Blackwell Publishers.

Divided No More. n.d. Website. http://dividednomore.ca (site discontinued).

Donegan, Moira. 2018. "How #MeToo Revealed the Central Rift in Feminism Today." *Guardian*, May 11. https://www.theguardian.com/news/2018/may/11/how-metoo-revealed-the-central-rift-within-feminism-social-individualist.

Eisinger, Peter. 1973. "The Conditions of Protest Behavior in American Cities." *American Political Science Review* 67 (1): 11–28. http://dx.doi.org/10.2307/1958525.

Flam, Helen, and Debra King, eds. 2005. *Emotions and Social Movements*. New York: Routledge.

Galloway, Gloria. 2013. "With Hunger Strike Over, Chief Spence's Polarizing Legacy." *Globe and Mail*, January 24. http://www.theglobeandmail.com/news/politics/with-hunger-strike-over-chief-spences-polarizing-legacy/article7760372/.

Gamson, William. 1975. *The Strategy of Social Protest*. Homewood, IL: Dorsey.

Gamson, William, and David Meyer. 1996. "Framing Political Opportunity." In *Comparative Perspectives on Social Movements: Political Opportunities, Mobilizing Structures, and Cultural Framings*, edited by Doug McAdam, John D. McCarthy, and Mayer N. Zald, 275–90. Cambridge: Cambridge University Press. http://dx.doi.org/10.1017/CBO9780511803987.014.

Gamson, William, and Gadi Wolfsfeld. 1993. "Movements and Media as Interacting Systems." *Annals of the American Academy of Political and Social Science* 528 (1): 114–25. http://dx.doi.org/10.1177/0002716293528001009.

Goffman, Erving. 1963. *Stigma: Notes on the Management of Spoiled Identity*. Englewood Cliffs, NJ: Prentice Hall.

Goodwin, Jeff, James M. Jasper, and Francesca Polletta. 2001. *Passionate Politics: Emotions and Social Movements*. Chicago: Chicago University Press. http://dx.doi.org/10.7208/chicago/9780226304007.001.0001.

———. 2004. "Emotional Dimensions of Social Movements." In *The Blackwell Companion to Social Movements*, edited by David A. Snow, Sarah A. Soule, and Hanspeter Kriesi, 413–32. Malden, MA: Blackwell.

Gould, Deborah. 2009. *Moving Politics: Emotion and ACT UP's Fight Against AIDS*. Chicago: University of Chicago Press. http://dx.doi.org/10.7208/chicago/9780226305318.001.0001.

Gusfield, Joseph R. 1994. "The Reflexivity of Social Movements: Collective Behaviour and Mass Society Theory Revisited." In *New Social Movements: From Ideology to Identity*, edited by Enrique Laraña, Hank Johnston, and Joseph R. Gusfield, 58–78. Philadelphia: Temple University Press.

———. 1997. "The Culture of Public Problems: Drinking-Driving and the Symbolic Order." In *Morality and Health*, edited by Allan M. Brandt and Paul Rozin, 201–30. New York: Routledge.

Hamilton, Graeme. 2012. "Hard to Claim Montreal Violence Isn't Tied into Wider Protest Movement." *National Post*, May 4. https://nationalpost.com/opinion/graeme-hamilton-hard-to-claim-montreal-violence-isnt-tied-into-wider-protest-movement.

Hochschild, Arlie. 1979. "Emotion Work, Feeling Rules, and Social Structure." *American Journal of Sociology* 85 (3): 551–75. http://dx.doi.org/10.1086/227049.

Jasper, James M. 1998. "The Emotions of Protest: Affective and Reactive Emotions in and around Social Movements." *Sociological Forum* 13 (3): 397–424. https://link.springer.com/article/10.1023/A:1022175308081.

———. 2011. "Emotions and Social Movements: Twenty Years of Theory and Research." *Annual Review of Sociology* 37 (1): 285–303. http://dx.doi.org/10.1146/annurev-soc-081309-150015.

Jenson, Jane. 1989. "Paradigms and Political Discourse: Protective Legislation in France and the United States before 1914." *Canadian Journal of Political Science* 22 (2): 235–58. http://dx.doi.org/10.1017/S0008423900001293.

Jenson, Jane, and Martin Papillon. 2000. "Challenging the Citizenship Regime: The James Bay Cree and Transnational Action." *Politics & Society* 28 (2): 245–64. http://dx.doi.org/10.1177/0032329200028002005.

Jenson, Jane, and Susan D. Phillips. 1996. "Regime Shift: New Citizenship Practices in Canada." *International Journal of Canadian Studies* 14 (Fall): 111–36.

Ladner, Kiera. 2008. "Aysaka'paykinit: Contesting the Rope around the Nations' Neck." In *Group Politics and Social Movements in Canada*, edited by Miriam Smith, 227–49. Peterborough, ON: Broadview.

Laforest, Rachel. 2011. *Voluntary Sector Organizations and the State: Building New Relations*. Vancouver: UBC Press.

Loewen, Peter, and Scott Matthews. 2013. "Op-Ed: Aboriginal Issues Are on the Agenda." *Ottawa Citizen*, March 4. http://www2.canada.com/ottawacitizen/news/archives/story.html?id=83b93aa7-8777-4a22-ae08-5546c2e76d8e&p=2 (link no longer active).

Marx, Gary T., and Douglas McAdam. 1994. *Collective Behaviour and Social Movements: Process and Structure*. Englewood Cliffs, NJ: Prentice Hall.

McAdam, Doug. 1985. *Political Process and the Development of Black Insurgency, 1930–1970*. Chicago: University of Chicago Press.

McAdam, Doug, John McCarthy, and Mayer N. Zald, eds. 1996. *Comparative Perspectives on Social Movements: Political Opportunities, Mobilizing Structures, and Cultural Framings*. Cambridge: Cambridge University Press. http://dx.doi.org/10.1017/CBO9780511803987.

McCarthy, John, and Mark Wolfson. 1992. "Consensus Movements, Conflict Movements, and the Cooptation of Civic and State Infrastructures." In *Frontiers in Social Movement Theory*, edited by Aldon Morris and Mueller McClurg, 273–97. New Haven, CT: Yale University Press.

Melucci, Alberto. 1988. "Social Movements and the Democratization of Everyday Life." In *Civil Society and the State*, edited by John Keane, 245–60. London: Verso.

———. 1994. "A Strange Kind of Newness: What's 'New' in New Social Movements." In *New Social Movements: From Ideology to Identity*, edited by Enrique Laraña, Hank Johnston, and Joseph R. Gusfield, 101–30. Philadelphia: Temple University Press.

Messer, Olivia. 2012. "Squarely in the Red: The History Behind That Felt on Your Lapel." *McGill Daily*, March 31. http://www.mcgilldaily.com/2012/03/squarely-in-the-red/.

Meyer, David, and Nancy Whittier. 1994. "Social Movement Spillover." *Social Problems* 41 (2): 277–98. http://dx.doi.org/10.2307/3096934.

Morton, F.L., and Rainer Knopff. 2000. *The Charter Revolution and the Court Party*. Peterborough, ON: Broadview.

Mueller, Carol. 1994. "Conflict Network and the Origins of Women's Liberation." In *New Social Movements: From Ideology to Identity*, edited by Enrique Laraña, Hank Johnston, and Joseph R. Gusfield, 234–63. Philadelphia: Temple University Press.

National Assembly (Quebec). 2012. *Bill 78: An Act to Enable Students to Receive Instruction from the Postsecondary Institutions They Attend*. http://www2.publicationsduquebec.gouv.qc.ca/dynamicSearch/telecharge.php?type=5&file=2012C12A.PDF.

Nevitte, Neil. 2000. "Value Change and Reorientation in Citizen-State Relations." *Canadian Public Policy* 24:S74–S94.

Offe, Claus. 1985. "New Social Movements: Challenging the Boundaries of Institutional Politics." *Social Research* 52 (4): 817–68.

Olson, Mancur. 1971. *The Logic of Collective Action: Public Goods and the Theory of Groups*. Rev. ed. Cambridge, MA: Harvard University Press.

Orsini, Michael. 2002. "The Politics of Naming, Blaming and Claiming: HIV, Hepatitis C and the Emergence of Blood Activism in Canada." *Canadian Journal of Political Science* 35 (3): 475–98. http://dx.doi.org/10.1017/S0008423902778323.

———. 2008. "Health Social Movements: The Next Wave in Contentious Politics?" In *Group Politics and Social Movements in Canada*, edited by Miriam Smith, 475–98. Peterborough, ON: Broadview.

Orsini, Michael, and Martin Papillon. 2012. "Death by a Thousand Cuts." *Mark News*, April 25. http://ca.news.yahoo.com/death-thousand-cuts-052241740.html.

Orsini, Michael, and Miriam Smith. 2010. "Social Movements, Knowledge and Public Policy: The Case of Autism Activism in Canada and the U.S." *Critical Policy Studies* 4 (1): 38–57. http://dx.doi.org/10.1080/19460171003714989.

Orsini, Michael, and Sarah Marie Wiebe. 2014. "Between Hope and Fear: Comparing the Emotional Landscapes of the Autism Movement in Canada and the United States." In *Canada Compared: Methods and Perspectives on Canadian Politics*, edited by Luc Turgeon, Martin Papillon, Jennifer Wallner, and Stephen White. Vancouver: UBC Press.

Phillips, Susan. 1999. "Social Movements in Canada: Past Their Apex?" In *Canadian Politics*, edited by James Bickerton and Alain-G. Gagnon, 3rd ed., 371–89. Peterborough, ON: Broadview.

———. 2004. "Social Movements, Interest Groups and the Voluntary Sector: En Route to Reducing the Democratic Deficit." In *Canadian Politics*, edited by James Bickerton and Alain-G. Gagnon, 4th ed., 323–47. Peterborough: Broadview.

Pickerill, Jenny, and John Krinsky. 2012. "Why Does Occupy Matter?" *Social Movement Studies: Journal of Social, Cultural and Political Protest* 11 (3–4): 279–87. http://dx.doi.org/10.1080/14742837.2012.708923.

Pinard, Maurice. 2011. *Motivational Dimensions in Social Movements and Contentious Collective Action*. Montreal and Kingston: McGill-Queen's University Press.

Pineault, Éric. 2012. "Quebec's Red Spring: An Essay on Ideology and Social Conflict at the End of Neoliberalism." *Studies in Political Economy* 90 (Autumn): 29–56.

Polletta, Francesca. 1998. "'It Was like a Fever …' Narrative and Identity in Social Protest." *Social Problems* 45 (2): 137–59. http://dx.doi.org/10.2307/3097241.

Prince, Michael. 2009. *Absent Citizens: Disability Politics and Policy in Canada*. Toronto: University of Toronto Press.

Samuel, Chris. 2012. "Throwing Bricks at a Brick Wall: The G20 and the Antinomies of Protest." *Studies in Political Economy* 90 (Autumn): 7–27.

Schwartz, Michael, and Shuva Paul. 1992. "Resource Mobilization versus the Mobilization of People: Why Consensus Movements Cannot Be Instruments of Social Change." In *Frontiers in Social Movement Theory*, edited by Aldon D. Morris and Carol McClurg Mueller, 205–23. New Haven, CT: Yale University Press.

Simpson, Leanne. 2013. "Idle No More: Where the Mainstream Media Went Wrong." Dominion, February 27. http://dominion.mediacoop.ca/story/idle-no-more-and-mainstream-media/16023.

Smith, Miriam. 2005a. *A Civil Society? Collective Actors in Canadian Political Life*. Peterborough, ON: Broadview.

———. 2005b. "Social Movements and Judicial Empowerment: Courts, Public Policy, and Lesbian and Gay Organizing in Canada." *Politics & Society* 33 (2): 327–53. http://dx.doi.org/10.1177/0032329205275193.

———. 2008. *Group Politics and Social Movements in Canada*. Peterborough, ON: Broadview.

Staggenborg, Suzanne. 2008. *Social Movements*. Don Mills, ON: Oxford University Press.

Tarrow, Sidney. 1994. *Power in Movement: Social Movements, Collective Action and Politics*. Cambridge: Cambridge University Press.

———. 1998. *Power in Movement: Social Movements, Collective Action and Mass Politics in the Modern State*. Cambridge: Cambridge University Press. http://dx.doi.org/10.1017/CBO9780511813245.

Tasker, John Paul. 2018. "Supreme Court Rules Ottawa Has No Duty to Consult with Indigenous People before Drafting Laws." https://www.cbc.ca/news/politics/tasker-indigenous-rights-consultation-parliament-1.4858321.

Vanhala, Lisa. 2011. *Making Disability Rights a Reality? Disability Rights Activists and Legal Mobilization in Canada and the United Kingdom*. Cambridge: Cambridge University Press.

Walcott, Rinaldo. 2017. "Black Lives Matter, Police and Pride: Toronto Activists Spark a Movement." Conversation, June 28. https://theconversation.com/black-lives-matter-police-and-pride-toronto-activists-spark-a-movement-79089.

Walia, Harsha. 2011. "2011: Reflecting on Social Movement Successes in Canada." Canadian Dimension, October 30. http://canadiandimension.com/articles/3976/.

White, Deena. 2012. "Interest Representation and Organization in Civil Society: Ontario and Quebec Compared." *British Journal of Canadian Studies* 25 (2): 199–229. http://dx.doi.org/10.3828/bjcs.2012.11.

nineteen
Acting in and on History: The Canadian Women's Movement

JACQUETTA NEWMAN

Introduction

In 2002, French sociologist and social theorist Alain Touraine (Touraine 2002, see also Touraine 1998) argued that the women's movement most closely resembled what he considered to be a true social movement, comparable to the labour movement in industrial society. According to Touraine, it was so important "that if there are some places in the world where elements of social movements exist, it is everywhere, in all countries and parts of the world where the women's movement exists, where the status of women appears to be the most important reason for opposing some trends" (Touraine 2002, 94). The women's movement questions not just economic interests but "the fundamental orientation, the social meaning and the social interpretation of modern individualism" (94). It does so most clearly by challenging a world based on a universalized idea of humanity as male, white, and middle class and highlighting the existence and inequality of women, or, those that are not (hu)men.

For Touraine, society is defined by social movement – that is, the structural and cultural conflicts between social groups over the organization of society and the "rules of the game" that define the type of society in which we live. As Cox and Nilsen (2014, 56) argue, social movements are the central "animating forces in making and unmaking the structures and needs and capacities that underpin [a] social formation" (56). They are by their nature historical actors and generally associated with projects of emancipation, liberation, and the challenging of forms of domination.

As an actor in history, the women's movement has been central to the struggles over social, cultural, and political life. This includes Canada, where from the late nineteenth century onward we can trace a clear social phenomenon or movement focused on women's emancipation, equality, and ending oppression through the advancement of women's social, economic, and political status. Thus, the purpose of this chapter is to explore the Canadian women's movement as a social movement and as a historical actor.

The Canadian Women's Movement as Social Movement

Social movements are expressions of collective action made up of heterogenous political, social, and cultural networks engaged in continual disputing, compromising, redefining, and adapting identities, strategies, and goals. It is a form of socio-political action where "the collective actor (1) invokes and is defined by a sense of solidarity and shared meaning; (2) makes manifest a social, political, and cultural conflict; and (3) within that conflict presents a vision that contains an immanent critique of society" (Melucci 1989). As such, they cannot be characterized as particularly unified or coherent entities. Cox and Nilsen (2014, 168), drawing on Touraine, argue for a view of social movements as social process rather as a specific organization, "not the fixed one assumed in the supposedly scientific social movements literature. It is one which, precisely, *moves* – wins or loses, falls back into particularism, becomes part of other movements, creates states, and so on." Thus, it is probably best to refer to "movement" rather than "*a* movement." This is particularly nebulous, but within such expressions of collective action, we can identify plural and heterogenous socio-political-cultural networks engaged in continual redefinition of movement and particular identities.

The Canadian women's movement comprises numerous groups and individuals involving different ideologies, grievances, and outlooks. Various segments of the movement express views about feminism, such as liberal, socialist, radical, and post-structuralist, while other segments express views that are not explicitly feminist, such as those concerned with anti-racism, LGBTQ+, and disability. Some even resist being called "feminist." What connects the segments is a vision of ending constructed hierarchies and structures of power that systematically disadvantage and limit one's autonomy on the basis of gender, class, race, age, and so on. And in some contexts, all of these actors coalesce in formal and informal networks or coalitions to work together, thus signifying a period of apparently unified mobilization.

... Action Made Up of Heterogenous Political, Social, and Cultural Networks

Adamson, Briskin, and McPhail's (1988, 9) description of the second wave of the Canadian movement is a good characterization of the heterogeneity and diversity of movement throughout its history including the first and third waves.

> To the extent that we define the women's movement organizationally, it is made up of hundreds of groups: some small, some large, some focused on single issues, some with a complex and wide-ranging

> political perspective. Some organize around legislative issues, some provide services, others focus on organizing women into unions. The constituency of some organizations is homogenous: immigrant women, lesbians, women of colour, business and professional women, women in trades. Others have a heterogeneous constituency and focus on specific issues such as day-care, or on supporting a political perspective.... Some are based in large institutions like universities and government ministries; some are located in small communities. Some use traditional methods of organizing themselves; others have developed unconventional organizational structures.... The diversity and political heterogeneity is enormous and is further complicated by the fact that the practice of the women's movement – the way it organizes for change – is also constantly being transformed through self-criticism, through experience, and by changing historical circumstances. (Adamson, Briskin, McPhail 1988, 9)

Although there is much overlap, we can divine four branches, comprising large and small groups, as well as individuals. First, equality feminists who focus on equal rights for women and campaign for equal opportunities in employment and politics. For example, during the first wave, Flora MacDonald Denison, president of the Canadian Suffrage Association from 1910 to 1914, referred to equal-rights feminists like herself as "the real-suffragists." She argued that "men and women should be born equally free and independent members of the human race" and entitled to equal rights (Adamson, Briskin, McPhail 1988 33; see also Strong-Boag 2016). In the second wave, the creation of the National Action Committee on the Status of Women (NAC) in 1972 to monitor implementation of the recommendations of the Royal Commission on the Status of Women was based on an understanding of equality rights and how that equality could be achieved by making good on the commission's 167 recommendations. These covered issues of economics, education, law, reproductive control, child care, needs of Indigenous, Inuit, and minority women, and women's representation in public life. Similarly, the Women's Legal Education and Action Fund (LEAF), founded in 1985 after the patriation of the Constitution and the enshrinement of the Charter of Rights and Freedoms, worked to ensure the substantive equality of women and girls as guaranteed in the Charter and women's "equality under the law" (leaf.ca). Today, as part of the third wave, organizations such as London, Ontario's Women in Politics focus on women's political equality by advocating for greater support for women in politics and getting more women into elected office. Nationally, the organization Equal Voice (equalvoice.ca) pursues similar ends, working to achieve equal political representation of women in federal and provincial governments and empowering young women to participate in politics through events such as Daughters of the Vote.

A second and more "traditional" branch comprises groups espousing social or maternal feminist goals that focus on bringing women's unique and private values, particularly their mothering and child-care capabilities, into the public world. This approach dominated the first wave. For example, the Women's Christian Temperance Union (WCTU) became a significant part of the Canadian suffragette movement because it saw political representation as a way to promote family moral values. This branch was much less prevalent in the second and third waves, although in the 1960s the focus on family and children is evident in the campaigns of the anti-war organizations such as the Voice of Women, the Women's International League for Peace and Freedom, and the Canadian Campaign for Nuclear Disarmament. These organizations were behind a campaign of knitting camouflage-coloured children's' clothes to highlight the aerial bombing of Vietnam and collecting children's milk teeth to test strontium levels as part of an effort by women peace activists to stop above-ground nuclear testing. Today as part of the third wave, this tendency can be seen in the continuation of the Federated Women's Institutes of Canada (fwic.ca). Formed during the first wave as an advocate for domestic science education and rural living, it continues today, having celebrated its centenary, to work on issues regarding violence against women, rural access to daycare, food and water security, and gendered international development.

A third branch focuses on the "self-determination" of identities and anti-racism. While the first wave was dominated by white middle-class women, ethnic women and women of colour were not absent. As feminist historian Veronica Strong-Boag (2016) points out, in the run up to the first wave, Mary Ann Shadd, a woman of colour and the first woman newspaper publisher in Canada, used her newspaper, the *Provincial Freeman*, to discuss women's rights along with the abolition of slavery. In Manitoba, Icelandic women were a significant feature in the campaign to achieve suffrage. However, the racism of the time did much to marginalize the contributions of such women, as did subsequent historical accounts. Women of colour, Indigenous women, and minority women would not receive full political rights until much later in the twentieth century. In the heat of the second wave, many small women's groups, given impetus by Black feminist and anti-colonial writers, came to voice concerns regarding specific identities based on race, ethnicity, sexual orientation, immigration status, and ability and started to challenge the perceived dominance of the movement by white middle-class women. In 1973, the Native Women's Association of Canada formed to promote the well-being and equality of First Nations and

Metis women, politically, economically, and legally and to protect Indigenous women's cultures. A corresponding organization for Inuit women, Pauktuutit, was established in 1984. In 1973, the Congress of Black Women was established in Ontario, evolving from the Canadian Negro Women's Association, itself established in 1951. Its mission was and is to provide a forum for Black women to identify and address issues that affect their lives, families, and communities.

In the third wave, the focus on intersectionality and difference, that is the recognition that gender, race, class, sexuality, age, ethnicity, ability, etc. cannot be understood in isolation and are woven together in more complex ways than just straightforward sexism, would come to define the movement. Indigenous women, women of colour, poor women, lesbians, and young women now highlight how peoples' lives are defined by intersecting and reinforcing identities rather than a homogeneous category of woman. For example, the DisAbled Women's Network (DAWN), works to end poverty, isolation, discrimination, and violence, which women with disabilities suffer at higher rates than men and white able-bodied women. In addition, intersectionality connects third-wave activists to other movements and their organizations, such as Black Lives Matter (BLM) or Gay Straight Alliances. In BLM, the focus is on ending racism and violence, particularly police violence against Black people in Canada, but it also highlights how the violence experienced by Black women is compounded by "sexism, cissexism, homophobia, transphobia, and racism" (Black Lives Matter – Toronto 2015). In the Gay Straight Alliance clubs that have emerged in Canadian high schools, students challenge heteronormative practices by school administrations that limit the expression of gender identities and result in student mental health and safety issues (Findlay, Newman, and White 2019; Stonefish and Lafrenière 2015).

The fourth branch consists of service providers: women's organizations whose primary purpose is to provide services to women, such as counselling, referral, reproductive health issues, or shelters. To an extent, such a branch was at work prior to and during the first wave, as the movement demands for political representation were based on the view that representation was a requirement to enhance charitable works and efforts at social reform. However, it was a significant feature of the second wave, when women and feminists holding anti-patriarchal and anti-institutional views argued against working through mainstream politics and instead created women-centred and women-only services. These included rape crisis centres, shelters for homeless women and women suffering spousal abuse, women's health centres focused on reproductive issues, contraception, and abortion, and centres for single mothers. There were also cultural endeavours such as magazines, journals, publishing companies, and art galleries run for women and by women.

Associated with this was the creation of Women's Studies departments within universities, starting with individual courses in 1970s and growing into full-fledged undergraduate programs offered by most universities, thirteen master's programs, and seven doctoral programs by the 2000s (Findlay, Newman, and White 2019). We cannot discount the significance of such programs in educating many of today's third-wave feminists. Reflecting the intersectionality of the third wave, many of these programs have become gender studies programs, offering an approach guided by diversity, difference, and intersectionality, and by doing so aiding the emergence of indigenous, disability, LGBTQ+, and even masculinity studies. In addition, the institutionalization of government support for women-oriented centres, while undermining their original rejection of the patriarchal state, has ensured their continuation. These shelters and crisis centres have not only provided protection for millions of women over the years, they also offer leadership and education for campaigns to end violence against women and the protection of bodily autonomy for women and other vulnerable persons.

Before we leave this far-from-inclusive outline of the functional branches of the Canadian women's movement, it is worth noting a further set of groups that have emerged as a counter-movement, campaigning for the maintenance of traditional divisions between men and women. Towards the end of the second wave, the emergence of REAL Women, Realistic, Equal, Active for Life (realwomenofcanada.ca), promoted an anti-feminist message focused on preserving the "traditional family" from the changing nature of Canadian society. Along with the Alberta Federation of Women United for Families and elements of the Canadian religious right, REAL Women pushed for legal and legislative protection of the "Judeo-Christian" understanding of marriage, the central role of women in the home, and the rights of the fetus. This helped to extend the influence of a Christian-Conservative movement in Canada (Dauda 2010). Gaining allies within conservative political parties, these groups became a significant feature of the backlash against Canadian feminism, in particular, and the equality gains made by the second wave women's movement more generally. Today, while REAL Women is less prevalent in the news, it continues to campaign against reproductive rights and against the expansion of gender identities and expressions.

Further to this is a geographical differentiation in the movement, most prominently the distinction between a francophone movement based in Quebec and an anglophone movement in the rest of Canada. Quebec women were active during the first wave, demanding access to the vote along with other women across Canada. However, the very traditional role afforded to Quebec women by the dominant conservative-Catholic provincial culture of the time meant that while the federal franchise was achieved, women in Quebec would wait until 1940 to be granted the provincial vote (see Baillargeon 2014). While the second wave of the women's movement in Quebec arose during the same period as in the rest of Canada, it also corresponded with Quebec's Quiet Revolution. During the Quiet Revolution a generation of Quebecers challenged the traditional Catholic-conservative culture and anglophone economic dominance of the province and worked to establish a modern, secular, francophone provincial state. Consequently, the association between Quebec's women's movement and the province-building nationalism of both Liberal and Parti Québécois provincial governments helped make the movement distinct, along with the issues and strategies it adopted (Cohen 2000). In the third wave, as with the movement in the rest of Canada, Quebec's women's movement has been much more diverse and intersectional in its outlook. This is highlighted not only by the participation of young women in the student and youth Printemps érable protests of 2012, but also in their rejection of the PQ's proposed Charter of Quebec values, which targeted Muslim women who wore the veil or hijab in public (see Frappier 2014; Seery 2015; Mayer and Lamoureux 2016).

Outlining the branches and pointing out significant actors within the women's movement highlights its heterogenous nature. It also draws attention to the variety of organizational forms, ranging from individuals to large national organizations, within the movement. In fact the distinction between social movement and advocacy organizations – such as interest groups, non-governmental organizations, service groups, protest groups, etc. – and the borders between the non-institutional character of social movements and the institutionalized politics of advocacy groups is hard to define. Social movements form organizational structures – social movement organizations (Obershall 1993) – which form coalitions with other organizations across social movements. As della Porta and Diani (1999, 19) point out, these organizations may in fact move from social movement characteristics to interest group characteristics and back again, depending on the political and social context in which they find themselves.

Within the history of the Canadian women's movement, we can see the dominance of particular branches and corresponding dominant forms of organizing. In the first wave, the struggle was conducted through large, national social reform organizations and unions, with communication between the activities facilitated by public personalities like Emily McClung, Emily Murphy, Emily Stowe, and Flora MacDonald Denison, who published their and other women's views and travelled town to town on speaking tours to spread the message. The second wave worked through small consciousness-raising and direct-action groups, which raised awareness and recruits who then came together through formal coalitions in national peak organizations such as the Federation des femmes du Quebec (FFQ) in Quebec and the National Action Committee (NAC) in English Canada. The greater movement often came together through national and international conferences of women, such as the UN's World Conferences of Women held in Mexico City (1975), Copenhagen (1980), Nairobi (1985), and Beijing (1985). The work was supported by professional staff funded by government grants and charitable donations. In the third wave, the movement has become much more diffuse, with work undertaken by mid-size and small non-profit civil society organizations like London, Ontario's Women in Politics (mentioned above) by associated movement organizations like BLM and GSAs, and by individuals on internet platforms. The social media aspect of the third wave is seen in the large-scale Twitter campaigns such as #MeToo or #TimesUp or in blogs that "began as simple websites and developed into communities of hundreds and thousands of people who needed a platform to express themselves" (Martin and Valenti 2012).

... Where "the Collective Actor Invokes and Is Defined by a Sense of Solidarity and Shared Meaning"

As the definition of social movement makes clear, it is the expression of collective action invoking a sense of shared meaning and solidarity that gives form to the heterogenous and nebulous nature of the phenomena. But what do we mean by solidarity?

Sally Scholtz (2015, 725) argues that solidarity "speaks to collective relationships that mediate between the individual and community, establishing commonality and agreement that neither subsumes the individual nor represents solely the community." It is an affective concept, a logic of affinity that is emotional and romantic and lacking ideological specificity and precision; something as hazy and indefinable as saying one is committed to "social justice," "freedom," or "equality." As Day and Montgomery (2014, 63) put it, solidarity is a relationship or attraction "oriented towards others who are on similar paths, an orientation that simultaneously engages with the other in relations of care and mutual respect ... that is not attempting to subsume the other in any relation of unitary transcendence." It is a form of political togetherness that is intersectional, multi-faceted rather than rooted in specific identities or group characteristics.

An idea-force – a belief or understanding that provides motivation – derived from the frustration and anger of multiple groups and individuals brings the disparate groups within a movement together as a collective *actor* (Hayward 1959). As Crossley and Taylor (2015, 75) point out, "The U.S. women's movement has never had a coherent collective identity, although feminist organizations, despite being composed of women of diverse backgrounds, sometimes organized around similar injustices." The same can be said of the Canadian women's movement, which, as outlined earlier, embraces multiple ideas and identities: social feminist, equality feminist (liberal, socialist, Marxist, radical) anti-racist, LGBTQ+, Indigenous, and disability. Nevertheless, as Dobrowolsky (2014, 152) shows, in different periods, the Canadian women's movement "has sought to achieve degrees of consensus and coordinated efforts to press for change. Certain perceived injustices served to focus the movement: suffrage as the defining feature of the so-called first 'wave' of the women's movement and abortion, violence against women and diversity concerns in the second and third wave."

For each wave of the women's movement, we can identify the idea-force that animated and brought together a movement of women and their allies. The first wave was motivated to achieve political rights, primarily the right to vote, and later in 1929 the legal recognition of personhood. In the second wave, while there was unfinished business from the first wave, particularly in achieving equal political representation, the socio-economic inequalities highlighted by the Royal Commission on the Status of Women animated and motivated the movement to action. In 1982, as in 1929, the enshrining of women's equality within the Charter of Rights and Freedoms confirmed the right of women to political and social equality and set a guide for pursuing equality. For the third wave, the recognition of the intersectional nature of women's lives and experiences is the basis of an idea-force on violence against women and other vulnerable communities. The disparate levels of violence against women and girls, particularly those marked as different and thus more vulnerable, has spurred the mobilization of women's groups and the emergence of a new movement. This is demonstrated in Canada by the expanding work and support of women's groups on behalf of Missing and Murdered Indigenous Women and Girls and the Sisters in Spirit campaigns, and, more widely, in the global work on violence against women and girls, and the #MeToo and #TimesUp movement.

... Makes Manifest a Social, Political and Cultural Conflict, and within That Conflict Contains an Inherent Critique of Society

In each of these periods, as Cox and Nilsen (2014, 170) point out, "what is defining is not any specific position but rather the argument itself and what it represents [i.e., political equality, socio-economic equality, equality of bodily autonomy] – a determined move beyond single-issue politics of any kind to challenging economic and political fundamentals, and the willingness to do so in alliance with other social groups and people elsewhere around the world." This is the nature of solidarity, according to Kolers (2012, 367), "essentially agonistic [conflictual and confrontational] in the sense that it involves political struggle, which is by definition struggle against other actors." This anti-systemic feature is at the heart of the disruption and challenge presented by social movements to societal norms. The movement's fundamental animus is not negotiable within the existing arrangement of social power; and in the women's movement that social power is patriarchal: the hegemonic power of men that determines all aspects of society.

The Women's Movement as Historical Actor

In 1988, Naomi Black (1988, 83–4) used the term *wave* to describe the Canadian women's movement, "reminding us that in social change as in oceans, calmer patches are followed by new and stronger peaks of activity." For Black, the second wave of the women's movement was "a tide pouring in, each wave going further up the beach, with a continuity of organizational and individual efforts over time and a hope of progress." The wave analogy is useful to describe social movement cycles and peaks. During the peak of a wave the movement is characterized by intense mobilization, which demonstrate the disruptive energy and capacity of social movement to bring about change. As Cox and Nilsen (2014, 174) point out, "In such waves, popular mobilization increases by one or two orders of magnitude, including normally passive groups. They [waves] are thus fundamental for restructuring popular agency, in that they reorganize the question of 'who is active?' in social movements, political parties, and so on – something which in routine times is normally more predictable; indeed, relatively few movement organizations survive such waves in anything like the form in which they entered." This view of "waves" helps describe the role of social movements as historical actors.

The trough of the wave and movement cycle appears when the mobilized peak loses momentum for various reasons. These can include movement success that attenuates goals, participant burn-out, loss of key allies, and/or state repression. This part of the cycle is characterized by abeyance or latency (see Taylor 1989; Staggenborg 1998; and Melucci 1989). During this period, the movement is not inactive, but working more "quietly" on public and self-education, often providing services in society, and sometimes cooperating with the state on public policy. The focus is on organizational sustenance and maintenance rather than confrontation (Crossley 2014, 10). This concept of abeyance/latency illustrates how movements are continuous phenomena and tie periods of mobilization together. The mobilizations of the first, second, and third waves did not emerge phoenix-like out the ashes of long-dead progenitors; they emerged from foundations set by women's organizations working steadily and quietly in society. This said, Crossley's (2014) characterization of "waveless" feminism, like "a river with shallows, deeps, rapids and diversions, a continuous flow rather than a series of disconnected diversions," underestimates the significance of the periods of intense mobilization as profound struggles over history.

It is the peak of the wave that truly demonstrates the power of movement as a historical actor. "Groups which have previously been resigned or had not yet become coherent political actors (re-)enter the political contest; some of those which had been unenthusiastic members of hegemonic coalitions detach themselves, and long-time opponents of the hegemonic order are able to make substantial alternatives visible to wide sectors of the population. The gains that are sought typically include *both* the unfinished business of earlier waves (reflecting the re-mobilization of the resigned) *and* new kinds of issues (reflecting the participation of new social actors)" (Cox and Nilsen 2014, 175, emphasis in the original). It is the large-scale mobilization that leads to opportunities for change and the possibility of realignment in the political system, as the conflicting claims presented during these periods of "episodic action" create uncertainty and a need for now visible social fault lines to be addressed (McAdam, Tarrow, and Tilly 2001, 9). Disruptions and protests motivate people to hope for and demand alternatives; they also bring issues to the fore and act as agenda setters. This is change not only in influencing public policy, but also by generally changing social attitudes and popularizing different understandings of political and social norms. This is nothing less than social and political transformation.

For example, in 1988 Adamson, Briskin, and McPhail described the fundamental changes to Canadian society brought about by the first wave of the women's movement. The work done by the feminists of the first wave was tremendously important in making the second-wave women's movement possible. "Although we are too often unaware of who they were and what they did, every day we reap the benefits of that work. Our right to vote and to own property, to participate in the world of politics and government, and our access higher education, divorce, and guardianship of our children, all owe much to those women" (36).

Organizations based on female private charity provided a foundation for action to formally establish women as equal persons politically and before the law. Thus, in 1921, Agnes MacPhail of the United Farmers of Ontario Party became the first woman to take a seat in the House of Commons, and in 1930 Liberal Party fundraiser Corrine Wilson was appointed to the Senate. The situation was far from perfect, but between 1920 and 1970 eighteen women were elected to the House of Commons; as well, women took positions in provincial legislatures and on municipal councils, even becoming mayors of major cities, most notably Charlotte Whitton in Ottawa in 1951 (although a woman has still to be elected mayor in Vancouver). Women's access to educational opportunities was expanded. During World War II, women entered the workforce to ensure the maintenance of the domestic economy and wartime production. While at the war's end most would return to domestic duties in the home – with the encouragement of both private employers and the state – not all did so, and others rejoined the labour market when their children reached school age.

The country had changed and so had the movement. The dominant social/maternal feminist view, strategically important in rationalizing the Military Voters and Wartime Elections Acts of 1917, and, eventually the 1918 extension of the vote to all women over twenty-one (with the exception of racialized and Indigenous women), became much less dominant. For example, by the end of the nineteenth century, the National Council of Women, a national network of women's organizations, had already developed a broader focus. It began to advocate not only for suffrage and temperance but also for better working conditions for female domestic and factory employees, the rights of married women to property, and measures related to public health (Burt 1994; Prentice et al. 1988).

Equality feminism gradually became the dominant form of feminism, particularly as women sought full inclusion in the professions, in the business world, and at universities. Such efforts included establishing the Canadian Teachers' Federation in 1920, the Federation of Business and Professional Women in 1930, and the Canadian Federation of University Women in 1919. All would become important organizations in sustaining women's networks and political interests during the period of abeyance and latency that followed the successful campaign for suffrage. This reflected the emergence of a "modern feminism" (Adamson, Briskin, McPhail 1988, 30) because it recognized the increasing heterogeneity and diverse loyalties among women, and it would be these women who would remain active in a variety of causes and issues throughout the years 1920–1960, after which they would come together again in the second wave. Therefore, when the second wave gained momentum in the 1960s, it was both old and new. As Adamson, Briskin, and McPhail (1988, 37) described it, "Although each of the major contemporary currents of feminism has a forerunner in the earlier women's movement, they are all, in a certain sense, new approaches. The world has changed enormously, and our analyses have become more complex. The second wave has been able to take for granted certain basic rights and build on those. Changes in women's work, an increasingly urbanized society, the growth of technology, and changes in family life have raised different problems and issues for contemporary women."

It is impossible to overestimate the changes brought about in Canada by the second wave of the women's movement. This wave, as with the first, emerged out of conflict between norms or the roles of women that were not adapting to the changing nature of society and the expanding role of women within it. Women were now much more active in both politics and the economy, but their advancement, security, and general access to higher positions, better wages and salaries, and more job and career opportunities were still significantly limited when compared to that of men. Women started to advocate across a broad range of political, economic, and social issues, pressing for better representation at all levels of government and in the bureaucracy. In the education field, they demanded curricula more appropriate for girls and women and equal opportunity in educational advancement. Women demanded equal pay for equal work, equality in career advancement, and an end to workplace sexual harassment. Issues of sexuality came to the fore, as women demanded the right to their own bodies and to birth control. Violence against women, domestic violence, pornography, and rape became lightning rods for women's activism.

Responding to women's demands, the creation in 1967 of the Royal Commission on the Status of Women to examine the status of women in Canada and make recommendations to the federal government on how to ensure women's equal opportunities provided an impetus and target for women's organizing while confirming that the personal grievances of many women were indeed political. It marked a point where many different segments of the movement and streams of feminist thought came together around a common set of goals. This grand coalition gained an organizational identity in 1972 with the establishment of the National Action Committee on the Status of Women (NAC) (Newman and White 2012).

Significantly, the efforts of the movement influenced the process of constitutional change, with most of the movement's demands for equality rights met in non-discrimination provisions (section 15) and the distinct gender equality provision (section 28) of the 1982 Charter of Rights and Freedoms. As Dobrowolsky (2000, 62, 71) points out, while the original vision of the movement had been "much grander," the provisions of the Charter set the foundation for subsequent policies to ensure women's equality. Further, it opened a new strategy for organizational action as women's groups turned to the courts to interpret and enforce implementation of equality guarantees. Such action would bring about new policies regarding employment equity and the expansion of reproductive rights, including expanded access to abortion. Work done in the federal Parliament, provincial legislatures and government bureaucracies by women politicians and "femocrats" would help establish new policies and practices regarding the workplace. These included pay equity, workplace harassment, and anti-discrimination policy. By demanding amendments to the Criminal Code, pursuing changes and protections through the courts, and by providing services for abused women and children, women politicians, public servants and women's groups were able to change the structures governing sexual harassment and violent behaviour toward women. As a result, by the twenty-first century, the idea that violence against women is unacceptable is widely understood, if not yet universally accepted as "common sense."

The discourse of this second wave was significantly different from the first wave. It was developed and led by a generation of women who were more secular and radical than the maternal/social feminists of the first wave (Adamson, Briskin, and McPhail 1988, see also O'Neill 2017). The second wave demonstrated how the "personal is political" and how women's oppression under patriarchy was founded on the control of women's bodies, their sexuality and their reproductive capacity, through the use and threat of male physical violence. The movement also demonstrated that this oppression was not a naturally given social reality because of a women's sex. Inequality was not the result of biology, but a function of the social construction of gender. As Simone de Beauvoir pointed out, "women were not born, they were made." Women's oppression was founded on social and cultural expectations and prescriptions of womanhood versus masculinity, neither of which were inevitable nor unchangeable. As these discourses became more prevalent during the second wave, the change in social attitudes was dramatic. It became clear that forms of inequality were not natural phenomena but created by institutionalized norms and values. It also became clear that social inequalities based on gender could be challenged and even eliminated through changes in attitudes, laws, and institutions.

The results of growing understanding of the "personal as political" and oppression arising from gender (not sex) was two-fold. First, as discussed earlier, was the rise of a counter-movement set on protecting the traditional differences between women and men and the hierarchical ordering of society based on those differences. Organizations such as REAL Women Canada adopted feminist language, strategies and venues of political engagement to combat the second wave, including making funding applications to the women's program of the federal Status of Women department (Dauda 2010; Newman and White 2006). In the 1990s, the counter-movement would find a receptive ally in Canada's conservative parties and both the Mulroney and Harper governments.

Second, the understanding of the socially constructed nature of oppression, combined with the politics of the personal, highlighted the complexity and ambiguity of the lives of many women. "Instead of being used to identify collective women's issues, feminists began to use it [the personal is political] to explain how individual acts can empower women as a group" (Van Deven 2009, 29; also see Arneil 1999, 189–90). As early as the 1980s, minority women's groups, such as the Native Women's Association of Canada and Black feminist groups had emerged to pressure for recognition of their multiple and intersecting oppressions by both the state and the women's movement itself. For example, the more critical women's voices in the constitutional hearings of the 1970s had been those of Indigenous women. As a result, by the 1990s, a cohort of women were setting their own agendas and exploring the conditions of their lived experiences not only as women but also in combination with their other identities.

All of this, as well as the cuts to social programs brought on by the austerity politics of neo-liberal state retrenchment in the 1990s, took on the appearance of a growing fragmentation and multiple schisms in the women's movement. The consolidation of a neo-liberal economic agenda by both Conservative and Liberal governments resulted in significant cuts in funding to equality initiatives and to women's organizations. As McKeen (2004, 74) points out, the mainstream movement came to focus not on specific "women's issues" like child care, abortion, affirmative action, and pay equity, but on struggling against more general economic and labour changes that had resulted from government pushes for free trade, privatization, deregulation, and deficit and debt reduction. Further, the shift of focus to social policies required an organizational shift to more locally based groups targeting provincial and municipal governments which had more direct influence on policies effecting women's everyday lives (Collier 2014). The NAC was the most obvious victim of this change. As Cheryl Collier (2014) relates, the decline of the NAC resulted from the closing of the political opportunity structure that had given the women's movement influence over public policy and a subsequent decline in the financial resources required to keep the organization running. The federal government was no longer interested in consulting or even debating women's issues; instead, the Canadian political agenda was focused on rolling back the welfare and participatory state through funding cuts, including to advocacy groups like the NAC.

It is very easy to argue that during this period the movement was its own worst enemy, disabled by "insurmountable tensions." It would be more accurate, however, to view this period as one of abeyance/latency where the movement was experimenting, debating, and negotiating its own transformation. This transformation was driven by the new discourses that had emerged during the second wave of the women's movement. On the one hand, older feminists (and some non-feminists) did accuse younger feminists who were active in identity politics and connected to other movements of being unfocused, self-obsessed, and not politically relevant. On the other hand, young feminists often criticized older feminists for their narrow focus and, frankly, for being out of touch. However, as Astrid Henry (2014) argues, it was a dispute based on a new generation of young feminists "announcing their arrival" and articulating how they would re-energize the women's movement within a new context (for examples, see Walker 1995; Baumgartner and Richards 2000; Mitchell, Rundele, and Karain 2001). In addition, the media were happy to dredge up gender stereotypes and characterize arguments within the movement as a "cat fight"; this was more dramatic, personal, and newsworthy than mundane reports of groups working cooperatively to craft legislation, lobby governments, and share skills and resources (Zeisler 2016).

After the second wave peak of mobilization, the status of women in Canada and globally was far from perfect, a fact that had become clear by the first decade of the new millennium. Disputes within the movement were replaced by a consensus that women's struggles were far from over. The movement regained its focus on the political and social inequalities that remained even after a century of women's struggles, though in the context of a changed Canadian and global economic, political, and technological environment. Brenda O'Neill's (2017) generational study of the Canadian women's movement demonstrates "evidence of change across subsequent generations of feminist recruitment. Importantly, however, they also reveal evidence of strong continuity. Canadian feminists are of one mind in the importance assigned to a range of issues and in their commitment to advocacy work and engagement with women's groups and organizations, despite increasing diversity among its members and significant changes over time in social and political contexts in which this is located" (456).

Thus, the feminism of the third wave of the women's movement is defined by the second wave, but filtered through the backlash of the 1990s, neo-liberal state retrenchment, and – for the "millennial generation" – the global financial collapse of 2008 and the growing precarity of employment and economic well-being (Garrison 2000; Milkman 2017). As was the case with the second wave, the third wave is both old and new.

Two features stand out in the third wave. First is an emphasis on the complexity and ambiguity of peoples' lives defined by intersecting and reinforcing identities. The third wave is underpinned by concepts of difference rather than sameness, particularity rather than universality (Arneil 1999, 87). There is no universal category of womanhood; rather, there is a sisterhood of solidarity between diverse and heterogeneous women. For the most part, there is an understanding that both feminism and the women's movement (1) cannot be a unified discourse and must acknowledge multiple perspectives; (2) are intersectional and inextricably tied to other social justice movements;

and (3) must be non-dogmatic and acknowledge the complexities and contradictions of lived experiences (Henry 2014). This view was illustrated by the response of the Quebec's women's movement to the Parti Québécois attempt to introduce a Quebec Charter of Values (Bill C-60) in 2013 that would ban Islamic veiling. Although the minority PQ government led by Pauline Marois advocated for the ban based on a universal view of women's equality, women quickly pointed out that the legislation discriminated against Muslim women, isolating them from public life and contributing to heightened discrimination and violence against them. There was tension within the movement and a small segment split from the FFQ, Quebec's main movement group, to form Pour les droits des femmes du Québec in order to support the legislation and a less intersectionally based view of patriarchal domination. However, young Quebec feminists were moving "not to create a unified discourse, but to accept a diversity of opinions and debate" and to be open to linking feminism to other social issues, groups, and movements (Seery 2015; Mayer and Lamoureux 2016).

Second is the dominance of digital technologies in third wave organizing. In the new millennium the internet has become a significant forum for the circulation of feminist ideas and organization. "The online 'eco-system' consists of blogs eZines, forums, newsgroups and journals where organizations run online campaigns, circulate petitions, and individual thought leaders ('influencers') express themselves on Twitter, Facebook, Tumblr, YouTube, and other social media platforms on a myriad of topics that relate to being women in the twenty-first century" (Findlay, Newman, and White 2019). Individual stories and interpretations of lived experiences combine with communities of readers to have global reach. These readers not only comment, they act. For example, the 2011 Slut Walk protest actions started in Canada when two York University students, Sonya Barnett and Heather Jervis, started a Facebook and Twitter campaign to respond to a Toronto Police recommendation that women stop "dressing like sluts" to avoid being harassed or assaulted. The protest marches were not confined to Toronto (which over three thousand attended) but spread to Australia, Brazil, India, Israel, Poland, and throughout the United States. As feminist blogger Jessica Valenti (Henry 2014) commented, this successful action "translated online enthusiasm into in-person action" and showed how the third wave online presence could be translated into "old school" street protests. In addition, the resulting online criticism by other women of these protests as foregrounding privileged cisgender, middle-class white women opened conversations, debate, and negotiation regarding the relationship between personal experiences and structural inequalities – an example, according to Baer (2016, 3), of "process-based political action."

The question we are left with at this point is whether this activity represents an emerging mobilization period – a peak in the third wave movement. Events during the second decade of the new millennium appear to indicate that there is a mounting tidal swell and renewed intense movement mobilization. The Arab Spring of 2010, the youthful European protests against austerity (particularly in Greece and Spain), and the worldwide Occupy protests can be identified as movement "early-risers" at the beginning of a protest cycle opening up opportunities for others to affect the political system (Staggenborg 2012). As Cox and Nilsen (2014, 161–2) argue, "Protests over climate change and against the energy companies, southern European *indignados*, 'Arab Spring,' Anglo-American Occupy, the gradual succession of the South African working class from the ANC's neoliberal hegemony, and other crises from Turkey to Thailand … represent a massive and sustained presence on the world stage of collective action from below of a very dramatic kind … [and] show a new confidence in street-based direct democracy and the formation of alternative bases of popular legitimacy."

Canada had its own signs of a fresh protest cycle with its own Occupy protests in the summer and fall of 2011, the Printemps érable (maple spring) Quebec student protests in early 2012, and the rise of Idle No More towards the end of 2012 (see Ancelovici and Dupuis-Déri 2014 and www.idlenomore.ca/articles). Regarding the women's movement, Idle No More was based on the frustrations and protest of Indigenous women elders not only against government policy towards First Nations peoples and the environment, but also against male-dominated Indigenous governance structures such as the Assembly of First Nations. This frustration was associated with the ongoing struggles at the time to get government action to combat the disproportionate levels of violence experienced by Indigenous women and girls. A national inquiry into missing and murdered Indigenous women and girls was launched in 2016, although within terms of reference and a timeline set by the federal government. Spearheaded by the Native Women's Association, community-based women's groups, both Indigenous and non, have been active in education and actions as part of the Sisters in Spirit and No More Silence campaigns and hosting art installations such as the "ReDress" and "Walking with Our Sisters."

The 2016 election of Donald Trump as forty-fifth president of the United States based on the antiquated and regionally biased Electoral College rather than the popular vote has given impetus for women's organizing not just in the United States but worldwide. That an admitted serial harasser and sexual predator could beat Hilary Clinton, an eminently qualified female opponent, clearly illustrated both the enduring persistence of women's political inequality and the lack of autonomous control of their bodies. The

Million Women's March organized in January 2017 spread around the world with "more than 600 'sister marches' held across the United States, Canada, and dozens of other countries," with a conservatively estimated turnout of three million worldwide (Enos and Brass 2017). The demands made at this time and in the follow-up march in 2018 included the enforcement of women's rights, the protection of women's reproductive rights, health care, and immigration, but also the revival of demands for equal pay and non-discriminatory hiring. Further momentum was given to the movement in 2017 when accusations of sexual assault and harassment against American film producer Harvey Weinstein went viral. What started as a campaign by female actors to highlight the levels of harassment and inequality in the movie industry quickly spread to an online consciousness-raising movement, as women around the world recounted experiences of abuse and harassment under the Twitter tag #MeToo. It became "the most high-profile example of digital feminist activism we have yet encountered; it follows a growing trend of the public's willingness to engage with *resistance* and *challenges* to sexism, patriarchy, and other forms of oppression via feminist uptake of digital communication" (Mendes, Ringrose, and Keller 2018; emphasis in the original).

The Women's Movement as Historical Social Movement

Whether we can say that the current activity is the beginning of mobilization or the peak of the third wave is an open question. These characterizations can be made only with the benefit of hindsight. However, we can say that a phenomenon we call the women's movement has acted and continues to act to fundamentally change what society deems acceptable and appropriate roles for women – it is acting to dismantle the patriarchal structures, norms, and values that oppress half the world. History is a struggle over such institutionalized social norms and values; it is about constructing ourselves as a society, politically, economically, socially and culturally. Historicity – the idea of our world as arranged by historical concepts, practices, and values determined by the most powerful – constructs oppressions and inequalities that are neither natural nor immutable. For over 100 years, a women's social movement has challenged those historical structures, often changing social norms, but at other times being thwarted and marginalized. Thus, we characterize this struggle as a series of waves continuously washing up against the shore, receding back into the sea, and then once more returning, but this time further up the shore. Each time the beach changes, at times subtly, but at others significantly. This is a continuous process, and the women's movement has been the most persistent and continuous in modern history. This is why Touraine describes the women's movement as a "true social movement" – it has been and is a continuous, broad-based participant in the struggles over historicity and defining what our society ought to be. Within Canada, the women's movement has been a central feature of political struggles over social, cultural, and economic life. When we look back on the twentieth century and the first decades of the new millennium, we can see a tumultuous, even revolutionary struggle, undertaken by diverse groups and networks of women. They have worked and are working in society to change lives, both theirs and everyone else's.

References and Suggested Readings

Adamson, Nancy, Linda Briskin, and Margaret McPhail. 1988. *Feminist Organizing for Change: The Contemporary Women's Movement in Canada.* Toronto: University of Toronto Press.

Ambrose, Linda. 2000. *Women's Institutes of Canada: The First One Hundred Years 1897–1997.* Gloucester, ON: Tri-Co Printing.

Ancelovici, Marco, and Francis Dupuis-Déri, eds. 2014. *Un printemps rouge et noir: regards croisés sur la grève étudiante de 2012.* Montreal: Écosociété.

Arneil, Barbara. 1999. *Politics and Feminism.* Oxford: Blackwell.

Baer, Hester. 2016. "Redoing Feminism: Digital Activism, Body Politics, and Neoliberalism. *Feminist Media Studies* 16 (1): 17–34.

Baillargeon, Denyse. 2014. *A Brief History of Women in Quebec.* Translated by W. Donald Wilson. Waterloo, ON: Wilfrid Laurier University Press.

Baumgartner, Jennifer, and Amy Richards. 2000. *Manifesta: Young Women, Feminism and the Future.* New York: Farrar, Straus and Giroux.

Black, Naomi. 1988. "The Canadian Women's Movement: The Second Wave." In *Changing Patterns: Women in Canada,* edited by Sandra Burt, Lorraine Code, and Lindsay Dorney, 80–102. Toronto: McClelland and Stewart.

Black Lives Matter – Toronto. 2015. "Black Voices Must Be Heard in the Conversation about Gender Violence." The Blog Black Lives Matter, March 9. Toronto. https://www.huffingtonpost.ca/black-lives-matter-a-toronto/black-voices-sexualized-gender-violence_b_8215922.

Burt, Sandra. 1994. "The Women's Movement: Working to Transform Public Life." In *Canadian Politics,* edited by James P. Bickerton and Alain-G. Gagnon, 2nd ed., 207–23. Peterborough, ON: Broadview.

Cohen, Yolande. 2000. "Chronologie d'une émancipation. Questions féministes sur la citoyenneté des femmes." *Globe: Revue international d'études québécoises* 3 (2): 43–65.

Collier, Cheryl. 2014. "Not Quite the Death of Organized Feminism in Canada: Understanding the Demise of the National Action Committee on the Status of Women." *Canadian Political Science Review* 8 (2): 17–33.

Cox, Laurence, and Alf Gunvald Nilsen. 2014. *We Make Our Own History: Marxism and Social Movements in the Twilight of Neoliberalism.* London: Pluto.

Crossley, Alison Dahl. 2014. *Finding Feminism: Millennial Activists and the Unfinished Gender Revolution.* New York: New York University Press.

Crossley, Alison Dahl, and Verta Taylor. 2015. "Abeyance Cycles in Social Movements." In *Movements in Times of Democratic Transition,* edited by Bert Klandermans and Cornelis van Straten, 64–88. Philadelphia: Temple University Press.

Dauda, Carol. 2010. "National Battles and Global Dreams: REAL Women and the Politics of Backlash." June 2010. Paper presented at the Annual Meetings of the Canadian Political Science Association, Edmonton, Alberta.

Day, Richard J.F., and Nick Montgomery. 2014. "Letter to a Greek Anarchists: On Multitudes, Peoples, and Finance." In *Radical Democracy and Collective Movements Today: The Biopolitics of the Multitude versus the Hegemony of the People*, edited by Alexandros Kioupkiolis and Giorgis Katsembekis, 45–72. Farnham, UK: Ashgate.

della Porta, Donatella, and Mario Diani. 1999. *Social Movements: An Introduction*. Oxford: Blackwell.

Dobrowolsky, Alexandra. 2000. *Politics of Pragmatism: Women, Representation, and Constitutionalism in Canada*. Don Mills, ON: Oxford University Press.

———. 2014. "The Women's Movement in Flux: Feminism and Framing, Passion and Politics." In *Group Politics and Social Movements in Canada*, edited by Miriam Smith, 159–80. Toronto: University of Toronto Press.

Dumont, Micheline. 1992. "The Origins of the Women's Movement in Quebec." In *Challenging Times: The Women's Movement in Canada and the United States*, edited by Constance Backhouse and David H. Flaherty, 72–89. Montreal and Kingston: McGill-Queen's University Press.

Enos, Elysha, and Emily Brass. 2017. "'More Than Just an American Issue': Thousands Protest Donald Trump in Montreal." CBC News, January 21.

Findlay, Tammy, Jacquetta Newman, and Linda White. 2019. *Women, Politics, and Public Policy: The Political Struggles of Canadian Women*. 3rd ed. Don Mills, ON: Oxford University Press.

Frappier, André. 2014. "The PQ's Secular Charter Divides the Quebec Women's Movement." *Canadian Dimension* 47 (7).

Garrison, E.K. 2000. "U.S. Feminism – Grrrl Style! Youth (Sub)Cultures and the Technologies of the Third Wave." *Feminist Studies* 26 (1): 141–70.

Hayward, J.E.S. 1959. "Solidarity: The Social History of an Idea in Nineteenth Century France." *International Review of Social History* 4: 261–84.

Henry, Astrid. 2014. "From Mindset to a Movement: Feminism since 1990." In *Feminism Unfinished: A Short, Surprising History of American Women's Movements*, edited by Dorothy Sue Cobble, Linda Gordon, and Astrid Henry, 147–226. New York: Liveright Publishing.

Johnson, Candace. 2016. "Transnational Reproductive Rights Regimes in the Context of Zika Virus." Paper presented at the Annual Meeting of the Canadian Political Science Association, Calgary, May 31–June 2.

Kolers, Avery H. 2012. "Dynamics of Solidarity." *Journal of Political Philosophy* 20 (4): 365–83.

Martin, Courtney E., and Vanessa Valenti. 2012. "#FemFuture: Online Revolution. New Feminist Solutions Series." http://bcrw.barnard.edu/wp-content/nfs/reports/NFS8-FemFuture-Online-Revolution-Report.pdf.

Mayer, Stéphanie, and Diane Lamoureux. 2016. "Le féminisme québécois comme mouvement de défense des droits des femmes." *Recherches féministes* 29 (1): 91–109.

McAdam, Doug, Sidney Tarrow, and Charles Tilly. 2001. *Dynamics of Contention*. Cambridge: Cambridge University Press.

McKeen, Wendy. 2004. *Money in Their Own Name: The Feminist Voice in Poverty Debate in Canada 1970–1995*. Toronto: Toronto University Press.

Melucci, Alberto. 1989. *Nomads of the Present: Social Movements and Individual Needs in Contemporary Society*. Philadelphia: Temple University Press.

Mendes, Kaitlyn, Jessica Ringrose, and Jessalynn Keller. 2018. "#MeToo and the Promise and Pitfalls of Challenging Rape Culture through Digital Activism." *European Journal of Women's Studies* 25 (2): 236–46.

Milkman, Ruth. 2017. "A New Political Generation: Millennials and the Post-2008 Wave of Protest." *American Sociological Review* 82 (1): 1–31.

Mitchell, Alyson, Lisa Brun Rundele, and Lara Karain. 2001. *Turbo Chicks: Talking Young Feminisms.* Toronto: Sumach.

Newman, Jacquetta. 2017. "Back to the Future: Encoding and Decoding Interest Representation outside Parties." In *Canadian Parties in Transition*, edited by Alain-G. Gagnon and A. Brian Tanguay, 4th ed., 250–76. North York, ON: University of Toronto Press.

Newman, Jacquetta, and A. Brian Tanguay. 2002. "Crashing the Party: The Politics of Interest Groups and Social Movements." In *Citizen Politics: Research and Theory in Canadian Political Behaviour*, edited by Joanna Everitt and Brenda O'Neill, 373–412. Don Mills, ON: Oxford University Press Canada.

Newman, Jacquetta, and Linda White. 2006. *Women, Politics, and Public Policy: The Political Struggles of Canadian Women.* 1st ed. Don Mills, ON: Oxford University Press.

———. 2012. *Women, Politics, and Public Policy: The Political Struggles of Canadian Women.* 2nd ed. Don Mills, ON: Oxford University Press.

Obershall, Anthony. 1993. *Social Movements: Ideologies, Interests and Identities.* New Brunswick, NJ: Transaction.

Offe, Claus. 2002. "1968 Thirty Years After: Four Hypotheses on the Historical Consequences of the Student Movement." *Thesis Eleven* 68 (February): 82–8.

O'Neill, Brenda. 2017. "Continuity and Change in the Canadian Feminist Movement." In "Finding Feminism," special issue, *Canadian Journal of Political Science* 50 (June): 443–59.

Pile, Stéphanie. 2017. "Celebrating 120 Years of the FWIC." Federated Women's Institutes of Canada. http://fwic.ca/news/fwic-blog/ (link no longer active).

Prentice, Alison, Paula Bourne, Gail Cuthbert Brandt, Beth Light, Wendy Mitchinson, and Naomi Black. 1988. *Canadian Women: A History*. Toronto: Harcourt Brace Jovanovich.

Scholtz, Sally J. 2015. "Seeking Solidarity." *Philosophy Compass* 10: 725–35.

Seery, Annabelle. 2015. "Les jeunes féministes et la valorisation du travail de reproduction: quelques réflexions sur le mouvement des femmes au Québec." *Recherches féministes* 28 (1): 151–68.

Staggenborg, Suzanne. 1998. "Social Movement Communities and Cycles of Protest: The Emergence and Maintenance of a Local Women's Movement." *Social Problems* 45 (2): 180–204.

———. 2012. *Social Movements.* 2nd Canadian ed. Don Mills, ON: Oxford University Press Canada.

Stonefish, Twiladawn, and Kathryn D. Lafrenière. 2015. "Embracing Diversity: The Dual Role of Gay-Straight Alliances." *Canadian Journal of Education* 38 (4): 1–17.

Strong-Boag, Veronica. 2016. "Women's Suffrage in Canada." *The Canadian Encyclopedia.* https://www.thecanadianencyclopedia.ca/en/article/suffrage.

Taylor, Verta. 1989. "Social Movement Continuity: The Women's Movement in Abeyance." *American Sociological Review* 54 (5): 761–75.

Touraine, Alain. 1998. *Catalysts of Change: Exploration, War, and Revolution.* VHS recording. Princeton, NJ: Films for the Humanities and Sciences.

———. 2002. "The Importance of Social Movements." *Social Movement Studies* 1 (1): 89–95.

Van Deven, Mandy. 2009. "Just Say Yes: Will a Pro-Sex Philosophy Be the Next Tool in the Anti-Rape Arsenal?" *Herizons* 22 (4) (2009): 29–31.

Walker, Rebecca. 1995. "Being Real: An Introduction." In *To Be Real: Telling the Truth and Changing the Face of Feminism*, edited by Rebecca Walker. New York: Anchor Books.

Zeisler, Andi. 2016. *We Were Feminists Once: From Riot Grrrl to CoverGirl, the Buying and Selling of a Political Movement*. New York: Public Affairs, Perseus Books Group.

PART SIX

Contemporary Issues

twenty

The Relationship between Canada and Indigenous Peoples: Where Are We?

NAIOMI WALQWAN METALLIC

Introduction

Owing in large part to the Truth and Reconciliation Commission's final report, we are having more discussions today about Indigenous issues, including establishing a nation-to-nation relationship and recognizing and implementing inherent rights and Indigenous laws (Truth and Reconciliation Commission of Canada 2015). These are not new subjects; some people have been discussing them for many years. It does seem, however, that there are more people joining the conversation today. This is a positive development. There are many questions that arise in these dialogues. What does reconciliation mean? What does a nation-to-nation relationship look like? How do we make meaningful change in this country over the next 150 years? In having these discussions, it is important for all of us to appreciate where the relationship between the Canadian state and Indigenous peoples stands at this moment.[1] I am a firm believer that knowing where you now are and where you have been is extremely helpful in figuring out how to get to your destination. Therefore, my contribution to this collection is to attempt to take stock of where we have been and where we are in the hopes of facilitating better dialogue on where we should be going.

In the Era of Renewal and Renegotiation

According to the 1996 *Report of the Royal Commission on Aboriginal Peoples* (RCAP), we are in the era of "renewal and renegotiation." In its comprehensive review of the relationship between Indigenous peoples and the Canadian government, the RCAP attempted to describe the changes in this relationship by organizing eras by major themes. Four were identified. "Separate Worlds" was the first era. It referenced the pre-contact period when for thousands of years Indigenous peoples lived on this part of the North American continent as fifty to seventy distinct nations with their own traditions, cultures, languages, and legal systems. Europeans lived across the ocean on their own continent, similarly made up of different nations with their own traditions, cultures, languages, and legal systems (RCAP 1996a, vol. 1, chap. 4). Following contact, the era of "nation-to-nation" relations lasts for roughly two hundred years (from 1600 to mid-1800s) (RCAP 1996a, vol. 1, chap. 5). This may come as a surprise to people who may have believed that, upon arrival, Europeans immediately set out to "conquer" and overwhelm the Indigenous peoples of these lands.[2] On the contrary, the themes animating this period include friendship, intermarriage, barter, and trade and military alliances. Further, the dealings between representatives of the British Crown and the Indigenous peoples they encountered, including the issuance of the Royal Proclamation of 1763 and the signing of treaties, are evidence of a clear recognition of Indigenous peoples' status as nations, their right to self-determination, and their legitimate claims to the territory (Truth and Reconciliation Commission of Canada 2015, 195–201; Borrows 1997b).

This long period of mutual coexistence was followed by a much darker period that the RCAP referred to as the era of "domination & assimilation." This period roughly coincides with the first 100 years of Confederation. Colonial governments, and later the federal government, segregated First Nations on small and less-than-desirable parcels of land (reserves). The aim and expectation was that they would disappear as distinct peoples as the result of disease and starvation or assimilation into mainstream culture (RCAP 1996a, vol. 1, chap. 6). As for the Métis, the Canadian government first claimed ownership of their traditional territory, then overwhelmed them militarily when they rebelled. Thereafter, their continued existence as a distinct people was essentially ignored. Canada's other Indigenous people, the Inuit, were left to fend for themselves in their northern homeland.[3]

On the newly established reserves, First Nations were barred from exercising their traditional subsistence livelihoods; government rations to alleviate starvation conditions were provided sparingly (Shewell 2004, 327–9). Later, the federal government pursued a policy of cultural genocide through sending thousands of Indigenous children – First Nations, Métis, and Inuit alike – to residential and day schools (Truth and Reconciliation Commission of Canada 2015, 37–135). In addition, the Indian Act and other assimilatory policies were used to revoke the "Indian status" of thousands of First Nations men, women, and children.

The RCAP tells us we started to turn the page on this dark era in the 1950s when relations shifted into the present era of "renewal and renegotiation." It describes this stage as a "time of recovery for Aboriginal people and cultures, a time for critical review of our relationship, and a time for its renegotiation and renewal" (RCAP 1996b). In the following sections, I will examine what I see as six milestones for this era: (1) amendments to the Indian Act in 1951; (2) the 1969 White Paper Policy; (3) the 1973 *Calder* decision; (4) section

35 of the Constitution Act, 1982; (5) the 1992 Charlottetown Accord; and (6) the 1996 RCAP report itself. My aim is to show how these events were improvements over the previous era of "domination and assimilation," but also to draw attention to the fact that significant problems remain. These shortcomings point us in the direction we need to go and indicate that there is much work left to do.

Amendments to the Indian Act

Following World War II, Canada – like many countries throughout the world – experienced a shift in its social outlook. Revulsion at the treatment of Jewish people and other groups persecuted by the Nazis spurred increased concern for equality and human rights in Canada and beyond. This can be seen through the passing of the United Nations Universal Declaration on Human Rights in 1948 (Shewell and Spagnut 1995, 1–2). As well, around this time, both the federal and provincial governments began paying greater attention to the basic right of individual Canadians to essential services, laying the legislative foundation for the social safety net (Van Harten, Heckman, and Mullen 2010, chap. 3–4, 8.17). With respect to the relationship with Indigenous peoples, this translated into a growing awareness of their impoverishment and a desire to do something to ameliorate their condition. A Joint House of Commons and Senate Committee on Indian Affairs was appointed with a mandate to inquire into the policies of the Department of Indian Affairs as well as the general conditions of First Nations peoples living on reserves (Shewell and Spagnut 1995, 3).

The committee's reports and recommendations consistently focused on the need to advance First Nations to full citizenship and equality (Shewell and Spagnut 1995, 3). At this time equality was defined in terms of "formal equality": the notion that everyone should be treated identically (Hogg 2007, para. 55.6e). In other words, First Nations ought to be treated the very same as other Canadians. Their separate legal status as "Indians," as well as their unique legal entitlements (treaties, reserves, the Indian Act, etc.) was blamed for the social and economic disparities that characterized their plight (as opposed to a century or more of colonial and assimilatory policies). Viewed in another light, while the policy goal was still assimilation, there was less outright denigration of Indigenous peoples and their cultures. However, mainstream Euro-Canadian culture was still viewed as the pinnacle of social ordering (Shewell and Spagnut 1995, 3).

The committee's recommendations influenced several amendments to the Indian Act. In existence since 1876, the Indian Act provided the legal basis for several assimilative policies. The 1951 amendments removed some of the more blatant forms of discrimination in the Act, including the prohibition of hiring lawyers to vindicate land rights and other collective claims, the prohibition against Indigenous spiritual practices, and the provisions that automatically disentitled a First Nations person from recognition under the Indian Act (and consequently the right to live on reserve) upon becoming a doctor, lawyer, getting a university degree, joining the holy orders, and joining the military (often called *compulsory enfranchisement*).[4]

Other highly problematic provisions in the Indian Act remained. Not least among these were the provisions on maintaining residential schools. Also left in the Act was the provision that robbed First Nations women who married non-First Nations men (and the children of these women) of their "Indian status." Moreover, the Act was revised to add a new provision disentitling First Nations people whose mothers and grandmothers were both non-First Nations (known as the "double-mother rule"). Both discriminatory provisions affecting First Nations women and their offspring were repealed in 1985 and replaced by new "Indian status" rules. Nevertheless, these rules maintain the Government of Canada's exclusive control over who is an "Indian" under the law, while introducing what is effectively a 50 per cent blood quantum rule, which continues to have an adverse impact on First Nations women and their descendants. This has been the subject of numerous Charter and human rights challenges over the last ten years.

One further major amendment was made to the Indian Act in 1951. The Joint Committee on Indian Affairs found that First Nations on reserves were excluded from many federal social programs and most provincial and territorial services that were provided to other Canadians. It recommended that provinces and territories be more involved in delivering and funding social services to First Nations. The federal government's initial response was to add section 88 (then section 87) to the Indian Act, which delegates any matters not covered by a treaty, the Indian Act, or its regulations to provincial laws of general application.[5] Provinces, however, were unwilling to extend their legislation and services to First Nations unless the federal government picked up the tab. This has resulted in a long-running game of "hot potato" between the federal and provincial governments in which neither wants to take responsibility for delivery of programs and services to Indigenous peoples (Wilkins 2000, 460–3). This explains the strong criticisms of section 88 and subsequent Supreme Court of Canada interpretations of section 91(24) that permit provincial laws to have broad impacts on Indigenous lands and resources. They have allowed (if not endorsed) the erosion of important protections for Indigenous lands, resources, and jurisdiction – protections promised in the Royal Proclamation of 1763 and the various treaties – from incursion by local governments (Borrows 2017). Finally, it bears emphasizing that except for a few minor amendments, the Indian Act largely remains in force today as it stood in 1951! Nor has the federal government significantly exercised its section 91(24) legislative jurisdiction beyond the Indian Act with a view to replacing it.

The 1969 White Paper

In June 1969, the Liberal government of Pierre Elliott Trudeau tabled its *Statement of the Government of Canada on Indian Policy*, known as "the White Paper." This policy paper recommended fundamental changes to the status of Indigenous peoples in Canada, notably the end of the distinct status for "Indians," the dissolution of the Department of Indian Affairs, and the repeal of the Indian Act and its replacement with an Indian Lands Act, all with the objective of facilitating First Nations' absorption into mainstream society. Consistent with the ethos of formal equality that earlier had animated the Joint Committee's recommendations, the federal government justified this proposal as a progressive move in tune with social reform and civil rights.

The significance of this milestone is not the proposal itself, but the reaction to it. Contrary to the Trudeau government, which viewed it as progressive, First Nations viewed the sweeping proposal to reset the relationship between Canada and First Nations as the ultimate attempt at assimilation. Anger towards the White Paper fuelled a national First Nations resistance movement and the creation of regional and national advocacy bodies, including the National Indian Brotherhood (which would eventually become the Assembly of First Nations). First Nations opposition was so strong that the federal government withdrew the proposal in 1971 and declared a formal end to its assimilation policy. However, the fire that was lit in response to the White Paper continued to burn strong; subsequent years would witness First Nations asserting Aboriginal title and treaty rights in the courts, as well as demanding seats at the negotiation table to settle outstanding land claims and secure agreements on self-government (Johnston 1983, 6–7).

While the Indigenous resistance and rights movement fuelled by the White Paper and Canada's subsequent disavowal of assimilationist policies are positive impacts of this milestone, it is important to understand that the slate had not been entirely wiped clean of assimilation. As noted in the previous section, assimilation in the guise of "formal equality" informed the attempts by the federal government to have the provinces assume responsibility for essential services on reserves. When these attempts largely failed, and faced with growing public outcry over poverty in First Nations communities (Shewell and Spagnut 1995, 4), Indian Affairs obtained Treasury Board approval in 1964 to spend federal funds for social assistance on reserves using the rates and standards enacted by the provinces (a practice often referred to as "comparability"). Indian Affairs staff subsequently adapted provincial laws and policies in order to create federal policy manuals to apply on reserves in different provinces. While Indian Affairs initially delivered these services, over time they were devolved to band governments and their staff through the introduction of funding agreements between Indian Affairs and First Nations. Although intended as a temporary measure, this practice of "regulating" via policy manuals modelled on provincial rates and standards has been expanded to virtually all essential services provided on reserve. Unless a First Nation has been able to negotiate a self-government agreement (and very few have, as discussed further below), the vast majority of day-to-day programs and services on reserves are provided in this manner.

Thus, in large measure, the assimilationist objective of having provincial norms apply to First Nations was achieved indirectly through what was intended as a stop-gap measure. This has become the status quo, despite Canada having declared an end to its formal assimilation policy nearly fifty years ago. The problem here is more than symbolic; the continued imposition of the "comparability standard" has been criticized as culturally inappropriate and contributing to high rates of child apprehension and welfare dependency, among other problems, in First Nations communities (Shewell and Spagnut 1995, 41–2; Johnston 1983, 68–71; Blackstock 2011). Indeed, a 2016 decision of the Canadian Human Rights Tribunal found the comparability approach to be discriminatory because it fails to result in services reflecting the distinct needs and circumstances of First Nations living on reserve. Yet despite these findings, Canada continues to impose this approach.[5] The tribunal also found that Canada knowingly funds child welfare services on reserve well below funding levels in the provinces, which has contributed to record numbers of First Nations children permanently taken from their families through the child welfare system. Government documents discussed in the case also revealed that Indian Affairs was well aware that the essential services on reserve that it funded fell well below levels funded by the provinces for similar services.

A final feature of this situation that is noteworthy relates back to an earlier milestone, the Indian Act. The Act is silent on the provision of essential services to First Nations (and, indeed, many modern developments in the Canada–Indigenous relationship, since it has not been amended since 1951), even though the provision of such services accounts for millions of dollars in transfers to First Nations each year. Although Canada could have amended the Indian Act in 1951, or any time afterwards, to provide for a proper regulatory framework for service delivery, the federal government has consistently resisted calls to do so. Numerous reports of the auditor general of Canada have criticized the lack of a proper legislative framework for such basic services, raising problems related to the lack of clarity around service delivery standards and the lack of transparency and accountability on the part of the government (Canada, Office of the Auditor General 1994, chap. 23, 2006, chap. 5, 2011, chap. 4, 2013, chap. 6). Some have also argued that the status quo gives the political executive and Indian Affairs staff too much discretion, which presents opportunities for abuse (Promislow and Metallic 2018; see also Borrows 2015a, 2015b). As we see below, regulation of Indigenous Affairs issues via *policy* instead of *legislation* is a recurring theme in the relationship between Canada and Indigenous peoples. In the summer of 2019, Canada passed some legislation that is a step towards addressing *some* concerns regarding lack of legislation in the area of essential services.[6]

The 1973 Calder Decision

The 1973 Supreme Court of Canada decision in *Calder v British Columbia (AG)*[7] is a milestone resulting directly from the Indigenous resistance movement fuelled by the 1969 White Paper. Although the members of Nisga'a Nation who brought the claim lost, it was nonetheless a watershed decision. Six judges found that Aboriginal title survived British assertions of sovereignty and continued at common law. Three of those judges found that such rights were never extinguished, while another three did; the remaining judge resolved the case purely on procedural grounds.

The possibility created by the ruling of the existence of inherent rights at common law, including Aboriginal title, triggered significant changes. First, the case caused Canada to reverse its long-standing policy not to negotiate First Nations land or treaty claims. Since this time, Canada has had policies to negotiate comprehensive land claims (also called modern treaties), as well as to settle what are called "specific claims" (i.e., First Nations grievances related to unfulfilled treaty promises and improper taking of reserve lands). These policies have resulted in the signing of twenty-six comprehensive claim agreements, with 100 comprehensive claim negotiations ongoing; as well, approximately 390 specific claims have been resolved.[8] *Calder* also spurred advocacy by Indigenous groups over inherent rights, ultimately leading to the recognition of Aboriginal and treaty rights in section 35 of the Constitution Act, 1982.

While being the catalyst for the modern recognition of inherent rights in Canada, *Calder* and the positive developments arising from it have their shortcomings. Most significantly, in reaching their finding that Aboriginal title exists at common law, the Supreme Court of Canada relied heavily on decisions made by Chief Justice Marshall of the US Supreme Court in a series of cases on the rights of American Indians decided in the 1820s and 1830s (Vicaire 2013). These cases, while finding that American Indians had inherent rights to land and self-government, were premised on the finding that the assertion of sovereignty by the British Crown had the legal effect of substantially *diminishing* their inherent rights, though not *extinguishing* them entirely. It has since been pointed out that Chief Justice Marshall's rulings were based on the doctrines of discovery and *terra nullius*: the racist argument that Europeans gained legal control over large territories and their peoples upon discovery of these territories because these populations were "savage" and inferior to Europeans. These doctrines have been completely discredited in international law and can no longer serve as a legal justification for colonization (Truth and Reconciliation Commission of Canada 2015, 191–5; Borrows 2017; Hoehn 2016).

Further, both the specific and comprehensive claims processes that arose from the *Calder* decision have been subjected to substantial criticism over the years. First, there are still hundreds of outstanding claims that have yet to be resolved through the specific claims process. Second, the process has been widely criticized as being biased, since Indian Affairs is at once the defendant and the judge and jury over these claims (Canada, Office of the Auditor General 2006). In response Canada attempted to improve this system in 2008 by creating a new tribunal to adjudicate specific claims, once Canada has rejected or failed to resolve a claim within three years of receiving it. However, this situation still gives Canada the balance of power in deciding these claims.[9] The government has recently announced that it will attempt to overhaul this system once again (Schmitz 2017).

The comprehensive claim process has also been charged with being exceedingly slow (in some cases taking two or three decades) and expensive, resulting in only a small number of groups with completed claims.[10] As a policy of the federal government – again, acting without a legislative framework – the process is often contingent on the attitude and political will of the government in power, and some governments have been very slow to proceed on land claims (Dalton 2006b, 31; Human Rights Council 2014). The process has also been criticized for excluding those Métis living south of the sixtieth parallel (Canada, Indian and Northern Affairs 2011, 35–6), as well as the signatories of the historic numbered treaties (Kleer and Rae 2014). There are also reports that some First Nations avoid the comprehensive claims process because Canada still insists on inserting clauses into modern treaties that extinguish or prevent their future reliance on inherent rights (Dalton 2006b, 50–3).

Section 35 of the Constitution Act, 1982

The recognition of Aboriginal and treaty rights in the Constitution Act, 1982, was a result of hard-fought lobbying by Indigenous groups (Joseph 2016). It was intended that future constitutional amendments would further specify the content of Aboriginal rights, but this did not occur. As a result, it has fallen to the courts to interpret the provision and tell us what is in the "section 35 box." Since 1990, the Supreme Court has released over thirty decisions interpreting section 35. This jurisprudence recognizes rights to hunt, fish, and gather for food, social, and ceremonial purposes,[11] and some rights to engage in commercial trading of fish and some other harvested items for the purpose of obtaining a moderate livelihood.[12] The Court has further fleshed out the nature and content of Aboriginal title – for instance, declaring it to exist with respect to land of the Tsilhqot'in Nation in the interior of British Columbia.[13] The Court has also found that governments have a duty to consult and accommodate when authorizing or engaging in activities that will affect these rights, even if they have not been legally proven but are credibly asserted.[14] The Court also has found that government can legally infringe such rights, but that such infringement must meet the justification test created by the Court (which in many ways resembles the section 1 *Oakes* test specifying reasonable limits on individual rights).[15]

While the Court's section 35 jurisprudence has led to positive developments for some Indigenous communities, the test for proving Aboriginal rights has been criticized as being unduly narrow, with a tendency to freeze Indigenous rights in the past by casting them as practices "integral and distinctive" to pre-contact cultures. The Court-applied tests for Aboriginal rights, treaty rights, and Aboriginal title have also been charged with placing a heavy onus of proof on Indigenous claimants, who must prove each right on a case-by-case basis (see Borrows 1997a; Barsh and Henderson 1997; Tokawa 2016; Gunn 2017). Likely because of this, so-called section 35 rights have not extended far beyond hunting, fishing, and gathering rights. The Supreme Court has even been reluctant to recognize self-government as a right protected by section 35. It has ruled that, if it is, the right must be linked to a pre-contact practice that is integral and distinctive to the culture.[16] Such an approach to self-government has been severely criticized for being far too restrictive (see Morse 1997; Vicaire 2013, 656–7; Dalton 2006a, 19–20; McNeil 2007, 13–14; Moodie 2003–4; Borrows 2013).

Increasingly, there have been questions about how effective a vehicle section 35 has been in transforming the relationship between Indigenous peoples and Canada. The Final Report of the Truth and Reconciliation Commission

(TRC) has suggested that section 35 has not furthered meaningful reconciliation because the case law remains anchored in the doctrine of discovery. Indeed, the Court continues to rely on the reasoning adopted in *Calder* (itself based on the aforementioned Marshall trilogy of decisions) that the inherent rights of Indigenous peoples were necessarily diminished by discovery and the assertion of sovereignty by the British. Indeed, in *R v Sparrow*, its first case interpreting section 35, the Supreme Court of Canada stated, "There was from the outset never any doubt that sovereignty and legislative power, and indeed the underlying title, to such lands vested in the Crown."[17] Again, the problem is more than symbolic. The concept of original Crown sovereignty has influenced the development of legal tests for Aboriginal rights, treaty rights, and title. This includes the heavy burden of proof placed on Indigenous claimants and a relatively forgiving justification test for governments (Truth and Reconciliation Commission of Canada 2015, 191–5; Hoehn 2016). Indeed, this convinced the TRC to conclude that section 35 has been used "as a means to subjugate Aboriginal peoples to an absolutely sovereign Crown" rather than "as a means to establish the kind of relationship that should have flourished since Confederation, as was envisioned in the Royal Proclamation of 1763 and the post-Confederation Treaties"(Truth and Reconciliation Commission of Canada 2015, 203).

The 1992 Charlottetown Accord

The Charlottetown Accord proposed to enshrine detailed provisions on self-government into the Constitution Act, 1982, and thereby brought about a national discussion on the inherent right of Indigenous self-government. This amendment would have specified Indigenous peoples' jurisdiction "to safeguard and develop their languages, cultures, economies, identities, institutions and traditions," and "to develop, maintain and strengthen their relationship with their lands, waters and environment." The accord favoured the negotiation of self-government agreements over unilateral implementation of the right by First Nations and denied direct judicial enforcement of the new inherent-right provision for five years to permit a reasonable period for negotiations. However, if an Indigenous nation had not negotiated an agreement within the five-year period, the right was, in principle, judicially enforceable without an agreement (Hogg 2014, chap. 28, 25–7). Although the accord, which included a wide number of amendments beyond Aboriginal self-government, ultimately failed, the momentum around self-government led the Liberal government of Jean Chrétien to pass a policy recognizing the inherent right to self-government in 1995 (known as the "Inherent Rights Policy") (Canada, Indian and Northern Affairs 1995).

The Inherent Rights Policy recognizes Aboriginal peoples' inherent right to self-government as an existing Aboriginal right within the meaning of section 35 of the Constitution Act, 1982. It describes this right broadly as encompassing "matters that are internal to their communities, integral to their unique cultures, identities, traditions, languages and institutions, and with respect to their special relationship to their land and their resources"(Canada, Indian and Northern Affairs 1995). Although it recognizes Aboriginal peoples' inherent jurisdiction over several areas, the policy does not contemplate Indigenous groups' unilateral exercise of these powers, even over areas that are internal to the group. Instead, the policy requires that all self-government powers must be negotiated (and agreed to) by both the federal government and provincial/territorial governments. This stipulation deviates sharply from the proposal in the Charlottetown Accord, which would have allowed unilateral exercise of self-government after five years. As such, it has significantly hampered the growth of Indigenous self-government in Canada.

Although the Inherent Rights Policy permits stand-alone self-government agreements, as well as agreements on the self-government of discrete subjects (known as "sectoral agreements"), in many cases self-government negotiations have been rolled into comprehensive claim negotiations (which can take decades to negotiate). The pace of these has been painfully slow, and contingent upon the political will of the governments in power to complete them. Only twenty-two self-government agreements have been signed: eighteen as part of comprehensive land claims agreements; three as stand-alone self-government agreements; and one sectoral agreement.[18] Once again, Canada's choice to proceed by policy as opposed to legislation severely limits Indigenous groups' ability to seek enforcement and accountability through the courts.

The leisurely pace of comprehensive land claims and self-government has meant that only a small minority of Indigenous groups have gained meaningful control over their own affairs and access to a land base beyond reserve lands. In the meantime, First Nations have continued to operate under the Indian Act and program devolution, with limited control over their lands or day-to-day lives. Again, the consequence here is more than symbolic. There is an obvious link between the exercise of meaningful self-government and improvement in Indigenous peoples' living conditions. This linkage is recognized in the academic literature (Hylton 1999; O'Neil et al. 1999, 130; Harris-Short 2012, 11–12), by the federal government itself (Canada, Indian and Northern Affairs 2011, 41) and has been demonstrated by those few instances where self-government has occurred in this country. On the other side of the coin, evidence also demonstrates that the status quo is hindering improvements in First Nations' quality of life. The community well-being index, tracked by Indian Affairs, illustrates a persistent twenty-point gap between First Nations and non-Aboriginal communities that has not changed in the last thirty years (Canada, Indian and Northern Affairs 2015).

The 1996 RCAP Report

Precipitated by the seventy-eight-day standoff at Kanesatake (Oka), Quebec, in 1991, which brought long-standing tensions between Indigenous and non-Indigenous peoples to national attention, the five-year Royal Commission on Aboriginal Peoples was intended to be a comprehensive study of the relationship between Indigenous peoples and Canada. Its five-volume final report contained over 300 recommendations on how to achieve a just and mutually respectful relationship. Despite its broad range of recommendations, key principles informed the direction proposed by the RCAP. Chief among these was the need for Indigenous peoples to be regarded as a third order of government, possessing rights of self-determination and self-government; entitlement to a more equitable share of this nation's lands and resources; a more equitable fiscal relationship with Canada; and the need for Indigenous peoples and governments in Canada to return to a nation-to-nation relationship.

To transform the current relationship to a nation-to-nation relationship, the RCAP first proposed a new royal proclamation committing Canada to a renewed treaty relationship in the long term and to adopting several new laws (RCAP 1996a, vol. 2, chap. 3, 296). On the heels of the proclamation would come a suite of new legislation (296–7), as well as the convening of federal, provincial, territorial, and Indigenous leaders to develop a Canada-wide framework agreement containing principles to guide the new nation-to-nation relationship (296, 305–9). The RCAP also put significant emphasis on the need for capacity building and support for Indigenous groups to become fully self-governing and called for the creation of a national Aboriginal Government Transition Centre to begin assisting Indigenous nations immediately (310–15). The plan was also that Canada and Aboriginal nations would devise a mutually acceptable long-term system of fiscal transfers (309–10).

The RCAP report had some important impacts. Primary among them was raising awareness of the impacts of the legacy of residential schools, which encouraged some very brave survivors to initiate individual and class actions against the government of Canada.[19] This litigation eventually led to the Indian Residential School Settlement and the creation of the Truth and Reconciliation Commission. Therefore, the RCAP report was the original catalyst for the TRC Report and its Calls to Action, which are having a significant impact on discussions across Canada on the need for transformation and reconciliation. For example, the RCAP report has impacted several Supreme Court of Canada decisions on Indigenous issues in the areas of sentencing and equality rights, and it continues to be a vital resource to inform "social context judging" as applied to the Indigenous context (Stack 2007).

On the political side of things, however, the RCAP report has had less impact. Generally, the Chrétien Liberal government was less than enthusiastic about the RCAP's proposals on self-government and a nation-to-nation relationship. In its response to the RCAP report, the government committed to providing Aboriginal communities with "the tools to guide their own destiny and to exercise their inherent right of self-government" (Stewart 1998). However, Canada remained unwilling to accept the unilateral exercise of inherent self-government, even over matters internal to Indigenous groups, and continued to define self-government as "well-defined, negotiated arrangements with rights and responsibilities that can be exercised in a coordinated way" (Serson 2009, 147; see also Assembly of First Nations 2006).

In addition to its unwillingness to embrace the RCAP report's recommendations on self-government, the government's attempt to reduce the deficit would also inhibit its ability to realize the RCAP's recommendation for a new fiscal relationship. Around this time, the government undertook a program review of all federal departments to find efficiencies in order to reduce the deficit. All departments were expected to reduce spending. The Department of Indian Affairs was reluctant to cut any core programs, given the rapidly growing First Nations population. Instead, it agreed to a compromise that funding increases for 1996–7 would be limited to 3 per cent and would be capped at 2 per cent thereafter. This funding cap – originally intended for a couple of years – remained for nearly twenty years, until March 2016. A past deputy minister of Indian Affairs has argued that the 2 per cent cap was the primary reason why the RCAP report's recommendations never got the attention from government that they deserved (Serson 2009, 149). The effect of the funding cap was to limit spending on core programs such as education, child welfare, income assistance, First Nations government support, housing, capital and infrastructure, and regulatory services programs. The result was that funding for these programs did not keep pace with the demands in First Nations communities, given population growth and inflation. By 2006 (ten years before the cap would finally be lifted), the Assembly of First Nations calculated that the cap had resulted in a 15 per cent decrease in real purchasing power for First Nations governments (Rae 2009, 27n107).

Conclusion

While there have been small changes during the twenty years after the RCAP, they have had minimal impact on transforming the Canada-Indigenous relationship beyond those events I have described here. Circumstances have stagnated and became worse in this period. In his 2014 report on the situation of Indigenous peoples in Canada, Special Rapporteur James Anaya stated that "the human rights problems faced by indigenous peoples in Canada … have reached crisis proportions in many respects" and "the most jarring manifestation of these human rights problems is the distressing socio-economic conditions of indigenous peoples in a highly developed country" (Human Rights Council 2014, 7). It has been only very recently – and primarily in response to the TRC Report and its Calls to Action – that we have started to see glimmers of the possibility of transformative change. It remains to be seen whether good words about transforming the relationship manifest in concrete action.

The six milestones that I have discussed tell us a lot about where we are in this era of "renewal and renegotiation." While there have been some improvements in the Indigenous-Canada relationship since the era of "domination and assimilation," the foregoing reveals many remaining problems that must be addressed for us to advance. We can see that some very damaging values continue to underlie and undermine the Canada-Indigenous relationship. For example, Canada continues to impose provincial rules and standards in areas of core services on First Nations, an approach steeped in assimilative assumptions. As well, our courts, and consequently Canada's whole approach to Indigenous inherent rights, take the sovereignty of the Crown – the power to make decisions over Indigenous peoples and their lands – for granted. This assertion of sovereignty, with its roots traceable to the racist doctrine of discovery, severely limits Indigenous claims to control over their own peoples and lands.

The stalling of progress on self-government and resolving claims to lands and resources has been extremely detrimental to moving towards a nation-to-nation relationship. The Canadian government has also consistently approached reforms to Indigenous relations in the last sixty years primarily through non-binding policies (as we have seen in essential service delivery, specific and comprehensive claims, and self-government). The failure to create a proper legislative framework has frustrated the development of clear norms and standards, transparency, and accountability. Nebulous policy approaches have allowed the government to knowingly underfund vital essential services in First Nations and maintain a 2 per cent cap on funding growth for many years. They have also kept relatively ineffective processes for the resolution of outstanding land and treaty claims and the negotiation of modern treaties and self-government. Meanwhile, conditions in Indigenous communities and Indigenous peoples' quality of life have not noticeably improved – and have possibly worsened. We need to learn from and address these problems if we want to achieve real progress during the next 150 years of the Canada-Indigenous relationship.

Notes

1 I generally use the term *Indigenous peoples* to refer to all peoples who descend from the original inhabitants of these lands, as this is the term gaining prominence internationally to refer to first peoples. It is synonymous with the term *Aboriginal peoples*, which was the terminology used by *Report of the Royal Commission on Aboriginal Peoples* (RCAP) in 1996 and is also the term used in section 35 of the Constitution Act, 1982, and defined to include "the Indian, Inuit and Métis peoples of Canada" (s 35(2)). While the term *First Nations* is now used instead of *Indian,* the latter term is still in use, given the continued existence of the Indian Act. When referring to RCAP or the Constitution Act, I use *Aboriginal* and *Indigenous* peoples interchangeably.

2 As noted by Chief Justice McLachlin for the Supreme Court of Canada in *Haida Nation v British Columbia (Minister of Forests)*, 2004 SCC 73 at paragraph 25.

3 In both cases, declarations from the courts were required for Canada to recognize any responsibility to these groups pursuant to s 91(24) of the Constitution. See *Reference re British North America Act, 1867 (UK),* s 91, [1939] SCR 104 and *Daniels v Canada (Indian Affairs and Northern Development)*, 2016 SCC 12.

4 See *Indian Act*, SC 1876, c 18, s 86(1).

5 *First Nations Child and Family Caring Society of Canada et al. v Attorney General of Canada (for the Minister of Indian and Northern Affairs Canada)*, 2016 CHRT 2 at para. 465 and paras 388–93 and 268.

6 "Making the Most Out of Canada's New Department of Indigenous Services Act," Policy Brief for Yellowhead Institute, August 12, 2019, Yellowhead Institute, https://yellowheadinstitute.org/2019/08/12/making-the-most-out-of-canadas-new-department-of-indigenous-services-act/; "The Promise and Pitfalls of C-92: An Act Respecting First Nations, Inuit and Métis Children, Youth and Families," Special Feature for Yellowhead Institute, July 4, 2019, https://yellowheadinstitute.org/bill-c-92-analysis/#analysis2 (with Hadley Friedland and Sarah Morales).

7 [1973] SCR 313 [*Calder*]. For reliance on decisions made by Chief Justice Marshall, see *Calder* above, note 55 at 320–1, 335, 346–7, 380–3, and 387.
8 For Indian and Northern Affairs Canada discussion on "comprehensive claims" see Government of Canada (n.d.). Discussion on "specific claims" be found at https://yellowheadinstitute.org/bill-c-92-analysis/#analysis2.
9 See *Specific Claims Tribunal Act*, SC 2008, c 22.
10 For a discussion of a results-based approach to comprehensive land claim and self-government negotiation, see Indigenous and Northern Affairs Canada (2015).
11 See, for example: *R v Van der Peet*, [1996] 2 SCR 507; *R v Côté*, [1996] 3 SCR 139; *R v Adams*, [1996] 3 SCR 101; *R v Powley*, [2003] 2 SCR 207; and *R v Sappier; R v Gray*, [2006] 2 SCR 686.
12 See *R v Gladstone*, [1996] 2 SCR 723; *R v Marshall*, [1999] 3 SCR 456.
13 See *Haida Nation v British Columbia (Minister of Forests)*, [2004] 3 SCR 511; *Mikisew Cree First Nation v Canada (Minister of Canadian Heritage)*, [2005] 3 SCR 388; *Rio Tinto Alcan Inc v Carrier Sekani Tribal Council*, [2010] 2 SCR 650; *Clyde River (Hamlet) v Petroleum Geo-Services Inc*, 2017 SCC 40.
14 See *Delgamuukw v British Columbia*, [1997] 3 SCR 1010; *Tsilhqot'in Nation v British Columbia*, 2014 SCC 44.
15 See *R v Sparrow*, [1990] 1 SCR 1075; *R v Gladstone*, [1996] 2 SCR 723; *R v Badger*, [1996] 1 SCR 771; *Tsilhqot'in Nation v British Columbia*, 2014 SCC 44.
16 See *R v Pamajewon*, [1996] 2 SCR 821.
17 See *R v Sparrow*, above, note 15. Note, in the more recent decision in *Tsilhqot'in*, above note 15, para. 69, the Court disavowed the doctrine of *terra nullius* but without addressing its relationship with the doctrine of discovery and how that doctrine has affected its interpretation of section 35.
18 Further Aboriginal self-government statistics are available through the INAC, "Fact Sheet: Aboriginal Self-Government," https://web.archive.org/web/20150913224833/http://www.aadnc-aandc.gc.ca/eng/1100100016293/1100100016294.
19 See, for example, *Blackwater v Plint*, [2005] 3 SCR 3.

References and Suggested Reading

Assembly of First Nations. 2006. *Fiscal Fairness for First Nations.* Ottawa: Assembly of First Nations.

Barsh, Russel Lawrence, and James Youngblood Henderson. 1997. "The Supreme Court's *Van der Peet* Trilogy: Naive Imperialism and Ropes of Sand." *McGill Law Journal* 42 (4): 993–1009.

Blackstock, Cindy. 2011. "The Canadian Human Rights Tribunal on First Nations Child Welfare: Why If Canada Wins, Equality and Justice Must Lose." *Children and Youth Services Review* 33 (1): 187–94.

Borrows, John. 1997a. "The Trickster: Integral to a Distinctive Culture." *Constitutional Forum* 8 (2): 27–32.

———. 1997b. "Wampum at Niagara: The Royal Proclamation, Canadian Legal History, and Self-Government." In *Aboriginal and Treaty Rights in Canada: Essays on Law, Equality, and Respect for Difference*, edited by Michael Asch, 155–72. Vancouver: UBC Press.

———. 2013. "Aboriginal and Treaty Rights and Violence against Women." *Osgoode Hall Law Journal* 50 (3): 699–736.

———. 2015a. "The Durability of *Terra Nullius*: *Tsilhqot'in Nation v British Columbia*." *University of British Columbia Law Review* 48: 701–42.

———. 2015b. "Legislation and Indigenous Self-Determination in Canada and the United States." In *From Recognition to Reconciliation: Essays on the Constitutional Entrenchment of Aboriginal and Treaty Rights*, edited by Patrick Macklem and Douglas Sanderson, 17–38. Toronto: University of Toronto Press.

———. 2017. "Canada's Colonial Constitution." In *The Right Relationship: Reimagining the Implementation of Historical Treaties*, edited by John Borrows and Michael Coyle, 474–505. Toronto: University of Toronto Press.

Canada, Indian and Northern Affairs. 1995. *The Government of Canada's Approach to Implementation of the Inherent Right and the Negotiation of Aboriginal Self-Government*. https://web.archive.org/web/20150913224833/http://www.aadnc-aandc.gc.ca/eng/1100100016293/1100100016294 (link no longer active).

———. 2011. *Final Report Evaluation of the Federal Government's Implementation of Self-Government and Self-Government Agreements: Project Number 07065*. Ottawa: Indian and Northern Affairs.

———. 2015. *Ministerial Transition Book: November 2015*. https://web.archive.org/web/20150913224833/http://www.aadnc-aandc.gc.ca/eng/1100100016293/1100100016294.

Canada, Office of the Auditor General. 1994. *1994 Report of the Auditor General of Canada to the House of Commons*. Ottawa: Office of the Auditor General of Canada.

———. 2006. *2006 Report of the Auditor General of Canada*. Ottawa: Office of the Auditor General of Canada.

———. 2011. *2011 Status Report of the Auditor General of Canada to the House of Commons*. Ottawa: Office of the Auditor General of Canada.

———. 2013. *2013 Status Report of the Auditor General of Canada*. Ottawa: Office of the Auditor General of Canada.

Dalton, Jennifer. 2006a. "Aboriginal Self-Determination in Canada: Protections Afforded by the Judiciary and Government." *Canadian Journal of Law and Society* 21 (1): 11–38.

———. 2006b. "Aboriginal Title and Self-Government in Canada: What Is the True Scope of Comprehensive Land Claims Agreements?" *Windsor Review of Legal & Social Issues* 22: 29–79.

Government of Canada. n.d. "Comprehensive Claims." https://www.aadnc-aandc.gc.ca/eng/1100100030577/1100100030578.

Gunn, Brenda. 2017. "Beyond *Van der Peet*: Bringing Together International, Indigenous and Constitutional Law." In *UNDRIP Implementation: Braiding International, Domestic and Indigenous Law – Special Report*, edited by Centre for International Governance Innovation, 29–38. Waterloo, ON: Centre for International Governance Innovation.

Harris-Short, Sonia. 2012. *Aboriginal Child Welfare, Self-Government and the Rights of Indigenous Children: Protecting the Vulnerable under International Law.* Burlington, VT: Ashgate Publishing.

Hoehn, Felix. 2016. "Back to the Future: Reconciliation and Indigenous Sovereignty after *Tsilhqot'in*." *University of New Brunswick Law Journal* 67: 109–45.

Hogg, Peter W. 2007. *Constitutional Law of Canada.* 5th ed. Scarborough, ON: Thomson Carswell.

———. 2014. *Constitutional Law of Canada.* 2014 student ed. Toronto: Thomson Carswell.

Human Rights Council. 2014. *Report of the Special Rapporteur on the Rights of Indigenous Peoples, James Anaya – Addendum – The Situation of Indigenous Peoples in Canada.* May 7, 2014 (advance unedited version), A/HRC/27/52/Add 2.

Hylton, John H. 1999. "The Case for Self-Government: A Social Policy Perspective." In *Aboriginal Self-Government in Canada: Current Trends and Issues*, edited by John H. Hylton, 2nd ed., 78–91. Saskatoon: Purich.

Indigenous and Northern Affairs Canada. 2015. "Report on Plans and Priorities." www.aadnc-aandc.gc.ca/eng/1420651340132/1420653980474.

Johnston, Patrick. 1983. *Native Children and the Child Welfare System.* Toronto: Canadian Council on Social Development in association with James Lorimer.

Joseph, Bob. 2016. "The Constitution Express and Its Role in Entrenching Aboriginal Rights." Working Effectively with Indigenous Peoples (blog). https://www.ictinc.ca/blog/the-constitution-express-and-its-role-in-entrenching-aboriginal-rights.

Kleer, Nancy, and Judith Rae. 2014. "Divided We Fall: *Tsilhqot'in* and the Historic Treaties." Olthuis Kleer Townshend LLP, July 11. https://www.oktlaw.com/divided-fall-tsilhqotin-historic-treaties/.

Lawrence, Bonita. 2004. *"Real" Indians and Others: Mixed-Blood Urban Native Peoples and Indigenous Nationhood.* Vancouver: UBC Press.

Lewington, Jennifer. 2012. "In Nova Scotia, a Mi'kmaq Model for First Nation Education." *Education Canada* 52 (5). https://www.edcan.ca/articles/in-nova-scotia-a-mikmaw-model-for-first-nation-education/.

McNeil, Kent. 2007. "The Jurisdiction of Inherent Right Aboriginal Governments." October 11. Research Paper for the National Centre for First Nations Governance. http://fngovernance.org/ncfng_research/kent_mcneil.pdf.

Metallic, Naiomi. 2019. "Ending Piecemeal Recognition of Indigenous Nationhood and Jurisdiction: Returning RCAP's Aboriginal Nation Recognition and Government Act." In *Redefining Relationships: Indigenous Peoples and Canada*, edited by Karen Drake and Grenda Gunn, 243–80. Saskatoon: Native Law Center.

Moodie, Doug. 2003–4. "Thinking Outside the 20th-Century Box: Revisiting *Mitchell*: Some Comments on the Politics of Judicial Law-Making in the Context of Aboriginal Self-Government since *Calder*: Search for Doctrinal Coherence." *Ottawa Law Review* 35 (1): 1–42.

Morse, Bradford. 1997. "Permafrost Rights: Aboriginal Self-Government and the Supreme Court in *R v Pamajewon*." *McGill Law Journal* 42 (4): 1011–44.

Napoleon, Val. 2001. "Extinction by Number: Colonialism Made Easy." *Canadian Journal of Law and Society* 16 (1): 113–65.

O'Neil, John, Laurel Lemchuk-Favel, Yvon Allard, and Brian Postl. 1999. "Community Healing and Aboriginal Self-Government." In *Aboriginal Self-Government in Canada: Current Trends and Issues*, edited by John H. Hylton, 2nd ed., 130–56. Saskatoon: Purich.

Palmater, Pamela. 2011. *Beyond Blood: Rethinking Indigenous Identity.* Saskatoon: Purich.

Promislow, Janna, and Naiomi Metallic. 2018. "Realizing Administrative Aboriginal Law." In *Administrative Law in Context*, edited by Colleen M. Flood and Lorne Sossin, 3rd ed., 87–137. Toronto: Emond Montgomery.

Rae, Judith. 2009. "Program Delivery Devolution: A Stepping Stone of Quagmire for First Nations?" *Indigenous Law Journal* 7 (2): 1–44.

Royal Commission on Aboriginal Peoples (RCAP). 1996a. *Final Report.* 5 vols. Ottawa: Canada Communication Group Publishing.

———. 1996b. "Highlights from the Report of the Royal Commission on Aboriginal Peoples: People to People, Nation to Nation." https://www.rcaanc-cirnac.gc.ca/eng/1100100014597/1572547985018.

Schmitz, Cristin. 2017. "Ottawa Pledges 'Complete Overhaul' of Specific Claims to Promote Reconciliation with Indigenous Peoples." *Lawyer's Daily*, September 7. http://www.thelawyersdaily.ca/articles/4586/ottawa-pledges-complete-overhaul-of-specific-claims-to-promote-reconciliation-with-indigenous-peoples-.

Senate of Canada. 2006. *Negotiation or Confrontation: It's Canada Choice: Final Report of the Standing Senate Committee on Aboriginal Peoples Special Study on the Federal Specific Claims Process.* Ottawa: Standing Senate Committee on Aboriginal Peoples.

Serson, Scott. 2009. "Reconciliation: For First Nations This Must Include First Fairness." In *Response, Responsibility, and Renewal: Canada's Truth and Reconciliation Journey*, edited by Aboriginal Healing Foundation, Gregory Younging, Jonathan Dewar, and Mike DeGagné, 165–74. Ottawa: Aboriginal Healing Foundation.

Shewell, Hugh. 2004. *"Enough to Keep Them Alive": Indian Welfare in Canada, 1873–1965.* Toronto: University of Toronto Press.

Shewell, Hugh, and Annabel Spagnut. 1995. "The First Nations of Canada: Social Welfare and the Quest for Self-Government." In *Social Welfare with Indigenous Peoples*, edited by John Dixon and Robert Scheurell, 1–53. London: Routledge.

Stack, David. 2007. "The First Decade of RCAP's Influence on Aboriginal Law." *Saskatchewan Law Review* 70 (1): 123–52.

Stewart, Jane. 1998. "Address by the Honourable Jane Stewart, Minister of Indian Affairs and Northern Development on the Occasion of the Unveiling of *Gathering Strength: Canada's Aboriginal Action Plan.*" Address given in Ottawa, January 7.

Tokawa, Kenji. 2016. "*Van der Peet* Turns 20: Revisiting the Rights Equation and Building a New Test for Aboriginal Rights." *University of British Columbia Law Review* 49 (2): 817–35.

Truth and Reconciliation Commission of Canada. 2015. *Honouring the Truth, Reconciling for the Future: Summary of the Final Report of Truth and Reconciliation Commission of Canada.* Winnipeg: Truth and Reconciliation Commission of Canada.

Van Harten, Gus, Gerald Heckman, and David Mullen. 2010. *Administrative Law: Cases, Text, and Materials.* 6th ed. Toronto: Emond Montgomery.

Vicaire, Peter. 2013. "Two Roads Diverged: A Comparative Analysis of Indigenous Rights in a North American Constitutional Context." *McGill Law Journal* 58 (3): 607–62.

Wilkins, Kerry. 2000. "Still Crazy after All These Years: Section 88 of the *Indian Act*." *Alberta Law Review* 38 (2): 458–503.

twenty-one
Immigration in Canada: From Low to High Politics

MIREILLE PAQUET

Introduction

Canada is a settler society. International immigration has been the primary source of its population and is now, more than ever, a contributor to its economic and social development. From the first European settlements to the postwar period, Canada's immigration program has grown in size and sophistication. It has also proven to be highly innovative and regarded with envy by other countries. Yet, despite its importance, immigration has not always figured as a topic of "high politics" in Canada. Contrary to debates over natural resources, fiscal federalism, or constitutional politics, issues related directly to immigration have remained in the background and have not been the object of strong national partisan cleavages.

In this chapter, I argue that immigration is now entering the terrain of "high politics" in Canada, but that this change is compounded with the specific institutional context and political divisions that make up the country's political life. Using the concept of "high politics" helps to convey the fact that immigration is now a topic of considerable salience in Canadian politics, something that is seen by most as having direct consequences for the survival of the state and for the continued existence of the political community (Teitelbaum 1994; Hollifield and Wong 2015).

In relation to this argument, this chapter starts by defining central concepts for the study of immigration in political science. It then goes on to identify the institutional foundations of immigration governance in Canada and to describe the main components of Canada's program. The chapter closes by discussing two contemporary political debates surrounding immigration in Canada – federalization and border crossings at the US border – and shows how they now attract more attention, involve more actors, and build into more central cleavages of national politics than ever before.

Immigration

Words like *immigration* and *immigrants* are politically and socially contested. Human movement across territories is constant and states have limited successes in curtailing it. According to the United Nations, the population of international migrants in 2017 was estimated at 258 million (United Nations 2017). While this number is high, it represents less than 4 per cent of the world population in 2017 (International Organization for Migration 2017). Most of the world's immigrants reside in the United States (48.9 million), Saudi Arabia (12.2 million), Germany (12.2 million), and the Russian Federation (11.7 million).

In that context, international immigrants are defined as persons who have changed their country of residence, either in the long term (over a year) or in the short term (at least three months but less than a year) (International Organization for Migration 2017, 15). This definition is translated by every government into different administrative categories for managing inflows, issuing visa and distributing rights or other entitlements. Since there is no universal and objective definition of the status of immigrant, it is crucial to consider how different labels – *economic immigrant, irregular migrant, humanitarian immigrant*, etc. – emerge out of time-bound and place-bound political processes.

This general definition does not account for the different reasons that people migrate, which can include a desire for economic mobility, the experience of insecurity or conflict, the maintenance of social and family ties, or, quite simply, the hope of living an adventure. Some international migration occurs through voluntary decisions, while a lot of movement is the result of forced displacement and persecution or as the consequences of natural disasters (International Organization for Migration 2017). In 2017, about 28.5 million persons were seeking asylum or had the status of refugees (United Nations High Commissioner for Refugees Canada 2018). Contrary to the term *immigrant*, the status of refugees rests on a shared set of international norms, including the 1951 Convention relating to the Status of Refugees and the related 1967 protocol, as well as several international law instruments that have regional focuses. It refers to "someone who is unable or unwilling to return to their country of origin owing to a well-founded fear of being persecuted for reasons of race, religion, nationality, membership of a particular social group, or political opinion" (United Nations High Commissioner for Refugees 2010, 3) and whose claim has been accepted by the state where resettlement occurs. Asylum seekers, on the other hand, are individuals who have formally requested protection as refugees but have yet to have their status determined (International Organization for Migration 2011).

Importantly, most human mobility occurs inside the boundaries of states. "Internal migration" refers to the movement of people towards settlement in another part of a country and "internal displacement" is used to describe the process of being obliged or forced to leave a place of residence in order to settle elsewhere inside the borders of the same state (International Organization for Migration 2011). Data on internal migration and internal displacement is harder to come by, as countries vary tremendously in their capacity and willingness to collect information on such movements (United Nations High Commissioner for Refugees 2018).

Immigration in Canada

In 2016, about 582,000 individuals entered Canada as international immigrants. Of this number, 296,000 settled permanently and about 286,000 were granted temporary status for work-related reasons (Canada 2018a). While these numbers may appear high, Canada is only the eighth world destination for permanent immigration. The total immigrant population is about 7.9 million persons and this represents 21.5 per cent of the overall population of the country (United Nations 2018). The main source countries of permanent immigrants are the Philippines (14 per cent), India (13 per cent), Syria (12 per cent), China (9 per cent) Pakistan (4 per cent), the United States (3 per cent), Iran (2 per cent), France (2 per cent), the United Kingdom (2 per cent), and Eritrea (2 per cent) (Canada 2018a). International immigration has been the largest contributor to population growth in Canada since the early 2000s (Bohnert, Chagnon, and Dion 2015). The country plans to maintain high levels of immigration in the years to come, as a way to contribute to the development of the labour force and to ensure population renewal in the face of aging citizens and low fertility rates (Canada 2017).

Because of its geography and the fact that it shares a border only with the United States – the largest country of settlement for international immigrants – Canada has been in an enviable position to manage a very effective and very selective immigration program. Central to Canadian discussions about immigration are thus administrative categories used to differentiate between different types of migrants. As noted, these categories reflect political decisions made by successive governments and not objective realities. In Canada, they have become terms that are used, often unquestioned, by governments, journalists, and citizens when they describe immigration. In addition to making a stark distinction between permanent immigrants and temporary residents, this program is structured upon three main administrative categories: economic immigrants; family immigrants; and refugees, protected persons, and humanitarian immigrants.

Economic immigrants include the individuals selected on the basis of their skills and work experiences, their education, their language proficiency, and their expected ability to adapt to Canadian societies. They may enter Canada through federal programs, such as the Federal Skilled Worker

Program, the Federal Skilled Trades Program, the Canadian Experience Class category, the Caregiver Program, and several businesses and investment streams. Economic immigrants can also be selected by provincial governments, either through the Provincial Nominee Program or Quebec's immigrant selection programs (Canada 2018a).

For social scientists, the administrative category of "economic immigrants" is misleading in two ways. First, it dismisses the direct and indirect contributions of other groups of immigrants to Canada's economy. Second, it does not account for the fact that the number reported under this category often also includes close family members of the principal applicant to immigration. It is important, from that standpoint, to contextualize properly that fact and its consequence that more than 53 per cent of the new arrivals to Canada are classified as economic immigrants (Canada 2018a). This percentage both underestimates and overestimates a complex phenomenon.

Immigrants entering through the family category are generally sponsored by the relatives already living in Canada as either citizens or permanent residents. Generally, relatives are understood to include spouses or partners, children, as well as parents and grandparents. There were 78,004 individuals who entered Canada in 2017 through immigration opportunities included in this category (Canada 2018a). Yet not all those with relatives in Canada and wishing to join them do so. Depending on their profile, they may be able to enter through other immigrant categories. On the other hand, having relatives in Canada does not guarantee entry into the country: there are several grounds for being refused family reunification.

Protected persons and refugees as well as humanitarian immigrants are individuals who are granted protection in Canada. They are identified and selected abroad, in collaboration with the United Nations High Commissioner for Refugees, in which case they are designated by the Canadian government as "government-assisted refugees" (Canada 2018a). It is also possible to apply for asylum from within Canada or at a point of entry to Canada (land border, airport, seaport, etc.). In those cases, government agencies and an administrative tribunal – the Immigration and Refugee Board of Canada (IRB) – will determine whether a person may receive asylum in Canada as a convention refugee or on the basis of other protection needs. Canada is also recognized internationally for its refugee sponsorship program. Under different streams, this program allows for Canadian citizens or institutions to provide "refugees with care, lodging, settlement assistance and support" during the first year of settlement in Canada (Canada 2018d). In 2016, the country welcomed 62,348 refugees, protected persons, and humanitarian immigrants, which accounted for 21 per cent of the new immigrant population (Canada 2018a).

Governing Immigration in Canada

The management of Canada's contemporary immigration program occurs through the country's specific institutional context and political conventions. Federalism, the parliamentary system, the centralization of executive powers, and the relative influence of different government departments all contribute to shaping the politics of immigration in Canada. These institutional forces constantly interact with social and political dynamics, such as changes in political party orientation and ideology towards immigration (Omidvar 2016) or "focusing events" that bring the attention of the Canadian public to immigration issues (Lawlor and Tolley 2017).

Immigration is one of only two formally shared jurisdictions in the Canadian constitution. Article 95 of the 1867 British North America Act (BNAA) states that provinces and the federal government may legislate on immigration matters but that, in case of conflicts between a provincial and a federal law, the Act of the Parliament of Canada will take precedence (Paquet 2014). In practice, this means that provincial legislative assemblies may vote upon immigration laws that will apply to their province only, while the federal Parliament may enact legislation that affects all of the country. Conflicts between provincial and federal immigration laws have been quite rare in Canada.

Despite this shared jurisdiction, prior to the 1990s most provinces, with the important exception of Quebec, were not very interested or active in immigration policy (Paquet 2014). In Quebec, beginning with the Quiet Revolution of the 1960s, successive provincial governments negotiated the decentralization and devolution of immigration powers. In 1991, Ottawa and Quebec signed a devolution agreement known as the Canada-Québec Accord Relating to Immigration and Temporary Admission of Aliens (sometimes called the Gagnon-Tremblay-McDougall Accord) (Quebec 2000). This unique intergovernmental agreement gives the provincial government the complete power to select economic immigrants and refugees abroad (once they are identified as such by Canada and UNHCR). It gives the sole responsibility to implement immigrant integration services in the province, which are partially funded by a federal grant to the province (in lieu of direct federal spending to provide these services).

Other provinces do not exercise this degree of autonomy, even if they have started to sign new immigration agreements with Ottawa in the early 2000s. In most cases, the agreements outline forms of collaboration between governments and allow provinces to establish small immigrant selection schemes, referred to as Provincial Nominee Programs or PNPs (Lewis 2010). These programs allow provinces to directly select a portion of the economic immigrants hoping to settle on their territories, according to the specific needs of their economies and labour markets. As of 2016, PNPs contributed 29.5 per cent of Canada's annual economic immigrant intake and for some provinces (e.g., Manitoba) confer the primary type of immigrant (Canada 2018a). Immigrant integration policies, interestingly, are not an area of jurisdiction defined in the 1867 BNAA.

Immigration-related laws also enable different actors in the governance of immigration. As such, they are the central pillars of Canada's immigration politics. The Immigration and Refugee Protection Act is the key law that organizes the procedures to grant and remove immigration statuses, including refugee status and other forms of protection (Canada 2013; Dauvergne 2003). It enables enforcement, such as deportation or loss of status, and creates arm's length institutions to deal with particular matters. It also provides government with the authority to make regulations that have to do with immigration. The Canadian Citizenship Act provides the rules and procedure for matters of naturalization in the country (Canada 2018b). These federal laws have consequences for a plethora of other laws in Canada, ranging from labour codes to the Extradition Act and the Criminal Code.

Three administrative institutions are centrally responsible for managing Canada's immigration program. Immigration, Refugee and Citizenship Canada (IRCC) is the only federal department dedicated to immigration. It manages the Canadian government's immigration responsibilities in collaboration with the Canadian Border Services Agency, which, in addition to its customs duties, is responsible for management of border services and enforcement of several dimensions of Canada's immigration program (e.g., immigrant detention). Another federal department, Employment and Social Development Canada, collaborates with IRCC to run the economic portion of the temporary immigration program and provides support for employment forecasting as it relates to new arrivals. Finally, the Immigration and Refugee Board of Canada is the main decision-making body for refugee status determination. As an administrative tribunal, it is expected to make decisions independent from pressures of the government of the day. Because immigration is complex and technical, these administrative institutions have been able to influence the content and implementation of Canada's immigration program at different times (Molloy and Madokoro 2017; Paquet 2015; Satzewich 2014).

The conventions and consequences of the country's political institutions also shape the politics of immigration management. In particular, the centralization of power with the political executive – first and foremost the prime minister and the minister responsible for immigration – have generally given to governments a large degree of freedom in designing immigration policies and programs. This is compounded by the conventions of responsible government and strict party discipline that limit the capacity of Parliament and its committees (such as the Standing Committee on Citizenship and Immigration) to affect the content of immigration policies. Parliament does remain in a potentially powerful position, however, in holding the government accountable. In particular, committee work has proven influential in identifying new policy challenges and providing stakeholders with a venue to voice their opinions about Canada's immigration policies. The power of the executive also has been reinforced by the creation of "ministerial instructions," following an amendment to the Immigration and Refugee Protection Act under the Harper government in 2008. These allow the minister to make important changes to immigration programs and policies through regulation-like orders that bypass the need for a vote in Parliament while also limiting other forms of oversight (Ferrer, Picot, and Riddell 2014; Kelley and Trebilcock 2010). In short, immigration has been, for the most part, a policy area dominated by the political executive in Canada.

Immigration as High Politics

Despite being intrinsically linked to state building, international immigration has never been considered a matter of high politics in Canada. Historically, it has been seen as an issue of less importance, as compared to economic development or constitutional politics. As a result, generally it has been left to administrative actors to manage, and the pattern of executive decision-making that is characteristic of this sector has not been heavily criticized by other political actors. Things are starting to change, however, as immigration becomes more politicized worldwide (Dauvergne 2016). Canada's dependence on international immigration and the growth of the country's immigrant population contribute to this change.

Immigration is consequently moving to the terrain of high politics: it is becoming an issue of high salience and political importance. Three trends are especially indicative of this change. First is the increased presence of immigration-related issues in national election campaigns, in parliamentary debates, and in the media. Canadians and their politicians are paying more attention to immigration and, relatedly, to what governments are doing about it. Second, the number of actors involved or interested in being involved in immigration-related issues is multiplying. From cities and provinces to private firms and public universities, a wide range of actors now see themselves as stakeholders in Canada's immigration policies and programs. Third, since the mid-2000s, the immigration minister has become more powerful within Cabinet. These trends are self-reinforcing and contribute to raising the profile of immigration in Canadian politics.

Immigration moving onto the terrain of high politics also means that new issues are now being considered through the prism of essential cleavages in Canadian politics. These include the practices of federalism, the issue of redistribution across Canada, and the tension between individual equality and the recognition of diversity. Two current debates effectively demonstrate the politicization of immigration and the continuing importance of traditional Canadian cleavages: the federalization of immigration and the burgeoning number of irregular border crossings from the United States.

The Federalization of Immigration

After Quebec gained more powers in immigration, several other provinces began to expect more autonomy in this policy sector. Not only have provincial governments demanded increased powers and more resources, they have also become much more active in immigration as it relates to their areas of jurisdiction (Paquet 2014). Indeed, immigration has direct and indirect consequences for some of the most important responsibilities of provinces: education, health care, and culture. Moreover, premiers and other provincial political actors have become adamant about the relationship between immigration and the future prosperity, in some cases the survival, of their provinces. Immigrants, they argue during election campaigns, speeches from the throne, and media releases, are needed more than ever to ensure economic growth and population renewal (Paquet 2019).

In earlier research, I have described this trend as the federalization of immigration: provinces have stopped being comfortable with Ottawa acting as sole decider and manager of immigration. As a result, the governance consequences of article 95 of the BNAA has slowly become a reality: Ottawa and the provinces both have a legitimate say on this issue and collaboration is required. This has been recognized by governments with the signing of bilateral agreements between the federal government and every province. Immigration now features as a regular topic in intergovernmental meetings – such as the interprovincial Council of the Federation – and new institutions have been created to further cooperation between governments (Schertzer 2015). The creation of the Provincial Nominee Program is also a direct consequence of this change. Provinces (including Quebec) now select 49 per cent of the total new economic immigrants arriving in Canada.

Federalization contributes to making immigration part of Canada's high politics. To start with, because it figures prominently on the political agenda of provinces, it has entered the mainstream federal-provincial-territorial relations, discussed in the same manner as energy or health care. More importantly, federalization feeds into a central cleavage of Canadian political life: the practices of federalism. Provinces' increased involvement in immigration raises the question of who within the federation should decide. Immigration has local and national repercussions: immigrants settle in provinces but are provided with mobility rights within Canada; both orders of government benefit from and invest in immigrants, but they do so with different capacities; provinces vary tremendously in the number of immigrants they receive and accordingly they diverge in the type of immigration policies they hope to implement. Recognizing these issues, two responses to federalization emerge.

Successive governments in Ottawa have often maintained that the country is better served by a centralized and unique immigration program. In 2012, Immigration and Multiculturalism Minister Jason Kenney perfectly summed up this position during an address to an immigration conference when he declared, "I believe there is a critically important ongoing role for federal selection of immigrants. Immigration is about nation-building. It's not just about addressing regional labour needs" (Canada 2012). From this standpoint, the direct involvement of provinces in immigration should be limited to providing insight on local dynamics, while the federal government should be in charge of implementing a standardized national immigration program from sea to sea. This view is reminiscent of the arguments of the advocates of a centralized model of federalism who consider Ottawa to be in a better position to ensure equality across the country.

Provinces, on the other hand, have generally argued that their substantive involvement is a precondition to a fair and effective immigration program. Indeed, the dramatic social, political, and economic differences between provinces requires place-based immigration policies (Bradford 2004). This can be achieved only if provinces are given both the jurisdictional autonomy and the fiscal resources to design their own policies. For example, New Brunswick welcomed 1.58 per cent of Canada's new permanent residents in 2016, whereas Ontario attracted 37.13 per cent of the total (Canada 2018a). In light of such huge differences, the argument goes that provinces need to be in a position to deploy different strategies to attract immigrants and to implement integration services that reflect their particular immigrant populations and their local labour markets. This position has often been identified with Quebec, since the province has historically advocated for the capacity to make policies that reflect its linguistic, political, and social distinctiveness. Yet, in the area of immigration this position has come to be adopted in one form or another by every province; it is not only a Quebec phenomenon. These arguments align with advocates for a decentralized model of federalism in Canada. It reflects the argument that provinces are in the best position to pursue a version of equality across the country that recognizes and accommodates diversity.

Border Crossings

Since the 2016 election of Donald Trump as the forty-fifth president of the United States, an unprecedented number of people have crossed the Canada-US border on foot in order to claim refugee status. This spike is driven by anti-immigrant policies and rhetoric in the United States, the closure of several avenues for status regularization in the United States and elsewhere, as well as reinforced by the social, political, economic, and environmental factors that contribute to the overall growth of the number of displaced persons in the world. Canada and the United States are party to the Safe Third Country Agreement, which came into force in 2004 (Canada 2016). Designed to ensure border coordination between the two countries and to limit the duplication of asylum claims, the agreement's central consequence is that individuals are required to claim refugee status in the country where they first arrive. Individuals arriving in the United States are required to make their claim to refugee status there and the same goes for Canada. Should their initial claim be rejected, they are not eligible to make a similar claim in the other country. There are several exceptions to this rule, including claims made by non-accompanied minors and claims made after non-land arrivals. The most important exception, however, is the one having to do with claims made by individuals who actually make it into Canada's territory. They are able to make an application for asylum in Canada, even though they are deemed to be arriving from the United States. This is more complicated than it seems; border agents at Canada-US points of entry (land border, airports, etc.) are entitled to stop and refuse entry to any individual they consider to be coming to Canada to claim status, on the ground that they may do so in the United States. As a result – with the political climate surrounding immigration in the United States creating fear for individuals and families with precarious residency status – a growing number are deciding to enter Canada away from official points of entry in order to make their asylum claim.

Over a twelve-month period in 2017–18, about 20,000 persons entered Canada through this irregular process (United Nations High Commissioner for Refugees Canada 2018). This represented an all-time high, and the rate of new arrivals has since decreased (Canada 2018e). The primary source countries of these claimants were Haiti and Nigeria. Having arrived in Canada, they were not granted refugee status automatically. On the contrary, as with any within-Canada claimant, they must submit their claim to the IRB. As of 2018, data on the success rate of these claims are too few to report but one thing is evident: the increased number of claimants is creating tremendous pressure on the administrative tribunal. As of March 2018, "15% of those who crossed the border irregularly in 2017 had their claims finalized"; of those, "47% … obtained refugee status" (United Nations High Commissioner for Refugees Canada 2018). Those who are denied status by the IRB might be deported to their country of origin or remain in Canada temporarily.

Irregular border crossings have attracted national attention in Canada and contributed to making immigration an issue of high politics. Their salience in the media, in political debates, and in everyday discussions has generated new anxieties about Canadian sovereignty and the country's capacity to determine its own immigration policies and procedures in the face of the United States. Irregular border crossings have also called into question Canada's reputation for being able to control immigration effectively, which is often touted as a prime reason for Canadians' generally pro-immigrant views.

In addition to these new fears, border crossings also play into cleavages in Canadian political life. Most irregular border crossings have occurred in Quebec, through a specific pathway in the Montérégie region. Most subsequently end up in Montreal and Toronto, two of the most common destinations for immigrants in Canada (United Nations High Commissioner for Refugees Canada 2018). This population requires housing and social services in the short and the medium term, as well as access to schools.

These developments have created tensions between orders of government when it comes to who should finance these services. Provinces and municipalities have argued that, since they are not in a position to effectively limit or stop border crossings, they should not be required to foot the bill for the help these asylum seekers require. For Quebec and Ontario, the issue at play is not whether or not the province should help. Instead, the debates are focused on fiscal equity and redistribution within the federation (Lecours and Béland 2009). It feeds into a broader conflict surrounding the vertical fiscal imbalance in Canada (Noël 2007; Saint-Hilaire 2005). Critics argue that the federal government generates more tax revenue than it needs to manage its areas of jurisdiction while provinces do not have enough to attend to theirs. There is a dual disequilibrium between the capacity to raise revenue and spending needs. This exists between the federal and provincial orders of government (vertical imbalance), as well as between provinces (horizontal imbalance). As a result, several mechanisms of territorial redistribution such as equalization and health transfer payments have been devised to fund most expensive provincial programs. Critics who cite a continuing vertical fiscal imbalance argue that these mechanisms are inadequate, that the sums transferred to provinces are too small, and that the calculations used to determine these sums are inadequate. The result, from this critical perspective, is that provinces are unable to provide appropriate services to their populations without running significant deficits, while Ottawa often generates a surplus.

The surge in border crossings feeds into this dispute, especially as Quebec and Ontario are, each in its own way, in the forefront of the battle over fiscal federalism (Courchene 2014). The increased fiscal pressure border crossings create for these provincial governments thus raises two quintessential federal questions: "Who is responsible?" and "Who should pay?"

Moreover, the local concentration of this population has revived debates about the role of cities in Canadian politics. Mayors, councillors, and local service providers have argued that border crossings increase the pressure on municipal and local services, such as shelters. They also highlight the fact that immigration has important consequences for public transportation, policing, and leisure services (e.g., municipal pools or libraries). In recognition of these realities, Montreal and Toronto have demanded to be allowed special powers and to receive more funding from both orders of governments (Canada 2018c). These requests reflect the general plight of cities in Canada. Since constitutionally they are "creatures of the provinces," cities and municipal governments have no protected area of jurisdiction (Andrew 2001). They depend on funding from other governments because they are limited in their capacity to raise revenue from taxes. Urban-dwelling citizens also tend to be less well represented in provincial and federal Parliaments, as their ridings generally include more voters than in rural areas. At the same time, the service demands and citizen expectations vis-à-vis municipal governments have expanded tremendously.

The institutional position of cities and the changing nature of Canadian governments have generated calls for a revision of the powers and resources allocated to municipalities. While several reforms have been implemented to address these challenges, local political actors, especially those in large cities, remain unsatisfied with their powers, particularly with their financial resources. The reaction of city governments in Toronto and Montreal to the growing number of irregular border crossers reflect this ongoing battle. In that sense, this new phenomenon feeds into the central debate over the role and capacity of different governments in Canadian political life, beyond the strict categories put forward by the Constitution. It raises the question of what political units today are most relevant for Canadians and why.

Conclusion

Immigration has been crucial to the establishment of Canada as a settler society and to its subsequent growth and character, and it remains vital for the survival and prosperity of Canada. International immigration is the primary contributor to Canada's demographic growth and is necessary to economic competitiveness. Relative to the country's population, Canada's immigration program is considerable in size; it includes "economic migrants," immigrants reunifying with their families, as well as refugees and protected persons. The political and administrative management of this stream of immigrants and refugees is affected by Canada's institutions. This chapter has highlighted how federalism, key laws and conventions, historical legacies, and challenges of public administration have shaped immigration politics. The defining feature of immigration policy-making is that those who hold executive power – especially the prime minister and minister responsible for immigration – have enjoyed a large degree of autonomous authority.

After being an issue relegated to the margins of Canadian politics, immigration is increasingly a topic of high politics. It is attracting more attention, generating more debate, and involving a growing number of actors. In this chapter, this change has been explored through two recent dynamics: the federalization of immigration and the sudden spike of irregular border crossings from the United States. As these developments demonstrate, more than ever debates over immigration are reflected through the prism of other long-standing cleavages in Canadian politics: fiscal federalism, decentralization and subsidiarity, as well as discussion about the contemporary relevance of different orders and scales of governments.

This move to centre stage of Canadian politics is likely to affect the substance of debates over immigration policies and programs for years. Indeed, the high politics of immigration runs counter to the pattern of executive autonomy that characterized policy-making in this area for most of Canadian history. The increasing number of actors involved in immigration politics – either as stakeholders, implementation agents, or members of the attentive public – will constrain the federal government's capacity to act unilaterally on these matters. Moreover, the growing salience of immigration issues may also create pressures for increased transparency and accountability in the immigration sector. It is becoming more complicated for Ottawa to act mostly alone in immigration, while leaving Canadians – including immigrants living in Canada – mostly in the dark.

References and Suggested Readings

Andrew, Caroline. 2001. "The Shame of (Ignoring) the Cities." *Journal of Canadian Studies* 35 (4): 100–10.

Bohnert, Nora, Jonathan Chagnon, and Patrice Dion. 2015. *Population Projections for Canada, Provinces and Territories, 2013 to 2063*. Ottawa: Statistics Canada.

Bradford, Neil. 2004. "Place Matters and Multi-level Governance: Paradigm on a New Policy Paradigm." *Policy Options* 25 (2): 39–44.

Canada. 2012. "Speaking Notes for the Honourable Jason Kenney, P.C., M.P., Minister of Citizenship, Immigration and Multiculturalism, Toronto, March 1, 2012."

https://www.canada.ca/en/immigration-refugees-citizenship/news/archives/speeches-2012/jason-kenney-minister-2012-03-01.html.

———. 2013. "Immigration and Refugee Protection Act (S.C. 2001, c. 27)." http://laws-lois.justice.gc.ca/eng/acts/I-2.5/FullText.html.

———. 2016. "Canada-U.S. Safe Third Country Agreement." Immigration, Refugees and Citizenship Canada. https://www.canada.ca/en/immigration-refugees-citizenship/corporate/mandate/policies-operational-instructions-agreements/agreements/safe-third-country-agreement.html.

———. 2017. "Notice – Supplementary Information 2018–2020 Immigration Levels Plan." Citizenship, Immigration and Refugee Canada. https://www.canada.ca/en/immigration-refugees-citizenship/news/notices/supplementary-immigration-levels-2018.html.

———. 2018a. "2017 Annual Report to Parliament on Immigration." Immigration, Refugees and Citizenship Canada. https://www.canada.ca/en/immigration-refugees-citizenship/corporate/publications-manuals/annual-report-parliament-immigration-2017.html.

———. 2018b. "Citizenship Act (R.S.C., 1985, c. C-29)." http://laws-lois.justice.gc.ca/eng/acts/C-29/FullText.html.

———. 2018c. "Government of Canada Providing Assistance to Toronto for Asylum Seeker Housing." Immigration, Refugees and Citizenship Canada. https://www.canada.ca/en/immigration-refugees-citizenship/news/2018/07/government-of-canada-providing-assistance-to-toronto-for-asylum-seeker-housing.html.

———. 2018d. "Guide to the Private Sponsorship of Refugees Program." Immigration, Refugees and Citizenship Canada. https://www.canada.ca/en/immigration-refugees-citizenship/corporate/publications-manuals/guide-private-sponsorship-refugees-program.html.

———. 2018e. "Irregular Migration Reaches Lowest Number in Past Year." Immigration, Refugees and Citizenship Canada. https://www.canada.ca/en/immigration-refugees-citizenship/news/2018/07/irregular-migration-reaches-lowest-number-in-past-year.html.

Courchene, Thomas. 2014. "Vertical and Horizontal Fiscal Imbalances: An Ontario Perspective." Montreal: Institute for Research on Public Policy. https://irpp.org/research-studies/presentation-2005-05-04/.

Dauvergne, Catherine. 2003. "Evaluating Canada's New Immigration and Refugee Protection Act in Its Global Context." *Alberta Law Review* 41 (3): 725–44.

———. 2016. *The New Politics of Immigration and the End of Settler Societies*. New York: Cambridge University Press.

Ferrer, Ana M., Garnett Picot, and William Craig Riddell. 2014. "New Directions in Immigration Policy: Canada's Evolving Approach to the Selection of Economic Immigrants." *International Migration Review* 48 (3): 846–67.

Hollifield, James F., and Tom K. Wong. 2015. "The Politics of International Migration. How Can We 'Bring The State Back In'?" In *Migration Theory: Talking across Discipline*, edited by Caroline B. Brettell and James F. Hollifield, 2nd ed., 227–88. New York: Routledge.

International Organization for Migration. 2011. *Glossary on Immigration*. 2nd ed. Geneva: IOM.

———. 2017. *World Migration Report 2018*. Geneva: IOM.

Kelley, Ninette, and Michael Trebilcock. 2010. *The Making of the Mosaic: A History of Canadian Immigration Policy*. 2nd ed. Toronto: University of Toronto Press.

Lawlor, Andrea, and Erin Tolley. 2017. "Deciding Who's Legitimate: News Media Framing of Immigrants and Refugees." *International Journal of Communication* 11: 967–91.

Lecours, André, and Daniel Béland. 2009. "Federalism and Fiscal Policy: The Politics of Equalization in Canada." *Publius: The Journal of Federalism* 40 (4): 569–96.

Lewis, Nathaniel M. 2010. "A Decade Later: Assessing Successes and Challenges in Manitoba's Provincial Immigrant Nominee Program." *Canadian Public Policy* 36 (2): 241–64.

Molloy, Michael J., and Laura Madokoro. 2017. "Effecting Change: Civil Servants and Refugee Policy in 1970s Canada." *Refuge: Canada's Journal on Refugees* 33 (1): 52–61.

Noël, Alain. 2007. "When Fiscal Imbalance Becomes a Federal Problem." In *The 2006 Federal Budget: Rethinking Fiscal Priorities*, edited by Charles M. Beach, Michael Smart, and Thomas A. Wilson, 127–43. Montreal and Kingston: McGill-Queen's University Press.

Omidvar, Ratna. 2016. "The Harper Influence on Immigration." In *The Harper Factor: Assessing a Prime Minister's Policy Legacy*, edited by Jennifer Ditchburn and Graham Fox, 179–95. Montreal and Kingston: McGill-Queen's University Press.

Paquet, Mireille. 2014. "The Federalization of Immigration and Integration in Canada." *Canadian Journal of Political Science* 47 (3): 519–48.

———. 2015. "Bureaucrats as Immigration Policy-makers: The Case of Subnational Immigration Activism in Canada, 1990–2010." *Journal of Ethnic and Migration Studies* 41 (11): 1815–35.

———. 2019. *Province Building and the Federalization of Immigration in Canada*. Toronto: University of Toronto Press.

Quebec. 2000. *Canada-Québec Accord Relating to Immigration and Temporary Admission of Aliens*. Quebec City: Immigration et communautés culturelles.

Saint-Hilaire, France. 2005. *Fiscal Gaps and Imbalances: The New Fundamentals of Canadian Federalism*. Kingston: Institut of Intergovernmental Relations, Queen's University.

Satzewich, Vic. 2014. *Points of Entry: How Canada's Immigration Officers Decide Who Gets In*. Vancouver: UBC Press.

Schertzer, Robert. 2015. "Intergovernmental Relations in Canada's Immigration System: From Bilateralism towards Multilateral Collaboration." *Canadian Journal of Political Science* 48 (2): 383–412.

Teitelbaum, Michael S. 1994. "Guest Editorial: International Migration: From Backwaters to High Politics." *Population and Environment* 15 (3): 167–71.

United Nations. 2017. *International Migration Report 2017*. New York: Department of Economic and Social Affairs, Population Division.

———. 2018. "International Migrant Stock: The 2017 Revision." Department of Economic and Social Affairs, Population Division.

United Nations High Commissioner for Refugees. 2010. *Convention and Protocol Relating to the Status of Refugees*. Geneva: UNHCR.

———. 2018. *Global Trends: Forced Displacement in 2017*. Geneva: UNHCR.

United Nations High Commissioner for Refugees Canada. 2018. "Irregular Arrivals at the Border in 2017: Background Information." Accessed Juy 30, 2018. https://www.unhcr.ca/wp-content/uploads/2018/12/IRREGULAR-ARRIVALS-AT-THE-BORDER-IN-2017-Final.pdf.

twenty-two
Canada and the Climate Policy Dilemma

DEBORA VANNIJNATTEN AND DOUGLAS MACDONALD

Introduction

In the fall of 2015, when the Trudeau Liberals formed a new majority government, the context for moving forward with its ambitious environment and climate agenda appeared highly favourable. Canada's turn toward pro-environmental policies seemed well-timed in terms of the growing international and continental consensus (Trudeau 2016). Within Canada, the Trudeau government's arrival also coincided with action already taken in the large provinces – BC, Ontario, and Quebec – and political party dynamics at the national and provincial levels that appeared to support concerted climate action. Moreover, public opinion appeared to be on the Liberals' side, swept along in the optimism of the "sunnier," more environmentally friendly future that the Liberals had promised (David Suzuki Foundation and the Environics Institute 2015). Environmental groups exulted in these new directions, and in Alberta the new NDP government was able to introduce a carbon tax and phase-out of coal-fired electricity with support from business. It seemed that finally, and for the first time – despite the many promises made over several decades – Canada might be able to meet its greenhouse gas (GHG) reduction targets.

Yet both international and domestic dynamics have evolved considerably since the fall of 2015, in ways that throw up several obstacles to climate change action. On the international stage, the impact of the Trump administration's foreign and trade policy since early 2016 can be likened to throwing a bomb into the established international and bilateral order, and this has spilled over into climate change policy, to the point where any kind of cooperation seems impossible. At home, the picture is even darker. During its first term in office, the Trudeau government managed to put in place a federal-provincial program, the Pan-Canadian Framework (PCF), which was centred on the goal of having a carbon tax in place throughout the country. If any province did not itself implement such a tax (or equivalent cap-and-trade system, discussed below), the federal government would introduce its own tax within that province. By the time of the federal election on October 21, 2019, five provinces (Alberta, Saskatchewan, Manitoba, Ontario, and New Brunswick), all led by right-wing governments, had dropped out of the PCF (and so the federal tax was applied within their borders) and three had gone to court, hoping to have the federal tax declared unconstitutional. Worse yet, climate change policy had become entangled with national unity. Two-thirds of voters in that election supported parties promising more effective climate action, but on the other side of the divide voters in Alberta and Saskatchewan did not elect a single Liberal member of Parliament, and angry voices in Alberta raised again the threat of possible separation from Canada. As of spring 2020, the obstacles to effective climate policy had become much greater than they were in the fall of 2015.

The first purpose of this chapter is to introduce readers to the climate change issue in Canada. This includes the nature of the issue, actions by business and environmental actors, public attitudes, party politics, and the workings of the federal system on climate change – namely, which level of government is responsible for what and how they do or do not work together to develop Canadian policy. A short history of government policy prior to election of the Trudeau government is also provided, along with a detailed presentation of the current program, the PCF. The second purpose is to provide thoughts on the perplexing question of why Canadian climate policy has continually failed to meet its internationally stated objectives and is not likely to attain these targets in the near future, even with the initiatives outlined in the PCF. We argue that climate change policy has always faced entrenched institutional and political constraints in Canada, and these have not for the most part been properly addressed by the Liberal government in order to secure a set of "winning conditions" for their climate policy aspirations.

What lies at the very core of Canada's climate policy dilemma is the fundamental difference of interest and policy actions between oil-producing provinces and other provinces. Emissions are increasing in the former and decreasing in the latter. What makes effective policy almost impossible is the plan by Alberta, already the largest-emitting province, to increase its emissions over the next decade, even while the country as a whole is attempting to reduce them. We argue that, at a bare minimum, all parts of the country must start moving in the same direction to reduce emissions between now and the Paris target date of 2030. This requires addressing the thorny political issue of how to share the emissions reduction burden. What portion of the emissions reduction effort will be shouldered by each of the major emitters (see table 22.1 on sources of emissions)? What portion of the total cost of this reduction will be borne by each province?

Table 22.1 Canadian GHG Reduction Targets

Year announced	International agreement	Reduction	Target for total Canadian emissions (Mt)
1992	UNFCCC, Rio summit	Stabilize emissions at 1990 levels by 2000	613
1997	Kyoto summit	Reduce emissions to 6% below 1990 levels by 2012	576
2010	Copenhagen summit	Reduce emissions to 17% below 2005 levels by 2020	620
2015	Paris summit	Reduce emissions to 30% below 2005 levels by 2030	511

Sources: Commissioner of Environment and Sustainable Development (2017); Environment and Climate Change Canada (2020a)

The Climate Change Policy Dilemma

What do we mean when we talk about climate change, and why is it such a problem? Climate change is the catch-all term used to describe both the increase in global average temperatures and the shifts in worldwide weather phenomena (e.g., more severe hurricanes, floods, and drought) associated with this increase. Global temperatures have been increasing for many decades but this trend has accelerated since the 1990s. The unprecedented increase in temperatures is being driven by rising concentrations of gases in earth's atmospheric "greenhouse" – the lower atmosphere that traps heat from the sun as it is reflected back from the Earth. Human activity, in particular the burning of fossil fuels and the consequent release of carbon dioxide, is currently generating an excess of greenhouse gases that is trapped in the atmosphere, resulting in a continuous build-up of heat.

As distinct from environmental effects that pose more local, immediate threats – such as invasive species, forest loss, and air pollution – it is difficult to link the environmental problem of climate change to specific impacts, including the extreme weather events just noted. Nor yet can a given impact be associated with any particular emission of greenhouse gases. Adding to this complexity, there is a time lag between GHG emissions and their associated impacts. Climate change impacts felt today are associated with past emissions, while today's emissions will cause impacts well into the future. What this means is that today's voters are being asked to pay a high cost in order to avoid future impacts – impacts that are predicted but not entirely understood – in order to safeguard future generations. This is, needless to say, a tough sell for politicians accustomed to jostling for partisan advantage over a short time horizon.

Countries such as Canada, which are heavily reliant on the production and use of fossil fuels, both of which generate large amounts of carbon dioxide, face a particularly daunting task when attempting to lower emissions. That task is made even more difficult by the fact that Canada is a fossil-fuel exporting country. Emissions caused by combustion of Canadian coal, oil, and natural gas outside the country do not count, under international rules, as part of Canadian emissions. However, considerable quantities of fossil fuels are needed to extract and transport those exported fuels. While oil and gas production (much of which is exported) is the largest source of GHG emissions, the need to heat buildings in our northerly climate as well as transport goods across large distances also contributes to our fuel use. Indeed, transportation is the second highest source of GHG emissions. Electricity generation, heavy industry, buildings, and agriculture are also significant emissions sources. While "carbon intensity" – which refers to the amount of carbon by weight emitted per unit of energy consumed – is falling in Canada, continued economic growth, increased production, and population growth, as well as the likelihood of increased production in the oil sands (with its associated emissions) are all working in the opposite direction, increasing Canada's overall emissions. The GHG reduction challenge is, by all measures, immense. Figure 22.1 shows the major GHG sources.

"Mitigation" efforts, which are policies and programs aimed at reducing GHG emissions, must encourage reductions across all of these sectors. This requires a full range of measures that change the way we produce and use energy: (1) *conserving energy* by increasing the efficiency of automobiles and other machinery so that they are more fuel-efficient as well as by encouraging more use of public transport and less of personal vehicles; (2) *fuel-switching*, whereby fossil fuels (coal, oil, and gas) are replaced with renewable technologies or nuclear power in order to power economic and residential activities; and (3) *placing limits on the amount of GHGs that can be produced* through economic activities, through absolute caps or intensity measures in specific sectors. As discussed below, such caps have existed at the national level since 1990 (although we have failed to stay within those limits). More recently, the Alberta government put a limit of 100 Mt (megatonnes) per year on oil sands emissions (most estimates put the figure now at about 70 Mt, although this is a matter of dispute between the federal government and Alberta). Governments are also working on programs that can help us "adapt" to the changes that climate change appears to be engendering, but such adaptation policies are not the subject of this chapter.

The other, very difficult aspect of climate change policy is that it requires actions by all levels of government, given that the impacts are widespread and

Figure 22.1 GHG Emissions Sources in Canada

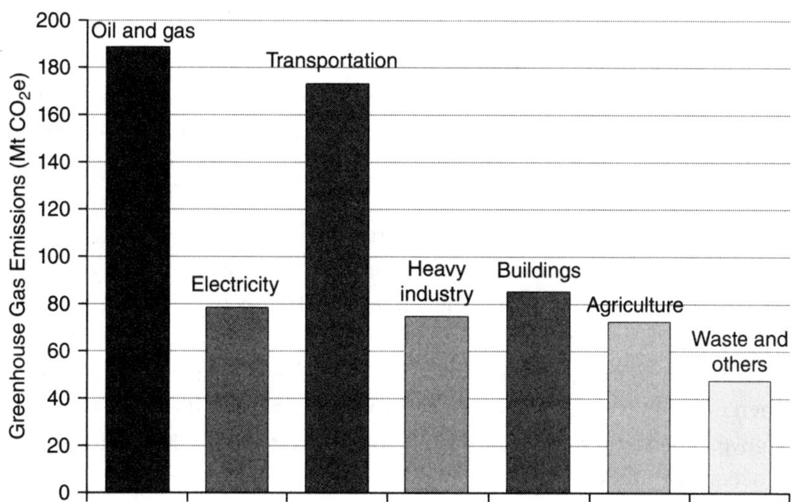

policy jurisdiction is divided and wide-ranging. Internationally, the United Nations Framework Convention on Climate Change (UNFCCC), which came into being in 1992, is an environmental agreement to stabilize GHG emissions in the atmosphere in order to prevent dangerous changes to the climate system. The framework supports the emission limits that individual countries set for themselves by promoting a range of partnership, technical, and financial support measures. Multilateral negotiating forums have resulted in several rounds of country commitments over the past decades. The 2015 Paris Agreement was the most recent round, and many argue the most successful, in engendering consensus for more ambitious action, because for the first time almost all the countries of the world committed to making reductions. That said, the Paris Agreement is based on voluntary commitments. While the Paris target is to hold global warming to no more than 2 degrees Celsius (and ideally 1.5 degrees), the sum of the Paris commitments seems more likely to result in 3 degrees of warming.

In Canada, implementation of GHG emissions reductions is complex, given that both the federal and provincial governments have constitutional jurisdiction to regulate GHG emissions. Alberta, Saskatchewan, and Ontario have challenged in court the federal authority to levy a carbon tax within their borders. Courts in Saskatchewan and Ontario, in split decisions, have found the tax to be constitutional. Conversely, the Alberta Court of Appeal has declared the tax unconstitutional. All three decisions have been appealed to the Supreme Court, which will rule sometime in 2020. Adding to the complexity, Indigenous actors have a constitutionally guaranteed say in such matters as pipeline approvals, and local governments are also important actors. The municipal level of government has no constitutional basis for engaging in mitigation and it possesses limited policy tools in this area. However, it can play a role in supporting public transportation, "green" building codes, and environmentally sensitive land use, as well as tree-planting, efficient water use, and other conservation initiatives.

The federal government has constitutional authority over international agreements, the international and interprovincial transport of energy, including pipelines, and nuclear power generation. It also has the power to levy taxes in almost any area of economic activity. However, the provinces own oil and gas resources, manage natural resource development and electricity generation, and regulate almost all point sources of GHGs. The two levels of government, therefore, must collaborate if effective GHG mitigation is to occur. The federal and provincial governments have engaged in intergovernmental decision-making to develop and implement environmental programs, but these agreements are non-binding; any government can opt out of a federal-provincial agreement at any time – as Ontario and some other provinces did in the summer of 2018 when they left the Pan-Canadian Framework agreement.

Negotiation in the process of intergovernmental relations operates on the basis of consensual decision-making, with no enforceable voting rules. This increases the veto power of the government least willing to act, which threatens to opt out, and drives agreement down to the lowest common denominator. The federal government can use its powers of persuasion, including promises of funding assistance and threats to regulate if provinces do not do so themselves (as did Prime Minister Justin Trudeau with his "backstop" carbon tax). Ideally, those powers would be sufficient to broker an agreement on an effective program. Experience, however, has shown that the regional interests of the western fossil fuel producing provinces, combined with a lack of political will and adroitness by the federal government, have frustrated any fully effective agreement that encompasses Ottawa and all provinces and territories.

The Failure of Canadian Climate Policy: 1990–2015

There have been four Canadian GHG reduction targets, expressed in megatonnes (one million tonnes) of carbon dioxide equivalent.

The first target was set by Prime Minister Brian Mulroney shortly after he had helped put the climate change issue on the international agenda. He did this by co-hosting the 1988 Toronto Conference on Climate Change with UN agencies. The federal and provincial governments began developing a coordinated national policy, but without the use of effective policy instruments. No legally binding requirements to reduce emissions were introduced; instead, voluntary action was the most prominent instrument employed. By the mid-1990s, emissions had substantially increased and it was clear the stabilization target could not be met by 2000. As a consequence, the government of Prime Minister Jean Chrétien, at the Kyoto summit, set a new objective roughly in keeping with the targets adopted by the United States and other industrialized countries. For the next five years, governments continued to develop programs, again with little use of effective instruments. A basic split developed when Alberta and other fossil-fuel provinces strongly resisted any actions that would reduce revenues flowing from the oil industry. In 2002, Alberta effectively withdrew from the national program and set its own, less ambitious target. Ottawa also effectively withdrew, as it developed plans to use its regulatory powers to bring about emission reductions, regardless of what the provinces did. When Ottawa ratified the Kyoto commitment in 2002 – despite objections from all provinces – the federal-provincial process effectively came to an end.

From 2003 to 2005, Paul Martin's short-lived Liberal government attempted to establish a federal policy without alignment with provincial actions. Under Stephen Harper's Conservative government (2006–15), the climate policy file languished. Concerns about escalating GHG emissions were crowded out by other priorities: a staunch commitment to make Canada an "energy superpower" through "responsible resource development"; a reluctance to make any international commitments that might impinge on this agenda (and hence Harper's decision to pull out of the Kyoto Protocol under which state signatories committed to reducing GHGs); and – even more fundamentally – an unwillingness to accept the findings of climate science. In 2010, the Harper government set the Copenhagen target shown in table 22.1, but took no action to achieve it. Some provinces, however, did take significant action, including introduction of a carbon tax in British Columbia in 2008 and ending of coal-fired electricity generation in Ontario. In 2015, shortly before losing power, the Harper government in Ottawa again set a target that was essentially plucked from thin air (though roughly in line with targets other countries were adopting), without any prior agreement by the provinces.

Yet, as critics frequently noted, Harper appeared little worse in actual actions taken than the preceding Liberal governments, who used pro-climate rhetoric but actually accomplished little – all previous GHG targets were missed, and by wide margins. The emissions level for 2017, the most recent year for which data are available, is 716 Mt (ECCC 2019). Notable here is that this is still not close to achieving the very first emissions goal set in 1990. To compensate for lack of effective policy, successive federal governments keep moving the target date further into the future. The obvious question here is why Canada has not been able to do better.

The Pan-Canadian Framework for Climate Action: 2015–2018

On the campaign trail in 2015, the Trudeau Liberals made it clear that, if elected, they would pursue an ambitious set of national climate and environmental policy goals in a manner that was both internationalist and meaningful. In fact, Canada's new federal leaders proposed a complete break with the previous Harper government in substance, approach, and instrument choice – most notably, they would set a GHG reduction target and meet it. Indeed, Trudeau committed the Liberals to re-engaging in international climate processes, and restoring Canada "as a leader in the world" (Liberal Party of Canada 2015), particularly in clean energy and climate multilateralism. Shortly after winning the election in December 2015, Trudeau attended the twenty-first session of the UNFCCC Conference of Parties (COP 21) in Paris and more firmly committed the country to reducing GHG emissions by 30 per cent below 2005 levels by 2030. This was the target actually set out by the previous Conservative government. The Trudeau government originally said that target was a "minimum" and that a more ambitious one would be set; some months later, however, that became the official Canadian target, without any consultation with the provinces.

At home, the commitment to environmental sustainability and climate change mitigation was to be thoroughgoing and collaborative (in federal-provincial terms) going forward. Federal and provincial environment ministers met in January 2016; first ministers (the prime minister, premiers, and territorial leaders) then met in Vancouver in March. After considerable wrangling, they issued the Vancouver Declaration on Clean Growth and Climate Change outlining a process to be followed to generate a national program capable of meeting the new Canadian target (Government of Canada 2016a). Although Saskatchewan Premier Brad Wall expressed skepticism, he and all other provincial and territorial leaders, along with Ottawa, signed the Vancouver Declaration. Four working groups proceeded to develop policy options, which were reported to federal and provincial ministers. On October 3, 2016, Prime Minister Trudeau announced in the House of Commons that his government would put in place a federal carbon tax in any province that had not already established a comparable carbon price. This unilateral action offended a number of provincial governments, most notably Saskatchewan.

Nevertheless, on December 9, 2016 all governments – with the exception of Saskatchewan and Manitoba (which refused due to a dispute over health care funding) – proceeded to sign the Pan-Canadian Framework (Government of Canada 2016b).

The national carbon pricing program, intended to encourage businesses and households to innovate and "seek out new ways to increase efficiencies and to pollute less," lies at the core of the PCF (Government of Canada 2016b). It sets out a national benchmark for pricing carbon pollution; as noted, the federal government applies that tax in any province that does not have a comparable GHG pricing measure in place. The federal tax comes in two parts. The first is a tax on fuels, such as gasoline and natural gas for home heating, which is passed on to consumers. The second is a tax on large industrial emitters. The carbon price is set at a minimum of $10 per tonne, rising $10 per year to $50 per tonne in 2022; provinces can establish their own carbon tax or set up a carbon trading program.[1] British Columbia, which has had a carbon tax in place since 2008, already met the national price benchmarks; Alberta had established a hybrid system combining a carbon levy with a performance-based system for large industrial emitters; Quebec was participating in a cap-and-trade system with California, which Ontario was about to join; Nova Scotia, using regulation instead of tax or trading, had already reduced its per capita emissions more than any other province, effectively meeting the Paris target.

Thus, various carbon pricing systems and other policy instruments were already being applied in provinces accounting for almost 85 per cent of the Canadian economy. These variations were recognized and allowed under the PCF as long as they consisted of either a tax or trading system (Nova Scotia was required to bring in a pricing system) and as long as the equivalent of the federal backstop price was achieved. For those provinces that did not set up a carbon pricing system, the federal government would put one in place. Finally – and critical to the political acceptability of the federal backstop tax – Ottawa indicated that any revenues generated in a province through the federal carbon tax would be remitted back to that province. At the time, the federal government did not say if these revenues would be transferred to the provincial government or go directly to citizens and firms within the province. However, on October 23, 2018, it was announced that Ottawa would impose its backstop carbon tax in four provinces and that all funds collected would go directly to citizens and businesses within the province.

The PCF also set out an array of "complementary actions" that were underway or would be taken in the electricity sector, transportation, forestry and agriculture, infrastructure, and across different industry sectors. These actions would deepen GHG mitigation efforts, as it was acknowledged that the carbon price set by the federal government was too low to achieve Canada's target. Analysis in 2017 suggested that with existing policies, the tax would have to be something like $150 to meet the target (Sawyer and Bataille 2017). Further, the federal government would provide hundreds of millions of dollars for infrastructure, for the Low-Carbon Economy Fund, and for other clean technology initiatives taken by provinces. In addition, intergovernmental machinery was put in place to support these efforts; federal, provincial, and territorial governments would work together under the auspices of the Canadian Council of Ministers of the Environment, through committees dealing with carbon pricing, emissions reporting, and complementary actions, and through relevant ministerial tables in different sectors, including energy and mines, transportation, forestry, agriculture, innovation, infrastructure, and finance/tax (46).

At the same time, however, it is critical to note that the Trudeau government – both on the 2015 campaign trail and in its governing speeches and policies – stressed that its approach would be "balanced," meaning that an ambitious GHG reduction approach would be balanced with support for new pipelines to facilitate the export of Canadian oil. For some time, both the Alberta government and the oil industry had been pressing for new pipeline capacity. They feared that existing capacity placed an upper limit on expansion of the Alberta oil sands. At the same time, they wanted a new pipeline to tidewater – either the Canadian west or east coast – to allow oil to be exported to Asian or other markets where it could be sold at a higher price than was available in the United States. Indeed, Alberta made federal approval of a new pipeline a condition of its participation in the PCF. Although the Trudeau government refers to it as a "balanced" approach, a better word might be "contradictory": simultaneously seeking to use the PCF to reduce GHG emissions *and* to approve (and now itself build, as discussed below) a new pipeline that will increase those emissions. This has created real difficulties for various actors who want to support the Liberals' climate policy.

During the first two years after its signing, the PCF encountered strong headwinds. The first problem was opposition by the NDP government elected in 2017 in British Columbia to the proposed twinning of the existing Trans Mountain pipeline to the west coast, which was the minimal condition imposed by Alberta for its participation in the PCF. In the spring of 2018, Kinder Morgan, the private-sector owner of the Trans Mountain expansion, informed the federal government that unless risk to the project arising from BC government opposition had been removed by May 31, 2018, it would cancel plans to build the pipeline. Ottawa initially offered to compensate the company against possible financial loss, but after further negotiation it announced instead its intention to go much further. The government of Canada would purchase the Trans Mountain pipeline and, for the price of $4.5 billion, take on the cost, estimated in early 2020 to be around $12 billion, of building the expansion, the twin pipeline to run beside the existing one. Ottawa, and all Canadians were now in the pipeline business.

The next problem to arise was the result of the Ontario election of June 7, 2018, which installed a majority Progressive Conservative government led by Premier Doug Ford. Ford had campaigned on a platform that included the elimination of Ontario's planned cap-and-trade program, effectively taking Ontario out of the PCF. Not only did the Ford government do so, it also initiated court action, similar to that of Saskatchewan, hoping to block the implementation in Ontario of the "backstop" federal carbon tax.

Third, the Federal Court of Appeal announced on August 30, 2018, that it had decided to disallow federal approval of the Trans Mountain twinning project. The court ruled that consideration of the potential impact of oil shipments on coastal whales had been inadequate; nor had government consultation with Aboriginal bands been fulsome enough. In response to the ruling, Alberta Premier Rachel Notley announced her government's withdrawal from the PCF. This was followed a month later by the withdrawal of Manitoba, which had originally stayed out, then subsequently joined the PCF (Tasker 2018).

Undeterred, the prime minister and his government vowed to stay the course. As noted, they announced that they would impose a federal carbon tax in four provinces deemed not to have a satisfactory pricing system in place: Saskatchewan, Manitoba, Ontario, and New Brunswick. After Jason Kenney was elected premier of Alberta in April 2019, it cancelled Alberta's carbon tax, and the federal tax was applied in that province, too. The prime minister stressed that citizens of those provinces would receive a rebate that in most cases would be higher than the costs to them of the federal tax. (This was because small businesses were also paying the tax but would not be receiving a rebate – in effect a monetary transfer from them to citizens.) The Trudeau government also said it would continue to work with the remaining provinces to implement other parts of the PCF. As well, the "balanced" approach would continue: everything possible would be done to proceed with the Trans Mountain pipeline project, including revisiting the issue of marine traffic effects on whales and launching a new round of Aboriginal consultation. The National Energy Board further studied impacts on whales and found these effects were real but acceptable in light of the economic benefits of the pipeline expansion. The federal government completed its consultations in June 2019 and again approved the pipeline. Indigenous actors again went to court, claiming the second round of consultations was still inadequate, but in early 2020 the Federal Court of Appeal ruled against them. Construction of the pipeline was restarted.

Despite provincial defections, the PCF is a more effective national program than anything preceding it. However, it too continues the familiar Canadian dynamic of climate policy failure. Government documents show emissions will be 19 per cent below the 2005 level (while the target is to be 30 per cent below), which means that it will miss the 2030 target by approximately 80 megatonnes (Environment and Climate Change Canada 2020b). Even to get to that point, the program relies upon new initiatives that are still being developed or have yet to be put in place. The real problem, however, is that it does nothing to address the gap between rising Alberta emissions and Canada's target of reducing total emissions by 30 per cent. It is impossible to believe that other provinces will be willing to offset Alberta's increasing emissions with further dramatic reductions of their own.

The Key Role of Regionalism and Federalism in Climate Conflict

We now will attempt to explain this Canadian policy failure. Canada's climate change policy dilemma is deeply rooted in the basic difference of interest between the oil and gas producing regions and the rest of the country. This dilemma finds it roots in Canadian "regionalism."

Regionalism and federalism are the two mainstays of, on the one hand, Canadian social and economic life and, on the other, Canadian politics and governance. Regionalism refers to the fact that Canada is made up of geographic areas with historically differing economies (e.g., fisheries in Atlantic Canada, aeronautics and forestry in Quebec, manufacturing in Ontario, agriculture on the Prairies), and distinct cultures and identities that are linked to these differences. Federalism is a system of government whereby two orders of government (federal and provincial) divide sovereignty between them; both have legitimate authority to govern over the same territory and people, and the system cannot be changed unilaterally by either order of government. Regionalism explains why Canada was created in 1867 as a federal state, first and foremost to accommodate Quebec's desire to protect its French-Canadian language, religion, and culture. Federalism, and more specifically "executive federalism" (which refers to negotiation among the heads of the Canadian federal and provincial governments), is the means used to broker agreement among differing regional interests. This is required whenever national programs – those spanning the entire country, delivered by both levels of government, with at least some intergovernmental coordination – are put in place.

The central fact of regionalism is difference. Different parts of the country have economies, cultures, and identities that differ from those found in other parts, and yet all must somehow find ways to work together as one country.

What are the differences dividing the oil-producing region of Alberta and Saskatchewan from other regions? The first is the existence of fossil fuel resources that have enormous potential to generate wealth. This wealth goes to the industry that extracts and processes the resources, provincial governments in the form of royalty revenue, the federal government in the form of various taxes, and the provincial economy as a whole (which benefits from the resulting jobs and economic growth). Although this regional difference may change as the result of advances in the new technology of fracking,[2] Ontario and Quebec, for instance, do not have those resources and their associated wealth potential. Figure 22.1 shows that GHG emissions from oil and gas extraction are Canada's largest single source, and they are located primarily in the two aforementioned western provinces. For that reason, effective national policy to reduce emissions poses a far greater economic threat to them than it does for other regions.

Another difference is that per capita reduction costs are much higher in Alberta and Saskatchewan than in other parts of Canada. Harrison and Bryant (2016) give data showing that per capita emissions in those provinces amount to over sixty tonnes per person, while it is only ten to fifteen tonnes in central Canada. This means the western economies are much more closely tied to high emissions than the rest of Canada, and as a result per capita reduction costs are much higher. This also means that those provinces are much more likely to resist national climate policy than the others.

A third regional difference is that GHG emissions in the two western provinces have increased considerably over the past twenty years, while they have declined in other provinces, as shown in table 22.2. This difference is explained in part by different climate change policies; in part by the fact that the flat Prairie provinces have negligible hydroelectricity and must generate electricity by burning coal or natural gas; and by the significant fossil fuel energy used to extract and transport oil and gas.

Beyond past performance, a fourth regional difference is apparent in announced plans for future emissions. The NDP government that took power in Alberta in 2015 brought in significant measures to reduce emissions, including a carbon tax and ending coal-electricity generation. However, a significant increase in future emissions is expected as the result of growing investment in the oil sands, facilitated by the expanded pipeline to the west coast that the Trudeau government has committed to building. Data supplied by the Alberta government (Government of Alberta 2017) shows that, with the provincial and federal policies now in place, emissions will *increase* to 9 per cent above the 2005 level by 2030. The catch, of course, is that the country as a whole is committed to a target that will *reduce* its emissions by 30 per cent below the 2005 level over that period. To accomplish this, other

Table 22.2 Emissions Changes (Megatonnes)

Provinces	1990 emissions	2017 emissions	Change (%)
Alberta	173	273	+ 58
Saskatchewan	44	78	+ 77
Ontario	180	159	−12
Quebec	86	78	−9
Nova Scotia	20	16	−20

Source: Environment and Climate Change Canada (2019). Percentages rounded to closest whole number

provinces would have to make significant reductions beyond their current plans to offset Alberta's failure to reduce its emissions (let alone its planned increase).

The combination of the Canadian Constitution, which gives us the complex governance system outlined above, and Canadian geography, which portrays the widely differing regional interests and policy performance outlined above, constitute the Canadian climate change dilemma. We will now review how well Canada has succeeded in addressing that dilemma.

Understanding Broader Political Dynamics

As noted at the outset, whereas it seemed in 2015 that Canadians were finally in broad agreement that the country needed to take steps toward a greener future, as of spring 2020 it is not entirely clear that the various levels of government and publics across the country are on the same page. First, the Canadian public seems to be losing its initial affection for the federal Liberal government and its agenda, as witnessed by the fact that Prime Minster Trudeau was able to secure only a minority government in the October 21, 2019, election. At the same time, the country has become even more regionally divided on the issues of climate change action and pursuit of the green economy. Strong majorities of Canadians in every province would prefer governments to put in place policies that support renewables and clean tech – with the exception of Alberta, where citizens want more support for fossil fuels (Anderson 2018). In addition, the major pillar in the federal government's climate action plan, carbon pricing, is the least favoured among policy options for reducing GHG (Anderson 2018).

For environmental groups, enthused by the Trudeau government's commitment to climate action yet dismayed at its continued support for pipelines, the climate policy framework has always been problematic. They find themselves conflicted, wanting to support the PCF but also feeling the need to push back against pipeline expansion. Yet these groups have not offered solutions to the basic dilemma of rising emissions in one part of the country undercutting progress made elsewhere.

Critically, large industry players must play a key role in achieving Canadian climate policy aspirations. Given the unpredictability of government and policy changes at the provincial level, more sustainable federal connections to business would help to build more resilient climate policy. Early in its mandate, the Liberal government did place a premium on bringing large business onto the climate policy scene; former Environment and Climate Change Minister Catherine McKenna worked closely with large corporations in Canada who chose to sign on to the Carbon Pricing Leadership Coalition. However, the impact of trade discord with the United States has altered the discussion with business, given the traditional desire of the private sector to see Canadian policy harmonized with that of the United States. As the gulf between the policy stances of the Trump administration and Trudeau government increases, this becomes a major political problem for the federal climate strategy.

It would be hard to underestimate the impact of President Trump's foreign policy on the international political and economic order (see Brawley in this volume), and this has spilled over into climate change cooperation. On the diplomatic front, the withdrawal of the United States from global environmental initiatives, such as the Paris Accord, the appointment of anti-environmentalists to key positions in the US administration, and the systematic dismantlement of the previous administration's climate programming (Jotzo, Depledge, and Winkler 2018) create a real challenge for Canada and other like-minded countries.

Indeed, there is a deeply rooted antagonism within the Trump administration toward any discussion of the climate change phenomenon. It refuses to accept the science of climate change and acknowledge any human role in inducing climate change. In October 2018, the Intergovernmental Panel on Climate Change warned that human activities had already caused global warming of approximately one degree Celsius since pre-industrial times and that this would cause further climate-related risks to health, livelihoods, food security, water supply, human security, and economic growth. In response to the report, Trump stated that scientists were pursuing "a political agenda" and that the United States would not be investing in climate programming that would result in the loss of "millions of jobs" (BBC 2018). As a result, his administration has moved to dismantle all national climate change programming put in place under the Obama administration. Done largely through executive orders, without the involvement of Congress, the affected policies include emissions reductions for specific industries, particularly the GHG-spewing coal-fired electricity plants; enhanced automotive fuel-efficiency standards; and support for renewable energy technologies and energy efficiency programs. Trump also cut funding for NASA's satellite-based climate change research program and attempted to eliminate a wide range of climate science programming; Congress, however, blocked most of the defunding attempts aimed at climate research and renewable energy programs (Noll and Krishnaswami 2018).

In Canada's relationship with the United States, the situation could hardly be worse, given the high level of personal animosity between Trudeau and Trump, serious ongoing trade frictions (despite having reached agreement on the 2018 USMCA trade agreement), and extreme diplomatic uncertainty. Given this suddenly difficult relationship (compared to historical norms), along with dramatically different stances on climate change policy, meaningful bilateral cooperation in this area seems nearly impossible. Not surprisingly, the kinds of environmental initiatives that Canada and the United States, along with Mexico, were contemplating prior to Trump winning the presidency – including continental collaboration on green energy and energy efficiency as well as GHG emissions reductions in the aviation sector, for "black carbon" and for short-lived climate pollutants, not to mention carbon pricing – are simply off the table.

It is also critical to note the ways in which Canada-US tensions are boiling over into federal environmental policy. Trump's punitive trade actions against Canada – on softwood lumber, steel, aluminum, and potentially other products – emboldened Canadian critics of climate and environmental policy, and particularly the Trudeau government's plans to implement a carbon pricing plan. While leading carbon tax critics – Premiers Moe of Saskatchewan, Ford of Ontario, and Kenney in Alberta – base their arguments against the tax primarily on the need to protect "average Canadians from a punitive tax," the difficulties of moving ahead with such a tax in the Trump era also figure into their calculations. In response, then federal Environment Minister Catherine McKenna announced a softening of the planned regime. The price levies on large industrial emitters were to be calculated on the basis of the emissions average for each sector – if a company's emissions are over the average, then the pricing kicks in. The government has announced that henceforth the pricing will kick in at a higher level of emissions for certain industries, particularly those hard hit by Trump's tariffs (Peyton 2018). This is an admission that the economic pain inflicted by Trump's actions is having an impact on other policy areas, particularly climate policy.

In addition to all these difficulties, there is a further challenge associated with the federal government's insistence that the focus remain on carbon pricing. While generally economists have established that it is more efficient, carbon pricing is also more vulnerable to political attack than are other policy instruments, for several reasons (see Rabe 2018 for discussion of this problem). First, it carries all the negative connotations of the word *tax*; for one thing, it acts as a catalyst in the division between the political left and right. "Tax and spend" is a common pejorative applied by right-wing parties to centre-left governments in general, whether Liberal or NDP, and this now extends to carbon pricing. Second, carbon pricing increases the cost of essential consumer goods, such as oil and gas for home heating and automobiles. Cigarettes and alcohol are subject to what are called "sin taxes," justified by the state because they target undesirable activity (because of associated social costs) resulting from an individual choice that is optional. The same cannot be said about carbon taxes. Finally, carbon pricing is open to attack because it cannot accomplish its goal at the current level anyway. A tax such as $50 per tonne of GHGs, as planned by the PCF, will reduce emissions, but not nearly enough to meet the target. All agree that it must be closer to $150 per tonne to be effective, as noted above, yet no government would dare introduce a tax at that level. The upshot is that citizens see a new tax (something they dislike), placed on goods they consider essential, and to what end? Since it cannot solve the problem, why impose the economic pain it will entail? Conservative politicians can safely attack the concept of a carbon tax without having to say they actually prefer not to do anything about climate change.

Concluding Observations

This chapter has highlighted the ways in which the most salient factors of Canadian political life – federalism and regionalism above all, but also interest group dynamics, public opinion and Canada-US relations – have contributed to the inability of successive Canadian governments to meet their international commitments and stated climate policy objectives. Overcoming these obstacles would require strong collaboration and a favourable political context, including supportive public opinion for action and a willing partner in the business community. These conditions do not fully obtain at present, and the current federal government seems likely to miss its announced targets as well – even with all the initiatives outlined in the PCF. The Pan-Canadian Framework, battered as it is, did survive the October 2019 federal election, simply because Andrew Scheer's Conservatives, who had pledged to cancel the program, did not win – but not because Canadians love the plan. Indeed, it is worth noting that the Conservatives won the popular vote.

Yet Prime Minister Trudeau has promised even more effective action, and during the election announced a new target, that Canadian emissions would be "net zero" by 2050. The term means emissions will need to be drastically reduced and any remaining emission will need to be offset by pulling carbon out of the atmosphere, such as by planting trees. By early 2020, the Trudeau government had not yet announced any new programs to achieve net zero, nor the new programs needed to achieve the 2030 target. And the Trudeau Liberals still need to win the constitutional challenge to the federal carbon tax, which is not assured, given the Alberta court decision. Much also depends on their ability to overcome provincial resistance, which has increased following the election of Jason Kenney's United Conservative Party; there is currently adamant western resistance to anything that stands in the way of steadily rising emissions from expanded oil and gas activity.

What should the federal government do now, then, in the face of continued domestic and international pressure to act, its new commitment to net zero by 2050, yet a strongly divided country where advocates and critics of climate action are in direct conflict? A helpful first step may be for the Trudeau government to prepare the ground by making a stronger case for its policies directly to the Canadian public. This would entail offering a much more fulsome economic and political package intended to prepare the country for a future that will inevitably require greener economies and technology, one that provides a stark contrast to an outdated, polluting-based economy that is not likely to offer the jobs of the future. Canadians, it might be argued, must get in the game now so as not to miss out on future dividends that will accrue to countries who are moving ahead quickly; public opinion data suggest this message would be well received by most Canadians (Anderson 2018).

Carbon pricing needs to be downplayed as only one item in a package that aims to provide all the necessary reductions, yet is considerate of the needs of different regions of the country. Moreover, relatively large-scale, tangible projects need to be showcased to make the point about the potential of this new, greener economy, with explicit plans for projects in those regions of the country that will suffer most from the transition to a green economy, including Alberta, Saskatchewan, and certain Atlantic provinces. Alongside this, political leaders in Ontario, Saskatchewan, Manitoba, and Alberta must be put under pressure to explain and justify their own approaches to the climate change challenge, particularly in how they expect to foster the transition to a green economy with job creation as a partner with the federal government or on their own initiative. In this respect, recent federal moves to partner with large cities on green economy projects are a good way to pressure provincial leaders by highlighting their comparative inaction. And the federal government can continue to push for – and tangibly support – efforts such as those by certain oilsands producers to achieve net-zero emissions by

2050. Provincial resistance will have less bite if the companies within their borders are on board with federal climate action.

Most important, Canadians need some sort of national reconciliation that ends the two very different pathways illustrated in table 22.2 – emissions steadily increasing in the western fossil-fuel provinces and decreasing elsewhere, with the increases in one region wiping out progress made by the others. All parts of the country have to start moving in the same direction, going down the same pathway of emission reductions. To do that, we need to address a major regional difference: the fact that per capita reduction costs are much higher in the fossil fuel producing western provinces than they are elsewhere. As a step toward addressing the thorny question of how to share the mitigation burden, then, we suggest the rest of the country give a guarantee to Alberta and Saskatchewan that they will not have to bear per capita reduction costs that are higher than those borne by other Canadians.

As we have seen, there are many obstacles to effective climate change action. To surmount them, we need our governments to act decisively to take the kinds of specific steps suggested above. We also need to reach across our regional divides with goodwill and understanding to close the widening gap that currently separates us.

Notes

1 Carbon trading – or cap-and-trade systems – are a market-based approach to controlling pollution that allocates "allowances to pollute" among corporations, and these allowances can then be bought and sold under an overall cap, or limit, on emissions. Over time, the cap is decreased and corporations are encouraged to reduce their emission so that they do not have to spend additional money on buying pollution allowances.

2 Fracking refers to the process of extracting oil and gas from shale rock, by injecting liquid (a mix of water, sand, and chemicals) at high pressure into the subterranean rocks and boreholes to force open fissures and extract resources. There are concerns that the process uses large amounts of water, may contaminate groundwater, and may cause earth tremors.

References and Suggested Readings

Anderson, Bruce. 2018. "Analysis: Carbon Pricing Could Stand a Little More Help From Its Friends." Abacus Data, April. https://abacusdata.ca/analysis-carbon-pricing-can-stand-a-little-more-from-its-friends/.

BBC. 2018. "Trump: Climate Change Scientists Have a 'Political Agenda.'" October 15. https://www.bbc.com/news/world-us-canada-45859325.

Carbon Pricing Leadership Coalition. https://www.carbonpricingleadership.org/.

Commissioner of Environment and Sustainable Development. 2017. "Report 1: Progress on Reducing Greenhouse Gases – Environment and Climate Change Canada." http://www.oag-bvg.gc.ca/internet/English/parl_cesd_201710_01_e_42489.html.

Craik, Neil, Isabel Studer, and Debora VanNijnatten, eds. 2013. *North American Climate Change Policy: Designing Integration in a Regional System*. Toronto: University of Toronto Press.

David Suzuki Foundation and the Environics Institute. 2015. *Focus Canada 2015: Canadian Public Opinion and Climate Change*. https://davidsuzuki.org/science-learning-centre-article/focus-canada-2015-canadian-public-opinion-climate-change/?nabe=6678838150168576:1&utm_referrer=https%3A%2F%2Fwww.google.ca%2F.

Environment and Climate Change Canada. 2018. *Pan-Canadian Framework on Clean Growth and Climate Change: Second Annual Synthesis Report on the Status of Implementation*, December. http://publications.gc.ca/collections/collection_2018/eccc/En1-77-2018-eng.pdf.

———. 2019. *National Inventory Report 1990–2017: Greenhouse Gas Sources and Sinks in Canada*. Executive Summary. http://publications.gc.ca/collections/collection_2019/eccc/En81-4-1-2017-eng.pdf.

———. 2020a. Canadian Environmental Sustainability Indicators: Progress towards Canada's Greenhouse Gas Emission Reduction Target, 5. https://www.canada.ca/content/dam/eccc/documents/pdf/cesindicators/progress-towards-canada-greenhouse-gas-reduction-target/2020/progress-ghg-emissions-reduction-target.pdf.

———. 2020b. *National Inventory Report 1990– 2018: Greenhouse Gases Sources and Sinks in Canada: Executive Summary*. http://publications.gc.ca/collections/collection_2020/eccc/En81-4-1-2018-eng.pdf.

Government of Alberta. 2017. "Climate Leadership Plan: Progress Report 2016–17." December. https://open.alberta.ca/publications/climate-leadership-plan-progress-report-2016-17.

Government of Canada. 2016a. "Vancouver Declaration on Clean Growth and Climate Change." March 6. https://itk.ca/wp-content/uploads/2016/04/Vancouver_Declaration_clean_Growth_Climate_Change.pdf.

———. 2016b. *Pan-Canadian Framework on Clean Growth and Climate Change: Canada's Plan to Address Climate Change and Grow the Economy*. http://publications.gc.ca/collections/collection_2017/eccc/En4-294-2016-eng.pdf.

Harrison, Kathryn, and Tyler Bryant. 2016. "The Provinces and Climate Policy." In *Provinces: Canadian Provincial Politics*, edited by Christopher Dunn, 3rd ed., 495–521. Toronto: University of Toronto Press.

Jotzo, Frank, Joanna Depledge, and Harald Winkler. 2018. "US and International Climate Policy under President Trump." *Climate Policy* 18 (7): 813–17.

Liberal Party of Canada. 2015. *Real Change: Canada's Leadership in the World*. Liberal Party of Canada. https://www.liberal.ca/wp-content/uploads/2015/10/New-plan-for-a-strong-middle-class.pdf.

Macdonald, Douglas, Jochen Monstadt, Kristine Kern, David Gordon, Asya Bidordinova, Alexey Pristupa, and Anders Hayden. 2013. *Allocating Canadian Greenhouse Gas Emission Reductions amongst Sources and Provinces: Learning from European Union, Australia and Germany*. Technical Report: University of Toronto, Technische Universität Darmstadt, and Wageningen University. https://tspace.library.utoronto.ca/bitstream/1807/77153/1/AllocatingGHGReductions2013.pdf.

MacNab, Josha, Erin Flanagan, Maximilian Kniewasser, and Sara Hastings-Simon. 2017. "Putting a Price on Carbon Pollution across Canada: Taking Stock of Progress, Challenges, and Opportunities as Canada Prepares Its National Carbon Pricing

Benchmark." Pembina Institute. http://www.pembina.org/reports/carbon-pollution-pricing-2017.pdf.

Noll, Elizabeth, and Arjun Krishnaswami. 2018. "Congress Rejects Trump's Dismantling of Clean Energy Funding." Natural Resources Defence Council, March 18. https://www.nrdc.org/experts/elizabeth-noll/congress-rejects-trumps-dismantling-clean-energy-funding.

Peyton, Laura. 2018. "Feds Easing Proposed Carbon Tax for Big Emitters." CTV News, August 1. https://www.ctvnews.ca/politics/feds-easing-proposed-carbon-tax-for-big-emitters-1.4036202.

Rabe, Barry. 2018. *Can We Price Carbon?* Cambridge, MA: MIT Press.

Sawyer, Dave, and Chris Bataille. 2017. *Taking Stock: Opportunities for Collaborative Climate Action to 2030.* Policy Brief 2: The Pan-Canadian Framework on Clean Growth and Climate Change. Decarbonization Pathways Canada, Climate Action Network Canada: Environmental Defense, Équiterre and the Pembina Institute.

Tasker, John Paul. 2018. "Ottawa Slams Manitoba's 'Flip Flop' on Carbon Tax after Pallister Pulls Out of Climate Plan." CBC News, October 4. https://www.cbc.ca/news/politics/tasker-leblanc-manitoba-carbon-tax-flip-flop-1.4850752.

Trudeau, Justin. 2016. "Leaders' Statement on a North American Climate, Clean Energy and Environment Partnership." June 29. https://pm.gc.ca/eng/news/2016/06/29/leaders-statement-north-american-climate-clean-energy-and-environment-partnership.

Zimonjic, Peter. 2018. "Nearly a Third of Canadians Don't Believe Humans, Industry 'Mostly' Cause Climate Change: Poll." CBC News, April 4. https://www.cbc.ca/news/politics/poll-abacus-carbon-tax-1.4603824.

twenty-three
Canada in the World

MARK R. BRAWLEY

Introduction

The twenty-first century promises to be a time of change in international affairs. Economic activity and political power is being redistributed in fundamental yet unpredictable ways. How well will Canada navigate this changing environment? Fifteen years ago, noted political scientist Jennifer Welsh wrote *At Home in the World* (2004), a reflection on Canadian foreign policy after the Cold War, as well as a guide for redirecting and refocusing the country's efforts in international affairs. Have Canadians followed Welsh's advice? What sort of international role has Canada pursued in recent years? What role can Canada play in the future?

The answer varies in some important ways, depending on the specific issues one concentrates on. Therefore the discussion below tracks a few different themes, flowing from traditional concerns about Canada's place in the global economy or in international alliances to broader considerations regarding global governance structures and the informal ties linking Canadians to other societies. In the 1990s, debates on the direction of Canadian foreign policy were quite optimistic about the role Canada could play in international affairs – though the specific means and methods for promoting positive change were not always obvious or clear. Three years prior to Welsh's book, the terrorist attacks of September 11 changed much of our thinking about how the world was evolving, and Welsh laid out several reasons for Canadians to rethink the way their government represents their country in international affairs, given the new challenges confronting key allies. Since her observations, concerns about the redistribution of economic and political power have only grown. The Trump administration's policy choices have added to the turbulence in international affairs, leaving Trudeau's Liberal government some surprising problems to confront.

Economic Ties

Canada has deep and profound ties to the international economy. The country is relatively rich, and Canadians are generally well aware of how much of their wealth is tied up with the activities of others. They recognize this in the aggregate sense ("national" wealth depends on trading with and investing in other countries) as well as on a personal level (individuals see how their own incomes or their own purchases rest on direct links to other countries). As Welsh noted in 2004, domestic opinion of Canada's engagement with the international economy had shifted significantly from where it had been only some twenty years before. When free trade with the United States was first debated in the 1980s, many Canadians expressed fears that such an agreement would threaten cherished domestic social welfare policies (such as national health care). Those fears worsened when the free trade agreement was expanded on January 1, 1994, to include Mexico. Economic performance over the last quarter century demonstrated those fears were largely ungrounded. That experience changed the nature of our discussions about international economic issues. As Welsh put it, Canadians have set aside their anxieties and embraced economic globalization (2004, 89).

Despite some of the fears associated with regional free trade in the 1980s and early 1990s – or perhaps because of those concerns – Canadian governments played a disproportionately large role in shaping the North American Free Trade Agreement. NAFTA currently represents the single largest free trade zone in the world (larger than the European Union). There's no question as to why – the United States remains the world's single largest national economy. While it may not hold onto that top position for much longer, the United States will be among the largest and richest states (judged on a per-capita basis) well into the future. For Canada, being next door to the United States is both an economic blessing and an economic curse. Proximity (coupled with social similarities) makes it easy for Canadians to do business with the United States, a major reason why Canada's exports remain tightly focused on the American market. Global Affairs Canada (2018) reported nearly 76 per cent of merchandise exports (by value) went to the United States in 2017. Merchandise imports were slightly more diverse, with about 51 per cent coming from the United States. That link to the United States is a blessing, because the US market is so wealthy, quite open to Canadian exports, made up of consumers very similar to Canadians, and oh so near.

The curse, however, is that Canada comes to depend too heavily on this single market. That dependence could be turned against Canada in a conscious fashion. Sylvia Ostry, a former deputy trade minister, warned long ago that the country could become too reliant on the American market, making itself vulnerable to pressure should the US government choose to exercise political leverage over Canada (quoted in Welsh 2004, 89). Such issues have now risen to the top of the agenda, as the result of Trump's nonsensical attacks on NAFTA. The Canadian government's defence of the agreement, and the public support for that position, show how deeply Canadians appreciate the country's trade ties.

Less obvious, but just as important, the Canadian economy has become lashed to the American. During the 1990s, the American economy worked like a locomotive, and Canadians were happily pulled along. In recent years, the experience has been more like a roller coaster ride. When the American economy rises, so too does the Canadian; when economic activity south of the border drops, the Canadian economy follows it down. Canada can do little to offset or avoid the gyrations of the American economy. Macroeconomic mismanagement originating in Washington, DC, necessarily means trouble here. This isn't good news, since the future will undoubtedly present Americans with daunting economic challenges. The American government's debt will weigh heavily on future decisions made there for years. Canadians will have to endure the unpleasantness of having their economic fate determined by fights in the halls of power in Washington rather than in Ottawa.

Canadian leaders have long recognized the need to diversify the country's economic connections. Liberal governments in the 1970s sought options for generating ties with other states, in what was then referred to as the "Third Option" (Muirhead 2007, 137). Recent governments have explored similar opportunities. The Harper government sought alternative markets for Canadian energy exports. Gas and oil exports should be directed towards Asia, the site of immense economic growth, Harper argued. He also proposed Canada pursue more free trade agreements in the future, to enhance opportunities to expand Canada's trade with a variety of other countries. This led to the Comprehensive Economic and Trade Agreement (CETA), liberalizing trade between Canada and the European Union, which was implemented by the current Liberal government. Meanwhile, Canada also participated in the negotiations for the Trans-Pacific Partnership (TPP), intended to liberalize trade among the countries of the Pacific Rim. The TPP may have been scuttled by the Trump Administration for the moment, but Canada's interest in a Pacific-wide agreement remains.

The energy sector itself has been the focus of debates. With the financial collapse of 2008, a series of policy decisions in Washington reshaped the economic calculations of investors and owners in a variety of settings. American policy-makers, worried about the health of their own financial institutions, pumped cash into their economy. The flood of dollars drove down interest rates in the United States, as designed; as an unintended consequence, however, the value of the US dollar slumped versus other currencies. Some foreigners decided it was better to spend cash now, either because their own currencies translated into more US dollars than before, or because the US dollars they held were losing value every month. Foreign investors went on spending sprees – especially those making decisions based on long-term calculations. These investors saw opportunities to buy up firms that were struggling during the economic slowdown that accompanied the financial meltdown of 2008.

To give a specific example, Chinese investors had accumulated substantial sums of US dollars, were calculating their needs for the decades to come, and had reasons to think it would now be wiser to spend dollars rather than hold onto them. Chinese investors began purchasing supplies of required imports, scanning potential sources around the globe. When the value of some Canadian firms slumped in response to the broader economic slowdown, Chinese investors saw opportunities. China National Offshore Oil Corporation (CNOOC) bid to purchase Nexen, a key company developing Alberta's oil sands. CNOOC offered slightly over $15 billion in December 2012. Nexen operates around the globe, but the tricky issues had to do with the resources it owns in Canada; the deal had to be approved by the federal government, since all such purchases by foreign firms are reviewed according to Canadian law. The more delicate matter, of course, concerns the true owners of CNOOC: the Chinese government. Should natural resources in Canada be owned by a foreign government? The Conservative government ruled that the assets could be sold, both in this agreement and in a similar purchase involving Petronas, an energy company owned by the government of Malaysia.

Diversifying trade ties would be one reason the Canadian government would approve these sales. As already mentioned, the government would like to see more energy exports to Asia. Consistency in policy practice would be another. Canada has long supported the notion that its own firms should be allowed to set up shop in foreign lands; foreign direct investment often involves buying up an existing firm in the foreign market. Since Canadian governments have long adhered to this principle for Canadian businesses seeking to enter China, it must take up a similar position when Chinese firms come to Canada seeking to purchase local businesses. Nonetheless, the decision sparked public debate over the tensions between private and potentially national interests.

In general, Canadian governments have been strong supporters of not only freer flows of capital for international investment, but of a broadly open international economic order. This stance has been true for decades and fluctuates little, depending on the party in power. Canada was the first state to join the Organisation for Economic Co-operation and Development (OECD), a founding member of General Agreement on Trade and Tariffs (which later became the World Trade Organization), and helped shape the International Monetary Fund (IMF) at its inception. Canada remains heavily involved in all these international organizations, and in promoting the principles these institutions were built on. The pursuit of CETA and the TPP demonstrate a consistency of goals, regardless of the party in office, as does the defence of NAFTA.

In economic terms, Canada will probably remain most intimately linked to the United States for a long time. Yet, as the discussion above has illustrated, the country will surely develop stronger trade ties to China and other Asian countries. Canadian governments – both under Liberal and Conservative leadership – have pursued opportunities to expand trade with Europe and other countries in the western hemisphere over the past two decades. Canada has also consistently sought to bolster the organizations that govern the international economy, as a way to boost and maintain open economic flows between countries. These will undoubtedly remain the country's long-term policy objectives. The chief question is how well Canada diversifies its economic relations away from the United States.

Military Ties

In security affairs, too, Canada remains tightly bound to the United States. Relations with the United States in this area were once consistently smooth – but that changed in the past decade (Clarkson 2008; Gotlieb 2003). In the aftermath of the 9/11 terrorist attacks, Canadian and American military (and civil) authorities worked quite well together as they struggled to comprehend what had taken place and then respond. Canada participated (via the NATO alliance) in the combat operations launched against the Taliban regime in Afghanistan, first by deploying special operations units, then with large-scale ground and air forces. Yet when the Bush administration chose to commit American forces against the government of Saddam Hussein in Iraq in 2003, Canada's Prime Minister Jean Chrétien declined to join the American-led "coalition of the willing." Canada's official position was that the United States and its allies needed new authorization from the UN Security Council before it would participate in a war against Iraq. Despite the Bush administration's efforts in front of the UN diplomats, no authorization was forthcoming, so Chrétien had Canada stand aside. American officials took this as a rebuff, with some sharp words uttered by politicians on both sides of the border.

Canadian officials (whether speaking for Chrétien's government, his Liberal successor Paul Martin, the Conservative government led by Stephen Harper, or the current Trudeau government) have taken pains to point out all the areas of increased cooperation between the United States and Canada on security matters since 2001. Canadian Forces supported the American mission in Afghanistan even after the end of Canadian combat operations in 2011, through personnel to train Afghan military and police. This can be seen, at least in part, as a way to affirm Canada's commitment to future cooperation with the United States on security matters (a point heavily emphasized in an in-depth analysis by Janice Gross Stein and Eugene Lang (2007).

The two countries' law enforcement and border patrol and policing agencies have coordinated their efforts to an unprecedented degree. The 9/11 attacks could have triggered American policies severely restricting the flow of goods and people over the US-Canadian border; instead officials from Canada seized the initiative to develop methods that would assuage American fears, yet maintain the relatively open border separating the two countries (Wark 2008). These efforts have included the introduction of new identification systems for travellers to use, greater information sharing between the two governments regarding people crossing their borders, cooperative training to ensure law enforcement agencies work well together on border-related issues, and a host of other measures. Canada even went so far as to introduce a permanent resident card, to help ensure landed immigrants in Canada would be able to cross the border as freely as Canadian citizens. In all these ways, the Canadian government found methods to prevent (or at least offset) side effects linked to the heightened security concerns of the United States in the wake of 9/11.

Canadian military forces did engage in combat alongside Americans, and participating in the war in Afghanistan took a toll on the Canadian military. Between early 2002 and 2011, 158 Canadian military personnel and five civilians died (via combat, accidents, or suicide), while more than 2,000 were injured. Canada deployed armoured vehicles, artillery, and helicopters, and eventually sent tanks into the field. These deployment operations were costly in military equipment, as well as exacting a heavy psychological and emotional cost on the troops. Moreover, the almost decade-long rotation of units in and out of Afghanistan meant fewer troops were available for use in other parts of the globe. The effort exposed some positive aspects of Canada's military, as well as some shortcomings. In the first decade after the Cold War, budget constraints led to difficult choices on equipment purchases. The more recent equipment served Canadian soldiers in the field well, though there were more than a few complaints about how the pieces complemented each other in action. (And Canadian soldiers lacked one or two key elements – medium lift helicopters, for example – which had to be resolved in the short term.)

The problems should not come as a surprise, since it was impossible to anticipate in the 1990s that Canadian soldiers would be sent on this kind of mission, or in this sort of terrain. Nor were the complaints heard from

Canadian Forces in Afghanistan uncommon; most NATO members were no longer capable of fielding the entire range of combat and support units in an integrated fashion. To an extent, European members of the alliance had therefore committed to specializing their military contributions, so that they could pool their smaller units into larger fighting formations. The disadvantage with that strategy, however, is that a government can then operate only when each of its allies agrees to contribute the specific units necessary. Without consensus amongst the partners, military deployments become impossible. (For a deeper discussion of these implications for Canada, see Jones and Lagassé 2012.)

As several recent operations have shown – particularly with NATO members engaged in North Africa – even the larger countries in the alliance (such as France) have difficulty gathering the entire package of combat and support units needed to pull off a small to moderate intervention. In comparison, Canadian units did well shouldering significant combat responsibilities in Afghanistan, as well as contributing to reconstruction in the country. Canada was a more effective participant in NATO's combat operations than several alliance members with larger populations.

On the downside, the smaller total size of the Canadian Forces – the number of regular personnel on the ground, naval and air units had fallen to below 60,000 by the end of the 1990s – limited the ability to send troops abroad for a sustained period. Normal policy is for a unit to spend a set amount of time deployed (typically, this would be for six to nine months). Since the stresses associated with being in the field build up over time, troops are then rotated back to Canada for an extended period (a year or more), before being deployed overseas again. This means, however, that no more than a quarter of the ground forces should be sent on operations at the same time, if there is an expectation for the commitment to be sustained beyond six months. These same principles govern troops serving on peace-keeping missions, since these count as combat operations. As the total number of military personnel fell, the ability to deploy units overseas rapidly diminished. This imposed constraints on when and where the government might be able to commit Canada to a military role.

To address these limitations and deal with the toll the Afghan mission took on equipment and general combat readiness, the Harper government developed an ambitious program for retooling and re-energizing the Canadian military. Recruitment targets were raised, in the hopes of increasing the number of regular personnel; militia recruitment was also expanded. The government chose to purchase new transport aircraft (both medium- and long-range), to construct an array of new ships for the navy, to buy upgraded fighting vehicles for the army, and most contentiously, to acquire a new fighter-bomber for the air force. (The air force bid is discussed in more detail below.) These purchases were justified in a planning document called *Canada First Defence Strategy*, released in 2008. As its title implies, the Conservative vision identified the priority for the Canadian Forces: the defence of Canada. Other goals follow. Of course, the purchasing programs indicated the desire to project power beyond Canada's borders, hence the decisions to buy new C-130 Hercules and C-17 Globemaster transport planes.

In 2017, the Trudeau government released its vision for the Canadian Forces, titled *Strong, Secure, Engaged*. The statement emphasizes the need to provide greater support for military personnel and their families. It also continues the previous government's commitment to procure new warships, though construction has only begun on patrol craft for the Arctic (the larger ships needed for ocean-going operations remain at the design stage). Likewise, the report reaffirms the commitment to replace Canada's aging fleet of fighter aircraft, though Trudeau's Liberals used the high cost of the Conservatives' planned acquisition of F-35s to their advantage in the last election. (There were important questions about the procurement process and the eventual cost of these planes.) The current plan is to acquire some used aircraft from Australia until a new procurement process can be undertaken.

Viewed overall, the coming challenges for the Canadian military remain quite similar to those confronted twenty-five years ago. It may be easy to recognize the need for forces capable of projecting power abroad, whether for peace-keeping, peace enforcement, or defeating a foreign threat, but it is difficult to know the precise location or timing when the Canadian Forces will be called upon. It would have been difficult to anticipate the types of missions they have been asked to execute: from air patrols over the deserts of North Africa to infantry slogging through the mountain valleys of Afghanistan, to search and rescue within the Arctic Circle. That makes choices about the form and equipment of the Forces difficult. Those challenges won't be any easier to resolve in the future, since Canada's Armed Forces will undoubtedly be asked to operate in a wide range of settings, some of which we haven't even thought of yet.

Global Governance/International Institutions

For most Canadians, the use of military force would be the last option for settling international disputes. The vast majority of Canadians would prefer problems between states be resolved through international mediation. Successful mediation requires having the appropriate international fora for states to deal with each other, as well as a full body of international law delineating rights and responsibilities. (States, either individually or through alliances, may still resort to the use of force as they interact, particularly when one state chooses to disregard international law.) Global governance is therefore central to Canada's future in international affairs, a point emphasized by Jennifer Welsh.

Given the relative decline of the United States from its overwhelming position of dominance, and the increasing role of other nations on the global stage, some aspects of the current international order may well be questioned; thus it makes perfect sense to be concerned with how the international community handles changing demands or clashing interests. (Donald Trump's actions also remind us the United States itself may undermine the international order.) In the past, Canadian governments have consistently followed the strategy that the institutions of global governance could be crafted or moulded to benefit Canada. The logic flows from the sense that Canada – as a country with a small population and a medium-sized, open economy – would suffer if international relations were to return to the "grab what you can" power politics of an earlier era. But the logic also flows from the notion that Canada derives disproportionate gains from multilateral cooperation in international affairs. Cooperation serves as a "force multiplier" for Canadian efforts to influence events elsewhere, regardless of the means selected, or the matter at hand. If well-designed international institutions help Canadians achieve their aims in international economic affairs, enhance the country's security, allow it to promote the values it cherishes, and so forth, the institutions themselves must be of concern to Canadian policy-makers. The more pressing problems looming, such as responding to global warming or limiting the proliferation of weapons of mass destruction, will demand greater international cooperation. As Welsh underscored (2004), Canadians – public and government officials alike – require little convincing when it comes to prioritizing the need for improvements in global governance.

The single most important body in global governance remains the United Nations. Canada played an important role in the establishment of the UN. Famously, Canadian John Peter Humphrey penned the first draft of the Universal Declaration of Human Rights; he would go on to be an advocate for developing the UN High Commission for Human Rights. While Canada's relationship with the UN has not always been easy or contented, Canadian governments have largely tried to work within the UN on most issues.

The UN Security Council presents some of the challenges the international system will be dealing with. When the UN was established, the Security Council had to be constructed to bring the world's most powerful states into a decision-making forum they would mutually accept. Accordingly, the United States, the Soviet Union, and the United Kingdom (along with France and China) were granted permanent membership on the Security

Council, as well as the ability to veto UNSC decisions. This privileged position meant that key issues were determined by the UNSC prior to consideration by the General Assembly of the United Nations. These necessary political compromises in the way the United Nations conducts its business ensured the major powers' participation, but also seriously hampered how often the UNSC would allow the UN to take decisive action.

Canada could make no claim for a permanent seat on the UNSC then, nor could it now. Permanent membership is based on military power and/or economic weight. Instead, Canada has routinely sought one of the rotating seats on the Council, which are chosen by the UN General Assembly. Canada has therefore been represented on the UNSC a number of times – about once every decade or so, beginning in the 1950s. In order to win broad approval, Canada traditionally promoted itself as a "good citizen" of the UN. There are two of the rotating seats reserved for Western advanced industrial countries; Canada ran for one of these seats in 2010, and for the first time, lost to rivals. There will be other chances, but the lost vote was a clear indication Canada's standing in the international community has fallen (Stairs 2011).

Of course, the other way to read the 2010 voting would be to recognize that other states seek representation too. The broader issue confronting the Security Council is whether it can be reformed to make room for more diverse voices. Canada is seen as one more Western country that speaks for itself, rather than representing the views of a number of other states. The bigger challenge for the UNSC, however, is the growing economic and military might of states such as Brazil or India – states representing large populations or regions of the world that do not have a permanent seat at the Security Council table. Those enjoying permanent status remain the key states who emerged victorious from World War II – including two from Europe (Britain and France). Germany and Japan, as the defeated states in World War II, have not held permanent seats, despite their economic or financial importance. With so many states jostling for a greater influence, it does not appear likely that Canada will achieve a greater role in the UN in the future.

Canada could be an important supporter of institutional change within the UN. As Welsh argued, "Canada's interests are best served if future superpowers are firmly embedded in international institutions and have been 'socialized' to co-operate with others in the management of common problems" (2004, 172). That statement may be even more true today, given that India and China have continued to close the economic gap with the United States. It is less clear how Canada can promote that change, however, if the current permanent members of the UNSC refuse to concede their power. This sort of challenge is replicated in other institutional settings, such as the IMF, World Bank, and so on.

Canada has successfully promoted reforms in other affairs, which might prove a useful strategy across institutions. In response to charges that the G8 economic summits were failing to represent large swaths of the world's population, let alone omitting significant economic players from the discussions, Canadian Prime Minister Paul Martin proposed the creation of a larger grouping that could meet alongside the summits. The G8 (now G7, minus Russia) meetings originated from efforts required to coordinate economic policy among the world's largest economies, beginning with ad hoc practices in the 1980s. These became regular affairs within a short amount of time, having proved their worth when resolving problems in exchange rate coordination. In 1999, Finance Minister Paul Martin proposed a wider number of states meet – the G20. (Note that the G20 is not made up of the largest economies, but is meant to draw on a different sense of representation, so that members reflect different regions, populations, etc.)

Critically, Martin and Foreign Minister Lloyd Axworthy did not advocate replacing the G8 with the G20, but encouraged the two to meet one after the other. In this way, the G8 could continue to function as it had, while the G20 meeting could then either bolster cooperation among those states along the same lines or at least allow the other states to voice their own perspectives on the matters at hand. While there are advantages to having the G20 alongside the smaller group, there might also be drawbacks to this strategy. When more than one institution can claim purview over an issue area, the possibility of "forum-shopping" arises. Forum-shopping describes the choice actors have in determining where a decision will be made. Each actor chooses the setting where it believes its perspective will prevail; it then pushes to have the decision made in its preferred arena. Forum-shopping can be problematic when a crisis occurs, which demands a rapid response. (This could be a financial meltdown, a genocide erupting, or any other instance where events require a group of states to react with speed if they are to limit the damage.) If actors run to different venues to deal with the crisis, then the reaction time by the group is considerably slowed. Thus, building more institutions to serve alongside existing ones may not be the best fix.

While Welsh noted that Canadians recognize the utility of institutions for global governance, she thought it was important that Canadians think more consciously about why international institutions are important. "We need to explain to others, and to ourselves, why we seek to work through international institutions such as the WTO and the UN," she wrote (Welsh 2004, 146). This was important for appreciating what international institutions can and cannot do, so that Canada is prepared to work around such institutions, if need be.

Canadians in the World

Another important trend Welsh identified, which has accelerated in the last decade, is the degree to which Canadians engage the rest of the world, not through their government, but as individuals, or through myriad private organizations. Technological advances ensure that wealthier countries such as Canada have a widening array of means to connect with foreigners. Canadians have been quick to take advantage of those new opportunities. This may be producing some interesting interactions – Canadians engage the world, but in the process change their own sense of themselves, who they are.

Beginning in the 1990s, both the government and Canadian society chose to invest in non-governmental organizations (NGOs). While data on NGO activity remains somewhat vague (making it difficult to compare across countries, for instance), Canadian NGOs have established a presence on every continent. Typically Canadian NGOs were created to address specific problems outside the country. Some target environmental issues, some economic development, others poverty, some aim to improve children's rights in other lands, and so forth. Canadian NGOs continue to grow in number, size, and sophistication. Anecdotal evidence suggests that a growing number of Canadian students are going abroad, either to attend school or to participate in volunteer work, which is probably changing the way the youngest generation of Canadians view the world (see Tiessen 2007).

At the same time, government funding for NGOs has fluctuated, in both amount and direction. Every time governments alternate in power, or budget situations change, public funding for NGOs shifts. Canadian NGOs have been particularly active in recent years in Iraq, Afghanistan, and Haiti, largely because the Conservative government redirected more of the development aid budget to these countries. NGOs respond to the money made available by designing programs to achieve targets set by donors. While the process works to keep Canadians involved, the ways in which NGOs have evolved in recent decades probably deserves more rigorous study and analysis. We know this is one of the many faces of Canada abroad, but we carry too many assumptions with us about how the actions of NGOs are viewed by others. NGOs come in many different shapes and sizes, with different levels of ambition, so they are not all perceived in the same way; nor are they all equally effective. Yet we can say little about these issues, because there has been too little analysis of NGO behaviour and its impact.

Many NGOs typically have a physical presence in other foreign countries, and improvements in communication and transportation have made it easier for them to execute their missions. Transportation costs have fluctuated over the past decade, but travel is in many ways easier than it has ever been. The number of Canadians making trips outside the country (defined as lasting more than twenty-four hours) hit record highs in 2012 (CBC 2012). This trend has continued; in fact, the number has risen every year since 2003 (Statistics Canada 2018). The strength of the Canadian dollar versus both the euro and the US dollar contributed to this trend. Nonetheless, statistics indicate Canadians enjoy a growing awareness of and exposure to other parts of the world.

The introduction of the option to hold dual or multiple citizenship has also created a trend towards Canadians not just visiting other countries, but being citizens of other states. This has prompted some interesting, if confusing episodes for consideration. Canadian citizens have sat in foreign parliaments, while a Canadian with dual citizenship has served as the leader of the official opposition here. (Since his mother emigrated to Canada from France, Stéphane Dion held French and Canadian citizenship. For a more in-depth look at these issues, see Macklin and Crépeau 2010.) In 2006, renewed civil conflict in Lebanon revealed that tens of thousands of Lebanese residing there also held Canadian citizenship. These examples demonstrate how Canadian identity has evolved, but also illustrates the implications these links might have on Canadian foreign policy.

Canadians have virtual links to the rest of the world as well. Canadians are wired to the web as much as any people, anywhere. An estimated 80 per cent of the population has internet access, and some 70 per cent have mobile phones. These figures are quite high when compared to most of the world. (Only Scandinavian countries and Iceland score higher.) Nearly two-thirds of Canadian adults have a social networking profile online. Canadians spend as much as seventeen hours online each week (Statistics Canada 2013). This presence on the World Wide Web complements the prominent role of Canadians in international cultural media, where they rank among the top celebrities in film, popular music, and other arts. These individuals also present a Canadian face to the rest of the world, as demonstrated so well by the opening and closing ceremonies of the Olympics in Vancouver in 2010. Of course, these same cultural channels allow Canadians to consume a growing diet of foreign-produced media content. In future, the global exchange of cultural goods and identities may have some curious and unexpected political consequences (Goff and Dunn 2004).

Canadian firms represent another dimension of the country's engagement with the rest of the world. The government has encouraged Canadian firms to find markets or other business opportunities abroad, by investing in support for their outreach via the Global Opportunities for Associations program. This program is on top of older forms of support, such as the Canadian Commercial Corporation and Export Development Canada. Many good economic arguments suggest Canadian firms need to have a growing presence in international markets if they are to remain vibrant and productive.

Sometimes Canadian international investments can be problematic. Canadian banks operating in the United States were caught up in the financial meltdown of 2008, and all were exposed to a certain extent. Our particular expertise in mining means that a growing number of Canadian firms have operations in developing countries, where their behaviour has often been more focused on profits than anything else. Canada places relatively few restrictions on how its firms do business abroad. As examples of environmental degradation or property rights disputes involving Canadian firms emerge, the demand may increase for more legal restraints on how firms engage in resource extraction abroad.

Of course, on the flip side of this international engagement, Canada remains quite open for foreign producers to set up shop here. Large numbers of foreign firms operate inside the country, and they include many of the country's most prominent and popular employers. There continue to be issues raised about the extent of foreign penetration of the Canadian market, though protective legislation such as laws to defend the use of French, or to ensure Canadian content in print, radio, and other media, seems to be working. One has to wonder, however, how the increased use of the World Wide Web will undercut the effectiveness of such laws. If anything, this is one more area where we might be looking at how Canada's engagement with the world may be changing Canadians' sense of themselves in new and unexpected ways.

Conceptualizing Canada in the World

Canadians have, for some time, tried to think about how Canada operates in the international arena, and struggled to come up with the appropriate labels to describe the country's aims and efforts. Since World War II, it was popular to consider Canada a "middle power." The term *middle power* conveyed that Canada was not a great power, but one that could still carry influence in world affairs; *middle power* also implied modesty in the range and nature of the goals the country set for itself. The term quickly came to be tied to a particular set of means to be employed in international affairs, perhaps as a consequence of the scale and form of power that countries such as Canada could effectively employ internationally (James and Kasoff 2008).

One acclaimed benefit of being a "middle power" was to be less threatening than a great power. Middle powers could not afford the ambitions of a great power, which affect how others perceive them. To paraphrase Welsh (2004, 133), middle powers are too weak to provoke suspicion or jealousy in the international system, but still capable of wielding adequate hard power to contribute to the success of multilateral efforts in addressing shared problems. This is supposed to explain why Canada places so much faith in alliances, international organizations, and multilateralism more generally: when operating alone, its chances of success are diminished, compared to when it cooperates with others.

Welsh noted, however, that the middle power label emphasized the *means* Canada was willing to employ in international affairs, rather than focusing on the country's *goals* (2004, 158). Middle powers build consensus, via coalitions and international institutions, as already noted. She suggested (citing the work of Denis Stairs [2005, 2011]) that the middle power tactics necessarily lend themselves to defence of the status quo; the example of the creation of the G20 suggests otherwise. The issue, however, comes down to how much the choice of means can constrain later choices about goals. In Canadian foreign policy, discussion or debate often focuses on means rather than thinking through goals. (For a nice discussion of the utility of the middle power concept, and the ways in which it describes ends as well as means, see Hynek and Bosold 2010).

Of course, a deeper discussion about Canada's goals brings us back to a point raised earlier: the need for more serious debates in domestic politics to address key questions about what the country's aims should be. We are missing that level of debate in Parliament, but also in the media. Despite widespread acknowledgment that Canada engages the world – indeed, a widespread agreement that Canada needs the rest of the world more than ever – we lack the tools and information to have meaningful exchanges over the formulation or elaboration of policy in this area. One hopes that situation will change in the near future.

Canada in the World as It Evolves

Writing more than a decade ago, Jennifer Welsh revealed several enduring insights regarding Canada and its place in the world. Despite the changes that have occurred since, and changes that will undoubtedly arise in the next decade, Canadians can expect to face vexing challenges in their relations with the rest of the world. Canada will always face difficulties in its interactions with the United States, because geography dictates such close and intense ties between the two, and we know Canada will never be as powerful as its primary international partner. In relations with the rest of the world, Canadians will need to identify the specific goals the country should seek to attain, as well as debate the proper means for pursuing those ends. Each of these areas has been a source of problems in the past and promises to present obstacles for Canadians to deal with in the future.

As for relations between Canada and the United States, Welsh (2004) argued Canada needed greater confidence in its dealings with America (2004, 19). The fates of the two countries are inextricably intertwined. That means Canadian governments must continually try to shape where the two are headed, even though it is exceptionally difficult for the smaller, weaker partner to influence either the direction or the pace of the trip! To its advantage, the Canadian government knows it must focus talent and attention on the United States; it must also continue to seize the initiative when opportunities to reconfigure the relationship present themselves.

The challenge in establishing foreign policy goals rests most intently on political processes, which do not always appear to be working well. Ideally, the government would reflect on policy-making via open public discussion, and deliberation in Parliament. This would mean building domestic consensus behind important decisions, enabling the country's leaders to act more effectively in the international arena. This would require leaders to articulate policies to the public and to Canada's allies – which they have generally failed to do in the last quarter century (Welsh 2004, 19–20). The process is equally important for clarifying to Canada's international partners just what Canada is – or is not – willing to do. Unfortunately, Canadian governments tend to make decisions solely within Cabinet, or even more exclusively within the Prime Minister's Office; opposition parties have done a poor job of anticipating issues, and thus have failed to provoke the sort of debates within Parliament that would benefit the public. Ultimately, then, the public needs to demand a more public airing of foreign policy issues, though such issues rarely rank high in either voter awareness or priorities.

Once goals have been established, then the appropriate means for achieving results have to be selected. Here, Welsh charged that Canada had too often failed to be strategic in its decisions (2004, 21). It had latched onto particular methods, and exploited certain openings to be sure; but it had also fallen back on the notion that being a middle power, or a niche player, dictated the policy instruments it should rely on. It makes much more sense, Welsh argued, to let the goal define what would be required. For every task, there is undoubtedly a preferred set of tools. Yet, two sorts of problems confront every state as it tries to establish its foreign policy strategies: matching goals and means. The first comes whenever goals shift; in parliamentary systems, foreign policy aims can vary widely and change rapidly, since these will reflect the party in power. With every election, new priorities can arise. The second comes as budgetary constraints become more pressing. Lack of funds demands that governments set priorities, but limited resources clearly constrict the policies governments can implement. These are problems for all governments. Canada cannot escape these restraints any more readily than others. Projecting budgetary issues in the near future, we can assume the formulation of foreign policy will be contentious, as the need to define clear objectives will be more demanding, as will the selection of effective means for attaining those goals.

Welsh's hope was that Canada can become a model citizen in the world (2004, 189). Canada should set the example for others, meaning it must hold itself to a higher standard. It must generate its "soft power" as well as the hard power discussed earlier. It must not only bring resources to bear in a way that is effective and meaningful (with or without allies), but also generate the ideas and norms that others will appreciate and follow. These are demanding goals, but ones that should be important to all Canadians.

References and Suggested Readings

CBC. 2012. "Canadian Travel Abroad Hits 40-Year High," August 21. http://www.cbc.ca/news/business/story/2012/08/21/canada-travel-june.html.

Clarkson, Stephen. 2008. "The Inconsistent Neighbor." In *Big Picture Realities*, edited by Daniel Drache, 107–22. Waterloo, ON: Wilfrid Laurier University Press.

Global Affairs Canada. n.d. "Annual Merchandise Trade." http://www.international.gc.ca/economist-economiste/statistics-statistiques/annual_merchandise_trade-commerce_des_marchandises_annuel.aspx?lang=eng.

Goff, Patricia, and Kevin C. Dunn, eds. 2004. *Identity and Global Politics, Empirical and Theoretical Elaborations*. New York: Palgrave Macmillan.

Gotlieb, Allan. 2003. "Foremost Partner: The Conduct of Canada-U.S. Relations." In *Canada among Nations 2003: Coping with the American Colossus*, edited by Norman Hillmer, David Carment, and Fen O. Hampson, 19–31. Toronto: Oxford University Press.

Government of Canada, Department of National Defence. 2017. "Strong, Secure, Engaged." http://dgpaapp.forces.gc.ca/en/canada-defence-policy/docs/canada-defence-policy-report.pdf.

Hynek, Nik, and David Bosold, eds. 2010. *Canada's Foreign and Security Policy: Soft and Hard Strategies of a Middle Power*. Toronto: Oxford University Press.

James, Patrick, and Mark J. Kasoff. 2008. *Canadian Studies in the New Millennium*. Toronto: University of Toronto Press.

Jones, Peter, and Phillip Lagassé. 2012. "Rhetoric versus Reality: Canadian Defence Planning in a Time of Austerity." *Defence and Security Analysis* 28 (2): 140–51.

Macklin, Audrey, and François Crépeau. 2010. "Multiple Citizenship, Identity and Entitlement in Canada." IRPP Study No. 6. https://irpp.org/wp-content/uploads/assets/research/diversity-immigration-and-integration/multiple-citizenship-identity-and-entitlement-in-canada/IRPP-Study-no6.pdf.

Muirhead, Bruce. 2007. *Dancing around the Elephant*. Toronto: University of Toronto Press.

Stairs, Denis. 2005. "Founding the United Nations: Canada at San Francisco, 1945." *Policy Options* 26 (7): 15–20.

———. 2011. "Being Rejected in the United Nations: The Causes and Implications of Canada's Failure to Win a Seat in the UN Security Council." CDFAI Policy Update Paper.

Statistics Canada. 2013. "Individual Internet Use and E-Commerce." http://www.statcan.gc.ca/daily-quotidien/111012/dq111012a-eng.htm.

———. n.d. "International Merchandise Trade for All Countries and by Principal Trading Partners, Monthly (x 1,000,000)." http://www.statcan.gc.ca/tables-tableaux/sum-som/l01/cst01/gblec02a-eng.htm.

———. 2018. "Travel between Canada and Other Countries, December 2017." https://www150.statcan.gc.ca/n1/daily-quotidien/180220/dq180220c-eng.htm.

Stein, Janice Gross, and Eugene Lang. 2007. *The Unexpected War: Canada in Kandahar*. Toronto: Viking.

Tiessen, Rebecca. 2007. "Educating Global Citizens? Canadian Foreign Policy and Youth Study/Volunteer Abroad Programs." *Canadian Foreign Policy* 14 (1): 77–84.

Wark, Wesley. 2008. "Smart Trumps Security: Canada's Border Security Policy since 11 September." In *Big Picture Realities*, edited by Daniel Drache, 139–52. Waterloo, ON: Wilfrid Laurier University Press.

Welsh, Jennifer. 2004. *At Home in the World*. Toronto: Harper Collins.

Index